SPADEFISH

On Patrol With A Top-Scoring World War II Submarine

Stephen L. Moore

© Stephen L. Moore 2006

Manufactured in the United States of America
All rights reserved

10 9 8 7 6 5 4 3 2 1

No part of this book may be reproduced or utilized in any form or by any means, electronic, or mechanical, including photocopying, recording, or by any information storage and retrival system withour permission in writing. All events, persons, locations, personal accounts and organizations are based on true accounts relayed to the author by the individuals who experienced them. Any resemblance to any other experience is unintended, and entirely coincidental. Inquiries or requests for permission to reproduce material from this work should be sent to:

Atriad Press LLC
13820 Methuen Green
Dallas Texas 75240

The paper used in this book meets the minimum requirements of the American National Standard for Permanence of Paper for Printed Library Materials, Z39.48.1984.

Library of Congress Cataloging-in-Publication Data

Moore, Stephen L.
Spadefish:On patrol with a top-scoring World War II submarine / Stephen L. Moore.
p. cm.
Includes bibliographical references and index.
ISBN 9781933177076
1. World War, 1939–1945—Naval operations—Submarine. 2. World War, 1939–1945—Naval operations, American.   I. Title

Library of Congress Control Number: 2006921557

Layout and typesetting by Stephen L. Moore. Cover photos of *Spadefish* crew and of *Spadefish* returning from her fifth patrol courtesy of Daniel D. Decker, Cdr., USN (Ret.). Author with battle flag photo by Michael Johnson. Cover art direction advice courtesy of Stephanie Shkolnikov.

SPADEFISH

Stephen L. Moore

Other Books by Stephen L. Moore

European Metal Detecting Guide: Tips, Techniques and Treasures. Garland, TX: RAM Books, 2009.

Last Stand of the Texas Cherokees: Chief Bowles and the 1839 Cherokee War in Texas. Garland, TX: RAM Books, 2009.

Presumed Lost. The Incredible Ordeal of America's Submarine Veteran POWs of World War II. Annapolis, MD: Naval Institute Press, 2009.

War of the Wolf: Texas' Memorial Submarine, World War II's Famous USS Seawolf. Dallas, TX: Atriad Press, 2008.

Savage Frontier: Rangers, Riflemen, and Indian Wars in Texas. Volume III: 1840–1841. Denton, TX: University of North Texas Press, 2007.

Savage Frontier: Rangers, Riflemen, and Indian Wars in Texas. Volume II: 1838–1839. Denton, TX: University of North Texas Press, 2006.

Spadefish: On Patrol With a Top-Scoring World War II Submarine. Dallas, TX: Atriad Press, 2006.

Eighteen Minutes: The Battle of San Jacinto and the Texas Independence Campaign. Plano, TX: Republic of Texas Press, 2004.

Savage Frontier: Rangers, Riflemen, and Indian Wars in Texas. Volume I: 1835–1837. Denton, TX: University of North Texas Press, 2002. Reprinted 2006.

Taming Texas. Captain William T. Sadler's Lone Star Service. Austin, TX: State House Press, 2000.

With William J. Shinneman and Robert W. Gruebel. *The Buzzard Brigade: Torpedo Squadron Ten at War.* Missoula, MT: Pictorial Histories Publishing, 1996.

For more information, visit www.stephenlmoore.com

Contents

Prologue vii
Acknowledgments xiii
World War II Muster Roll of *USS Spadefish* 1

Commissioning and Training
1. Mare Island and Luau 7
2. Uncle Charlie's Secret Weapon 37

First Patrol
3. Typhoon 59
4. "First Blood for *Spadefish*" 85
5. Cat and Mouse Games 99
6. A Double Barreled Patrol 113

Second Patrol
7. Underwood's Urchins 131
8. "Shaken Up" 143
9. *Jinyo*'s last "Banzai!" 155
10. Luau's Litter 175

Third Patrol
11. Friendly Fire 189
12. "A Good Working Over" 201
13. Icy Hunting in the Yellow Sea 215

Fourth Patrol
14. Guam and Germershausen 235
15. "Beyond Test Depth" 253
16. "Like Pirates of Old" 275

Fifth Patrol
17. Operation Barney 303
18. Hell's Bells 321
19. "It Was a Real Turkey Shoot" 335
20. Transbalt 349

21.	Mighty Mine Dodgers Return	.365
22.	"Cease Offensive Operations"	.391
	Epilogue	.403

APPENDICES:
A. Top U.S. Subs of World War II by Tonnage Sunk 417
B. Top U.S. Subs of World War II by Ships Sunk 418
C. Efficiency Rating of Top U.S. Subs of World War II 419
D. Other *Spadefish* Top 10 Statistics 420
E. Best War Patrols by Number of Enemy Ships Sunk 421
F. *Spadefish* Sinkings: Claims and Credit Given 422
G. Awards Given to *Spadefish* and Crew 425
GLOSSARY 428
CHAPTER NOTES 433
BIBLIOGRAPHY 447
INDEX 453

Arriving in Pearl Harbor following her fifth war patrol, *Spadefish* flies the Stars and Stripes, Japan's Rising Sun flag, and one "meatball" flag for each merchant ship sunk. Her thin 1944 commissioning pennant is also flying alongside the American flag. *U.S. Navy photo, courtesy of Thomas Miller.*

Prologue

Of the 258 American submarines participating in World War II, only five were successful enough to sink more than twenty enemy ships that were officially credited to them. Better analysis in recent years has added a few more boats to this list, but it remains an elite few nonetheless. To achieve such an impressive feat, some of these proud submarines spent up to 701 days at sea on war patrol in enemy waters, scouring the horizon for the sight of enemy ships.

Two U.S submarines managed to make the top of the list by racking up their sinking totals in less than 250 days on war patrol—*Tang* (SS-306) and *Spadefish* (SS-411). By sinking verifications established immediately post-war, the Joint Army-Navy Assessment Committee (JANAC), credited *Tang* with the sinking of 24 enemy ships in 203 days on patrol. JANAC officially credited *Spadefish* with 21 "kills" in 220 days on patrol. By these standards, *Tang* ranked No. 2 in total sinkings and *Spadefish* tied for fourth. JANAC did not assign credit for smaller vessels under 500 tons, thereby not officially crediting U.S. submarines with the countless smaller ships destroyed with their deck guns.

More recent analysis by retired Navy Commander John D. Alden and researcher Roger Allan, however, more accurately shows that *Spadefish* sank a total of 30 ships and *Tang* sank 27 total vessels. *Spadefish*'s 30 total sinkings came in 220 days on patrol, or one ship sunk every seven and one-third days. *Tang* destroyed her 27 vessels in 203 days on patrol, averaging one ship sunk for every seven and one-half days out.

Of the top boats which sank sixteen or more vessels, only four cracked the single digit kills-per-days-on-patrol ratio—*Spadefish*, *Barb*, *Tang* and *Wahoo*. In sinking efficiency by total kills, *Barb* came in second place with 73.33 vessels destroyed in 545 days on war patrol. Of these sinkings, 54 were trawlers and other small vessels were sunk by

Barb's rockets, gunfire or other means. Behind *Spadefish*, *Barb* and *Tang*, *Wahoo* was the fourth most efficient U.S. submarine of World War II, sinking an enemy vessel every 9.73 days she was on patrol.

Tautog, credited by JANAC with the most ships sunk, did so in thirteen war patrols. *Silversides* spent nearly 500 more days on patrol than *Spadefish* did in order to take the third spot on JANAC's list. *Flasher*, tied with *Spadefish* for fourth, took an extra 110 days on patrol to achieve 21 confirmed sinkings. The exploits of *Tang* were well chronicled by her Congressional Medal of Honor winning skipper, Commander Richard Hetherington "Dick" O'Kane. Another Congressional Medal of Honor recepient, Gene Fluckey, has written of his command patrols during *Barb*'s glory days. As for America's most efficient World War II submarine, comparatively little has been published on the successes of *USS Spadefish*.

Spadefish's accomplishments were many. Only seven U.S. submarines managed to sink a Japanese aircraft carrier during the war. On her second patrol, *Spadefish* torpedoed and sank the 21,000-ton carrier *Jinyo* (also known as *Shinyo*) on 17 November 1944. Of the 1,682 war patrols conducted by U.S. submarines, *Spadefish* turned in the fifth best patrol with six ships sunk during her very first patrol. Her first war patrol also ranked as the eighth best in terms of tonnage destroyed, with 31,542 tons of enemy shipping sunk.

Her second war patrol also cracked the top ten in tonnage, when *Spadefish* sank four Japanese ships for 30,421 tons. This patrol was ninth best of the war in tonnage. Recently, the research of submarine veteran John Alden credits *Spadefish* with sinking an additional 6,600-ton tanker during her second patrol. Allowing this extra tonnage would have made *Spadefish*'s second patrol the fifth best in total tonnage. For sinking ten confirmed ships and 61,963 tons on her first two patrols, *Spadefish* was awarded the Presidential Unit Citation, which was given to only 34 of the 258 U.S. submarines taking part in World War II.

By 1945, Japanese shipping targets had become very scarce and many boats returned to base having made "dry" runs, where no enemy ships were destroyed. *Spadefish*, however, continued to be productive, sinking another nineteen enemy vessels with her torpedoes and guns. On each of her five war patrols, she destroyed at least four ships of varying size.

During her fifth war patrol, *Spadefish* was part of a nine-boat wolf pack which penetrated the minefields of Tsushima Strait to enter the Sea of Japan. The pack sunk or damaged more than 55 Japanese ships in a three-week span. *Spadefish* had been the first U.S. submarine to be equipped with frequency-modulated (FM) sonar, which allowed her to penetrate enemy minefields while submerged.

For the above reasons, my interest in bringing the *Spadefish* story to life can be understood.

Amazingly, no man who ever served on *Spadefish* was killed in action or subsequently lost on another submarine. More than 3,500 other U.S. submariners remain on "eternal patrol" aboard 52 boats lost during the war. In comparison, the Japanese lost 128 submarines and the Germans lost more than 700 U-boats. *Spadefish*'s first executive officer, Ted Ustick, lost sixteen of his class of 1939 U.S. Naval Academy fellow graduates aboard subs in World War II. "Of the roughly 16,000 men who fought in those combat boats, a little over 20% were lost," Ustick reflected in 1999. "Odds were 20-25% you wouldn't come home."

Unlike other United States Navy ships, submarines were often affectionately referred to as "boats" by the proud crews that manned them. "The first submarine was a boat that could be paddled," said Ustick. "Even the big modern nuclear submarines are still called boats."

U.S. submarines in World War II sank 1,113 Japanese merchant ships, totaling 4.8 million tons, and another 201 Imperial Japanese Navy vessels, adding up to 541,000 tons. This makes a total of 1,314 Japanese ships sunk for a 5.3 million gross ton total. U.S. submarines accounted for 55 per cent of all Japanese vessels sunk in World War II, although the submarine service only accounted for 1.5 per cent of the U.S. Navy.

Submarine skippers traditionally received the glory for the work of the crews they commanded. Selective wartime press helped promote the names of such brave skippers as Mush Morton, Dick O'Kane, Slade Cutter and Sam Dealey, among others. Equally daring but less quickly remembered were the two excellent wartime skippers of *Spadefish*: Gordon Waite Underwood and William Joseph Germershausen. Any good skipper would admit that he was only as good as his crew. For Underwood and Germershausen, they were truly blessed with one of the fighteningest crews in the Navy.

Both men were among the war's best skippers. Gemershausen and Underwood each turned in one of the 26 war patrols in which a U.S. submarine destroyed five or more enemy vessels whose individual weight was more than 500 tons. Underwood turned in two of the top ten best war patrols for tonnage sunk and ended up third highest U.S. submarine skipper of World War II in enemy tonnage destroyed, with the 14 ships for 75,386 tons he was credited.

The *Spadefish* crew was a tight knit family which operated well in very close quarters. Many commendations were handed out, to officers and enlisted men alike, for key contributions during the successful patrols. As former chief radioman Paul Majoue—who was awarded the

Bronze Star while aboard *Spadefish*– pointed out, however, "We didn't talk too much about medals. Anything we got, the whole boat had something to do with earning it."

In tribute to the brave men who manned and fought *Spadefish*, this book draws heavily upon both the ship's officers and crewmen to paint a picture of life aboard a submersible combat vessel that was one of the war's best. *Spadefish*'s triumphs are brought to life through the personal reflections contributed by more than four dozen of the men who took her to sea. They told their stories via personal and telephone interviews, correspondence, newspaper clippings, and newsletter stories. Family members of some of those now deceased also contributed photographs, audiotapes, military papers and even a private journal.

Although none perished aboard *Spadefish* in World War II, some of her escapes had been close. One particular close round of depth charges slammed *Spadefish* far below her test depth. During another patrol, anti-submarine vessels dragging chains with grapneling hooks made contact along her hull, trying to snag and destroy the underseas raider. On another patrol, *Spadefish*'s skipper steadfastly drove his submarine toward a Japanese harbor on the surface one night. *Spadefish* was within sight of an enemy airfield and she was overflown by an enemy aircraft with its landing lights on as it approached the airfield. *Spadefish* also narrowly escaped several Japanese destroyers and sub chasers on the surface which were firing shells over her conning tower. Several brave men remained topside to coordinate a torpedo attack against her pursuers–even as a miscommunication caused *Spadefish*'s engines to be shut down in the face of onrushing warships.

Aside from the many merchant vessels she sent to the bottom, *Spadefish* fearlessly attacked men of war. She destroyed a 21,000-ton aircraft carrier, a destroyer-type frigate, a submarine chaser and a patrol craft. She played a deadly game of cat and mouse in a bay on the coast of Luzon, stalking a Japanese destroyer that was guarding a crippled tanker already hit by *Spadefish*. Her crew manned her deck gun and bridge guns to sink five other smaller vessels. Four Japanese prisoners of war were transported back by *Spadefish* for intelligence purposes and five members of her crew even boarded an enemy vessel to seize maps and classified documents.

Prior to her commissioning, several crewmen brought a small dog aboard *Spadefish* to serve as the ship's mascot. Luau, the lovable beer drinking little terrier, gave birth to six puppies on the second war patrol. The dark-colored little male pup, named Seaweed, remained aboard *Spadefish* with Luau for the rest of the war.

Even periods ashore between patrols came with certain risk. *Spadefish* used new advance bases in the Pacific such as Saipan,

Majuro and Guam for several of her refits. During one such refit, five submariners from *Sea Fox* were killed by Japanese soldiers still prowling the jungles on Guam.

The sailors who manned *Spadefish* and made her one of America's top World War II submarines are not a boastful lot. They are immensely proud of the fine record their boat amassed. Many of them went decades without speaking much at all about their war experiences. Former *Spadefish* torpedoman Bert Spiese said," I went forty years before I could even read our Presidential Unit Citation."

The *Spadefish* crew has stayed in touch with each other via their quarterly newsletter, named "Luau" after the first ship's dog. Started by radioman Ken Powers, the "Luau" is now edited and distributed by Thomas "Buck" Miller and his girlfriend Peggy Ellis. One topic the *Spadefish* shipmates jestingly debated in the Luau concerned which department aboard ship did the most to help win the war. Miller prodded, "Auxiliarymen did. How you fire a fish without air pressure?" Quartermaster Bob Maxwell replied in another issue: "We always had the right time—knew where we were going and, let's face it, quartermasters steered you straight!" Even Captain Bill Germershausen added his opinion to the debate: "I'd say it was the pinup girls—Rita Hayworth, Betty Grable and those three anonymous bimbos displayed in *Spadefish*'s wardroom!"[1]

Rather than a narrative which just follows the submarine skipper through the pressure he faced in sinking ships, this story is told as often as possible by the common sailor as well as her officers. Every man aboard *Spadefish* had a job and each depended upon each other's ability to carry out his duties. An operational mishap could cost the lives of the eighty-five men aboard just as easily as an enemy counterattack could.

"I wouldn't take a million buck to have missed the experience," recalled former motor machinist's mate Charles Griffith. "But I wouldn't do it again for ten million!"

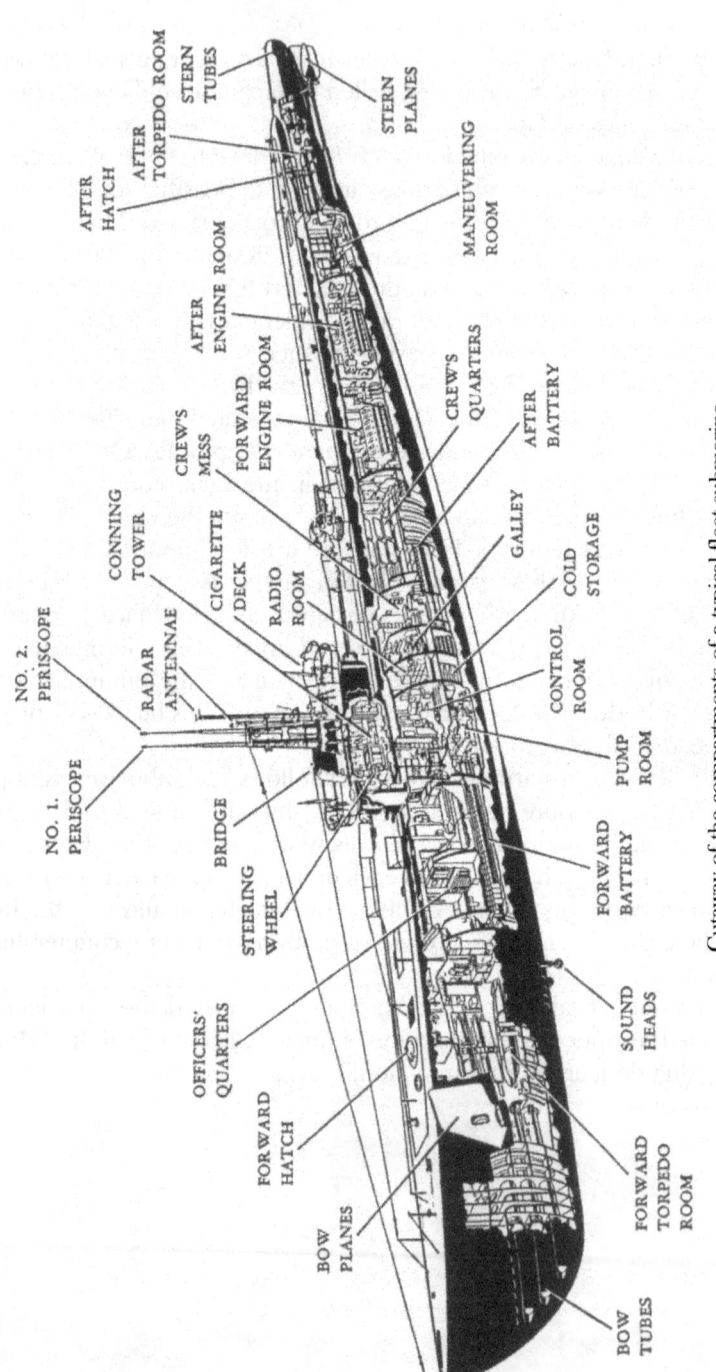

Cutaway of the compartments of a typical fleet submarine.

Acknowledgements

The story of *Spadefish*'s successes in the Pacific War would not have been possible without the participation of her brave crew. Their personal testimony is the heart and soul of this submarine story, just as they were the lifeblood of their ship sixty years ago.

I must thank all of the enlisted men and officers of *Spadefish* who openly shared their memories, papers and photographs from World War II. The direct contributors were, in alphabetical order: Don Anderson, Willard Battenfield, Harry Brenneis, John Brewer, Jim Casey, Dr. Harry Buncke, Jim Cole, Dan Decker, Willard Eimermann, Jack Gallagher, Dick Gamby, Alvin Gibson, Wayne Greening, Charles Griffith, Pat Kelley, Al La Rocca, Gus Laundy, Paul Majoue, Joe Marasco, Bernie Massar, Wallace McMahon, Thomas Miller, Olaf Olson, Neal Pike, Charles Rolf, Don Scholle, John Schumer, Mike Sergio, Ken Sigworth, Bert Spiese, and Perry Wood. From past experience in interviewing World War II veterans, I was honestly amazed at how openly each man shared his personal experiences with a stranger, particularly a non-submariner.

The sources for material throughout this book are well annotated in the chapter notes with the exception of the above *Spadefish* veterans. Their stories are intertwined on every page and precluded me from citing them dozens or even hundreds of times. The dates on which I interviewed each man are listed in the bibliography.

The children, grandchildren and siblings of other *Spadefish* veterans were equally supportive. Clair Ustick Bagley and Commander Perry W. Ustick, USN (Ret.), supplied speeches, audiotapes and photographs for personal input from the late Ted Ustick, the first executive officer of *Spadefish*. Don and Maury Martin provided photos and stories they had collected from their late grandfather, Carl Schmelzer. Copies of torpedoman Hugo Lundquist's journal, personal papers and photo collection were generously reproduced by his son, William A. Lundquist, courtesy of Mrs. Jeanne Lundquist. Bill also handled a number of my follow-up requests for images without hesitation. Ilona

Rymer shared the recollections and photos of her late husband Robert Rymer, a photographer who made a patrol aboard *Spadefish*.

Lucille Butchofsky, Argyle Charles, Honey Snider and Margaret Strong shared papers, photos and stories concerning their late husbands. Thanks also to the contributions of Robert Ives (son of Victor Ives), Sandra Powers Wilson (daughter of Ken Powers), and to Kathy Ware Grant (daughter of Bill Ware). My apologies to anyone I have neglected to mention.

Thomas "Buck" Miller and Peggy Ellis were kind enough to copy ten years worth of the "Luau" newsletter, the *Spadefish* quarterly which held priceless recollections from many former crewmen and officers. Captain Richard M. Wright's oral history was made available by East Carolina University's J. Y. Joyner Library. John Waggener of the University of Wyoming American Heritage Center went the extra mile to successfully locate a 1970s interview with the late Captain William J. Germershausen, taped by Clay Blair Jr. for his superb book on the U.S. submarine war, *Silent Victory*.

Steven Trent Smith, author of *The Rescue* and *Wolf Pack*, put me in touch with the first few *Spadefish* veterans I interviewed. My brother-in-law, David L. Hunt, assisted greatly by searching out addresses and phone numbers for *Spadefish* veterans. Naval historian Anthony P. Tully kindly shared much of his research on Japanese convoys HI-71 and HI-81, as well as vital Japanese ship data. Wendy Gulley of the Submarine Force Museum in Groton, Connecticut, helped research and scan photographs of *Spadefish* and her crew. Patrick R. Osborn of the National Archives and Records Administration's Modern Military Records division went above and beyond in pulling copies of commendation citations for the submarine's officers and enlisted men. Artist Diane Rome Peebles kindly granted permission to include her illustration of an Atlantic spadefish.

Dan Decker, Bernie Massar, Buck Miller and Bert Spiese provided their eyewitness and technical expertise in reading through draft versions of this manuscript for accuracy. This group helped me "keep a zero bubble" throughout the process. Dan and Bernie, in particular, each fielded endless questions and mailed me dozens of letters to ensure that events were reported accurately. Dan and his daughter, Julie Decker, made a first-rate editorial team, typing up extensive notes, corrections and suggestions for each chapter. Finally, I must thank my family, particularly David H. and Patsy Hunt, for their patience and support in bringing the *Spadefish* story to life.

To all of those valiant submariners who allowed me to witness World War II through their experiences, this book is dedicated.

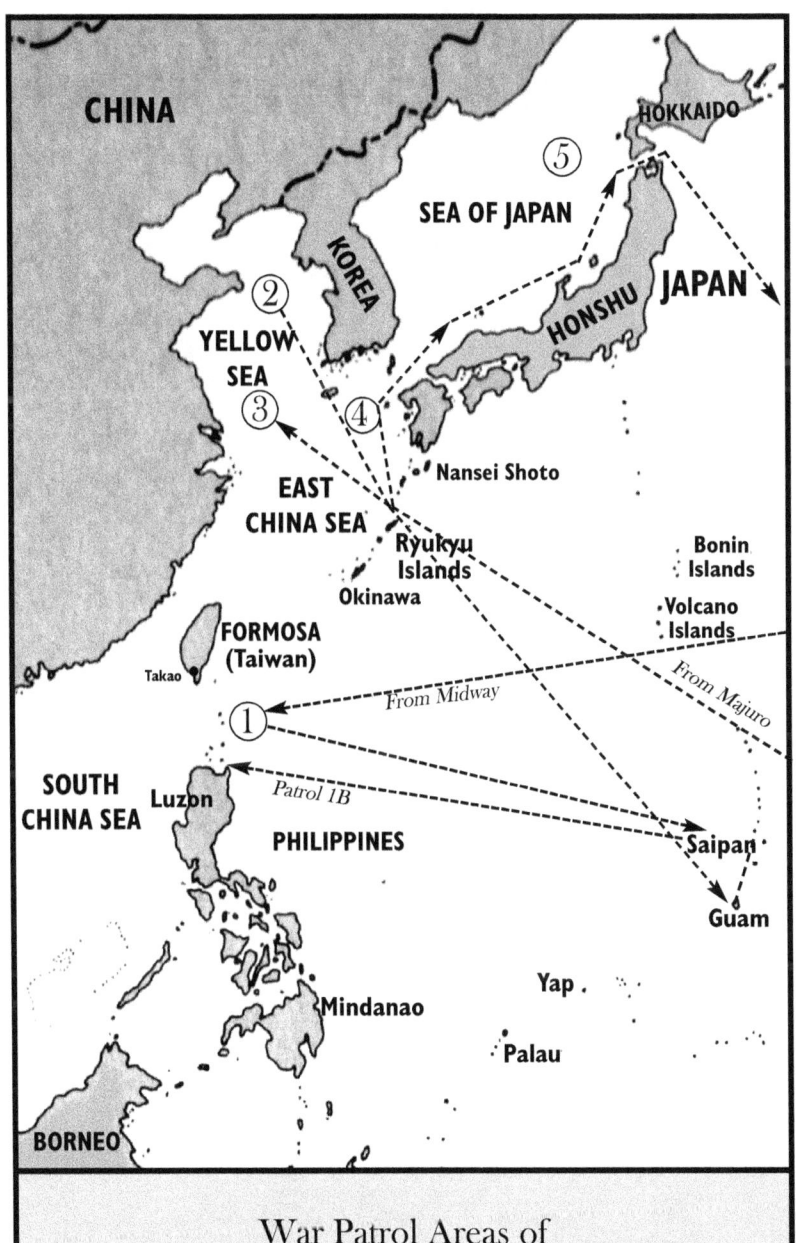

War Patrol Areas of
USS Spadefish (SS-411) in World War II

23 July 1944–4 July 1945

USS Spadefish World War II Roster
Commissioning through Fifth Patrol: 9 March 1944 - August 1945

Note: The first rank or rate for officers and crew indicates highest held during *Spadefish*'s fifth war patrol. Previous ranks and rates held are also shown.

1c	First Class	Lt.(jg)	Lieutenant, Junior Grade
2c	Second Class	MoMM	Motor Machinist's Mate
3c	Third Class	PhM	Pharmacist's Mate
BM	Boatswain's Mate	QM	Quartermaster
C	Chief Petty Officer (CPO)	RM	Radioman
CCS	Chief Commissary Steward	RT	Radio Technician
Cdr.	Commander	S	Seaman
Ck	Cook	SC	Ship's Cook
EM	Electrician's Mate	SM	Signalman
Ens.	Ensign	ST	Steward
F	Fireman	StM	Steward's Mate
FCS	Fire Controlman, Surface Weapons	TM	Torpedoman's Mate
		WM	Warrant Machinist
GM	Gunner's Mate	Y	Yeoman
Lt.	Lieutenant		

* Indicates sailor aboard at time of commissioning. If no further number is shown, he left before start of first patrol.
** Sailor who joined at Mare Island before first patrol.

OFFICERS

Name:	Rank:	Patrols:
Underwood, Gordon Waite	Cdr.	*1-3
Germershausen, William Joseph Jr.	Cdr.	4-5
Ustick, Theodore Montanye	Lt. Cdr./Lt.	*1-2
Alvis, Frank Ryals	Lt.	*1-2
Cook, George Carlton	Lt.	3-4
Laundy, Henry Howard, Jr.	Lt.	*1-3
Decker, Daniel Delos, Jr.	Lt./Lt.(jg)	*1-5
Fellows, Richard Decatur	Lt.	4-5
Wright, Richard Morgan	Lt.	5
La Croix, Edward J.	Lt.(jg)	3-5
Wood, Perry Satterthwaite	Lt.(jg)/Ens.	*1-5

Name	Rank	Patrols
Ware, William James	Ens.	*1-5
Buncke, Harry Jacob, Jr.	Ens.	5
Dix, Raymond E.	Ens.	5
Johnson, Charles C.	Ens.	3-4
Martin, Donald Ernest	Ens.	1-4
White, Ray Curtis	Ens.	*1-2
Falconer, LeRoy Douglas	WM/CMoMM	*1-5

ENLISTED MEN:

Name:	Rank:	Patrols:
Anderson, Benjamin Herschel	RT3c	*
Anderson, Donald Carl	TM3c/S1c	2-4
Armstrong, Edward Richard	PhoM2c	5
Asher, Warren Jay	EM3c/F1c	2-5
Babb, Maurice Lee, Jr.	F1c	5
Barger, Clarence Randolf	CQM	*
Barnes, Silas Marion	TM1c/2c	*1-4
Barton, Thad Ralph	TM2c/3c/S1c	*1-5
Bassett, Richard Harold	EM3c/F1c/2c/S2c	*1-5
Bieberdorf, Carl Christopher	CMoMM/1c	**1-3
Bird, Donald William	TM2c/3c	*1-2
Brenneis, Harry Jerome	MoMM3c/F1c	2-5
Brewer, John Belton, Jr.	MoMM3c/F1c	2-5
Brooks, Sie (n), Jr.	StM1c	3-5
Butchofsky, Richard David	TM2c	*
Bynum, William Thomas	St3c/StM1c	4-5
Carney, Hugh Patrick	TM3c/S1c	3-5
Case, Joseph Bennion	RT1c/2c	**1-5
Casey, James David	EM3c	5
Charles, Walter Joseph, Jr.	FC3c	4-5
Chiavacci, Louis Joseph	S1c/2c	*1-2
Cohen, Solomon (n)	RT2c	**
Cole, James Douglas	F1c	5
Cooper, Samuel (n)	QM2c/3c	*1
Cruze, Herman Franklin, Jr.	EM2c/3c	*1-5
Cunningham, Edwin William	MoMM2c	4-5
Cuthbertson, John Marshall	TM2c	*1-5
De Loney, Adam (n)	Ck3c	**
Dependahl, Leonard Edward	EM1c/2c/3c	*1-5
Drew, Wesley Arthur	EM1c/2c	*1-3
Dunleavy, Anthony (n) Jr.	MoMM3c/F1c	2-5
Eimermann, Willard Christ	CBM/1c	*1-5
Fautley, James Walter	F1c	2

Fletcher, James Wallace	QM2c	3-5
Frazier, Dale Wayne	SM2c/3c	*1-2
Gallagher, Jack Ambrose	EM3c/F1c	*1-4
Gamby, Orville Richard	MoMM2c/3c	*1-5
George, Harry (n)	CTM/1c	**1-3
Gibson, Alvin Wilson	S1c	3
Gouker, Zelbert (n)	SM2c/3c	4-5
Graf, Edward Frank	SC2c/3c	*1-5
Graff, Benjamin Pennybaker Jr.	EM3c/F1c	2-4
Graff, Charles Alfred	S1c	5
Gregory, Earl Owen	CEM	*
Griffith, Charles Clain	CMoMM/1c	*1-5
Harbison, Joseph Albert	MoMM2c/3c/F1c	*1-5
Hatch, Carlton (n)	S2c	4
Hobbs, Jessie Burl	EM3c	**
Holeman, Victor Rolla	MoMM1c/2c	*1-5
Hord, Cleveland Maybee	F1c	4-5
Ingberg, Norval Owen	QM3c/S1c	3-5
Ives, Victor Leon	CPhM(AA)/1c	**1-5
Jackson, Robert Franklin	MoMM2c	*1
Jerolmon, Walter Edward	MoMM3c	2-4
Keeney, William Jackson, Jr.	RT2c	4-5
Kelley, William Patrick	MoMM2c/3c	*1-5
Kite, Vernon Joseph	TM1c	5
Kreher, Emery Andrew	TM1c/2c	*1-5
Kreinbring, Irwin Henry	Y1c/2c	*1-5
LaFose, Murphy (n)	F1c/2c	5
Larkie, Arthur Edward	StM1c	*
La Rocca, Albert George	EM3c	5
Lester, Clifford Robert	MoMM3c	4-5
Lewis, Edgar Lycurgous	CGM/1c	*1-5
Lundquist, Hugo Carl	TM2c/3c	*1-5
Mainard, Bill Jack	RM2c	3-4
Majoue, Paul Henry, Jr.	CRM/1c	*1-5
Manson, Robert Thomas	SC3c	3-4
Massar, Bernard Adam	GM2c/3c	*1-5
Maxwell, Robert Elmer	QM3c/S1c/2c	*1-4
McLaughlin, Paul Francis	MoMM2c	*1-2
McMahon, Wallace Francis	TM3c/S1c	*1-5
Melstrand, Howard Walfred	S1c	5
Mikesell, Robert Edward	S1c/2c	5
Miller, Thomas Harry	MoMM2c/3c	*1-5
Mitzel, Joseph Emanuel	CMoMM(T)	*1-2
Moody, Roy Hubert	EM1c/2c	*1-5

Morrison, James Walter	RM3c/S1c/2c	4-5
Mullen, Melvin "C"	MoMM3	**1-5
Nesnee, John (n)	TM2c/3c/S1c	*1-5
Newton, Gerald Arthur	RM1c	*1-2
Noonan, Maurice Anthony	GM3c/S1c/F2c	*1-5
Nordstrom, Edwin George	F1c	**1
Nudd, Alton George	GM1c	**
Olah, Andrew (n)	FCS1c/2c/3c	*1-5
Olsen, Norman Androus	EM1c	*1-2
O'Neil, Thomas Patrick	RM3c/S1c	3-5
Ordway, Emerson Locke	CEM/1c	*1-5
Panek, Edmund Edward	RM3c	*1
Parker, Billy Rice	CPhM(PA)	*
Parscale, James Stewart	SM2c	**1-2
Partin, Doyle Burline	TM2c/3c	*1-3
Paulson, Roger Francis	F1c/S1c/2c	5
Peel, John Richard	CMoMM/1c/2c	*1-5
Pelliciari, Nicholas John	MoMM2c/3c/F1c	*1-5
Pierce, Sam Henry	MoMM1c	3-5
Pigman, Billy Bob	EM2c/3c	**1-5
Pike, Neal (n)	CRT/1c	*1-5
Pirrung, Edward Nicklous	SC1c	**1-2
Pizzini, Fabian Frank	EM2c	**1
Portwood, William Marshall	StM1c/2c	**1-2
Potting, Roy Christian	Y2c/3c	4-5
Powell, Wayne Hobart	EM2c/3c	*1-3
Powers, Kenneth Clyde	RM2c/3c/S1c/2c	*1-5
Price, James Edward	S1c/2c	*1
Randall, Augustus Lockhart	EM3c	**1
Rewold, Radford Crowell	CMoMM/1c	*1-5
Riley, Thomas Gordon	SC1c/2c/3c	*1-5
Ring, Joseph John	MoMM2c	5
Roberts, William Arthur	F1c	3-4
Rolf, Charles Frederick	S1c/2c	2-3
Rymer, Robert Hamilton	PhoM1c	4
Sandleben, Olaf Bernard (Olson)	TM3c/S1c	3-5
Scheerer, Robert Allen	MoMM1c/2c	3-4
Scherman, Francis Julian	CCS(PA)	*1-5
Schmelzer, Carl Thomas	CEM(PA)	*1-5
Scholle, Donald Joseph	QM3c/S1c/2c	*1-3, 5
Schuett, James Shirley	SM1c	*1-5
Schumer, John Martin	TM3c	2-4
Sergio, Michael (n)	RM1c/2c	*1-5
Shaw, Thomas Eugene	EM3c/F1c	3-5

Sigworth, Kenneth Leroy	EM2c/3c	*1-5
Simms, William Wallace Jr.	CTM(T)	**1
Snider, Cameron Frederick	S1c	2
Solomon, Henry Lewis	St3c/Ck3c/StM1c	*1-3
Spiese, Albert Lewis	TM3c	*1
Stanford, Jack (n)	MoMM2c/3c	**1-2
Taylor, John Wright	MoMM1c	5
Terboss, William Frederick	TM3c/S1c	3-5
Waleszonia, Alexander John Jr.	CTM(AA)	*
Weidner, Delbert Clinton Jr.	MoMM3c/F1c	*1
Wells, Francis Arthur	CTM	4-5
Yates, Palmus Lamar	MoMM1c	*1
Yocum, David Pier	MoMM1c/2c	*1-3

Forty officers and men that commissioned *Spadefish* made all five runs. Four other men who joined after her commissioning made all five war patrols. Six that commissioned her made no runs.

NEW HANDS RECEIVED PRIOR TO WAR'S END

Name:	Rate/Rank:	Date:
Battenfield, Willard Elvas	TM1c	8/22/45
Brinkman, Gerald Adelbert Jr.	F1c	7/26/45
Clawson, Meredith Thomas	S1c	7/26/45
Code, Thomas Joseph	S1c	7/26/45
Ericson, Robert Alfred	S1c	7/26/45
Gillespie, Robert Wayne	CPhM	7/26/45
Greening, Wayne Albert	F1c	7/26/45
Hamilton, Paul Jackson	TM2c	7/26/45
Houser, Gordon Lee	F1c	7/26/45
La Croix, Alvin Maurice	TM1c	8/11/45
Larkin, Alfred Lawrence Jr.	MoMM1c	7/26/45
Marasco, Ralph Joseph Jr.	RM3c	7/26/45
Noblit, William James	GM1c	7/26/45
Prast, James Leroy	S1c	7/26/45
Schraft, William Ernest	RM1c	7/26/45
Shearer, Everett (n) Jr.	EM3c	7/26/45
Sherman, Vernon Fred	F1c	7/26/45
Smith, Raymond Charles	S1c	7/26/45
Stephenson, Arnold John	MoMM1c	9/1/45
Strong, Louis Edward	CCS	8/3/45
Wall, James D.	Lt.(jg)	7/7/45
Way, Angus Park	F1c	7/26/45

PASSENGERS:
J. C. Casey   Rep. of Fairbanks Morse
F. F. Flaig   General Electric Rep.
(Both men sailed on 11 May 1944 from Mare Island Navy Yard aboard *Spadefish* to San Diego.)

USS Spadefish (SS-411), stern view off Mare Island Navy Yard, with lookouts on her periscope shears, taken on 11 May 1944. *Official U.S. Navy photo.*

Mare Island and Luau

Commissioning   *January–March 1944*

By all expectations, the new submarine's first deep dive should have been uneventful.

The reassuring thump of valves slamming shut indicated that the main induction was properly sealed, shutting off the oxygen supply to the big diesels that drove the ship. When open, the main induction took in oxygen from the sky through a pipe that ran up through the superstructure. Parallel to the main induction, a smaller tube ran the length of the submarine to supply ventilation to all compartments. The air passages to both of these inductions were sealed by hydraulic valves upon diving.

The roar of the diesel engines had ceased and battery power took over the ship's propulsion underwater. In the control room, the senior chief petty officer, Chief Electrician's Mate (CEM) Earl Owen Gregory, watched the hull opening indicator light panel known as the "Christmas Tree." Having enlisted in the Navy on 23 December 1941, immediately after Pearl Harbor, Chief Gregory was well qualified in submarines. Only two months after putting his new sub into commission, he had been promoted to chief of the boat, or senior enlisted man aboard, to replace his predecessor.

Each of the lights on the panel in front of Gregory changed from red to green, showing that all hull openings on the submarine were properly closed. In order to check for leaks, a blast of compressed air was blown into the sub. The barometer rose, a good sign that the ship was watertight.

"Green board," called Gregory. "Pressure in the boat."

It was a customary process, but one that meant the difference between life and death. The *Squalus* (SS-192) had been in the process of making a trial dive on 23 May 1939, off Portsmouth, New Hampshire, when disaster struck. Her main induction valve failed to close, and her Christmas tree had shown a safe green. As she submerged, however, the open valve caused massive flooding which had caused her to sink to the bottom, 240 feet below. Twenty-six sailors drowned. Incredibly, 33 of the *Squalus* submariners were rescued thanks to an experimental McCann diving bell and the ingenuity of Lieutenant Commander Charles B. "Swede" Momsen. He was co-inventor of the McCann rescue bell and the "Momsen lung." Momsen had gone to great risk to personally test helium-oxygen breathing air mixtures for ascending from depths. Worn around one's neck and filled with oxygen, the vest he designed was planned to allow a man to exit a sunken submarine from around 200 feet below the surface. It was not until October 1944 that some of the survivors of the *USS Tang* successfully escaped from the bottom of the ocean with a Momsen lung.[1]

In May 1944, five years after the *Squalus* mishap, the possibility of how such a simple mechanical or human error could end in death was never far from the minds of the crew manning the new United States submarine *Spadefish* (SS-411). "Your life literally depends on each other," said Lieutenant Ted Ustick, *Spadefish*'s executive officer. "One guy opens the wrong valve and it can cost you the whole boat." The men had made many successful dives already, but this was the day to test the ship's strength at depth.[2]

In the cold Pacific waters off San Francisco, *Spadefish* was to descend to 425 feet to test the integrity of her watertight hull. The ship had already performed extensive maneuvers while still in contact with the escort vessel which had accompanied her out to sea. Finally, it was time to do the deep dive.

With pressure in the boat, Captain Gordon Underwood began with *Spadefish* at operating depth, under the watchful eyes of shipyard superintendents. The skipper began to take her down, issuing orders to diving officer Frank Alvis in the control room. There was no crash dive this day, but instead a slow and methodical deep submergence. Another officer, Dan Decker, remembered: "At 100 foot intervals, we went deeper, checking at length the integrity, buoyancy and performance of all systems."

As *Spadefish* passed the 400 foot mark, the men watched closely for any abnormal signs of strain. "There were all sorts of little leaks, which was expected," recalled Ensign Perry Wood. Senior petty officers manned phones in all compartments to report leaks or signs of any severe stress. They made note of any little imperfections that would need further yard work later.

Deep submergence was critical, as the Imperial Japanese Navy was known to be setting depth charges deeper in 1944. This was thanks in large part to Congressman Andrew Jackson May, a 68-year-old member of the House Military Affairs Committee. Returning from a war zone junket in June 1943, he boasted in a press interview that the Japanese were setting their depth charges too shallow to destroy U.S. submarines. After the press ran the story, Admiral Charles Lockwood, in charge of the Pacific submarine fleet, wrote his boss that Congressman May "would be pleased to know the Japs set 'em deeper now." Lockwood bitterly wrote postwar, "I consider that indiscretion cost us ten submarines and 800 officers and men."[3]

After this blunder, Japanese depth charges increased from 242 pounds of high explosive to 357 pounds. They had generally been set to detonate at 100, 200 or 300 foot depths. By 1944, the more powerful explosives, known as "blockbusters" to submariners, could also be set to detonate at 400 or 500 feet.[4]

The earlier *Gato* class World War II submarines had 11/16" steel hulls and were test rated at 312 feet. Being of the newest *Balao* class, *Spadefish* had a thicker pressure hull, made of 7/8" of high-tensile steel. Her test depth was officially listed at 400 feet, meaning that she had a 100 percent safety factor at that depth. The deeper the ship dove, the more the tremendous pressure of the sea compressed her hull. In theory, a "thick-skinned" *Balao* class submarine was strong enough to descend hundreds of feet beyond her test depth without her pressure hull imploding, but few skippers found the desire to test their boat to extremes.

Spadefish's steel hull was designed to compress as it encountered more severe pressure at extreme depths. When *Spadefish* surfaced later, her hull would return to its normal shape, just as designed.

The escort vessel accompanying *Spadefish* with her diving tests off San Francisco tracked her via sonar from the surface. During the dive, she passed under a water temperature gradient that terminated communications with the surface. "This gradient, which we always recorded, was a submariner's best friend," recalled Lt.(jg) Decker. "It was a place to hide but it was not always available." When being hunted by enemy surface ships, such a temperature gradient could be a true lifesaver. Ensign Wood further explained, "The temperature inversion acts like a mirror that the surface craft can't hear through, so they lost contact with us."

Such a gradient should not have been unexpected. "At each level, much time was spent with all the observations and tests," said Decker. *Spadefish* was fine and went about her lengthy testing, oblivious to the fact that the escort above was concerned.

Spadefish reached 425 feet and operated as expected, checking out fine. Although the surface contact had been lost, the crew went on about its tests. She stayed down for some time and slowly returned to the surface later. When Captain Underwood brought his ship back to the surface, he found that his escort ship was long gone.

While heading back toward port, one of the lookouts, Gunner's Mate Third Class (GM3/c) Bernie Massar, found several boats looking for *Spadefish*. The ship's history notes:

> Surfacing a few hours later, they found the escort had departed. The *Spadefish* proceeded to port, discovering she had been reported sunk in 1200 feet of water. Blimps, planes, and small craft had been ordered out to search for survivors, boat, or wreckage. This was only one of the times the *Spadefish* was reported sunk.[5]

The Japanese propagandist Tokyo Rose would later make claims to have sunk *Spadefish*, but it was the first time the U.S. Navy had believed her to be lost!

SS-411 had been launched four months earlier on 8 January 1944. Dignitaries stood on the christening platform, including the wife of the Navy yard's captain, Mrs. Francis W. Scanland. She had been given the honor this day to officially name the United States Navy's newest submersible warship. Topside on the submarine were a number of the yard workers who had helped build her thus far. With them were four officers, three chief petty officers and a handful of other sailors who were charged with manning and fighting this ship upon its completion.[6]

Beside Mrs. Scanland was thirty-three-year-old Commander Gordon Waite Underwood, the prospective commanding officer of the new vessel. From her periscope shears, commissioning pennants were stretched forward to her stem and aft to her stern. Upon the signal of a yard whistle, she smashed the bottle of champagne against the ship's stem, proclaiming, "I christen thee *Spadefish*."

Like all new subs, *Spadefish* was named for a fish. An Atlantic *spadefish* (chaetodipterus faber) was a deep-bodied, spiny-finned food fish found in the warmer parts of the western Atlantic from Cape Cod to Cuba to the northern Caribbean Sea around the Cayman Islands. A spadefish is a reef dwelling fish characterized by barred black and white markings.

Spadefish then began to move and rapidly gained speed as she rolled down the ways toward the water. Once afloat, she was powerless, pulled back to a dockside berth by yard tugs. She was a long way from complete, but was beginning to take shape.

For Gordon Underwood, *Spadefish* was to be his first command. He had only recently been promoted to full commander in December 1943 while *Spadefish* was under construction. Born in Jamestown,

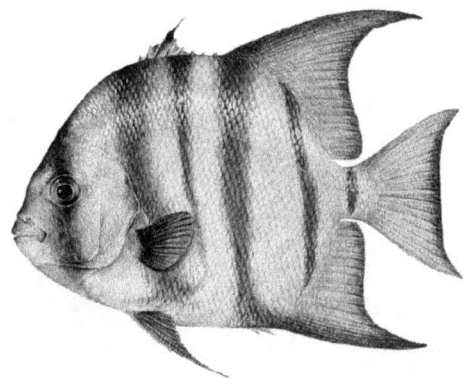

Like all U.S. Navy submarines, *Spadefish* was named for a fish, the Atlantic spadefish shown here. *Illustration courtesy of Diane Rome Peebles.*

New York, on 3 June 1910, he had entered the Navy on 9 July 1928 to attend the U.S. Naval Academy. A member of the Navy's football team, he had been rated an All-American by *Liberty* magazine. Underwood was the starting center for Annapolis in the big Notre Dame game and had been nominated as the best center. "He was not really a big guy, but he was tough," recalled one of his fellow *Spadefish* officers, Gus Laundy. He was commissioned an ensign upon graduating on 2 June 1932 and reported aboard the battleship *Oklahoma* as an engineering and gunnery junior officer. Underwood spent three months at the Naval Academy in the fall of 1932 as assistant football coach.[7]

Ensign Underwood served in the gunnery division aboard the battleship *Colorado* from March to June 1934. He married Marion Outerson of Los Angeles in 1934 and the couple would later have two sons. Following his battleship duty, Underwood then reported to submarine school at the Submarine Base, New London, Connecticut. While there through December of 1934, Underwood also coached the football team.

In January 1935 he joined the *S-27*, an older submarine that had been launched in 1924. Underwood served on *S-27* until August 1936, rising to the rank of Lieutenant, junior grade (j.g.) while aboard. During the next three years, he returned to surface ships, serving aboard the *Mississippi* and *USS Vega*. He returned to Annapolis in July 1939 to attend U.S. Naval Postgraduate School. Underwood then went on to Massachusetts Institute of Technology (MIT) from July 1941 to May 1942 to study Naval Engineering.

While serving as Division Engineer for Submarine Division 110, he was promoted to Lieutenant Commander in August 1942. Underwood also served as Squadron Engineer for Submarine Squadron 10 through May 1943, before finally heading out on his first submarine war patrol. Underwood reported aboard the submarine *Tunny* (SS-283) as

With commissioning pennants streaming, *Spadefish* rolls down the ways at Mare Island on 8 January 1944, and floats freely for the first time with officials and members of her crew topside. *Top: courtesy of Cdr. Perry W. Ustick, USN (Ret.). Right: Carl Schmelzer collection, courtesy of Donald Martin and Maury Martin.*

Executive Officer to Captain John Addison Scott. *Tunny*, making her third patrol, sunk one 1,964-ton Japanese converted gunboat off the Marianas on Lt. Cdr. Underwood's first patrol. On her fourth patrol, she was assigned to the area of Palau, but managed only to claim damage to three freighters.

Upon returning from this patrol in September 1943, Underwood was transferred to the New London Submarine Base for additional instruction. There, he was promoted to Commander and notified that he was to report to the construction of *USS Spadefish* at Mare Island.

Because of his time coaching football at Annapolis and at New London, a few of the sub force commanders, such as Admiral Lockwood, had nicknamed Gordon Underwood "Coach." But, aboard his new submarine *Spadefish*, he was never called "Coach." The only names that his men or wardroom officers addressed him as were "Captain" or "Skipper."

Commander Gordon Waite Underwood was the first skipper of *Spadefish*. He was a highly decorated World War II skipper and finished with the third highest tonnage of enemy ships sunk. *Official U.S. Navy photo, courtesy of USS Underwood.*

Commander Underwood's crew began to learn more about their new CO during their days of training at Mare Island. His command style and daring nature would cause his crew to respect him deeply.

Having been launched, *Spadefish* was scheduled to be commissioned into the U.S. Navy in two months. A considerable amount of work remained to be done, installing everything from the 252 cells of the two main electrical batteries, which would drive her while submerged, to all kinds of sophisticated new equipment.

Spadefish was one of seventeen fleet-type submarines built at the Mare Island Naval Shipyard in Vallejo, California, during World War II. Established in 1854 in the San Francisco Bay area, the naval shipyard at Mare Island had first been commanded by Commander David Farragut. In order, the attack submarines constructed at Mare Island and commissioned during the second world war were: *Silversides*,

Trigger, Wahoo, Whale, Sunfish, Tunny, Tinosa, Tullibee, Seahorse, Skate, Tang, Tilefish, Spadefish, Trepang, Spot, Springer and *Stickleback*. Eight of these submarines would be among the top 20 producers in terms of enemy shipping sunk during World War II.

A fleet submarine was the only U.S. Navy attack vessel commonly referred to as both a "ship" and a "boat" without invoking the ire of its crew. "We called submarines boats," second officer Ted Ustick later explained. "The first submarine was a boat that could be paddled. Even the big modern nuclear submarines are still called boats." The Navy allotted hull number SS-411 to *USS Spadefish* and her keel was laid at Mare Island on May 27, 1943. She was destined to be one of the *Balao* class submarines.

She displaced 1,870 tons surfaced and 2,391 tons submerged, with her extra ballast. She was 311'7" with a 27'4" beam. Her normal complement of officers and crewmen was listed as 81. *Spadefish* was capable of making 20 knots with her four Fairbanks Morse diesel engines. She had one 5-inch, .25-caliber deck gun mounted on her after deck, plus two 20-millimeter (mm) machine guns, one mounted forward and one aft on her bridge. *Spadefish* also carried two spare 20mms that could be remounted topside during patrol. Once one of the mounted guns began to show the effects of salt water corrosion, it would be replaced and taken down below for cleaning.

In addition to her deck guns, she could carry 24 torpedoes, each 21 feet long and weighing more than 2,000 pounds. She carried sixteen torpedoes in her forward torpedo room, which had six tubes from which to launch the deadly missiles. In her tail end, *Spadefish* had another four tubes and eight torpedoes in her after torpedo room.

Although Commander Underwood had a core group of his crew aboard at *Spadefish*'s christening, the majority of the ship's company began arriving in January and February. Among the crewmen on hand during the early weeks at Mare Island was eighteen-year-old Torpedoman's Mate Third Class (TM3c) Albert Lewis Spiese, who had enlisted in the Navy in February 1943. Bert came from the small town of Columbia, Pennsylvania, where he grew up with seven brothers and five sisters. "We knew what poor was!" Assigned to *Spadefish*'s forward torpedo room, he found the early days lacking for action. "There were very few of us when they mustered us in those days," recalled Spiese. "They would pick us to stand fire watches under the superstructure while they were welding it."

One large group of men had been off the Florida Keys receiving valuable training aboard an old World War I era boat, *R-20*. Gunner's Mate 3/c Bernard Adam Massar was part of the recent New London graduate group which had just reported from training aboard the old

R-20. Massar says, "There were about 15 of us who went down to Key West and got aboard the *R-20* for practice. It was an old clunker from World War I. The *Spadefish* had just launched and they didn't need us yet, so they kept us down there." Electrician's Mate 3/c Kenneth Sigworth was another of the new hands who had trained on *R-20*. "We came cross-country aboard a train from Key West to San Francisco to join *Spadefish*," he said.

While the work continued aboard ship, *Spadefish*'s new crew took the time to learn every inch of her. Their ship was moored alongside a dock at Mare Island while the shipyard workers swarmed over her 24 hours a day to keep schedule. Across the street from the dock was a building where Underwood's crew was allowed to operate. There was a large, locked storage area on the ground floor to house incoming gear that was to eventually be installed on *Spadefish*.

On the second floor were several rooms, including a large classroom. Underwood's second senior officer, 28-year-old Lieutenant Theodore Montanye Ustick, was in charge of seeing that those men who manned their submarine were properly qualified. "Ted" Ustick, a 1939 Naval Academy graduate and veteran of nine war patrols aboard the submarine *Tarpon*, had reported aboard as Underwood's Executive Officer and Navigator. Known to the crew as the "Exec" or "XO," Ustick was responsible for carrying out all of the CO's orders.

During his teen years, Ted Ustick acquired a love of ships while working at Long Beach, California. Perry Ustick, who followed Ted into a Navy career, found his older brother to be a continual source of inspiration. "Ted strove to achieve the highest position he could in whatever organization he entered. He was an Eagle Scout in the Boy Scouts and a Quartermaster in the Sea Scouts." Ustick entered the Naval Academy in September 1934 but suffered from appendicitus in December and had to return home. He assisted in the production details of the Clark Gable movie "Mutiny on the Bounty" by acquiring and renting boats to the movie crew the next summer.

In September 1935, Ted Ustick was able to return to Annapolis to complete his appointment. Like Gordon Underwood, Ustick played varsity football while a midshipman at the Academy. He was also a member of the crew and rifle team for one year. Following his graduation in June 1939, Ensign Ustick served for a year aboard the battleship *Arizona* in the engineering division.[8]

After less than a year, Ustick put in for a transfer to avoid the "spit and polish" of battleship life. "I didn't go more than a quarter of a mile to go from one ship to another in Pearl Harbor," he said. He served as the torpedo and gunnery officer and first lieutenant aboard the destroyer *Alwyn* (DD-355) through December 1940. Ustick reported to New London for sub school and was subsequently assigned to *Tarpon* in August 1941, which he was aboard at Cavite in the Philippines when World War II commenced. During his nine war patrols on *Tarpon*, Ustick held the positions of Gunnery, Torpedo, Communications and finally Executive Officer. He was awarded the Silver Star for his work as the TDC operator on *Tarpon*'s sixth patrol in sinking two very large merchant ships.[9]

Once ordered back to Mare Island, Ustick married a Navy nurse, Claire Marie Parsons of Vallejo, in December 1943. Upon reporting to *Spadefish*, Lieutenant Ustick worked with the new and unqualified *Spadefish* crew members. Part of becoming qualified as a submarine sailor was knowing all there was to know about the ship. "We had work books to complete, and went daily aboard the boat to observe and learn in detail," recalled Bernie Massar. "We'd go aboard the boat and trace the lines." They would also talk with the Mare Island workmen about specific parts of the installations, as they followed *Spadefish* through her final construction. "We studied the whole ship—everything about her."

Lieutenant Theodore Montanye "Ted" Ustick speaking at *Spadefish*'s commissioning party. A veteran of nine previous war patrols, Ustick was second in command of *Spadefish* during her first two patrols. *Courtesy of Cdr. Perry W. Ustick, USN (Ret.).*

Of course, the school room had an endless supply of coffee to keep the sub students alert. "There was always one guy assigned to making it," Massar remembered. "Tom Miller never drank it, so he made about the lousiest coffee!"

Training on a World War II fleet submarine was on-going. "School of the boat" would continue even on war patrols as newer men tried to qualify as true submariners. Only when a sailor could demonstrate knowledge of all operations of the ship was he able to earn his dolphins. Officers wore a gold twin dolphin pin while wartime enlisted men earned a cloth twin dolphin patch which was sewn on their right forearm just above the wrist.

When the crew did have down time during the early training days, they could travel from Mare Island to Vallejo via a small ferry. Tom Miller and his buddies would bring back a couple of hamburgers for electrician Herman Cruze. "We hurried, but it was close to impossible to bring hot hamburgers back," recalled Miller. "They were lukewarm at best." When the time came for Cruze to reciprocate during his Vallejo visit, the burgers he brought back were "stone cold. He must have went via Seattle." Bernie Massar agreed that Cruze would "return to the barracks and wake us up at 2 or 3 in the morning with cold and soggy burgers. He must have walked all night with our burgers."[10]

Ted Ustick's right-hand man in training the crew was Chief Torpedoman Alexander Waleszonia, the chief of the boat. This key position, equivalent to an Army top sergeant, was often filled by the most senior rated enlisted man aboard. The skipper and Exec chose this man based largely on his ability to lead, and not solely on his rating. The chief of the boat served as a go-between with the XO and CO. Those aboard *Spadefish* would learn that the chief of the boat was not always a chief petty officer.

The enlisted men Ustick and Waleszonia began shaping into watch sections had already been to Submarine School at New London, where they had studied diesel engines, torpedoes, electric batteries, and torpedo fire control. Each student had also been trained in escaping a sunken submarine in a 100-foot water tank, using the Momsen lung underwater breathing device.

When *Spadefish*'s senior radioman Paul Henry Majoue Jr. had entered New London's diving tank, he was not alarmed at all. As a kid in Louisiana, he built a diving helmet out of a hot water heater and went down 35 feet in a canal. His buddies were afraid to try it, but offered to pump air into his tank through 50 feet of welding hose. "My first dive in the tank didn't bother me after going through that," he says. "But I was short, so when they filled up the escape tank, I had to stand on my toes!"

Gunner Bernie Massar similarly found little discomfort with the diving tank. He had long been fascinated with the idea of being underwater. In the summer of 1940, he and two teenage buddies had walked on the bottom of Binghamton, New York's Chenango River with diving apparatus they had constructed. "The three of us made two diving helmets. The first was strictly an exploratory one," wrote Massar. "We decided on an old hot water tank. I also rigged up two-way phones in this helmet." A year after the Binghamton newspaper featured the local divers, all three enlisted into World War II.

Majoue and Massar's fascinations with deep sea diving would have to be satisfied with deep dives made by *Spadefish* for the time being. Massar was later designated as the *Spadefish* ship's diver, after he attended underwater damage control school with an officer. "We did have shallow water diving gear on the sub," he wrote.

One of the exercises Lieutenant Ustick took his new submariners through was proper procedures for lookouts in clearing the bridge for an emergency dive. He also went through disaster drills, where those on the bridge may have been injured and could not sound the diving alarm. "In this case," said Massar, "the helmsman, being near and almost under the conning tower hatch, was to sound the diving alarm."

Another key part of the training was learning all of the internal machinery that would drive *Spadefish* both above and below the water. Organizing these key crew members fell upon the shoulders of the Engineering Officer, Lieutenant Frank Ryals Alvis. The third senior officer aboard, he had also reported aboard before his new ship's christening. Alvis came from the submarine *Sculpin*, which he had reported aboard in late May 1943. *Sculpin* had stood by her sister submarine *Squalus* in 1939 when the deadly main induction flooding disaster had occurred. Aboard *Sculpin*, he had served as her commissary officer, assistant communications officer, first lieutenant, and finally gunnery officer while making five patrols aboard her. Fair-skinned, Alvis' wardroom mates had nicknamed him "Meatball" for the tones he would burn while standing watch on the bridge.[11]

Alvis was fortunate to have left *Sculpin* after her eighth patrol. Badly damaged by Japanese depth charges, she was forced to surface and fight it out with an enemy destroyer with her little deck gun. One of the destroyer's first salvos had hit the submarine's bridge, killing several officers. Division Commander John Cromwell was later awarded the Congressional Medal of Honor for electing to go down with *Sculpin* versus being captured, where he might give up vital intelligence under torture. The damaged *Sculpin* was scuttled and the surviving crewmen took to the water. Forty-one of 84 men were fortunate enough to be taken back to Truk by the Japanese destroyer. Half of the *Sculpin* survivors would be killed several weeks later while being transferred to Japan aboard the carrier *Chuyo*. She was torpedoed and sunk by her own former submarine *Squalus*, renamed *Sailfish* after she had been raised off the ocean floor.[12]

Unaware of the fate of his *Sculpin* buddies, Lt. Alvis now presided over *Spadefish*'s auxiliary gang and her engine rooms. Almost one third of the new crew were rated either motor machinist's mates or firemen. Alvis worked in coordination with the fifth officer to report aboard *Spadefish*, Lt.(jg) Daniel Delos Decker, Jr.

Dan Decker came from surface duty originally. Upon graduation from the Naval Academy in June 1942, he had requested destroyer duty to become qualified as an officer of the deck, "a requirement in those days before one could apply for submarine school." He was assigned to the new destroyer *Coghlan* (DD-606) in San Francisco. "I married Jean Duncan (a Navy Junior) in September just before we sailed for the Aleutians. We were just in time for the Battle of Komandorskies and initial attacks on Attu and Kiska," he recalled.

After serving aboard *Coghlan* into 1943, "I requested submarine duty or flight training. Immediately, I was ordered to Submarine School in New London." Upon graduation from New London, Decker had received orders to report to Mare Island to help bring *Spadefish* into commission.

"When I reported aboard, the ship was tied to the waterfront with hundreds of workers and hundreds of cables, in great activity to complete construction and outfitting." Lt.(jg) Decker was assigned as *Spadefish*'s first lieutenant. In this position, he was in charge of deck and auxiliary maintenance that was not covered under other specific departments. Once on war patrol, actual officer assignments would matter little, as men shifted about and learned each other's roles. Decker would also serve as diving officer, officer of the deck and as part of the conning tower tracking party for ship attacks.

"I think we were all impressed with the talented workmen assigned to fitting out the boat, and by all the latest equipment being installed," he remembered. "Our job was to procure charts, data, and instructions for study, filling and organizing the crew into departments as the chiefs and enlisted personnel continued to arrive. We had a host of things to learn."

Decker soon became close friends with Frank Alvis, and helped him work on qualifying men for the engine rooms and auxiliary gang. Chief Motor Machinist's Mate Joe Mitzel was the auxiliary boss, in charge of a small group of highly qualified machinists. Raised in an orphanage with his siblings, Mitzel had joined the Navy before the war. After completing sub school, he had served aboard the big *Argonaut* and had made his first war patrol aboard *Silversides* back in April 1942. Aboard *Spadefish*, Mitzel was in charge of a select group of highly trained men.

"I was asked, along with Whitey Harbison, by Lt. Dan Decker, to serve in the auxiliary gang," recalled MoMM3/c Thomas Harry "Buck" Miller, who had been among the group which had reported aboard from training on *R-20*. "We had one auxiliaryman for each watch, whose main duties included watching over the high pressure air manifold. We were assigned to this gang based on our qualifying knowledge. We had to know all systems, beyond just general knowledge."

Fireman 2/c Joseph "Whitey" Harbison had joined the Navy in August 1941, from Cleveland, Ohio. He gained experience aboard the light cruiser *Savannah* (CL-42) during her support of the November 1942 invasion of North Africa before he volunteered for sub duty. Nicknamed for his tight, curly blond hair, Harbison knew his ship

After engine room of *Spadefish*. Hugo Lundquist collection.

thoroughly. His love for guns soon made him a top recruit to help man the 20mm guns on *Spadefish*'s bridge.

Chief Mitzel's auxiliarymen were Miller, Harbison, Johnny Peel, and Orville Richard "Dick" Gamby. "We were the auxiliary gang," recalled Gamby. "The engine men had their own rooms. We were mainly in the pump room or the control room." Located directly below the control room, the pump room contained machinery for transferring air or water from one tank to another, or into and out of *Spadefish*. The pump room was a mass of equipment, including the main hydraulic plant, the air conditioning equipment, a fresh water tank, and the fresh water distiller.

Gamby had signed up at the beginning of the war and had done boot training at Newport News. He was then shipped aboard the old carrier *Hornet* down to the sub base at Panama for training, where he was assigned to the old training boat *S-17*, a real pigboat. "For the first few days, we were just cleaning that ship. It was a mess," he recalled.

Gamby rode *S-17* back through the Panama Canal into the Pacific, where she made extensive training dives to break in the new submarine recruits. *S-17* made seven to ten-day patrols "to chase U-boats away from the lighthouses." *S-17* made seven war patrols in the Atlantic, but did not receive credit for any ship destruction. Gamby went through the new sub school at New London and continued serving on the old boats along the East Coast. "Everybody was trying to get new construction, but they didn't want to let us go. We were told, 'We need you guys to run these old boats and train new guys.'" Gamby finally got the welcome orders to new construction at Mare Island.

Gamby and his fellow auxiliarymen learned all of *Spadefish*'s inner workings as she was completed. The motor machinist's mates (motormacs) would run the ship's engines while she was surfaced, while the electricians' mates would run the electric generators which drove the boat while submerged. The upper portion of the forward battery compartment held the sleeping quarters for the officers and CPOs. Each compartment was no longer than a Pullman roomette aboard an old train car. The forward storage battery held 126 rechargeable cells. Further aft, beyond the control room, was the after battery compartment, below which lay another 126 battery cells, watched over by the electricians.

Spadefish had two chief electrician's mates, Earl Gregory and Carl Thomas Schmelzer. Their electrical gangs worked in the maneuvering room handling the power from the generators and that of the batteries when submerged. They directed power to the main motors, as ordered by the conning tower, which drove the propellor shafts. Thirty-three-year-old Scmelzer, a veteran of seven war patrols, was combat experienced but short on temper. His buddies called him either "Smiley" or "Stinky." When Schmelzer first enlisted in the Navy, he wanted to be a ship's cook. He was instead assigned to the "black gang," cleaning the bilges in the engine rooms below decks, where he worked his way up the ranks as an electrician's mate.[13]

Schmelzer was in charge of the main power unit, while Gregory, assisted by electrician Emerson Ordway, had the IC crew. Electrician striker Jack Gallagher, a native of San Francisco, had joined *Spadefish* from sub training off Key West. "I worked for Ordway in the IC crew," said Gallagher. "The intercommunications of the ship included just about everything else electrical on the boat aside from the main battery power. Schmelzer had the main power crew."

Ordway, a twenty-six-year-old from Maine, had spent two years in Key West aboard the training boats *R-20* and *R-14* before receiving a transfer to new construction. Another of Schmelzer and Ordway's experienced electricians was EM2c Wes Drew, a twenty-four-year-old also from Maine. Before being assigned to S*padefish* in late 1943, Drew had served nearly three years and six war patrols aboard the old *Nautilus* (SS-168), which had fired on a damaged Japanese aircraft carrier at the battle of Midway.[14]

Surfaced, *Spadefish* ran on her diesels, which generated electrical power to turn her screws. Submerged, her powerful storage batteries could drive the boat nearly two days at the crawling speed of 3 knots or would last only about an hour at full submerged speed.

In addition to the auxiliarymen and electricians, *Spadefish* had a large number of motormacs and firemen who called themselves the "black gang," those in charge of keeping the four diesel engines running. CMoMM Leroy Douglas Falconer, known to all as "Dutch," was over the motormacs and firemen who ran the engine rooms. "Dutch was a real sharp man, a pre-war sailor who had already been in for a few years," recalled motormac William Patrick Kelley. "Back when most of us kids were 18 or 19 years old, Dutch was 31 years old." Falconer had entered the Navy in 1935, served as a signalman striker aboard the battleships *New York* and *Texas*, and then went through New London's Sub School in 1937. Following diesel school, he worked his way through sub tenders and the submarine *Tambor* prior to America's entry into World War II. Once hostilities had commenced with Japan, Dutch had made three war patrols aboard *Finback* and *Halibut* before being assigned to *Spadefish*.[15]

"Pat" Kelley had prior experience on the old R-boats and was already familiar with the inner workings of the engine rooms and maneuvering room. He quickly made a connection with engineering officer Frank Alvis, whose hometown of Richmond was not far from Kelley's small Virginia home.

Spadefish would be driven by four 1,600 horsepower Fairbanks Morse diesel engines. A dozen new fleet boats in 1943 had been equipped with HOR (Hoover-Owens-Rentschler) engines, which were soon found to be poorly designed and subject to frequent breakdowns. The motormacs cursed the lousy HOR engines, dubbing them "whores" and worse. The HORs were eventually removed and were no longer being installed by the time Mare Island reached this stage with *Spadefish*.

Pat Kelley became a member of the forward engine room, which was also home to MoMM1/c Charles Clain Griffith, a highly-seasoned sailor from *Silversides*, the same submarine Chief Joe Mitzel had started the war aboard. Griffith had joined her fresh out of New London, made seven war patrols on *Silversides*, and had then put in for new construction. "I was first class motormac when I joined *Spadefish*," he recalled. "When we commissioned her at Mare Island, I got the forward engine room on her."

Twenty-two-year-old Ensign Perry Satterthwaite Wood, born in San Francisco and a February 1943 University of California at Berkeley graduate, had been another of the officers who reported to Mare Island during December 1943. "When I was leaving sub school," he recalled, "I had a friend at Mare Island. I communicated with him to see which submarine I should request, which would be here the longest. He said, 'The *Spadefish*. She hasn't been launched yet.' So, I requested the *Spadefish* and was assigned to her."

Perry Wood rode his new ship down the ways at her launching and then became immersed in his new billet as *Spadefish*'s communications officer. He was in charge of all of the boat's electronics gear, including radio, sonar and radar. With his parents' home in nearby Berkeley, Wood was fortunate to be able to work at Mare Island all week and then commute home on the weekends.

Wood's electronics gang originally consisted of three radiomen and one radar technician. Other men, such as Seaman 2/c Kenneth Clyde Powers, would become "strikers," or unrated sailors working toward the rating of their choice. To become qualified and advanced in rating, the men had to train with the senior petty officers within their field. K. C. Powers had paid a quarter to go aboard his first submarine, an old S-boat, on the shores of Lake Erie in Cleveland in the summer of 1936. Eight years later, Powers fulfilled his childhood dream by finishing sub school and being assigned to a new fleet submarine, *Spadefish*.[16]

RM1c Paul Majoue, a self-professed "real, 100 percent coonass," had been born and raised in New Orleans. He was nicknamed "Hamhocks" by his football buddies because of the size of his legs. The nickname, shortened to just "Hocks," followed him aboard *Spadefish*. He was musically inclined, master of many instruments. He had been in the National Guard, part of the 108th Cavalry Band, before joining the Navy. Majoue decided to follow in his father's footsteps and join the Navy. At the time, radar was a very secret thing, and Majoue was found to be an amateur radio operator, or ham.

"They sent 50 of us hams to New York. The other 50, which I was part of, were sent to the University of Houston. We got nine hours of college credit in three months—a real crash course! I believe only 22 of us graduated." From the University of Houston, Majoue and the other graduates were sent to Treasure Island to learn about radar. "That was when radar was very hush-hush," he says. "You'd say 'radar,' and about three people would go, 'Sssshhhh!'"

Aboard *Spadefish*, Hocks Majoue was the leading radioman. The radio gang also included RM1c Gerald Newton, RM3c Edmund Panek and RM2c Michael Sergio. Majoue and Sergio had gone through sub school together and had grown quite close. Sergio had served on surface destroyers pre-war in the North Atlantic and continued on destroyers during the invasion of Africa, Sicily and Italy before going to sub school in 1943. As one of the shortest men aboard, Sergio could easily scamper through the hatches without a worry of banging his head. One of his *Spadefish* buddies, motormac Radford Rewold, hung the nickname "Little Fox" on him. "He said I reminded him of the little fox he used to hunt back home in Alabama," related Sergio. "Then the crew added the name 'Fox Hole,' and from that day on everyone called me 'Fox Hole.'"[17]

Majoue worked closely with RM1c Newton, whom he found to be concerned with good luck charms. "In civilian life in Oregon, he had been a mortician," Majoue recalled. "He was very superstitious. When we used to get ready to leave to go on patrol, he would put on a pair of black socks. He would never take 'em off until we got back. Like walking under a ladder or something; very superstitious, but he was a good radioman."

While Newton may have been superstitious, other crewmen had their own forms of good luck charms. Among such items were "lucky" pin-up girls and signed movie star photos. In the officers' wardroom, Betty Grable and Rita Hayworth soon appeared among the pin-up girls. In the forward torpedo room, Jeannie Crane was the autographed poster girl of choice.

The sixth officer to arrive aboard *Spadefish* in January was Lieutenant (jg) Henry Howard Laundy. He had worked in residential real estate before completing his education at Northwestern and moving on to the war. As a youth, Laundy had acquired the nickname "Gus" from his best friend in high school. "My close friend's name was Harry, and we didn't like our names," Laundy recalled. "So, I called him Steve, which was a name I liked, and he called me Gus. My name stuck from there." From that point, everyone except his family called him Gus, and so it remained when Laundy reported aboard *Spadefish*.

After finishing midshipman school at Northwestern, Gus Laundy had gone to New London for his sub school training in January 1942. From there, he was assigned to the old training submarine *S-20*, which was commanded by Lt. Cdr. Samuel David Dealey. Sam Dealey, of course, would go on to command the new boat *Harder* and become the famed "Destroyer Killer." His tactics for firing "down the throat" at an enemy warship and for sinking four Japanese destroyers in one patrol made him legendary in the service. According to Laundy, "He was aggressive even then."

From *S-20*, Laundy had moved on to *Tuna*, aboard which he made her seventh through ninth war patrols from May to December 1943. His *Tuna* was admittedly "not very successful," sinking only one merchant ship that was credited to her post-war. Laundy was the torpedo and gunnery officer at the time he left *Tuna*, and his experience would qualify him for the same position aboard *Spadefish*. He was happy to get aboard his new ship. "Because I was ordered to the *Spadefish*, at Mare Island I was left with many duties when the *Tuna* returned for her overhaul there," wrote Laundy.

Laundy found Underwood, Ustick, Alvis, Decker and Wood there before him. As a bachelor, he spent much of his time aboard ship, while the other married officers spent most of their personal time ashore with their families. Laundy was impressed with the new 5-inch, 25 caliber gun aboard *Spadefish* and its stainless steel linings. He was also in charge of the torpedomen, and he had some experienced ones aboard. TM2c Emery Kreher of Illinois had prior submarine service aboard *Haddock* (SS-231), *Tuna* (SS-203), *Nautilus*, *Drum* (SS-228) and *Finback* (SS-230). The leading torpedoman was Chief Waleszonia, the chief of the boat, and he soon received TM1c Harry George, a San Diego native who had been serving at the Navy's torpedo factory in Newport, Rhode Island, where new electric torpedoes were in continual development. George was assigned as the senior petty officer in charge of the after torpedo room crew.

In the forward room, TM3c Donald William Bird was eager to get to war. In 1940, he had commissioned and served aboard *USS Yukon* (AF-9), "a seagoing grocery store." In 1942, while standing lookout duty in a convoy en route to the States, Don Bird spotted a torpedo on his ship's port quarter. He reported this to the bridge and it missed his ship by thirty feet. His *Yukon* did take torpedoes on two other occasions, "but refused to go down." Tired of being fired upon, Bird transferred to submarine duty to dish out the torpedoes.

His first service was aboard an old sub school boat "making sixteen dives a day out in the Long Island Sound." He moved on to the old *O-4* for a while, but Bird longed to see torpedo action aboard a more modern submarine. "I requested a transfer to any fleet boat. The request was granted," he wrote. "I could have the *Tang* or *Spadefish*. I picked the *Spadefish*, and lucky I did."[18]

There were also unrated sailors who joined the torpedo gangs to begin earning their ratings. Seaman 1/c Wallace Francis McMahon from Massachusetts reported aboard *Spadefish* with his buddy, S1c Thad Ralph Barton, from Buffalo, New York. The two had attended sub school and torpedo school together. Barton was sent to the after torpedo room and McMahon was assigned to the forward room, where both would work on the torpedo reload gangs until earning their TM3c ratings.

Another of the veteran torpedomen Lieutenant Laundy had was TM2c Richard David Butchofsky, who had made five war patrols aboard the successful *Haddock*. During the early days of fitting out *Spadefish*, Butchofsky's future wife came to visit him. Lucille Carpenter took a train across country from El Paso with her best friend. Lucille, her friend and Richard attended a fancy party in San Francisco one night. Afterwards, he asked the ladies, "How would you like a tour of the *Spadefish*?"[19]

Somewhere around midnight, Butchofsky brought the two ladies aboard ship to show them the forward torpedo room where he worked. Some of the crew were asleep, but others were still working.

As they started down the ladder into the submarine, Butchofsky called down to his shipmates below, "You all look down!"

But, as Lucille Butchofsky later recalled, "Of course, all the guys looked up the ladder, because here comes two ladies in high heels and dresses!"

Captain Underwood found security in some of the more seasoned enlisted men who joined *Spadefish* during her early days. Those who had actually been out on war patrols would help break in the green recruits he would also receive.

The wardroom included two "mustang" officers, Ensigns Ray Curtis White and William James Ware. Both were experienced former enlisted men who had been promoted up into officers' country. Ware, thirty-one, already a veteran of six war patrols, had lied about his age and entered the Navy at age 15 as a seaman. When he enlisted in the Navy on 1 June 1928, no birth certificate was required and no questions were asked. Bill Ware started as a fireman third class, but was later promoted to yeoman third class. He first served on *S-17* at the Sub Base, Coco Solo, before moving on to *S-13* and *S-14*. Ware then went to surface duty in an aviation squadron aboard the carrier *Lexington* for three years. Returning to sub duty, he commissioned *Searaven* (SS-196) and made her first six war patrols as her chief yeoman. After fifteen years' Navy experience, Bill Ware was promoted to ensign and ordered to *Spadefish* at Mare Island.[20]

Ray White had been similarly promoted up and came to *Spadefish* from war patrols aboard the successful boat *Snook* (SS-279), which had destroyed eleven Japanese ships in 1943 alone. Unlike many of the "90-day wonders," ensigns fresh out of school with little experience, mustangers White and Ware were considered seasoned sailors. Ray White became Frank Alvis' assistant engineering officer, while Bill Ware was given the commissary officer billet. The commissary officer was responsible for requisitioning, receiving, storing and accounting for all of the ship's stores.

Seaman 2/c James Price was the newest man in service, having only enlisted in the Navy six months prior on 10 August 1943. The chief petty officers had many years of experience in the Navy, most having joined before the war. CTM Waleszonia was the man with the most years experience in the Navy, followed by CEM Gregory.

Those men reporting aboard with actual war patrols under their belts were given a certain level of respect. One of the men who reported at Mare Island was 28-year-old BM1c Willard Christ Eimermann, who was already an old hand both on surface ships and subs as a coxswain and boatswain's mate. He was a plank owner of the old destroyer *Henley* (DD-391), commissioned at Mare Island in 1936. Eimermann's last destroyer was *Patterson* (DD-392) during the pre-war. After his four years were up, he went back home to a restaurant job, where he made $15 a week. Eimermann then went to West Bend Aluminum in Wisconsin, working on a punch press. The superintendent and the super's brother-in-law loved to coerce Eimermann to tell "girlie stories" from his Navy days. Finding himself short of fascinating tales, Eimermann "was doing some mad lying" to impress his bosses. Taking advantage of the situation, Eimermann asked for a raise.

He got one, but found the move from forty cents an hour to 42¢ an hour not quite enough in 1940. The naval bureau was after him to reenlist for more destroyer duty. "No way," he thought. "Not another destroyer." Eimermann reenlisted, but wanted something with a little more adventure, hoping for a PT boat or a dirigible. He instead found himself in sub school at New London.

He made eight war patrols aboard the large *Barracuda* in 1942 and 1943. The old B-boats were then used as training boats on the East Coast. After many months of running to sea on *Barracuda*, Eimermann found himself wanting to see some action. While ashore having a beer one day, he ran into a fellow who offered him a plan. "You go see the Admiral's yeoman, and grease his palm with a $10-er," he was told. "Before the week's over, you'll be heading for the West Coast."

Eimermann figured he had nothing to lose, so visited the yeoman and slipped him ten dollars, to see if he would truly get the magic transfer out of the B-boats. "You know," he later laughed, "that's exactly what happened!"

He shipped out aboard a passenger train across the United States, bound for California. "My back was killing me by the time we got to Mare Island." Once aboard *Spadefish*, he found that they were excited with his experience. "You had to put down how many runs you had," he recalled. "The old *Barracuda* had made eight runs, but I didn't tell 'em we didn't sink no ships, you know."

Eimermann soon found himself on good terms with the Exec, Lt. Ted Ustick. The XO brought his bulldog from home occasionally to wander about with him.

"What do you call him?" asked "Boats" Eimermann.

"Boats," replied Lieutenant Ustick.

"That must be a damn good bulldog with a name like Boats!"

Ustick smiled. "That must have been the right thing to say," Eimermann later recalled, because he maintained good relations with the *Spadefish* Exec from that moment on.

Luau, brought aboard from a Vallejo bar, became *Spadefish*'s mascot and made all war patrols. Traveling topside or below decks was not a problem for the little dog with helping hands such as RT2c Bill Keeney. *Courtesy of Joe Marasco.*

Luau joined *Spadefish* in February before commissioning.

Motormac Pat Kelley recalled that "there was about seven or eight *Spadefish* boys there" at the Barrel Club, including himself, Shaky Jake Lewis, "Rebel" Rewold and Roy Moody. It was only natural that the story of how Luau came to be part of the *Spadefish* crew involved some of the ship's more storied characters.

"Rebel" Rewold was MoMM1/c Radford Crowell Rewold. Rewold had enlisted in the Navy on 6 November 1939. His father had owned the only Cadillac dealership in Montgomery, Alabama, during the 1920s but had lost the business during the Great Depression. Rebel, who favored growing a long mustache while on patrol, was serving aboard the submarine *Pompano* (SS-181) when Pearl Harbor was attacked on December 7, 1941. His ship was en route from Mare Island to Pearl Harbor, and arrived three days after the "day of infamy." *Pompano* was mistakenly bombed twice by eager Navy pilots during the early weeks of war, but was fortunate enough to survive both attacks. Rebel Rewold served on the first three war patrols of *Pompano*. She was aggressive, sinking several smaller ships with gunfire and being credited with the sinking of five larger Japanese ships during her early patrols. Rewold eventually received new orders shortly before *Pompano* was lost with all hands in early September 1943 off Japan.

Aboard *Spadefish*, his Southern style and wild nature made him an instant hit with his fellow crewmen. Very little seemed to faze him. While *Spadefish* was being fitted out alongside the Mare Island dock, Rewold had the deck watch one evening and wore his 45-caliber pistol on his hip. Alongside the submarine was a harbor barge loaded with

Luau came to *Spadefish* from The Barrel Club, located at what was Highway 40 (now 80) and Benicia Road in Vallejo. *Courtesy of Betty Fletcher.*

food, snacks and coffee for the civilian construction workers who still swarmed over the ship. Gunner Bernie Massar recalled: "Several civilian workers were talking to Radford, and asked him if the gun was loaded. He took out the .45 and shot out the light in the barge. Needless to say, the workers took off to parts unknown."[21]

Another of the *Spadefish* sailors ashore with "Reb" Rewold was his buddy, Gunner's Mate 1/c Edgar Lycurgous Lewis, who was known as "Shaky Jake" to all of his friends. Rewold's wife, Denise Rewold, later wrote that her husband and Shaky Jake Lewis "had a friendship that never ended."[22] Asking his former shipmates the origination of his "Shaky Jake" moniker incites many different versions. "After every liberty ashore, he had the shakes," recalled one officer. Others, like Pat Kelley, recalled that Lewis was a lightweight champion boxer in the pre-war Navy, and that "Shaky Jake" was his ring name. Gunner Bernie Massar recalled: "When he walked, it was something like a duck."

Edgar Lewis, a native of Frankford, Kentucky, had served on battleships before entering sub school. Lewis and another of his *Spadefish* buddies, EM2c Roy Moody, had both commissioned the submarine *Whale* and made her first five war patrols. Both had endured a seventeen-hour depth charge attack aboard *Whale* in late 1942 which had severely damaged their sub.

On this particular February evening, Lewis, Rewold and their shipmates had gone for dinner and drinks at a local bar called the Barrel Club, located on old Highway 40 (now Highway 80) in Vallejo. It was there they first found the alcohol-loving dog that soon won their hearts.

"We took her away from some Marines," recalled Pat Kelley. "They were trying to give her a drink of whiskey." The *Spadefish* sailors managed to get the little dog away from the Marines without a fight. The dog was young and small of size. She seemed to have some

Jack Russell terrier in her. She had brown ears and a brown patch over her right eye. "Shaky Jake was having a steak," recalled motormac Charles Griffith, "So, he cut the dog a piece of steak and fed her with the same fork he used."

Lewis became quite fond of the little dog and, after a few more drinks, decided he would bring her back to *Spadefish* with him. His drinking buddies went along with the idea and the dog was smuggled aboard ship that night.

Of course, the presence of a dog was quickly found out by Captain Underwood. Much to the pleasure of Shaky Jake Lewis and his buddies, the skipper did not throw the dog off his ship. He figured if she was good for morale, what harm was she doing?

The little dog was given the name "Luau" at Mare Island and she became the ship's mascot. Exec Ted Ustick considered Lewis' dog "a little mongrel pup," but he soon came to love Luau. She later proved her worth. Captain Underwood would write months later, "The dog, Luau, contributed greatly to the morale with her ready playfulness with all hands."[23]

Luau would be present for the ship's commissioning. Once at sea, Lewis and Rewold would find plenty of help taking care of Luau. She became an instant favorite. Some of the crew trained her to use the crew's shower to take care of her "business." A bed was made for her in the forward torpedo room, although she had the run of the ship. When the crew took her ashore for leave, she was not afraid to sip a little beer with them.

Two days before the Navy formally commissioned *Spadefish*, Captain Underwood threw a commissioning party for his entire crew on the night of 7 March. Held at the Women's Club in Vallejo, each man could bring a date for drinks, music, and dancing to a live band. It was the last big party held while the Mare Island Navy Yard still officially had control of *Spadefish*.

Seaman 1c Wallace McMahon later recalled that the ship's party "was quite a night. We all got to know each other better that evening. There were many new meetings: noses with fists, necks with choke holds, heads meeting heads, and bodies meeting the floor." After the buffet, consumption of spirits led to "overzealous camraderie" among shipmates. En route home to the barracks, McMahon took a fall that broke his nose. "After that evening, the Vallejo Womens' Club voted never again to host a submarine commissioning party!"[24]

The ship's party carried into the early morning hours. "When the party broke up very late that night, everyone was gathered in front of

"Spade 'Em Under" was the theme of the 7 March 1944 invitation to the ship's party to celebrate *Spadefish*'s commissioning. *Courtesy of Bernie Massar.*

the dance hall, going their different ways," recalled radioman Mike "Fox Hole" Sergio. "Pat Kelley and I had a disagreement over some foolish thing and we got into a good fight."[25]

Both returned to the barracks, where the crew was staying until *Spadefish* was commissioned, to sleep off the effects. The next morning, Sergio was in the washroom, cleaning up and shaving. Three of his shipmates ran in and yelled, "Run, Little Fox Hole! Pat Kelley is looking for you!"

Before Sergio could do anything, Kelley was standing in the doorway to the washroom.

> He looked as big as a giant to me, and boy was he sporting a big black eye! Needless to say, we were both sober now. I figured, now I am about to die. Here is Pat coming toward me–a huge man, six foot three, 230 pounds, and here I was five foot four and 130 pounds. I was scared stiff.
>
> Pat bellowed, "You're just the man I am looking for, Little Fox Hole!"
>
> He walked up to me very slowly, put out his big hand and said, "Put it there Little Fox Hole. You are a helluva sailor!"
>
> From that day on, Pat Kelley and I were the best of friends.

Spadefish's Captain Gordon Underwood addresses his crew at ship's commissioning party in Vallejo, 7 March 1944. *Courtesy of Dan Decker.*

Spadefish's day of commissioning came on 9 March 1944, two months after she had been christened and launched, and less than ten months after her keel had been laid. On this date, responsibility and authority for *Spadefish* passed from Captain Scanland to prospective commanding officer Gordon Underwood. Seventy-three officers and crewmen, plus the little dog Luau, were present, lined up on deck, for the commissioning ceremony. Five more men would report aboard her within weeks, bringing the complement to 78 men aboard. With a simple, solemn service at the Navy Yard, Mare Island handed the boat over to the United States Navy.

Commander Underwood read his orders from Secretary of the Navy Frank Knox, placing him in command of *USS Spadefish*. As he finished, Chief Quartermaster Clarence Barger hoisted the commissioning pennant and the national ensign up the main mast.

Acknowledging his command, Captain Underwood turned to Lieutenant Ustick and ordered, "Post the watch." The Exec had one of the crew take position at the gangway, as *Spadefish* officially become a part of the U.S. Navy.

Best of all, the crew commenced drawing their additional 50 per cent pay for submarine duty. The extra money was well appreciated ashore at San Francisco in the days before the ship's shakedown began. On the weekends, the locals returned home often. Ensign Perry Wood often had the use of his family's car on the weekends. "There was gas

USS *Spadefish* (SS-411) 9 March 1944
Original Watch Sections of Commissioning Crew

CPO Watch List
Gregory, Earl O., CEM *
Schmelzer, Carl T., CEM
Falconer, Leroy D., CMoMM
Barger, Clarence R., CQM *
Parker, Billy R., CPhM *
Mitzel, Joseph R., CMoMM
Waleszonia, Alexander J. Jr., CTM *
Scherman, Francis J., CCS

First Section
Schuett, James S., SM1c
Griffith, Charles C., MoMM1c
Holeman, Victor R., MoMM2c
Weidner, Delbert C. Jr., F1c
Ordway, Emerson L., EM1c
George, Harry, TM1c (3/15)
Maxwell, Robert E., S2c
Panek, Edmund E., RM3c
Riley, Thomas G., SC3c
Price, James E., S2c
Dependahl, Leonard E., EM3c
Lundquist, Hugo C., TM3c
Kreinbring, Irving H., Y1c

Second Section
Cooper, Samuel, QM3c
Bieberdorf, Carl C., MoMM1c (4/12)
Harbison, Joseph A., F1c
Nordstrom, Edwin G., F1c (3/13)
Moody, Roy H., EM2c
Cruze, Herman F. Jr., EM3c
Kreher, Emery A., TM2c
Massar, Bernard A., GM3c
Chiavacci, Louis J., S2c
Eimermann, Willard C., BM1c
McMahon, Wallace F., S1c
Olah, Andrew, FC3c

Third Section
Lewis, Edgar L., GM1c
Frazier, Dale W., SM3c
Rewold, Radford C., MoMM1c
Pelliciari, Nicholas J., F1c
Olsen, Norman A., EM1c
Gallagher, Jack A., F1c
Cuthbertson, John M., TM2c
Spiese, Albert L., TM3c
Barton, Thad R., S1c

Sergio, Michael, RM2c
Larkie, Arthur E., StM1c (3/28)
Bird, Donald W., TM3c

Fourth Section
Yocum, David P., MoMM2c
Noonan, Maurice A., S2c
Drew, Wesley A., EM2c
Barnes, Silas M., TM2c
Nesnee, John, S1c
Majoue, Paul H. Jr., RM1c
Solomon, Henry L., StM1c
Bassett, Richard H., S2c
Newton, Gerald A., RM1c
Kelley, William P., MoMM3c
McLaughlin, Paul F., MoMM2c

Fifth Section
Butchofsky, Richard D., TM2c *
Sigworth, Kenneth L., EM3c
Gamby, Orville R., MoMM3c
Jackson, Robert F., MoMM2c
Miller, Thomas H., MoMM3c
Scholle, Donald J., S2c
Powers, Kenneth C., S2c
Pike, Neal, RT1c
Peel, John R., MoMM2c
Graf, Edward F., SC3c
Powell, Wayne H., EM3c
Yates, Richard L., MoMM1c
Partin, Doyle B., TM3c
Pirrung, Edward N., SC1c (3/29)

Officers
Underwood, Gordon W., Cdr., USN
Ustick, Theodore M., Lt., USN
Alvis, Frank R., Lt., USNR
Laundy, Henry H., Lt.(jg), USNR
Decker, Daniel D., Lt.(jg), USN
Wood, Perry S., Ens., USNR
Ware, William J., Ens., USN
White, Ray C., Ens., USN

* *Transferred before first patrol.*

Note: All men aboard for commissioning unless later reporting date is shown beside their name.

Officers table at *Spadefish* commissioning party. Back row, left to right: Perry Wood and date, Frank and Libby Alvis, Ted (with cigar) and Clair Ustick, Marion and Gordon Underwood. Front row (left to right): Jean and Dan Decker, Mrs. and Ens. Ray White. *Courtesy of Dan Decker.*

rationing," he related. "So, if I could get some crew to sign up as my passengers, then that gave me extra gas stamps."

Nearly half of *Spadefish*'s enlisted men were motor machinist's mates, electrician's mates and firemen. Another quarter was comprised of torpedomen, radiomen, and seamen. The rest were more specialized: one pharmacist's mate, one boatswain's mate, a fire controlman, yeoman, radio technician, cooks, steward's mates, quartermasters, and signalmen. Once at sea, many of these men would take turns standing watches as a lookout, helmsman, duty chief, soundman, diving planes operator, or on radar duty. Six of the eight officers would rotate as officer of the deck (OOD), junior officer of the deck (JOOD), or diving officer. The only exceptions to standing regular watches would be Captain Underwood, his executive officer and navigator, Ted Ustick, and Ustick's assistant navigator, CQM Barger.

The ship's trials now began. The engines and all mechanical systems were first tested dockside under the watchful eyes of both *Spadefish* and Mare Island engineers. Next came the first underway trials to see how the new submarine would act at sea.

Spadefish exercised in San Francisco Bay for a few days, conducting maneuvering drills from practice dives to man overboard drills. The first shallow dives were a little apprehensive for all. Men hoped that nothing had been missed. "We'd let the sub go down until the deck was awash," recalled gunner's mate Bernie Massar. "Then, we would go a little deeper, checking, checking, checking everywhere for leaks and problems."

The officers became close to each other, as they would depend upon each other when on war patrol. Dan Decker soon found Frank Alvis to be his closest friend. Alvis, like Underwood, had previous wartime patrol experience. "My education would not have been complete without him," wrote Decker.

No enlisted man in the Navy had as much responsibility and latitude as a submarine's chief of the boat. Sometimes the wide range of latitude worked against the chief, however. When Chief Waleszonia tried to cover for another man's poor judgement on 12 April, Captain Underwood was not in favor of Waleszonia's choices. "He covered for a couple of whitehats who were late coming back," recalled one *Spadefish* sailor. "He did a no-no, covering for them." A second class motor machinist's mate involved was tried by a summary court martial before Underwood. The motormac remained aboard, but Chief Waleszonia was transferred off *Spadefish* the next day. CEM Earl Gregory succeeded him as chief of the boat. *Spadefish* received a new chief petty officer, CTM William Wallace Simms Jr., a few weeks later on 24 May.

Spadefish returned to Mare Island at the beginning of May for her final fitting out, to repair anything that was found to have problems during the early exercises and testing. On 8 May, after all fitting out was completed, the first three days of trial runs were conducted in San Francisco Bay.

Executive Officer Ted Ustick, newly promoted to Lieutenant Commander, trained his lookouts on the war patrol procedures he had been lecturing about in his Mare Island classroom. Gunner's mate Bernie Massar was on the helm in the conning tower for one of the practice dives. He remembered Ustick's emergency training had called for the helmsman to sound the diving alarm in the event that the bridge crew was unable.

Ustick was on deck with Frank Alvis as officer of the deck (OOD) and junior officer of the deck (JOOD) Perry Wood, preparing the lookouts for a diving drill. "The colors were brought down, so I knew we were about to dive," related Massar. "I asked the quartermaster if I should sound the alarm if none was heard. He didn't answer."

Next instant came the command, "Clear the bridge!"

Almost instantly, the lookouts came dropping down the ladder, the lookouts passed on below to the control room. Massar was concerned that no one had bothered to sound the diving alarm.

"I remembered our instructions during training the unqualified men," he wrote. "So, I sounded the diving alarm as told and trained."

USS Spadefish (SS-411), port side view off Mare Island Navy Yard, taken on 11 May 1944. Note her deck gun mounted aft. *Official U.S. Navy photo.*

Alvis and Wood dropped down the ladder, followed by the Exec, who was "boiling mad."

"Who the hell sounded the alarm?" demanded Lt. Cdr. Ustick.

"I did," replied Massar.

"You almost got me washed overboard!" snapped the XO. Busy watching his lookout crew clear the bridge, he had barely made the hatch before the waves washed over.

Lieutenant Alvis later quizzed Massar on why he had pulled the alarm. "I explained that the Exec had instructed us helmsmen to do this in case no alarm sounded. I assumed this was just a test and did as instructed."

The XO's anger subsided and Bernie Massar's hurt pride healed, but the orders on when a helmsman should pull the diving alarm underwent some further discussions for all involved.

After a few days of sea trials, Captain Underwood was eager to move on to the next stage. It was time for the shakedown cruise of *Spadefish*, to test out the five watch sections and to train his crew thoroughly for attack situations. To do, *Spadefish* would move from San Francisco down to San Diego.

Aboard for *Spadefish*'s departure for San Diego were two civilian observers to monitor the performance of her diesels, generators and main motors for endurance while at speed en route. For this passage, she took J. C. Casey, a Fairbanks-Morse representative, and F. F. Flaig of General Electric.

She sailed from the Mare Island Navy Yard on 11 May, passing under the Golden Gate Bridge, one step closer to war.

Uncle Charlie's Secret Weapon

Shakedown   *April–22 July 1944*

Gunnery officer Gus Laundy and his two gunners mates, Jake Lewis and Bernie Massar, were thrilled that their boat would be among the first to receive a more sophisticated deck gun. While most subs currently in the Pacific War were equipped with a 3-inch or 4-inch deck gun, the Mare Island Navy Yard installed on *Spadefish* a new 5-inch/25 caliber deck gun. Some boats were fitted with their deck guns forward and others aft. *Spadefish*'s gun was mounted aft of the conning tower by Gordon Underwood's request, giving her the ability to maneuver to fire on enemy vessels but to also be able to fire back at a pursuing ship should things become so desperate. Most submarines had to keep a plug in the deck gun's barrel and a cover over the breech to protect it from the salt water. "Our new 5-inch had an alloy liner, so you didn't have to have a plug," said Bernie Massar. "The water would run right through it and didn't hurt it one bit."

Spadefish's 5"/25 deck gun was actually a rifled cannon which fired a 5" diameter shell from a 125-inch barrel. The 25 indicates the length of the barrel in calibers, with one caliber, in this case, being the bore diameter of 5 inches. Although the barrel was relatively short at 125 inches (25 total 5" calibers), the rolling of a submarine's deck at sea made a longer barrel of little use. Each 65-pound 5-inch shell had an effective range of 8,000 yards, or more than 4.5 miles. Strong men were required to be on the ammunition passing team to bring the shells up through the hatches from below decks. While on war patrol, *Spadefish* would carry a total of one hundred rounds of 5-inch shells aboard.[1]

With practice, a well-trained crew could fire one round every five seconds, or about twenty rounds a minute. Leading gunner's mate Jake Lewis would serve as gun captain for *Spadefish*'s 5-inch gun. His role as supervisor included opening the breech and inspecting the mechanism and bore prior to firing to insure that there were no obstructions.

Two other men actually sat on either side of the gun to operate it. The trainer, motormac Rebel Rewold, sat in the right hand seat, moving the gun from side to side with hand wheels, which connected the traverse ring around the mount's base via a gear system. Rewold was responsible for aiming the gun in the horizontal plane. Across from Rewold sat Chief Francis Scherman, the commissary steward, who served as the deck gun's pointer. From his left hand seat, Scherman learned how to aim the gun in the vertical plane, elevating and depressing the barrel. Scherman was the one who would actually fire the gun by stepping down on the right foot pedal, which was hydraulically connected to the firing plunger on the left side of the breech.

Another special instrument installation at Mare Island had been the target bearing transmitters (TBTs). This instrument received binoculars for the transmission of bearings to the tracking party and the torpedo data computer in the conning tower. One was mounted forward and one aft on *Spadefish*'s bridge. On moonless or very dark nights, the TBT would help make up for the poor visibility through the attack periscopes.[2]

Upon reaching San Diego in May, *Spadefish* received a new piece of equipment which was destined to shape her future for a secret mission drafted by the Navy's top leaders. Its creation had been in the works for some time and was presided over by ComSubPac himself, Vice Admiral Charles Andrews Lockwood Jr.

Spadefish was the first submarine to be mounted with a frequency modulated (FM) sonar, which was capable of detecting mines and similar objects. The FM Sonar and its purpose had been in the works long before *Spadefish* received the first set. Rear Admiral Lockwood, soon to become a three-star vice admiral, set the pace for his submarine force, establishing doctrine.

Lockwood, from the class of 1912, had served in submarines since 1914. A World War I veteran, he had also commanded five different submarines. During the late 1930s, he fought for changes that he felt would greatly improve the fighting abilities of fleet submarines. He pushed for larger deck guns and insisted on adding air conditioning to the newer boats being built. Lockwood had become Commander Submarines Pacific (ComSubPac) in early 1943 when his predecessor, Rear Admiral Robert E. English, was killed in a plane crash.[3]

Known as "Uncle Charlie" to his submarine force, Lockwood was an avid supporter of anything that would enhance the ability of his sub skippers to sink more enemy shipping in World War II. During one of his inspection trips, he had stopped over at San Diego during April 1943. While there for his visit to the San Diego Submarine Squadron, Lockwood accompanied base commander Captain Gordon Campbell to the San Diego Naval Research Laboratory. This lab at Point Loma was headed by Dr. Gaylord Probasco Harnwell, Director of the University of California Division of War Research (UCDWR). Harnwell's immediate research associates introduced to Lockwood were Dr. Franz N. D. Kurie, Dr. R. O. Burns, and Dr. Malcolm Colby Henderson. These four scientists took great delight in showing ComSubPac all the latest gadgets that were in the works to help shorten the Pacific War.[4]

It might have been right out of a more modern James Bond movie, with agent 007 being shown all the latest spy gadgets before his next great mission. Admiral Lockwood had his own secret mission in mind, with a goal to end the war quicker. The crew of the new *Spadefish*, fitting out in nearby Mare Island, had no idea of how this little visit would figure prominently into their own history.

Vice Admiral Charles Andrews Lockwood, Jr. served as Commander, Submarines, Pacific (ComSubPac) from February 1943 through the end of the war. Known affectionately to his fellow submariners as "Uncle Charlie," Lockwood took a personal interest in the development of the first FM Sonar unit that had been installed aboard *Spadefish* at Mare Island. *Official U.S. Navy photo.*

Dr. Harnwell finally took Lockwood down San Diego harbor's entrance channel in a small motor boat to demonstrate a new device called Frequency Modulated Sonar (FMS). Aboard the boat was a Position Plan Indicator (PPI) screen, which looked something similar to an old television set. This monitor would indicate the distance and directions of the sides of the channel through which the little boat was passing. This underwater radar also showed other passing motor boats as blobs on the screen.[5]

The FM Sonar system was known as "Fampas," short for Frequency and Mechanically Plotted Area Scan, and the first set that Lockwood saw this day had been dubbed Fampas Mark I.

Lockwood later wrote of how the other passing boats showed on this prototype FM sonar screen:

> Their steel hulls gave back a clearly audible, bell-like tone, a tone which I was destined to hear many hundred times in the far reaches of the Pacific in the years to come, a chime which our submariners learned to call Hell's bells because of the sinister, death-dealing enemies from which they echoed.

Dr. Harnwell's scientists had been asked in 1943 to develop the Fampas sonar for Mediterranean minesweepers, but it had proved unsuitable in rough waters for detecting enemy mines. He believed that a submarine, however, could use this new gear beneath the surface to safely slip into mined enemy harbors.

The set's early performance did not impress Admiral Lockwood, but he did see enough potential with this sonar to give the scientists a chance to further pursue it. Through the rest of 1943, the Fampas gear, soon renamed as just "FM Sonar," continued to test with the scientists and a number of enhancements were made. Dr. Malcolm Henderson and the UCDWR scientists used their lab boat, *Torqua*, a 56-foot twin engined glass-bottomed former sight-seeing boat, to test the FM gear. They found that not only could the gear detect metallic objects, but also could track whales and even seals quite well.[6]

Testing continued into the winter of 1943-1944. Plans were put in motion to install an FM set on a school submarine at San Diego. In January, 1944, however, UCDWR received a request from the Navy Mine Warfare Training Station at Charleston, South Carolina, to review the set for use in detecting moored mines. In late February 1944, the original FM set was tested aboard the old submarine *S-34*, under former *Wahoo* officer Lt. Cdr. Roger Warde Paine Jr. A dummy mine field was established in San Diego Bay, and *S-34* tested the FM gear during March 1944. Although the gear did detect mines, Captain Paine was not pleased that the FM only detected the mines about 85 per cent of the time.[7]

Testing proceeded, and on 21 March 1944, Cdr. Edwin Robinson Swinburne, commanding Submarine Division 41 to which *S-34* belonged, wrote a note to Admiral Lockwood. "It is understood that *Spadefish* will be in San Diego for torpedo and machinery trials in May," Swinburne wrote. He recommended to ComSubPac that orders be given "to install FM sonar with PPI screen in this vessel for test and further delivery to Force Commander."

When Lockwood presented his findings to his boss, Admiral Chester Nimitz, he was relieved to get the go-ahead. "The Big Boss told me to go ahead and explore the matter."[8] Lockwood approved Commander Swinburne's proposal on 18 April, and thereby changed the destiny of the new boat *Spadefish*.

Thus, the gears had been set in motion for the University of California's Division of War Research scientists to provide *Spadefish* with the first FM sonar set for testing. Once *Spadefish* moved from Mare Island down to San Diego, UCDWR technicians, under the direction of Dr. Franz Kurie, completed the final FMS installation.

Mare Island's yard teams had made modifications to *Spadefish* to accept the sonar unit. The actual sonar head was mounted on a motor-driven column that penetrated the ship's hull near the forward torpedo room door on the ship's port side. The FM equipment stack was mounted on the deck close by. This steel box, standing nearly four feet tall and protruding up from the main deck, was filled with electronics. Cables were run from this box into the control room via the ship's bulkheads. From the control room, the cables went up into the conning tower, where the PPI scope and speaker were mounted.[9]

Spadefish conducted trials and preliminary training in the San Diego area from 13 May to 2 June, 1944. Her crew had been divided up into watch sections. Once her shakedown was complete, each watch section was expected to handle all of the routines of diving, surfacing and fighting a fleet submarine. When battle stations was sounded, each man had a specific spot aboard ship where he would be stationed. Chief of the boat Gregory set these stations for all enlisted men and posted them on the Watch, Quarter, and Station Bill for all to see.[10]

From San Diego, *Spadefish* went through the usual shakedown testing. This included tracking and simulated torpedo firing runs. After the fire control and tracking parties were thoroughly trained, *Spadefish* fired actual exercise torpedoes at an escort target, each set to pass harmlessly under the "target." Simulated attacks were conducted both during the daylight and at night.

"The shakedown created the heart of *Spadefish*," according to auxiliaryman Buck Miller. "The creation, input and coaching background of Captain Underwood really made the boat function as a unit under all the drills. Checking equipment and machinery went with the drills, constantly one after another."

The threat of losing the submarine was just as possible due to human error or operational mishap as it was to enemy attack. *Spadefish* had one such close call during her trials off California. "She was a brand new boat and things don't always work just right," recalled Ted Ustick. "We were doing a crash dive, which means you are going 15 knots on the surface and then you suddenly sound the diving alarm and see how fast you can get her under."[11]

This time, however, something went wrong during the crash dive. "The stern planes went out of commission," said Ustick. *Spadefish*'s bow took an alarming down angle and plunged for the ocean's depths, throwing men off their feet. She raced past 400 feet and still kept diving. Ustick recalled that the diving officer, Frank Alvis, "kicked her in full reverse and saved the ship, no doubt." Lt.(jg) Perry Wood said that this errant crash dive was one he would not forget. "We went below test depth and had to shift from hydraulic power to hand power to stop her. It was enough to make people need to wash their underwear!"

In addition to her other trial runs during the shakedown period off San Diego, *Spadefish* conducted a lengthy series of tests on her new

Ken Powers standing on the stern planes of *Spadefish* while in dry-dock. During her early training dives, the stern planes of *Spadefish* stuck and caused the ship to dive sharply for the ocean's bottom. *Courtesy of Bernie Massar.*

FM sonar device. Among these tests was whether or not *Spadefish* could penetrate an enemy mine field. Dummy mines were strung out in the pattern to simulate a mine field. Under the watchful eye of Professor Malcolm Henderson, Captain Underwood's crew had had some success in detecting and locating these mines.[12]

Twenty-two-year-old RT1c Neal Pike was the only radio technician aboard *Spadefish* during her early days. Prior to joining the Navy Reserves in August 1942, he had worked three years in a lumberyard in Emmett, Idaho. Pike had been through extensive electronics training after boot camp, including three months at the University of Houston. Then, it was on to Mare Island, where he spent another six months of training on underwater sound gear and the top-secret radar. Graduating in the top ten per cent of his class, he had the option to choose his assignment. "I had never seen an ocean," recalled Pike. "I was raised in Idaho. My best buddies in the school were choosing submarines, so I chose submarines, also."[13]

After sub school and further schooling at New London on the special electronics gear of submarines, Pike was assigned to *Spadefish*. Being the only radarman aboard, the experimental gear that soon came aboard became his special project. The FM sonar was developed by the Naval Electronics Laboratory in San Diego, as he recalled.

> Its object in the development was to try to reduce the detectability of this equipment on the then standard single fre-

quency echo ranging equipment, the QC sonar. The Japanese Navy had the identical single frequency equipment, since they had purchased it from the Submarine Signal Co. right up until the war started with Japan. The idea of the frequency modulated equipment was that its frequency would sweep past the single frequency of the standard equipment so fast that it could not be heard on that equipment and therefore it would not be detectable. Therefore, it was reasoned the new equipment could be used in enemy waters without detection by the Japanese warships. If we turned on our single frequency equipment, it could be heard for 40 to 100 miles, depending on water conditions.[14]

XQLA serial number 1 was now Neal Pike's pet project to learn and understand. "Scientists from the Naval Electronics Laboratory accompanied us on our initial trial run and trained me on the operation and maintenance of this equipment," he wrote.

The Navy officially called the equipment the QLA Small Object Detector, but the crew knew it as FM Sonar. The sonar operator could see the blobs on the eight-inch PPI screen. Thanks to the speaker, anyone within range could hear the clear bell tone known as "hell's bells" when a mine was detected.[15]

The first tests of *Spadefish*'s new FM Sonar did not go as smoothly as Dr. Kurie's team would have liked. In fact, radio tech Pike considered them to be a failure. The set howled and screeched through the speakers when it was turned on. After five days of sea trials, Dr. Kurie's team had no success and removed the FM gear.[16]

The set was placed aboard the wooden hulled surface craft *Torqua*, and the problem was quickly found to be faulty wiring. Once the technicians had this fixed, the gear worked brilliantly. Dr. Kurie had to reserve his enthusiasm however, as the inner workings of the steel submarine had much more equipment to interfere with the FM's performance than did the *Torqua*.

By the time Dr. Kurie's scientists were happy enough to try another test of the FM gear aboard *Spadefish*, their time was just about up. After the training period was completed on 2 June, *Spadefish* returned to the Mare Island Navy Yard for final repairs and alterations. Captain Underwood celebrated his 34th birthday en route on 3 June. This post shakedown repair period at Mare Island was from 5 June to 14 June.

One of the old traditions in submarines was to celebrate the promotion of fellow crewmen. This was often done by tossing the newly-promoted sailor overboard into the "drink." During early June, eleven *Spadefish* sailors were notified of changes in their ratings, among them Steward's Mate 1/c Henry Lewis Solomon. As of 6 June, he would be

Cook 3/c. The tradition of throwing him overboard was about to take place from *Spadefish*'s deck at Mare Island.

Solomon protested that he could not swim. "Nobody paid any attention, and off he went flying into the drink," remembered Bernie Massar. "He started to flounder and cried for help and was going under. The tide was strong and was running, carrying him away from the sub."

Quartermaster Sam Cooper, a former life guard, removed his shoes, watch and wallet, and then dove in. Cooper hauled poor Solomon back to *Spadefish* and helping hands. According to Massar, this little event did not slow the promotion festivities. "The next man to go overboard also could not swim. A life line was tied to him and over he went. He was then hauled in like a fish!"

The FM set was trucked up to Mare Island and was reinstalled in *Spadefish*'s conning tower during the final days of her repairs in early June. *Spadefish* was ready to depart for war, and Captain Underwood reluctantly gave Dr. Kurie's scientists just another half day to check out their new electronics gear. Outside of San Francisco Bay, the gear worked perfectly this time. Off the Farallon Islands, the PC-boat which had accompanied *Spadefish* acted as a target. From underwater, the new sonar could pick up the PC at 800 yards. Dr. Kurie felt that the results were excellent and in his report, the physicist wrote that his FM gear "abundantly justified all confidence placed in the system's abilities."[17]

During the final preparations to depart, CPhM Parker became sick and was transferred to the Mare Island Naval Hospital on 11 June for treatment. Fireman Jack Gallagher remembered that *Spadefish*'s Chief Pharmacist's Mate Billy Parker "was one of those guys who could hypnotize people. He could take a deck of cards, go through it once and then tell you where every card in the deck was." Torpedoman Bert Spiese was another "victim" of Parker's hypnosis. "He would hypnotize me every week just for fun. I would be playing pinochle later and he would come up and use that post-hypnotic suggestive stuff on me. He would have me right back in that state again!"

Gallagher found the doc's magic vanished when it came time to go to war. "When we got ready to go to sea, he developed some kind of skin rash." In Parker's place, *Spadefish* received a new "doc," PhM1c Victor Leon Ives, a 24-year-old Texan whose childhood buddies had once nicknamed him "Diddle." He had joined the Navy a year before the attack on Pearl Harbor and his experience was welcomed aboard *Spadefish*. Medical services during torpedo attacks would not be need-

Lt. Cdr. Ted Ustick, the newly promoted executive officer of *Spadefish*, receiving the Silver Star at the San Diego Naval Repair Base for one of his prior war patrols aboard *Tarpon*. Rear Admiral Wilhelm Lee Friedell, Commandant 11th Naval District, pins Ustick as Cdr. Gordon Underwood (far right) looks on. *Courtesy of Cdr. Perry W. Ustick, USN (Ret.).*

ed, so Vic Ives would become an integral part of the conning tower attack team. There was a saying among submariners that few of them were ever awarded the Purple Heart. *Spadefish* would either come out of her enemy engagements intact or not at all.[18]

Doc Parker was not the only crew member to suffer an ailment. During the days in California, ship's mascot Luau managed to break her leg while jumping from the boat. Although the lovable little terrier was set in a leg cast, some feared she would not fully recover. The leading gunner's mate, "Shaky Jake" Lewis, finally gave up on her when the little dog became despondent, listless and refused to eat. Bernie Massar, the other gunner's mate aboard *Spadefish*, noticed Lewis taking Luau into the superstructure near the forward escape trunk.[19]

Noting that Lewis was carrying his .45 pistol, Massar called, "What are you going to do with her?"

"I'm going to put her out of her misery," Lewis replied.

"Jeez, why don't you wait a couple of days and see what happens?" Massar pleaded.

Shaky Jake agreed to give her a little more time. "In those few days," wrote Massar, "she snapped out of her mood and once again became the frisky Luau."

Spadefish departed Mare Island on 14 June 1944, proceeding down the channel into San Francisco Bay and out under the Golden Gate Bridge. Her destination was Pearl Harbor. As the men passed under the Golden Gate Bridge, they did not know when—or if—*Spadefish* would pass under this bridge again.

When *Spadefish* entered Pearl Harbor on 23 June 1944, she was already something special.

She was so special that ComSubPac himself, Vice Admiral Lockwood, was eagerly awaiting her arrival. For the crewmen topside on *Spadefish* for deck detail this day, it was their first view of Pearl Harbor, where Japan had started the war on 7 December 1941. *Spadefish* eased along the twisting channel past Hickam Field, Hospital Point, Ford Island and the tall Navy Yard cranes before reaching the sub base. Much of the wreckage and destruction had been cleared, although the hulls of the battleships *Oklahoma* and *Arizona* remained as testaments to the day of infamy. It was hard for Exec Ted Ustick—who had served on *Arizona* in 1941—to view the wreckage.

Once *Spadefish*'s maneuvering watch had secured her into the Submarine Base at Pearl Harbor, "Uncle Charlie" came aboard to greet Captain Underwood and to inspect the new FM Sonar gear. Lockwood later wrote, "I was on hand with a lot of questions for her commanding officer and his technicians." He had hopes that the new FM sonar could be used to actually chart mine fields and eventually penetrate them.[20]

Four of the scientists from UCDWR, including Dr. Franz Kurie, had flown from California to await *Spadefish*'s arrival as well. "When we got into Hawaii, the technicians were like ants crawling all over the boat to get to the FM sonar," said torpedoman Bert Spiese. "We had to stand watch at the gangplank while we were at the sub base because of that sonar." Dr. Kurie's team went over *Spadefish*'s FM equipment and found that it had received damage to the receiving transducer, apparently the result of a heavy storm *Spadefish* had encountered en route from California. A spare head was swapped with the non-working unit, and Kurie found that the FM set showed positive signs again.[21]

Spadefish was put into a drydock at Pearl Harbor to repair the FMS and other minor voyage issues that had developed. Repairmen regasketed her torpedo tube outer doors. They also installed a new APR-1 non-directional enemy radar detector, an RBH receiver, and a new type of SJ radar reflector. The *Spadefish* wardroom also received a new officer, who would help fill out the watch list as a junior OOD. Thirty-two-year-old Ensign Donald Ernest Martin, USNR, a veteran of two previous war patrols, was assigned as the new Radar Officer.

The most popular change during this refit was the installation of an air conditioning unit in the forward battery compartment. This AC unit, per Captain Underwood, "made a great improvement in the livability of that usually hot spot."

Upon arrival at Pearl Harbor, *Spadefish* began an intensive training period which was not terminated until nearly a month later. At that time, each man was capable of performing his job with almost automatic precision.²² She would make day and night simulated attack approaches on warships to cover the situations her crew would most likely encounter on patrol.

Spadefish's first sea test came on 26 June. An additional sonar operator, RT2c Solomon Cohen, had reported aboard ship to take part in this training. *Spadefish* operated with the destroyer escort *USS Seid* (DE-256) off the coast of Oahu that day. Dr. Kurie was not happy with the performance of the FM during submerged tests with the tin can. Neal Pike and the FM team could barely pick up *Seid*, even when the destroyer was as close as 600 yards. "Things run good in the laboratory," recalled Lt.(jg) Perry Wood, the communications officer, "but they don't always run right at sea."

Spadefish went out again on 28 June, this time to try and pick up a dummy minefield moored off Oahu. The Japanese "planted" their minefields with minelaying ships which worked at specified distances apart. A typical enemy minefield would consist of two or three rows of mines which spanned certain shipping lanes, straits or channels. The rows were generally widely spaced, with distances apart from four hundred to 1000 yards between rows. Within their respective rows, the mines were planted from 75 to 100 yards apart, this to keep one explosion from setting off a whole chain reaction.²³

The most typical mine which the U.S. was most familiar was their Type 93, a moored contact mine. It was a spherical, chemical horn-type that exploded when an acid in a horn was released through the breaking of the horn. These mines could be planted as deep as 250 feet or more, but were rarely planted below 100 feet. Even then, the norm was for the Japanese to plant them at elevated tiers from ten feet to forty feet to seventy feet. The draft of a surfaced submarine was eighteen feet when the boat was in standard trim. The top row of shallowly planted mines would thus offer a menace to submarines surfacing through a mine field.²⁴

Moored mines, known as "hell pots," were supposed to be armed only when the pull and weight of the cable provides tension on the mooring spindle. A drifting mine which separated from its cable over time was supposed to be harmless, as the tension could not pull it, but no sailor trusted a drifting mine. It is possible that the United States lost three submarines and as many as eight submarines to enemy mines during World War II.

As *Spadefish* moved submerged into the dummy minefield off Oahu on 28 June, the results were somewhat unnerving. RT1c Pike, despite his best efforts, was unable to detect a single mine this day. One of the UCDWR experts took over the set, but did not have much better luck. The lab technician had more experience, but was able to pick up the dummy mines only through sheer perseverance.²⁵

After 28 June, Dr. Kurie and his scientists then had to step aside so that ComSubPac could finish preparing *Spadefish* for war. She then began an intensive three-week combat training program to give her crew and equipment its final checking out. During the "Convoy College" exercises, the experimental FM set was left aboard, but was never turned on.

Spadefish conducted numerous torpedo exercises, making simulated attacks on anti-submarine surface vessels. Tough senior officers rode aboard to critique Captain Underwood's crew under pressure. The scrutiny was tough, and at the end of the first session, the sub was either recommended for patrol or another practice patrol was prescribed.

The gun crews got in some practice training. Gunnery officer Gus Laundy coached his gunners on deck as they fired. "We tested them out by firing into a hill that was vacated," he recalled. "There was nobody living there, I think on the west side of Oahu."

After the first few days of Convoy College testing, the FM set was again damaged during heavy seas. *Spadefish* pulled back into Pearl and the UCDWR men surveyed the latest damage. Neal Pike recalled that the three-inch steel shaft that rose from the hull to support the transducers had been bent by the storms. Intended to revolve a full 360° during normal operation, the unit was frozen solid. The UCDWR engineers, unable to free the shaft, asked the Navy Yard to fabricate a temporary shield that would take the brunt of the wave action. They further recommended that future FM units be protected by a more rugged five-inch shaft.[26]

On 4 July, *Spadefish* made more trial runs against a dummy field that had been laid 2,000 yards off Brown's Camp on Oahu's north shore. This time, the results were more encouraging. The telltale hell's bells would begin ringing at 400 yards, but only about 30 per cent of the time. Dr. Kurie considered this to be pleasing performance. Captain Underwood decided to test the FM gear further during the next three days of convoy exercises. With Neal Pike monitoring the PPI, *Spadefish* tracked a destroyer with improved consistency.

The FM testing was thorough. Precision with this equipment, as well as faith in its ability, was crucial. On 6 July, *Spadefish* received a new sonar tech, RT2c Joe Case from Phoenix, Arizona, to replace the technician who had recently come aboard at Pearl to help train on the new sonar. Leading technician Pike found Case to be a solid new assistant and together the two would operate as a team for all patrols.

Spadefish conducted her training period from 28 June to 20 July, including the sound gear tests and participation in two rounds of convoy exercises. Generally, the testing prior to a new submarine's first war patrol was for two weeks only, but *Spadefish* ended up doing four.

Moored mines such as this one were planted in a test field off Oahu. *Spadefish*'s FM sonar set, the first installed in the U.S. Navy, made a particular ringing when a mine was detected. This ringing became known to submariners as "hell's bells" and the explosive sources as "hellpots." *Author's photo.*

Operating out of Pearl, the senior squadron commander rode aboard *Spadefish* for her testing and did not pass her after the first convoy exercise. Captain Underwood took this in stride, noting in his first patrol report, "No better training could have been obtained than the two convoy exercises in which this ship participated." *Spadefish*'s return for a second round of Convoy College exercise had not been anticipated, according to Lt.(jg) Decker.

> We were found lacking, for reasons I was too inexperienced to understand. I thought we were perfect. Frank Alvis, my closest friend, had considerable submarine experience. He was very disturbed when we were held at Pearl for another two weeks of training and inspection. He knew we were not ready for patrol, but I certainly did not. But I guess we showed 'em later![27]

During the final days of *Spadefish*'s training period, Admiral Lockwood went to sea with her to observe the FM sonar testing first-hand for the first time. "I was beset by cross-currents of thoughts and emotions," he recalled of coming aboard her on 13 July 1944.[28]

Aboard *Spadefish*, "Uncle Charlie" took the time to speak to the enlisted men and acknowledge the responsibilities each was entrusted with. "That guy was a sailor's admiral," recalled radioman Mike Sergio. "He'd always speak to you."

Out from Pearl, Admiral Lockwood stood on the bridge with Captain Underwood, anxious to test out his new toy. "Say, Skipper, do you think we could speed her up a bit?" he asked impatiently.

The use of high speed was discouraged in such an area. Underwood tried to suppress a thin grin as he leaned toward the open conning tower hatch and ordered, "All ahead full!"

Spadefish sped westward along Ewa Beach, a couple of miles offshore. Lockwood noted the rubber sphere of the FM transducer which jutted up from the forward deck. It was mounted on a short and slim steel shaft that rose from the deck slightly abaft the bow-planes. This shaft extended down through *Spadefish*'s hull into the forward torpedo room where gears, operated by electric motors, turned the shaft right or left as Neal Pike in the conning tower might direct. Lockwood later described his first impressions of this new equipment.

> Contrary to the procedure used on minesweepers, the device had been installed on deck. As I studied it, it occurred to me that—from a submariner's standpoint—it might be preferable to place the sonar set in the keel of the sub rather than on the deck. If mounted in the keel, the set might not only give a better signal but might even prove usable on the surface. So mounted, it would not be affected by the noise of water gurgling through the deck gratings and the superstructure.[29]

In the field, there were twenty hellpots planted in two rows with some 150 feet between mines and about 300 yards between the rows. The rows ran at right angles to the coast. The mines were planted at a uniform depth of thirty feet in order that Hawaiian Island shipping could pass safely over without hitting them.

When about 1200 yards south of the buoys that marked the nearest row, Underwood ordered, "Clear the bridge!" The bridge watch scrambled down the hatch. As the raucous echo of the diving alarm sounded, Lockwood eagerly headed toward the spot on the starboard side in the conning tower where the FMS receiving set was installed.[30]

Radio technician Neal Pike was seated at the FM Sonar. His set looked something like an old television set. It had a circular scanning plate with a diameter of about sixteen inches. From its center extended a series of concentric circles with range markings that rose from 100 to several 1000 yards. Bearing lines extended from the center of the screen to all points on the compass, like spokes in a wheel. These bearing lines helped Pike relate the position of a hellpot he saw as related to *Spadefish*'s position.

A hair-line thin luminous sweep ran from the center of the screen and covered the compass area designated by Pike to search. He usually selected the sweeping beam to map out an area left to right over a zone of about 90 degrees, ahead of the ship. When the beam did not find an object ahead, it ran from the center to the edge of the screen as it swept the desired area. But when the tranducer's beam hit a mine or some other solid object, the luminous sweep formed a light blob on the sonar screen at that precise point. Pike or other operators could then report the distance from *Spadefish* to the mine, or other object, and its bearing from the course currently being steered.

The trouble with these blobs was that any number of things could cause the transducer's beam to bounce back. In addition to mines, Pike and his operators would find that a reef, a school of fish, a mass of colder water, or even the wake of a vessel could cause enough deflection to give them a blob on their FM screen.

While approaching the minefield, a loudspeaker was switched on in the conning tower above Pike's sonar set. The intensity of the sound depended upon the quality of the blob on screen. A hellpot registered as a small but almost pear-shaped blob on the screen. The loudspeaker would emit irregular, scratchy noises if the blob was a poorly-defined light image. When the pear-shaped blob of a true mine appeared on the PPI screen, the loudspeaker produced a full, clear sound of a tiny bell. "A skilled operator might fail to guess the source of flickering light blobs and their cacophony of sounds," wrote Lockwood. "But even the greenest hand would know the meaning of pear-shaped blobs and tolling chimes—the bells that heralded the presence of hellpots and no doubts about it."[31]

With Admiral Lockwood in the conning tower, *Spadefish* dove to 62 feet for periscope depth. She had barely reached this depth when hell's bells rang clearly from the FM speaker.

"Contact!" announced Pike at the sonar. "Bearing –zero-three-zero, sir!"

This meant that Pike's FM sonar had detected the blob of a planted mine slightly to the right of *Spadefish*'s course.

An immense "tidal wave of triumph" swept through ComSubPac at this announcement. Since giving approval a year before to begin the work on FM gear being placed aboard one of his subs, he had gambled much that this prototype would work. Now, Pike's screen had a light blob for a hellpot and hell's bells were ringing clearly in the conning tower. For Lockwood, it was "truly heavenly music."[32]

Cautiously at a 3-knot pace, Captain Underwood took *Spadefish* through the planted mine field. During the morning, he made a dozen trial runs, testing and practicing with the new FM set. They probed for the limitations of the gear, and found some. "I soon realized that the efficiency of a sonar set could not rise above the ability of the men who operated it," wrote Lockwood.

It took operators who were properly trained on how to distinguish the different sounds with only a light touch on the volume control. Lockwood sensed that "Underwood's faith in the sonar device had been on the low side. Of course, the set was far from perfect. But even miracles fall short of absolute perfection. That FM sonar set was at least within range of perfection if we gave the device the time and study and patience it deserved."[33]

The UCDWR scientists got *Spadefish* again for one last full day of FM trials on 15 July. Another destroyer escort was provided to be the target. On this date, the detection ranges were stretched out as far as 1,200 yards. Dr. Kurie, however, found that there was an area of silence directly above *Spadefish*. In this "blind spot," *Spadefish*'s FM gear would simply not pick up any target of any size or shape.[34]

By Dr. Kurie's calculations, the FM gear's minimum range "is approximately six times the submarine's depth. Thus, for 150 feet, targets within 300 yards will not be detected." This meant that *Spadefish* had to submerge where she knew she had clear water, for the area immediately ahead of her would be completely blind for the first distance of travel.

This, added to the screeching sound the FM sonar made in conjunction with her other gear, was enough to dissuade Underwood from using it.

While *Spadefish* went off to war, Lockwood worked on and received permission to install more FM sets on at least a dozen other subs. Based on his trial run with *Spadefish* this day, he would have all future FM sets keel-mounted instead of deck mounted.[35]

Neal Pike and *Spadefish* would be intimately associated with their top boss during that year as he worked on plans to conduct a secret mission involving subs equipped with this FM gear. When *Spadefish* returned to the sub base for voyage repairs, Admiral Lockwood requested the UCDWR boys to leave the FM gear aboard *Spadefish*. Dr. Kurie was happy to oblige in loaning this equipment to the Navy for an "indefinite period, asking in return only that we be kept informed of the results of its further use."[36] She would thus be the first U.S. submarine in the fleet to go into the war zone with this new top-secret electronics apparatus.

There was one problem, however. Although the FM had proven its ability to detect mines and other targets, it did not play well with *Spadefish*'s other gear, as Pike explains.

> We discovered that when it was turned on simultaneously with the single frequency equipment, far from being silent and undetectable, it sounded like a chamber of horrors on the single frequency equipment, emitting howls and squeals, rendering

the single frequency equipment useless until the new equipment was turned off. Further tests revealed that it was detectable at long distances on the standard equipment [contrary to what the scientists had believed]. Therefore, the decision was made by ComSubPac *not* to use the new equipment in the war zone.[37]

The FM sonar remained aboard, mounted topside, but was left off. *Spadefish* would depend upon her single frequency sonar in the war zone, where the ear-splitting squeals and howls of her FM gear would be a deadly giveaway.

With training finally completed on 20 July, *Spadefish* spent the next few days preparing to depart on her first war patrol. BM1c Willard "Boats" Eimermann was selected by Captain Underwood and Lt. Cdr. Ustick to become the new chief of the boat.

His predecessor, Chief Earl Gregory, had received orders on 15 July that he had been promoted to warrant officer and was being transferred to new construction back in the States. Gregory returning to the States proved to be a good thing for Eimermann. "I had a hot run with cards and I was buying my wife a diamond and a wedding ring," he recalled. The problem of how to get it back home was solved. Eimermann worked a payment with Gregory to take his jewelry back Stateside and mail it to his wife. "Sure as heck he did," Boats said. "So, I got that off my hands."

It was somewhat unusual for a first-class bosun's mate to be selected as *Spadefish*'s chief of the boat. It probably did not hurt that he had clicked with Exec Ted Ustick since first meeting him. With more than seven years collective service in the Navy, however, Boats Eimermann was now the senior enlisted man aboard ship. Although the chief of the boat was technically exempted from standing watch duties, Eimermann opted to keep himself on the schedule.

Eimermann had to spring several of his men from the base brig shortly before *Spadefish*'s departure for war patrol. "I was on the shore with four other swabbies," recalled crewman Bert Spiese, who had trained a little as a boxer before joining the Navy. While out "hunting for fun" after some drinks, Spiese and his buddies "got into a fight with some Marines and we ended up in the brig." Spiese felt that submarine sailors "had some pretty good immunity. The Skipper sent the new chief of the boat to the brig to get us out. They told him to pick out his *Spadefish* guys, and I almost didn't get out, because the new chief hadn't met me yet!"

Another early challenge for Boats Eimermann also occurred just before *Spadefish*'s first patrol. Following the last ship's party prior to departing Hawaii, veteran torpedoman Richard Butchofsky got into a disagreement with one of the signalmen, Dale Frazier, a smaller man in size. Captain Underwood did not tolerate misconduct among his crew and on 22 July, the day before departing Pearl Harbor, Butchofsky was transferred to the sub base. Frazier's nose was set and he remained aboard ship. Although the incident is one her crewmen still do not like to mention, the impression of this event insured that such behavior would never be repeated aboard *Spadefish*.

Butchofsky did not let the incident deter him. He quickly made it aboard another brand-new Mare Island boat, *Trepang*. She was commanded by Commander Roy M. Davenport, a veteran of the early patrols of the successful submarine *Silversides* and Butchofsky's former skipper aboard *Haddock*. "I considered myself extremely fortunate to have some of my *Haddock* personnel join the crew of the *Trepang*," wrote Davenport, among them "good old 'Butch,'" who would make five more successful war patrols aboard her.[38]

Aboard submarines, fighting was absolutely not allowed. "If you got into a fight," recalled motormac Pat Kelley, "they would kick you off the submarine." In 32 years of Navy service, mostly on subs, Kelley never saw a fight aboard ship. "Guys would get mad at each other on subs, but there were no fistfights. If something had to be settled, you waited until you got into port."

After the departure of CEM Gregory at Pearl Harbor, Chief Carl Thomas Schmelzer was the leading electrician aboard. Dedicated and experienced, Schmelzer was also prone to salty outbursts. "If Carl Thomas spoke six words, he swore five of 'em!" said motormac Pat Kelley. Schmelzer had a way of making his point: he was direct. One morning, while going through the serving line in the galley, ship's cook Ed Graf asked, "Chief, how many eggs you want?"

"I want a clutch," said Schmelzer, who had originally joined the Navy in hopes of being a ship's cook.

"What's a clutch, chief?" asked Graf.

"Any damn fool knows a clutch is four!" snapped Schmelzer.

The other chiefs had a good time with "Stinky" Schmelzer and loved to see him get riled up. The cooks took a fair amount of teasing from the enlisted men they served, but it was all in good spirits. It was no secret that the submarine service managed to garner the finest food in the fleet. Those who served aboard her could boast not only of their extra hazard pay for undersea duty but that they were the best fed men in the service. "We ate like family," remembered electrician's mate Ken Sigworth. "When we had steak, you didn't just get a steak on your plate. The cooks let you order it the way you liked it."

Within the tight space of *Spadefish's* galley, Chief Scherman and his three cooks prepared meals for 85 men three times a day. *Courtesy of Bernie Massar.*

During the final days of stocking up for patrol, Ensign Bill Ware and his chief commissary steward, Francis Scherman, were busy ashore securing the best cuts of meat and stores to be brought aboard *Spadefish*. Scherman had been a first class ship's cook aboard the destroyer *Stewart* (DD-224) before moving on to the old submarine *Narwhal* and making five war patrols. Aboard *Spadefish*, Chief Scherman presided over the galley and crew's messroom. His leading cook was SC1c Edward "Buckwheat" Pirrung, who was ably assisted by SC2c Tom Riley and SC3c Graf. Pirrung, Graf, and Scherman took the crew's ribbing in style.

Tom Riley, however, was another story. A tough New Yorker and a good fry cook, Riley was considered by shipmate Wallace McMahon to be "one of the best cooks I ever met. He was a little guy, and everytime he went ashore, he was always getting restricted for getting into a fight. So, Captain Underwood assigned Riley to a bakery in Vallejo and he became the ship's baker." Tom Riley became the biggest morale booster aboard *Spadefish* behind Luau, the ship's mascot. "Evidently, most ships' bread was not too good," said fireman Jack Gallagher. "One of Riley's claims to fame was that he was able to put out some great bread."

His cakes, pies and bread were beloved by many. Some of the crew teasingly nicknamed him "Mother" Riley for his baking. His monicker certainly did not soften his demeanor, however. Crewmen coming off watch at 0400 to the aromas of freshly baking pastries were cautioned against pilfering by a stern Riley warning: "Touch any of those pies and I'll kill you!"

The only African Americans who served aboard were the two mess attendants, Henry Solomon of Des Moines and William Portwood from Cincinnati. Blacks in the U.S. Navy of World War II were integrated with white crews, but in the submarine service were restricted to service roles. Solomon and Portwood's primary duties included serving meals to the wardroom and keeping duty officers in the conning tower and on the bridge supplied with fresh coffee. During attacks, the mess attendants took station in the galley and crew's berthing quarters, manning the battle phones.

Spadefish's "fuel king," MoMM1c Charles Griffith, oversaw the topping off of the fuel tanks. At the Base chart pool, navigator Ted Ustick drew the charts he and his quartermasters would need en route and while on their patrol station. The location of the first war patrol was kept confidential, with only Captain Underwood and Lt. Cdr. Ustick aware of the destination. By the captain having advance knowledge of the patrol area, he was able to read up on patrol reports from submarines who had been in the same area previously.

Lieutenant Gus Laundy and Chief Torpedoman Simms supervised the final loading of live torpedoes aboard at Pearl Harbor. The after torpedo room took on eight new Mark 18, Model 1 (18.1) electric torpedoes. Bars and straps were installed at Pearl Harbor in order that charging the electric torpedoes in their tubes would be safer. Charging the Mark 18.1 was accomplished by pulling them partially out of the tube and then securing them with the straps. Each charge took between two and three hours and was repeated weekly to keep the torpedoes in good firing condition.[39]

The jury was still out on the reliability of the Mark 18 electric torpedo. Although wakeless due to its electric propulsion, the Mark 18s ran a slower rate of 29 knots. Lt.(jg) Decker wrote that, "Our skipper was reluctant to accept them, untested as they were, but finally took eight, all loaded aft."[40]

Spadefish's forward torpedo room was loaded with sixteen of the longer range Mark 23 steam torpedoes. The Mark 23, driven by a steam engine, was an improved version of the Mark 14, which was in heavy use during the war. Each torpedo was twenty feet in length and weighed more than a ton and a half. The "war fish" required routine maintenance by the torpedomen each week to insure proper performance upon firing.

The Mark 18 electric torpedo now loaded in *Spadefish*'s after room had been an utter failure during its early development in 1942. In September 1943, Captain Dudley "Mush" Morton's famous *Wahoo*

Original Officer Assignments: May 1944
USS Spadefish

Cdr. Gordon W. Underwood, USN	Commanding Officer
Lt. Cdr. Theodore M. Ustick, USN	Executive Officer
Lt. Frank R. Alvis Jr., DE-V(G)	Engineering Officer
Lt. Henry H. Laundy Jr. D-V(G)	Gunnery Officer
Lt.(jg) Daniel D. Decker USN	First Lieutenant
Lt.(jg) Perry S. Wood, DE-V(G), USNR	Communications Officer
Ens. Ray C. White, USN	Assistant Engineering Off.
Ens. Donald E. Martin, D-V(S), USNR	Radar Officer
Ens. William J. Ware, USN	Commissary Officer

(SS-238) had taken a load of Mark 14 torpedoes into the Sea of Japan. Morton, one of the war's hottest skippers with 19 confirmed sinkings, was frustrated with torpedoes that missed, broached or failed to explode on impact with target ships. "Damn the torpedoes," he noted in his patrol report. Subsequent testing carried out on the Mark 14 torpedoes would show Admiral Lockwood that those fired straight-on into an enemy ship often failed to explode on impact.

After only four frustrating days in the virgin waters of the Sea of Japan, *Wahoo* received permission to return to base for a torpedo reload. Faulty torpedoes reduced the kills that sister submarine *Plunger* could have made in the area at the same time. Six submarines had entered the Sea of Japan during July and August, but they had only turn in a disheartening five confirmed ship sinkings for 13,500 tons.[41]

Mush Morton, still smarting from his luckless patrol, asked for permission to return immediately to the Sea of Japan. Admiral Lockwood granted his request, sending *Wahoo* and sister sub *Sawfish* through La Perouse Strait with a mixed load of Mark 14s and the brand new Mark 18 electric torpedoes. *Sawfish* had pitiful luck with both torpedoes types, suffering dud hits, erratic runs and even one Mark 18 which plunged straight to the bottom of the ocean. *Wahoo* fared much better, sinking four confirmed ships.[42]

Wahoo never returned from the Sea of Japan, however. Recently translated Japanese military documents show that search planes found her departing the Sea of Japan through La Perouse Strait on 11 October 1943, running on the surface and trailing oil from damage she had previously suffered. A Wakkanai (Oonuma) Base pilot dropped two bombs, further damaging *Wahoo*. The three available scout planes at this base made fourteen total bombing attacks against the damaged U.S. sub throughout the day. The location was in Soya Strait. Although she was submerged, *Wahoo* trailed a heavy oil slick which made her an easy target. The planes then directed in patrol vessels in the afternoon which finished off one of the war's most famous submarines.[43]

Although the Sea of Japan was among the most prime of targets for shipping, the loss of *Wahoo* and her famous crew stung Charles Lockwood deeply. His staff would spent considerable energy on solving the torpedo problems. For the time being, though, his staff declared any further war patrols into the Sea of Japan forbidden.

3

Typhoon

Patrol 1A   *23 July-19 August 1944*

A prolonged blast of her whistle announced to all that *Spadefish* was getting underway. Her diesels had already been rumbling for some time as Admiral Lockwood's staff saw her off on war patrol. The usual "good luck and Godspeed" farewells were exchanged. Shortly before casting off, Yeoman Irv Kreinbring passed the completed sailing list to the command staff. In the event of *Spadefish*'s loss while on war patrol, this muster roll gave a final accounting of all 83 souls—nine officers and 74 enlisted men—who had gone on war patrol aboard *USS Spadefish*. The final item to go over the gangplank, the sailing list included each man's rank or rate, their next of kin and home address.[1]

The deck watch cast off the lines and *Spadefish*, newly painted in a light gray camouflage color scheme, backed out of her slip. Boatswain's mate Eimermann moved about on deck, directing the sailors who were securing the gangway to the side of the superstructure. Giving two-thirds speed to one screw, Captain Underwood made his boat twist away from her slip while almost stationary. "All ahead two-thirds." Both screws bit into the water and pushed his submarine forward and away from Pearl Harbor's submarine base. The maneuvering watch was secured and deck hatches were slammed shut as the sub headed past Ford Island and moved down the channel for the harbor's exit.

At 1330 on 23 July 1944, *Spadefish* was thus underway from the sub base, headed out on her first war patrol. Early U.S. fleet boats had been painted black, which was good concealment in deep water. On the surface in bright light, however, it was much more obvious than a lighter gray color. *Spadefish* filed out of Pearl Harbor in company with two other boats, *Redfish* (SS-395) and *Picuda* (SS-382). Together, the trio had orders to form a wolf pack, operating in concert with each other to effect greater shipping losses against their enemy.

Command of the wolf pack was given to Commander Glenn Robert "Donc" Donaho, skipper of *Picuda*. With six previous war patrols, he held seniority over *Spadefish*'s Captain Underwood and Lt. Cdr. Louis Darby "Sandy" McGregor of *Redfish*. Like *Spadefish*, *Redfish* was a brand new boat making her first patrol. *Picuda* had been out, but her captain voluntarily stepped down after his last patrol.

Taking a nod from the success of the Germans with their Atlantic U-boat wolf packs, the U.S. Navy had adopted the submarine wolf pack method in late 1943. The first such pack consisted of *Shad*, *Cero* and *Grayback*, commanded by staff officer Swede Momsen, who had helped rescue the sunken *Squalus* crew in 1939. Momsen's pack went into the East China Sea in October 1943. Although postwar analysis showed that they destroyed only three ships, they returned claiming five ships sunk for 38,000 tons and damaging another eight ships for 63,000 tons.[2]

Admiral Lockwood considered the pioneering wolf pack run to have been a success. He next sent out Commander Freddy Warder in charge of the second wolf pack, which comprised *Harder*, *Snook* and *Pargo*. Although these subs accounted for seven confirmed ship sinkings, *Harder*'s Captain Sam Dealey and the other two skipper were sour on the whole wolf pack concept. Poor communications had plagued the trio throughout the patrol, leading Warder to recommend that future wolf packs be commanded by the senior skipper versus a staff officer making the ride.[3]

When the third ever U.S. wolf pack departed in December 1943, the senior skipper was indeed in charge of the group. Communication was improved via the three boats rendezvousing at sea on patrol. Other than the sinking of a 500-ton tender, however, the only success this pack could claim was damage to the Japanese escort carrier *Unyo*. In March and April 1945, Admiral Lockwood sent out two more wolf packs. Some of the newer packs created a pack name, usually a twist on the senior skipper's name, such as "Fenno's Ferrets," "Blair's Blasters," and "Wilkin's Wildcats." Wolf Pack Four sank seven confirmed ships for about 35,300 tons, while Wolf Pack Five had very little success.[4]

Wolf Pack Six in June 1944 was the most successful yet, and produced the most successful war patrol of the entire war. Commander Dick O'Kane, former Exec of the sunken *Wahoo*, and his submarine *Tang* were credited postwar with sinking ten Japanese ships. Collectively, *Tang*, *Sealion* and *Tinosa* sent sixteen Japanese vessels to Davey Jones' locker.[5]

Another of the early wolf packs was that of *Parche*, *Hammerhead* and *Steelhead*, known as "Park's Pirates." While pursuing a Japanese convoy, *Parche*'s Captain Lawson Paterson "Red" Ramage made one of the war's most aggressive attacks against it on the night of 31 July

1944. Clearing his bridge except himself and an officer on the TBT, he steamed *Parche* into the convoy's midst, firing nineteen torpedoes. Under gunfire, Red Ramage twisted *Parche* through the convoy, narrowly avoiding a collision with one ship that tried to ram his submarine. For his bravery, he was credited with sinking four ships this night and damaging another and was awarded the Congressional Medal of Honor for this patrol. Postwar analysis reduced the number of ships that had actually gone down, but certainly Ramage's *Parche* had done considerable damage to this convoy.[6]

In spite of mixed results on some patrols, the U.S. wolf pack tactic was thus firmly in operation by the time *Spadefish* joined the war effort in mid-1944. Admiral Lockwood and his staff clearly saw a value in multiple submarines converging upon prime target areas, operating in union to make impactful attacks on convoys.

Spadefish was part of the thirteenth ever organized U.S. wolf pack which was sent out against Japan. *Spadefish*, *Picuda* and *Redfish* were collectively known as "Donc's Devils," after pack commander Donc Donaho of *Picuda*. Donc's Devils were ordered to patrol Luzon Strait in the Philippines, between Formosa and Luzon and in the area northeast of Formosa. ComSubPac's operations officer, Dick Voge, had carved up the Western Pacific into numbered patrol areas. Area Eleven was Luzon Strait, extending from northern Luzon north to the southern tip of Formosa, and west to the China coast. Voge dubbed this large wolf pack area "Convoy College," in honor of Captain John Herbert "Babe" Brown, who had run the Convoy College wolf pack training program from Pearl Harbor.[7]

The UCDWR scientists and technicians had flown back to California, leaving *Spadefish* with her experimental FM Sonar gear. They had high hopes that Captain Underwood's electronics team would find time to conduct further tests. It was probably the last thing on Underwood's mind, however.

Spadefish departed Hawaii and headed for Midway with *Picuda* and *Redfish*. They were escorted by a small patrol craft, *PC-1077*. The three boats officially commenced operations as Task Group 17.12 (Coordinated Attack Group) in accordance with ComTask Force 17's Operation Order No. 253-44, dated 22 July 1944. Commander Donaho of *Picuda* was Commander Task Group 17.12.

Spadefish made a trim dive at 1700, and at 2015 her escort, *PC-1077*, departed. Dick Voge's Operation Order spelled out the general patrol area in Convoy College, but left some latitude to the wolf pack commander to delegate to his subordinate skippers. While surfaced, Perry Wood's radio gang always monitored radio traffic called Fox schedules for any changes in orders. The Fox schedules were a system of serialized messages that were transmitted by Commander Submarine Forces, Pacific Fleet from his submarine headquarters.

Spadefish would always maintain radio silence and only acknowledge orders directed to her call sign when asked to do so. Foxes were broadcast across a network of relay stations set up in Hawaii, the United States, Australia and other locations. To prevent a submarine from missing a key message while she was submerged, the Foxes were repeated at varying times on different frequencies.[8]

The radio gang--Paul Majoue, Gerald Newton, Mike Sergio, Edmund Panek, and striker K. C. Powers--alternately guarded the Fox network while *Spadefish* was surfaced. The radiomen normally copied Morse code into five-letter groups. Communications officer Perry Wood or the duty officer would then use an electric coding machine (ECM), which housed decoding wheels, to type out what the radio gang had copied. If *Spadefish* was operating in particularly shallow waters while on patrol, the ECM would be substituted for a strip cipher system instead. The strip cipher consisted of twenty numbered strips, which had the full alphabet in scrambled orders.[9]

Captain Underwood kept the patrol orders under tight wraps until after *Spadefish*'s refueling stop at Midway Islands, the most advanced Pacific submarine base during the early war years. The captain ran his crew through the paces of ship and fire control drills, training dives and other practice exercises while underway to Midway from July 24-27. The radio and radar gangs also practiced communications tests with *Picuda* and *Redfish*. Wood's radio gang practiced with their JP-1 and JK sound gear, practicing counting the propeller turns on their sister subs and "pinging" them to determine ranges. *Spadefish* also had a WCA-2 sound head which was used while she was submerged. This sound head was lowered from the hull and listeners were stationed in the forward torpedo room.

Ensign Don Martin, the newest officer aboard, found that his ship's SD-4 aerial search radar functioned consistently, but had its limits. It often did not pick up aircraft until after they had already been sighted by lookouts. The SJ-1 surface-search radar proved very dependable in tracking *Picuda* and *Redfish* en route to Midway. Martin's radar gang also had the new APR-1 radar detector. The watch standers listened over headphones and monitored the unit's SPA-1 screen, which also plotted out radar signals visually.

In his patrol report, Captain Underwood described how *Spadefish*'s radarmen could signal *Picuda* and *Redfish* via "keying" their radar.

> During wolf pack operations and when encountering friendly submarines, the interference on the SJ "A" scope has proven

to be a valuable item. This interference can usually be noticed when the other submarine is within 15 miles. By keying own SJ so that a pulse is sent out just as the interference sweeps by, you can usually call the other submarines' attention to you, if he hasn't already steadied on you.

Then. recognition can be established by recognition signals, a system of pre-arranged pulses, or by sending Morse code, usual visual signals, and receiving with ear phones.

Underwood and Lt. Cdr. Ustick drilled their watch sections. "Once we headed for the war zone, the crew was divided into only three watch sections, so we all stood watches with familiar faces," recalled Lt.(jg) Dan Decker. Only Underwood and Ustick, who doubled as navigator, would not stand watches out of the eight officers. The others paired in teams of OOD and junior OOD teams to supervise the lookouts on duty. Frank Alvis, Gus Laundy, and Dan Decker were OODs, with Perry Wood, Bill Ware, and Ray White serving as their junior OODs. Ensign Martin had not yet been fully qualified by Captain Underwood as a deck officer, but would be trained as such while on patrol. Frank Alvis and Perry Wood had the 0400 to 0800 morning watch, which would almost always allow the diving officer to handle his morning trim dive.

Spadefish made her approach to Midway on 27 July. Entering her tricky shoals was never taken for granted. Two submarines, *Flier* and *Scorpion*, had grounded themselves on rocks and reefs off the atoll during approaches. The masts of *Macaw*, a submarine rescue vessel that had been wrecked during a storm while trying to pull *Flier* off the rocks, were visible to approaching skippers of the care that was needed in entering Midway.

Spadefish twisted into Midway's channel at 0944 and proceeded to her assigned berth, mooring her port side to Berth S-2. There, she took on food, stores, and 17,000 gallons of fuel oil. Midway was known to sailors as "Gooneyville," named for its most abundant inhabitants, the gooney birds.

The *Spadefish* sailor were amused by watching Midway's gooneybirds, the Laysan albatross. "Guys that were stationed there could watch them every day for five years and still laugh," said Bert Spiese. "They come in and put their wings out for a landing. As soon as their feet hit the ground, they would bounce and fall. To take off, they would run like hell. They'd get four or five inches off the ground and then they would crash."

That afternoon, a conference was held ashore for all three submarines' commanding officers, executive officers and communications officers. Underwood, Ted Ustick and Perry Wood went ashore to map out their patrol plans with the other officers. Each boat had specific call signs and radio frequencies and procedures for how to communicate with each other that were agreed upon. Radio silence was to be maintained as much as possible, using the boats' radar to key messages to each other in most cases.

During the stopover, *Spadefish* had one change of personnel, when Chief Quartermaster Clarence Barger received transfer orders. From Midway's relief crew, SM2c James Parscale came aboard on 27 July as Barger's replacement. SM1c Jim Schuett became the senior member of the quartermaster gang and thus Exec Ted Ustick's assistant navigator. As such, he would take star readings with the XO to constantly maintain proper navigation. "The moment we surfaced at night, the navigator got out and started shooting the stars, while we still had a horizon, to find out where we were," Ustick explained.[11]

Spadefish was underway from Midway at 0730 on 28 July, in company with *Picuda* and *Redfish*. Shortly out from Midway, Captain Underwood got on the 1MC overhead address system and informed his crew as to the wolf pack's destination.

In the forward torpedo room, TM3c Hugo Carl Lundquist made note of the skipper's address. Lundquist had attended Sampson Naval Training Station on Seneca Lake in New York and then completed Sub School in November 1943 before being assigned to *Spadefish*. Although forbidden to do so by Navy regulations, he nonetheless made brief notes of significant events while on patrol in a private journal. Lundquist's entry for 28 July: "Left Midway. Cross 180th Meridian. Capt. told us we were headed for 'Convoy College'—Bashi Channel in Luzon Strait."

Upon crossing the 180th Meridian, *Spadefish* changed her time aboard to reflect zone-12. This meant that at 0000 on 29 July, she lost a complete day due to crossing the International Date Line, and thus the date jumped ahead to 30 July. Upon recrossing this meridian en route home, she would actually repeat a date to return to the proper time zone.

By 30 July, *Spadefish* was 500 miles north of Wake Island. The third day out from Midway, 31 July, *Spadefish* rendezvoused with *Picuda* and *Redfish* to receive changes to the communication code from Commander Donaho. During the next five days en route to station, Underwood conducted training dives, fire control and tracking drills.

Ted Ustick trained his OODs and lookouts carefully, now that the war patrol was underway. The lookouts were picked for their vision and their ability to be free of duty. This included electricians, seamen,

Gunner's mate Edgar "Shaky Jake" Lewis, an eagle-eye on lookout duty, on duty atop *Spadefish*'s periscope shears. *Courtesy of Thomas Miller.*

firemen and the gunners' mates. "You didn't see a ship when you were on lookout duty," explained Fireman 1/c Jack Gallagher, one of the regular lookouts in the first watch section. "You would just see a little tip of a mast on the horizon or a puff of smoke. If you were looking for airplanes, you would just see a little dot about the size of a pinhead at first."

Back at the New London Submarine Base, many of *Spadefish*'s lookouts had been thoroughly trained on the necessity of precise reporting. The bow of *Spadefish* was always on course 000° to a lookout, regardless of which direction the ship was heading. Bearings of objects sighted were reported by measuring around from the bow in a clockwise direction. Lookouts going on duty at night wore red goggles before going onto the bridge in order to adapt their eyes.

"The duty messenger woke us up for our watches," said Gallagher. "At night, the conning tower used only red lights when we were surfaced. If the red lights were on, that was the only way you ever really knew if it was day or night." The new watch section came up on deck a few minutes before the change of the watch to allow their eyes to get used to the darkness.

Many of the black gang never had a chance to stand lookout duty, due to the demand of maintaining the engine rooms. "I never stood lookout watch in my life, and I put in 30 years in submarines," motormac Pat Kelley recalled. He and some of his fellow auxiliarymen did, however, take rotation on the bow and stern planes in the control room and helped stand sonar watches on the WCA sonar in the forward torpedo room.

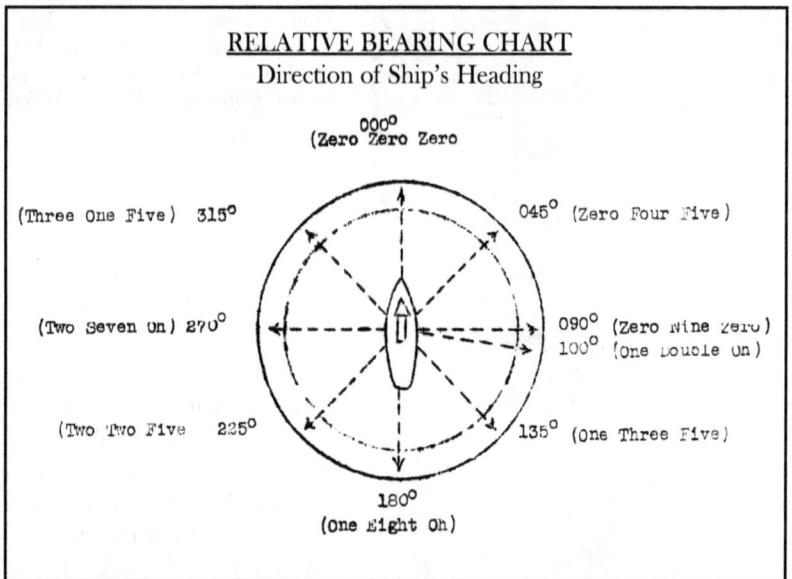

This lookout training diagram, used by the New London Submarine Base, helped teach new *Spadefish* lookouts how to properly report the bearing of a visual contact. For ease of reporting, the bow of the ship was always 000° regardless of which direction the ship was heading. *Courtesy of Bernie Massar.*

Chief of the boat Eimermann had enlisted gunner's mate Bernie Massar to assist him in keeping up the ship's special gear. "He took care of the fire extinguishers and foul weather gear." Massar also was charged with destroying the ship should she have to abandon ship to prevent her from falling into enemy hands. "We had two 55-pound blocks of TNT with a time clock on each. I was supposed to put one in each torpedo room and blow the things up to prevent the ship from falling into enemy hands."

One of the few entertainment options for the crew was the nightly movie when patrol conditions allowed. The forward torpedo room would be converted into the movie room. "You'd get fifteen or more guys in there," recalled Paul Majoue, "and before you know it, the boat is leaning down forward." The control room would have to pump from the bow buoyancy tank forward to aft to trim out the boat due to the weight imbalance. It made for very close quarters. The same movie was often shown numerous times, and could only be exchanged when *Spadefish* returned to port or rendezvoused with another sub of her pack.

More often than not, Hopalong Cassidy movies ended up as the films received by *Spadefish*. "As one of those who ran the projector, I

The forward torpedo room aboard *Spadefish* contained bunks for its torpedomen and doubled as the crew's movie viewing area. In this photo from the fifth war patrol, Bernie Massar prepares to feed dimes into the ship's slot machine. Seated below Massar is TM3c Olaf (Sandleben) Olson. Kneeling is TM1c Vernon Kite. Seated to right is TM2c Hugo Lundquist. *Courtesy of Bernie Massar.*

can't recall the number of times the film broke, with no splicing machine to assist," wrote auxiliaryman Buck Miller. "I caught hell for the breaks, too!"[12]

Radioman Majoue became the unofficial ship's photographer once at sea. Prior to the war, he had purchased a cutting edge German Leica III(F) camera. Manufactured between 1933 and 1939, the III(F) was the first model with slow shutter speeds, controlled by a dial on the front of the body. The Leica camera had been presented to the public in 1925, and it revolutionized the aesthetics of photography, elevating the instant "candid" portrait photo to art form. "When we were on the surface, I'd shoot pictures from the periscope shears or through the periscope when I was in the conning tower."

Other than movies in the forward room, the crew played card games such as pinochle and acey-deucy, the Navy's form of backgammon, in the crew's mess. "You could play cards if you wanted," said Torpedoman 3/c Bert Spiese. "There was no actual money aboard, so you couldn't spend any if you wanted to." Debts were collected once the boat returned to port and the crew was paid. Radioman "Little Fox" Sergio enjoyed gambling and playing poker. "The sub's officers never bothered you if you gambled and money was on the table," he said. "Even our captain let us gamble for money. This was unheard of on surface craft."[13]

The other popular gambling attraction aboard *Spadefish* was the slot machine mounted in her forward torpedo room. This had come aboard at Mare Island, courtesy of the local California sheriff's department. "When they confiscated illegal slot machines, they used to dump them into the ocean, unless a ship wanted it," recalled Bernie Massar. *Spadefish* took on a dime machine for the crew's entertainment while in port or out of the war zone. Lt.(jg) Perry Wood became the casino master, adjusting the machine for how loose or tight it would be on paying out jackpots. "We used the proceeds from our slot machine to fund ship's parties," said Massar.

"We lived like a close family," recalled auxiliaryman Dick Gamby. In the messroom, four tables seated two dozen men for meals or for recreation time. Off duty sailors drank hot coffee from the 10-gallon urn in the mess, exchanged rumors, smoked cigarettes or studied their books for rating advancements. Chief Scherman and his cooks put some of the non-rated sailors to work each day, assisting in the galley as messcooks. The galley's ice cream mixer found plenty of good use. Ship's mascot Luau had the run of the boat. She found many handouts in the galley and many welcome bunks in the crew's quarters, which held thirty-six bunks above the after battery compartment.

Torpedoman Hugo Lundquist's journal entry for 3 August notes, "Notified of Task Force attack on Bonins, so we speeded up to get out of area." On 6 August, *Spadefish* passed within 15 miles of Sofu Gan, a landmark in the Ogasawara Islands group south of the Japanese island of Honshu. Sofu Gan, which means "Lot's Wife," was a submariner's navigational landmark, a vertical rock pinnacle about 400 feet in height and roughly 350 miles off Honshu. Passing Lot's Wife was generally accepted as entering into Empire waters.

Here the boat began encountering some rough weather. The weather "confirmed the opinion that this design of ship is a one engine room ship in rough weather."[14] *Spadefish* was "pooped" in the afternoon by a high wave which struck the boat from behind and swept over her exposed bridge. As low to the waves as the bridge was, Frank Alvis, Perry Wood and their lookouts held on for dear life when such a monster wave pooped the bridge. This particular wave sent a slug of water down the main induction, grounding out both evaporator stills in the forward engine room. The water grounded out or shorted all the instruments on the instrument panel to the No. 2 main engine. No serious damage was done other than to create much cleaning and drying work for the electricians and motormacs.

Ahoogah! Ahoogah!

The diving klaxon sounded two raucous blasts as OOD Gus Laundy shouted, "Dive! Dive!" The lookouts dropped down through the conning tower hatch as *Spadefish* began to nose underwater.

Two days of uneventful cruising toward the Convoy College patrol station was finally shattered by the shout of a lookout at 1449 on 9 August.

"Aircraft! Bearing zero-two-zero degrees."

A Japanese patrol plane had eluded *Spadefish*'s searching SD radar, which was used only sparingly to avoid detection by the enemy. The aircraft slipped to within 15 miles before an alert lookout spotted her. Although the distance was too great to identify the plane any better than being a monoplane, *Spadefish* submerged to avoid detection. The plane was later believed to be a "Sally," the nickname for a Japanese Army Mitsubishi twin engined medium bomber. For more than half the crew—new, untested men—this dive to avoid enemy attraction was their first realization that they were part of war.[15]

A little more than a half hour later, *Spadefish* resurfaced at 1521 and resumed course and speed. The diesel engines were used during the night to recharge the ship's main batteries. Also at night, a little housekeeping was done as the ship's garbage was brought topside to be given the deep-six in weighted gunny sacks. The ship was close enough to Japan that the radio shack could pick up the propaganda newscasts of Tokyo Rose for all to hear in the mess hall. "She said just enough specific things to make you a little nervous," said Bert Spiese. "She would name how many submarines were in a certain area. Where she knew that stuff, I'll never know." The radio on 9 August brought news of a U.S. Army B-29 raid on Japanese mainland.

At 0535 on 10 August, diving officer Frank Alvis took her down for a morning trim dive. At first light each morning possible, *Spadefish* made a dive to compensate for changes or shifts in her weight since the last dive. During war patrols, such changes would come from torpedoes or ammunition expended, fuel burned, water and stores consumed, and even changes in salinity or seawater temperature. Fuel oil was lighter than water, so consumption affected the boat's trim as much as salinity. A cubic foot of water weighs about 64 pounds, or about ten pounds more than a cubic foot of diesel oil.[16]

After monitoring the trim at periscope depth, Lt. Alvis made a daily dive to 300 feet to take a bathythermograph (BT) card reading. The bathythermograph was a temperature measuring device. Using a stylus that traced a vertical wiggling line on a lamp-blackened card, the BT visually recorded every water temperature change encountered as depth was increased. By taking a BT reading in the morning, the diving officers of the day would know where they could expect to find a friendly underwater temperature gradient layer that would deflect enemy sonar.[17]

Spadefish resurfaced at 0611 and resumed course and speed. At 1234, there was a momentary contact on the SD at 30 miles. At 1259, one of the lookouts spotted a Japanese Sally bomber bearing 170° True (T) at a distance of about 10 miles. *Spadefish* slipped below for half an hour to be safe.

At 1500 on 10 August, *Spadefish* crossed another meridian and changed time to -8 zone time. At 2300 on 10 August, she officially entered her patrol area and commenced a surface patrol on a north and south line in accordance with her operating orders. *Redfish* and *Picuda* both patrolled a similar line, at 20 mile intervals to the westward of *Spadefish*.

Most of the morning hours of 11 August were spent at periscope depth, patrolling along on battery power. At 1150, the periscope watch sighted the persistent Sally bomber, distance about 10 miles. *Spadefish* went deep to avoid detection. "Three days in a row we have had to dive for this fellow," Underwood noted in his report. "Don't think he has sighted us yet."

By 2200 that night, *Spadefish* converted her Number 4 Fuel Ballast Tank into a Main Ballast Tank (MBT) as fuel was burned up. This process involved someone going topside and down into the superstructure through an access grate to carry out the procedure. This person was the "fuel king," the motormac responsible for fueling the ship in port and controlling the fuel situation while at sea for the engineering officer. *Spadefish*'s fuel king was MoMM1c Charles Griffith.

"When a fuel ballast tank ran dry, you had to go up and take the blank flange off of the piping topside and reconnect the flapper valve to the hydraulic system," Griffith explained. Working in the dark with only a two-cell red flashlight made this process a little trying at sea. "Before you went up there, you got all the nuts and bolts cleaned up so everything would go together just fine." Holding the flashlight alternately under an arm and in his teeth, Griffith worked quickly to thread the nuts and bolts as he switched the fuel tank to a ballast tank capable of taking in sea water to help control buoyancy. Fortunately, no enemy aircraft appeared during this dangerous conversion and *Spadefish* was not forced to dive.

The seas were far from calm through the rest of this particular night. *Spadefish* submerged at 0449 on 12 August for her trim dive and BT card. The wind began picking up all day, shifting from the east to the northeast. "It looks as if we are in for a bit of a blow," recorded Captain Underwood.

Off the southeastern tip of Formosa, *Spadefish* was approaching the area of a typhoon, the Pacific equivalent of a Caribbean hurricane. The seas became very rough. Hugo Lundquist noted in his journal that *Spadefish* "surfaced in a typhoon—rough as hell."

Standing watch with Frank Alvis, Lt.(jg) Perry Wood noted the deep troughs between the waves. The stronger the wind became, the higher the waves grew. As the wave heights increased, the distance between crests and troughs increased also. "We would go partway through the middle of the waves, and then the bow would drop down and made a huge splash. Sometimes the water just dogged us, and everybody held on tight."

Being neutrally buoyant on the surface, *Spadefish* did not have to contend with her screws broaching the surface, as would a destroyer's during such rough seas. The increasing wave height, however, was another concern to the water personnel.

TM3c Bert Spiese, a member of the forward torpedo room, stood daily lookout watches. "Being a rookie, that was my duty most of the time. Going into the storm, it was rough. The waves must have been 30 feet high." Another lookout, fireman Jack Gallagher, later said, "Up in the shears, the spray hit you just like pebbles."

Gunner Bernie Massar recalled, "Those waves were tremendous. The guys were hanging on for dear life topside." After standing a watch as lookout, Massar went below for his turn on the helm. He was on standby for twenty minutes in the conning tower, where he found one of his buddies, EM3c Herman Cruze, struggling to maintain the designated course due to the heavy seas. "I looked at the ship's heading while Herman was helmsman. He was 180° off course! The OOD on the bridge was not aware of this, as everyone topside was hanging on because the huge waves were breaking over the bridge." Massar quickly helped Cruze get the boat back on the right course gradually during his twenty-minute break. "The OOD never realized we were completely off course," he related. "The waves would hammer the boat at least 15° each way, off our main heading while trying to hold our course."[18]

The typhoon built through the night into 13 August. *Spadefish* submerged at 0536, as Gordon Underwood wrote in his patrol report:

> The storm is of such intensity as to make useless any surface patrol. Had intended to patrol submerged today anyway. Found that we broached if we got any higher than 75 feet, so went to 150 feet. Sound range exceeded visual range anyway.

At 1000, *Spadefish* came back up to periscope depth for a look and quickly broached again. The wind had shifted to the north at about 60 knots (69 mph). Diving officer Frank Alvis took the boat back to 150 feet. At that depth the 2,400-ton submarine had a consistent roll of 15 degrees with an occasional 20-25 degree roll. "When you get down that deep and you're still rolling more than 15 degrees, you know it's a big, big typhoon!" said motormac Dick Gamby.

In the control room, BM1c Willard Eimermann watched his planesmen struggle to maintain control. "You had to be on the ball with the planes," he recalled, "trying to keep her stabilized. You could feel the seas grabbing us."

The control room was centrally located and included all the diving mechanisms. Manifold levers were used to flood ballast tanks with seawater to submerge the boat. Blowing the ballast tanks with compressed air caused *Spadefish* to rise. The ship maintained an even keel while submerged by two large wheels which controlled her bow and stern planes. The diving officer on duty ordered the desired up or down angle for the ship. Two enlisted men, one seated in front of the bow planes wheel and the other in front of the stern planes wheel, physically wrestled the large wheels to maintain the proper angles. An arc-shaped glass tube called the inclinometer was located before the planesmen. Its air bubble shifted, similar to a carpenter's level, to show the planesmen the steepness of *Spadefish*'s angle. The phrase "Keep a zero bubble!" was made nearly impossible under the typhoon seas that were rolling the boat even at depth.[19]

"We were accustomed to smooth sailing submerged," agreed Lt.(jg) Dan Decker. "When a submarine rolls and tosses at depth, it is kinda scary."

Evening chow was challenging in the stormy seas. Items note secured slid from one side of the mess tables to the other. "In the center of each table was a strip about eight inches wide where food dishes could be placed," recalled electrician's mate Ken Sigworth. "Each had a lip around the sides to keep the food from sliding or spilling." One particularly rough roll of the boat sent a massive container of green peas slamming to the deck. "We had peas rolling around in the after battery for the next month!" said Sigworth.

The storm put a beating on *Spadefish* at depth, but would be far more severe if she tried to ride it out on the surface. U.S. fleets did encounter several typhoons during the Pacific War. Months later, on 18 December 1944, Admiral William "Bull" Halsey's Third Fleet would encounter a severe typhoon in the Philippine Sea near Luzon. Howling winds exceeding 100 knots and massive waves caused some of the destroyers to roll as much as 75 degrees. Many ships were damaged and three destroyers—*Spence* (DD-512), *Monaghan* (DD-354) and *Hull* (DD-345)—capsized and were lost. and On 4 June 1945, another typhoon with winds exceeding 70 knots and waves towering over 100 feet ripped the bow section off the heavy cruiser *Pittsburgh* (CA-72).[20]

Whenever the boat rose to periscope depth for an observation, the heavy waves caused her to broach. At 1400, Underwood took another peek and broached his sub again. The heavy winds had now shifted to the northwest. "The flying spray gave the appearance of a heavy blizzard," he noted. "Went back to 150 feet."

After another four-plus hours, *Spadefish* surfaced to head north, only to find that the wind had swung around to 180. So, Underwood changed course to 170 to head into it and prepared to ride out the storm. "Received ComSubPac dispatch telling us we were in the vicinity of a typhoon. We know!"

With ComSubPac's "warning," *Spadefish* and her packmates rode out the storm without suffering material damage. It was proof that "Mare Island boats were rugged and well built."[21]

Some men found their appetites wane from the constant rolling and pitching. Dishes, coffee mugs and anything not lashed down or forcibly secured were subject to breaking. Some found it tough. Bernie Massar noted one seasick sailor watching the radar screen while the ship was surfaced in the fierce storm. "When he was on the radar watch, he kept a bucket beside him. The boat was rocking that much." Massar recalled that one of his buddies also could not keep his food down while standing lookout duty atop the pitching periscope shears.

Others had been through rough weather. Dan Decker, a former destroyer sailor felt, "I had been through worse in the Aleutians." Radioman Mike Sergio, another veteran of destroyer duty, also took it in stride. "It was rugged, but we made out all right."

Captain Sandy McGregor of *Redfish* estimated the winds at 100 knots (115 mph).[22] The one piece of equipment which did not fare well in the typhoon was the newly-reinforced FM sonar head which was mounted on the forward deck. Although Captain Underwood had no intention of using it on this patrol, the head would be found to be damaged later.

Spadefish stayed on the surface during the night as she battled the rough seas created by the typhoon. At 2135, she exchanged signals over the SJ radar with *Picuda*.

At 0504 on 14 August, *Spadefish* submerged. "Seas had subsided to where we could almost stay at periscope depth." Underwood brought her up at 0904 so navigator Ted Ustick could get a sun line. The ocean was still far too rough to go the direction Underwood wanted to go, so he submerged again at 0916. At 1147, boat surfaced and proceeded to patrol station off Koto Sho (Formosa), and proceeded to patrol eastward between that island and Kasho To. Radar contact was made on Koto Sho at 1850, distance 25 miles, bearing 295° T.

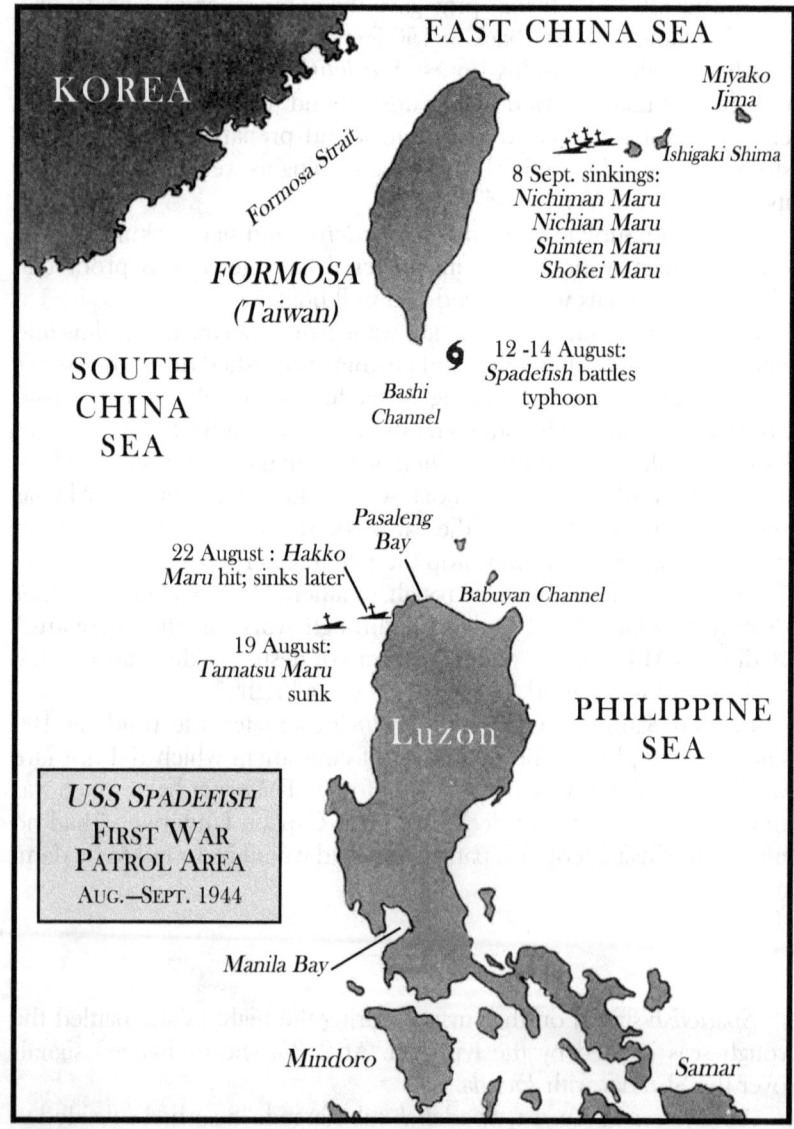

The following morning, at 0430 on 15 August, radar contact showed Kasho To to be bearing 308° T, distance 20 miles. *Spadefish* submerged at 0500 and commenced submerged patrolling eastward of and between Koto Sho and Kasho To. "Frequent rain squalls made visibility poor," noted Underwood.

Spadefish surfaced at 1900 and ran on the surface through the night. At 0302 on 16 August, radar contact was made on Y'ami Island, distance 19 miles. At 0457, she surfaced to begin another day of submerged patrolling in the southern part of Bashi Channel. After sunset, she surfaced at 1907. The first days on patrol station had been devoid of targets.

At 0212 on 17 August, radar contact was made on the southern tip of Formosa at a distance of 70,000 yards. Underwood took her down at 0512 to begin yet another day of submerged patrolling off the southern tip of Formosa. Fortunately, the watch standers quickly found more activity brewing in this area.

At 0815, the periscope watch sighted a squadron of 11 Betty bombers headed south, distance about 8 miles. Two hours later, at 1005, a small fishing sampan crossed ahead of *Spadefish* about 2 miles distance. At 1204, the periscope watch spotted a "Topsy," a Japanese transport plane that was headed south, distance 8 miles.

No shipping targets other than the sampan had appeared, so *Spadefish* surfaced at 1902 to recharge her batteries. After sunset, the radar gang could not contact Formosa on the SJ radar, so Underwood headed in that general direction until contact was made at 1949, range 60,000 yards (30 miles). This report notes: "We had experienced a westerly current whereas we had expected an easterly one in this area. However, we now know where we were. Overcast skies had prevented any celestial navigation for the last three days."

At 2010, word finally came of action. *Picuda* send a message saying that *Redfish* had made contact with a convoy of 13 ships, plus many escorts. *Spadefish* immediately bent on all engines as they became available and commenced searching based on the *Redfish* report. At 2112, SJ interference indicated another radar ship ahead. This was quickly identified as *Picuda* by exchanging signals. At 2219, *Redfish* was also picked up by SJ interference and identified with signals. Underwood noted in his report that where he found *Redfish* "doesn't agree with his reported position."

Underwood's frustration with the position of his packmates would only increase. At 0048 on 18 August, SJ radar interference was picked up on bearing 306. This should have been *Redfish* from his report, but turned out instead to be *Picuda*. "At this time discovered the SJ was not operating properly," he logged. Radar officer Don Martin and radio technicians Neal Pike and Joe Case went to work on the SJ to effect repairs. They found that it would transmit enough to give interference for an object, but not its range. "Should have been in front of convoy at this time although we had not contacted it yet," wrote Underwood, "so took convoy base course until radar was reported in working order, at 0318."

Captain Sandy McGregor's *Redfish* had picked up a very large southbound convoy and passed the word to *Spadefish* and *Picuda* before attacking.

McGregor had found Japanese special convoy HI-71, which was bound for Manila in the Philippines and Singapore. HI-71 had started from Moji on 8 August 1944. It originally comprised eleven large, heavily laden merchant ships—troop transports, the 18,300-ton tanker *Hayasui*, and the food supply ship *Irako*. Screen protection was supplied by the modern destroyer *Fujinami*, the 1920s vintage destroyer *Yunagi*, and five smaller *kaibokan* (coastal defense vessels, or CDs).[23]

The 17,830-ton escort carrier *Taiyo* provided air cover for Rear Admiral Kajioka Sadamichi's HI-71. These nineteen vessels represented the convoy's core, although other escorts and merchant vessels would join or leave during its voyage. During a stopover at Mako in the Pescadores, *Yunagi*'s sister destroyer *Asakaze* and four other *kaibokan* joined the convoy as escorts, as Rear Admiral Sadamichi sortied from Mako. The carrier *Taiyo*, also known as *Otaka* (Japanese for "great eagle"), had been attacked unsuccessfully thus far by other U.S. submarines.

Redfish fired unsuccessfully at one of the convoy's ships before spotting the aircraft carrier. He shifted targets quickly and fired two more at the carrier, but was not successful with either. *Redfish* was able to fire at another tanker four hours later, but missed again.

While Captain McGregor cursed his own bad luck, his convoy report had brought other submarines converging on HI-71 like wolves to sheep. His packmates, *Spadefish* and *Picuda*, were frustrated in trying to close on the convoy with all engines on the line.

While the radar gang struggled to repair the SJ, *Spadefish* continued to follow the convoy's route. At 0330, she picked up word that *Redfish* was making an attack on the convoy from the starboard flank. *Picuda* was contacted again via SJ radar interference at 0426, but she had been unable to make an attack on this convoy. Spirits rose briefly at 0511, when RT1c Pike sang out that he had a contact. Instead of a convoy, however, this blip turned out to be some small islands south of Balingtang Channel.

Spadefish continued her pursuit of the convoy throughout the day on 18 August. She dived briefly at 0547 to avoid a Sally bomber which appeared at a 10 mile distance, but she resurfaced as quickly as possible and continued a surface run toward the convoy. In the meantime, another three U.S. subs had picked up the alert and were closing from the south. *Raton*, *Rasher* and *Bluefish* all pursued.[24]

At 0636, four more Sallys were sighted through the periscope at 8 to 10 miles distance. Lieutenant Alvis also announced a periscope off the port quarter, so *Spadefish* turned away and submerged. "Periscope not definitely identified. Nothing heard on sound," wrote Underwood. "Safety uppermost on our minds at this moment."

Redfish continued her assault against convoy HI-71 on 18 August, finally managing to damage one oiler, the 8,673-ton *Eiyo Maru*. Two destroyers, *Yunagi* and *Asakaze*, were detached to accompany the crippled tanker back to Takao. *Spadefish* would have her own encounter with these two tin cans in due time.[25]

Captain Underwood remained frustrated through the early morning hours of 18 August, unable to find the large convoy.

> In retrospect, it appears that failure to make contact was due to the uncertainty of the *Redfish* position, and hence convoy position, with respect to our position. The *Redfish*, being to the westward, had not the opportunity to fix her position as we did by radar contact on Formosa. If her DR position was out as much as ours was, this is understandable. It would have been a wise move to have headed down the bearing of the *Redfish* SH interference at 2219 until contact with her had been made, thus correlating our positions. Failure to make contact with such a promising group of targets was, needless to say, disappointing.

Spadefish sighted six airplanes at 1034 to the eastward, circling in the vicinity of Balintang Channel, so she was submerged to avoid detection. Shortly, the JP sound man, radioman Mike Sergio, picked up the sound of screws. A minute later at 1049, the JK soundman, Paul Majoue, heard pinging from three or four ships from the direction of the channel. "Apparently a convoy is coming through the channel, hence all the plane activity."

Five minutes later, *Spadefish* sighted the smoke of at least three ships under these circling planes. The range of this first ship contact was still extreme, as far out as 20,000 yards. A careful periscope search at 50 feet failed to disclose anything but smoke, yet the JP and JK sound operators heard the escorts for this group. "Very commendable performance," wrote Underwood of his sound gang.

RM1c Majoue was the leading soundman on the number one set, the JK long range search set, in the conning tower for the approach. "Little Fox" Sergio was on the number two, JP, set. Majoue would take a single ping on a target ship "to make sure that all of the tracking party's ranges were equal to mine." In the meantime, Sergio would zoom around with his sound gear, looking for the rest of the escorts and other ships.

Fate of Japanese Convoy HI-71
Convoy College: August 1944

Ship Name	Type	Tonnage	Attacks Against/Notes
Hayasui	AO	6,500	Sunk 8/19 by *Bluefish*
Irako	AK	9,570	
Teiyo Maru	AO	9,849	Sunk 8/18 by *Rasher*
Eiyo Maru	AO	8,673	Damaged 8/18 by *Redfish*
Teia Maru	AK	17,537	Sunk 8/18 by *Rasher*
Awa Maru	AK	11,249	Damaged 8/18 by *Rasher*; sunk 8/19 by *Bluefish*
Noto Maru	AK	7,191	
Hokkai Maru	AK	8,416	Lost 9/23/44 to *Bowfin* mine
Tamatsu Maru	AP	9,589	Sunk 8/19 by *Spadefish*
Noshiro Maru	AP	7,184	Damaged 8/18 by *Rasher*; beached
Mayasan Maru	AK	9,433	Sunk 11/17 by *Picuda*
Taiyo	CVE	17,830	Sunk by *Rasher* on 8/18
Fujinami	DD	2,000	
Yunagi	DD	1,270	Attacked by *Spadefish* 8/23; sunk by *Picuda* 8/25
Hirato	CD	940	
Kurahashi	CD	940	
Mikura	CD	940	
Shonan	CD	940	
CD-11	CD	630	
Asakaze	DD	1,270	Sunk by *Haddo* 8/23
Sado	CD/PF	870	Sunk by *Haddo* 8/22
Etorofu	CD/PF	870	Damaged by *Pintado* 8/6
Matsuwa	CD/PF	870	Sunk by *Harder* 8/22
Hiburi	DD	940	Sunk by *Harder* 8/22

Sources: Research of Anthony P. Tully, author of "Convoy HI-71 and *USS Harder*'s Last Battles." Se also Alden, *U.S. Submarine Attacks During World War II*.

Majoue's dual-head JK-QC sonar was trained using hydraulic motors. The JK sound heads could be retracted into protective trunks in the forward torpedo room when not in use to prevent damage to them. The JK was used for listening and for echo-ranging to determine a target's distance. Sergio's JP sonar was newly developed by the Navy's Underwater Sound Laboratory in New London. The JP's T-shaped hydrophone protruded from the main deck, forward of *Spadefish*'s noisy machinery aft. The JP gear, sonic and manually trained, was not used for echo-ranging but for listening.[26]

Convoy HI-71 was headed south for Luzon from the change in bearing of the smoke, which soon disappeared from *Spadefish*'s view. The planes were still in the vicinity, so Underwood brought his boat to a southerly course and trailed the ships submerged. "The Commanding Officer received a thrill at this time by looking at the belly of one of the planes at about 2000 yards distance when starting a periscope sweep." Fortunately this plane did not drop her bombs.

At 1630 of 18 August, *Spadefish* surfaced and headed for Cape Bojeador on Luzon, trying to estimate a possible convoy route. At 2045, *Spadefish* was off Cape Bojeador, headed down the possible convoy route. At 2158, *Spadefish* had radar contact, range 16,550 yards. Perhaps this was a ship that had changed course following one of the wolf pack's attacks.

"Battle stations submerged," ordered Underwood.

Bong! Bong! The chimes, known as the Bells of St. Mary's, sounded the battle alarm throughout the boat, sending men scurrying to their assigned stations.

Underwood changed course to put his contact astern. It soon developed into a single ship, unescorted and thought probably to be a destroyer or escort vessel. Underwood commenced tracking this target, who was zig-zagging at a speed of 13.5 knots. The SJ radar's "A" scope picked up interference on this target's bearing, indicating that this ship had radar equipment.

Underwood noted in his patrol report:

> The target was sweeping with his radar at all times except at one instance when the range decreased to 7,500 yards and the interference was steady. Range soon opened to above 8,000 yards and he commenced to sweep again. Kept use of our own radar at a minimum. There was no indication that he detected it.

By 2303, *Spadefish* obtained position ahead of this target, with a range of 12,500 yards. Underwood turned his boat in, intending to dive for a submerged radar attack. The target, however, suddenly zigged radically to the left. "He had changed his base course to 270, leaving us out in the cold again, so commenced another end around. Visibility was about zero so we hadn't seen target at all." There was also the thought that this vessel might be patrolling for subs, but it had been dismissed due to the fact that his speed was too high for listening and that he wasn't pinging.

Shortly after midnight on August 19, Captain Underwood was still pursuing this lone ship, doggedly intent on bettering his own luck. The conning tower was crowded with those working on making the attack. Several of the quartermaster gang would be present to assist. SM1c Jim Schuett served as the skipper's "scope jockey," operating the controls to the periscopes as requested by Underwood. He would also aid assistant attack officer Ted Ustick in calling out bearings in degrees from the dials on the periscope during observations.

"Up scope," said Underwood. Schuett pressed on the white button and the periscope began rising up out of the conning tower floor. The skipper pulled down the handles, pressed his face to the viewing lens and slowly rose up with the periscope to a full standing position. After a brief sweep, Underwood called, "Down scope," as he backed away from the lens and slapped the handles against the sides. The cables whined as Schuett held down the black button which pulled the periscope back down into its well.

At the wheel, forward of the scope, was QM2c Jim Parscale. As helmsman, he would handle speed changes and call out the log speeds. Depending upon the time of day or night, the quartermaster on duty for that shift—QM2c Samuel Cooper, SM3c Dale Frazier, or striker S1c Bob Maxwell—would enter all commands, course changes, speeds and relevant data into the detailed Quartermaster's Notebook.

Behind the quartermaster were Paul Majoue and Mike Sergio, manning the sonar gear. RT1c Neal Pike's battle station for a submerged attack was in the forward torpedo room, manning the JP hydrophone. For surface attacks, Pike and radar officer Don Martin would often be present on the port side of the conning tower, ready to take readings as needed. Exec Ted Ustick, assisting the skipper, would handle the centrally located firing panel when the time came. As the ship's navigator, Ustick was also instrumental in figuring the target ship's base course, despite any zigzag pattern it was making.

Moving aft, Lt. Gus Laundy was seated at the torpedo data computer (TDC). Seated at the little plotting table was Lt.(jg) Dan Decker to plot out the enemy's course. Lt.(jg) Perry Wood flipped through the recognition manuals for profiles of the enemy ship that was being described to him. He also backed up the plot by checking ranges and bearings on the Mark 8 angle solver, a slightly more modern version of the prewar Mark 6 circular slide rule, which had been commonly known as a "banjo."

Lieutenant Decker explains the role that the plotting team played in conjunction with the TDC's solutions.

> The TDC, an analog computer, cranked out only the instant attack situation, sending the correct gyro angles to the torpedoes to be fired. As an aid to the Skipper and the TDC, it was important to calculate the base course of the target and its zig-zag plane. By plotting the range and bearing after each observation, with luck we could estimate when the convoy or target might change course again. A turn away might mean an escaped target, and a turn toward might mean an instant good firing position. It was a team effort from beginning to end.[27]

The battle stations talker was chief pharmacist's mate Victor Ives, who manned headphones to communicate orders to the rest of the ship. When the order came to fire torpedoes, this was done electrically in the conning tower. Ives would pass the orders to either the forward or after torpedo room, where the leading torpedoman also hit the manual firing plunger, just in case the electrical control should fail. "Everything was worked by time," explained Paul Majoue.

By 0039, Underwood had again obtained position ahead of this ship, with the range now at 7,500 yards. He dived *Spadefish* and commenced his attack in a very bright moonlight. The target had been zigging 30 degrees either side of his base course, staying five minutes on the diverting legs and ten minutes on the base course leg. "We had him plotted so well we could tell when his helmsman used too much rudder and made a bad turn," logged Underwood.

This target ship could just be seen as a dark shape from the bridge when the skipper took her down. Mike Sergio, monitoring the other ships, at 0045 reported target screws as heavy, and at a speed of about 100 rpm. "Decided it wasn't a DD or a patrol craft after all," logged Captain Underwood.

"Open the forward doors," he called.

Talker Vic Ives repeated the order to CTM William Simms' forward torpedo gang, where Simms was overseeing his able crew crew in their first combat torpedo firing. Simms' position was at the blow and vent manifold, while Hugo Lundquist and Emery Kreher manned the flood valves, each controlling three of the six torpedo tubes. Gus Cuthbertson manned the sound-powered battle phones, relaying the orders from Ives. Bert Spiese was between the tubes to handle the gyro setter, matching the pointers from the conning tower's TDC solutions. He also stood ready to operate the interlocks, which had to be aligned to open the outer doors and flood the tubes. Other members of the torpedo reload gang, such as S1c Wallace McMahon, stood ready to assist with reloading new torpedoes into the tubes once they had been fired.

All of these men had specific duties, crowded into the small room. Only when the skipper was certain that an attack was imminent would he order his torpedomen to crank open the tube doors and flood the torpedoes with seawater for firing. "If something happened and we couldn't fire the tubes, it became a lot of work for us," said TM3c Spiese. "We had to get the water out of the tubes, get the inspection plates off the torpedoes, dry everything, make inspections, and so forth."

In the conning tower, "Hocks" Majoue took a final ping to check the range. "My job at the end of the approach, right before we fired the fish, was to take a single ping to make sure that the torpedo data computer, the banjo, and everything else agreed," Majoue explained.

Decker worked out the plot and Laundy cranked out the TDC solutions. Everyone was happy with the setup.

"130 degrees, starboard track," Underwood estimated aloud as he took his final periscope observation. This data was the angle on the bow of the target ship, or the angle between the target's axis extended forward and the crosshairs on the periscope's viewing lens.

Scope jockey Jim Schuett called out the relative bearing from the ring above and surrounding the periscope.

"Set!" called Gus Laundy, signifying that the angle called by the skipper was exactly the same as the bearing generated by his TDC solutions. The average gyro angle for the torpedoes was 354, meaning that the torpedoes would turn 6° to the left to make a proper intercept. Everything checked out as Underwood took his last peek at the oncoming ship.

"Fire one!" the captain ordered at 0110.

Ted Ustick hit the firing button just as Chief Ives repeated the orders to Chief Simms' forward room.

At 0110, *Spadefish* fired tube No. 1 from a range of 3,040 yards.

As the first war fish was fired, a loud *kawoof!* announced the sound of the escaping torpedo. *Spadefish* shuddered as she belched forth her first 2,800-pound war fish into the open sea. The torpedo's propellers began giving it propulsion even before the torpedo had completely cleared the tube.

Everything with firing a torpedo was a matter of precision. Before the tail of the torpedo had left the tube, torpedoman Simms would open a vent valve called the poppet valve. This allowed the compressed air to be forced back into *Spadefish*. Allowing this huge bubble of air to escape would send a signal to the surface. Simms then quickly closed the poppet valve before an excessive amount of sea water entered. The sea water which did enter helped to compensate for the lost weight of the torpedo. Firing a full forward spread of six fish would be the equivalent of losing almost 17,000 pounds.[28]

After firing, torpedomen Lundquist and Kreher closed the outer doors. Next, they opened the drain valves which connected the tubes to a special holding tank. Then, air was released under pressure into the tubes, forcing out the remaining water into the holding tank. When the water was forced out and the air pressure equalized to that in the boat, it was safe to open the inner tube door for reloading.

Bert Spiese, standing between the tubes on the angle setting knobs, turned the handles to match the commands coming from the TDC relay from the conning tower, putting the proper commands directly into the torpedo guidance systems. At the "Fire one!" order, Chief Simms smacked the firing plunger with the palm of his hand. Gus Cuthbertson, on the talker set, then called back instantly to the conning tower, "Number one fired!"

Eight seconds later, there came, "Fire two!"

Spadefish shuddered again as torpedo tube No. 2 spit forth its fish. Eight seconds later, she fired tube No. 5, followed eight seconds later by a fourth torpedo from tube No. 6. Each torpedo was fired in a spread with a slight variation, hoping to insure that despite any slight miscalculations, at least one or more torpedoes would still hit. By firing such a spread, at least one of the torpedoes was fully expected to miss the target.

In the conning tower and torpedo room, the quartermasters and torpedomen counted the seconds down from the time of firing to the expected moment of an impact explosion.

It was disheartening when the time passed where the first torpedo should have exploded. Still more seconds and no explosions. *Spadefish*'s war fish had missed. Captain Underwood offered his explanation in his log entry for 19 August 1944.

> No hits! Radar bearings after we had fired showed target had changed course to about 220. He may have seen the torpedo wakes as the water was highly phosphorescent. There is a possibility that he noticed the wake of our radar antenna and turned away, although at that range this is considered doubtful. The radar interference had not steadied so don't think he had detected us.

Lieutenant Laundy was certain that this ship had not seen the torpedo wakes, but made a turn "just by chance." He recalled, "As soon as we fired, I noticed she had changed course. Immediately, the plot officer, Dan Decker, also noticed that she had changed course." Laundy was certain that *Spadefish* was simply the victim of bad luck, with the target ship taking an unexpected course swing at the most inopportune moment.

At 0114, four minutes after firing, the *Spadefish* crew clearly heard two explosions, which they decided must be depth charges. Not knowing what countermeasures might be expected, Underwood turned away and took his boat to 400 feet. As no more explosions were heard, he realized what the crew had heard were probably torpedo end of run explosions. "This going deep was probably unnecessary. Should have stayed at periscope depth until out of radar range, then surfaced and given chase."

Thus, *Spadefish*'s first potential victim of the war had been pursued for hours and had been given four torpedoes, but no damage. In return, the sound of *Spadefish*'s own exploding torpedoes had been enough to make her dive. "This was not the only 'miss' registered during the remaining patrols," relates *Spadefish*'s unofficial history, "but it was surely the most disappointing; the first contact, the first fish fired —all for nothing!"[29]

"First Blood for *Spadefish*"

Patrol 1A 19-22 August 1944

At about the same time that *Spadefish* was making her first unsuccessful torpedo attack, Captain Hank Munson's *Rasher* was making an attack on Rear Admiral Sadamichi's convoy HI-71. The carrier *Taiyo* was hit by two *Rasher* torpedoes at 2225 on 18 August. Even as the CVE burned and exploded, *Rasher* next picked off the 17,537-ton freighter-turned-transport ship *Teia Maru*—the second largest merchant ship sunk by U.S. submarines in World War II.[1]

After *Rasher*'s first two sinkings, Sadamichi split his convoy into two or more distinct groups. Continuing his dogged attacks on HI-71, Munson expended all of his torpedoes and sank two more large merchant vessels from the convoy. In terms of tonnage of enemy shipping destroyed, *Rasher*'s fifth patrol had become the most successful single patrol of the war to date, with 52,600 tons of Japanese shipping destroyed.[2]

Bluefish (SS-222) was next to kill, slamming torpedoes into the large tanker *Hayasui* during the early morning hours of 19 August. In spite of his woes thus far, Admiral Sadamichi's convoy HI-71 had not yet escaped the clutches of the U.S. wolf packs stalking it. War school was in session in the patrol zone known as Convoy College!

The *Spadefish* crew did not have long to dwell on missing their first torpedo target. The ship had eased back up to periscope depth at 0128, just eighteen minutes after firing. With a clear radar screen, Captain Underwood ordered his boat to the surface at 0158 on 19 August to give chase. Gus Laundy, Bill Ware and their lookouts took their positions on the bridge. The Fairbanks Morse diesels roared to life and *Spadefish* was off to the races, making up lost ground. Minutes later, radar picked up a target again, distance 20,500 yards. The target's range was shown to be decreasing, so Underwood put his tracking party back to work.

Neal Pike's radar blips indicated that this was a new and apparently larger target. The original target was not showing on the screen. The crew's disappointment at missing their first target was quickly cast aside by the zeal to better things with this second target.

At 0214, another contact was made on the SJ, range 22,650 yards and decreasing. The size of this pip and its range gave evidence that this was also not the first ship that had escaped *Spadefish*. At this point, the fact that *Rasher* and *Bluefish* had shredded into convoy HI-71 was not yet known to *Spadefish*'s tracking party.

"Couldn't understand where all these single ships were coming from," noted Underwood in his patrol report, "but wasn't complaining about it." The captain ordered battle stations at 0218. The latest target was coming in at 16 knots, zigging 80 degrees, and "running like hell." From the size of his pip on the radar at 15,000 yards, Underwood "decided he was a big one, also unescorted—a gift from the gods these days."

The same type of sweeping radar interference was noticed on *Spadefish*'s SJ, so Underwood planned for a submerged radar attack. At 0317, *Spadefish* received a dispatch from ComSubPac telling of *Rasher*'s attack on the convoy off Luzon. "This explained the mystery of unescorted ships running all around the ocean," the captain wrote. "This convoy was the one whose smoke we had seen and which we were chasing yesterday."

Spadefish reached position 7,500 yards ahead of her target at 0321. The target's radar sweeping had not settled on his ship, so Underwood felt good that he had not yet been picked up. From the bridge, Underwood's tracking party was able to see the target well enough to decide she was a large AP, or transport ship. With the range closing nicely, he was ready to set up for the attack approach.

"Take her down," Underwood ordered the OOD.

"Clear the bridge!"

As the lookouts and officers piled down through the conning tower hatch, *Spadefish* was already easing down. As soon as the duty chief in the control room saw all green on the engine indicator lights, he knew it was safe to shut the main induction valve. As the hum of the diesels abruptly halted, the electricians in the maneuvering room arranged the propulsion control levers to put battery power to the screws. The bow planesman in the control room stood by his chrome plated wheel until the "rigged out" indicator light showed that his bow planes were properly outstretched into the ocean to influence the ship's depth. The normal actions of diving the ship took mere seconds as each room carried out their particular task.

The entire submerged run against convoy HI-71 was made at radar depth. Radio technician Pike only keyed his SJ set when a range was taken. The enemy ship's sweeping interference was consistent, not settling on *Spadefish*'s bearing to indicate contact had been made.

JK soundman Paul Majoue picked up target screws at 0324 and reported about 112 rpm. As Underwood and assistant approach officer Ted Ustick took peeks at the approaching Japanese ship, they estimated her to be a 10,000-ton troop transport. Japanese records show their identification to be right on, for this ship was a large transport, the 9,589-ton passenger-cargo ship *Tamatsu Maru*.

The tracking team had *Tamatsu Maru*'s zig zag plan down and knew when to expect her next move. Suddenly, however, she zigged about 20 degrees further to the left than she had before. The whole setup had changed in an instant.

Underwood could see the dim outline and long, high superstructure of his target. He estimated her length to be about 600 feet.

"Bearing—mark!" he called. Jim Schuett called out the bearing from the scope's dials, as the skipper esimated the target's ship's angle: "One three five, starboard track."

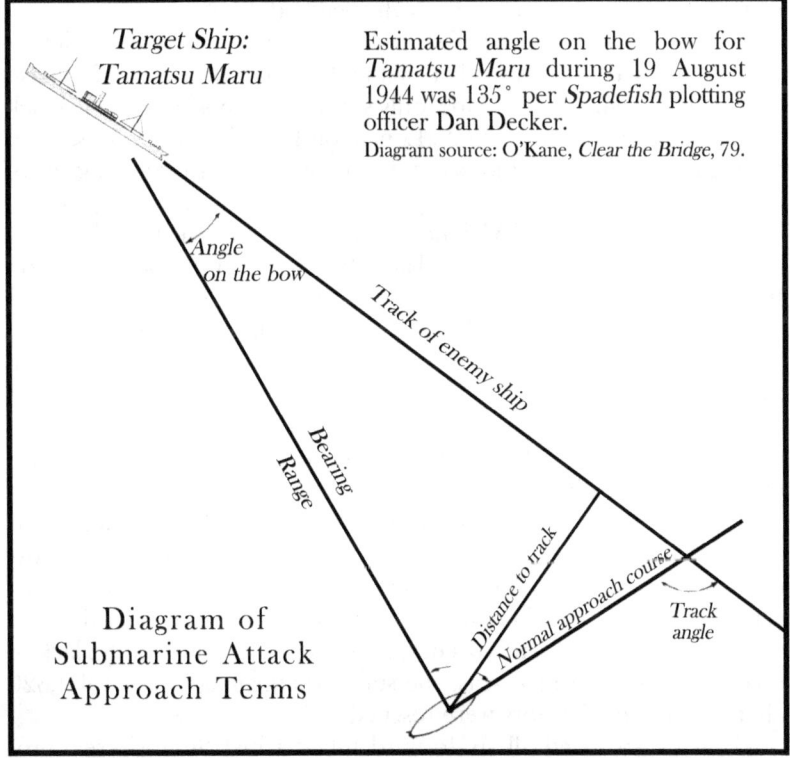

This often-published periscope photograph shows a Japanese merchant vessel sinking stern first after being torpedoed by USS Aspro (SS-309) in 1944. Spadefish achieved her first "kill" on 19 August 1944. Official U.S. Navy photo.

"Range—mark!" Underwood ordered.
"Range two-five-oh-oh."

The gyro angle for the torpedo settings was 335, a small angle for the setting. From the recognition books, Perry Wood called out important data on this ship. The plotting team determined that Tamatsu Maru had a draft of 16 feet, and was on course 270, making 16 knots. Spadefish herself was on course 251, making 6 knots at 45 feet. Underwood called for a six-foot depth setting on his Mark XIV torpedoes and had them set on high speed, 46 knots.

At 0333, Spadefish fired all six of her forward tubes. Three minutes later they timed the hits for her first and second torpedoes. No flash was seen through the periscope, only smoke. The position of the attack was logged as Latitude 18-48 N, Longitude 119-47E. "Cheers sounded throughout the boat and looks of disappointment gave way to grins of satisfaction."[3]

Mike Sergio and Paul Majoue on sound reported the target's screws to have stopped. Three minutes later, they heard a very loud explosion from the target. "Radar pip died down and disappeared," logged Captain Underwood. "No doubt about this fellow." Sonar continued to hear the breaking up noises for a few minutes. The patrol report triumphantly announced, "First blood for Spadefish!"

Imperial Japanese Navy (IJN) sources show that Tamatsu Maru was hit at about 0430 (0330 as time was being logged on Spadefish) by two torpedoes amidships on the starboard side. She quickly listed over, spouting out steam. Ten minutes later, she heeled over and plunged to the bottom. Keeping convoy HI-71's war diary aboard the new destroyer Fujinami, Rear Admiral Sadamichi says that Tamatsu Maru simply vanished and her "whereabouts became unknown." She did not respond to radio calls and was never seen again. Because of the lack of escort vessels and rough seas, she suffered appalling losses. Of 4,820 aboard, a mere 65 sailors were rescued.[4]

Having dispatched all six forward tubes, Chief Simms' crew pro-

Torpedoman's Mate 3/c Bert Spiese, shown here on the deck of *Spadefish*, suffered four broken fingers while reloading torpedo tubes on the first war patrol. *Courtesy of Albert L. Spiese.*

ceeded to reload with new torpedoes. "The work for our men came after an attack," recalled TM3c Bert Spiese. Using block and tackle, the torpedomen worked new torpedoes into each tube. Moving 2,800-pound war fish did not always go without incident. "I got four broken fingers loading the tubes. The submarine pitched and I wasn't holding the torpedo right. I broke two fingers in one hand and then had two more broken in the other hand, just like that," related Spies. "Being a rookie, these things happened." *Spadefish*'s "doctor," Victor Ives, used wooden tongue applicators to tape up the broken fingers. "The pharmacist's mate taped me up," said Spiese, "and that's about all he could do."

Eleven minutes after smashing her first maru, *Spadefish* blew ballast and surfaced to survey the situation. Captain Underwood was eager to chase after *Rasher*'s reported position of damaged ships.

> A strong odor of pyrotechnics and fuel oil was in the air. Passed through wreckage and oil slick of our target. Too dark to identify anything but believe one or two lifeboats were afloat. Heard a few cries as we headed past. We had about 35 miles to go and only one and a half hours of darkness left to get to the reported position of the *Rasher* contact so didn't slow to investigate further.

Due to the approach of dawn, no attempt was made to pick up a survivor for interrogation. This troopship was undoubtedly heading to the Philippines to face General Douglas MacArthur's troops. All that remained was wreckage and an oil slick.

After *Spadefish*'s kill, convoy HI-71's remnants took temporary refuge at San Fernando. Thanks to *Rasher*, *Bluefish* and *Spadefish*, the convoy had lost an aircraft carrier, a tanker, and four transports.

Two other troop ships had been too heavily damaged to continue. Once regrouped, the remnants of Sadamichi's troops ships and escorts ran to Manila without further assault, arriving on 21 August.[5]

Two hours later, at 0535, the radar watch had picked up Luzon at a distance of 64,000 yards (32 miles). At 0548, a ship was sighted over the horizon and the crew went back to battle stations. Lt. Gus Laundy had the deck when this ship was sighted. "It was pitch dark. We couldn't see anything," he recalled. "All of a sudden, I sighted a ship ahead of us, which we were approaching quickly. I finally recognized it as one of our submarines at 1,350 yards."

Incredibly, radar had not seen this other submarine. "Then, the radar man announced a contact. It seems our radar had not been 'in' all that time," wrote Laundy. "I'm glad I never knew who was 'on' radar at that time. I think I would have committed a crime!"[6]

Lieutenant Laundy was fortunate to spot the submarine, friendly or not. His lookouts had not reported it up until *Spadefish* closed the distance considerably. When one lookout finally made an announcement, it was, "There's a submarine signaling to us, sir." Another of those on lookout duty, F1c Jack Gallagher, recalled: "The skipper got so damned mad that he went down below. It was kind of a good lesson for us, because it was one of our own submarines on the way back in from patrol. We realized that if it had been a Japanese submarine, we would have all been toast."

Battle stations were secured at 0556, once the other submarine was postively identified as friendly. Underwood closed on the boat and exchanged calls by keying the SJ surface radar. It was *Rasher*. *Spadefish* closed to within signaling distance of *Rasher* and received Captain Munson's report of the convoy attack.

Munson reported that a destroyer or cruiser was behind him on course 045. *Rasher* was headed for home, out of torpedoes. "We headed over to see if we couldn't find it," logged Underwood. At 0701, *Spadefish*'s periscope watch sighted an unidentified Japanese DD, distance about 15,000 yards (2,000 yards to a nautical mile). *Spadefish* turned away and started tracking, keeping the tin can's tops in sight.

At 0721, there was more radar interference from the bearing of this target. *Spadefish* had a new APR-1 radar detector that could pick up enemy signals, showing if *Spadefish* was being tracked by the Japanese. Captain Underwood's patrol report explains:

> The Japanese seem to have progressed with the installation of a radar of a frequency close to our SJ [surface radar] on a lot of their ships. Our APR doesn't go high enough to pick up the SJ band so no definite information could be obtained other than the appearance of interference on the SJ "A" scope.

Ten minutes after sighting the destroyer, the periscope watch lost the target. He had been tracked at a speed of 15 to 16 knots. For the next two hours, *Spadefish* chased this destroyer in and out of rain squalls off the coast of Luzon, trying to get into position. Underwood tried to get ahead a couple of times only to have the destroyer suddenly turn to another course. "We finally decided to get astern of him and wait for him to come back to us."

Underwood believed that the radar interference indicated that his opponent was aware of *Spadefish* and would likely have called for aircraft support. A "long expected plane contact" soon showed up at 7 miles, moving in. Underwood thus "terminated this ring-around-the-rosy performance" and submerged. Being only about 20 miles off the coast of Luzon, *Spadefish* remained submerged and headed south to try to intercept the patrolling DD. He wasn't sighted again.

At 1550, Underwood decided to take a chance at surfacing during daylight "as it was a long way back to where we belonged." *Spadefish* thus surfaced and headed for Formosa. The three lookouts scurried up to their platforms on the periscope shears. A fourth man of the watch stood by to relieve one of the three for helm duty. Using powerful 7x50 binoculars, each covered a sector of 120 degrees so that there was an overlap of areas scanned. "The stern 180 degrees was reinforced by the JOOD and the OOD augmented the search for the forward half," noted Lieutenant Decker. "There was really nothing much else for the two officers to do."

The telltale smudge of "smoke on the horizon" could give away an enemy ship long before its masts could be seen. With the SD aircraft warning radar being used sparingly to avoid Japanese detection, the lookouts became doubly important.

At 1622, one of the bridge lookouts spotted a Sally bomber astern, at a distance of 15 miles. The plane did not change course. They were not noticed, and *Spadefish* remained on the surface to make up ground. At 1918, the duty radar operator picked up SJ radar interference while *Spadefish* was surfaced. It resembled the ship's own SJ radar interference, indicative of one of her wolf pack mates, but attempts to establish identification failed.

At 0510 on 20 August, a small patrol boat was sighted, west of *Spadefish*'s position by about 7 miles. She had remained on the surface throughout the night hours, closing on Formosa. "An unexpected southerly drift (current) had put us behind position," wrote Captain Underwood. "The patrol boat blinked at us so we drew out of sight to the eastward, then headed south."

Spadefish submerged for the day at 0540. The next few hours were quiet, except for enemy aircraft contacts. At 0853, the periscope watch spotted a Nell, a land-based Japanese Mitsubishi medium bomber, at a distance of 9 miles. A Mavis, a Japanese Kawanishi flying boat, patrol plane was sighted at 1125, patrolling the area. It was *Spadefish*'s fifteenth aircraft contact of the patrol.

The periscope watch sighted smoke on the horizon at 1204 and headed in that direction, but the smoke got further away. The watch decided it was probably another patrol boat. At 1400, *Spadefish* attempted to notify *Picuda* of the smoke sighting by sending with her SD mast raised, but could not contact *Picuda*. "Probably they are too close in to risk raising the mast and listening for five minutes on even hours, as had been scheduled," noted Underwood.

Another Mavis patrol bomber was sighted through the periscope at 1455, distance about 5 miles. "This fellow was a little close and headed our way, so went to 90 feet for about 20 minutes," notes *Spadefish*'s patrol report. An hour later, at 1555, smoke was sighted in the same vicinity as had been sighted earlier. It soon disappeared, however, and was later determined to be the same patrol boat on his southerly patrol leg of his patrolling plan.

After sunset, *Spadefish* surfaced at 1909 and set course for the next day's patrolling area, southwest of Balintang Channel. Prior to sunrise on 21 August, *Spadefish* submerged for the day, going deep to take a BT reading. The welcome water temperature change was found to be at 300 feet. If attacked and forced deep, the boat could simply drop down below the change and enemy sonar would be unable to detect her.

Between 0845 and 1033, *Spadefish* had three Japanese plane contacts. The closest one was a Sally bomber at 6 miles, which turned and headed in. *Spadefish* therefore dove to 90 feet and stayed there for fifteen minutes without incident. At 1124, the periscope watch sighted the masts of a ship and upon closing it was identified as a small converted trawler. After sunset, *Spadefish* surfaced at 1909 and headed for the north coast of Luzon for the next day's patrolling.

At 0425 on 22 August, *Spadefish* submerged about 7 miles off Mayroira Point on the north coast of Luzon. The daily deep dive was made to check the BT card. Lieutenant Alvis reported excellent sound conditions due to a thermocline.

By 0538, visibility was good enough to see the coast clearly. Throughout the day, various and sundry sailing craft came in and out of sight. At 0553, the periscope watch sighted the masts of a ship and began closing. Once again, it turned out to be nothing more than a good-sized sampan heading out to sea.

A Mavis patrol bomber passed at 5 miles at 0839. At 1240, sound reported faint pinging bearing 086. Screw noises were heard a few minutes later, so *Spadefish* went to battle stations. At 1252, the masts of two ships were sighted at a distance of about 15,000 yards. A third set of masts soon appeared. This was apparently a convoy that had come through Babuyan Channel in column and was now opening out into a line of cruising formation. Pinging was heard from two escorts, but they must have been farther to seaward as they were not seen. *Spadefish* came to normal approach course.

The targets appeared to be zig-zagging by constant helm, on a base course of 270. As the ships came closer they were identified with the ONI-208-J recognition book as large tankers, riding empty, similar to *Kurosio Maru*, 10,519-ton class. "We found ourselves in an excellent position on the base course," noted Underwood, "between the second and third ships, so we waited for them to come by."

This group of ships included warships originally part of the HI-71 convoy. The remnants of Rear Admiral Kajioka Sadamichi's convoy had entered port at Manila on 21 August. Three of his frigates—*Sado*, *Matsuwa* and *Hiburi*—had remained behind for two days to hunt the U.S. submarines which had torn up his convoy. Sadamichi ordered them to suspend their searches and return to Manila. They were just approaching the entrance to Manila Bay on 22 August when Captain Sam Dealey's *Harder* put torpedoes into all three destroyers. Sister sub *Haddo* finished off *Sado*, one of Dealey's crippled frigates.[7]

Admiral Sadamichi received the distressing news of the loss of these three men of war the same day. His surviving troop ships offloaded their cargo at the coast port of Manila, located on the southern end of Luzon. On the southeastern side of Manila Bay was the Philippine naval base of Cavite, where Exec Ted Ustick had been stationed at the beginning of the war.

Sadamichi prepared to move his remaining vessels on to Singapore but was ordered to await the arrival of additional vessels before proceeding. These vessels were departing from Takao. Two destroyers, *Asakaze* and her sister *Yunagi*, were both originally part of convoy HI-71. They were now ordered to escort two new large tankers, the 10,023-ton *Hakko Maru No. 2* and the 10,022-ton *Niyo Maru*, to join Admiral Sadamichi.

The quartet, officially convoy TAMA-24A, departed Takao for Manila at 0900 on 21 August. Command of the convoy fell to Lieutenant Commander Iwabuchi Goro, captain of *Yunagi*. Captain Goro found making progress was very fitful, as the new *Hakko Maru No. 2* was plagued with mechanical breakdowns. For the approach to Manila, Goro chose for his four-ship convoy to hug the shore of Luzon. By the time the convoy had the first inkling that an American submarine was tracking them, it was too late.[8]

"We've got a couple of nice, fat tankers," mused Gordon Underwood as he studied the approaching convoy in his scope.

His *Spadefish* had the two large tankers coming west through Babuyan Channel, off Mayraira Point on the northern coast of Luzon. He found that one of the two escorting destroyers was trailing the tankers. The other tin can was out of sight to seaward, with only its stack smoke visible on the horizon. The setup was beautiful, as Underwood found himself between the columns of ships. *Spadefish* had only to lie in wait until the tankers passed by before opening fire.

Underwood selected *Hakko Maru No. 2*, the second tanker in column, as his first target. Through the periscope, he noted that one of the two tankers, *Niyo Maru*, was "very rusty," perhaps having been scraped in preparation for a new paint job. The second tanker, *Hakko Maru*, had a fresh paint job. Holding at 66 feet and making 6 knots, *Spadefish* opened her outer torpedo tube doors as the conning tower tracking party made a final check of bearings and ranges.

At 1314 on 22 August, she commenced firing her third-ever torpedo attack against enemy targets. Estimating *Hakko Maru*'s draft at 11 feet, Underwood ordered Chief Simms' crew to set their torpedo depth at six feet. *Spadefish* shuddered three times as three forward torpedoes were fired from a range of 1,960 yards. As soon as all three had cleared, Underwood was swinging his boat to fire upon the second tanker.

Boom! Boom! Two of *Spadefish*'s torpedoes slammed into the tanker in quick order. Stealing a quick look through the scope, Underwood saw "that the first hit was amidship. The second hit must have been near the stern, as it was spread to the right. Didn't wait to see this hit as were then getting the set-up for the stern tubes."

Destroyer *Yunagi*'s action report shows that a *Hakko Maru* lookout spotted a torpedo trace "70 degrees to port, 800 meters distant." Her skipper ordered a hard turn to avoid, but it was too late. *Spadefish*'s first torpedo exploded with violent force against *Hakko Maru*'s midships section. Seconds later, "a second torpedo hit near bow."[9]

As *Spadefish* swung to bring her rear tubes to bear, Paul Majoue reported that the target's screws had stopped. In the after torpedo room, TM1c Harry George and his gang—TM2c Si Barnes, TM2c Don Bird, TM3c Doyle Partin, and S1c Thad Barton—were eager for their first chance to fire at the enemy. At 1316, their time had come. *Spadefish* fired three torpedoes from her stern tubes at the number three ship, *Niyo Maru*, at a range of 1,120 yards. Underwood wisely held back his fourth war fish. "Had four tubes ready, but withheld the fourth torpedo as it was reasonable that the target would maneuver radically when observing its neighbor being torpedoed. He finally awoke and swung sharply left," presenting a 140° port track.

The tracking team put in a new setup quickly and at 1318, the fourth stern tube was fired at a range of 1,800 yards with a zero gyro. Just as the word to fire was given, an explosion indicated that one of the first three torpedoes had hit. The time was correct for the torpedo fired first. No explosion was seen as the periscope was being swung forward to see where the escorts were. This target was the *Niyo Maru*, but despite the timed hit, *Niyo Maru* claimed no damage in this attack and none was noted in *Yunagi*'s action report.

The trailing destroyer *Yunagi* was now bearing down on *Spadefish*'s position. "This was the first sight of any escort. As the periscope was swung past the first target, it was observed to have a heavy port list. No further details were observed as the escort was getting all the attention right then. This, plus the probability of arrival of planes prompted us to go deep without further glance at the targets."

Leaving the crippled *Hakko Maru No. 2*, Captain Goro turned his destroyer *Yunagi* after the American submarine that had wrecked his little convoy. He "went at full speed to ram," forcing the submarine down. Lookouts on *Hakko Maru* also sighted *Spadefish*'s periscope and the wounded merchantman also fired on the American ship.[10]

Captain Underwood had just given the order to fire the last torpedo when he swung the periscope and caught sight of *Yunagi* turning to race toward the submarine that had just launched it.

"Take her deep! Rig for depth charge!" he called.

During the submerged firing approach, *Spadefish* had been in a state of neutral buoyancy, just as a scuba diver strives to achieve. In such a condition, her depth was easily adjusted via propulsion motors and the diving planes on her hull. The stern planes controlled the angle while the bow planes influenced her depth. To dive rapidly to escape an incoming angry destroyer, diving officer Frank Alvis flooded the ship's "negative tank." The negative tank was vented inboard, and air howled into the control room, working as a vacuum to rapidly suck sea water into the midship's tank.

Spadefish achieved negative buoyancy quickly and began dropping like a rock. Rigging the ship for depth charge meant that all hatches were secured and all noisy equipment, motors and air conditioning alike, were shut down. The bow and stern planes were shifted from hydraulic power to hand control while at silent running, making the giant chrome plated wheels quite a task to turn. Yeoman Irv Kreinbring and gunner Jake Lewis, the battle stations planesmen, had taken over the seats in the control room before the wheels. Lieutenant Alvis kept an eye on the inclinometer—watching the little bubble just as a carpenter might watch his level—to insure his men kept a "zero

One of the Japanese ships attacked by *Spadefish* on 21 August 1944 was the 10,020-ton freighter *Hakko Maru No. 2*. This view taken from the Naval Intelligence 1944 Japanese merchant ship recognition manual used aboard *Spadefish*.
ONI 208-J (Revised).

bubble," keeping the boat steady and buoyant. Nearby at the Christmas tree, Boats Eimermann monitored that all the hull opening indicator lights continued to show a safe green color.

As *Spadefish* clawed for depth, the angry swishing of the destroyer's propellors began to be heard. The sound operators listened as the roar of the approaching warship grew closer by the second. Just forty seconds after the last torpedo had been fired, *Yunagi*'s first depth charge exploded. "It was a blockbuster for sure," noted Underwood, "fortunately, not close."

He ordered his boat to evade at two-thirds speed, turning away from the destroyer as it raced by overhead. Men braced themselves for the next explosions. In the control room, gunner's mate Bernie Massar stood by to relieve Chief Jake Lewis on the bow planes. He later related the duty of his battle stations submerged station.

> We shut down everything and put on the emergency lights. The hydraulic power was also shut off on silent running. The bow and stern planes were then turned by hand to push the hydraulic fluid by hand. I relieved Shaky Jake on the bow wheel when he was tired and Maurice Noonan relieved Kreinbring on the stern planes when he was tired. The air conditioning was also shut off during silent running. Of course, the heat from the engines would go through the whole boat. It would get hotter than hell.[11]

Jack Gallagher was another who put in some hours at the planes station during battle stations. "The main problem during silent running was turning the rudder without power," he said. The skipper often called out "full left rudder" or "full right rudder" as a destroyer's screws came racing in for a depth charge approach. "In order to crank the rudder over manually—especially if you had been submerged for a long time and the air in the boat was bad—we had to rotate guys on the wheels," Gallagher stated.

Evading depth charges was a process that spawned two common phrases among submariners. "Keep a zero bubble," was the phrase often uttered by the diving officer to his planesmen. "Run silent, run deep," was an expression most often used during evasive tactics. Lieutenant Decker explains this effort to escape enemy counterattack.

> Running silent required very slow and quiet screw revolutions. Once we reached the ordered depth and gained a zero bubble on the inclinometer, we knew we weighed the same as the water we displaced. The skipper could then slow down and order the electricians to make turns for two knots. This made depth control tricky since the bow and stern planes had little bite.[12]

Another round of depth charges, "ash cans" to the submariners, exploded with a fury, sounding like thunder rolling below the water's surface. Fortunately, they were again not extremely close.

In the forward torpedo room, Bert Spiese would never forget his first depth charge attack.

> I thought it was average. I didn't know it could get worse than that. But, of course, it did. I could always judge every other depth charge attack by that first one. It was like lightning and thunder. If you heard the detonators go off first—click! click! *Wham!*—then you were safe. Ones that you didn't hear click would be the lightning hitting you. Those were the ones that got you.

Three minutes after firing on the second tanker, the crew heard another explosion at 1321. Although ash cans were still exploding, this separate explosion was believed to be the last torpedo hitting. Aboard *Spadefish*, eleven depth charge explosions were tallied. *Yunagi*'s records actually show that she dropped 20 depth charges, so a number of them must not have been very close, or some may have been heard as the same explosion.[13]

"Apparently the DD didn't know where we were and assumed we were to seaward of the first target," a relieved Underwood recorded in his report. "No attempt to search for us was made. This ended a rather busy half-hour."

At 1347, sound operators Paul Majoue and Mike Sergio reported explosions in the direction of *Spadefish*'s targets. Several loud explosions were heard by the topside sonar (JP) and both conning tower sound operators. *Spadefish* had crippled the 10,000-ton *Hakko Maru II*. "There's nothing like the sound of a ship breaking up," remembered Bert Spiese. "That's a beautiful sound."

Spadefish had three sonars, which were all located in the forward part of the boat. While at battle stations torpedo, all three were manned. Two were operated electronically by sound operators in the conning tower. The other was operated by hand from the forward torpedo room by either radio technician Neal Pike or Joe Case.[14]

During normal submerged running, only one of *Spadefish*'s three sonars was manned, this one being in the conning tower where the officer of the deck was located along with the two periscopes. This sonar was lowered hydraulically out of the bottom of the pressure hull. The JP sonar, on the other hand, was a permanent topside sonar, mainly for use when lying on the bottom.

Captain Underwood decided that one of his two targets must have sunk. "If the first target had been damaged only, it undoubtedly would have also headed for Pasaleng Bay with the damaged second target, in order to have the protection of the DD escort." Due to the size of the explosion he had witnessed when the first torpedo slammed home, plus the damage aft from the fourth and final torpedo, Underwood did not believe it possible that this ship could have cleared the area.

Spadefish had crippled the 10,000-ton tanker *Hakko Maru* with two torpedo hits, but she had not gone down. If the second spread of torpedoes fired at *Niyo Maru* did any damage, it went unrecorded by the Japanese. At 1530 (1430 by the time *Spadefish* was keeping), *Niyo Maru* was ordered on to Manila with the destroyer *Asakaze*. Bad luck continued to plague the Japanese, for the submarine *Haddo* found *Asakaze* the following day, sinking her at 0800 off Lingayen Gulf.

Hakko Maru was crippled, her mid section buckled and her bow dangerously low in the water. Her watertight compartments had saved her for the moment. After a short depth charging against *Spadefish*, *Yunagi* had turned back to protect the crippled tanker. The pair was only able to make 4 knots as *Hakko Maru* limped toward Pasaleng Bay, located on the northeast corner of Luzon.[15]

The sound operators kept tabs on the sounds of ships growing more distant. Once Captain Underwood felt it was safe enough to assume the enemy destroyer was not lying in wait above, he planned to slip back to the surface and try to pick off another ship from this convoy.

5

Cat and Mouse Games

Patrol 1A 22 -31 August 1944

Spadefish cautiously eased back up to periscope depth at 1421, just one hour after enduring *Yunagi*'s depth charge attack. A quick sweep of the scope showed no enemy ships. Smoke could be seen in the direction of Luzon's shore. Sonar pinging indicated that one of the two escorting destroyers was near this smoke. Assuming that the tin can was guarding a wounded maru, Captain Underwood conned his boat toward the smoke. En route, a Sally bomber and a Zeke fighter plane were sighted. Both were circling in the vicinity of the smoke, further indication that something worth attacking lay ahead.

Limping along to Pasaleng Bay at 4 knots, *Hakko Maru* was beached while emergency repairs were made on the damage caused by her two torpedo hits. Her escorting destroyer would keep up an anti-submarine sweep to ward off American predators while the damage control was attempted. "Vigilant patrol of bay entrance begun for enemy submarine," recorded *Yunagi*'s Captain Goro.[1]

At 1530, *Spadefish* passed through considerable wreckage, consisting of mainly boards, splinters and oil. She closed the Luzon shore close enough to see that the ship's smoke and pinging were coming from the direction of Pasaleng Bay, a small cove on northern Luzon. "Apparently one of the targets managed to make the beach, and one of the two escorts stayed behind to guard him," wrote Underwood.

At 1920, *Spadefish* surfaced and cleared the coast. Underwood sent word to *Picuda* of the day's happenings. *Spadefish* received orders back from Donc Donaho to patrol the same sector tomorrow. Prior to sunrise on 23 August, *Spadefish* submerged at 0425 while 5 miles off the entrance to Pasaleng Bay. She headed in to investigate the smoke and pinging that had been heard the previous evening before surfacing. At 0429, sound reported pinging in the direction of the bay.

At 0530, Captain Underwood found what he judged to be a *Mutsuki*-class destroyer patrolling the entrance to this bay. "He was

Spadefish stalked and fired on the IJN destroyer *Yunagi* in Pasaleng Bay on the northern coast of Luzon. Shown here is one of *Yunagi*'s sister destroyers, *Harukaze*, also of the *Kamikaze* class, fitted with 4.7-inch guns and six Long Lance torpedo tubes. Author's collection.

doing the pinging. He looked like the escort that had been trailing the convoy of tankers yesterday."

Rather than be deterred by the tin can guarding the bay, Underwood turned to Ted Ustick and announced, "Sound battle stations." The Bells of St. Mary's announced to the crew that their skipper fully intended to find out what the Japanese destroyer was protecting. With his tracking team in position, Underwood approached the same DD which had depth charged *Spadefish* the previous day. "He was patrolling a roughly triangular shaped area, varying his speed between zero and 13 knots, alternately pinging and listening."

At 0601, *Spadefish* sighted the damaged *Hakko Maru No. 2* beached at the head of the bay. Lt.(jg) Wood noted in the deck log, "Sighted ship, bearing 174°T, beached with tug alongside, identified as second tanker that was fired at yesterday." *Spadefish* dove to 90 feet at 0640 to avoid being sighted by four sailing craft that were headed her way. Conditions were not in *Spadefish*'s favor this day. TDC officer Gus Laundy recalled, "That bay's surface was as calm as a mirror."

Nonetheless, Gordon Underwood kept *Spadefish* nosing into the edge of the harbor, hoping to pick off the destroyer before going in to give the death shot to the tanker. The ensuing hours would prove to be a tense cat and mouse game with the alert *Yunagi*.

The 1,270-ton destroyer and her crew of 240 officers and men were on high alert for American submarines. At 320 feet in length, *Yunagi* was heavily armed with three main batteries of 4.7-inch guns, plus .50 calibers, two anti-aircraft machine guns and six 21-inch torpedo tubes. *Yunagi* was of the *Kamikaze* class destroyers, originally launched 23 April 1924 and christened as *No. 17*. On 29 November 1941, she had been rechristened as *Yunagi*. Early in the war, she participated in the fall of Wake Island and later fought in naval battles around the Solomon Islands in 1942 and 1943. Most recently, she had participated in the Battle of the Philippine Sea in June 1944.[2]

Spadefish kept tracked of the DD's movements by the bearing of his pinging. At 0725, she eased back up to periscope depth. The DD was now at the end of his run to the south. His range was over 10,000 yards [5 miles]. Five minutes later, the destroyer was suddenly headed back on his northeast leg. Underwood hoped to get into position to use the stern tubes with wakeless Mark 18 torpedoes on him, and save the three remaining longer ranged Mark 23's forward for the tanker. "This was a difficult job as he hadn't followed the same course twice. We couldn't afford to be caught broadside to him under 4,000 yards for fear of being contacted on sound."

Underwood hoped to narrow the range to 2,000 yards or less before firing on this man-of-war. At 0752, the *Yunagi* had started on the westerly leg of his patrol route, this time on course 270. "His range was now 4,800 yards. Saw we couldn't swing the stern tubes to him without presenting a broadside. Also we would be too far off his track, so swung to keep bow pointed at him and let him go by. Needless to say, we were at silent running by this time."

At 0759, the destroyer passed ahead of *Spadefish*, at a range of 2,300 yards, pinging steadily. In his report, Underwood shows his concern.

> What we wouldn't have given for Mark 18 torpedoes forward at this moment. In the glassy sea, he would have spotted the Mark 23's in time to avoid. He went by without detecting us. What little hair the CO has left certainly should have turned gray at this moment. Had he detected us, we would have been in for a very uncomfortable time.

At 0806, *Yunagi* now turned for his southern leg. Lieutenant Laundy on the TDC had fed countless solutions into his computer as Underwood and assistant approach officer Ted Ustick called out ranges and bearings, trying to obtain a good firing position on this destroyer. "The speed and distance was difficult to gauge," recalled Laundy. "He was pinging us all the time. You'd get the distance right, but the speed would be wrong. We had a hell of a time trying to get a fix on her. The setup on that destroyer just kept changing."

While maneuvering to get the tin can into a favorable firing setup, Underwood continued to peek occasionally at his beached tanker. At 0815, he made a startling discovery.

"Our cripple is getting underway!"

The oiler's damage control crew was apparently making some progress, for they now began to ease her back off the beach. Underwood believed that this ship was the second one in column that he had fired on the day before "by its new paint job." Unknown to him,

Niyo Maru had actually escaped being hit by *Spadefish*'s second torpedo attack the previous day. Driven down by *Yunagi*, Underwood had been unable to confirm the damage he believed his ship had made. Through the periscope, he could see that the beached *Hakko Maru*'s "port quarter side was all black from the fire started by the last torpedo. She has about a 15 to 20 degree list to port. She apparently moved off the beach about 2 miles and anchored."

Underwood's decision to attack a destroyer was bold. During the early years of the war, Japanese merchant shipping was the primary target. Only two days before, Sam Dealey's *Harder* had slammed three Japanese frigates that had been part of convoy HI-71, making his boat something of a legend in the submarine force. Apparently, Gordon Underwood and Sam Dealey shared the same beliefs on destroying enemy destroyers. Neither was afraid to take them on, as evidenced by the fact that *Spadefish* had already tracked one other destroyer on this patrol. *Harder*, however, would be lost to enemy attack on 24 August, the day after *Spadefish* took on *Yunagi*.

At 0840, the destroyer now started his northeast leg. This time, Underwood thought that he was far enough into the bay for *Spadefish* to get in her attack. Luck was not on his side, however. At 0858, the unpredictable tin can turned again. Instead of coming west, he went southwest on course 225, "leaving us out again."

An hour later, *Yunagi* had started back on his northeast leg again at 0952. "This time on course 060. We were just inside his triangle by now. If he came back on 270 we had him," thought the skipper.

At 1005, the DD turned west on course 260, just ten degrees off what had been hoped for. This time, however, he continued on his northeast leg longer than the time before. "We headed for him as long as we dared, and then put our stern to him and waited for him to come by," Underwood wrote. "He was further away than we would have liked, but after playing games with this guy for five hours, we decided to take a chance."

Spadefish fired her last four aft torpedoes at 1015, at a range of 2,600 yards, with a 4-foot depth setting. Each of these $10,000 torpedoes missed. The warship turned away at the last moment, and she now knew where *Spadefish* was. *Yunagi*'s Captain Goro had been fully aware of *Spadefish*'s presence. He had maintained his vigilant patrol over Pasaleng Bay's entrance while *Hakko Maru* effected her emergency repairs. "Enemy submarine known to be present," Goro logged. *Spadefish* had been detected multiple times over four hours. When *Spadefish* did finally attack *Yunagi*, Goro reported, "Torpedoes fired at us, but hit shallows and exploded." More likely, these were end of run explosions as the torpedoes sank and detonated.[3]

Now it was time to pay. The angry destroyer raced toward *Spadefish* as she sought out deep water. Through their sonar, Paul Majoue and Mike Sergio could hear the angry swishing of the DD's screws as she headed in to attack. Even for the veterans, the moments waiting for the ashcans to fall were always anxious. Eyes invariably looked upward as they followed the sounds of the approaching ship. For the sake of the new hands, they had not long to wait.

When depth charges exploded very close aboard, the men could actually hear the ashcan's detonator explode with a click before the massive explosion of TNT followed. The sound operators removed their headsets when the splash of depth charges hitting the water could be heard. The roar of an exploding ashcan would be deafening through the headsets.

Click—*wham!* Click—*wham!*

At 1019, four minutes after her torpedoes had been fired at the destroyer, *Spadefish* was rocked with four blockbusters. Loose objects stored in the overhead rained down and light bulbs were granulated in some compartments. Reverberating in this small bay, these explosions sounded louder than any ever heard aboard *Spadefish*. No damage was sustained, however, and *Spadefish* continued on down to 450 feet. In the forward torpedo room, TM3c Hugo Lundquist would note in his journal for 23 August: "Can passed us 5 times, dropping blockbusters. Damn close."

Captain Goro's first depth charges had been very close. Unknown to him, *Spadefish* quickly pulled away from the area. *Yunagi* remained in the vicinity of *Hakko Maru*, charging about the bay entrance, pinging for the American sub. On four different occasions, *Yunagi*'s soundman thought he had a strong sub contact, and depth charges were dropped. "Only dead fish were brought to surface in quantity," logged Goro.[4]

Captain Underwood kept *Spadefish* running at standard speed submerged out of Pasaleng Bay. Astern, *Yunagi*'s depth charges continued to explode, but thankfully at farther distance. As the range increased, Underwood eased back to two-thirds speed. "The DD didn't follow us. We headed out the eastern side of the bay, while he was searching on the western side."

Once the thunder of the depth charges had fallen far astern, the process of evaluating the damage began. Electrician Ken Sigworth recalled, "We used sound powered phones to contact each compartment to check for damage." The only casualties *Spadefish* had suffered were some light bulbs, which were quickly replaced by Chief Schmelzer's electricians.

An hour later at 1115, *Spadefish* came back to periscope depth. The destroyer was still on the western side of the bay about 6,000 yards away, so Underwood secured from battle stations and continued away from the bay. "Whew!" he wrote in relief of the escape.

At high noon, after having a breather and some food, Underwood decided to try his luck again with his destroyer friend. He hoped to bore straight in this time, bypassing the destroyer and using up his last three torpedoes on the crippled tanker. *Spadefish* would have to penetrate Pasaleng Bay while submerged.

Suddenly at 1212, there was an explosion from one depth charge. The explosion was assumed to be a bomb from a plane, so the skipper ordered his boat down to 200 feet. Three more depth charges quickly exploded, close enough to rattle *Spadefish*.

"Take her to 400 feet!" Underwood called out.

Three more ashcans went off. All seven charges were "blockbusters," the more powerful Japanese weapon. Fortunately, none were close enough to do damage. "The DD either made a false contact or just dropped them to discourage us," wrote Underwood. "He did accomplish the latter. We headed north and cleared the area."

At 1240, *Spadefish* came to periscope depth and found nothing in sight. The boat was rigged for normal submerged running and course was set as 000, due north. Four hours later at 1630, an observation from 55 feet showed the tanker in the same position. The persistent pinging still audible on sonar made it clear that the destroyer was still lurking around the bay.

After sunset, *Spadefish* surfaced at 1914 and tried to get a message off to *Picuda*, giving her attack results and Captain Underwood's intention to go to Saipan for more torpedoes. The radio gang, however, had trouble with their receivers. Return messages were garbled by poor reception, which delayed getting the messages understood.

Although discouraged in not being able to finish off the crippled *Hakko Maru*, *Spadefish* had fatally damaged her. The crew of *Hakko Maru No. 2* had continued to make repairs on their damaged ship throughout the day, while *Spadefish* and *Yunagi* played cat and mouse. The crew worked throughout the night and all of 24 August, struggling to make her seaworthy. At 0800 on 25 August, convoy TAMA-24 was sighted passing Pasaleng Bay. Captain Goro of *Yunagi* turned over the duty of escorting *Hakko Maru* to *CD No. 25*, another escort vessel. "Decision made to abandon *Hakko Maru*, total loss," logged Goro. He directed *CD No. 25* and *Genaki Maru* to come alongside and remove *Hakko Maru*'s crew, passengers and equipment. While the crew was transferred, *Yunagi* proceeded on with TAMA-24 as a screening vessel.[5]

Spadefish's victim, *Hakko Maru*, finally broke in half and sank, and *Spadefish* would receive full credit for her demise in postwar analysis. The determined destroyer *Yunagi*, which *Spadefish* had tried to attack, did not survive 25 August. Shortly after leaving *Hakko Maru*, one of

Yunagi's marus was torpedoed by *Picuda*. Seeing the torpedoes coming from starboard, Captain Goro turned and charged. At 1025, *Yunagi* was hit by a *Picuda* torpedo which broke her back and caused heavy flooding. Captain Goro immediately ordered abandon ship. Ten minutes after being hit, *Yunagi* jackknifed and disappeared, taking 38 crewmen with her. Captain Goro and 201 other *Yunagi* crewmen were rescued by escort *CD-32*.[6]

For *Spadefish*'s crew, it had been a long two days. Lieutenant Gus Laundy, who normally stood the midnight to 4 a.m. watch (the "0 to 4" or "midwatch" in Navy jargon), had gotten very little sleep. After his watch, he would normally have to go down and decode messages. Most nights, he was able to catch an hour of sleep before 0800, when he made his daily torpedo room inspections. The torpedo crews were required to service the torpedoes daily and part of Laundy's job was to be sure the work was properly performed. The leading torpedoman in each room led his crew in checking the torpedo gyroscopes, air pressure, igniters, engines and propellers. Following his morning rounds, Laundy and Bill Ware then stood the 1200 to 1600 afternoon watch.

Aside from Laundy's daily routines, the added action of enemy contact further complicated sleep aboard a submarine. "I was so damned tired most of the time from lack of sleep," he recalled. "I would actually fall asleep doing the decoding!"

After several hours of garbled messages, *Spadefish*'s radio gang did finally receive a clear message at 0036 on 24 August from wolf pack leader Donc Donaho in *Picuda*, requesting an 0400 rendezvous. Course was set for the appointed meeting.

At 0340, *Spadefish* picked up SJ radar interference dead ahead, indicating a friendly radar. Attempts were made to establish identification as the ship headed down her bearing. Finally, by 0432, Don Martin's radar gang had identified the SJ interference as coming from packmate *Redfish*. Two minutes later, *Redfish* was sighted ahead.

At 0435, *Picuda*'s SJ radar interference was picked up. At 0448, she sighted *Picuda* and *Spadefish* stopped to allow her to come alongside to starboard. At 0516, *Picuda* made an unusual exchange. "We sent over a HP air compressor 3rd stage head that she needed," Captain Underwood wrote. In return, *Picuda* sent over a Japanese prisoner the sub had picked up from the ocean. The prisoner was an old rice farmer from Taiwan who had been pressed into the merchant marine service. He had a badly wounded foot from a gunshot that he had suffered prior to his ship's loss. The pharmacist's mate aboard *Picuda* had been forced to take off one of his mangled toes.

At 0533, *Redfish* approached *Spadefish*'s port side and sent her Japanese prisoner over, "also by the water route." In his journal, torpedoman Hugo Lundquist made note. "Rendezvous with *Redfish* and *Picuda* to pick up two Nip prisoners. One from *Redfish* was on troopship we sank. Other was on bombed supply ship near Bonins."

Auxiliaryman Buck Miller had heard that the Japanese considered it a disgrace to be captured and that some would even consider hari-kari, a Japanese form of suicide, over the alternative. Miller therefore found it incredulous that these men would actually swim between U.S. submarines. "If it was a disgrace to be captured, why not just stop swimming and drown?"

Commander Donaho had decided to put the prisoners aboard *Spadefish*, as she was preparing to return to Saipan for more torpedoes. There, the enemy could be put ashore and properly handled. BM1c Willard Eimermann, chief of the boat, supervised the prisoner transfer. He found that his new Japanese prisoners could speak very little English. "We'd ask the wounded guy, 'How'd you get hurt?' He would go, 'Airplane. *Tat-tat-tat-tat,*' making the sounds of a machine gun." Eimermann felt that pharmacist's mate Vic Ives "did the best he could" to care for the soldier's wounds until he could be taken off *Spadefish* to better care.

The *Redfish* prisoner was the man retrieved from the troop transport *Tamatsu Maru* that *Spadefish* had sunk on 19 August. This soldier "was a sergeant in the Japanese Army," recalled motormac Dick Gamby. "He was an arrogant son-of-a-gun. He had that arrogant, never-lose fighting mood." He was kept closely watched during the run into Saipan. This feisty prisoner was taken to the forward room.

The hostility of this prisoner did not sit well with all. "We'd show him the pictures on the torpedo tubes for the number of ships we'd sunk," recalled gunner Bernie Massar. "We had to keep a close watch on him." This forward room prisoner was shackled to TM3c Bert Spiese's bunk for safekeeping.

"He would have killed you if he got a chance," said Spiese. "We had to keep a guard on him." Both prisoners could see the Rising Sun emblems for the three marus that *Spadefish* claimed as sunk or damaged on her first patrol. "Every time we sunk a ship we painted it on three big shiny cabinets we had in the forward room," said Spiese. "The prisoners knew what they meant."

Per seaman first class Don Scholle, the forward torpedo room prisoner's attitude did not help his condition. "One of the guys in the torpedo room tried to have fun with this prisoner," Scholle said. "He offered him a knife, saying, 'Hari kari?'"

The wounded prisoner from *Picuda* was no trouble. He was secured to a bunk in the after torpedo room, where PhM1c Ives continued to look after his wounds during the return run to Saipan. Paul Majoue remembered that for the longest time "neither one knew the other was in the boat." They were kept isolated, but intelligence was hard to come by, since *Spadefish* had no interpreter aboard. Instead, "they were taught the most obscene sailor language, of course!" recalled Lt.(jg) Dan Decker.

With her prisoners stowed below, *Spadefish* departed the rendezvous at 0536, heading toward Balintang Channel. At 0924, the duty watch sighted a flight of five Japanese Betty bombers at a distance of 10 miles and submerged to avoid detection. Returning to the surface at 0958, she soon passed through an area covered with a large number of empty oil drums.

At 1107, the watch spotted the masts of two ships and *Spadefish* dived again. She commenced a submerged approach, only to find at 1130 that the targets were two fishing sampans. Underwood broke off the approach and continued through Balintang Channel submerged, sighting several more of these sampans during the afternoon.

At 1856, *Spadefish* surfaced and began to run for Saipan on all four main engines, as she had plenty of fuel oil remaining. At 2127, she turned away at flank speed from what was reported as a submarine, at a range of about 6,000 yards. A quick radar fix was made on the "target," which proved to be the tip of Balintang Island, distance 35,000 yards. Captain Underwood noted of this error: "In the peculiar visibility of a dark night, this was an easy mistake to make."

Spadefish continued her run to Saipan over the next few days. On 25 August, she closed and exchanged information with the submarine *Sailfish*. At 1002 on 27 August, the watch spotted a friendly Coronado patrol plane coming out of the sun, at a distance of 5 miles. To be safe, *Spadefish* quickly dove to avoid detection. The following day, another friendly Coronado patrol plane was sighted at 0758 at 8 miles distance, and *Spadefish* again dived to be safe.

At 0633 on 29 August, she sighted her escort, *USS Downes*, bearing 097, distance 12 miles. At 1048, *Spadefish* sighted a periscope on her starboard quarter, distance 1,500 yards. She immediately turned away at flank speed and notified her escort, who went back to investigate. *Spadefish* continued on alone to Saipan, passing through the protective coral reefs into Tanapag Harbor.

Saipan had been held by some 32,000 Japanese soldiers when U.S. troops first stormed ashore on 15 June, following heavy bombardments and carrier air strikes to soften up the invasion. The "Great Marianas Turkey Shoot" carrier battle had followed the next week. During this pivotal carrier clash, the Japanese Navy lost more than 400 aircraft. *Spadefish* had been active attacking Japanese shipping during late August just prior to the American landing on Leyte, therefore entitling all hands aboard her to wear a star on their Pacific Area Ribbon for having participated in the Battle for the Philippines.[7]

Saipan was not declared secure until 9 July, after which time invasion forces landed on nearby Guam and Tinian, where fighting was also fierce. The United States lost 5,000 men killed and 20,000 wounded before all three islands were declared under U.S. control on 10 August. With the permission of Fleet Admiral Nimitz, ComSubPac began to move sub tenders into Saipan's Tanapag Harbor and Guam's Apra Harbor during the next few weeks.[8]

The advance base at Saipan was brand-new when *Spadefish* arrived on 29 August. At 1145, *Spadefish* moored to the starboard side of the submarine tender *Holland* (AS-3), which had arrived only days prior. Saipan's Tanapag Harbor would only be used initially for topping off or for emergency repairs. Complete refits would be made at Guam, Majuro, Midway or Pearl Harbor for Lockwood's subs.

Army engineers were working to expand Isley airfield into a base where B-29s could fly bombing raids against Japanese mainland targets. The Japanese airfield of Aslito was renamed Isley Airfield, in honor of Cdr. Robert H. Isley, who was killed in action attacking Saipan with his Avenger squadron from the carrier *Lexington* on 13 June. Amazingly enough, less than two weeks later, Avengers from the carrier *Enterprise*'s VT-10 squadron landed on Saipan to see the captured Japanese aircraft and facilities ashore firsthand.[9]

Once secured alongside *Holland*, first aboard *Spadefish* was an armed Marine detail to retrieve the two prisoners she had picked up from *Picuda* and *Redfish*. Motormac Dick Gamby remembered that the feisty Japanese sergeant in the forward torpedo room had lost his will to fight by this time. "He had to climb out through the hatch. Once he climbed up and saw those four Marines standing there, he almost fell back down the ladder! His fight was over. He must have met Marines before, maybe on Guadalcanal or somewhere."

The boat spent two days alongside *Holland*, making preparations to return to her patrol station. During this time, *Spadefish* was given a fresh coat of paint. To the chagrin of some, the paint color was lighter than what had been her normal color. The skipper would soon find the new lighter paint to his liking during night action in the next two weeks. The crew took advantage of this time to complete some minor voyage repairs and to look over the destruction that the Marines had wrought during the previous weeks.

"There was still fighting going on ashore," recalled Lt. Cdr. Ustick. "I went ashore and watched them bomb one of the enemy's caves. I also brought a couple of Marine officers out to the boat for dinner." Ustick found the Marine officers stunned to be sitting at *Spadefish*'s wardroom table with a white linen cloth and the mess attendants,

Spadefish would carry four different Japanese prisoners of war back for interrogation during the course of her war patrols. In this view, Marine guards are escorting POWs over the *Spadefish* gangplank at Pearl Harbor following the ship's fifth patrol. These three prisoners were actually picked up by sister wolf pack sub *Skate*. Note *Spadefish*'s battle flag flying from her No. 1 periscope.
Courtesy of Bernie Massar.

Henry Solomon and William Portwood, serving them. "They had been eating nothing but K-rations so long that they didn't know what food tasted like," said Ustick.[10]

Proud of their accomplishments on the first leg of this double-barreled war patrol, the *Spadefish* crew posed for a picture topside. They proudly held their new battle flag, which showed a spade riding a toothy torpedo. Seaman Don Scholle recalled that the skipper had wanted a battle flag created during the first patrol. "The leading signalman, Jim Schuett, asked me to make him a flag," said Scholle. "I just sat there for a couple of hours, but couldn't decide what to do with it." At length, the quartermaster gang enlisted leading radioman and able illustrator Paul Majoue to assist with the original illustration. In the upper left corner, three stars were sewn on to represent the three Japanese merchant ships torpedoed thus far. With each future war patrol, the battle flag would be revised.

Under the supervision of fuel king Charlie Griffith, *Spadefish* took on 51,279 gallons of fuel. She also topped off her fresh water tanks. Lieutenant Gus Laundy and the torpedo gangs oversaw the loading of twenty-one more Mark XIV torpedoes, to bring the ship back to a full load of twenty-four torpedoes. "We didn't load our own torpedoes," forward room torpedoman Bert Spiese related. "The tender did all

After firing 21 torpedoes during her first war patrol, *Spadefish* returned briefly to newly captured Saipan to reload. Taken alongside a submarine tender, this 1945 photo shows crewmen loading a Mark 14 torpedo into their submarine. *Official U.S. Navy photo.*

that for us. We more or less just sat around and drank a few bottles of 'near beer' which the tender had for us. Saipan wasn't totally secure yet, so going ashore for the crew was out of the question."

During the layover at Tanapag Harbor, the *Spadefish* crew had a beer party on the beach. The Marines, who had just taken Saipan three weeks before, were still on full alert. While ashore, electrician Roy Moody managed to come up with a skull as a souvenir. "I don't know where the hell he got the skull," said Wallace McMahon, "but he mounted it right there in the maneuvering room—until the captain found it, and that was the end of that."

From the tender *Holland*, *Spadefish*'s crew also received welcome news on current events. Torpedoman Hugo Lundquist acquired a copy of the 30 August 1944 edition of the *Holland Herald*, a typed up summary of war and worldly news. The U.S. Third Army was "smashing enemy resistance on the Seine below Paris." In Rome, "Allied troops roamed virtually at will over southern France Sunday." In the Pacific, Army Liberator bombers had blasted Iwo Jima in the Volcano Islands, 750 miles south of Tokyo. Back home in baseball standings, the St. Louis Browns held a five game lead over New York in the American League. The other St. Louis team, the Cardinals, commanded the National League with a seventeen game lead over Pittsburgh. Such news helped bring everyone up to speed on the war and life back home. Senior radioman "Hocks" Majoue's gang would eventually type up their radio intercepts and start their own newsletter aboard *Spadefish*, dubbing it "Maru's Bull Sheet."

Even on a newly-captured island far out in the Pacific, personal encounters proved that it was indeed a small world. Gus Laundy had only received one letter from his brother, Ens. Jim Laundy, during the

Spadefish crew with their early battle flag, viewed at end of first patrol 1A alongside sub tender *Holland* at Saipan on 29 August 1944. Note the three stars on the flag for three Japanese vessels torpedoed during patrol 1A. Officers standing in second row are (left to right): Ens. Bill Ware, Lt. Cdr. Ted Ustick, Captain Gordon Underwood (wearing his campaign cap, directly beneath the flag) and Lt. Frank Alvis. Officers kneeling in front row are (left to right): Ens. Perry Wood, Lt. Gus Laundy, Ens. Don Martin, Lt.(jg) Dan Decker (directly behind ship's mascot Luau), and Ens. Ray White. *Courtesy of Dan Decker.*

war. He was pleased to find that his brother was now stationed ashore at the ammunition dump on Saipan, and he was allowed to go ashore for a reunion with him.

Lt. Dan Decker also managed to make it ashore with some officers to survey the scene of the recent battles.

> Naturally, we had to go rubber-necking in the hills of Saipan. The place was really torn up. We came across what appeared to be their recreation center. The building had taken a hit or two and ten yen notes were scattered about the yard, some still in bundles. Maybe it was the paymaster's shack. We all took about a dozen or so of the notes for souvenirs and

mailed them to friends and family. After the war, all Japanese currency was redeemed at face value. How could we guess?

While in Tanapag Harbor, Paul Majoue was below in the radio shack, when he got an unexpected call from topside that somebody up there knew him. "Who the hell knows me in Saipan?" he thought.

Topside, he found an Army soldier named D'Angelo, whose sister from New Jersey he was dating. She had sent her brother a letter, telling him that her boyfriend Paul was aboard the submarine *Spadefish* and that he should look him up if he ever had the chance. When Majoue went topside, he encountered the "scraggly-looking" Army soldier whom he had never met.

"Would you like to come below?" Majoue offered. D'Angelo and his fellow soldier took the offer to tour a submarine. The submariner then asked if they had eaten. Majoue related:

> That's when he told me, "We've been eating K-rations for the past few weeks." Like a jackass, not thinking, I said, "But all we have right now are steaks."
>
> He says, "Steaks!" So, we go into the galley and I asked the cook, Riley, to fix them up a couple of steaks and a potato each. Riley looks up and says, "How do you want 'em?"
>
> D'Angelo said, "We don't give a damn how you fix 'em! Just cook 'em any kinda way. We'll take 'em."

Riley proceeded to cook up the steaks and potatoes for Majoue's new Army buddies. About the time they sat down to eat them, the alarms began sounding for an incoming Japanese plane. Around Saipan, the *Spadefish* crew quickly became accustomed to Japanese fighters or patrols planes passing nearby. Whenever an enemy plane was spotted, the subs would go out and submerge until the all-clear was given. The airplane drills were more precautionary than any real danger they posed.

"Stay where you are," Majoue said calmly. "We're just going to go out for about a half hour, submerge, and then come right back."

D'Angelo snapped, "Submerge my ass! I'll eat on this thing, but I won't ride on it!"

As *Spadefish* prepared to pull away from the sub tender, the Army boys scrambled topside. "The last thing I saw was those two boys going up with a steak in each pocket and a potato in the top pocket of their fatigues!" Majoue laughed. "I have never seen them again."

6

A Double-Barreled Patrol

Patrol 1B   *1-24 September 1944*

While *Spadefish* was en route to Tanapag Harbor, her packmates made another attack on a convoy on 25 August, sinking a small transport, a destroyer and a 6,000-ton maru. Following this attack, Donc Donaho took his *Picuda* and *Redfish* toward Saipan to also reprovision. They would not depart Saipan until September 5.[1]

Spadefish had departed the sub tender *Holland* and Saipan's Tanapag Harbor at 1000 on 1 September for her patrol area, being escorted out by the destroyer *Ellet* (DD-398). Upon arrival in the submarine safety lane, the escort departed and *Spadefish* was again on her own, starting the second leg of her double-barreled war patrol.

At 0257 on 2 September, *Spadefish* picked up a very close radar contact at 330 yards. It was a bright moonlit night and nothing could be sighted. The contact moved out to 1,600 yards and then continued out, being lost at 2,600 yards. "The birds around this area must be full of buckshot," Captain Underwood noted wryly in his patrol report.

"It was sensitive enough to pick them up," recalled radar tech Neal Pike. "They may have been in the water. If their feathers were wet, we could get an echo on them."

Underwood kept his boat running on the surface back toward her patrol area in Luzon Strait, diving once in the morning for a Liberator bomber and again in the late afternoon for a submarine that could not be confirmed as a friendly. *Spadefish* resurfaced at 1847, but nothing was in sight or on radar. At 2144, she sighted *USS Billfish* (SS-286), and exchanged identification by radar interference. During the night, numerous SJ contacts were made on birds, ranging from 900 yards to 3,000 yards. The birds could occasionally be seen in the moonlight.

3 September passed quietly en route to the patrol station. At 1257 a plane contact was made on the SD radar, range 20 miles. The plane was using IFF but, as it was not sighted, and the range decreased rapidly to 9 miles, *Spadefish* dove at 1300 to avoid detection. The lookouts

received good practice clearing the bridge with these bird and plane contacts. Bernie Massar later explained the various functions of the lookout duty section.

> We had five men when we stood watch. Three were topside lookouts, one man was on the helm in the conning tower and the fifth man was on standby on a twenty-minute rest period. Every twenty minutes, the lookouts rotated to stay fresh. When the sub submerged, the lookout on the helm remained at his post. The three lookouts and the man on twenty-minute rest dropped down to the control room. They took over the bow planes, stern planes, trim manifold and phone set to receive calls from all departments reporting that they were secured and normal.[2]

On 4 September, the radar gang continued to practice tracking bird contacts on the SJ. One bird was followed out to 6,300 yards! At 1220 on 5 September, *Spadefish* reentered her assigned patrol area. She was to work the area off the northeastern corner of Formosa, including the adjacent waters of Nansei Shoto.

Nothing about operating an attack submarine in enemy controlled waters could be taken for granted. Every function of the men on watch aboard was vital to insure the sub's safety. A slack periscope, sonar, radar or bridge watch could allow an enemy aircraft or ship to make a fatal attack on the ship. Aside from enemy predators, *Spadefish* and her crew could just as easily be lost to operational error.

One such episode occurred on her first war patrol as the ship was making a dive. Auxiliary boss Joe Mitzel was the duty chief in the control room. Instead of the proper sequence being followed on the hydraulic manifold, the main induction was opened and the diesel engines were started as *Spadefish* descended.

With *Spadefish* below the surface, the open induction allowed sea water to pour into the pipe. "We took water in the hull engine supply through the battery and hull exhaust," wrote Bernie Massar. "Only the line systems were flooded, but it gave us negative buoyancy." On the surface, the mighty diesels would pull air at gale force through the open conning tower hatch and through the main induction line. With all hatches secured and the main induction flooded, the diesels immediately began sucking the air from within the boat at a rate that caused an ear-popping vacuum.

Auxiliaryman Buck Miller was on the air manifold, and "felt the suction on my ears." Electrician's Mate 2/c Len Dependahl was on the headphones directly in front of Miller. Dependahl saw what was happening and, without orders from a superior, calmly called over the intercom, "Maneuvering room—secure those engines."[3]

"My personal view is that he saved our butts," thought Miller. Quartermaster Don Scholle recalled Dependahl's swift thinking.

> I was in the conning tower with the Exec when the main induction was flooded. We had the hatch closed, so we really couldn't feel the suction in the conning tower. But I heard Dependahl call out, "Maneuvering room, secure those engines!" Captain Underwood later awarded Dependahl a commendation for saving the crew.

Chief of the boat Willard Eimermann was just leaving the chief's quarters at the moment the engines began pulling the negative pressure through the boat. "Holy man!" he thought. "We always used to discuss this happening. Would the suction pull your eardrums out or not?" Instantly sensing what was wrong, he shouted to Buck Miller to use the air manifold to ease the pressure. "I got the auxiliaryman to put a little air in the boat—about 600 pounds—because it was really pulling," said Eimermann.

The error was quickly corrected but not soon forgotten. "What happened?" Captain Underwood quizzed Engineering Officer Frank Alvis, who reluctantly admitted that Mitzel had erred in flooding the No. 4 main engine. "Nobody said anything to him," remembered fireman John Brewer, "but they all felt bad for him."

The black gang went to work on the Number 4 engine right away. "We dried it out and pumped the bilges," said motormac Charles Griffith. "Then we put the lube oil purifier on and ran it through to pick up any moisture in the engine." Captain Underwood's report notes: "After clearing of water, the engine was started and found to be out of timing. The vertical drive shaft assembly was broken down and the engine re-timed. Time out of commission, 24 hours."

Spadefish patrolled submerged between Yonakuni Jima and Iriomoto Jima, Formosa on 6 September. Fishing sampans provided the only item of interest for watchstanders. As *Spadefish* withdrew from the vicinity of Yonakuni Jima on 7 September, Captain Underwood found that the starboard forward wing antenna had carried away due to faulty construction. He sent a repair party on deck to weld a 50-foot jury antenna mast aft from the conning tower to a life stanchion. "Reception on the jury rig was excellent," he noted.

Such repairs at sea were crucial, and by 0830, the antenna repair was completed and *Spadefish* set her course for Formosa. At 1453, a Japanese Mavis patrol plane was sighted and *Spadefish* dived to avoid detection. Upon surfacing at 1526, the watch found that the morning's welding job on the antenna had broken loose again. At 1900, the radar gang made an outstanding SJ contact on Formosa again. This time the second pulse echo was an actual range of 168,000 yards! "Formosa is a good radar target."

Ens. Don Martin's radar gang had its own challenges and unique remedy on 8 September when the SD radar's blower motor failed, due to a lack of lubrication. A ship's fan was mounted on the door to the SD transmitter with a canvas sack leading the air from it into the blower louvers.

Captain Underwood took his boat down at 0448 to begin the day's patrol, his third day back on station. He used the prevailing 2-knot southwest current of 2 knots to maintain position off Kusoan To.

"Smoke on the horizon! Bearing zero-zero-five, sir," came the welcome call from starboard lookout at 0958.

Junior OOD Ray White sent word below to have the captain come to the bridge. MoMM2c Buck Miller, the duty auxiliaryman in the control room, was sent to wake the skipper, who had been awake most of the night. Regardless, he was ever ready for the call to dispatch more war fish. He had barely called, "Smoke on the horizon, Skipper," when Gordon Underwood flew into action. "He raced right by me in his skivvies," said Miller. "You had to move out of his way or get bowled over!"

At 0958, smoke was sighted bearing north. Sound picked up pinging from the direction of the smoke. The smoke developed into a convoy of eight cargo ships and at least three escorts. All the ships were smoking heavily, intermittently. The convoy, visible only by its masts and stacks, came down the northeast coast of Formosa and took departure off Samucho Kaku [Point] on course 105, speed 8 knots.

Spadefish, unable to close any more than about 18,000 yards, set course to trail this convoy. Underwood became impatient and surfaced at 1652, chasing the convoy on the surface. He slowly began overtaking the smoke from the Japanese ships. At 1850, an SJ contact on a ship at 7,000 yards was thought to be a trailing escort ship, but it turned out to be a fisherman headed for Formosa. At 1853, SJ contact on this convoy showed their range at 17,000 yards.

Underwood set a tracking party and commenced an end around, moving around the convoy at high speed to get ahead and lie in wait near the base course to the south. The end-around run, derived from football terminology, kept *Spadefish* within visual sights of her convoy while minimizing her chances of being spotted. The plotting team now determined the convoy to be zig-zagging 20 to 30 degrees either side of the base course of 105, at a speed of 8 knots. The radar pip sizes indicated eight good-sized ships and three escorts.

"During these long end-arounds, Gus Cuthbertson would be the battle stations talker in the forward torpedo room," recalled seaman Wallace McMahon. Pre-war, Cuthbertson had been a radio actor out of San Francisco, where he had acquired a wonderful range of vocals with his deep bass voice. "We'd be at battle stations for hours, but Gus would keep us from falling asleep," said McMahon. "He would go into these long soliloquies about gangster life or do perfect impersonations of President Roosevelt to keep us entertained."

At 1922, Underwood sounded battle stations. The convoy had come into sight at 9,000 yards. Radar encountered interference of a sweeping type, at a rate of 20 sweeps per minute, similar to that encountered with the Japanese ships off Luzon. "Decided to disregard their radar and make attack on the surface."

At 2030, *Spadefish*, making 11.5 knots on the surface, headed in for the attack on the starboard flank of the convoy. The convoy was arranged in two columns of four ships each. One escort was ahead, one on the starboard bow and one astern. As the range narrowed, lookouts could make out more details of the Japanese merchant ships. From his observations, Underwood felt that six of the freighters were "good-size, well-deck, composite superstructure. Two were larger, more flush-decked appearing, split superstructure type." This convoy was officially known as TAKA-808, which had departed Keelung for Okinawa on 8 September and consisted of eight ore carriers and four escorts.[4]

Underwood called Chief Simms' forward torpedo room gang to prepare its Mark 14-3As with 6-foot depth settings. On the bridge, Ens. Bill Ware took final bearings on the target ships with the TBT, which transmitted the data down to Gus Laundy's TDC. With the skipper on the bridge, Exec Ted Ustick orchestrated the actions of the well-practiced conning tower attack team. Fire controlman Andy Olah stood by Lieutenant Laundy to tackle any adjustments to the computer. Near plotting officer Dan Decker, assistant Perry Wood continued to look up ship silhouettes in the ONI-208J book as new information was called down. Sonarmen Majoue and Sergio monitored both the target ships and the escorts through their headsets while Neal Pike and radar officer Don Martin took occasional SJ radar sweeps to keep tabs on the convoy.

Selecting the last ship in the far column, the skipper ordered tubes 2, 3 and 4 fired forward. At 2033, Underwood then ordered the other three forward tubes fired at the last ship in the near column, which was

500 yards closer at 2,100 yards. The first target was the 1,922 freighter *Nichiman Maru*. The closer ship in the near column was a much larger freighter, the 6,197-ton *Nichian Maru*. *Spadefish*'s patrol reports gives the torpedo results from Underwood's perspective.

> This second target was one of the largest in the convoy. His range on firing was about 2,100 yards. He was long, about 500 feet, split superstructure and heavily loaded. It was too dark to see more details. One hit was observed on the first target, which seemed to disintegrate, throwing sparks and smoke high in the air. Two hits were observed on the second target, one amidships and one aft. He was last seen smoking heavily and settling rapidly.

The bridge crew was ecstatic. Six torpedoes had been fired, and two Japanese marus (merchant ships) were on their way to the bottom. The smaller *Nichiman Maru* was ripped apart by the Mark 14's Torpex explosive, which killed fifty-three of her crewmen. The larger *Nichian Maru* was sunk in mere seconds, with a loss of fifty-one men, from her two direct hits.[5]

A mere five minutes after firing at his second target, Captain Underwood had swung *Spadefish* into position to fire her rear tubes. Using radar, he picked the "closest large pip of convoy, ahead of previous targets and was probably the next to the last ship in near column." He fired four torpedoes at 2036 at a target in the middle of the convoy, using radar ranges and bearings, firing range 3,000 yards.

Two hits were heard, with times corresponding to the first and fourth torpedoes. "Convoy was now smoking so heavily it was hard to determine where the torpedoes exploded, other than sudden additions to the puffs of smoke."

Neal Pike reported that only nine pips showed on the radar where there had been eleven. The first two ships had certainly gone to the bottom. At 2044, depth charges began going off in the vicinity of the attacks. "As we were astern of the convoy and crossing to the port side, we could afford to laugh at them."

Once the torpedoes had been fired from both torpedo rooms, Chief William Simms and Harry George's torpedomen had gone to work reloading. The racks holding the torpedoes were on tracks, which were used to force each new torpedo into a position which lined it up with the tube. A block and tackle system of ropes and chainfalls was used to manually force the torpedo partway into the tube.

At 2120, *Spadefish* was in position on the port flank of the convoy, so she headed in for another attack. Underwood was eager to hit this convoy again, although he found that its ships had still not quite settled down into stable disposition again. The enemy's base course was now 113, with the ships zigzagging radically at a speed of 8 knots. "We were within 10,000 yards of the convoy at all times after the first attack and could determine that no ships scattered from the convoy," reported Underwood. A small ship astern, taken for an escort, began moving up the port flank. "We got in to a range of 1,900 yards from the fellow when it was decided to pull out and try again. This ship could be seen to be a small, well-decked, inter-island freighter, about 150 to 200 feet long, probably acting as escort."

Two PC-type escorts were on the port bow of the convoy. Pike picked up radar interference was coming from their bearings, but the Japanese apparently didn't pick *Spadefish* up as their sweeping did not stop, even when *Spadefish* had closed to 1,800 yards of them. One of the freighters was smoking quite heavily aft, and was obviously a wounded *Spadefish* victim. With so many escorts on the port side, Underwood decided to go around the stern of the convoy and attack from the starboard side again.

At 2208, *Spadefish* charged in under moonlight for another attack from the starboard flank. Fortunately, the convoy was between *Spadefish* and the moon, keeping conditions in her favor, so she continued in. Underwood made his second attack of the night running at 15 knots on the surface, beginning to fire at 2223 on 8 September, less than two hours after first firing on this convoy.

Underwood picked out two targets silhouetted by the moon and fired three torpedoes at each, with a range of 2,300 yards. The convoy was still making 8 knots, but the second target was possibly as far back as 3,400 yards. Two hits were seen and heard on the first target. He was later seen to blow up and sink. The second target was missed. "Radar had trouble getting on the right target and possibly a faulty range was given," logged Captain Underwood.

Having dispatched all six forward fish again, *Spadefish* swung quickly to bring her rear tubes to bear, making two full rounds of attacks for each torpedo room this night!

Using the TBT (target bearing transmitter), on each end of the bridge, the bridge crew fed true bearings to the plotting party, in addition to the relative observed bearings being called by the lookouts and the radar ranges that were being called out. From a range of 2,450 yards, Underwood fired four of his stern torpedoes. The SJ radar was right on the money this time. At the proper time on SM1c Jim Schuett's stopwatch, two torpedo hits were observed on the target freighter. Underwood wrote, "Target was low in the water and then obscured by smoke as we withdrew from the vicinity."

Lt. Cdr. Ted Ustick, seen holding ship's mascot Luau on the cigarette deck. Captain Gordon Underwood gave Ustick the Silver Star Medal for his role in helping *Spadefish* sink four Japanese merchant ships in one night. *Courtesy of Cdr. Perry W. Ustick, USN (Ret.).*

Beginning at 2229, indiscriminate depth charging was seen and heard in the vicinity of the attack for the next fifteen or so minutes. Some forty to fifty depth charges thundered off in the distance as escorts attacked what they imagined was a U.S. submarine below. Still running on the surface, *Spadefish*'s bridge crew saw some gunfire from the Japanese vessels, but was not threatened by any fire her way. There was much flashing of searchlights. Flames and explosions continued to erupt from the convoy's vicinity for some time. *Spadefish* drew away aft of the convoy, and as the range increased to 6,500 yards, Neal Pike's radar screen showed a beautiful sight. There were clearly only seven pips out of the convoy's original eleven.

Spadefish had sunk four ships in two back-to-back attacks, one of the most successful single assaults on a convoy of the war!

Spadefish's crew felt certain from the visual evidence and the radar screen's testimony that they had sunk four Japanese ships on the night of 8 September. Indeed, of the five enemy ships fired upon with twenty torpedoes, four did sink this night. The latest two victims of this convoy were the 2,557-ton well-deck, composite superstructure freighter *Shokei Maru* and the smaller 1,254-ton *Shinten Maru*. *Spadefish* had become something of a one-boat wolf pack, ripping four marus from this important convoy in just under two hours. *Shokei* was hit in her port side aft by one torpedo which killed two men. *Shinten* was hit in her starboard side aft, killing six men and sinking her in twelve minutes.[6]

Spadefish kept within a range of about 10,000 yards, as she circled around to the south to make an end run down moon. In the deck log, JOOD Ray White wrote that *Spadefish* "retired when escorts commenced firing deck gun and [we] commenced end around for position ahead of convoy." In his patrol report, Underwood noted the conditions that had helped make this night so successful.

> Visibility was excellent. We could see the dark shapes and smoke plainly. They couldn't see us with our light color. The paint job received in Saipan was lighter than normal, but at this time we were glad it was.

The success of these two night attacks was in large part due to the work of the Executive Officer, Lt. Comdr. T. M. Ustick, USN, in coordinating the fire control party in the inherent noisy and crowded conning tower of a night radar attack.

Twenty minutes after the last attack, another ship was picked up at 2241 at a range of 9,350 yards, coming from the west at 16 knots. It was another escort joining up. The convoy could be plainly seen to consist of only four big ships now. The last in column was having a hard time keeping up and was guarded by two of the escorts. The other two escorts were seen with the leading three ships. The convoy was headed on course 113, at a speed of 6 to 7 knots, headed for Naguro Wan in Ishigaki Jima. At 2253, Ensign White logged, "Heard numerous explosions far away in direction of convoy."

At 0002, a southerly zig by the convoy forced *Spadefish* to speed up to pull away. "Our wake must have been sighted, as one of the escorts flashed a searchlight in our direction, so we submerged and started in for a submerged radar attack," wrote Underwood.

At 0023 on 9 September, one of the escorts with the trailing ship headed in *Spadefish*'s direction and started dropping depth charges. The escort's range was 4,200 yards when the first four went off. The sound men heard the splashes of depth charges dropping and quickly removed their earphones to avoid the deafening explosions, which would be further amplified. The second group of four depth charges were dropped at a range of 3,000 yards, with the escort still closing.

With the range of 2,100 yards, Underwood decided to give up and go down, so went to 400 feet. The escort passed close astern as *Spadefish* turned away. He was pinging, but didn't pick her up. The last ship in the convoy and the other escort also passed close astern.

Captain Underwood was not afraid to push test depth, as his patrol report relates. "Evasion tactics used were clearing the area at 2/3 speed, at a depth of 450 feet, endeavoring to keep the stern pointed at the searching ship or ships. Speed was increased at times when depth charges were being dropped."

Spadefish resurfaced at 0148 and started chasing the convoy again. One of the escorts could still be seen at the spot where *Spadefish* had dived. The remaining units of the convoy were headed into Naguro Wan, too close to the beach for another attack.

Underwood secured his crew from battle stations and commenced patrolling about 10 miles off the beach of Isigaki Jima. As dawn approached, the boat submerged and headed in to investigate this harbor. The sound operators soon picked up enemy pinging, which continued intermittently throughout the day. One or two patrol vessels remained in sight, patrolling off the entrance to Nagura Wan. At 1112, numerous columns of smoke were sighted inside the harbor, believed to be coming from the ships of the convoy. At least one of the escorts was putting off heavy smoke, so it was hard to distinguish them. At 1243, Frank Alvis and his JOOD, Perry Wood, picked up smoke on the horizon at 15,000 yards initially. Wood noted that it was "identified as a Japanese patrol boat, PC-13 class." Headed in for the harbor, the PC passed about 3,000 yards ahead of *Spadefish*.

At 1705, heavy smoke was sighted and then the masts of a ship coming in from the east, headed for the harbor at a speed of 14 knots. The Bells of St. Mary's bonged through the ship, as the now familiar call of, "Battle stations, torpedo!" went out.

Spadefish commenced an approach on the target ship. As the range closed, it was found to be a small inter-island freighter similar to one of the escorts seen with the convoy. Underwood decided he was a worthwhile target, so he ordered the remaining torpedoes to be set at four feet and headed in.

At 1731, *Spadefish* fired her final three forward torpedoes, with a firing range of 1,470 yards, the enemy's angle on the bow 83, and gyro 359. All missed. The target had not changed course, so Underwood sent out his last torpedo. It missed also. "The target draft must have been less than four feet or the Mk 14 torpedoes ran too deep. The set up was too good to miss at that range. Saw the Japs running to battle stations, so we went deep."

With the SESE fathometer, nicknamed "Susie," Frank Alvis was able to find the 100 fathom curve and head for very deep water. At 1741, the depth charges began exploding, falling astern and fairly close. A total of twelve were dropped as *Spadefish* withdrew from the area at high speed. She returned to periscope depth at 1818, and spotted her target 4,000 yards astern, headed away. Six more depth charges were heard, all distant.

As silent running, diving officer Alvis was careful not to allow his men to blow any ballast tanks when changing depths. "A bubble the size of your hand released at 400 feet would be the size of a house when it hit the surface," explained TM3c Bert Spiese. "If you blew any bubbles, the escorts would know exactly where you were."

Spadefish surfaced at 1850 and commenced a night patrol, keeping within 10 miles of northwest coast of Ishigaki Jima. Underwood sent dispatches to Donaho and McGregor, who were en route back to station from Saipan. He also sent reports to Admiral Lockwood back at Pearl Harbor, reporting on expending all twenty-four of his torpedoes in a twenty-four hour period.

Out of torpedoes, Underwood notified ComSubPac of the convoy's position and the fact that his boat was "riding herd on it. Didn't like opening up on the radio so close to land but had no alternative if possible radar contact range was to be maintained. The Japs knew we were there anyway." Hugo Lundquist wrote in his journal for 9 September: "Depth charged at 450. Nice pattern—close. All fish expended, but Com-Sub-Pac radioed us to stick around and keep the convoy holed up."

During the night hours, Japanese patrol vessels were seen to remain active outside the harbor entrance and along the coast of Ishigaki Jima. Radar picked up the ships at about 10,000 yards, so there was no trouble in avoiding them. *Spadefish* managed to evade them and still keep inside a 10 or 11-mile line from the coast so as to insure being within radar range of the convoy if it came out.

At 2349, activity commenced in the vicinity of the harbor. Numerous depth charges were heard to explode and flashes of light were seen. Searchlights blinked back and forth. Another strong light, resembling a flickering carbide light was placed in the water about 3 or 4 miles off the beach. Patrol vessels could be seen moving back and forth, both inshore and seaward of the light. "Apparently they thought we were in closer and were trying to silhouette us against the light," wrote Underwood. *Spadefish*'s recent success had obviously put a strong fear into these surviving Japanese sailors.

Spadefish remained about 4 miles off the harbor at Ishigaki Jima, monitoring the movements of the enemy convoy inside. During the night, all the activity within the harbor made Underwood think that the convoy might be coming out now that the moon was coming up. "We trailed a contact out to eastward of the island, but he turned and came back to the harbor, so we resumed our patrolling." Spadefish submerged before dawn on 10 September ton continue patrolling the harbor mouth again. The enemy was well aware that Spadefish was lying in wait. A Kate bomber, distance 5 miles, was spotted headed in the direction of the harbor at 0700. The first of the patrol vessels came out of the harbor at 0755 and started his rounds, "pinging as usual."

At 1034, the first of about two dozen depth charges was heard in the distance. At 1400, a PC-13 class patrol vessel gave Spadefish "a few anxious moments when he patrolled about 2,000 yards astern of us. This patrolling in the midst of a lot of patrol vessels, with no torpedoes, was no fun. This PC would have been a good target with a shallow running torpedo," wrote Underwood.

At 1456, a float-equipped Zeke fighter was seen to head in and land in the harbor. At 1833, Spadefish surfaced and "commenced our night game of hide and seek." Underwood received word that Redfish and Picuda, fresh from Saipan, were on their way back to station.

Radio contact was made with Redfish and Picuda on the wolf pack frequency during the night. The exchange of information required considerable transmission on the part of Spadefish. Captain Underwood could not afford to clear the coast, for fear of getting out of radar range. "We fully expected to be DF'd," he wrote. The enemy had become quite proficient at using multiple land radar sets for direction finding (DF) to pick up an American submarine's radar transmissions and box in her location.

At 0330, the results of being DF'd began to show themselves. The Japanese radar operators had Spadefish's location and three patrol vessels were headed toward her. She had just finished a radio transmission, and had changed course towards the beach. At 0410, one of the incoming patrol vessels fired a yellow rocket. Four minutes later, Underwood took Spadefish deep to 450 feet, rigged for depth charge and silent running and headed for the 100 fathom curve. In his report, he recorded:

> Five or six ships passed over and astern, some pinging, some stopping and listening. As one sound operator expressed it: "There was pinging and screwing all around." Two or three of the screws were heavy and slow. It was thought at the time that part of the convoy had come out. They didn't make con-

Homeward bound. Torpedoman 3/c Hugo Lundquist on the bridge of *Spadefish*, in a photo taken en route to Pearl Harbor after the first war patrol. Although against Navy regulations, Lundquist kept a secret journal while aboard ship. *Hugo Lundquist collection, courtesy of Jeanne Lundquist.*

tact but headed on up the coast to eastward.

We made use of the SESE fathometer in locating the 100 fathom curve and following it.

He returned to periscope depth at 0551, expecting to see the smoke of the convoy having departed the harbor. There was none, however. The one thing in sight was the mast of a PC boat in the direction that the ships had passed. *Spadefish* headed in that direction to determine his course, but quickly found that this escort was circling.

At 0702, a Kate bomber was spotted flying low over the water at 3 miles distant. At 0719, four patrol vessels were seen heading back for the harbor, from the east, "probably our friends of the early morning coming back." It seemed that the convoy had not departed after all. Three of these returning vessels were PC boats and one was the small converted freighter.

During the rest of the morning the plane and the patrol vessels were usually in sight. At 1317, depth charges commenced going off in the distance, a total of twelve being dropped. At 1745, eighteen more depth charges went off in the distance. "Heard distant depth charges," wrote torpedoman Lundquist in his journal. "*Redfish* was getting worked over." At 1846, *Spadefish* surfaced and cleared the coast for her expected rendezvous with the rest of wolf pack. At 1957, she exchanged identification over the SJ with *Redfish*.

Soon after midnight on 12 September, SJ interference identified *Picuda* and at 0138, *Spadefish* rendezvoused with her sister ship. Captain Underwood exchanged information and found that a very welcome bag of mail had arrived in Saipan after *Spadefish* had left. Within sight of the harbor off Ishigaki Jima, the mail was transferred in two sacks via a rubber boat from *Picuda* over to *Spadefish*.⁷

The mail exchange was handled by BM1c Willard Eimermann, the chief of the boat. In his previous life on destroyers, he had been coxswain of some of the ship's launches. Before *Spadefish* had departed Pearl Harbor, he had determined that his ship needed a good rubber raft. "We were supposed to pick up zoomies if they got shot down," he reasoned. So, he went to aviation authorities and told them his sub needed a proper boat if she were to save their flyboys.

So, in the early hours of 12 September, Boats Eimermann got to break out his new rubber boat and paddle over to *Picuda* to retrieve the mail. They tossed over a large mail bag and he paddled back to *Spadefish*, all the while nervous that they were clearly within sight of the Japanese. Once aboard, Eimermann and his men had to struggle to get the inflatable boat below again. "I had to jump on the damn thing to get it down the hatch. It wouldn't bend at all."

Another important part of the exchange between boats was the opportunity to pick up movies that the crew had not seen. The *Spadefish* crew had seen more that their fill of Hopalong Cassidy at this point. "How I remember those exciting shows—"Hoppy Serves a Writ"—and others," wrote Buck Miller, who often ran the projector in the forward torpedo room. "We thought we outsmarted other subs by transferring movies at sea. We slipped our Hopalong movies over and when we got theirs, we got in return–Hopalog Cassidy movies! Who outfoxed whom?"⁸

Eimermann turned over the mailbag to Shaky Jake Lewis, the *Spadefish* mailman, for delivery. While aboard ship, *Spadefish*'s officers helped censor outgoing letters during the war. For his letters to his wife, Chief Carl Schmelzer learned to cut them up to appear to be censored. The officer who would inspect his letter would thus think it was already handled.⁹

At 0202, *Spadefish* set course to clear the area. She dived at 0730 to avoid detection of a Kate torpedo bomber that was 7 miles distant. She resurfaced 40 minutes later and continued to clear the area. A group of five planes, distance 20 miles, crossed astern of *Spadefish* at 0900. When another SD contact was made at 8 miles at 1245, she submerged. At 1246, one bomb went off astern of the ship. At 1249, another bomb went off astern of the ship. *Spadefish* returned to the surface again at 1355, her crew feeling that the Japanese did not want them to leave the area in one piece.

The course home was "zero-nine-zero," the submariner's favorite return course, which meant heading well south out of Japanese waters. *Spadefish* was bound for Pearl Harbor. Standing procedures called for subs making their first patrol to return to Midway or some other advance base for refitting. A return trip to Pearl Harbor was more of a luxury reserved for subs that had made consecutive patrols. But *Spadefish* still carried the prototype FM sonar gear, a pet project of Admiral Lockwood's. So, she was ordered back to Pearl so that the secret gear could be inspected.[10]

In the ensuing week, as *Spadefish* was en route to the Hawaiian Islands, Donc's Devils added more Japanese shipping to their already impressive bag. Captain McGregor's *Redfish* sank another large tanker and troop transport ship, while Donaho's *Picuda* downed two more marus. *Spadefish*'s return was fairly uneventful, save several encounters with Japanese patrol boats.

At 0902 on 13 September, *Spadefish* submerged to avoid detection of a Betty bomber, distance 8 miles. She had to dive again at 1254 to avoid an unidentified plane that was spotted at 13 miles distance. *Spadefish* was en route to Pearl Harbor from 15 - 23 September, making trim dives, holding drills and conducting personnel training. *Spadefish* had to dive twice for a Navy PBY patrol plane that was headed in her direction. "He wasn't using IFF and was again headed for us," recorded Underwood.

At 0630 on 24 September, *Spadefish* met her escort, *PS-483*, and was escorted in to the submarine base at Pearl Harbor. Donc's Devils had proven itself to be one of the most successful double-barrel Allied wolf packs of the war. In two forays during this thirteenth ever U.S. wolf pack, Underwood, Donaho, and McGregor's boats had sunk 13 confirmed ships for almost 65,000 tons. *Spadefish* alone had accounted for six of these ships, for 31,500 tons, plus another ship damaged. *Picuda* had sunk four ships for 11,270 tons, including one Japanese destroyer, and *Redfish* had tallied another three ships for 21,800 tons.[11]

The advance base at Saipan had been priceless in allowing the three boats to refuel and reload during patrol. *Spadefish*'s first patrol had been for 63 days, including twenty days in her patrol area and eighteen days hunting submerged.

By the time *Spadefish* returned to the Submarine Base at Pearl Harbor, she had made a name for herself on her maiden war patrol. Of the 1,682 war patrols conducted by U.S. submarines, this was the eighth best for tonnage (31,542) and fifth best for ships sunk, six.

Admiral Lockwood was waiting at the Sub Base dock. He came aboard for a cup of coffee and to congratulate Captain Underwood on his successful patrol. "His congratulations were most welcome," recalled Lt.(jg) Dan Decker. "I cannot imagine a more capable, professional, and friendly person. The Submarine Force was indeed fortunate to have a commander of his stature."

The lab technicians came aboard *Spadefish*, as well, to inspect her FM sonar. The UCDWR boys found that the typhoon encountered in early August had bent the shaft on which the sonar transducer was mounted. This was the strengthened shaft that they had improved upon in July, but it was no match for the typhoon's power. Once again, the deck-mounted sonar head's shaft would have to be strengthened.[12]

The technicians were also not happy to find that Captain Underwood and Neal Pike had not even turned on the noisy unit during this patrol. The lessons learned thus far from *Spadefish* proved important in the ongoing installation of FM sets. The second submarine to receive the FM gear, in September 1944, was *Tinosa*, another Mare Island-constructed boat. Her set was keel-mounted to avoid the damage that *Spadefish*'s set had encountered. The new sonar gear would allow their sub to navigate right through mine fields. *Tinosa*'s skipper, Richard Latham, soon found that over half his crew wanted to leave the ship before she went out looking for mines. Upon *Tinosa*'s arrival at Pearl Harbor in November, Captain Latham received permission from ComSubPac to transfer 35 of his enlisted men and chiefs. In sad irony, most of those transferred went to *Shark*, which was lost with all hands on her next patrol.[13]

Spadefish was tied up alongside another Mare-Island constructed fleet boat, Captain Dick O'Kane's *Tang*. She was already one of the war's hottest boats, having set the record war patrol with ten confirmed sinkings with twenty-four torpedoes. Now, *Tang* was preparing to depart at 1300 on 24 September for her fifth patrol. "Bernie Massar and I heard her skipper address the crew, and I will never forget him telling his crew, 'We will be home for Christmas, or not at all,'" recalled Buck Miller. "They needed one more successful patrol to get back home."

Much later, Miller and Massar would come to realize how prophetic Dick O'Kane's vow would prove to be. While *Tang* did manage to sink another nine ships on her fifth patrol, she was sunk by her final torpedo, which made a circular run and struck the submarine. Only O'Kane and eight of his men were picked up by the Japanese and spent the remainder of the war as POWs.

In his first war patrol report, Captain Underwood noted the positive effects that *Spadefish*'s mascot had had on his crew.

Nothing but praise can be expressed for the fine performance of the entire crew, both officers and men. The high morale and cool attention to duty, even after long hours of battle stations on repeated days, was outstanding. The dog, Luau, contributed greatly to the morale with her ready playfulness with all hands. She was a bit perturbed by the depth charges, but soon recovered with only a slight case of 'depth charge nerves.'

Captain Thomas Michael Dykers, Commander of Submarine Division 282 to which *Spadefish* belonged, wrote the initial endorsement to Captain Underwood's patrol report. "The patrol was characterized by a spirit of aggressiveness," he wrote. "The commanding officer, officers and crew of the *Spadefish* are to be congratulated on an extremely aggressive and well conducted patrol."

Charles Frederick Erck, Commander of Submarine Squadron Four, concurred with Dyker's endorsements on *Spadefish*'s "tenacious aggressiveness" and for the sub's "heavy toll on enemy shipping."

Underwood would be awarded the Navy Cross for his first patrol. Early in the war, decorations were so slow in being presented that some of the recipients had been killed before their medal arrived. Admiral Nimitz issued a directive in 1943 to hasten submariners' awards. The submarine division commander would review the patrol report and question witnesses to ship sinkings. As commander of the ship, the skipper generally received the highest award, one for which the entire crew was responsible. For at least one confirmed enemy ship sinking, the skipper could receive the Secretary of the Navy's Letter of Commendation. For two ships, his decoration could be the Silver Star Medal and for three of more enemy ships destroyed, the Navy Cross could be awarded.[14]

USS *Spadefish* First Patrol Summary	
Patrol Area:	Luzon Strait
Time Period:	23 July - 24 September 1944
Number of Men Aboard:	83: 74 enlisted and 9 officers
Total Days on Patrol:	59 at sea
Day Submerged:	20
Total Miles Steamed:	16,548 miles
Fuel Burned:	170,952 gallons
Number of Torpedoes Fired:	45
Ships Claimed as Sunk:	6 ships/40,000 tons
JANAC Postwar Credit:	6 ships/31,500 tons
Shipping Damage Claimed:	10,500-ton tanker

For achieving the Navy Cross on his first war patrol, Gordon Underwood was then able to recommend some of his officers and men for subordinate awards. Earlier in the war, the issuance of a Navy Cross would allow the commanding officer to issue two Silver Stars and two Bronze Stars. By 1944, the Navy was more generous with its commendations for highly successful war patrols. The fact that *Spadefish* had destroyed six enemy ships and damaged others during a two-pronged patrol allowed Underwood to issue additional medals. To his assistant approach officer Ted Ustick, he gave the Silver Star, later presented to Ustick as a Gold Star, in lieu of a second Silver Star Medal. Diving officer Frank Alvis and TDC operator Gus Laundy would each also receive a Silver Star.

In addition to the three Silver Stars, Underwood awarded four Bronze Stars. For these medals, he recommended plotting officer Dan Decker, signalman Jim Schuett, radar operator Neal Pike, and senior after room torpedoman Harry George. Finally, the skipper selected several other enlisted men for the Secretary of the Navy's Letter of Commendation, including Paul Majoue, Francis Scherman and Len Dependahl.

While each of these men were proud when later pinned with his award, most chose to remain modest about it. "We didn't talk too much about medals," Hocks Majoue later explained. "Anything we got, the whole boat had something to do with earning it."

Underwood's Urchins

Refit and Second Patrol   *24 September–7 November 1944*

The motor scooter that came aboard *Spadefish* was top secret. The secret was so well kept, in fact, that only a handful of the crew ever knew about it for some time. Most were ashore at the Royal Hawaiian on leave at the time. Few things got past the ears of chief of the boat Willard Eimermann, however. Knowing that his crew deserved to let off some steam after putting their lives at stake on war patrol, he was not opposed to looking the other way occasionally when his guys wanted to have a little fun.

Eimermann heard the whine of a little engine and the beeping of a horn as a motor scooter approached the dock where *Spadefish* was moored. "I thought, 'What the hell?' All of a sudden, here's this motormac on this little scooter!" recalled Eimermann.

Auxiliaryman Dick Gamby "acquired" the little motorcycle from the sub base late at night after a little nightlife ashore. At the time, taking the scooter back aboard *Spadefish* into his pump room seemed to be the thing to do, and his buddy Whitey Harbison agreed to help.

"We disconnected the front and back sections and took the engine off," Gamby later admitted. "We walked it over the gangplank and had it disassembled in about ten minutes. We took it down the gun hatch through the control room and into the pump room below."

With the benefit of most of the crew being ashore, Harbison and Gamby were able to stash the parts, including wheels and handlebars into the overheads of the pump room. They did so well that their fellow auxiliaryman Johnny Peel would go weeks before he happened to find some of it. Only those aboard this night knew anything about Gamby's scooter for some time. When the Shore Patrol made rounds the next day, each ship was questioned. "The word was that a chief had built the motor scooter himself and was looking all over for it," said Gamby. When Chief Eimermann was asked if his crew knew anything about the missing scooter, his reply was, "No, not us."

Spadefish sailors enjoy Oahu's Waikiki Beach in front of the Royal Hawaiian Hotel after their first war patrol. *Hugo Lundquist collection, courtesy of Jeanne Lundquist.*

"A message came out and they wanted to know about the disappearance of a motor scooter," recalled motormac Charles Griffith. "Of course, nobody knew anything about that."

Those "in the know" were wise enough to keep this little episode tightly under wraps for the time being.

R&R for the crew was at the "Pink Palace," the Royal Hawaiian Hotel on Waikiki Beach. Constructed of sandstone in 1927, this hotel was expertly stained to resemble a huge pink palace of royalty. Expecting the Gooneyville Hotel following their first patrol at best, this was a real treat, and the ensuing partying showed that none took their leave for granted. They were replaced aboard ship by a relief crew from Sub Division 282. Admiral Nimitz had requisitioned the Honolulu hotel as a rest camp exclusively for naval aviators and submariners. Despite the posted price of $105 per day, submarine officers could rent rooms for $2 per day, food included. Twenty-five cents a week covered the cost for an enlisted man's fresh linens.[1]

"The girls ashore had learned right away what those dolphins meant that we wore on our uniforms," recalled torpedoman Bert Spiese. "Them dolphins meant this guy has been out at sea for three months and he has three months' pay, wondering how to spend it!"

The brothels that once operated without shame in Honolulu early in the war had been shut down by 1944. More adventurous souls, however, could still find an occasional house in business. The *Spadefish* crew felt it was only fair to let their ship's mascot search out companionship as well.

After many weeks aboard a tightly confined ship, the crew found that Luau enjoyed the party life as much as they did. "She was a lush," said Paul Majoue. "She loved beer!" After a few drinks, some of the

R&R at the Royal Hawaiian following the first war patrol. Left to right are MoMM3c "Buck" Miller, S2c Bob Maxwell, TM3c Hugo Lundquist, EM3c Ken Sigworth and GM3c Bernie Massar. *Courtesy of Bernie Massar.*

crew decided to find canine partners for the ship's mascot. "Shaky Jake, the gunner's mate, and Rewold, one of the motor machinists, took Luau ashore and got her drunk," recalled electrician Ken Sigworth. "They found some other ship that had a male dog on it and fixed her up." Lewis and Rewold's efforts ashore were successful, as noted by the unofficial "Ship's History" of *Spadefish*: "The ship's dog, Luau, enjoyed several suitors there, the effects of which appeared during the next patrol."[2]

The partying was a way to vent steam from the patrol. Some wondered during the depth charge attacks or weeks in the engine rooms if they would even see the sun or stars again. Two weeks ashore in Hawaii helped restored mental health.

"They had brown-out conditions, versus total blackout," remembered auxiliaryman Dick Gamby. "You had to be off the streets at 10:30p.m. Our hotel was right on the beach, so we'd just go out and lay on the beach all night."

The room Gamby's bunch was staying in at the Royal Hawaiian had a small patio with two chairs by the railing. Seaman Maurice Noonan actually fell over the railing one night. "We raced down the stairs, figuring that he was dead," said Gamby. "He was drunker than a hoot owl, but he had hit the soft ground and was fine. He just sat up and said, 'What happened?'"

During refit periods, submarines underwent changes of personnel. This was a necessary process where qualified submariners were transferred on to other submarines and newer men were brought aboard in their place. Some men received orders to report on to other particular duties. Others were transferred by orders of the captain, Exec or chief of the boat. In those cases, a similarly-rated sailor was sought out from the relief pool to cover the loss. The number of new subs coming into the fleet necessitated such a turnover rate.

Twelve to fifteen percent of the crew was expected to be rotated after each war patrol. In *Spadefish*'s case, eleven men were transferred following the first patrol: QM2c Cooper, MoMM2c Jackson, F1c Nordstrom, RM3c Panek, EM2c Pizzini, S1c Price, EM3c Randall, CTM Simms, TM3c Spiese, MoMM3c Weidner, and MoMM1c Yates. Eleven new men were received—S1c Anderson, F1c Asher, F1c Brenneis, F1c Brewer, F1c Dunleavy, F1c Fautley, F1c Graff, MoMM3c Jerolman, S1c Rolf, TM3c Schumer and S1c Snider—keeping yeoman Irv Kreinbring's sailing list at 83 men.

During the inbound run to Pearl, Paul Majoue's radio shack had received news of some of the crew's rating increases, effective 2 September. Among the seven *Spadefish* sailors with rate increases was RM1c Majoue to Chief Radioman. Also officially joining the CPO quarters would be chief of the boat Willard Eimermann, advancing from BM1c to Chief Boatswain. During *Spadefish*'s refit period, Harry George was also promoted to Chief Torpedoman on October 9.

Among the transferees was RM3c Edmund Panek. Lt.(jg) Perry Wood did not get another rated radio operator from the men available at Pearl Harbor. Fortunately, striker Ken Powers was quickly promoted to RM3c, and seaman first class Charles Rolf was among the new hands received from the sub base. "I had radar and sonar training," Rolf recalled. "I had spent about nine months aboard an S-boat at Pearl." Once on patrol with *Spadefish*, Rolf would rotate in as a watch stander on the SG surface and SD air search radar sets. Chief Eimermann, in fact, added several other new hands, such as fireman Harry Brenneis, to the lookout pool. Eimermann reorganized the Watch, Quarter and Station Bill, working up a new training schedule with Lieutenant Commander Ustick for the upcoming weeks.

Among the new members of the black gang was Fireman 1/c John Belton Brewer Jr. A farm boy from Georgia, he had worked in a Brunswick shipyard during the early part of the war until being drafted. After boot camp at Green Bay, diesel school at Chicago, and sub school at New London, Brewer was working in the relief crew at Pearl Harbor when *Spadefish* returned from her first war patrol. During that time while servicing her engines, he got to know chiefs Joe Mitzel and Dutch Falconer. "I volunteered and asked them to let me on." Brewer was assigned to Charlie Griffith's forward engine room, where he soon became buddies with motormacs Nick Pelliciari and Melvin Mullen. Although a long way from his farm in Georgia, Brewer was ready to see some action at long last.

The torpedo gang lost Chief Simms and TM3c Bert Spiese to transfers. In their place, Emery Kreher (now promoted to first class) took charge of the forward room and *Spadefish* received TM3c John Schumer and Seaman 1/c Don Anderson, a torpedoman striker. Anderson, fresh out of sub school, was assigned to the forward room, where he joined Kreher, Gus Cuthbertson, Hugo Lundquist and another striker, Wallace McMahon. As a "learnee," Anderson was also assigned regular watch duties as a lookout.

John Schumer joined the after room, now run by TM1c Si Barnes since the promotion of Harry George. The after room included Don Bird, Thad Barton, Doyle Partin, and John Nesnee, the latter newly promoted to torpedoman third. "We were a small bunch in the after room," Schumer recalled. "We kept eight torpedoes aft on the ready, four in the tubes and four in the racks." Schumer's early days at war had been aboard the sub tender *Sperry*. "I put in quite a long time as a seaman," he recalled. "They kinda liked to let me handle the paint brush!" Schumer had finally managed to get aboard *Silversides*, making her ninth and tenth war patrols and rating torpedoman third in the process. When not on duty in his torpedo room on *Spadefish*, Schumer handled planesman duty and lookout watches.

Chief George, in addition to supervising both torpedo rooms, was added to the duty chief watch list. "If Chief George had any time to hang out, it was in our forward room sometimes," said McMahon. "Most of the chiefs hung out in the 'goat's nest,' the chief petty officers' area. We called it the goat's nest, because that's what it smelled like." The chiefs' quarters was a small compartment with sliding curtains for a door, two rows of bunks and a big locker in the rear for their uniforms.

Seaman first class Don Scholle of New Jersey found that he was now rated quartermaster third class. "I had gone to signal school prior to sub school," he reflected. "I had applied for signalman, but they made me quartermaster. I didn't stand watches after I was rated. There was no difference between quartermasters and signalmen aboard *Spadefish*. Our quartermasters could handle signalmen duties." Scholle joined the quartermaster's gang, replacing QM2c Sammy Cooper, who had been transferred.

Together with SM2c Dale Frazier and Jim Parscale, he would work four hours on and eight hours off keeping the quartermaster's log notebook while on patrol. "We had the log in the conning tower," Scholle said. "We would go up, check the conditions above, such as wind and water conditions, and put them in our log book." Leading signalman Jim Schuett did not regularly stand this watch, as he continued to serve as Exec Ted Ustick's assistant navigator.

Leading petty officers in each department worked to help qualify the new hands in submarines in order to wear the coveted "dolphins" —an insignia that symbolized the fact that a man was "qualified" in submarines. As recommended by Captain Ernest J. King in 1923, the qualification process meant that each officer and crew member must be fully able to operate every pipe, switch, valve and operating system in the boat, and be able to draw each from memory.[3]

Even the instructions for flushing the head were not simple. To flush the head in *Spadefish*'s after torpedo room, a "simplified" seven step process was posted there:

1. Close flapper valve.
2. Open sea and stop valves to flood bowl.
3. Secure sea and stop valve. Use head.
4. Open flapper valve. Empty contents. Close flapper valve. Hold flapper valve closed.
5. Open discharge valve to sea. Charge volume tank to 25 lbs.
6. Open quick opening valve. Blow head. Close quick opening valve.
7. Close discharge valve. Secure air. Check to see all valves closed before leaving.[4]

Failure to follow these steps in the proper sequence could result in the head's contents being blown onto the operator.

Following the leave at the Royal Hawaiian, *Spadefish* underwent another intensive training period to break in her new hands and to rotate them into the watch sections.

The last few days at Pearl Harbor's sub base were spent preparing to go out on war patrol again. Commissary officer Bill Ware and his chief commissary steward, Francis Scherman, saw to it that *Spadefish* was packed with only the finest meats, fresh produce and baking goods. "The quality of the meat was better than that received last patrol from Pearl Harbor," Skipper Underwood would write of his commissary department. The only disappointment was the absence of frozen fruit and berries, the absence of which "was keenly felt" from Scherman's galley on the upcoming patrol.

Lieutenant Gus Laundy's torpedo gangs oversaw the loading of replacement torpedoes, both Mark 18.1s and Mark 14.3s. Admiral

Lockwood had his submarines by July 1944 routinely carrying a 75/25 mix of Mark 14 steam and Mark 18 electric torpedoes. The electrics, which could travel up to 30 knots, depending on water temperatures, were loaded only in *Spadefish*'s after torpedo room.[5]

For her second war patrol, *Spadefish* would once again operate as part of a wolf pack, which had proven to be successful on her maiden run. This time, Commander Gordon Underwood was the senior skipper and wolf pack leader. He would lead Cdr. Edward Ellis Shelby's *Sunfish* (SS-281) and Cdr. Robert Hugh Caldwell Jr.'s *Peto* (SS-265). The pack was to be called "Underwood's Urchins."

Heading out at the same time and operating also in the Yellow Sea was another wolf pack, consisting of the boats *Queenfish*, *Barb* and *Picuda* (*Spadefish*'s senior packmate on her first patrol). Captain Elliott Loughlin in *Queenfish* would command this second pack. Both wolf packs would operate largely between southwest Korea and Shanghai, informing each other of enemy contacts and attacking the same convoys.[6]

Spadefish departed the submarine base, Pearl Harbor, at 1130 on 23 October in company with *Sunfish* and *Peto*. Together, the three boats comprised Coordinated Attack Group 17.13 in accordance with ComSubPac Operation Order 354-44, with Commander Underwood in command. Upon clearing the harbor entrance, they set course for Midway Island. At 1400, all three boats made a trim dive. They resurfaced at 1420 to learn that *Sunfish* had problems. Underwood received a message from *Sunfish* that she had suffered a leak in the compensating water line in her forward battery that had caused partial flooding of that compartment. The wolf pack proceeded at slow speed while *Sunfish* repaired her leak, made another trim dive and then rejoined the group. Course was set for Midway.

At 1900, the escort ship returned to Pearl Harbor and the trio of submarines proceeded to Midway. The next few days were spent conducting training dives, exercises and communications drills with the other submarines of the group.

The morale was good. One of the favorites in the galley area was a record player that had been brought aboard. The only trouble was in agreeing on what records to play. One of the western records that was played incessantly aboard *Spadefish* during the war was "Look Who's Talking," a favorite of motormac Rebel Rewold, Oklahoma native Billy Bob Pigman and several other Southerners aboard. Chief of the boat Eimermann had to break up one disagreement in the galley one day, when one of the crew grew tired of hearing Rewold's western songs. Eimermann ended the argument with, "I'll throw that damn record player over the side if you guys are gonna argue about it! We have a war to fight!"

Spadefish joined packmates *Peto* and *Sunfish* on the surface early on 27 October, and sighted Midway at 0810. She approached the main channel a half hour later, and there received a harbor pilot aboard, who relieved Gus Laundy of the conn through the tricky channel. *Spadefish* moored at pier Sail 3 and began topping off with 17,000 gallons of fuel oil. Commander Underwood held a conference ashore for his wolf pack. With Ted Ustick and Perry Wood, he drew up communications plans with the skippers, Execs and communications officers of the other two boats. Plans were made for future rendezvous and for operations en route to and in the patrol area.

In his second patrol report, Captain Underwood noted that a "lack of motion pictures was keenly felt this patrol." Where the *Spadefish* forward torpedo room had been a favorite spot when conditions had permitted on the first patrol, the crew had found nothing new available at the Pearl Harbor sub base. Fortunately, "Midway gave us three films from their scant supply," Underwood wrote.

At 1545, *Spadefish* and company departed Midway and set course to clear Kure Island. At 2100, a knocking developed in the starboard shaft. Officer of the deck Frank Alvis ordered the starboard screw stopped. He then stopped the port screw and tried backing both screws to free the debris, but to no avail. A piece of mooring line had been thrown over the side earlier in the afternoon at Midway. Although the ship was stopped at the time, the line somehow had gotten caught in the screw. Underwood directed the other two subs to proceed. He sent a message to Midway telling of the reason for *Spadefish*'s need to return to port. He headed his boat back to Gooneyville at standard speed (10 knots) on her port shaft.

At 0858 on 28 October, *Spadefish* returned to Midway. A diver soon cleared the line from the starboard propeller. By 1030, *Spadefish* had departed Midway and set course to overtake the rest of the group. Upon crossing the International Dateline, she once again lost a day. Hugo Lundquist, making notes in his forbidden journal, recorded: "Crossed 180th. Capt. told us our area was around Yangtze R[iver]. Entrance in Yellow Sea."

At 1754 on 1 November, *Spadefish* exchanged calls over the SJ with *Sunfish*. At 2230, she exchanged calls with *Peto*. Underwood's Urchins were reunited and the attack group proceeded, conducting training exercises and communications drills en route to the patrol area.

At 0109 on 4 November, radar contact was made on two targets, distance 7,000 yards and 10,000 yards. Underwood closed to investigate.

One blip turned out to be a patrol boat, patrolling on station. The second contact disappeared from the radar screen before visual contact could be made. "Suspecting an enemy submarine with the patrol boat for bait, cleared the area," wrote Underwood. *Spadefish* sent notice of this potential trap to her pack mates and hauled clear.

On 5 November, *Spadefish* had her first aircraft contact of the patrol, an SD contact at 6 miles distance. The boat dived at 1439 and resurfaced at 1503 after no attack was made. At 1605, the watch sighted Sofu Gan at distance of about 25 miles. The radio gang received a message from *Sunfish* at 1930 stating that she had been forced down twice by planes.

The next enemy contact came on 7 November, when the bridge watch sighted a patrol bomber at 0729. The enemy plane was coming out of the clouds, distance 3 miles. "Clear the bridge!" shouted ODD Dan Decker. The lookouts poured below and *Spadefish* made a crash dive to escape. No bombs were dropped, but the airplane hung around the area. At 0757, just prior to surfacing, a quick look with the SD radar showed the contact at one mile still. "Changed my mind about surfacing," recorded Captain Underwood.

He kept his boat down another half hour, surfacing at 0829. At 0915, a Betty bomber was sighted heading straight in for *Spadefish*, distance about 8 miles. Gus Laundy called, "Clear the bridge!" The lookouts and officers piled below and *Spadefish* made another crash dive, remaining below until 1006. Underwood secured the SD radar, assuming that it was bringing in the aircraft. He opted instead to post two additional lookouts on the bridge.

The day passed uneventfully until 1700, when a lookout sighted a floating mine. Underwood decided to give his gunners some practice by exploding it. The bridge crew opened up on the target as the boat circled the bobbing mine a few times. The men fired at it with small arms. "Bounced a few rifle bullets off it but it didn't go off. The mine was very rusty in appearance." Underwood finally called off the shooting on account of darkness and went on his way.

The bridge gunners enjoyed this chance to shoot, however. It was such things that helped a crew gain confidence in their skipper. Captain Underwood was well respected by his *Spadefish* crew, not just for the success he had achieved on his first patrol, but for all the little things. Up one night on the midwatch in the radio shack, Mike "Little Fox Hole" Sergio was greeted by the skipper, who was coming in to check on messages.

"Fox Hole, how about a cup of coffee?" Underwood asked.

The skipper went out and returned to the radio shack with a cup of coffee for his radioman.

"I will never forget that as long as I live," Sergio later wrote. "That is why submarine men in time of war would follow their skipper right into hell if he so asked. They cared for their men."[7]

Such little events helped endear Gordon Underwood to his crew. Mutual respect and trust went a long way in making a successful boat. One event which required a great deal of trust was the conversion of fuel tanks to ballast tanks while at sea in enemy waters. For *Spadefish* fuel king Charlie Griffith, the process was old hat to him, but certainly never boring.

While making one such conversion on the second patrol, he was accompanied topside with MoMM2c Pat Kelley and F1c Tony "Red" Dunleavy. "We had to go topside at night while we were underway to convert a fuel tank into a regular ballast tank so that you could blow the ship up higher to get more speed on the surface," recalled Kelley. The group went below the main deck through a hatch into the actual tank to access the necessary bolts. "We used a little red flashlight to locate the nuts and bolts," said Kelley, "but almost everything was done by feel in the dark."

As Griffith's crew was finishing the conversion, the OOD on the bridge, Gus Laundy, made a sudden sharp turn, forgetting that he had the fuel king's men down below in the superstructure. "I heard one of the valves pop open as we bent on another engine, and then he changed course," said Griffith. "I guess Lieutenant Laundy had a radar contact and ordered a course change. It bounced me around like a fish in a live box! Water was hitting me and driving me all around up there."

The water rushed over the men with tremendous force. "Red Dunleavy and I were very fortunate," said Pat Kelley. "We were right under the deck gun down through an opening in the deck. I grabbed Dunleavy by his hair and hung onto his head with the water rushing against us."

Kelley was ready to confront the OOD as he and Dunleavy scrambled back onto the main deck and headed for the conning tower. "Captain Underwood had reached the bridge before I got there, and he was screaming, 'We've got men in the superstructure!'"

Tightening his last bolt, a dripping wet Charlie Griffith also emerged from the superstructure, stomped to the bridge and angrily announced to Lt. Laundy, "The fuel king is going below!"

At 1843 on 7 November, radar contact was made on Suwanoshe Shima, distance 75,000 yards. At 2046, another radar contact was made on a target at 8,000 yards distance. This was soon identified as a

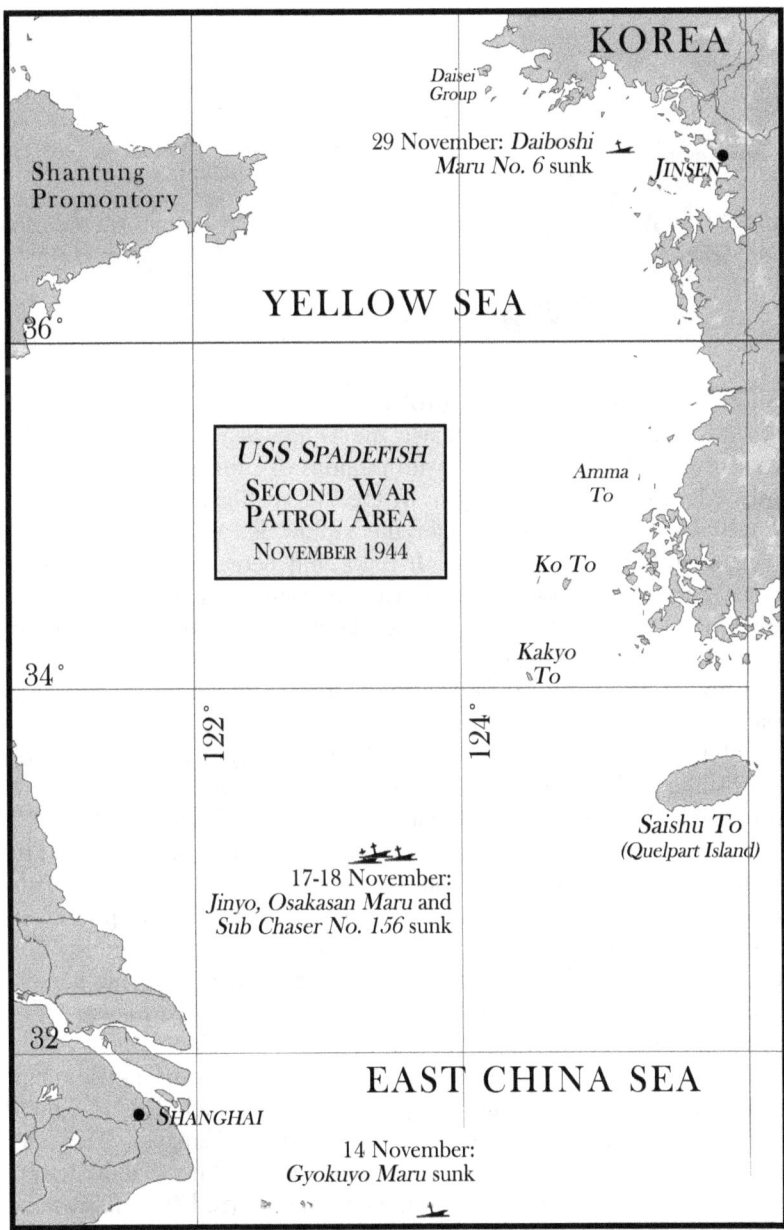

friendly submarine of her pack by SJ interference. At 2100, *Spadefish* passed Suwanoshe Shima abeam to starboard, distance 12 miles. At 2305, she exchanged calls over the SJ with *Sunfish*, ahead of *Spadefish*, and *Peto*, behind *Spadefish*. The group passed through the Nansei

Motor machinist's mate Charles Griffith, a veteran of seven war patrols before joining *Spadefish*, was the ship's original "fuel king." Griffith, promoted to chief petty officer, is seen receiving a Letter of Commendation from Captain Lewis S. Parks, Commander of Submarine Squadron Twenty, aboard *Spadefish* on 3 March 1945 at Guam. *Courtesy Submarine Force Museum, Groton, Connecticut.*

Shoto and headed for their patrol area.

The men soon began to see why the Yellow Sea was so named. The waters were shallow and dirty, with millions of cubic yards of sediment washed into the ocean each year by the Yellow River of China. A western division of the Pacific Ocean, the Yellow Sea area is vast, covering roughly 156,000 square miles. It is located between China's eastern coast and Korea. South of the Korean peninsula, the Yellow Sea becomes known as the East China Sea, with the 34th parallel of latitude dividing the two seas.

Captain Mush Morton's *Wahoo* had been the first submarine to patrol to the extreme northern reaches of the Yellow Sea, in the vicinity of Dairen and the Yalu River. Postwar analysis credited *Wahoo* with sinking nine ships in March 1943 in this virgin territory, causing the Japanese to believe a wolf pack was operating in the area.[8]

Such prime hunting grounds came with a certain risk, however. The Yellow Sea was notoriously shallow, averaging only 120 feet (20 fathoms). To submariners, it was little more than a "wading pond." In April 1943, *Snook* had temporarily become stuck in the muddy bottom at 60 feet as she approached the Yangtze River. Freeing herself, *Snook* managed to sink three freighters with her torpedoes and two sampans with her deck gun.[9]

In 1943 and into 1944, the Yellow Sea continued to be a major shipping lane for warships and merchant vessels which linked China, Manchukuo (Manchuria) and Korea to Japan. Tsingtao, Tientisin, Dairen and Seoul were among the major ports. The shallow waters were not conducive for submariners who preferred to run silent at deep depths to escape anti-submarine attacks.

Underwood's Urchins could only hope that the prospects of plentiful shipping targets would far outweigh the inherent dangers.

8

"Shaken Up"

Second Patrol   *8-18 November 1944*

Soon after reaching her patrol station in the Yellow Sea, *Spadefish* was detected by enemy radar stations ashore. She spent 8 November submerged as she approached the tiny Japanese islet of Danjo Gunto. After dark, *Spadefish* surfaced and dodged a small fishing vessel. The APR1 radar detector showed indications that night of a sweeping radar located on Maro To off southwest Saishu To, a mountainous island of volcanic origin near the Korean coast.

Spadefish remained submerged during the day on 9 November, sighting some 25 or 30 different fishing craft. *Spadefish* surfaced after dark and headed west to clear Saishu To. Captain Underwood directed *Sunfish* to take the plane guard duty that had been scheduled for 11 November. Captain Elliott Loughlin's *Queenfish* was the first of the two wolf pack boats to find the enemy. She sank two freighters during the night of 8 November, and added a third Japanese freighter during the early morning hours of November 9. Captain Gene Fluckey's *Barb* managed to down a 10,400-ton maru next.[1]

10 November was another day of submerged patrolling off the northwest corner of Saishu To, dodging only fishing craft. *Spadefish* recharged her batteries that night, running on the surface until diving at a point 13 miles south of Kwaku To at 0610 on 11 November. "A number of fishing craft, some with lights on them, were sighted just prior to diving," noted Captain Underwood. "This shallow water is good for the fishermen, anyway."

Diving officer Frank Alvis encountered some spots of water throughout the day that reacted like fresh water. The ship would become unaccountably heavy and would sink rapidly, making for some tense moments in the control room for the planesmen.

Spadefish surfaced again at 1838 on 11 November. At 2230, she received word of two friendly planes being down in her area. She also received a message from the wolf pack to her east, telling of a convoy headed her way. *Barb* and *Queenfish* had already attacked. As the attacks proceeded, Underwood picked up Loughlin's original contact report. Intent on first handling the downed fliers, he sent *Peto* to intercept this convoy and search for the nearest of the downed planes. *Peto* found this convoy and charged in, firing ten torpedoes, but only netting one sinking that was confirmed in postwar analysis.[2]

Spadefish was unable to contact *Sunfish*, which was apparently submerged. "With reluctance, [we] turned our back to the convoy and headed for the coast of China to look for the downed plane in that vicinity," wrote Underwood. *Spadefish* had no luck with the downed aviator, but did sight another floating mine at 0815 the following morning. Less than an hour later, the watch sighted another floating mine at 0910. "Pleasant waters, these!" wrote Underwood.

At 0930, *Spadefish* had reached the reported position of the downed plane. She commenced searching the waters, considering the possible 24-hour drift of a life raft. Lookouts sighted at least three Chinese junks sailing around this vicinity. At 1202, a plane was sighted at a distance of about 8 miles and Lieutenant Alvis made a crash dive in only 90 feet of water. *Spadefish* stayed down an hour, resurfacing at 1332 to continue her search for the downed aviator.

At 2000, after "having covered an area of all possible locations of a life raft in this vicinity, abandoned search. Notified ComSubPac of negative results." Underwood set course for a position east of Shanghai to spend the day there. The watch at 0413 contacted the first of numerous fishing boats. Prior to sunrise on 13 November, *Spadefish* submerged between Two Brothers and Lukon. She stayed on the deep side of the 20 fathom curve. "This seemed like deep water after playing around in 15 fathoms yesterday," wrote Underwood.

During midmorning, several distant explosions were heard. At 1157, the periscope watch sighted smoke and headed for it, moving from the "deep" water of 120 feet into waters that were 90 feet (15 fathoms) and shallower as *Spadefish* moved toward Shanghai. At 1230, the sound watch heard pinging in the direction of the smoke and commenced an approach on what was judged to be a converted ore carrier with one PC escort.

At 1258, a flashing light was seen from the patrol craft, apparently flashing recognition signals toward *Spadefish* to identify herself. Captain Underwood remained on the surface, hoping the escort would remain confused and keep its distance long enough for *Spadefish* to fire. "No other escorts in sight," he later recorded. "He may have been signaling to an unseen plane that had seen us."

The range on the ore carrier was now down to about 5,000 yards. Soon afterwards the escort hoisted a signal. Underwood's tracking

"Run silent, run deep" was a familiar phrase to submariners who were avoiding enemy counterattack. Auxiliaryman Thomas "Buck" Miller is shown here in *Spadefish*'s control room manning the ballast valve controls which helped level out the boat at various depths. Miller's nickname can be seen stenciled on his belt.
Courtesy of Bernie Massar.

party was almost to the firing position when the target ship suddenly zigged 90 degrees away at 1301. The PC, now about 1,000 yards distant, turned for *Spadefish*. Underwood had his team work on a fast setup, still hoping to get in the attack.

The escort, however, was hellbent for *Spadefish* and the skipper had to give up the attack. "Take her to 90 feet!" he ordered.

Spadefish had edged out from the 15 fathom curve, but the ocean depth at this point in the Yellow Sea was only about 130 feet. "We went deep—to 90 feet," the skipper wrote. "All of a sudden the 23 fathoms didn't seem to be very much." *Spadefish* was an easy target in the very shallow water, as the wash from her screws was churning up a trail of light brown mud as she fled for deeper water.

At 1303, the patrol report shows that depth charges started falling, thick and fast...Nineteen depth charges in all were dropped. All in a period of two minutes, all close! The depth charge direction indicator (DCDI) looked like an electric sign on Broadway. The only helpful indication being that they were falling every place. We already knew that anyway! The depth charges made the electricians happy by reducing the grounds by about 40 volts.

Electrician's mate Ken Sigworth had a close call during this depth charging. Just before the escort ship had charged *Spadefish*, he was sent below decks down into the forward battery compartment. The batteries depended upon the distilled water made by the ship's Kleinschmidt stills. "There was a sight glass between the tanks that was used to see how much good water you had for the battery cells," Sigworth explained. "Someone had to lean over the batteries, outboard of the wells, to turn off the valve to the sight glasses so they wouldn't break during depth charging and lose the battery water."

The forward battery compartment housed 126 batteries, each weighing nearly a ton. The crawl space was tight around them and Sigworth found it was not a place to be when enemy depth charges began exploding directly overhead.

> Each of our batteries was 16 inches wide, 19 inches long and six feet high. They were arranged in six rows, varying in height. The second set of cells stood about one and a half feet higher than the first one. The third set was another foot and a half higher than the previous one, with a board running over the top of them all. I had to crawl over the boards above the third row of cells to get to the water tanks.
>
> I was down there, reaching out to get to them just as the first depth charges exploded. All I could see was sparks! Sparks were shooting through my fingers, from my eyes, from the batteries, and from the floor to the batteries. I thought to myself, "Sigworth, you're done for!"

Surprisingly intact, he managed to shut off the valve that would protect the sight glasses and scrambled out. "I came out of the battery white as a sheet," said Sigworth. "I was really shaken up."

In his journal, torpedoman Hugo Lundquist considered this to be a very close depth charging. "P.C. came over and laid a good pattern of 18 depth charges around us. We were at 90 feet because water was 100-120 ft. deep. Nips gave very good performance."

Seaman Wallace McMahon, part of the forward torpedo room's

reload crew, found that there was very little he could do during silent running. "We just sat there and smoked cigarettes," he said. "The first thing you did as soon as you rigged for silent running was put one guy on the battle phones and then out comes a carton of cigarettes."

In the forward engine room, new hand John Brewer received his first depth charge indoctrination. "That was the worst thing I've ever been through in my life," he said. "We didn't have but about 85 feet of water. You talk about a boy being scared!"

After such a close depth charging, the cork insulation would rain down. "They would shake all the dust out of the corners," recalled Lt.(jg) Perry Wood. "Anybody that had hid something somewhere, it came falling down from wherever they hid it."

In this case, there were Dick Gamby's hidden motor scooter parts that were discovered by auxiliaryman Johnny Peel in his pump room. After the attack, he confronted fuel king Charles Griffith.

"Did you store anything in my pump room?" demanded Peel.

"No, why, John?" asked Griffith.

"Well," said Peel as he held up a piece of evidence, "I found these handlebars, an engine and a couple of wheels in there!"

Griffith was just as bewildered. Peel soon got the story out of Gamby about stealing the motor scooter at Pearl Harbor after the first patrol. Nothing was said about this event and Griffith, along with the auxiliary gang, kept the parts hidden away from the officers.

Spadefish evaded the attack at two-thirds speed at 80 to 90 feet in the shallow Yellow Sea, clearing the area, with a healthy respect for the patrol craft that had shaken her. Two friends of the escort soon arrived to join the hunt. Fortunately their luck was not good, thanks to poor sound conditions. At 1338, *Spadefish* came to periscope depth for a look. The escorts were still all astern, milling around in the vicinity of the depth charge attack. There was no sign of the target. Well after sunset, *Spadefish* surfaced at 1849 to survey her damage.

Captain Underwood went topside first. Only minor damage had resulted, including some bent deckplates. On the conning tower, the bridge repeater gimbal rings were broken and the bridge speaker was cracked. The use of the TBT on the bridge for night attacks would be hindered somewhat without the speaker. "The bearings could still be shouted down the open conning tower hatch easily," said plotting officer Dan Decker.

"Electrician to the bridge," Underwood called. The duty electrician happened to be Ken Sigworth, who had just recently survived the depth charging in the forward battery. Topside, he found that the directional repeater "was gone. So were the cells. I looked around the hull and found where the cable came out." Following the cable, he found that the bridge repeater was knocked clear out of its gimbals. "I had to make new gimbals and put it back together."

More disturbing than the minor damage topside was the sight and smell of the mire that covered the boat. Considerable amounts of mud and fish remains covered the topside of *Spadefish*, indicating just how shallow the Yellow Sea was. Depth charges had obviously gone off quite close aboard, blowing mud and disintegrated fish parts against the decks and hull of the sub. "Up under our 5-inch gun, there was a great big ball of mud," recalled Sigworth. "It was called the Yellow Sea for good reason."

According to Lieutenant Decker, "The stench of rotten fish was too much for the bridge crew. It was impossible to stay on the bridge. We dived at high speed—twice—to try to wash away the mud and dead fish smell."

Following the October 1944 Battle of Leyte Gulf, the fight to control the Philippine Islands was raging heavily in early November. Chief Paul Majoue's *Spadefish* newsletter, "Maru's Bull Sheet," gave the latest information on Japanese efforts to continue landing more troops from Mindanao, Cebu and other neighboring islands.

The "Maru's Bull Sheet" announced a shipwide tournament in cribbage, acey deucy and checkers, top payout being $10.00 in each category. The newsletter even let shipmates advertise their services. A torpedoman from each torpedo room offered his services as a barber for a nominal fee. "When you finally gather enough nerve, see either Cuthbertson or Barnes (the fish peddlers) . . . a quarter an hour or less," proclaimed the editor. One of Majoue's second patrol November issues announced "for the benefit of all late and hard sleepers, 'We have just been depth charged.'" Majoue then took the chance to poke fun at two of his fellow radiomen.

> Here' a little ditty that I thought was pretty funny, especially since it happened to a couple of the fellows on our own maru. Powers and Newton, whose battle stations is the radio shack, was shooting the crap the other day, and just out of nothing at all, Newton asked Powers if he shook very much when they were being depth charged. "Hell, yes," said Powers. "Well," returned Newton, "You'd better get the hell out of here and find another place to stay during battle stations. There isn't room enough for the two of us in this little radio shack, to be shaking at the same time.

During the night, an Ultra (short for ultra secret message) was received from ComSubPac. By May 1943, U.S. intelligence had cracked both the Japanese naval and merchant marine codes, enabling submarines to be deployed with very accurate information. When an Ultra was received, junior officers were required to stop decoding the message with that first word: "Ultra." On most submarines, only the commanding officer decoded the actual message, and then had the cipher strips burned. Many of the crewmen aboard had no idea that intelligence was occasionally directing their boat exactly what time and place to intercept a key enemy ship or convoy. Ultra was not declassified until the 1970s. In *Spadefish*'s case, Captain Underwood never acknowledged in his written patrol reports that his sub had even received an Ultra.[3]

"We were breaking the Japanese secret codes for the entire war," recalled Ted Ustick. "Many times we were told to be at a certain place at a certain time out there in the Pacific." Ustick found the Ultras to be very precise and vitally confidential. "It was very important that we keep our mouths shut so as not to divulge that one big secret. The codebreakers had a lot to do with our winning World War II. We submariners were called the Silent Service, and happily so."[4]

Although Ultra gave him a specific place to find the enemy, it was still up to Captain Underwood and his crew to actually destroy the target. In this case, Underwood was tipped off via Ultra that a damaged tanker was being towed by the escort vessel *CD-8* into Shanghai near the Yangtze River. The night hours thus far had been filled with nothing but numerous contacts on fishing boats. Most of these were usually picked up at about 8,000 yards distance and avoided. With a hot Ultra in hand, Underwood sent *Spadefish* to the races.[5]

"We bent on all four mains, not worrying about the mines that we knew could be in the area," recalled Ken Sigworth. "We got there in the early morning."

At 0001 on 14 November, radar contact was made at 17,150 yards on the expected ships. *Spadefish* went to battle stations and commenced tracking. This contact developed into one large ship, which was being towed by a smaller ship about 500 yards ahead of it. Three escort vessels were also seen to be milling around the towed ship. The base course was judged to be 270, the vessels apparently destined for Shanghai at a speed of 6.5 knots. The towing ship was zigging every ten minutes, but the tow had a hard time following the zigs. The night was dark and overcast.

Postwar analysis would later show that this ship was the 5,396-ton freighter *Gyokuyo Maru*. She had been hit by one torpedo from the submarine *Barb*, in a neighboring wolf pack, on 12 November. *Barb* had actually penetrated more than 100 miles into the area of Underwood's Urchins while looking for a ditched plane. Captain Gene Fluckey torpedoed two Japanese marus this night, disintegrating one. The second freighter, *Gyokuyo Maru*, was caught by a fish in the overlap. Fluckey's crew heard this as a timed hit, but he was forced deep by escorts. Packmate *Peto* came upon the attack area and found "a burning ship" from *Barb*'s attack.[6]

Although claimed as a kill by *Barb*, *Gyokuyo Maru* did not sink after this hit. Postwar analysis and the research of Japanese records by Roger W. Allan found that *Gyokuyo Maru* was disabled and abandoned by her crew. When *Spadefish* found her during the night of 13-14 November, she was under tow for port by escort *CD-8*.[7]

As *Spadefish* approached the ships on the surface, SJ interference was detected from one of the escorting vessels. Captain Underwood noted that the enemy radar "steadied down on us when the range had closed to 8,500 yards, so [we] opened out and crossed to the other side. Only one of the three escorts had radar."

Frank Alvis had the deck watch, as Ens. Bill Ware, the battle stations JOOD, was on the bridge TBT checking the bearings. Battle lookouts Kreinbring, Massar, Bassett and Lewis had taken their respective stations on the shears and at helm. Captain Underwood was also on the bridge to direct the attack, calling orders to Exec Ted Ustick, who was supervising the conning tower tracking party. It was 0102 as *Spadefish* headed in for the attack on the little convoy's starboard flank, making 10 knots on the surface. One escort ship was on the freighter's starboard bow, one astern, and one off the port beam. The bridge watch could now see that their target was a large freighter, with long well decks, and a composite superstructure, fairly well loaded. Although damaged and under tow, she was on an even keel. The closest escort in view was judged to be a PC-13 class.

Once all available data was fed to Gus Laundy's TDC, Underwood commenced firing his bow tubes from a range of about 3,000 yards at 0108. Five Torpex-loaded Mark 14s sped toward the freighter. The officers and lookouts on *Spadefish*'s bridge saw and heard four of the five torpedoes hit *Gyokuyo Maru*.

"The first torpedo fired must have run a little slow, and the second a little fast–or a combination of both–as they were seen to hit the target in an interval of not more than one second," wrote Underwood. The fish had been fired from the forward room at 8-second intervals, making it hard to explain the 1-second apart explosions.

"The hits and fires were plainly seen," recalled Bill Ware. "My battle station on the attack was manning the Target Bearing Transmitter (TBT) and I was able to observe everything as it happened through this piece of highly magnifying optical equipment."[8]

The towed freighter exploded and commenced burning fiercely. Postwar data would indeed show that *Gyokuyo Maru* was finished off by a *Spadefish* torpedo which exploded in her engine room. The vicinity was too well lighted for comfort, so *Spadefish* cleared the target at flank speed area to watch the results. *CD-8*, the escort towing *Gyokuyo Maru,* had promptly dropped his line and gone racing after the attacking submarine. Along with the other two PCs, they dropped depth charges for the next two hours on imaginary submarines. Secure as she pulled away surfaced, *Spadefish's* crew could now breathe easier.[9]

At 0220, the fire on the target freighter went out suddenly. The SJ radar showed three escorts and one smaller pip, probably the tug. "Our target was gone!" wrote Underwood. "Must have sunk!"

Nearly two hours later, at 0400, the last bunch of depth charges was heard to explode in the distance. Years later, there was some controversy over whether *Spadefish* or *Barb* had sunk *Gyokuyo Maru*. Roger Allan's research in Japan found that the freighter had been hit and abandoned. Thus, *Barb* certainly damaged this ship, and her crew and her escorts ships apparently believed she would sink. Efforts were obviously made to save her, for *Spadefish* found her under tow. There was little doubt as to her sinking. Three officers and three lookouts on the bridge witnessed four torpedo hits, and the target burning. She then disappeared from sight and from radar.

Spadefish cleared the area after celebrating her first kill of her second war patrol. At 0801 on 14 November, a floating mine was sighted about 4,000 yards ahead on the port beam. At 0934, an SJ radar contact was made at 10,000 yards, "coming in fast," bearing 225, the direction of the rain squall. *Spadefish* dove to avoid detection. She resurfaced soon at 0956 and spent the day passing over the Yangtze Banks, headed for Saishu To. The watch sighted a total of nine floating mines during the day. "The middle of the Yellow Sea is literally covered with them," recorded Captain Underwood. "The circular currents in this center portion of the Yellow Sea makes this area a 'Sargasso Sea' for floating mines."

All of the drifting mines sighted on the second patrol, thirty-five counted in all, were of the horned type. "These were old moored mines that had broken away or rusted away from their cables," wrote Dan Decker. "With a strong northerly flow into the Yellow Sea and the Tsushima Straits, those in the Yellow Sea stayed there, caught in a counterclockwise flow, some probably from as far away as the South China Sea."¹⁰

At 1838, *Spadefish* intercepted a *Queenfish* report of a convoy headed west. Underwood flashed the news among his Urchins. Together with *Sunfish* and *Peto*, *Spadefish* set course to search out the reported convoy, but without luck. *Spadefish* patrolled on the surface the following day about 60 miles west of Saishu To.

At 1230 on 15 November, *Spadefish* set course to investigate the western Yellow Sea, north of Shanghai. Two floating mines were sighted in the late afternoon and avoided. At 1844, she received a message from *Queenfish* reporting the convoy sighting at 1200 in position Latitude 33-14N, Longitude 128-19E, on a westerly course. "We were too far to the west to return for the convoy," noted Underwood. *Sunfish* and *Peto*, who had spent the day submerged in the vicinity of Saishu To, joined in the hunt.

At 2322, *Barb* reported contact with an aircraft carrier and four escorts. After being attacked by *Barb*, the carrier group headed back for home. *Sunfish* and *Peto* headed back for the next day's patrol station. An important convoy, labeled HI-81, was transporting the Japanese 23rd Imperial Army Infantry Division to the Philippines. It included landing ships and tankers, escorted by six destroyers, and the 21,000-ton *Otaka*-class aircraft carrier *Jinyo* (also known as *Shinyo*). *Jinyo* was carrying a load of aircraft to Manila for use against the Allies. *Jinyo*'s convoy had originated at 0600 on 14 November from Imari Bay in Kyushu, Japan, bound for Manila in the Philippines.¹¹

Codebreakers found out about this important sortie and passed the intelligence to Admiral Lockwood. He in turn flashed Ultras to his two wolf packs in the Yellow Sea, sending six U.S. subs best positioned to intercept into high alert mode for this delicious prize.

HI-81 made an overnight stop off Goto Island in Ukishima Channel before continuing toward Manila on 15 November. Elliott Loughlin's *Queenfish* had made the contact with the carrier convoy on 15 November. Japanese escort vessels and aircraft made the area very dangerous. Loughlin closed on what he believed to be the carrier *Jinyo*, and fired four stern tubes from 1,500 yards. As escorts drove him deep, he heard two hits in the carrier. His hits were true enough, but this target proved not to be *Jinyo*, but instead another valuable prize, the 9,200-ton aircraft ferry ship *Akitsu Maru*. She sank in three minutes with 2,150 lives lost.¹²

Gene Fluckey pursued the convoy next with *Barb* and made an attack on *Jinyo* in the late minutes of 15 November. He could only manage to close to 3,500 yards before dispatching five torpedoes at her. Although he believed he scored one hit, there was no record of this. *Barb* continued to pursue *Jinyo*'s convoy into 16 November, sending out contact reports continually for both wolf packs to hear. *Barb* finally expended her last two war fish against a freighter, before turning for the barn.

Spadefish and her packmates were frustrated at not being able to catch up with this prime convoy. During the morning hours of 16 November, Underwood's boat sighted nothing more than two floating mines and a Chinese junk. He remained on the surface, diving for only half an hour at 1259 to dodge an enemy aircraft that was sighted at 5 miles. In the afternoon, lookouts spotted a distant waterspout and a sampan.

After enjoying a wealth of kills on their double-barrel first patrol, the *Spadefish* crew was becoming anxious for more action. Around the mess tables, the scuttlebutt was that a big convoy was in their neighboring wolf pack's area. While Underwood's Urchins had been deprived thus far, the pack's luck was about to change for the better.

Spadefish ran on the surface through the early morning hours of 17 November, still unable to pick up any of the convoy action that seemed to permeate the radio messages lately. Her amazing radar operators picked up Kokozan To at 0442, distance 64,000 yards. At 0606, SJ interference from a friendly submarine was picked up, but the sub was not identified. At 0632, *Spadefish* submerged southwest of Kokuzan To. At 1354, her crew heard the first of six depth charges in the distance and knew that someone must be attacking.

On the bridge, fireman Harry Brenneis, a new hand assigned to the forward engine room who also stood lookout, spotted the distant smoke of ships on the horizon at 1434. The OOD, Frank Alvis, called the control room to have the captain summoned. As *Spadefish* pushed her nose toward this prospect, the distant thunder of depth charges could be heard. Between 1543 and 1546, two dozen explosions were counted as some escort hunted another U.S. submarine.

Brenneis' contact began to look more encouraging, for at 1642, *Spadefish*'s watch had five distinct columns of smoke. An airplane was also soon seen to be seen circling over the convoy. The JK sound watch picked up pinging on bearing 051 and screws could be heard on the JP sonar. At long last, here came a convoy.

This was indeed the same important carrier convoy that *Barb* had fired upon and chased into the early hours of 16 November. Her pack mates of "Loughlin's Loopers," *Queenfish* and *Picuda*, had continued to pursue convoy HI-81 down into the territory of Underwood's

Urchins. As the Loopers and Urchins both converged upon the same convoy, Loughlin's pack took the next licks at the Japanese ships.

Nine minutes after picking up enemy screws and pinging, *Spadefish* at 1651 sighted the masts of at least four ships, bearing 059. Junior officer of the deck Perry Wood noted in the deck log that they had visual sighting of "one carrier, identified as *Otaka* class, on the horizon, and two airplanes [were] above the convoy."

This was indeed a prized convoy, one that submariners could dream about an entire war. Very few of them would ever actually be in position to potentially fire upon a Japanese aircraft carrier. "The convoy was headed right for us," wrote Captain Underwood. "We decided to let it go by, as it was only an hour and a half to sunset. We planned to surface and attack at night."

In the galley, Chief Scherman and his cooks—Ed Graf, Buckwheat Pirrung and baker Tom Riley—worked on feeding the crew quickly and quietly, knowing that it might be a long night of standing at battle stations without food.

Spadefish went to 150 feet. "The Skipper elected to stop and settle into the mud to await a more favorable position for a night surface attack," recalled Lieutenant Dan Decker. The enemy convoy passed directly over *Spadefish*. "There were numerous escorts, pinging loudly. We could hear the screws of a very large ship pass almost overhead."[13]

In the forward torpedo room, Hugo Lundquist scribbled in his secret journal, "Went to silent running and let convoy pass over us."

At 1729, twenty-two more depth charges went off. "Not so distant this time," noted Underwood. As the churning of numerous screws passed overhead, men silently prepared for the attack, not needing any prompting. They were a veteran crew now, and their reason for being was rumbling by up above, ripe for the picking.

The thus-far charmed carrier *Jinyo* had escaped approaches or direct attacks upon her by three different U.S. subs in as many days. So far, she had waltzed through unscathed. But then, she had not yet danced with *Spadefish*.

Jinyo's last "Banzai!"

Second Patrol   17–18 November 1944

"Condor" was the name the Imperial Japanese Navy had given its newest aircraft carrier on her commissioning on 15 December 1943. *Shinyo* would also be known in the IJN as *Jinyo*, and it was this name that she more commonly became known as.

Truth be told, *Jinyo* had originally been known to the world as the German passenger ship *Scharnhorst*. She was a twin-screw turbo-electric ship, originally launched 30 April 1935. After the start of World War II, the Nord-Deutscher-Lloyd liner *Scharnhorst* had taken refuge in Yokohama, Japan. She was eventually purchased by the Imperial Japanese Navy on 7 February 1942, for conversion to an escort aircraft carrier. *Scharnhorst*'s gross weight was 18,000 tons. Her steam turbines did not need re-engining, as she was capable of 21 knots already.[1]

Conversion then began at the government shipyards in Kure to convert her to an aircraft carrier. A hangar box was placed where her upper superstructure had been. A 590-foot steel flight deck was also added, some of the steel coming from a fourth *Yamato* class battleship that had been abandoned in March 1942.

The new carrier would have but a single funnel, located on her starboard side, exhausting downwards. Her flight deck was flush, with the navigating bridge located at the forward end of the hangar structure, under the flight deck overhang. *Jinyo* had four twin 12.7cm (5-inch) anti-aircraft guns mounted below her flight deck on each side. By 1944, she also sported ten triple 25mm (1-inch) AA guns, and twenty additional 25mm barrels, in single and double mountings.

Jinyo's weight was listed as 20,900 tons. She could carry a crew of 948 men and her normal aircraft complement was 21 attack planes and eleven fighters. *Jinyo* had not been used in combat to any great extent. She served more as a deck-landing training carrier for Japanese naval aviators in the months leading up to the battle of the Philippine Sea.

Since departing from Kyushu on 14 November, *Jinyo*'s convoy HI-81 had been stalked by two of Admiral Lockwood's wolf packs. Already the convoy had lost one heavy troop ship and *Jinyo* herself had been fired on by *Barb*. The other two boats of Elliott Loughlin's wolf pack, *Queenfish* and *Picuda*, stayed with convoy HI-81. Captain Shephard in *Picuda* attacked the convoy in the late afternoon of 17 November, damaging the 6,925-ton tanker *Awagawa Maru* and sinking the 9,433-ton troop transport *Mayasan Maru*. Loaded with 4,500 troops of the Imperial Japanese Army's 23rd Division from Manchuria, *Mayasan Maru* capsized in seconds—taking 3,437 men, more than two hundred army horses and other material down with her. Escort frigates *Daito* and *Shinan* dropped behind to give *Picuda* a good working over—the explosions from which could be heard miles away from *Spadefish* as she lay in wait.[2]

One of Captain Underwood's pack, *Sunfish*, was next to find *Jinyo*. Unable to get into position to fire against her, he chased her, sending out contact reports to his pack mates. Captain Ed Shelby was finally forced to break off and attack some of the freighters traveling with *Jinyo*, sinking another troop transport and a freighter. Finally, *Spadefish*'s other pack mate, *Peto*, tore into this luckless HI-81 convoy and downed two more freighters.[3]

The two wolf packs had taken a toll on HI-81 and MI-27, but the big prize of the sister convoys still steamed ahead toward Manila in the Philippines with her cargo of aircraft. With frustrated United States submarines in her wake, *Jinyo*'s silhouette was now, however, beginning to fill the periscope lens of Commander Gordon Waite Underwood's *Spadefish*.

At 150 feet, the Japanese convoy sounded like a freight train rumbling by overhead as *Spadefish* lay in wait. As soon as sound reported that the convoy had passed, Captain Underwood brought her back up to periscope depth at 1754. He could count five big ships, trailed by an aircraft carrier.

In his patrol report, he noted the ships he could see.

> It was too dark to see the convoy clearly. One appeared to be a large modern tanker, the others good-sized AKs. There were numerous escorts, DDs and PCs. The CVE resembled the *Otaka* class closer than any other. However, the bow wasn't quite right. The flight deck extended out to almost the tip of the bow, with only a small amount of open grillwork forward.

The carrier had three objects, possibly stacks, just showing above the flight deck, on the starboard quarter. There was no island. The flight deck extended almost to the bow with one or two supporting members under the overhang. The open part below the flight deck at the stern was short. It resembled the *Otaka* class with the exception that the flight deck extended further forward.

At 1811, an explosion was heard. This was followed by the sight of smoke billowing from a large freighter ahead of the carrier. "Guess some other sub decided not to wait for dark. Couldn't see what happened to the target." This was *Picuda* sinking the large auxiliary *Mayasan Maru* and damaging the tanker *Awagawa Maru*. Aboard *Spadefish*, the crew could hear the explosions of *Picuda* being treated to seventeen depth charges at 1813. "They sounded close in the shallow water," wrote Underwood.

Gordon Underwood decided it was time to go on the offensive. Other subs were licking at this precious convoy, and he was not about to let this most coveted prize—a Japanese aircraft carrier—slip by without at least putting up a fight.

Battle stations bonged throughout *Spadefish* at 1816. Men relieved those men not normally assigned to that spot for battle stations. Ten minutes later, *Spadefish* was preparing to surface. In the conning tower, OOD Dan Decker and Perry Wood stood ready, binoculars in hand. The battle lookouts, wearing their red goggles to protect their night vision, stood by the edge of the ladder as Jim Schuett spun the wheel and cracked the hatch. The air pressure in the boat caused a momentary release on the ears. Salt water pouring through the opening drenched the watchstanders. The rush of air escaping from the boat helped push the first men up the ladder not unlike a cork being propelled by the pressure escaping from a bottle.

At 1834, *Spadefish* had surfaced to commence tracking the convoy and her four diesels coughed to life. Bending on all four engines, she began her run to get into attack position. Don Martin's radar gang took quick radar impulses to keep track of the ranges. Underwood preferred to attack on the surface, using the cover of darkness to his advantage. The closest targets were only 12,000 yards away. This turned out to be two escorts that had remained behind to heckle the sub that had made the attack. The convoy was 22,700 yards away. Radar interference was obtained from the two escorts.

At a range of 10,000 yards, the interference steadied on *Spadefish*. Upon opening the range, it started sweeping again. The APR radar detector had radar contact at 160 megacycles. "This promised to be an interesting night if any more of the escorts had this radar. Fortunately, these two escorts remained in the vicinity and we left them behind as we went after the convoy," wrote Underwood. "Intermittent depth charging was heard from the direction of the two escort vessels."

At 1856, *Spadefish* now received a radar contact report from *Sunfish* telling of two convoys, the one that she was in contact with, and an eight ship convoy three hours behind. *Sunfish* was preparing to work on the latter convoy, MI-27.

A contact report was received which stated that the convoy with the CVE (HI-81) had five DD escorts and nine other ships. This data was from a Chinese Air Force reconnaissance plane which had overflown the convoy. Underwood could count only five other marus with the aircraft carrier. "The number of escorts was correct," he wrote, "but believe at least two were PC, as they were smaller."

The escorts with *Jinyo* at this point were the new 1,260-ton destroyer *Kashi*, and PC-type escorts *Kume*, *Tsushima*, and *Etorofu*. Two other *kaibokans*, *Daito* and *Shinan*, had dropped back to depth charge *Picuda*. If Underwood's count of five escorts was correct, this would lend credence to another escort having joined the convoy along its course.[4]

Spadefish tracked the carrier to be zig-zagging by constant helm superimposed on a regular zig-zag plan, with base course 225, varying speed from 11 to 16 knots. The convoy could be plainly seen from a distance of 10,000 yards. "The CVE was the last ship, with two escorts on the beams and two more on the bows. The rest of the convoy was in two columns ahead. The escorts appeared to be pretty good-sized, probably DD's."

The changing speeds kept everyone on the tracking party busy. Mike Sergio, on the JP sonar gear, kept the skipper informed every time a turn count was called for. Sergio explains how a trained ear could figure a ship's speed by the turn count of its screws.

> The skipper would say, "Soundman, get me a count."
> I would figure how many times the propellers were turning. I'd hold the palm of my left hand out with my fingers together. I'd take my right index finger and synchronize it with the turn count. As the propeller is rotating, there was always a definite flat sound when it completed one revolution. I would synchronize my index finger with that flat sound and give the proper count as "One-two turn count" or "One-three turn count." Then the gunnery officer, Lieutenant Laundy, would put this count right into the TDC and it would figure the speed of the enemy.

At 2119, *Spadefish* headed in for the attack on the CVE from the starboard beam. The escort that was on the beam 2,600 yards from the CVE had now fallen back to the quarter. At a range of 4,600 yards, the CVE zigged away, so Underwood turned around and headed out again for another try. "Was relieved to find no radars from the escorts picked us up," he wrote.

At 2130, *Spadefish* received a radar contact report from *Sunfish* that she had attacked her convoy and it was scattering. RT1c Neal Pike was on the SJ radar. Underwood drove his boat in for another try at 2258 on 17 November. "Was a little more on the bow of the CVE this time. The beam escort was further forward and we passed astern of him successfully. Radar interference was present, but it didn't steady on us, and there was no indication that they had us spotted."

Pike reported radar presence while RM2c Sergio stayed tuned to his sonar gear for other ships that might be heard before being seen.

Spadefish remained on the surface for the carrier attack. During the attack the officer of the deck and those topside could see the intermittent fires from the ships attacked by *Sunfish* some 30 miles away.[5] *Sunfish* had torpedoed the transports *Seisho Maru* and *Edogawa Maru* of convoy MI-27. One went down right away, and *Sunfish* tenaciously pursued her cripple until she had also put it under the waves. Packmate *Peto* teamed up with *Sunfish* to hound this convoy.

Chief of the Boat Eimermann, technically exempted from watchstanding by nature of his billet, kept himself available as a battle stations lookout for attacks. The five-man battle stations watch section included Y1c Irv Kreinbring, GM3c Bernie Massar, GM1c Shaky Jake Lewis, S1c Maurice Noonan, and newly promoted EM3c Dick Bassett. Eimermann generally substituted in for one of these men. For an attack on an aircraft carrier, he was certainly not planning on spending his time below decks this night.

Dan Decker and Perry Wood, normally on watch during this time period, had turned over their duties to Ensigns Ray White and Bill Ware so that they could drop down into the conning tower to handle the battle plot details. White and Ware each manned one of the TBTs at each end of the bridge. Junior OOD Ware served as the bridge talker this night and was later commended by Captain Underwood for "his expert navigation and his accuracy in transmitting information to his commanding officer."

Underwood ordered his boat flooded down to reduce her topside radar profile. Her decks were awash with just the bridge structure exposed. "An overcast made it quite dark but soon the ships could be identified," recalled Dan Decker, "and accurate range, bearing and speed could be set in the TDC."

The forward bridge TBT fed info directly into the TDC, where Gus Laundy used his analog fire control computer to tackle the complex firing data. Plotting officer Decker continued to track the base course changes of the convoy relative to *Spadefish*'s own maneuvers.

At 2303 on 17 November, all was in sync as Gordon Underwood called down from the bridge, "Fire one!"

In the conning tower, Ted Ustick hit the firing plunger. In the forward torpedo room, Chief Harry George also fired the torpedo manually as a precaution. There was a momentary zing of the torpedo's propellers, and a slight pressure to the men's ears forward as the poppet valve vented the residual air in the torpedo tube back into the boat.

"One fired, sir," came back the reply.

At eight second intervals, *Spadefish* fired her full bow nest, sending six torpedoes racing toward *Jinyo* with a 150% spread. At least two war fish were thus expected to miss in order to insure several direct hits. At the time of firing, the target carrier was at the long range of 4,100 yards, with a 65° starboard track. *Spadefish* was on the surface, making 14 knots on course 175 at time of firing. In the course of completing the turn to fire, *Spadefish* had slowed to 7 knots.

At 2304, *Spadefish* turned to port and Bill Ware put the after TBT on the tanker ahead of the carrier for stern shots. With radar ranges to fire a divergent spread, Underwood ordered the firing of all four after torpedoes from Si Barnes' room at a range of 2,980 yards, track 132 starboard. The time was 2304, one minute after firing the forward tubes.

At 2305, the first torpedo hit in the stern of *Jinyo*. "When they hit her, you could see fire go up every time a torpedo hit," recalled Chief Eimermann. *Wham!* Two more quick hits were seen to follow, logged as tubes 2 and 3. *Wham! Wham!* From the bridge, Underwood, Eimermann, Ware, White, Bassett, and Massar could see the torpedoes strike home. The succeeding explosions walked forward from her stern toward her island structure. The next two torpedoes appeared to miss, and then a fourth explosion was seen and heard —either torpedo No. 6 or a large internal explosion aboard *Jinyo*.

Commander Underwood wrote: "The carrier burst into flames and started settling by the stern. The fire could be seen spreading the length of the ship below the flight deck."

After the firing of the second after torpedo, *Spadefish*'s target tanker had zigged. At 2307, a timed hit was heard for one of the stern torpedoes but no explosion was seen. Japanese convoy records for HI-81 leave room for interpretation on which submarines hit which vessels. Researcher Anthony Tully says that *Spadefish* may have caused damage to the 8,170-ton landing ship *Shinshu Maru* with her second salvo with one of the four torpedoes. *Shinshu Maru* was fully able to proceed but was reported "damaged for unclear reasons" in Japanese reports.[6]

In his updated analysis of all U.S. submarine attacks, Cdr. John Alden credits *Spadefish* with sinking the 6,600-ton tanker *Osakasan Maru*, which presumably had scattered from convoy MI-27 after it had come under attack. His research of Japanese convoy records show that *Osakasan Maru* took a torpedo in her No. 2 hold at 2340 (Japanese time). At an unknown time, this tanker took another torpedo hit under her bridge and sank with 142 lives lost. With lack of evidence of a sinking in this case, Captain Underwood would only claim damage to a 10,000-ton tanker.[7]

Attention on the *Spadefish* bridge and in her conning tower had turned to the Japanese aircraft carrier that was now burning brilliantly before her. "Everyone was watching the CVE burn up," wrote Underwood. "The carrier was loaded with planes that could be seen rolling off the deck as the ship settled aft and took a starboard list."

"After we fired and hit *Jinyo* with four of six fish, I went topside and watched her burn and settle," recalled Executive Officer Ted Ustick many years later. "That scene is still very clear in my mind."[8]

Chief Eimermann watched as "the airplane wings just curled up" from the intense heat and flames. With Captain Underwood's permission, he then allowed members of the *Spadefish* crew to come topside. Battle lookout Bernie Massar, scanning the rear 180° as the stern lookout, felt "the whole thing was a mass of flames." He distinctly recalled watching the escort ships racing around dropping depth charges near the sinking carrier, "probably killing their own men," as they attempted to find the submarine.

Lieutenant Dan Decker, the plotting officer, clearly recalled the crew being allowed topside to view *Jinyo*'s demise. The crew seldom ever had a chance to see a sinking. The fact that the escorts had not located *Spadefish* gave skipper Underwood the incentive to reward his men.

> The crew, five at a time, were allowed on the cigarette deck of the bridge for a few minutes each group. Binoculars for all were used, at that distance, to watch one aircraft after another catch fire (must have had fuel aboard), burn through their tiedowns and slide aft or over the side. I think *Jinyo* stayed afloat, at least its bow section, for close to 30 minutes.

In his private journal, scribbled that night as brief notes, torpedoman Hugo Lundquist agreed with the length of time *Jinyo* stayed

Japanese aircraft carrier *Jinyo* (also known as *Shinyo*), seen during her trial runs in 1943. The 21,000-ton *Jinyo* was sunk by four torpedoes from *Spadefish* on the night of 17 November 1944, with a heavy loss of lives. *Courtesy of Anthony Tully.*

afloat. "4 hits on aircraft carrier. Blazed up right away and went down burning in 1/2 hour. Also damaged an A.K. on same run. Banzai!"

Captain Underwood ordered his tubes reloaded as his ship pulled clear of the attack scene. Underwood allowed all possible hands to come topside "to watch the carrier burn and vanish" as she cleared the area. Escort vessels were racing around dropping depth charges on the area where they thought *Spadefish* to be.[9]

Signalman striker Don Scholle, keeping the quartermaster's notebook, was among those allowed topside briefly. "You could see the planes rolling into the water. I think they had 55 planes aboard. She was aflame from stem to stern. We looked at her with binoculars from the bridge."

While small groups of men were allowed up the conning tower ladder onto the bridge, others were allowed to take quick peeks through the periscope. "Everybody was looking through the periscope in the conning tower," stated Don Anderson, who was preparing to go on lookout duty. "I just got about a five second glance." He took the helm briefly so the helmsman could take a look. From the maneuvering room, Ken Sigworth was also "relieved to go up into the conning tower to look through the periscope quickly." Like the others, he saw "a lot flames and planes sliding off her tilted deck."

Lt.(jg) Perry Wood, who had been on the plotting team for the *Jinyo* attack, also took a proud moment to look through the periscope. "I could see aircraft rolling off the deck and flames going high into the sky. It was very spectacular."

The carrier was upended, with her bow pointing skyward, her stern digging into the ocean bottom 23 fathoms (138 feet) below. The carrier was last seen around 2330, as *Spadefish* pulled away from the scene and pursued convoy HI-81 to the west. Underwood's report says: "When last seen, the bow was sticking up in the air, still burning. The stern was on the bottom in 23 fathoms of water."

Some reports would indicate that *Jinyo* went down very quickly due to the very heavy loss of lives she suffered. The *Spadefish* crew all agreed that her bow was still visible thirty minutes after the attack. Motormac Dick Gamby, one of those allowed to take a peek at her, remembered, "I think it took her about 20 or 25 minutes to sink." Boats Eimermann says, "She was down in a half hour." The massive explosions and raging fires aboard her no doubt added to her casualty rate. Her own escort vessels may very well have taken other lives by racing about dropping depth charges and failing to immediately stop and pick up survivors.[10]

The Imperial Japanese Navy listed the ship sunk as 17,500 ton *Shinyo*, although JANAC called her the 21,000-ton *Jinyo*. Survivors of this ship, as related to *Spadefish* crewmen, called her *Jinyo*. After the war, Nobuyuki Okamura contacted "Buck" Miller, editor of *Spadefish*'s "Luau" newsletter. Okamura stated that of 1,164 people on board *Jinyo*, including 834 officers and crewmen, only 60 men survived the *Spadefish* sinking. There were obviously some 300-plus other military personnel aboard the carrier bound for the Philippines.[11]

In further coincidence, Dan Decker would later live in Japan for a short period of time. In 1959, he was serving as operations officer to the rear admiral commanding Naval Air, Far East, headquartered in Atsugi, Japan, about 20 miles west of Yokohama. He lived in a home near the station and hired a Japanese maid and gardner to take care of his residence.

> The maid spoke English quite well and eventually told me her husband was a naval aviator, but was lost when his ship was sunk. I asked her what ship, and she replied, the *Jinyo*. I gave her a hug, told her I was very sorry, but said no more.

Even after blasting convoy HI-81's prized aircraft carrier, *Spadefish*'s action was far from over this night.

Commander Underwood remained on the bridge as he readied his boat for a second attack on this convoy. The blazing *Jinyo* had long since fallen astern. The remainder of the convoy was now zigging by constant helm on a zig-zag plan with a base course 270, speed 12 to 16 knots. The wounded tanker had been able to keep her speed and move out of range.

The night of 17 November slipped into 18 November as *Spadefish* moved in to attempt another kill. "On 18 November, we were in position on starboard bow of convoy," wrote Underwood. "Headed in for attack before convoy had time to reform its escorts."

Once again one of the *kaibokan*'s radar was giving interference, but did not steady on *Spadefish*. Just as with the carrier attack, Lt. Cdr. Ustick would direct the plotting team. "I was in the conning tower, with the Skipper on the bridge," he recalled.[12]

At 0003, a green light was seen from the closest escort, range 2,000 yards, on the starboard bow of convoy. This was answered by a green light from a ship out of radar range to the north. At this time, the convoy zigged about 60 degrees toward *Spadefish*, causing the range to close rapidly, "and putting us in a doubtful position."

One minute later, at 0004, two red lights flashed on the closest escort. She then immediately opened fire on *Spadefish* with her 40mm guns. "I saw the Japanese escorts were flashing the lights in their masts, and then they started shooting at us," recalled port side lookout Bernie Massar.

In order to protect his men, Captain Underwood called, "Left full rudder! Clear the bridge!"

Radioman Ken Powers later reported: "The Captain ordered the bridge cleared to protect the lookouts and in the same breath, passed the word, 'We will *not* dive! We will *not* dive!'"[13]

Underwood, electing to con his ship under fire by himself, remained on the bridge. The shells were now whining over the bridge as the escort rapidly closed the range. Ensign Ray White requested permission to remain topside. Below decks, Bernie Massar heard White call out, "Should we open up with the 20mm and return their fire?"

"No!" hollered Underwood, who knew the flash of *Spadefish*'s gun would only serve as a perfect aiming point for the Japanese gunners.

Electrician Dick Bassett, up on the starboard lookout station in the periscope shears, failed to hear the order to go below and thus remained topside with White and Underwood. White's offer to stay and the fact that both men stayed topside under gunfire to assist their captain resulted in decorations for both men. Battle lookout Bassett was later awarded the Silver Star and White received the Bronze Star.[14]

Chief Eimermann and Bernie Massar were only too happy to get the hell below at the skipper's first order. "Tracers were going right over our head into the wake," recalled Massar. "Bassett didn't hear the command, and he stayed up there. The captain gave him a Silver Star later."

Bassett would later tell his buddies that his staying topside was less voluntary than Ensign White's action. Bassett was still sweeping the horizon when he happened to notice that there was no one else on the periscope shears with him. As the tracers grew closer he thought, "I'd better get out of here!"

Just as Bassett started to swing down, he saw Captain Underwood standing around on the other side of the conning tower. "Jesus! I don't know what the hell to do now!" he thought. He kept his post and continuing calling out the bearings of escorts that were now coming after *Spadefish*. Dick Bassett was from Macon, Georgia, and he had a heavy, monotone drawl.

One of his buddies, Jack Gallagher, later recalled:

> I was on the stern planes in the control room at the time, beside Whitey Harbison on the air manifold. I remember seeing the lookouts coming down below and assuming that *Spadefish* would dive. But Bassett didn't come down and we didn't dive. I don't know if Bassett's slow, Southern drawl calling out the ships' bearings calmed the captain down—or if it was just the comfort that someone else was up there with him—but, anyway, the skipper gave Bassett the Silver Star when we got back.

When the skipper remained on the bridge, hoping to still get in a shot at the turning convoy, his action sparked some confusion below decks. The order to "clear the bridge" was almost invariably followed by the words, "Dive! Dive!" This time, however, Underwood simply passed the word below, "We will *not* dive."

In the conning tower below, helmsman Jim Parscale only heard "dive," and assumed from the tracers flying overhead that the skipper was certainly taking the boat down. "The helmsman, in the confusion, seeing the lookouts clear the bridge, misunderstood the captain's orders and pressed the diving alarm, at the same time ringing up 'all stop' on the engine order telegraph," wrote Ken Powers. Parscale's shift on the annunciators signaled the maneuvering room personnel to shift to battery power and stop the diesel engines.[15]

Down in the maneuvering room, electrician Ken Sigworth felt instantly that something was wrong. "The quartermaster, if he rang up All Ahead Full, this meant to us that we were going to dive." Sigworth just knew that *Spadefish* should instead be running flank speed on the surface. As the signal came up, the electricians looked at Carl Schmelzer, "What do we do?"

"That's what they say," replied the chief.

This photo shows the forward end of the conning tower of a World War II submarine. In front of the helmsman's wheel are the annunciator and other engine order control displays. A misunderstanding by the *Spadefish* helmsman caused the ship's engines to be shut down as Japanese escort vessels raced toward her. *Courtesy of Bernie Massar.*

Sigworth recalled, "We went ahead with stopping and dumped all four main engines." The motormacs immediately shut down their Fairbanks Morse engines. *Spadefish* quickly lost headway as she slowed to a coast. Topside, Underwood felt his ship coming to a halt under his feet and realized that Parscale had misunderstood his words. He hollered below to restart the engines.

"Where the hell's my main engines?" Captain Underwood shouted from the bridge. "Give us all you've got if you want to live!"

Sigworth didn't need Chief Schmelzer to tell him what to do with his controllers. "You could hear the Old Man's yell from up on the bridge."

Radioman Ken Powers remembered the skipper also ordering over the 1MC: "Left full rudder! Make ready the stern tubes and fire when ready!"[16]

In a tense spot on the bridge, Captain Underwood could see the Japanese warships racing toward his slowing submarine. He later wrote in his patrol report:

Before the error could be rectified and the engines started again, we had slowed to 8 knots, and the escort had closed to 970 yards, shooting with 20-mm and 40-mm, and with a few heavier caliber shots [5-inch caliber]. He hadn't detected our turn yet, so all shots were astern of *Spadefish*.

Ted Ustick, in the conning tower, found these moments to be "scary as hell" in an area with only 120 feet of water. He later related:

> All I can remember is hearing those diesels stop, one by one, exhaust valves clang shut...and the racket of rapid-fire cannon shooting at US. Looking up through the conning tower hatch, it looked like a string of red-hot footballs were whizzing over us, all glowing red in the night. That was pretty scary stuff because all they had to do was hit us once and we probably would have been lost. One hole in the hull and that's it. As we rapidly slowed, that magnificent engine-room gang got those diesels back on line.[17]

The engines could not be restarted quickly enough for most. "An effort was made to start all engines at once and a tremendous vacuum was created in the boat. According to procedure, on the sound of the diving alarm, the main engine air induction was closed and the conning tower hatch secured," wrote Ken Powers.[18]

One of the new hands aboard *Spadefish*, seaman Charles Rolf, had been assigned to man the talker's headset at the quartermaster's cubby in the control room during the torpedo attack. Luau, the very pregnant ship's dog, was seated in his lap at the time.

The sudden vacuum had negative effects on more than just the ears of some crewmen, as control room talker Rolf found. "It pulled a negative pressure in the boat, or a vacuum in the boat, when those diesels started," he said. "Luau was on my lap when this happened, and she pissed all over me."

The intense pressure was quickly handled, according to Powers.

> Now realizing that nothing could be opened until the vacuum was reduced, an auxiliaryman in the control room jammed open the spare air connection and a great rush of air filled the boat, relieving the vacuum but putting the ship under pressure as the valve froze open. When the conning tower hatch was finally opened, the navigator and the quartermaster, with the help of the escaping air, reached the bridge without touching a rung of the ladder.[19]

Spadefish could not come up to speed quick enough for the three desperate men on her bridge. "The total time elapsed from the sound of the diving alarm to the time the engines were back on line was one minute and 27 seconds!" wrote Powers. "For the crew of *Spadefish*... an eternity!"

The nearest destroyer had closed to within 1,000 yards after the engines were cut. Fortunately, this destroyer did not detect *Spadefish*'s turn, so his gunfire was not on the mark. *Spadefish* quickly opened up the distance again, as her dark silhouette was not easily spotted by the destroyer's skipper.

The escort that had been on the starboard quarter of the convoy had picked her up, though, and he now also opened fire. His shots crossed astern of *Spadefish* and landed on her port quarter. "Those 40-mm tracers certainly light up the night, and also make a hell of a racket," wrote Underwood. In the after torpedo room, Si Barnes and his crew opened the outer doors to the torpedo tubes and prepared to fire as *Spadefish* clawed for speed.

One of the escorts firing on *Spadefish* was the large destroyer *Kashi*. A new *Matsu*-class warship, *Kashi* had only been able to rescue a handful of *Jinyo* survivors before keeping pace with the remaining merchant vessels of HI-81. According to her records, she attacked an American submarine around midnight. The research of Anthony Tully shows that another one of the ships firing on *Spadefish* this night was a transport, the large 10,564-ton ex-tanker *Mirii Maru*.[20]

In the conning tower keeping the log, Don Scholle recalled that he could see but could not hear the shells over the noise aboard ship. "I could look up the conning tower hatch and see the streaks of shells going over continuously."

The nearest destroyer was chasing *Spadefish* at an uncomfortable distance as Gordon Underwood hoped to make at least one more strike against this convoy as he cleared the area. "I had the destroyer on the radar and he was gaining on us very rapidly," said radio technician Neal Pike. On the bridge, Captain Underwood asked for range and bearing to this nearest target.

"We only had one thing to do, and that was to run like hell and hope to sink one of those cans," recalled Lt. Cdr. Ustick. "One of them was galloping up our track and shooting like crazy."[21]

The stern tubes were ready, so the after TBT was turned on at 0007 on 18 November. Ustick, looking through the periscope, had a large warship all lined up astern. The convoy vessels and escorts racing about gave gunnery officer Gus Laundy some tough moments on the TDC. "I gave the captain three different solutions, because the ship was changing speed and course all the time." In his patrol report,

This illustration shows a typical Japanese submarine chaser, a smaller vessel armed with depth charges and at least one deck gun. Ultra intelligence led JANAC to credit *Spadefish* with sinking *Submarine Chaser 156* on the night of 18 November 1944. Author's collection.

Underwood wrote of his target destroyer, "This was a large escort in line with two ships of the convoy, range 2,800 yards, so we tracked him for a couple of minutes and fired four torpedoes from the stern tubes on a 100° starboard track."

Exec Ustick had his skipper's full confidence and fired the stern tubes. "I fired those torpedoes without any further orders from anybody, with a slight spread," he related. "If we couldn't get him, that was going to be the end of the patrol and the end of a boatload of sailors on the *Spadefish*."

The depth setting had been dropped to 4-feet to allow for a shallow-running escort. Just over one hour after firing on *Jinyo* and the tanker, *Spadefish* had thus launched four more war fish toward the pursuing Japanese warships of convoy HI-81.

As soon as the fourth tube was fired, Ted Ustick raced up the ladder onto the bridge. He saw heavy billowing smoke in the direction of the target destroyer. "I had binoculars on the leading escort coming up our kilts, a huge bow-wave and guns flashing away, until the first fish hit with a big puff of smoke, visible in the dark hazy night," recalled Ustick. "And then, thank God, the other two escorts slowed and turned away...and we lived to fight again."[22]

Three timed explosions were heard. Neal Pike's radar clearly showed the pip of this target warship to disappear in short time. It had been a close call, but *Spadefish* had survived to fight another day. "I was very proud of those TDC solutions," said Lieutenant Laundy.

Postwar records for convoy HI-81 and MI-27 do not show any large destroyer being sunk this night. JANAC would later determine the warship which disappeared from radar this night was the small, 100-ton *Sub Chaser No. 156*. Clearly, *Spadefish* had destroyed an escort this night, although the Imperial Japanese Navy says *No. 156* was sunk on 29 March 1945 at Takao by U.S. aircraft. Independent researcher John Alden questions JANAC's attribution of this little sub chaser to *Spadefish*, but gives no further indication of what ship might have been destroyed.[23]

Fate of Japanese Convoys HI-71 and MI-27
November 1944

CONVOY HI-81 (one carrier, ten marus and six escorts)

Ship Name	Type	Tonnage	Attacks Against/Notes
Jinyo (Shinyo)	CVE	21,000	Sunk by *Spadefish* 11/17/44
Arita Maru	AO	10,238	Later sunk by *Flasher* 12/22/44
Akitsu Maru	XAPV	9,186	Sunk by *Queenfish* 11/15/44
Hashidate Maru	AO/AP	9,000**	
Kibitsu Maru	AP	10,000**	
Kiyokawa Maru	XAV	6,863	
Mayasan Maru	XARL	9,433	Sunk by *Picuda* 11/17/44
Mirii Maru	XAO	10,564	
Otowasan Maru	AO	9,204	Later sunk by *Flasher* 12/22/44
Shinshu Maru	LS	8,170	
Toa Maru	AO	9,997	
Kashi	DD	1,270	
Daito	PF	870	
Shinan	PF	870	
Etorofu	PF	870	
Kume	PF	900	Later sunk by *Spadefish* 1/28/45
Tsushima	PF	870	

CONVOY MI-27 (eight marus and five escorts)

Ship Name	Type	Tonnage	Attacks Against/Notes
Aisakasan Maru	AK	6,923*	Sunk by *Spadefish* 11/18/44
Awagawa Maru	AO	6,925	Damaged by *Picuda* 11/17/44
Chinkai Maru	AK	2,827	Sunk by *Peto* 11/18/44
Edogawa Maru	AP	6,968	Sunk by *Sunfish* 11/17/44
Enki Maru	AO	6,968	
Koshu Maru			
Seisho Maru	AP	5,463	Sunk by *Sunfish* 11/18/44
Shoho Maru	XAP	1,358	Sunk by *Pomfret* 11/25/44
CD-61	PF	810	flagship of convoy
CD-134	PF	940	
Minesweeper 101	WA	175**	
Sub Chaser 156	SC	100***	Sunk by *Spadefish* 11/18/44
Sub Chaser 157	SC	130	

* Per Alden, *United States and Allied Submarine Successes in the Pacific*, D-280. *Aisakasan Maru* also known as *Osakasan Maru*.
** Approximate tonnage.
*** JANAC credit only. *Spadefish* crew believed escort ship to be larger.

Sources: Research of Anthony P. Tully to author; Clay Blair, *Silent Victory*, 2:750; Alden, *U.S. Submarine Attacks During World War II*. Per Tully, some ships of this convoy split off at various times from convoy MI-27.

For the *Spadefish* crew, the name of this sub chaser or destroyer meant nothing at the time. After inadvertently shutting down their diesels in the face of onrushing Japanese warships, the crew's kill this night was merely a special bonus on top of escaping with their lives.

Lieutenant Commander Ustick actually believed that Jim Parscale's annunciator error error this night had saved *Spadefish*:

> It has always been my theory that we saved our ship that night when we shut down the engines, because all the shooting was too long in range. They must have used our top speed for range settings, while we were crawling along on the batteries—as the shells went over us or beyond us on either side. Whatever the reason, we were not hit and got safely away. Such are the fortunes of war and the roll of the dice in a game of life and death.
>
> Our first son, Teddy, was born Oct. 17, 1944, and almost lost his old man one month later.

After leaving a wrecked warship in her wake, *Spadefish* continued to run like hell with Japanese escorts on her tail. Shells continued to pass overhead, but her emergency speed soon began to build some distance. At maximum power, as the electricians put it, they "bent on everything including the washing machine," attaining a shaft speed of 305 turns on a 1400KW load from the motors for a pit log speed of 22.8 knots—the fastest that *Spadefish* was ever to be driven while fully loaded![24]

The engines were on overload and the strain quickly showed. Motor machinist's mate Charles Griffith in the forward engine room became very concerned. "The engine rpms would trip out an overload at about 720 rpms. They were bouncing up on that."

Griffith called back to feisty Chief Schmelzer in the maneuvering room: "Schmelzer, you're going to burn them engines up!"

"Crackerass, it's burn 'em up or get shot up!" Schmelzer, struggling to keep the breakers from tripping, fired back.

With that, Griffith "pulled the stops off the governors" and let *Spadefish* run full out.

"We disconnected the governors on the four engines, and got two extra knots out of her," remembered Ted Ustick. Chief Electrician Carl Schmelzer was later awarded the Navy Letter of Commendation for his efforts in bringing *Spadefish* to her fastest speed. "Schmelzer and Roy Moody went right into the cage in the maneuvering room and held the goddamn breakers in with their feet so they wouldn't kick

For his quick thinking in keeping *Spadefish* running at full speed following the *Jinyo* attack, Chief Electrician's Mate Carl Schmelzer receives a commendation on 3 March 1945 in Apra Harbor, Guam, from Captain Lewis Parks, Commander SubSquad Twenty. *Carl Schmelzer collection, courtesy of Don and Maury Martin.*

out," said crewman Wallace McMahon. "I don't know how they ever did it."[25]

Spadefish didn't dive since the water was only 22 fathoms. The escort certainly had her located, with plenty of other angry escorts in the area to help if he found her. Not until 0028 did Underwood have his boat slow from emergency speed to normal flank speed, under which she continued to clear the area.

Commander Underwood's report shows how hard his boat raced to clear the enemy warships.

> By this time, we were going all ahead emergency flank, getting considerably more than the rated horsepower out of our 10-cylinder engines. It was sufficient to pull away from the escort. He had discovered us by this time and his tracers were spraying first one side and then the other of us, only once passing overhead. His gunners were blinded by their own tracers so they would fire a few bursts, then stop and pick up our wake,

then open up in its direction. Whey they stopped shooting, we would zig about 10 degrees one way or the other, so he wasn't successful in getting on [us].

The *Spadefish* paint job worked in her favor also. The most prominent part of her visibility was her wake. When the range was opened up to about 2,500 yards, the closest pursuing destroyer turned away and dropped a string of depth charges. In his patrol report, Captain Underwood wrote, "Believed he did that to 'save face.' His story would be he lost us because we submerged."

Auxiliaryman Buck Miller later wrote that the engines "gave more emergency knots than they were designed for." As *Spadefish* finally eased up on her speed, Miller vividly recalled the "engine room gangs came out of the engine rooms looking like they fell overboard—wet, and I mean wringing wet, with sweat."[26]

While still clearing the area at normal flank speed at 0043, Japanese radar interference was picked up by *Spadefish*'s radar team. Contact range on this vessel was initially 14,000 yards distance. This ship came in fast, tracked at 30 knots. He narrowed the distance to 10,000 yards before turning toward the other escort. He then proceeded to drop about fifteen depth charges, apparently coached on by his fellow *kaibokan* and then headed off to the south. Underwood wrote, "Lucky break for us he hadn't been in the vicinity a half-hour earlier!"

This new approaching escort was likely the smaller frigate *CD-61*. Underwood's Urchins were slamming two convoys on the night of 17 -18 November, HI-81 and MI-27. *CD-61* was apparently dispatched from her convoy to search for *Jinyo*, which had "broken off from the convoy." She had not broken off, but was broken—belching flames and wracked with explosions that were consuming her as her convoy steamed on without her. Convoy records show that *CD-61* also made an attack on a submarine during the night.[27]

The Japanese convoy was by this time about 12 miles south of *Spadefish* and due to turn for Shanghai. The location of the escort vessels prevented Underwood from turning for a direct chase. "With the convoy making between 15 and 16 knots, decided time did not permit making the long wide end run, so headed for the vicinity of the carrier attack, hoping to pick up a cripple or a stray from *Sunfish*'s convoy."

All told, this convoy had lost eight ships sunk from the two wolf packs. The most severe losses had been the *Jinyo*, the aircraft ferry and two troop transports. It is unknown how many troops of the Japanese 23rd Division perished or were knocked out of action, but the number was certainly in the thousands. In addition to the two full loads of aircraft lost, other field guns, ammunition, supplies, and crucial military equipment had gone to the bottom. By failing to make the Philippines, this made General MacArthur's job easier in the coming weeks.[28]

At 0129, an explosion lighted up the horizon eastward. This was believed to *Sunfish* working on her convoy. *Spadefish* headed in that direction and sighted another glow on the horizon at 0315. At 0430, three distant depth charges were heard. Another submarine of *Spadefish*'s wolf pack, *Peto*, reported her position at 0440 and said she was chasing one ship with one escort. *Spadefish*'s SJ radar picked up interference at 0445 from another U.S. radar. Although this boat was not identified by *Spadefish*, she was believed to be *Peto*.

Peto had managed to sink two marus from Convoy MI-27 during the early hours of 18 November. Following her first transport sinking on 17 November, *Sunfish* had managed to finish off another crippled MI-27 transport. Underwood's Urchins had destroyed an aircraft carrier, an escort ship, two freighters and two troop transports in less than eight hours.

Spadefish made radar contact with another ship at 0530, range 14,000 yards. Commander Underwood closed to investigate, finding a small escort searching the area. He elected to turn away and leave this escort alone, as daylight was approaching and one running fight with escorts for one morning was enough.

Underwood assumed this to be the remains of *Peto*'s contact. At 0610, he ordered *Spadefish* submerged about 60 miles southwest of the Ko To light. "All hands needed a quiet day to recuperate."

As Paul Majoue recalled, the captain allowed Chief Pharmacist's Mate Ives to go through the boat and offer a shot of the medicinal whiskey to any willing hands as celebration. "The medic had a key to the cabinet and passed out an ounce of bourbon to all of us to celebrate," recalled fireman John Brewer.

After a long night of sinking two Japanese men-of-war and a near fatal mishap under the blazing guns of a Japanese escort vessel, there were many willing partakers happy to see Chief Ives.

10

Luau's Litter

Second Patrol   *18 November–12 December 1944*

    The quiet hours of patrolling submerged on 18 November were much appreciated by all hands. The motormacs surveyed their engines and found them none the worse for wear after the life or death emergency flank speed running.
    Throughout the day, the sound watch picked up distant depth charges. *Spadefish* surfaced at 1815 and at 1840 picked up SJ interference from another sub, but could not identify her.
    Radar contact was made on Ko To at 0359 on 19 November. One minute later, the APR radar detector picked up sweeping radar on 160 megacycles. This was believed to be a land-based radar set on Ko To. At 0600, this radar set steadied onto *Spadefish*, so the sub dived 18 miles northwest of Ko To for the day.
    She resurfaced that evening and ran throughout the night without any contacts. She submerged at 0611 on 20 November, 15 miles northwest of Kokuzan To. Two distant explosions were heard during the morning and an enemy aircraft was sighted at 10 miles distance. The plane did not close and *Spadefish* remained surfaced. At 1252, a ship's mast was sighted, bearing 100°T, range about 10,000 yards.
    By 1312, the sound watch could hear pinging in the direction of the ship sighted. At 1400, the mast was no longer in sight, and pinging was no longer heard. Captain Underwood decided "it was a patrol boat sweeping the area." At 1750, two masts were sighted by periscope just as dusk was falling. By the next scope observation, however, the darkness was enough that the masts could not be observed again. At 1807, there was nothing in sight at 55-foot depth, so Underwood decided to surface early.
    Spadefish rose to the surface 13 miles southwest of Kokuzan To and sighted two ships bearing 070T, distance 11,000 yards. Although it had been too dark to see them through the periscope, they were plainly visible on the surface. Underwood turned away from them,

hoping they hadn't sighted his submarine. The SJ had radar contact at a range of 26,500 yards in the direction of the masts that had been first sighted at 1750. This first contact was lost as *Spadefish* drew out of sight range of the close ships.

At 1830, Japanese radar interference was picked up at 080°T. *Spadefish* changed course at 1835 to regain contact with the target contacted at 26,000 yards. The radar team was unable to make contact on this target again. They did, however, pick up radar interference from this direction which drew rapidly to the right, indicating a high speed target headed southwest. *Spadefish* pursued at high speed but was unable to overtake this target. She then sent contact reports to *Peto* and *Sunfish*, then headed back to the position of her original sight contact.

A frustrated Gordon Underwood was unable to make any further contacts this night.

> Decided we had surfaced in the vicinity of two convoys; one a high speed group that headed SW, the other apparently turned back, heading east past Kokuzan To. During the whole of the above operations the radar at 160mc, on Kokuzan To, had been steadied on us. This radar seems to steady on us at any range up to 25 miles.

Captain Underwood had to give up on ship chasing at 2158 and head for *Spadefish*'s plane guard station for the following day. She arrived on station at 0430 on 21 November, 30 miles south of the west tip of Saishu To. At 0956, the watch spotted a group of B-29s passing overhead.

At 1118, one of the lookouts sighted planes in the clouds overhead. Lieutenant Gus Laundy sounded the diving alarm. As he was clearing the bridge, he identified the plane as a B-29 headed back. *Spadefish* returned to the surface quickly. Captain Underwood advised his watch officers to "identify planes before diving." Buck Miller, one of the lookouts who had been topside with Laundy, fully agreed with his OOD's decision. "Precaution came first," Miller thought.[1]

Spadefish was surfaced at 1123, and during the next hour several groups of B-29s passed overhead. Torpedoman Hugo Lundquist was standing watch on the conning tower shears this day. His journal entry for 21 November reads: "They came over us about 10 a.m. and back at 11:30. Quite a beautiful sight. Tokyo Rose said 85% shot down—very bum dope."

At 1215, in response to plane number 394, *Spadefish* was sent "his course and distance to us. He apparently was in trouble." Ens. Bill Ware would later find out that these B-29s were part of the 40th Bomb

Group. On 21 November, the 28 planes from the 40th (in conjunction with 31 other B-29s) had made a daylight bombing mission against industrial targets on Kyushu Island, bombing the aircraft factory at Omura. Major Donald W. Roberts' B-29 sustained damage from Japanese fighters and headed out over the Yellow Sea to try and shed the fighters and nurse his crippled B-29, called "Last Resort," back to base. Major Roberts made contact with *Spadefish*, whose call signal that day was "Funny People."[2]

Auxiliaryman Buck Miller recalled "Little Fox" Sergio, with his heavy New England accent, using direct voice radio to try and bring the pilot in. "The pilot probably thought we were Japanese trying to trick them, as only Japs would give an exact position," thought Miller.

The crew of "Last Resort" was: Major Roberts, co-pilot Lt. John C. Harvell, bombardier Lt. Harold W. Dickerson, navigator Lt. Raphael V. Ford, flight engineer F/O Elmo Gray, radio operator Staff Sergeant Howard T. Anderson, central fire control gunner SSgt Rolland W. Geisler, left gunner SSgt Irving W. Smith, right gunner Sgt Everett J. Nygard, radar operator SSgt Charles W. Sullivan, and tail gunner SSgt Jack L. Mueller.

Last Resort had lost her number 4 engine and had suffered damage to two others, one of which failed for a time. While Major Roberts struggled to move out from Kyushu, radio operator Howard Anderson attempted to raise *Spadefish*, as he recalled:

> Major Roberts told Ford to try to get us headed to the area of the Yellow Sea where the submarine *Spadefish* was on lifeguard air rescue duty, as it looked doubtful for us to stay airborne on only two engines to get back to China.
>
> I attempted radio contact with the sub on the emergency frequency. I encountered some difficulty because the gunners had shot away the fixed wire antenna leading up to the vertical stabilizer for use with main liaison radio. I set the emergency frequency up on the high frequency 274N command radio, as it utilized a different antenna.
>
> I started contacting "Funny People" (the call sign of the submarine). There was some confusion at first in proper code authorization; however they gave us their coordinates using the grid map system and informed us to "Come on down; we will pick you up."
>
> It was evident that he was surfaced and eager to help us as he gave the distance and bearing to fly to his position. Now, that was a good feeling to us because by now there were no other B-29s in sight. At least we weren't all alone out there.[3]

Major Roberts ultimately decided to try to make friendly territory in China, but his radio operator was unsuccessful in alerting *Spadefish* as to this fact.

Spadefish's patrol report notes that at 1242, "after much heckling over identification and authentication, plane 394 decided we were friends and asked for another course and distance to us from his position. He apparently didn't like our position, too close to Saishu To, and headed over towards *Peto* and *Sunfish* position."

At 1331, Underwood directed *Peto* to send her position to the B-29 pilot. At 1335, *Spadefish* heard *Peto* send her position to the plane. At 1354, the plane, through *Peto*, requested that *Spadefish* transmit. At 1409, *Spadefish* could hear *Peto* talking with the plane. "We could not hear plane. Nothing more was heard," noted the patrol report. "We didn't know if plane had ditched or not, and if so, where."

At 1559, *Spadefish* left her plane guard station and headed in *Peto*'s direction in case the B-29 had crashed in between their areas. At 1839, *Spadefish* sighted a green flare on the horizon and headed in that direction. Upon reaching the approximate location, she searched the area, firing green flares at various times. No more flares or lights were seen. Still unaware that the B-29 crew had not ditched in the ocean, *Spadefish* patrolled in this area during the night.

Captain Underwood finally began clearing this area at 0645 on 22 November. He had not received any word of an aircraft being down, so he headed west to clear the vicinity. "After all the radio activity of the last 18 hours, the Japs must know we were there."

Spadefish headed for surface patrol about 60 miles southwest of Kokuzan To. During the day she sighted a large amount of wreckage, life belts, a dozen or so dead Japanese sailors, and two empty life boats. Two paravanes were seen. Only one mine was sighted this day. Her gunners also got in some target practice, destroying "one well equipped life boat with 20mm fire."

At 2133, *Spadefish* exchanged calls with *Sunfish* over the SJ. At 0049 on 23 November, the SJ picked up a different radar interference. It appeared at first to be Japanese, but further closing it turned out to be another SJ, identified as being *Peto* further off shore than she had been expected.

At 0530, a radar contact was made at 2,800 yards. This small dark shape was tracking at only 2 or 3 knots, and was determined to be a fisherman. *Spadefish* conducted a surface patrol west of Kokuzan To and her lookouts sighted a total of seven mines. Underwood allowed his bridge gun crews to have a little more target practice on floating mines this day. They riddled two with bullets, but the mines simply sank without exploding.

At 1105, the watch sighted a ship bearing 196°T, distance 15,000 yards. It was identified as a small patrol boat, a converted yacht type. OOD Gus Laundy put it astern and drew out of sight from this vessel, which appeared to be headed for Kokuzan To. Chief Scherman's cooks served up their Thanksgiving best on 23 November, complete with "Mother" Riley's signature holiday pies.

Spadefish did not submerge again until 0621 on 24 November, having run on the surface nearly 24 hours. She slid under in the midst of a fog bank off Ko To. At 1045, sound picked up screws on the JP sonar, bearing 297°T. Nothing was in sight through the periscope however, as visibility was down to only about 500 yards.

The fog did not lift much until 1209, when it raised just enough for the watch to spot two motor sampans. From their actions it was believed they were patrolling the area, likely in search of American submarines. *Spadefish* surfaced at 1820 and at 1848 exchanged calls with *Sunfish* over the SJ. "In exchange of information in view of possibly rendezvous, it was found that the *Sunfish* was over 90 miles from us," wrote Underwood. "A good record for communication by SJ interference."

The next four days passed with little to speak of. *Spadefish* dived at 0625 on 25 November and spent the day submerged off Rashu Gunto. Her only luck was the sighting of sailboats and sampans during the day. She returned to the surface at 1815 and ran through the night without sightings.

Underwood patrolled on the surface west of Kokuzan To on 26 November. His lookouts found only six floating mines and considerable wreckage during the day. *Spadefish* ran surfaced through the night and into the early hours of 27 November. At 0440, radar contact was made on Mansoi To, bearing 340, distance 20 miles.

In the early morning light, lookouts made an uneasy discovery this morning. "There's an object in the water," announced the port side lookout. A minute later, F1c Jack Gallagher, standing watch on the starboard side of the shears, heard his buddy clarify, "The object is a man!"

Spadefish closed the distant man and Chief Boats Eimermann came up with a grapneling hook. As the distance narrowed, he could see that the man was dead. Soon, other bodies were spotted, some draped over squares of cork and other wreckage they had tied together. "They were all laying back with their faces up to the sky," recalled Gallagher. "It made you realize what kind of damage you did when you saw all these dead people." Another lookout, Hugo Lundquist, made the following entry in his journal for 27 November: "Ran through an area lousy with dead Japs and wreckage. Sank a mine with 20mm."

At 0615, *Spadefish* went under to patrol submerged this day, as fog and rain had made visibility very poor. The ship ran silent until returning to the surface at 1822. Captain Underwood, frustrated with his luck, sent a message to *Peto* and *Sunfish*, changing the patrol area.

On 28 November, the pack patrolled on the surface west of Dai Kokuzan Gunto, heading north for a new area. At 1007, the masts of a ship were sighted bearing 029. *Spadefish* started an end around. The watch identified this ship at 1120 as a catcher type patrol boat, too small for torpedoes. Since Ko To was only 17 miles away, *Spadefish* turned away and cleared the area. At 2330, *Spadefish* sent a message to *Peto* and *Sunfish*, changing the patrol area again.

Commander Underwood was now not of the mind to waste his precious days in unproductive areas. His pack would seek out targets of opportunity.

Moving toward a new area, *Spadefish* found better luck quickly on 29 November. She received a single ship contact report from *Sunfish* which stated that a contact was 80 miles south of *Spadefish* on a southerly course. She continued her surface patrol at the entrance to Sekimo Suido, a few miles west of the 10 fathom curve.

At 0755, radar contact was made on Tosan Kan, bearing 000, distance 48,000 yards. Navigation for Ted Ustick and quartermaster Jim Schuett was not taken lightly in this area. The chart for this locality showed that the depth was close to a mere 10 fathoms but the ship's SESE fathometer, known as "SUSIE," said otherwise, reading depths up to 34 fathoms at times. Readings were taken at half hour intervals during the patrol. In water of 20 fathoms or less, readings were taken every fifteen minutes. On this day, inside the 10-fathom curve, *Spadefish*'s SUSIE was used continuously. After a quick trim dive at 0842, *Spadefish* spent the morning patrolling on the surface. Visibility was poor due to rain and mist.

"Radar contact! Range 19,400 yards."

The dull morning finally picked up as the SJ watch found a shipping target at noon. Frank Alvis called the skipper, who in turn soon stationed his tracking party in the conning tower as *Spadefish* swung in the enemy's direction. This vessel, still unseen through the misty conditions, was tracked to be zig-zagging along a base course of 160 at a speed of 7.5 knots. As the range narrowed to 13,000 yards, Captain Underwood decided to not risk being spotted.

"Clear the bridge! Take her to radar depth."

At 1225, *Spadefish* submerged to 55 feet, where the tracking party could keep tabs on this ship with the radar. Radio technician Neal Pike called out the ranges from his radar scope until the distance between attacker and prey closed to 7,000 yards. The enemy ship was still

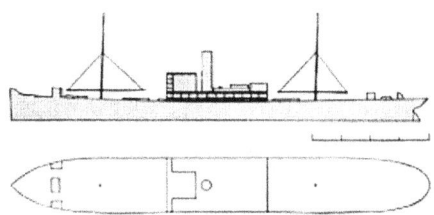

Recognition book image of *Daiboshi Maru*, a 3,925-ton freighter disintegrated by two *Spadefish* torpedoes on 29 November 1944. *ONI 208-J (Revised).*

obscured by fog at this time but Underwood eased down to 65 feet at 1243.

He and assistant approach officer Ted Ustick would take peeks at her through the periscope and not risk excessive radar use. As the potential victim continued to close, she was sighted at 3,500 yards. Underwood could only make out enough detail to classify her as a medium-sized well-decked Japanese freighter. She appeared to be proceeding alone down the coast of Korea with no escorts anywhere to be found. The persistent fog and rain made more accurate identification of this maru impossible for the moment.

"Make ready the bow tubes," Underwood called.

When the range had closed to 1,750 yards, *Spadefish* fired four Mark 14-3A torpedoes from the bow tubes at 1305. The first and fourth torpedoes were seen through the periscope and heard to hit. The target disintegrated and sank one minute after the second hit.

The tracking party estimated this freighter to be 4,000 tons. Postwar analysis by JANAC would show her to be the 3,925-ton *Daiboshi Maru No. 6*, while *Taisei Maru No. 6* was the name given her by Imperial Japanese Navy records.[4]

With no escorts in sight, Captain Underwood was prepared to surface to try and pick up prisoners. Fourteen minutes after firing on *Daiboshi Maru*, *Spadefish* hit the surface with her bridge gunners standing ready. Underwood proceeded to the point of the sinking, nosing his boat through the oil, wreckage and Japanese sailors who were scrambling to find flotsam to sustain them.

In his journal, torpedoman Hugo Lundquist wrote for 29 November: "Surfaced and invited Nips aboard. They refused. It was cold as hell and raining." In his patrol report, Underwood also noted the enemy sailors' reluctance. "Several survivors were seen. They all played dead when we came near. The sea was too rough to take any aboard forcibly, so abandoned the idea of taking a prisoner."

An hour after bypassing the freighter's wreckage, *Spadefish* had a new radar contact at 1444 on the SJ, bearing 067, range 19,420 yards. The tracking team was back to their stations again. The ship was tracked and was determined to be zig-zagging by constant helm on a northerly course. Captain Underwood doggedly pursued this ship, passing over some dangerously shallow 6 fathom water in the process. The enemy ship finally changed its base course to 040 and headed in to Kaishu Wan, forcing *Spadefish* to break off.

The shallow water was teeming with targets this day.

"Radar contact," came the next call at 1641. "Bearing 000. Range 12,000 yards."

With *Spadefish* still in water only 8 to 10 fathoms deep on the average reading, Underwood elected to head "for deeper soundings." The tracking team continued to plot the target vessel as their own sub sought safer depths from which to attack. The target was making 10 knots on a course of 230. Contact was lost at 1707. Now outside the 10 fathom curve, *Spadefish* changed course back toward the shallower waters to try to intercept the contact.

"Contact was not regained," recorded a dejected Gordon Underwood. "Target must have changed course to the NW and headed for the channel east of Daisei Gunto."

At 1815, the skipper abandoned his search and pursuit of this lone ship. Having only one torpedo remaining aboard ship, he set course to the south to clear the area. At 2213, *Spadefish* exchanged calls with *Sunfish* on the SJ. Underwood was informed that *Peto* had expended all of her torpedoes and was headed for the barn. *Sunfish* reported that she still had eight torpedoes remaining. He informed Captain Shelby of his own recent hunting grounds and wished *Sunfish* luck. *Spadefish* continued to haul clear of the 10-fathom curve. At 2255, her efficient radar made contact on Kakureppi Retto, distance 36,000 yards.

Spadefish continued to run on the surface on 30 November in search of targets worthy of her last torpedo. The watch sighted a ship at 1115, distance 15,000 yards. She was quickly identified as a patrol boat. Another engine was put on the line to draw out of sight of her. During the afternoon hours, three more floating mines were sighted.

Captain Underwood received permission from ComSubPac to return for a refit. At 0300 on 1 December, *Spadefish* departed her patrol area. Instead of the luxuries of Pearl Harbor, she had been assigned this time to the new advance submarine base at Majuro in the Marshall Islands chain. She ran on the surface, sighting nothing more than a Rufe fighter seaplane at 1501. The plane contact drew no closer than 15 miles, so *Spadefish* continued her surface run. At 1930, she passed through Tokara Kaikyo and set course for Majuro.

At 1958, SJ radar interference indicated another ship dead ahead. Moments later, *Spadefish* passed another friendly submarine, sighted from bridge at 3,500 yard range. No identification was made on her.

South of Honshu, *Spadefish* sighted the navigational landmark of Sofu Gan at 1245 on 3 December. Passing the tall rock pinnacle at 20 miles distance, she was now exiting Empire waters. Another Japanese fighter seaplane bid *Spadefish* good-bye, closing from 14 miles at 1253 and forcing her to dive to avoid detection.

Captain Underwood had cautioned his OODs to "identify planes before diving," after Gus Laundy had dived for a B-29 the previous week. Lt. Dan Decker and Lt.(jg) Perry Wood had the deck watch this early afternoon with auxiliaryman Buck Miller on the periscope shears portside and Shaky Jake Lewis on the starboard side. Lewis, one of the best lookouts aboard, called out this aircraft from a long distance, believing it to be a Japanese Zero fighter.

"Confirm identity," called Lieutenant Decker.

"It's Japanese!" called Lewis, as the enemy floatplane approached. "I can see the meatballs!"

Buck Miller had been anticipating the order to dive long before Lewis could plainly make out the red balls painted on the plane's wings. After "what seemed forever," Decker called, "Clear the bridge!"

Although the skipper's clear identification orders had been followed, Miller was much relieved at the welcome, "Dive! Dive!" calls. "I swear, as the diving alarm sounded, I was already swinging down from the lookout shears!"

Spadefish returned to the surface twenty minutes later and continued to head for the Marshalls. At 1500, a small ship was sighted at 16,000 yards. Commencing an approach, Captain Underwood soon found her to be a patrol boat or a large sampan. Hopeful that he could use his last torpedo on this vessel, he made an end around to head off the target. *Spadefish* submerged at 1622 for a final approach, but the target was obscured by a rain squall. Twenty minutes later, the target reappeared from the storm. Reluctantly, Underwood decided that the opportunity of making a deck gun attack against this vessel was not worth the risks.

> It is a shallow draft patrol boat. He had what appeared to be a 3" gun forward and several machine guns. Decided he wasn't worth a torpedo even if it would have hit. Would have had to fire across a heavy sea. It was getting dark so decided against a gun action.

In his journal, Hugo Lundquist recorded, "Almost battle surfaced,

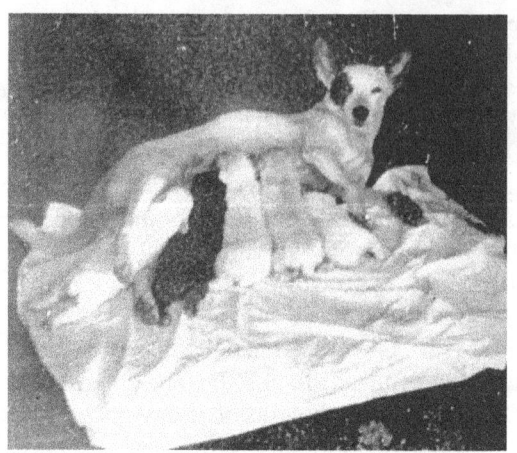

Ship's mascot Luau gave birth to six puppies on 11 December 1944, during the return from *Spadefish*'s second war patrol. The youngest male pup would also be adopted by the crew and make the future war patrols.
Hugo Lundquist collection, courtesy of Jeanne Lundquist.

but 'sampan' had radar and all guns manned, so we stayed down."

Spadefish surfaced at 1716 and proceeded on her course. During the next week, she ran uneventfully from Empire water toward the Marshalls. The newest officer, Ensign Don Martin, was rotated into the watch schedule by Ted Ustick. Martin paired with Dan Decker for the 8 to 12 and 20 to 24 watch schedules. Aboard ship, the new hands worked on their qualification notebooks, hoping to earn their dolphin pins as a fully qualified submariner. The leading petty officers continued schooling unrated men who were striking for specific ratings.

Returning from the patrol area, Chief Scherman and his cooks found that much of the food stores were running thin. Seaman Wallace McMahon found the usually excellent menu somewhat lacking at this point.

> By the end of the patrol, we were eating a lot of rice. All the fresh veggies were gone or rotted, especially the potatoes, so we ate a lot of rice. Captain Underwood loved Indian lamb currie, so we had quite a bit of that, whether we liked it or not. It looked green when it was on your plate. Of course, you could always make yourself a tuna fish sandwich.

As *Spadefish* approached friendly waters on 11 December, the radar contacts became more frequent on both shipping and aerial targets. One of the highlights of the second war patrol occurred this day as she neared Majuro. The lovable little ship's dog, Luau, finally gave birth to the puppies she had been carrying since leaving Pearl Harbor in October. Captain Underwood noted the event in his patrol report: "FLASH NEWS. Ship's dog, Luau, gave birth to the first of six pups."

The ship's history later documented, "During the night, Luau gave birth to a complete sextet of howling pups!"[5]

Junior OOD Don Martin logged at 2242, "First pup born by ship's mascot, Luau." The crew had made a little box for the expectant mama to rest in, and it was there that she began giving birth to her pups. "She delivered the dogs in a locker," recalled motormac Charles Griffith. Gunner Bernie Massar remembered, "The whole ship was awake for the birth, waiting for the results." Lieutenant Commander Ustick felt the birth of the puppies "added a little excitement to our activities that night."[6]

As the birth proceeded during the night, the drama was played out for all hands on the 1MC. "Now, Luau has number one," the talker relayed. The running commentary went on, as she gave birth to four more little white pups, all looking similar to mom.

And then, came the announcement, "It's a black one!" Luau's sixth and final pup was dark in color, looking something like a police dog. "It looked like a German shepherd," thought Boats Eimermann. "So, Luau had gotten pregnant from two dogs!"[7]

The following morning, *Spadefish* rendezvoused with her escort ship off the Marshalls at 1030. They steamed in company until 1330, when she reached Majuro Atoll. Majuro had been seized early in 1944 with the Marshalls. The submarine tender *Sperry* had arrived there on 12 April to begin handling submarine refits, now 2,000 miles closer to Japan than Pearl Harbor had been. Shortly thereafter, the newer sub tender *Bushnell* had joined *Sperry* at Majuro to service the increasing number of subs needing refits.[8]

The second patrol ended on 12 December, forty-nine days after departing Pearl Harbor. *Spadefish* had spent twenty-two days in her patrol area, twelve of which were submerged. Throughout the patrol, Don Martin's radar gang had given excellent results with their SJ radar. Twice, ranges over 90,000 yards had been obtained on Saishu To. Using radar keying, operators had also been able to communicate with *Sunfish* at a range of more than 90 miles on one occasion.

Her first war patrol under Gordon Underwood had ranked fifth best of the war in terms of ships sunk. *Spadefish*'s second war patrol ranked ninth best patrol of the war's 1,682 U.S. war patrols in terms of tonnage, with 30,421 tons sunk. As a result of both the first and second war patrols, the ship would be awarded the Presidential Unit Citation. Postwar analysis would show that *Spadefish* had sent a collective ten Japanese ships weighing 61,963 tons to the bottom of the ocean.

Spadefish crew alongside the submarine tender *Bushnell* at Majuro following their successful second patrol, during which they sank the Japanese carrier *Jinyo*. Note Luau on deck in foreground with her litter of pups. Holding the sign behind the dogs are Lt.(jg) Perry Wood and Lt. Dan Decker. Lt. Gus Laundy is right of Decker, with his arm across his knee. Officers standing are (left to right): Lt. Cdr. Ted Ustick, Captain Gordon Underwood, Ens. Ray White, Ens. Bill Ware (leaning forward) and Lt. Frank Alvis. *Courtesy of Dan Decker.*

This citation was given by the Secretary of the Navy, in the name of the President, to any ship or unit for outstanding performance in action against an enemy of the United States. The Presidential Unit Citation ribbon was regulation size, and consisted of three horizontal stripes of equal width in the colors of the Navy and the Marine Corps. From top to bottom, the stripes were Navy blue, gold, and scarlet. A star was authorized for each subsequent award of the citation.

In terms of confirmed sinkings, these two wolf packs under Loughlin and Underwood would prove to be among the most successful of the war. Their grand total of ships destroyed was 19 ships for roughly 110,000 tons.

Gordon Underwood would receive his second Navy Cross, allowing him to recommend awards for his *Spadefish* crew. The skipper spread the wealth, recognizing different men in every case from those whom he had selected for the first successful war patrol. Silver Stars went to electrician Dick Bassett, Lt.(jg) Perry Wood, and to Ensign Don Martin. Bronze Stars were awarded to chief Vic Ives, torpedoman Emery Kreher, and to Ensigns Ray White and Bill Ware.

During the refit period at Majuro, Captain Underwood received the confidential endorsement to his patrol report. He was credited with sinking four ships for 33,200 tons, including two freighters, a 20,000-ton carrier and a 1,700-ton destroyer. Through two patrols, *Spadefish*

USS *Spadefish* Second Patrol Summary	
Patrol Area:	Yellow Sea
Time Period:	23 October - 12 December 1944
Number of Men Aboard:	84: 75 enlisted and 9 officers
Total Days on Patrol:	49
Days Submerged:	12
Miles Steamed:	13,194
Fuel Used:	129,557 gallons
Number of Torpedoes Fired:	23
Ships Sunk, ComSubPac credit:	4 ships/33,200 tons
JANAC Postwar Credit:	4 ships/30,421 tons, including an armed sub chaser and the 21,000-ton aircraft carrier *Jinyo*
Shipping Damage Claimed:	one 10,000-ton tanker
	John Alden's 1999 research adds 6,600-ton tanker *Osakasan Maru* to *Spadefish*'s score (see appendix F for more details).

had been given credit for sinking ten ships for 73,200 tons and damaging three other ships for 24,500 tons. Unlike many World War II submarines' claims, those of *Spadefish*'s first two patrols would actually hold up very well to JANAC's analysis. Against ComSubPac's credit kill totals of ten ships for 73,200 tons, JANAC would list *Spadefish* as having sunk ten ships for 61,963 tons. Her crew was also awarded the Submarine Combat Insignia for this successful patrol.

Admiral Lockwood's endorsement, forwarded by Admiral Nimitz, said in part:

> This alert, aggressive patrol was one of the outstanding patrols of the war to date. Five expertly conducted attacks were made which resulted in four enemy ships sunk and one damaged. The series of three aggressive attacks made on the convoy the night of 18 November in the face of most severe enemy anti-submarine measures, which resulted in a CVE and a large escort being sent to the bottom and damage to a large tanker, was a feat deserving of the highest praise. The two other attacks made were equally successful and resulted in the sinking of two AKs.

Friendly Fire

Refit and Third Patrol   *12 December-6 January 1944*

The prospect of spending Christmas ashore on an island in the middle of the Pacific was not first choice in the minds of many a *Spadefish* sailor. Six months had passed since their ship had departed California, leaving all friends and family far behind. With the blistering tropical sun, the most appropriate holiday spirit found on Majuro was of the liquid variety.

Yeoman first class Irv Kreinbring was generally the last to leave *Spadefish* for R&R after a war patrol, as he tended to the necessary paperwork. Pay day upon arrival in port was anticipated by all. Kreinbring also prepared the paperwork for those who were being transferred, as he recalled.

> It seems we all "cliqued" together in groups of four when we left for rest camp. In my case, it was Vic Holeman, Johnny Brewer, and "Moon" Mullen that made up my group. It was always Vic who took my things with him and saved a bunk for me. I would have to stay aboard at least one day to transfer the "departees" and at the end of the

Yeoman Irv Kreinbring at work in his "office." In addition to handling the ship's payroll, personnel and administrative paperwork, Kreinbring served as one of *Spadefish*'s battle stations lookouts for night attacks and as a battle stations planesman when submerged. *Courtesy of Thomas Miller.*

Following two highly successful war patrols, the *Spadefish* crew enjoys a beer party ashore at Camp Myrna on Majuro Atoll in the Marshall Islands. Pictured are (l-r) Ens. Ray White, F1c John Brewer and TM2c Gus Cuthbertson. *Hugo Lundquist collection, courtesy of Jeanne Lundquist.*

rest period come back a day early to bring on the new men and get their names on the Watch Bill, to replace those who left.[1]

At the start of the second patrol, forty-seven *Spadefish* sailors had been qualified to wear the submariner's dolphins. By the end of the patrol, the ongoing school of the boat had successfully qualified an additional nineteen enlisted men. Irv Kreinbring also spread the welcome news that six men had been advanced in rating during the patrol, allowing them to draw additional pay.

The sub tender *Bushnell* and a relief crew from Submarine Division 141 began the refit while *Spadefish*'s crew departed for two weeks of R&R at the local submariners' camp. The men were ferried over to Myrna Island, where the rest camp was located. Auxiliarymen Dick Gamby and Whitey Harbison were dejected to find that there would be no easy place to reassemble the motorbike they had smuggled aboard the sub at Pearl Harbor.

Ashore, there was no Royal Hawaiian like Pearl had boasted. Captain Underwood did make the most of the available amenities of Camp Myrna, holding beer and barbecue parties for his crew. Among the palms and picnic tables, officers and enlisted men alike downed cold beers, played craps and toasted *Spadefish*'s recent successes.

Majuro was a coral atoll and lagoon in the Marshall Islands chain just 400 miles north of the equator. The vast lagoon inside this ring of coral islands could hold the entire Pacific fleet, if necessary. A narrow entry passage to the open sea was easily defensible against Japanese submarines. The islands offered visiting submariners lush varieties of coconuts, breadfruit, papaya, and other tropical delights to sample.[2]

The officers had a club on the beach and a recreation area. Lieutenants Frank Alvis and Dan Decker got to be pretty good horse shoe pitchers while in camp. One of the first nights after arriving, some of the *Spadefish* officers invited the chiefs down to their quarters to celebrate the success of the past patrol, with the sinking of a Japanese destroyer and an aircraft carrier. Boats Eimermann and his fellow CPOs found the "regular booze" to be quite effective. "We got plastered to the gills and began throwing records around their Quonset hut," Eimermann recalled. Not appreciating this reciprocity, the officers sent the chiefs back to tear up their own quarters.

The enlisted men had just as much of a chance to let loose. Radioman Mike "Little Fox" Sergio, the smallest man aboard *Spadefish*, spent many of his shore leaves with buddies Shaky Jake Lewis and Rebel Rewold. "How those two loved to get me loaded!" After a few beers, the "Little Fox" stretch contest became a favorite of some of the crew, as Sergio relates.

> I was the shortest sailor on board, at 5' 4" tall. After they would get loaded up on beers, Shaky Jake and Radford Rewold would grab hold of me for the "stretch test." My other good shipmates would each grab hold of a leg or an arm and pull like hell to stretch me out. I would scream bloody murder. The crazy things we would do for a few laughs!
>
> As soon as my shipmates turned me loose, over came Herman Cruze, who I believe was about 6' 4". Cruze would shout, "Hey, Little Fox, I believe you grew a quarter inch!"
>
> Herman would laugh like hell and say, "If they keep stretching you out like that, by the time the war ends, you'll be as tall as me!"[3]

Chief Paul Majoue and some of his buddies found another diversion. "We went sport fishing with hand grenades," he recalled. They took a borrowed rig that the refit crew loaned to them while their sub was being reprovisioned. "We'd go out in the rig, throw grenades over the side, and when they'd blow up, the fish would come to the surface."

Electrician's mate Jack Gallagher earned a new nickname during one of the ship's parties ashore at Majuro.

> We would take the torpedo alcohol ashore into the rest camp. One night, we had a big alcohol party around a bonfire. So, I was a young kid and I really got drunk on the alcohol. I staggered down to the beach and just passed out down there.

Spadefish crew enjoying a beer party at Majuro following second patrol. *Front row (l-r):* Roy Moody, Don Scholle, TM3c Thad Barton, S1c Bill Terboss, and CBM Willard Eimermann. Standing (l-r): MoMM1c Charles Griffith, FCS2c Andy Olah, QM3c Bob Maxwell, MoMM3c Walter Jerolmon, F1c John Brewer, GM3c Bernie Massar (white cap), TM2c Doyle Partin, TM3c John Schumer, TM2c Gus Cuthbertson, and EM3c Jack "Zombie" Gallagher (walking in distance). *Courtesy of Bernie Massar.*

The next morning, the Marine guards were driving by in a jeep and they saw me laying there. I guess some flies were crawling on me and they thought I was dead. They went up to the dispensary and got a doctor. When they came back down they discovered I was just passed out.

In the meantime, the word got around the rest camp that there was a dead man on the beach. When Gallagher's *Spadefish* buddies found out that the "dead man" was one of their own, he received no mercy from the ribbing.

Shaky Jake Lewis declared, "Look, it's the living dead man! It's the zombie." And from then on, he was "Zombie" Gallagher to the *Spadefish* crew.

A few of the crew would return to the sub sporadically to check on the ship and the work of the relief crew. One day in port, fuel king Charlie Griffith and his oiler, David "Pappy" Yocum had the battery charge duty in their forward engine room. Both men were pre-war sailors. Griffith had joined the Navy in 1939 and Yocum in June 1941, although Yocum was much older than Griffith. They had to wait out the battery charge with the one diesel left running. "Old 'Pappy' got tired," said Griffith. "He sat down against the secured engine, which was nice and warm, and he just dozed off. When the charge finished, I just shut down the other engine and left him sleeping."

A few days before Christmas, Captain Underwood and Ted Ustick were invited to visit another island. Several times each year, the Red Cross made inspection tours of the islands to see how the natives were being treated. The *Spadefish* senior officers and two other submariners were invited along with the Red Cross this day. Underwood and Ustick were accompanied by Commander John Howard Maurer and Lieutenant Commander Paul R. Schratz, skipper and XO of the submarine *Atule*, which was also at Majuro for refit.[4]

Schratz and Ustick were 1939 Academy classmates, so the day was like a reunion for them. On the little island, they found that the native people and their way of life was little changed. At noon, the villagers assembled in a town square to sell trinkets they had made since their last market day. Passing the local laundry, Ustick and Schratz saw a group of women beating their laundry with sticks.

Schratz found one young woman staring at him. "She began using her charms, including lowering her dress to bare a small, shapely breast, which she waggled at me shyly," he wrote. "I nudged Ted, but as soon as he looked she called off the show and became a prim maiden again. He claimed that she recognized he meant business."[5] To submariners, the tease was alluring, but the group moved on. The conditions on the islands were very primitive, and a tropical variation of syphilis was known to be widespread.

Spadefish crewmen spent their time at the rest camp, enjoying the beer parties, swimming, or playing softball. The island was only several hundred yards wide by perhaps a half mile long. On the main dock at Majuro, the water was crystal clear and men could watch octopus and other ocean life on the floor below. Softball was a favorite sport. Chief Eimermann served as pitcher of the team, which would prove to be consistently victorious against other sub teams during refits. The *Spadefish* crew was also challenged to a tug of war contest by another boat. "Our Captain Underwood was the anchor man," recalled participant Bernie Massar. "We won that, also."[6]

Motormac Dick Gamby, who joined one of the softball games as a second baseman, found himself very much out of shape.

> I got up to bat in the first inning. When you don't get any exercise on patrol, it's tough. I swung and hit the ball. It bounced to the short stop and I came running hard to first. I got a Charlie horse in both legs. That sudden exercise! I was cramped up and sore for weeks.

For Christmas, a midnight mass was held aboard the tender *Bushnell* for those interested, presided over by a padre who had been with the Marines in the forward areas of fighting only recently.[7]

"At Majuro, stale donuts and coffee by the Red Cross was our Christmas gift, and I don't drink coffee," wrote MoMM2c Buck Miller. Since he didn't care for coffee, Miller requested Chief Commissary Steward Scherman for tea bags. "To my surprise, he said, 'Let me see what I can do.' He delivered enough for the balance of the war and it was really appreciated."

For many, it was their first holiday season away from wives, kids or girlfriends. "We had a white Christmas, all right," reflected Paul Majoue. "White sand!" Despite the lack of a winter feel, Majoue and his buddies soon found some real Christmas "spirit."

> One of the boats came in while we were there. They had one torpedo tube that was filled with bourbon. We had a great Christmas, from what I can remember. One of the cases was buried, to be sure that after we got all crocked up, we would have some toddy again the next day if we wanted it. When we woke up the next morning, there were bulldozers out there leveling the sand. We had taken markings on trees to be sure we knew exactly where we had buried the case of booze. But nothing was there in the morning. It had been rolled over by the bulldozers. I guess the birds had a wonderful time!

By the time *Spadefish* was ready for sea again, Luau's puppies had grown considerably. One dog aboard ship was great for the crew's morale, but a whole litter was out of the question. One pup was left on Majuro, one was given to *Bushnell*'s crew, and three to other submarines on refit at the time. "Every other sub there knew we had the pups and they all wanted them," recalled Bernie Massar.

The runt of the litter, the dark colored male with the German shepherd features, was named Seaweed. "Seaweed was the funniest looking thing, with little two inch legs," said seaman Wallace McMahon. "He was faithful to his mom. Wherever Luau went, he was there. The guys in the forward torpedo room looked after them both." With the skipper's blessings, the crew was allowed to keep both Luau and Seaweed for the next patrol.[8]

One of those reporting back aboard following R&R was in rough shape. During a crew's party ashore at Majuro, "Little Fox Hole" Sergio overindulged with his partners in crime, Jake Lewis and Rebel Rewold. "They got me so drunk I couldn't even stand up. The yeoman, Irv Kreinbring, carried me aboard like a sack of spuds over his shoulder," recalled Sergio.[9]

Captain Underwood apparently witnessed Kreinbring hauling the drunken radioman aboard, but chose not to say a word. The next morning, he stopped by the radio shack, where Sergio was busy copying messages. "Fox Hole," said Underwood. "You are all dog on liberty, but you sure are all sailor on board ship. Be a little more careful on the beach."

"Aye, aye, Skipper." Sergio took his CO's advice as a friendly warning, instead of the severe dressing down he might have received from a less compassionate officer. "I always respected Captain Underwood for that."

One of the highlights of the R&R at Majuro was an awards presentation by newly-promoted Rear Admiral Babe Brown, the Deputy Commander, Submarines Pacific Fleet. A number of the *Spadefish* officers and crew were pinned with commendations earned for their actions on the first war patrol. Among those pinned was Captain Gordon Underwood, receiving the Navy Cross.

Bushnell's relief crew had finished *Spadefish*'s refit by 27 December. Post repair trials, sound tests and training exercises were conducted from 29 December to 3 January 1945. A coordinated night exercise was also conducted on New Year's Day with three other boats, *Pompon, Atule* and *Jallao*.

The early days of January were spent reprovisioning the boat for her next patrol. The *Spadefish* wardroom had remained intact for the first two runs, but Captain Underwood lost three key officers to transfers before his third patrol: Lt. Cdr. Ted Ustick, Lt. Frank Alvis and Ens. Ray White. Alvis was transferred to *Pompon* (SS-261), which would be operating with *Spadefish* on her upcoming patrol. Ustick, now a veteran of eleven war patrols, reported to PCO school to prepare for his own command. He commanded *Searaven* (SS-196) and later the newer submarine *Rock* (SS-274) before the war ended.

When Ustick left the boat, Boats Eimermann noted a couple of things missing. "We had $200 in case an enlisted man had to get home quick. When he left, all our big ashtrays left, and the $200." Eimermann sought out Captain Underwood to see if this met with his approval. "I'll handle it," the skipper assured his chief of the boat. "Those Academy guys!" thought Eimermann.

In place of the wardroom's losses, three new officers were received prior to the final training before leaving Majuro. Reporting aboard on 3 January as the new Exec was Lieutenant George Carlton Cook, a tall reservist from Quincy, Massachusetts with eight prior war patrols. Cook, 25, had graduated from the Massachusetts Nautical School in 1938 and was appointed ensign in the U.S. Naval Reserves in 1940. He served as an officer in the Merchant Marine before beginning active duty in February 1941 aboard the *USS Otus* for submarine instruction. After the outbreak of war, Cook joined *Searaven*, Ted Ustick's new boat and Ens. Bill Ware's former submarine.

On *Searaven*'s third patrol, she successfully evacuated a group of thirty-one Royal Australian Air Force aviators from the island of Timor in the Netherlands. *Searaven* spent the nights of 18 and 19 April 1942, landing rubber boats on a jungle coastline of the Japanese-held island. Ensign Cook was in charge of one boat and was awarded the Navy Cross for swimming ashore, and contacting the aviators. "Subsequently making several additional trips through the surf, he efficiently supervised the transfer of the sick and wounded men to his own ship and rescued two of them from drowning."[10]

George Cook made five patrols on *Searaven*, serving as her first lieutenant and communications officer. Transferred to the new boat *Guavina* (SS-362) in August 1943, he served as her engineering and electrical officer, earning the Bronze Star during his first patrol. He then served as executive officer and navigator of *Sargo* (SS-188) from July to December 1944. Much to the *Spadefish* crew's delight, Cook had a layed-back nature and did not restrict friendly wagering going on during the usual messroom games in off hours.[11]

Although the role of engineering and diving officer usually fell to a senior lieutenant, Ens. Ware—a mustang with nine war patrols under his belt—took over this post. On 4 January, Ens. Charles C. Johnson and Lt.(jg) Edward J. La Croix reported aboard. As the new "George," or lowest rated officer aboard, Johnson assumed the duties of commissary officer and assistant communications officer. La Croix became Bill Ware's electrical and assistant engineering officer. Dan Decker remained first lieutenant and plotting officer. George Cook set the watch schedules, using his three officers with the most war patrols under their belts—Decker, Gus Laundy and Ware—as OODs. Their JOODs would be La Croix, Lt.(jg) Perry Wood and Ens. Don Martin. Ensign Johnson, fresh from sub school, would work into the watch schedule only after being qualified.

The painful but necessary process of transferring qualified officers and men to other boats took twenty per cent of *Spadefish*'s crew prior to her third patrol. MoMM1c Rebel Rewold and SC2c Tom "Mother" Riley, the baker, were two of the more popular men who were transferred off on 13 December. With a little creative paperwork, Chief Eimermann managed to receive both men back aboard as replacements on 22 December. In the end, sixteen men were transferred off *Spadefish* and seventeen new faces arrived, bringing the ship's complement to 84—nine officers and 75 enlisted men.

Chief Radioman Majoue lost his first class radioman, Gerald

Newton, but gained two new men—Bill Mainard and radioman striker Thomas O'Neil—to fill in his watch schedule. "Little Fox" Sergio, promoted to radioman first class, became the senior member of the radio gang on Majoue's watch schedule.

Almost one quarter of the crew was advanced in rating during the refit period. Electrician Emerson Ordway, gunner's mate Jake Lewis, pharmacist's mate Victor Ives and motor machinist Carl Bieberdorf all moved into CPO country as newly promoted chief petty officers. Bieberdorf, a man of few words, was known to his buddies as "Silent Running Carl." He was in charge of the after engine room, while Charlie Griffith had the forward room. "Carl and I had the watch together sometimes when we were submerged," recalled Griffith. "We would sit there and talk for four hours. All Carl would say was, 'Yeah.' That's why we called him, 'Blabbermouth.'"

In Si Barnes' after torpedo room, TM2c Don Bird was transferred, replaced by seaman first class Bill Terboss, a torpedoman striker. Emery Kreher's forward room received S1c Olaf Bernard Olson on 13 December as a replacement torpedoman striker. Actually, his name when he reported aboard *Spadefish* was Olaf Bernard Sandleben, as he later explained. "My father died when I was in diapers. My mother remarried when I was two years old, so I always went under the name of Sandleben." After the war, he changed religion to Catholicism, and the priest asked him for a copy of his birth certificate. "So, I gave him the birth certificate that said my name was Olaf Bernard Olson." The priest was confused. "You told me your name was Sandleben," he said. "This says you are Olson. Who are you?"

Olaf promised to get a copy of his adoption papers from his mother, only to find out from her that he had never been legally adopted by his stepfather. He therefore went before the city of New York to legally change his last name back to his birth name of Olson. The papers came through two days before he was married.

Aboard *Spadefish*, Olson was assigned to the forward torpedo room. He also stood sound watches, topside watches, periscope watches, helm duty and bow and stern planes watches. He found that being a lookout required sharp senses and keen vision. "They had a contest going to see who could spot the most planes during the run," he remembered. "Shaky Jake was fantastic at that. I guess he was an old squirrel hunter, because he had an eagle eye. He could spot 'em before radar picked 'em up." Captain Underwood helped such new lookouts learn the art of clearing the bridge rapidly. "He was a big man," said Olson. "When you'd come down off the bridge on a dive, he would grab you by the shoulders, spin you around and drop you down through the hatch."

For her third patrol, *Spadefish* was going out in her third wolf pack. With ten confirmed sinkings under his belt from his first two runs, Captain Underwood would again command this pack. Operation orders called for Underwood's Urchins to return to the Yellow Sea, where shipping prospects remained hot.

For this foray, the Urchins would consist of *Spadefish*, Lt. Cdr. John Howard Maurer's *Atule* (SS-403), Lt. Cdr. Stephen Gimber's *Pompon* (SS-267) and Lt. Cdr. Joseph Bryan Icenhower's *Jallao* (SS-368). Underwood's Urchins were underway from Majuro at 0930 on 6 January 1945. Gordon Underwood was Group Commander of Coordinated Attack Group 17.23, in accordance with ComSubPac Operation Order 4-45. The destroyer *USS Ramsey* served as escort for the four-boat wolf pack as it put out to sea.

At 1420, *Ramsey* returned to Majuro. At this point in the Pacific War, the skies were so literally filled with aircraft that it became more commonplace for Allied submarines to come under attack by overzealous flyboys. *Pogy* was strafed by a U.S. Army Liberator while lifeguarding near Tokyo Bay. On April 8, 1945, *Bullhead* had another Liberator drop three bombs about 75 yards astern of the boat.[12]

Just six hours out of Majuro on 6 January, it was *Spadefish*'s turn.

For Seaman 1/c Alvin Gibson, a twenty-year-old from Tulsa, it was one hell of a welcoming aboard experience. Gibson had been the last man aboard *Spadefish* on 6 January, a last minute replacement hand from Submarine Division 141 who had been added to Yeoman Kreinbring's roster. "I came aboard that morning from the submarine tender *Bushnell*," he recalled. "They put me in the quartermaster gang as a striker, because I had been training as a signalman on the tender." Al Gibson was in the conning tower, learning the ropes with Jim Schuett's gang on his first afternoon out on a submarine war patrol. "All of a sudden, we did a crash dive and got down as quick as we could," said Gibson. "This was my first time to be bombed, but it felt pretty close to me!"

Running on the surface at 1615 in the safety zone, *Spadefish* was approached by two unidentified low wing monoplane aircraft. Gus Laundy had the watch at the time the planes were sighted. When the lookouts shouted a warning, the planes were coming straight in for the ship from 000°T, range 6 miles.

Lieutenant Laundy decided their action was unfriendly and dived. Attempts at raising these planes via IFS and radio signals were unsuccessful. "Our doctrine was, dive first, because all aircraft represent danger," Lieutenant Dan Decker related. In Laundy's haste to pull the plug, no bridge flares were initially fired.

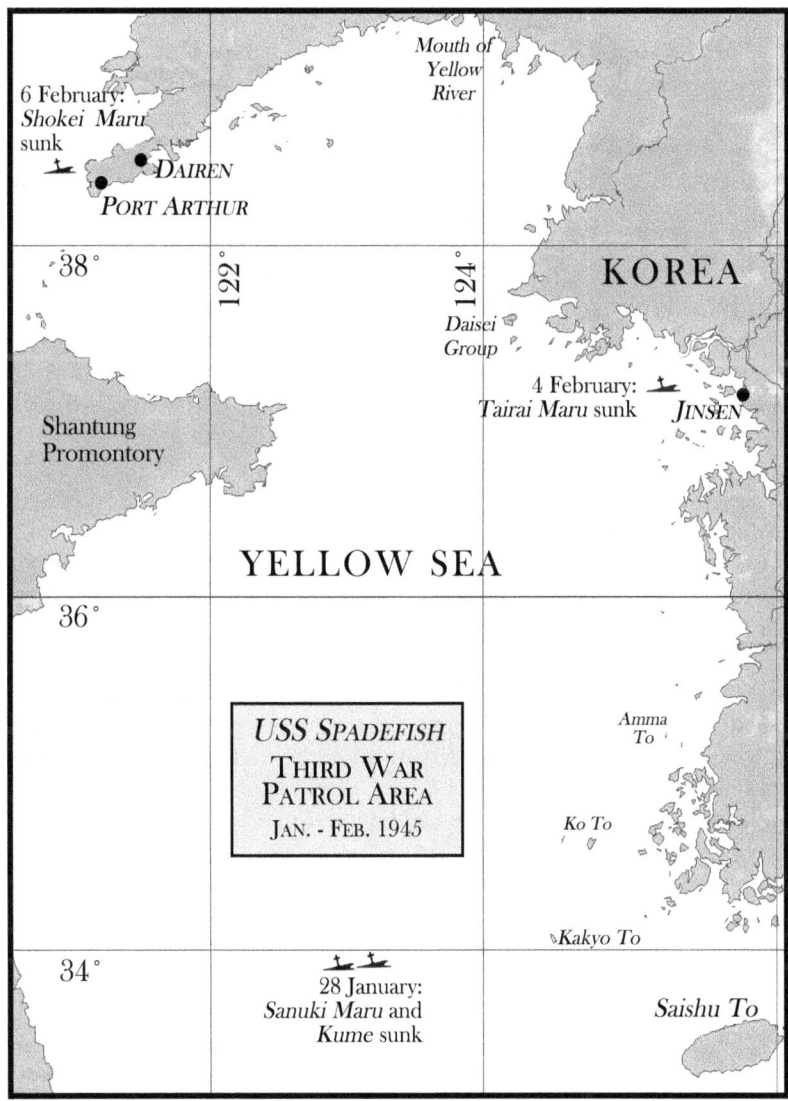

As she was going down, *Spadefish* was rocked by an explosion. Motormac Charles Griffith, on duty in the forward engine room, recalled, "By the time I shut the throttle down and closed the exhaust valves on the hydraulics, it was only a matter of a few seconds before this explosion went off right right over my head."

"We were down about 45 feet when the first bomb went off. The explosion felt close in the forward room, because the water is a tremendous acoustic transfer," said torpedoman striker Olaf Olson.

Captain Underwood then ordered one red smoke bomb to be fired from the after torpedo room as a recognition signal. The naval aviator, however, wasn't convinced of this submarine's nationality, and instead used the smoke signal as a point of aim for the next run. His second bomb exploded much closer to *Spadefish*.

The next sub in line, *Pompon*, made a crash dive upon sighting the Navy planes to avoid a similar attack as *Spadefish* had suffered. Captain John Maurer in *Atule* witnessed the entire attack. According to his Exec, Paul Schratz, the culprits were two low-flying Navy TBM Grumman Avenger torpedo bombers, which bracketed *Spadefish* with two aerial bombs. When the planes overflew *Atule*, Maurer's signalmen successfully exchanged recognition signals with the pilots to avoid a similar pasting. According to the *Spadefish*'s ship's history, first written in 1945, the two planes were U.S. Marine Corsairs.[13]

Certainly the aviators had been eager to make a kill in the safety zone and had not thoroughly challenged their "enemy" sub. In return, some felt that the failure of *Spadefish* to fire her emergency recognition flare as they first approached was an error. Chief Boats Eimermann counseled his bridge crew with, "What do you guys want us to do—get down and play with the fish?"

Although shaken mightily, *Spadefish* had not suffered any serious damage from the two bombs. At 1654, she surfaced and reported the incident to command at Majuro. The only damage sustained was a cracked bridge speaker and a few more specks in the periscope. "*Atule* was in sight when we surfaced," wrote Captain Underwood in his patrol report. "She asked if we had been bombed and stated the planes were friendly."

According to *Spadefish* history, the U.S. aviator responsible for attacking the ship was later confronted in Hawaii.

> A fitting end to the incident was the encounter between the ship's officers and the aviator at the Officer's Club in Pearl Harbor weeks later. The aviator professed to a conviction of the *Spadefish*'s enmity because she dove, offered his apologies, and ordered drinks all around.[14]

At the moment, however, the *Spadefish* crew was not in the mood to buy this persistent pilot a drink. "At that time, if we could have caught him, I think we would have killed him," said Bernie Massar.

"A Good Working Over"

Third Patrol 7-28 January 1945

Following the potentially deadly bombing attack, *Spadefish*, *Pompon*, *Atule* and *Jallao* proceeded en route to Saipan without incident during the next week, conducting the usual training dives and tracking exercises with each other along the way.

The wolf pack rendezvoused with their escort, *PC-1126*, at 0527 on 14 January. At 1144, *Spadefish* moored to the port side of the sub tender *Fulton* in Saipan. Captain Underwood received word that *Bang* (SS-385) would replace *Jallao* in his task group. *Spadefish* took on fuel, putting just enough fuel in the No. 4 fuel ballast tank so that it would run dry before reaching the Nansei Shoto. "Did not put blanks on the main vents of the ballast tank," noted Underwood. "Once the blanks were installed—the main vent for the No. 4 fuel/ballast tank—operated from the control room, could not be used," explained Lieutenant Decker. "When the fuel was used, the main vent to that tank could be opened and flushed out, making it a ballast tank."

At 0959 on 15 January, *Spadefish* was underway from Saipan en route to her patrol area in company with *Bang* and *Atule*. Together, these boats comprised Task Group 17.23, under command of Gordon Underwood. Another new boat, *Devilfish* (SS-292), was to accompany the pack until 17 January and then depart for her own area. *Pompon*, delayed in Saipan one day for repairs, was scheduled to catch up with the pack and patrol as part of Underwood's Urchins. *Spadefish*, *Devilfish*, *Bang* and *Atule* were escorted out by *PC-1126* until 1645, at which time she departed and the submarines proceeded independently toward their stations.

As the night passed to 16 January, the ship's clocks were set to -9 time to accommodate the time zone that *Spadefish* would be working in soon. At 1430, Hocks Majoue's radio gang received a dispatch telling of a life boat with one survivor in the water about 130 miles west of her position. *Atule* sent word that she was heading that way.

Underwood sent a message to CTG 17.7 asking if he wanted the entire group to search. A correction to the position of the life boat placed it northeast of the group, so Underwood ordered *Atule* to rejoin the formation. Several B-29 planes were sighted searching to the northeast, so it was decided that a rescue by plane would be affected.

Underwood's Urchins continued on their way, but at 2245, another dispatch was received. This one directed the wolf pack to make a 24 hour search for the raft in the first reported position. Underwood navigated his task group for the corrected position. *Bang* received the word from *Spadefish*, but *Atule* couldn't be raised. Underwood then asked Saipan for a verification of the corrected position.

At 0300 on 17 January, a new dispatch was received, directing *Spadefish* and her sister subs not to go east of Longitude 140E. As the location of the raft was considerably to the east of 140, the dispatch directed the task group to stop their search and proceed toward their patrol area. Sadly, the lack of good navigational data from the search planes may have cost the life of an aviator lost at sea. *Spadefish* again failed to raise *Atule*. The circuit guarded, 4155 kilocycles, was very heavily loaded. "A continuous jamming of the circuit by the Japs added to the difficulties," noted Captain Underwood in his patrol report.

Devilfish departed for her own patrol area on 17 January, leaving *Spadefish* with *Atule* and *Bang* to carry out their wolf pack patrol. The pack continued running on the surface on 18 January. The only encounter during this day was a friendly plane bearing 228, distance 13 miles. Although monitored with a higher degree of caution, this "friendly" did not close enough to warrant alarm. At 1644, an unusually high wave broke over the bridge, washing the port lookout, TM3c Thad Barton, out of the lookout platform. "Fortunately, he hit the life line and bounced back on the cigarette deck," *Spadefish*'s patrol report recorded. OOD Gus Laundy called for Chief Pharmacist's Mate Ives, who took Barton below to dress the lacerations in his face.

At 0651 on 19 January, *Spadefish* made a short trim dive and flushed out the No. 4 MBT. This tank was only partially filled with fuel at Saipan and had not been rigged as a fuel ballast tank. Fuel king Charlie Griffith went topside with motormac John Brewer, whom he was training to take over his position. "The captain told us that if a plane was spotted, we would have to dive," remembered Brewer. Although the process of crawling around in the superstructure with only a little two-cell flashlight took less than a half hour, Brewer felt "it seemed like forever." Sloshing around in cramped quarters and cold sea water, he was much relieved to finally go back below. "I was glad to get into my bunk."

At 1235, the watch spotted a flight of a dozen B-29s, bearing 100, distance 15 miles. *Spadefish* made VHF contact with them, and Captain Underwood had his wolf pack man the lifeguard frequency for the next six hours in case any of the aircraft needed assistance. During this time, the air search radar had friendly planes all over the screen.[1]

Spadefish dove for a day of submerged patrol at 0651 on 20 January. That evening, Underwood's Urchins began a surfaced transit of Nansei Shoto, the island chain dominated by Okinawa. At 1940, SJ contact was made with Yaku Shima, bearing 334, distance 82,000 yards. A weak signal was picked up on APR at 154mc. This was likely a radar station on Tanego Shima or Yaku Shima. Throughout the transit, various Japanese radar stations attempted to locate *Spadefish* by the signal given off by her SJ radar. "Believe they detected our SJ and steadied on the bearing, trying to pick us up," wrote Captain Underwood. By 0300 on 21 January, two Japanese radar stations were sweeping with their radar. "They don't steady as long as the SJ is not trained in direction of land," Underwood noted.

At 0820, the first of many floating mines that would be encountered on this patrol was sighted. Each mine, roughly thirty inches in diameter, was spherical, with four to six horns protruding from its upper surfaces. The remainder of the day brought only two more contacts, a Rufe plane at six miles and a patrol craft, sighted by high periscope and avoided.

At 0300 on 22 January, *Spadefish* entered her patrol area. She used her SJ radar at 0340 to exchange calls with *Pompon*, which had left Saipan one day late. Around sunrise, four small white lights were sighted on the horizon. *Spadefish* changed course to avoid. At 0850, the watch sighted the smoke of two patrol boats—distance 16,000 yards—through the high periscope. She changed course and speeded up to draw out of sight. At 0945, Underwood wrote that his watch had "sighted our two friends again. Changed course and speed to draw out of sight again. They seem to be patrolling same area we want to."

Spadefish sighted various lights on the horizon during the early morning hours of 23 January and avoided them. "These may be fishermen, but doubt it, as it is too far from shore," recorded Underwood. "Suspect picket boats, but why the lights? Estimated range 10,000 yards, but no radar contact, so they are small. Changed course to avoid."

At 2300, *Spadefish* sent a dispatch to *Atule*, directing her to shift area to the vicinity of Latitude 37N.

While at sea, the radio shack could pick up Tokyo Rose while surfaced. Her propaganda was very poor, and yet often quite entertaining for the crew. There were actually twenty-seven different female disc jockeys who worked on Japanese radio stations during the war, such as

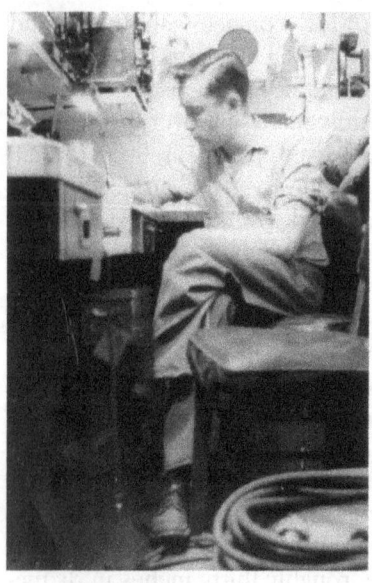

RM3c Ken Powers works on copying messages in the *Spadefish* radio shack. Tokyo Rose was a source of amusement for the crew while patrolling near Japanese waters. *Courtesy of Joe Marasco.*

NHK Radio Tokyo. They were all dubbed "Tokyo Rose," and their efforts to destroy the morale of the American servicemen close enough to pick up the frequencies on which they transmitted often had the opposite effect. Most submariners found her threats and sarcasm to be quite entertaining.[2]

On some occasions, Tokyo Rose would be put on the loudspeakers and pumped into the crew's mess. She knew enough to occasionally name the areas where certain subs were operating, naming them. On at least one occasion, Tokyo Rose broadcast claims that the submarine *Spadefish* had been destroyed.[3]

Lieutenant Gus Laundy carried out the morning trim dive at 0701 on 24 January. At 0802, she sighted a mine and let the gunners sink it with 20mm gunfire. At 1044, another mine was sighted, and again Underwood let his 20mm gunners sink it with gunfire.

"The gunners' mates and others were issued rifles and ammo for some target practice," recalled Lieutenant Decker, who had the deck watch with Lt.(jg) La Croix. *Spadefish* moved in to close range and the sharpshooters cut loose. Some mines would sink eventually, while others exploded, blowing icy water and hot mine fragments toward the ship. "About half exploded to the cheers of those on deck. Removing these mines was probably a wise thing to do, and it was great fun for the crew," said Decker. "A welcome change from the daily routine below decks!"

Whitey Harbison, who manned the after 20mm gun, had gotten to be an eagle-eye shot with his gun. "Harbison had real curly little blond hair, like he was gonna be bald," recalled Boats Eimermann. "He always looked like he was half asleep, but he'd get on his gun and he'd go *"Bah! Bah! Bah!* BOOM! 'What else you got?' he would ask."

Zombie Gallagher handled the forward 20mm. "We had an ammunition locker in the superstructure where we stored some of the big, round 20mm magazines," he recalled. "My loader put the magazines in my gun while I fired." Gallagher enjoyed the chance to shoot up the mines. "Some of them would just sink. Every once in a while, you'd get in a good burst and one of the mines would explode." Harbison brought his own energy into firing his gun. "Whitey would take his spot on deck and scream as he fired his gun. The captain really loved the show!" related shipmate Dick Gamby.

At 1450, a pip appeared on the SJ radar. "Radar contact at 10,000 yards, and lost same instant," noted Ens. Bill Ware in *Spadefish*'s deck log. He cautioned the lookouts to keep a sharp eye out and two minutes later, a Sally bomber was sighted bearing 100°T, distance 4 miles. "Clear the bridge!" Ware shouted.

Spadefish dived and stayed down until 1609. Enemy aircraft remained in the area as Gus Laundy and Perry Wood took the bridge with their lookouts. At 1735, another enemy plane was spotted, this time without warning from radar.

"Aircraft! Bearing 070, distance 10 miles!" called a lookout.

This plane was heading right for *Spadefish*, so Laundy pulled the plug again. A splash and a small explosion was heard at 1737, just after submerging. This was believed to be a smoke float hitting the water and setting off. Twelve minutes later, at 1749, one depth bomb exploded, but not too close. The plane had apparently circled before making another attack run later.

Spadefish resurfaced later and ran through the night without event. Lookout duty was tough on 25 January. Temperatures had fallen some sixty degrees in two days and snow flurries began falling this day. The four hour watches on the bridge were a far cry from the hot tropical sun of Majuro from two weeks earlier.

Spadefish spent the day of 26 January on the surface, patrolling about 50 miles west of Saishu To. During the early morning hours a heavy snow was falling, with strong winds which made lookout duty pure hell. Six mines were sighted during this day. The gunners exploded two and sank three with 20mm fire. The winds gusted up to 30 knots, driving sleet and snow into the miserable watch standers. Heavy ice began to accumulate topside from the freezing salt spray.

Lieutenant Decker explains how salty ice accumulated:

> Fresh water from all the rivers from China and Korea flowed over the top of the heavier, salt-saturated water underneath and continued to circulate counter-clockwise. Salinization was slow but much of the fresh water remained close to the surface, where it could be blown upwards by the winds. This spray, combined with the cooling effect of evaporation, was enough to make our boat accumulate serious amounts of ice. This ice added many precious seconds to our dive times in the Yellow Sea.

Spadefish moved in toward Kokuzan To during the early morning hours of 27 January. Japanese radar operators on the island were sweeping the area as *Spadefish* moved in toward her patrol station. At 0703, *Spadefish* submerged 20 miles south of Kokuzan To. During the morning, visibility was somewhat reduced by snow piling on the periscope windows. *Spadefish* stayed submerged throughout the day and surfaced at 1839 in the bitter cold. At 1915, she received a message from *Pompon* giving information on a six-ship convoy headed west across the Yellow Sea. Captain Underwood immediately set course to intercept. At 2132, a floating mine was sighted and avoided.

At 2315, the watch sighted smoke bearing 302. At 2318, radar made contact at 18,000 yards with three ships on the bearing of the smoke. *Spadefish* also picked up SJ interference. "*Pompon* must be getting ready for an attack," wrote Captain Underwood. By 2354, *Spadefish* had determined that *Pompon* was on the starboard flank of this convoy and Underwood commenced an end around to port.

Bill Ware and Don Martin took over the watch at midnight. Ten minutes later, three large ships and one smaller one were sighted, range 16,000 yards. "There was a full moon and it was directly overhead," Underwood reported. "What we wouldn't have given for a dark night. Commenced getting indication on our radar of several Japanese radars." Underwood much preferred the maneuvering options he had with a surfaced night attack to a periscope attack.

At 0011 on 28 January, *Spadefish* sighted several small lights on the horizon. These must be lighted picket boats again. "We had to pull out away from them." They were about 10,000 yards off the convoy track (base course), which was now 250 degrees.

At 0025, radar had contact on a single ship at 22,000 yards. *Pompon* sent a message stating that she was attacking a convoy from starboard. This message was erroneously reported to Captain

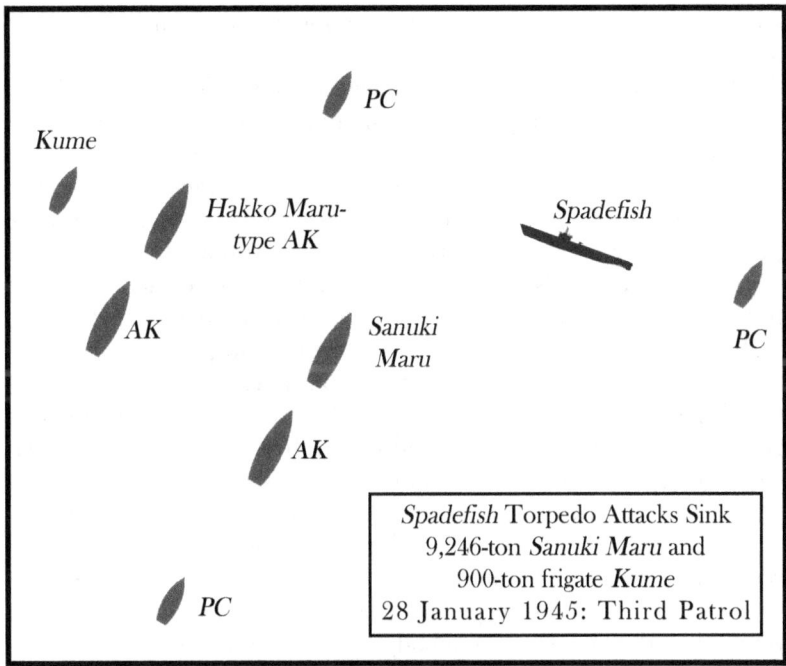

Spadefish Torpedo Attacks Sink 9,246-ton *Sanuki Maru* and 900-ton frigate *Kume*
28 January 1945: Third Patrol

Underwood on the bridge as *Atule*, leaving him with the belief that both *Pompon* and *Atule* were after this convoy, as well as *Spadefish*.

At 0054, the convoy suddenly reversed course. *Pompon* had evidently been detected. At 0114, the *Spadefish* lookouts saw signals from the convoy. They then changed course and came back to the base course 250, speed 13 knots.

At 0134, *Spadefish* sent a message to *Pompon* and *Atule* that she was attacking from the port side. During the approach, *Spadefish* received a message from *Atule* at 0143 asking for the position, course and speed of this convoy. Thinking that *Atule* was already making an approach, Underwood only had the course and speed sent out.

At 0159, *Spadefish* dived at a position about 5,000 yards off the base track, at a range of 16,000 yards to target. The nearest escort was at about 14,000 yards. Underwood continued his approach at radar depth, going to periscope depth at 7,200 yards range. Pinging could be heard from four separate escorts.

At the time of diving, the convoy was in two columns of two ships each, distance between columns 2,400 yards; interval between ships 1,000 yards. The leading ship in the starboard column was the largest. Two escorts were ahead. Two others were astern somewhere, but they could not be located. The convoy, apparently four freighters escorted by four escorts, made two zigs to the left and then back to the base course. "This placed us right in front of the convoy, almost broadside to the two escorts," wrote Underwood.

One of the two escorts passed ahead of *Spadefish* by about 1,000 yards. The other passed astern at a mere 500 yards as the submarine ran silent, waiting for the setup to fire on the unsuspecting marus. The conning tower was dead silent as the men of war bracketed *Spadefish* on both ends with their echo-ranging gear clearly audible. "Both were pinging horribly," wrote Underwood, but they continued on by.

In Emery Kreher's forward room, the tubes were made ready to fire. His newest trainee, S1c Olaf Olson, worked the gyro angle setter, making sure that the TDC's angle setup was properly cranked into each torpedo. Kreher, Wallace McMahon, Hugo Lundquist and Gus Cuthbertson stood at the ready to make any other adjustments that ship's talker Vic Ives might call down from the conning tower. Torpedoman 3/c Don Anderson, making his second patrol, had been selected to wear the headset to take the orders from the conning tower. "I think they chose me because I didn't have any Southern accent," he recalled. "I was a little more easy to understand."

"We'd write on the torpedoes just before we fired them," Olson remembered. "We'd put somebody's name on one, or 'Here's to you, Hirohito!' and that kind of stuff." Anderson also recalled that, "Once in a while somebody would put their girlfriend's name on the torpedo."

Spadefish was making 4 knots, submerged at 65 feet depth. Captain Underwood and his assistant approach officer, George Cook, made their final preparation for firing.

"Up scope," the skipper called. He dropped the handles and rode the scope up from the deck. "Bearing—mark!" called Underwood.

"Two-seven-oh," Jim Schuett read from the rings.

"Range—mark!"

Schuett read 1,500 as the skipper estimated the angle on the bow of the target ship.

"Set!" called Gus Laundy, indicating that the TDC's analyzer section and angle solver were both static, as were the gyro angles on the torpedoes.

"Fire one!" called Underwood.

As Chief Ives relayed the order over the battle phones, Lieutenant Cook pushed the electric firing button in the conning tower. As Anderson relayed, "Fire one!" from the headset in the forward room, Kreher manually fired as well. Anderson then repeated back to the conning tower, "One fired."

Two more torpedoes were fired from tubes 2 and 3 in the forward room, all three aimed at the large cargo ship which was leading the star-

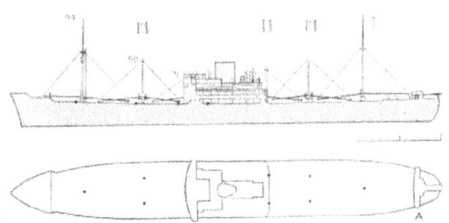

Sanuki Maru, a 7,158-ton seaplane tender converted into a 9,246-ton merchantman in 1942, was sunk by *Spadefish* on 28 January 1945 during her third war patrol. *ONI 208-J (Revised)*.

board column. The tracking party had estimated her range of 1,500 yards, but the count on the torpedo run had only reached twenty seconds when—*boom*! The first torpedo exploded with a resounding detonation, indicating that the target was much closer than had been estimated. The distance was timed to be half what was originally thought, or 750 yards! All three torpedoes hit. "When last seen, target was listing heavily to port, surrounded by smoke and flying debris."

As soon as the third forward tube was fired, Captain Underwood swung his boat around to bring his stern tubes to bear. Keeping his depth setting at 6 feet, he ordered all four of Si Barnes' after tubes fired at 0233. The second freighter targeted was the leading ship in the port column, an engine aft cargo ship. From the ONI-209J book, this AK was determined by the conning tower identification team to be of the *Hokko Maru* type.

Although his first target ship was clearly seen to be sinking, Captain Underwood did not have the luxury to monitor his second target for long. The second ship in the convoy's starboard column turned with a zero angle on the bow toward *Spadefish*. She was at 1,000 yards and coming on fast.

"Take her down!" the skipper hollered.

With the enemy escorts fully alerted and charging down her throat, the normal protocol for *Spadefish* would be to "run silent, run deep." In the wading pond known as the Yellow Sea, however, she had a mere 180 feet of water to hide in. Underwood had Bill Ware take her to 120 feet and evade. The boat was now "rigged for depth charge, awaiting our turn."

As *Spadefish* descended, there was "one definite hit and explosion" that was noted on this second ship. This was timed to be the No. 9 torpedo exploding. A second torpedo was believed to hit but failed to explode. Firing in a spread, misses were expected in order to achieve at least one good hit. Captain Underwood attributed the other two misses to this ship making evasive maneuvers after her sister ship exploded nearby.

The track was large and target may have started turning due to torpedoes hitting target of Attack Number 1, causing misses with other torpedoes. A sharp crack was heard by everyone in the boat at the time Number 7 should have hit. There was no explosion and this may have been a dud.

There was no time to curse torpedo performance, as the angry swishing of enemy screws could be plainly heard. *Spadefish* reached 120 feet at 0235, just two minutes after firing her after tubes. In the control room, Irv Kreinbring and Jake Lewis operated the planes by hand, with the hydraulics shut down for silent running. Bernie Massar and Maurice Noonan stood by to relieve them, as the heat increased throughout the boat. Rigged for silent running, the tense sailors were not the only ones perspiring from the heat. "Them old walls would just sweat," remembered torpedoman John Schumer in the after room. "Water would just pour off of them."

Spadefish did not have long to wait. At 0238, the first depth charge detonated with shaking force. "They were big ones, dropped singly," Underwood wrote. "Three escorts were working on us. One pinging, one listening, and one doing the dirty work." He considered this trio "a very efficient hunter-killer group." Sound conditions were not good in this vicinity, put these three escorts would prove to be quite successful. They used their depth charges sparingly, waiting until the listening ship had a good fix on the enemy sub.

Even the old hands found depth-charging to be a tense experience. Chief Carl Schmelzer had already survived some fierce ashcan explosions during his seven war patrols prior to joining *Spadefish*. "One time we were depth charged so much that a filling fell out of my tooth," he recalled. His submarine had taken such a beating "that all the tobacco in my cigarettes was shaken out." Schmelzer found that there was little to do but "sit and sweat and pray" as the ashcans thundered overhead. The really close explosions sounded to him like "ten thousand hammers hitting the hull all at once." As soon as one exploded, however, his concerns immediately shifted to "worrying about where the next one will fall."[4]

Each time one of the escorts raced in to deliver another ashcan, the screws of the attacking ship could be heard through *Spadefish*'s hull. At her shallow depth of 120 feet, she was particularly vulnerable. "The captain had made a wise choice of depth," notes the ship's history, "for the escorts were setting their charges to explode near the bottom."[5]

Another saving grace for *Spadefish* was Underwood's effective maneuvering of his boat. He often used a "knuckle" system to create false echoes for the attacking destroyers. "The echo ranging was loud

Spadefish's torpedoes also found the 900-ton destroyer-type frigate *Kume*, which had been one of the escorts for the carrier *Jinyo* in November 1944.

and clear," recalled Dan Decker. "When the destroyer shifted from long range to short range echo signals, we knew the depth charges would shortly follow." As soon as the escort went to short range echoing, Underwood would order a speed increase and then make a sharp turn at the last second. "This sharp, fast turn created what we called a knuckle—a very turbulent area on which the attacker could echo range," explained Decker.[6]

The thoroughness of these escorts was an indication of how effective *Spadefish*'s torpedoes had been. Postwar intelligence would show that she had sunk *Sanuki Maru*, a former seaplane tender that had been converted in August 1942 to a troop transport. JANAC credit officially gave *Spadefish* 7,158 tons, although Imperial Japanese Navy had *Sanuki Maru* listed as 9,246 tons in 1952. Japanese convoy records showed that *Sanuki* sank at 0313, Japanese time, with many casualties. The second ship torpedoed by *Spadefish* during the early morning hours of 28 January was no merchant ship at all, but one of the escorts! The No. 9 torpedo had found the 900-ton frigate *Kume*, the same escort which had been part of the carrier *Jinyo*'s convoy on the previous patrol. The sound of the dud torpedo hit was likely against the hull of the original freighter target. *Kume* burned for some time and eventually sank, taking 140 sailors to the bottom with her.[7]

The loss of a large troop transport and the sight of sister frigate *Kume* belching smoke and fire gave passion to the Japanese men of war working *Spadefish* over this night. After the fourth depth charge, the sound operators picked up some odd noises. "Several times a group of noises were heard that sounded like the splash of objects thrown into the water," wrote Captain Underwood. "No explosions were heard, however."

Just prior to the fifth depth charge's explosion, everyone aboard figured out what was causing the splashing sounds. A series of metallic sounds indicated that the escorts were dragging something along the ocean's bottom, which was just 180 feet. The depth charging ceased for the moment as the enemy screws above continued to crisscross the area. The dragging noises drew closer and a loud *clank!* was heard as something slammed against *Spadefish*'s hull.

"We thought we were hung up on something at first," recalled Don Scholle, who was busy keeping the quartermaster's notebook.

The chilling realization suddenly hit home. "They're dragging for us!" someone called out.

The initial metallic *clank* against the hull was followed by lesser grating sounds as the metal object bounced along the starboard side of *Spadefish*'s hull. Believed to be a chain or heavy wire, the scraping sound could be heard plainly in all compartments. "You could hear it rubbing up against the side of the boat," recalled Chief Paul Majoue. "You could hear it clearly without the sound gear."

Seaman Al Gibson was in the control room when he heard the chains dragging on the hull. "We knew then that they had us located and would be dropping more depth charges," he said. "There was not much we could do except say a few prayers and try to get the hell out of their way as best we could."

In the maneuvering room, electrician Ken Sigworth listened as the cable scraped by on the pressure hull within six feet of where he sat. "It was pretty scary hearing them scratching on our hull." The biggest fear was if these wily Japanese could actually snag an obtrusion with their grapnel hooks. If the grapnel would hold against a deck rail or some equipment protruding from the conning tower, the depth charging process would become a cake-walk. In gunner Bernie Massar's mind, it would be the kiss of death. "We'd be like a fish with a bobber. Wherever we went, they could follow us and drop depth charges on us. The sound of the grapnel scraping along us made my hair stand on end."

This grapnel-dragging technique was not unheard of. On 6 May 1944, a group of anti-submarine vessels had pinned down *Crevalle* after she sank a huge 16,800-ton tanker under their charge. Lying silent on the bottom in 174 feet of water, *Crevalle* was actually snagged by one of the sub chasers' grapnels. Being neutrally buoyant, she was literally dragged along the bottom of the ocean. Her skipper eased her off the bottom and then ordered flank speed to snap the grapnel. Upon return to port, her crew found a one-inch iron ladder rung on the starboard side of the fairwater had been straightened out and fractured at one end.[8]

Fortunately for *Spadefish*, these escorts were unable to snag her with their grapnel. By brushing her with his cable, however, one escort was able to determine a good fix on his prey. The next depth charge, the fifth dropped, was another blockbuster. It was set to explode on the bottom, for it went off directly beneath *Spadefish*, shattering light bulbs in some compartments.

In the forward torpedo room, Olaf Olson felt his first depth charge experience was very close. "Believe me, you held your breath, being among all these torpedoes," he later said. "Some of the depth charge explosions would knock cork off the overhead, and make our torpedoes bounce in their racks!"

One of his fellow torpedomen, Hugo Lundquist, scribbled in his journal this night: "Nips started dropping depth charges and used cable and grappling hooks. One cable dragged across our bow as ship went over us."

Underwood: "There were no serious damage resulting from the depth charges. Again, hats off to Mare Island-built subs! The biggest howl was heard from the baker [Riley]. The depth charges flattened out his rising bread."

Motormac John Brewer recalled that few things upset ship's cook Tom Riley more than someone ruining his baking. "He would do all of his baking at night, making cakes, bread and hot apple pies. When we dove, the pressure changed and his pies and bread would fall," said Brewer. "He would raise hell about those pies!"

Luau, as was her normal routine, had taken the depth charging fairly well. She generally crawled under a bunk to wait it out. "Whenever the battle stations bells would ring, both dogs hauled rear ends toward the after torpedo room and stayed there until everything was over," recalled Wallace McMahon. "As soon as a depth charge went off, they were gone!" The dogs both somehow knew to keep quiet during the silent running, but poor little Seaweed was terrified of the powerful explosions. He would shake uncontrollably as the blasts shook *Spadefish*, but then resume scampering about once the quiet returned.

A survey of the boat later revealed no threatening damage. "We got a good working over that time. Some of the deck plating was warped from the depth charges," recalled Bernie Massar. "They had cables around the deck gun to protect the personnel, and some of them had snapped off."

At 0320, *Spadefish* returned to periscope depth. There were three escorts visible astern, distance about 5,000-6,000 yards. A ship was burning, with explosions and high columns of smoke, in the vicinity of the attack. "Must have been the second target," noted Underwood. "There wasn't enough left of the first one to stay up that long."

The burning ship in the distance was one of the two earlier torpedo victims. *Spadefish* surfaced at 0430 to charge batteries and remained in the vicinity for a daylight investigation of the burning ship. At 0526, she exchanged radar signals with *Pompon*, bearing 346. An hour later, radar interference bearing 130 degrees indicated another submarine's presence. This was believed to be *Bang*, returning from her station off Saishu To, although she could not be properly identified via recognition signals. *Spadefish* submerged at 0745 about 16,000 yards from the burning ship, which had not moved from the attack location.

Through the periscope, two heavy columns of smoke were plainly visible at 0755. Captain Underwood felt that this ship might have actually been a tanker instead of an engine aft cargo ship due to the heavy smoke. "The size of the 'booms' seen in the dim light gave the impressions of a cargo ship."

By 0800, the smoke from the cripple had disappeared. Pinging from two ships was heard on the bearing of the smoke. "This fellow must have sunk," theorized Underwood. "All that smoke couldn't have died down and disappeared in five minutes otherwise." *Spadefish* continued to close the scene where the burning ship had been. The simple fact that it had been burning fiercely for five and a half hours meant that there couldn't have been much left of whatever it was.

At 0934, *Spadefish* heard a distant explosion. By 1120, the escorts' pinging had died out, so Underwood surfaced. Nothing was in sight as he ran toward the scene of his attacks. As she drew closer, *Spadefish* passed numerous empty life boats with their oars out. One that was passed close aboard had the numerals "773" on the bow. The scene was covered with fuel oil and all kinds of wreckage.

Although this fresh debris was a strong indication that *Sanuki Maru* had gone to the bottom, it was not considered solid enough evidence. Generally, ComSubPac needed the attacking submarine to actually have witnesses see the ship sink. Sometimes a ship sinking was credited to a submarine by what the intelligence people overheard. In other cases, many submarines chose to pick up a prisoner from their "kill" to verify its sinking.

The surface wreckage was not enough to count *Sanuki Maru* as sunk. Captain Underwood claimed damage against another 7,500-ton freighter, having no idea that the torpedo explosion he had heard was the sound of frigate *Kume*'s last moments. In this case, *Spadefish*'s official wartime score for her third patrol would have to stand at one ship sunk and one damaged. ComSubPac would, however, allow *Sanuki Maru*'s sinking as a 7,500-ton freighter, when sister sub *Pompon* verified the sinking as a *Spadefish* kill.[9]

13

Icy Hunting in the Yellow Sea

Third Patrol   *28 January–13 February 1945*

Spadefish headed south at high speed for two hours in case the target had been towed away, but nothing was sighted. Reluctantly, Captain Underwood headed east for his own patrol area.

Lookouts sighted another patrol boat and three floating mines during the afternoon and evening of 28 January, all of which were successfully dodged. *Spadefish* submerged at 0705 on 29 January, 20 miles southeast of Kokuzan To. In his journal, lookout Hugo Lundquist noted that it had been "cold as hell and ice [was] on deck."

Kokuzan To's radar picked up *Spadefish* at a range of 25 miles that evening, but soon resumed its regular thirty-second sweeps. *Spadefish* remained surfaced on 30 January, patrolling 40 miles west of Kokuzan To. Lookouts sighted two mines during the day, both of which the skipper allowed his sharpshooters to sink with 20mm fire.

At 1430, a message was received from one of the China-based search planes which had sighted a convoy of three ships with four escorts heading out from northeast of Kokuzan To. "We'd get a message from a spy system up in China that would tell us what certain ship would be leaving and approximately what it was carrying and what course it was taking," recalled Chief Radioman Paul Majoue. This group was called SACO, the Sino-American Cooperation Organization. Based in Chungking, China, under Commodore Milton E. Miles, the group operated a top-secret intelligence organization to track Japanese shipping for Allied subs.[1]

Spadefish headed north to intercept the China plane's reported convoy. By 2100, she had covered all possible convoy positions from the reported 5-knot speed up to 12 knots. No contact was made, so she headed across the Yellow Sea to the usual turning point for Japanese convoys, in the vicinity of Latitude 34-30, and Longitude 122-30. At 2108, the radio gang sent a message to *Pompon*, giving *Spadefish*'s current position and requesting theirs. Although *Pompon* should have been in good position to intercept the convoy, efforts to raise her went unanswered.

At 0206 on 31 January, *Spadefish* was near the convoy turning point by the 20-fathom curve off the China coast. No contacts had been made, so Underwood changed course to the north. Two hours later, at 0345, a radar contact was made, bearing 063, range 17,800 yards. *Spadefish* sent a contact report to her task group at 0400. "Began maneuvering to make night attack," logged radar officer Don Martin.

Three ships of the convoy soon came within visual range. The sky was overcast, but the full moon still lit up the sky so that the ships were in sight at 16,000 yards. This convoy consisted of three merchant ships with four escorts, crossing the Yellow Sea from a position between Kokuzan To and Ko To. Underwood found the light cloud overcast and the full moon to his disliking. Visibility was so good that a surface attack was out of the question. It was just poor enough, however, to make a submerged attack difficult.

By 0420, two of the convoy's escorts were within sight. *Spadefish* dove to radar depth as the range to the targets came down to 9,800 yards. Dan Decker on the plotting table, working with navigator George Cook, found that the base course of the convoy appeared to be about 240, with speed varying from 9 to 14 knots. They did not have sufficient time to track the targets, as the 20-fathom bank was only 6 miles ahead. With dangerously shallow water fast approaching, it was attack at once or let these choice targets slip by.

Approaching the 20-fathom curve, the convoy had formed into two distinct columns. There were two marus in the starboard column and one in the port. The distance between each column was 1,500 yards. One escort was ahead, between the columns, and another was in sight on the port flank. The other escorts were not seen.

At 0440, *Spadefish* came to periscope depth of 65 feet. She attained position on the port bow of convoy, about 2,000 yards off the track of the port column. Torpedoman Emery Kreher's forward room readied their tubes, with depth settings at 6 feet. The welcome order to fire came and *Spadefish* shot all six forward fish at the overlapping targets. The time was 0452 on 31 January 1945.

Jim Schuett counted off the seconds in the conning tower from the first torpedo being fired.

"Eighteen, nineteen, twenty...."

Boom! The unmistakable smash of a torpedo hitting home was heard by all, only one-third of a minute after the No. 1 torpedo had been fired. Underwood was surprised until Decker and Perry Wood informed him that the escort ship that had just passed was in a position that was in line with the torpedo track. Quick work on the plotting

Icy Hunting in the Yellow Sea

table showed his range to check with that of the torpedo run.

"Sound had just reported screws in this direction slowing down," recorded Captain Underwood. "It probably hit him."

Underwood did not see the source of this explosion, as he was still training his attack scope on the target ships when the No. 1 torpedo exploded. Mike Sergio and Paul Majoue continued to hear breaking up noises on this bearing for a short time. The explosion of the first torpedo caused the rest to miss, as Underwood details.

> The targets were seen to have changed course, probably due to the first torpedo explosion. Also it is believed that the target speed was less than that used. They had been tracking at 13.8 knots at the time of going to periscope depth. The bearings did not check too well and poor visibility prevented giving good bow angles. Time did not permit complete analysis by bearings only.

This was one of the few times that Gordon Underwood was not successful with a full spread of fish. Following this patrol, *Spadefish* was credited with sinking an escort vessel of 500 tons. Postwar analysis, however, failed to show an enemy vessel lost at this location or date, and was not allowed by JANAC. This unsuspecting escort had walked into one of *Spadefish*'s torpedoes, sparing her charges from certain destruction. Whatever her name was, it went down with her. Ultra intelligence showed that the freighter *Nanshin Maru* reported a torpedo track from *Spadefish*, but suffered no damage.[2]

At the moment, Underwood was more concerned with evading a now thoroughly alerted enemy. At 0455, a red flare was seen from the leading escort. "Take her deep!" he ordered.

Spadefish went to 120 feet and started evasion tactics with her stern towards the position of attack. One of the escorts raced up from astern while two others came in from the port beam. These latter two escorts had not been sighted previously, but accounted for the four seen by the China plane. The ship went to silent running and everyone braced for the inevitable shockwaves and thunder from the rain of ashcans.

Incredibly, this time nothing happened. The escorts raced around pinging for their attacker, but did not press home their attacks. By all appearances, their sonarmen were unable to get a good read on *Spadefish* and they held their fire. Underwood was pleased: "They were a tame trio compared with the three encountered three nights ago. Maybe sinking one of their comrades damped their ardor a bit."

At 0529, *Spadefish* returned to periscope depth, but nothing was in sight. She surfaced at 0545, and sent a message to *Atule*, giving her the convoy's position, course and speed at the time of attack. *Atule* did not answer, so the message was sent twice, blind before *Spadefish* set course back across the Yellow Sea. "Will spend the day shooting up mines," decided Underwood. "Maybe we can hit them."

During the late afternoon, the masts of a patrol boat were sighted and avoided. *Spadefish* spent the night charging her batteries and searching for prey. At 0609 on 1 February, SJ contact was made on Amma To, distance 47,000 yards. The ship dived for a submerged patrol off this island, but the only contact was another pesky patrol boat in the afternoon, which passed about 6,000 yards from *Spadefish*. Upon surfacing at 1846, the bridge watch found that a strong wind was blowing from the northwest. The sea had started kicking up angrily and the already cool temperature was dropping down.

The temperature grew colder during the night as *Spadefish* entered the northeastern corner of the Yellow Sea, off the port of Jinsen. "I stood lookout duty quite a bit," said S1c Al Gibson. "We got into a storm in that area and liked to froze our balls off. It was very bitter. Ice and snow accumulated on deck, but we stayed on the surface most of the time. I had five suits of clothes on when I went on watch."

After daybreak on 2 February, *Spadefish* submerged to melt the ice off the boat. The temperature of the water was now 35 degrees and the temperature of the air about 22 degrees. Needless to say, this made for some discomfort while on the bridge. Inside the ship, the hull felt as cold as the outside water. Upon surfacing at night, the open conning tower hatch helped create a small gale as the diesel engines angrily sucked in air as they came to life. The arctic blast of air ripped through the boat each night, sucking the stale air out of the ship, blowing loose papers everywhere, and putting a chill through anyone who was not dressed for the cold weather. "When the hatch was first opened at night, it created a cold air vacuum," said Gibson. "We tried to stay dressed as warm as we could, but it was damn chilly below." Topside, however, it was bitter. "We just put on all the clothes that we could wear and still be able to fit through the hatch," recalled Lt.(jg) Perry Wood of his OOD watches.

At 0827, *Spadefish* surfaced and headed for the 10 fathom bank of Tokuseki Gunto. Dan Decker and Ed La Croix took their positions on the bridge with three lookouts above them in the periscope shears. At 1124, one of the bitterly cold lookouts sighted smoke on the horizon. This was quickly followed by radar contact with two ships, bearing 030, range 16,000 yards.

Spadefish commenced an end around to the south to get ahead of them. Although it was cold, the surface visibility was about 16,000 yards. One of the ships made a turn up the channel heading to Sekimo

Suido, the other proceeding down the coast, crossing over the 10 fathom bank. *Spadefish* managed to get ahead and entered the small channel just west of Tokuseki Gunto, where there was a strip of 20-fathom water. The battle stations plotting team had figured the target ship to making 9 knots and tracking on course 100. Although she was unescorted and not zig-zagging, the target ship was hard to distinguish by her heavy stack smoke, being blown forward by a strong tail wind.

By 1318, the ship was identified as a medium-sized freighter. She now changed course to about 140, giving a zero angle on the bow. *Spadefish* had turned for a stern tube shot and opened out on a starboard track. The tracking party decided that the enemy had slowed to 7 knots. *Spadefish* had to make 2/3 speed to hold depth, and this speed was opening her out too fast against the enemy's track. A setup for a 2,800 yard torpedo run, small track shot, with Mark 18 torpedoes, was rejected by Underwood due to the uncertain speed performance of the Mark 18s at the low water temperature of 35°.

At 1340, Underwood swung his boat around for a bow shot. The target ship had now opened out sufficiently to identify it as a composite superstructure, rake bow, counter stern, high stack freighter. She was fairly well loaded, but was apparently an old type ship with two newer tripod masts.

As the range closed to 2,400 yards, *Spadefish* fired four bow tubes at 1348. The torpedoes had a 112 starboard track, near zero gyro, and 8-foot depth settings. Majoue and Sergio on sound tracked the torpedoes to run normal. They reported them on a bearing that, after the correct torpedo run time, merged with the sound of the target screws. The setup on the target kept checking right on.

"Everything was just right," wrote Commander Underwood, "except no torpedo explosions. No explanation unless temperature of water affected depth setting of the Mk 14 and Mk 23 torpedoes. A very disappointing performance to say the least."

In testing as early as 1942, the Navy had found that the Mark 14 torpedo often ran ten or more feet deeper than its prescribed setting due to an improperly designed and tested depth-control mechanism. By early 1945, many of the serious torpedo problems had been cured that had allowed countless Japanese ships to escape during the early war years. During all of 1944, Pacific submarines had fired 6,092 torpedoes during 520 war patrols—more than all the submarines had fired in both 1942 and 1943 combined.[3]

Through the periscope, Underwood could only watch in disgust as their unsuspecting target maru lumbered along on her way, now inside the 10-fathom curve. Everything on Gus Laundy's TDC still checked out perfectly, but this one had gotten away due to the torpedoes.

Spadefish surfaced at 1747 following the disheartening torpedo attack. "The seas were now mountainous," Underwood wrote. Several big waves crashed over the bridge, drenching the watchstanders and forcing every man to hold on for dear life.

The boat faced a fresh northwest gale with very high seas during the first days of February. The skies were cloudy with periodic snow flurries. The average air temperature logged by *Spadefish* in the North Yellow Sea was 25°. The lowest air temperature during this time was 17° with a 31° sea temperature.

The boat rode out the rough weather and bitter cold through the night. At 0530 on 3 February, the radio antenna mast, which had been coated with ice for days, suddenly broke from the weight of the ice on it and the waves' force. *Spadefish* turned away from the sea and took down the antenna. Don Martin's radar gang used the SD mast to copy the Fox schedule and found the reception to be good.

At 0615, a repair party had completed work on the antenna. *Spadefish* turned and headed back into the tall seas toward the position off the 10 fathom bank where the previous day's contact was made. At 0918, *Spadefish* dived in the relatively deep 33 fathom Yellow Sea channel between the 10 fathom banks at the end of Sekimo Suido. At 1230, she surfaced for Lieutenant Cook and Jim Schuett to take a sun line.

At 1302, a lookout sighted smoke, bearing 343. Four minutes later, *Spadefish* nosed under to begin an approach. When forty minutes of submerged running had not brought the smoke any closer, she resurfaced. Smoke was then picked up on the high periscope, bearing 094. This ship was apparently heading across the 4 to 5-fathom bank and was at very slow speed. *Spadefish* dove again at 1414. The shallow water would not permit chasing this ship. Due to the slow speed and heavy amounts of black smoke billowing from this target, it was presumed to be a small tugboat with a tow. Underwood secured his crew from battle stations.

To top off the day's broken mast, the SUSIE fathometer went out of commission at 1537, forcing Underwood to return to the surface. "This vicinity was no place to run around without that instrument," he noted. At 1617, the watch sighted a small boat. Upon closing to investigate, *Spadefish* found a small native sampan, anchored, with three very cold-looking natives in it. With seas was too rough to investigate further, she cleared the area. At 1800, a repair party came up on deck to rig a jury antenna. Despite the rough waters, the repair crews successfully completed work on the new antenna by 1926.

While these repairs continued, *Spadefish* suffered injury to a crewman on the afternoon of 3 February. In the forward torpedo room, TM3c Wallace McMahon was off duty, reading a book. Someone else came along and removed a deck plate to work in the bilges below. "He forgot to replace the deck plate and I didn't pay any attention to it," said McMahon. "Naturally, when I got up, I fell right down into the bilges and struck my lower back on a protrusion."

In great pain, the torpedoman crawled out of the bilges and stumbled back toward the control room in search of the pharmacist's mate.

"Is the doc topside?" McMahon asked the duty chief in his thick Massachusetts accent.

According to the way McMahon spoke, the duty section thought he had asked, "Is it dark topside?"

"No, it's daylight!" someone announced.

"At the point, I passed out," recalled McMahon. Doc Vic Ives rushed to assist and McMahon was carried back to his bunk. When he came to, he found Ives checking out his badly bruised back. "The doc kept sticking needles in my legs and I couldn't feel them. I was a little worried, but everything came back to normal in a few days."

Having found something in the same spot every day, Underwood reasoned that he should spend another day west of the port of Jinsen. Rain swept back and forth through the channel on 4 February, forcing the OODs to keep position by radar fixes. Between showers, the visibility was only somewhat limited by haze. At 1503, the afternoon watch sighted smoke bearing 140 degrees. About fifteen minutes later, the watch made another smoke sighting, bearing 000. This smoke plotted in on the 4-5 fathom (24- to 30-foot) bank. The latter contact was disregarded in favor of the more southerly contact, which was moving up the steamer lane.

At 1532, the shape of a ship could now be seen in the haze, so *Spadefish* submerged. This ship tracked at 9 knots, not zigzagging, and unescorted. Captain Underwood's report detailed the target setup.

> We were in middle of channel, being set up the channel at about 3 knots. The target was not affected by this current as yet. He was bucking a 1 knot, southeast current. We maintained a constant bearing ahead of target until range of 6,000 yards, then turned to move off the track for stern tube shot. Before the firing position was reached, the target entered the channel, catching the 3 knot current. This changed the setup, target speed now about 7 knots, making the torpedo run around 2,000 yards. This was too long a run for Mk. 18 in this cold water so swung around for bow shot.

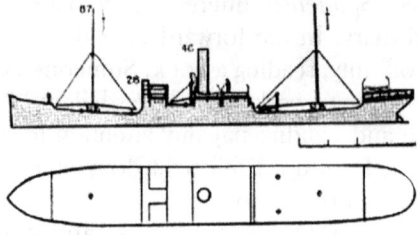

Tairai Maru, a 4,273-ton passenger/cargo ship sunk by *Spadefish* on 4 February. One of this maru's survivors was taken aboard *Spadefish* as a POW. *ONI 208-J (Revised)*.

This target ship was now plainly seen and was decided by the identification crew to be similar to *Anzan Maru* in their ONI 208-J book, with the exception of her masts, which were narrow and high, goal-post type. Underwood found his periscope visibility to be very poor. The muddy Yellow Sea water left a scum on the window so that a clear picture could not be seen. Also, the target's light gray color blended in very well with the slight haze.

The target appeared to be riding empty, so the skipper called for a mere 4 feet on the torpedo depth settings. The seas had calmed considerably from the previous days, leaving only small waves. With a near zero gyro, Underwood ordered tubes 2, 1 and 4 fired at 1654 as the range reached 1,500 yards.

The steam torpedoes, set at their normal high speed of 46 knots, were seen through the periscope to broach several times. Two fish missed their mark, but the third slammed home into the stern of the 4,273-ton Japanese freighter *Tairai Maru*. "We had a few anxious moments waiting for that torpedo hit," wrote the skipper. "Were afraid we were in for a repetition of our last attack."

Tairai Maru was seen to stop and swing around, as she began to settle slightly by her stern. Two life boats were seen to pull away from the ship. At 1707, the ship stopped settling so Underwood swung *Spadefish* for a stern tube shot. This time he had Si Barnes' crew fire only one Mark 18 electric torpedo from tube No. 7, set for 28 knots speed. The torpedo run was a mere 650 yards, considered point blank range for a submarine.

The Mark 18 hit *Tairai Maru* at the count of 58.5 seconds on Jim Schuett's stopwatch, giving a torpedo speed of 20 knots. The periscope range was checked with a ping range just after firing. The height of the freighter's stack, used during periscope observations to determine the distance, proved to be accurate. "The angle between the waterline of the target and the top of its highest mast or stack gave the plotting team the ability to know the range," related plot officer Dan Decker. The temperature of the batteries in the torpedo was about 44°, while the

Although poor in quality, this photo through *Spadefish*'s periscope shows the final moments of *Tairai Maru* as her stern settles under the waves. This 4,273-ton freighter became the unlucky thirteenth torpedo sinking victim of *Spadefish* on 4 February 1945. Sailors climb her mast, hoping to be the last to jump free as she goes under. *Courtesy of Submarine Force Museum, Groton, Connecticut.*

temperature of the sea was 32°. Again set at 4 feet, this torpedo ran as expected—albeit 8 knots slower than its setting—and exploded amidships, causing *Tairai* to settle aft again.

Periscope pictures were taken of this sinking. At 1728, *Tairai Maru* went down with her bow sticking straight up. There were now four life boats in the water. Periscope observations showed no enemy aircraft or surface vessels, so Captain Underwood decided to give his crew the chance to witness a ship sinking during the daylight.

For confirmation of the ship's sinking, additional witnesses helped insure *Spadefish* would receive proper credit for this kill. For the crew, it was a rare moment of pride to see the results of their coordinated efforts. In the conning tower, control room, maneuvering room and elsewhere, men spelled each other from watch so that each could go to the conning tower for a quick peek.

"The entire crew was allowed to view the slow sinking via periscope," recalled auxiliaryman Buck Miller. "I was the last witness and saw nothing."

Underwood noted Miller's puzzled looked and asked, "Gone?"

A disappointed Miller affirmed that *Spadefish*'s target ship had indeed fully "submerged."

The area remained clear of enemy activity, so Underwood elected to bring his boat to the surface at 1736. *Spadefish* headed for the scene of *Tairai Maru*'s sinking to look over the survivors. Executive Officer George Cook led an armed party out on deck to inspect the survivors, hoping to bring aboard a useful prisoner who might yield some intelligence. From the bridge with Captain Underwood, Ensign Bill Ware noted that most refused to come aboard.

Torpedoman John Schumer was amazed. "When you got topside after a sinking and saw the group in the water, you felt sorry for them. You'd know they weren't going to last very long." In this bitterly cold water, Schumer was "surprised at how many wouldn't come toward the boat. They would swim away from it."

Chiefs Shaky Jake Lewis and Boats Eimermann, both armed with .45 caliber Thompson machine guns, motioned for one of the survivors to come aboard. When he did not at first take the heaving line that was thrown his way, Eimermann became frustrated. "I let loose with that old machine gun," he recalled. "I didn't bullet him, but I gave him the idea, you'd better pay attention!"

Spadefish nosed right up against one of their lifeboats which held several men. A couple of the Chinese men did come aboard via a rope ladder draped over the submarine's side. The youngest youth approached the armed sailors.

"I think that's a woman!" stammered Chief Lewis.

A closer inspection revealed the terrified youth to be a male. "He had real pink cheeks from being in the water," recalled Eimermann. Lieutenant Cook hauled the youngster back toward the conning tower, where Captain Underwood could inspect him. Submarine skippers had been encouraged by Admiral Lockwood to bring back Japanese prisoners if they could do so without significant risk.

During a hasty inspection where the youth used broken English, the skipper found that the men in this boat were not Japanese. "A couple of men were taken aboard," wrote Underwood. "They claimed to be Chinese, so put them back in the boat."

As junior OOD Bill Ware recalled, Underwood—remembering his fishing days—jokingly told his Exec of one of those men brought aboard, "It's too small. Throw it back." Without a second thought, Cook ordered the man to be tossed overboard to swim back to his lifeboat. "They interrogated him and threw him back overboard," remembered Neal Pike. "I don't think they were successful in getting anything out of him." Afterwards, Ware began calling the Exec "Killer

Cook," and threatened to tell Cook's wife when *Spadefish* returned home.[4]

Shaky Jake Lewis was holding the poor youngster who had to be returned to the sea. "He had to throw him over the side," recalled motormac John Brewer. "Boy, I think that really got to ol' Jake."

Another of the Chinese men was taken below as a POW for interrogation. *Spadefish* continued to nose among the other boats in search of a higher-ranking Japanese survivor who might yield more intelligence. At length, a lone man was sighted on some wreckage. This survivor "waved and started sending semaphore with his arms, so we picked him up. His uniform resembled that of a naval cadet," recorded Underwood. EM3c Jack Gallagher, standing by as part of the forward 20mm crew, recalled, "This guy had binoculars around his neck, so we thought he would have more information." The survivor grabbed the line thrown to him and was hauled aboard.

This young man was Japanese and was soon found to be the third officer of the freighter which had been sunk. Eimermann and Lewis took him below for dry clothes and a new home in the after torpedo room. Finding an officer for a POW likely meant better intelligence for *Spadefish*, but it also meant a return to the ocean for the first sailor who had been taken below. Jack Gallagher noted that after the Japanese officer was brought on board, "the other prisoner was brought back up on deck and thrown over the side."

Captain Underwood decided that his crew did not need the extra challenge of guarding two prisoners from the same ship, particularly the Chinese sailor. The officer that was kept aboard "was real polite," according to John Brewer. "He had a wallet and showed us pictures of his folks." Seaman Al Gibson was among those who took the Japanese prisoner to his new quarters. "I searched him for anything he might have on his body, and I managed to get a little bit of Japanese money off the prisoner. We took him up to the forward torpedo room, where he could be watched." Now out of torpedoes, Emery Kreher's forward room became the prisoner's quarters for the balance of the patrol. "They got all kinds of information from this guy after we took him prisoner," said Boats Eimermann. He identified his ship as the 4,375-ton *Taidai Maru*. JANAC postwar credit would list the vessel to be the 4,273-ton *Tairai Maru*.

In his journal for 4 February, Hugo Lundquist wrote, "Surfaced and ran among 4 full lifeboats and one raft. Some very young Nips aboard. Accidentally rammed one lifeboat. Took one Nip aboard and threw 3 or 4 others back. Weather freezing—ice and snow on deck."

Motormac Harry Brenneis had been topside, standing by with the deck gun crew. Orders were to only take Japanese prisoners, so to him it was gut-wrenching to see the Chinese survivors being returned to the sea. The sight of leaving the poor young men to face the elements with very little probability of rescue was one that would bother Brenneis for many decades. Such was the harsh reality of war and the living hell it could truly be for all involved.

Spadefish cleared the area at 1828. This area at the mouth of the channel leading to Sekimo Suido had been a good hunting ground. A contact had been made almost every day, unescorted, following about the same routing along the edge of the 10-fathom curve. During her second patrol, *Spadefish* had sunk a ship in about the same spot. Underwood decided he would have to wait until the next day for this area to be productive again. *Tairai Maru* certainly had enough time to get out radio distress signals that would have diverted traffic.

Spadefish had three Mark 18 torpedoes left aft and nothing forward, where all sixteen fish had already been fired. Wallace McMahon was still confined to his bunk in the forward room, where he was recovering from the injuries he had sustained in his fall the previous day. "While I was laid up in the rack, they had our Japanese prisoner in the bilges up forward." Congenial in nature, this Japanese sailor was given blankets and was taken back to the crew's mess to eat. "He loved sugar," said McMahon. "He'd eat sugar by the spoonful. His nickname became 'Sugo,' which I guess was Japanese for sugar."

Captain Underwood sent a message to ComSubPac at 0030 on 5 February, relating his boat's results and the poor torpedo performance. After a quick trim dive at 0731, she surfaced to patrol off the 10-fathom curve again. The day was clear and visibility was excellent. The air temperature was about 25 to 30 degrees. *Spadefish* now headed into the northernmost part of the Yellow Sea to patrol between Port Arthur and Dairen, where the bitter weather was even colder. The increased severity of the weather resulted in large accumulations of ice topside, which hampered the ship's ability to dive because of the added buoyancy.[5]

At 0940, smoke was sighted, bearing 177 degrees. This target was tracked and found to be on course 260, speed about 8 knots. *Spadefish* made an end around, keeping the smoke and masts in sight. From the size and position of these masts and stack, the target was judged to be either a patrol boat similar to the type seen before in this area, or possibly a very small freighter.

At 1135, *Spadefish* was in position ahead of this ship, but the smoke had disappeared. She headed back to the last true bearing until the ship was again sighted. Navigation plot showed the ship had headed back to the east. It was headed back for the northwest corner of the 10-fathom bank. By 1218, this patrol boat had gotten nearer, showing a course of north. The shallow water he had entered made this target off limits. Underwood had already planned to shift patrol areas this night, so he set course early for his new area south of Dairen. "We now have only three torpedoes remaining, and those aft," he wrote.

At 2020, a navigational light was sighted on Shantung Promontory, showing two flashes every 17 seconds. At 2354, the lights of two small boats were sighted on the horizon. Upon closing, side lights and several white lights were visible on each boat. Being very small in size, these craft were avoided.

Despite the added difficulties of operating the boat with all the ice on her, *Spadefish* was able to find new targets soon after entering her new area on 6 February. At 0433, SJ radar contact was made on Rotetsuzan Seikaku, bearing 330, range 72,000 yards. Gus Laundy took her down at 0703, 15 miles south of Port Arthur. It took the boat 75 seconds to submerge due to the layers of ice on the deck. At 0859, sound picked up pinging bearing 333. Possible smoke was soon sighted on the same bearing. At 1001, sound picked up pinging bearing 065.

"JP believed to have picked up churning screws at 066°T," noted Ed La Croix in the deck log at 1005. *Spadefish* turned toward this direction, and ten minutes later sighted a mast. This contact was soon lost, but it was apparent that some sort of patrol vessel was working this area. The crew could only hope the PC was there to protect a worthwhile target.

"Captain, we've got smoke, bearing one-five-five." The duty messenger was sent for Underwood at 1208 to notify him of the latest contact.

Spadefish commenced an approach and by 1302, she had two ships in sight. Both were medium-sized freighters, steaming along without escorts and not maintaining any zig-zag patterns. They were heading from the direction of Dairen, through the Pohai Straits toward Tientsin on course 235, speed 7 knots. *Spadefish* maintained position in front of the outboard ship, which was apparently the faster of the two. He appeared in sight later but had now passed the first ship.

As Underwood and George Cook took peeks at this AK, they called out her details. The identification party flipped through the Office of Naval Intelligence books and decided this ship resembled the *Genzan Maru* in construction, particularly in the shape of her well deck. This ship, estimated to be 4,000 tons, was not as large as *Genzan* showed to be. Her draft was figured to be 10 feet, so Underwood ordered Si

Barnes' after room to set their Mark XVIIIs at 4 feet, just to be safe. She appeared to be riding empty, high in the water.

At 1312, *Spadefish* came left to bring the stern tubes to bear and pull off the track. At 1315, she commenced firing her last three after torpedoes at a range of 1,480 yards, with a 100 starboard track. The first torpedo from tube 8 missed, as the target speed was now judged to be higher than the 7 knots used. The No. 9 tube's torpedo slammed home in the stern of this small freighter and she immediately began to settle.

The other ship turned away as soon as she saw the explosion and she reversed course back for port. "Could have used some torpedoes forward," wrote Underwood. With his ship only 5 miles from Port Arthur, he "expected trouble sooner or later" and cleared the area to the south. This little freighter, later identified as the 1,092-ton *Shohei Maru*, took five minutes to sink, plenty of time to give out her position for the scouting planes and escorts that could be expected in the area soon.

Sure enough, at 1503, a Rufe plane was sighted fairly close through the periscope. *Spadefish* was cruising at 90 feet in this relatively shallow area of the Yellow Sea. At 1639, a depth charge exploded fairly close aboard, startling everyone. The bottom was both rocky and sandy. The pressure waves from the depth charge could be heard reverberating off the bottom for some seconds after the explosion. "Not a very pleasant sound," wrote Underwood. "The boat would rock and roll as the waves went underneath."

Following this first blast, *Spadefish* immediately went deeper, in search of safety. "Went *deep* to 130 feet," Perry Wood wryly recorded in the deck log. "Commenced maneuvering at various course and speeds, avoiding depth charges." The fathometer showed the depth of water was only about 28 fathoms (168 feet). During the next hour and a half, a total of seven charges were dropped, none very close. No screws were heard so they must have been dropped by planes. The crew made a careful check on all possible air leaks but did not turn up any culprits. The number of depth charges dropped indicated multiple aircraft, so the Rufe sighted at 1503 must have noticed *Spadefish*'s periscope and called for help.

The ship remained down until 1915, before surfacing and clearing the area to the east at high speed. At 2110, *Spadefish* sighted the lights of a small boat, bearing 020. The side lights of three more small boats were spotted ahead during the evening. The SJ radar soon picked them up as well and these ships were avoided.

The prospect of returning to warmer weather and the anticipation of R&R at the Royal Hawaiian Hotel was inviting to all. Torpedoman

Lundquist wrote on 6 February, "Going home—very happy." After receiving ComSubPac orders during the night that disclosed *Spadefish* would not receive her refit in Hawaii, Lundquist wrote the next morning, "Headed for Guam. Not so happy now."

———

During the early morning hours of 7 February, *Spadefish* again sighted the lights of various fishing boats on the horizon and steered clear of them as she headed out of her patrol area. Gordon Underwood kept his boat on the surface aside from a morning trim dive and an afternoon crash dive to avoid a Nell bomber. *Spadefish* returned to periscope depth at 1421 and found that the Nell was still in the area, flying low over the water. At 1454, a distant explosion was heard, assumed to be a depth bomb from a plane.

Spadefish returned to the surface a half hour later and exchanged calls over the SJ with pack mate *Bang*. During the early morning hours of 8 February, she also communicated with *Jallao*, announcing her own intention to retire from the Yellow Sea, out of torpedoes. At 1136, three Rufe seaplanes were sighted at a distance of 10 miles. *Spadefish* submerged to avoid detection, surfacing after lunch in the midst of a "very welcome fog." She proceeded southeast out of the area toward Tokara Kaikyo. She dove again at 1459 according to her patrol report "to kill some time. We were close to the Nansei Shoto."

Spadefish surfaced at 1831 and passed through Tokara Kaikyo that evening. The radar gang was careful to keep the SJ trained away from known Japanese radar stations. No enemy signals were picked up on the APR. During her last run through this area on the second patrol, at least three stations had been detected. Thoughts of Pearl Harbor were long gone as she made her way toward Guam.

En route the next several days, she ran mainly on the surface, making only daily trim dives. The usual backgammon and acey-deucy games were lively in the crew's mess this patrol. In CPO quarters, Hocks Majoue and Dutch Falconer played cribbage routinely after finishing their watch shifts each night. They spent the early morning hours playing, "payable when we got in. On the way in, we always did double or nothing, so we ended up owing each other nothing," recalled Majoue.

Many of the others were not so fortunate. In fact, quite a bit of future pay passed hands in the acey-deucy and poker games. Mess attendant Sie Brooks made out well in one game. The games were a favorite pastime, and the men ribbed the cooks continually. "They took quite a hazing," recalled torpedoman striker Olaf Olson. He

Mess attendant Sie Brooks (right), lucky at poker, was also awarded the Navy Letter of Commendation on 3 March 1945, following *Spadefish*'s third war patrol.
Courtesy of Submarine Force Museum, Groton, Connecticut.

wasn't much of a gambler, but did get into a blackjack game with messcook Brooks one day. "Neither one of us had enough money to take the deal," said Olson. "So, we pooled our money and took it together, and we won fifteen hundred bucks. This kid, Sie Brooks, he was a lucky son-of-a-gun. He'd hit twenty and still get twenty-one!"

During the return run, Captain Underwood had his officers practice new roles aboard ship. The newest young ensign, Charles Johnson, was the assistant communications officer. Lookout "Buck" Miller recalled an incident involving Johnson.

> He was a very thin and very small officer and was backup to Communications Officer Wood. When officers rotated positions coming in off patrol, he made his first dive as diving officer or officer of the deck. He didn't have enough weight or strength to secure the hatch on way down. When I received the order for pressure in boat from air manifold, I yelled, "Hatch! Hatch!" several times, as I didn't have a green board. Captain Underwood was standing a few feet from me, eyeball to eyeball with me.
>
> He realized the danger and flew up the ladder. Don Scholle advised me that the Exec pulled the hatch closed, not the Captain, but I will never forget Captain Underwood's eye contact. It was not of fear, but of concern. I had a little of both.[6]

At 0445 on 13 February, *Spadefish* made contact with her escort out from Guam. *Spadefish* circled on station until the submarine *Devilfish* was contacted at 0640. They then proceeded into Guam, arriving 39 days after the boat had left Majuro. She pulled alongside the tender *Holland*, waiting for *Proteus*, her scheduled refit tender. A Marine guard soon came aboard to remove "Sugo," the sugar-loving Japanese POW from *Tairai Maru*.

During this patrol, *Spadefish*'s three packmates had less than stellar luck. Captain Stephen Gimber's *Pompon* made a dive with its hatch open and flooded the pump room, damaging equipment. Gimber was forced to leave station early to make repairs. Captain Gallaher's *Bang* made a number of attacks, but was stripped of any kills in postwar accounting. Only Captain Jack Maurer's *Atule* was credited with sinking one nice freighter.[7]

Spadefish had been by far the most productive ship of Underwood's Urchins. She claimed four ships sunk and in postwar analysis was credited with sinking four ships for 13,423 tons. Her crew had also sunk seven drifting mines and exploded two with 20mm fire during the third patrol. Through his first three patrols on *Spadefish*, Gordon Underwood had been credited with sinking sixteen Japanese ships, including an aircraft carrier and a destroyer. In fitting tribute to his successes, he was one of the very few skippers who would actually be given credit postwar by JANAC for sinking the exact number of ships he had been credited with during the war.

Underwood was awarded his third consecutive Navy Cross for his third war patrol. This award, of course, allowed him to select others for commendations. Underwood awarded the Silver Star to Exec George Cook for his work as assistant approach officer, another to diving officer Bill Ware and the third to Dan Decker for his work as battle stations plotting officer. Bronze Stars were recommended for torpedo and gunnery officer Gus Laundy, yeoman Irv Kreinbring, torpedoman Emery Kreher and radioman Mike Sergio.

For the third consecutive patrol, *Spadefish*'s FM sonar had not been used. At the start of the patrol, the FM's head would not train. Upon investigation, the radar gang found that the shaft was sprung. No repairs were attempted.

Yeoman Irv Kreinbring had finished typing up the skipper's patrol report upon reaching Guam. Captain Underwood detailed each attack and gave a summary of his boat and crew's performances during the third war patrol.

> The food was good and well prepared. The excellent products of the baker [Tom Riley] were again appreciated by all hands.
>
> The dog, Luau, was again the most popular member of the crew. However, her standing as such is in danger of being usurped by her young son, "Shaky" [also known as Seaweed], a born and bred submariner!

Remarks: Six or seven submarines are about the right number to cover the Yellow Sea. This allows a concentration of three or four boats in the central eastern side to cover convoy routes, with the other boats covering shipping in the northern part of the sea and one to cover approaches to Shanghai. The convoys encountered this patrol crossed westward from

between Ko To and Kokuzan To to a position about Latitude 32-30N, Longitude 122-30E; and then cut south. During late November, they went south of Kokuzan To and headed for same turning point. The China planes were helpful in spotting one convoy apparently making up southeast of Ko To.

Use of radio should be kept to a minimum in this area. On several occasions when the radio had been used, it was noted that either a patrol boat or a plane searched the area in the vicinity the next day. Numerous close Japanese radio stations seem to DF the submarines quite accurately. The radio should be used for necessary contact and attack information.

The health of all hands was unusually good, considering the cold wet weather encountered throughout the patrol. There were no serious colds. The bridge personnel suffered much discomfort from icy winds and spray, but due to sufficient clothing, no ill effects resulted.

OPPOSITE PAGE: Spadefish crew and her mascots following the third patrol, prior to Captain Gordon Underwood being transferred.

Seated across the front row (left to right) are: Chief Emerson Ordway, Chief "Jake" Lewis (with hands on Seaweed), Chief Carl Schmelzer, Chief Dutch Falconer, Ens. Bill Ware (with hand on Luau), Ens. Charles Johnson (with pipe), Ens. Don Martin, Lt.(jg.) Perry Wood (legs crossed), Chief Carl Bieberdorf, Chief Harry George, Chief Paul Majoue, and Chief "Boats" Eimermann.

Second row (l-r): Bob Maxwell, Roy Moody, John Nesnee, Thomas O'Neil, Lt. Dan Decker, Lt(jg) Ed La Croix, Captain Underwood, Lt. George Cook, Chief Vic Ives, Wally McMahon, Dick Gamby, Joe "Whitey" Harbison, and Henry Solomon.

Third row: Bill Pigman (in white hat, leaning forward), Don Scholle (no hat), Ken Sigworth, Pat Kelley, Jack Gallagher (white hat), Thad Barton, Ed Graf (white hat), Joe Case, Tom Riley, Ken Powers, Radford "Rebel" Rewold (with mustache), John Peel, and Mike Sergio.

Standing, fourth row (l-r): Charles Griffith, Emery Kreher, Tony Dunleavy, Jim Schuett, Melvin Mullen, Irv Kreinbring (white hat), Dick Bassett, Charles Rolf (white hat), Tom Shaw (no hat), Norval Ingberg, Don Anderson, Maurice Noonan (white hat), Hugh Carney (hatless), Wesley Drew (white hat), (unknown behind Rewold), Warren "Pappy" Asher, Olaf (Sandleben) Olson, David Yocum (beard), Silas Barnes, Jim Fletcher, and Neal Pike.

Cigarette deck (l-r): Sie Brooks, Bill Terboss (holding flag), Ben Graff (holding flag) and Bill Mainard. Upper bridge (l-r): John Cuthbertson, Vic Holeman, unknown, Doyle Partin, Hugo Lundquist, Andy Olah, Herman Cruze, Walter Jerolman (center, no hat), Wayne Powell, Nick Pelliciari, Francis Scherman, Harry Brenneis, John Brewer, Leonard Dependahl, and Bernie Massar (background).

Courtesy of Dan Decker.

The ship was quite cold most of the time. This is to be expected with a water temperature averaging 35 degrees and air temperatures from 17 to 35 degrees. An air conditioning unit was operated most of the time to keep the moisture down.

The new men received during the last two refits have rapidly fitted themselves into the efficient, close-knit organization that this ship has always had. The loss of three experienced officers was felt at first. However, the manner in which the previously junior officers accepted their new responsibilities was such that the loss was soon overcome. This was particularly true of the Engineering and Diving Officer, Ensign Ware. The new Executive Officer, Lt. George C. Cook, USNR, new to the ship and her organization, took hold in such a commendable fashion that the organization was soon running smoothly and efficiently as before.

USS Spadefish Third Patrol Summary

Patrol Area:	Yellow Sea
Time Period:	6 January - 13 February 1945
Number of Men Aboard:	84 (75 enlisted and 9 officers)
Total Days on Patrol:	39
Days on Station:	17
Days Submerged:	6
Miles Steamed:	9,569
Fuel Used:	91,129 gallons
Number of Torpedoes Fired:	24
Ships Sunk, ComSubPac credit:	4 ships/16,400 tons
JANAC Postwar Credit:	4 ships/13,423 tons
Shipping Damage Claimed:	one 10,000-ton tanker
Limiting Factor of Patrol:	Torpedo performance

14

Guam and Germershausen

Refit at Guam   *13 February–16 March, 1945*

    Memories of the ice and snow in the Yellow Sea quickly melted away as *Spadefish*'s crew came topside to soak up the balmy rays of the Mariana Islands. Signalman striker Al Gibson was feeling the ill effects of standing so many topside watches in the ice and snow during the previous weeks. "By the time we got back to Guam, I was very sick," Gibson said. "I came down with pneumonia and ended up in sick bay. I didn't even make R&R with the crew."

    The refit was conducted by Submarine Division 201 and the tender *Proteus* (AS-19). Once the refit crew had come aboard, the men had two weeks of rest and relaxation at Guam's new submarine rest camp. Camp Dealey had been named in honor of Samuel David Dealey, the fearless "Destroyer Killer" skipper who had been lost with his boat *Harder* on 24 August 1944 to a depth charge attack west of Luzon. Once ashore on Guam, the crew had a ninety-minute truck ride from the tender across the island to Camp Dealey.

    Marines had stormed ashore on Guam in July 1944 and declared the island secured after three weeks of fighting. Major General Henry L. Larsen took over the island on 15 August. Some 1,300 U.S. soldiers died while taking Guam and another 5,600 were wounded. They had killed more than 10,000 Japanese soldiers by 1 September, but the jungles on Guam held more enemy soldiers. When General Larsen took command of Guam, at least 9,000 Japanese troops were at large in the jungle. Mopping up activities would continue until after the war.[1]

    When *Spadefish* arrived on 13 February 1945, pockets of these Japanese soldiers remained on Guam. "We were told there were 5,000 Japanese still running around the jungle there," recalled Chief Neal Pike. "The afternoon we were trucked around to the rest camp, we found out that guys from the *Sea Fox* had been killed."

    Electrician's mate Ken Sigworth, who played on the *Spadefish* softball team, recalled that *Spadefish* was scheduled to play against the *Sea*

Fox (SS-402) team. Tragedy struck that day when seven crewmen from *Sea Fox* went on a forbidden trip through the scrub jungle with a Guamanian constabulary officer. The visiting submariners had been warned not to handle ammunition or dud shells and to beware of booby traps left in Japanese "souvenirs." Less than a mile from Camp Dealey, a group of about thirty Japanese soldiers attacked the party. "I was told they set up a machine gun and some rifles around a clearing and a massacre ensued," related Lieutenant Dan Decker. "Most probably, the Japanese were not just intent on killing Americans. They needed, and were willing, to expose themselves–but they wanted the money the sailors were carrying for many reasons, including buying the same girls the sailors planned to visit."[2]

Six men, including the guide, were killed. *Sea Fox* lost CEM Gilbert S. Snyder, CTM Theodore L. Goodhue, EM1c John E. Brey, MoMM2c Edward J. Counsell and S1c Anthony Trupis. Two other *Sea Fox* sailors, badly wounded, managed to crawl to safety and survive.[3]

"Some of those killed were senior petty officers, and they didn't grow on trees out there," remembered *Spadefish* torpedoman Don Anderson. "That caused some consternation, to lose a leading petty officer in any department, I would suppose."

The *Sea Fox* tragedy ended any and all from leaving the compound of Camp Dealey. The crew and the officers had Quonset huts right on the beach among the palm trees. "You didn't move away from the bivouac area," recalled radioman "Little Fox" Sergio. "There were a lot of Marines around and you could still hear 'em shooting at times."

Camp Dealey was blacked out at night. "We didn't even light a smoke after dark," said Don Anderson. Quartermaster Don Scholle recalled that "we had Marine lookouts for us at night" to protect against potential snipers. Each submarine was also required to keep one crew member on duty as a sentry for every 25 crewmen ashore.

"I was asked to return to the *Spadefish* and obtain .45-caliber pistols, holsters and spare clips, to issue to each Quonset hut at night for persons standing guard watch," recalled gunner's mate Bernie Massar. The pistols were kept locked up during the day. "My bunk was near the door of the hut," wrote Massar. "I had a .45 for myself and kept it under my pillow during the night. I told the person on watch to wake me up if anything should happen and I would assist him with my gun."[4]

"We were sleeping there with a sailor with a gun on one end of the area and another guard on the other end, but otherwise we weren't protected," recalled Neal Pike. "We were in mostly thick jungle. So, we spent two weeks there gritting out teeth. I was glad to finally get back on war patrol!"

R&R at Camp Dealey, Guam, in February 1945 for the *Spadefish* crew. *Left:* Enjoying a little fun in the sun are (l-r) Hugo Lundquist, Joe Case and Bob Maxwell. *Right:* Sammy Cooper (putting seaweed on Seaweed), "Rebel" Rewold, Jim Schuett and "Shaky Jake" Lewis (right of Luau) with the ship's mascots. *Hugo Lundquist collection, courtesy of Jeanne Lundquist.*

Despite the stern warnings of what had happened to the *Sea Fox* sailors, a small group of *Spadefish* sailors ventured out into the jungle looking for a reported village contained females. "As soon as we reached Camp Dealey, they told us not to go over that fence," said torpedoman Wallace McMahon. "So, they told us that, and what do you think we were going to do? Myself, Thad Barton, Ken Sigworth and Tony Noonan took some .45s out of the gun locker and damned if we didn't go over the fence!"

The quartet hiked uphill through the jungle to a little native village on a high hill. "We had no idea about the road we were on," recalled Sigworth. "It wasn't really much of a road, all surrounded by bushes and jungle." Fortunately, the submariners eventually made their way back to Camp Dealey without any enemy encounters and without any *Spadefish* officers finding out. "We never found any girls," said McMahon. "The only thing we found was this native with a water oxen plowing his field. Talk about idiots!"

Fresh from being depth-charged on war patrol, and with gunfire occasionally heard on Guam, some found their nerves still on edge. "When the wind would blow a coconut loose and make it fall on the Quonset hut," recalled motormac Charles Griffith, "you ought to see all the guys move!"

Across the blacktop road from the Quonset huts was the head, which had a six-holer. "To take a crap at night, you had to take a flashlight and a .45 with you, because the Japs were still around," said

Griffith. Some of the Japanese holdouts on Guam moved about through the jungle, reportedly even stealing clothes and food at night from the area around Camp Dealey. One brazen Japanese soldier dressed in stolen garments actually entered the chow line.

Guam had become an important forward refit station for U.S. submarines operating in the Pacific. Shortly after the island had been declared "secure," Rear Admiral John "Babe" Brown had Seabees use their bulldozers to level off a site in a coconut grove on the windward side of the island. There, working parties from the sub tenders *Sperry* and *Apollo* had set up dozens of Quonset huts for the use of submarine officers and men recuperating between patrols. White coral dust was everywhere as the Seabees continued to add on to the runways and build up the base for the Army's big B-29s.[5]

In spite of the dangers, motormac John Brewer and his buddies collected Japanese paraphernalia. "We got all kinds of souvenirs," he recalled. Brewer found the most interesting artifact on Guam to be a captured Japanese mini-submarine that was put out on display near Camp Dealey. It was the same type of mini-sub that had been used against Pearl Harbor during the attack on 7 December 1941.

Guam had strict operating orders for naval personnel whose vessels were stationed temporarily in Apra Harbor. Specific recreation areas had been designated, including a small area on Orote Peninsula known as Gab Gab Beach. The Seabees had even blasted out enough of the coral, with a metal shark net to seaward, to make a fine swimming hole at the camp. A fleet canteen was established where off-duty sailors could purchase beer, soft drinks, cigarettes, cigars, pipe tobacco and candy. Rationing limits kept the sale of beer to two cans per individual per day.[6]

Sailors were warned to avoid bootleg liquor, left over from the Japanese forces, that was peddled by the local islanders. Part of this liquor had been poisoned by the Japanese and a number of service personnel had died from drinking it.

There was also a volleyball court and four softball fields. The *Spadefish* crew had become quite good at softball. "They would almost cry if they made an error in softball," recalled Boats Eimermann, the pitcher and team manager. "Each run we made, we played for plaques. We won five plaques." Aboard ship, Chief Carl Schmelzer proudly kept track of the *Spadefish* plaques. The crew also excelled in volleyball, tug of war and other sports. "We had quite an athletic bunch," proclaimed Eimermann.

An officers' club had also been erected at the rest camp. "Our small officers' mess had a bar with a very limited supply of whiskey," recalled Dan Decker. "Plenty of beer, of poor quality, was furnished to all." The chief petty officers decided that they needed their own club and

Spadefish chief petty officers in photo taken May 1945 alongside the tender *Holland* in Apra Harbor. *Front row (l-r):* CPhM Victor Ives, CTM Red Wells and CRM Paul "Hocks" Majoue. *Rear (l-r):* CMoMM John Peel, CEM Emerson Ordway, CMoMM Charles Griffith, CEM Carl Schmelzer, CGM "Shaky Jake" Lewis, CRT Neal Pike, and CBM Boats Eimermann. Not shown: CMoMM Rebel Rewold and CCS Francis Scherman. *Hugo Lundquist collection, courtesy of Jeanne Lundquist.*

set about to create one. "The way we got a chiefs' club was using the shack that closed up the heads," explained Paul Majoue. The screened-in shack had been put in place to cover two rows of toilets that had been installed in the camp. "What we did was all get together and pick up the shack and moved it over about 50 yards. I made a sign that said, 'CPO club,' and that was our club."

Aboard ship, there was no drinking during patrol. Between patrols was another story. Lt.(jg) Perry Wood found that Guam had plenty of welcome beer to drink. "It seemed like just shiploads of beer came to that rest place. Some people got smashed out of their minds."

As with all U.S. subs, there was a natural desire to use some of the torpedo alcohol for parties. Most who did so will not readily admit it to this day. "As soon as we came in, we set up a still," recalled torpedoman John Schumer. "We had some boys aboard from the South, and they knew how to make them stills, I'll tell you that!"

While on patrol, the still was kept hidden away from inspections by the officers. Only when *Spadefish* came into port would the torpedo gangs and their allies set it up once most of the crew had gone ashore. According to Schumer, the stillmaster in charge of the "gilly juice" then "brewed it up and took it ashore."

"The presumption was that the torpedo alcohol would poison you," related Wood. "They put a red die, supposedly a poison, in it so people wouldn't drink it. So, we would take a loaf of bread and pour the torpedo juice through the bread, hoping that the bread would filterize all of the poison. None of us went blind!"

The "torpedo juice" was methyl alcohol, the combustion fuel in the torpedo chambers. The Navy had tinted the alcohol pink, thus earning the nickname "pink lady," to warn sailors not to drink it. Once it was cooked through a home-made still, the resulting crystal clear pink lady was called gilly. Potatoes or loaves of "Mother" Riley's bread proved to be acceptable strainers to sponge out most of the methyl. The resulting batch was still highly potent and was generally cut down by mixing it with orange, pineapple or grapefruit juices to make it comparable to a very powerful screwdriver. Bottles of gilly brewed during patrol were carefully tucked away until *Spadefish* ended her patrol run.[7]

The torpedo gang was careful to leave enough juice in the fish to prevent the torpedoes from having problems. This, of course, was never passed on to the captain or Exec, although Wood suspected the skipper was in the know. Wood was in on the gilly juice because he had once caught his chief of the boat in the act of running a batch of the alcohol through bread during a refit period. "I was sitting down in the dining room, running it off and drinking," recalled Boats Eimermann. The incident was kept quiet, but only after a few drinks were shared with Perry Wood and Stinky Schmelzer, the other chief who happened to be aboard at the time.

Guam also had a Naval Hospital ashore to handle the casualties of the fighting that still went on in the island chain. "One of our officers knew a nurse at the naval hospital. He invited a carload of nurses with a day off to visit us at the camp," recalled Lieutenant Decker. "They enjoyed the day and we certainly did." There had been little opportunity to see a woman since departing Pearl Harbor.

One of the nurses had been awake on duty all night, but did not want to miss the chance to visit Camp Dealey this day, as Decker recalled.

> Now she was falling asleep in her chair and asked me if she could lie down somewhere for a short nap. I offered my bunk in our sleeping quarters next door and she said, "Fine." As we walked from our small rec center to our Quonset, one of the crew members spotted us. She lay down in my bunk and was sound asleep in seconds. I read a book, much to the disappointment of several of our crew peeking in the windows at both ends of our Quonset hut.[8]

EM3c Jack Gallagher made a trip back to *Spadefish* with Lieutenant Decker during the refit period. "Our boat was in drydock and they were rigging in and rigging out the bow planes. There were two cables from the bow of the boat to the end of the bow planes," said Gallagher. "There was a lot of welding going on at the back of the boat. They were putting big flanges around the propellers to allow us to go through minefields without us snagging the mine cables."

In addition to the screw guards, all of *Spadefish*'s structural protrusions were carefully rigged to prevent mine cables from snagging on anything. "Cables were rigged from the bow to the bow planes; from the bow to both sides of the conning tower, and similar cables aft so that the stern planes would not snare," recalled Dan Decker.

The relief crew had to be overseen occasionally by some of the crew, who had been trucked out to Camp Dealey. Two of the auxiliaryman, Johnny Peel and Dick Gamby went back to *Spadefish* every couple of days to check on the progress of the jobs of the relief crew. While aboard ship, Gamby took the chance to finally reassemble the motor scooter he had brought aboard from the Pearl Harbor Sub Base before the second patrol.

He had left it aboard ship for some time to let things cool down. "I heard later that the chief at Pearl was looking all over the Pacific for his scooter. The captain did inspections through the boat, but he never found it. After the second run, we were at Majuro but didn't get a chance to bring it ashore."

This night, Gamby and Peel rode it back to Camp Dealey. "I didn't tighten up all the parts to the carburetor, though, and it wouldn't run right," he recalled. After fussing with it awhile the next day, Gamby opted to take the motor scooter back to *Spadefish*. "I tried to ride it back to the ship, but the carburetor would crap out every few miles."

He was able to restart it a few times, only to have it die out a little while later. Gamby finally came across a civilian worker who was walking along the blacktop road. Frustrated with the engine, still a little worried about being caught with a stolen motorcycle, and knowing the bike would have to be disassembled again before going aboard *Spadefish*, he asked, "Hey, you want this thing?"

Gamby explained that all the man needed to do was find somebody to fix the carburetor and it was his for the taking. "I walked the rest of the way back to the sub base!"

The crew returned on 26 February from two weeks' leave at Camp Dealey to find changes in store for them. First, they would not be heading out immediately upon patrol, but would instead be spending the next two weeks preparing for a special mission. Furthermore, they would be doing so with a new skipper. After three highly successful war patrols in command of *Spadefish*, Commander Underwood had new orders to report to the Bureau of Ships for duty. The move was sorely felt aboard ship. "Skippers didn't come any finer than Gordon Underwood," recalled motormac Pat Kelley. "I would have hated to try and fill his shoes."

The crew gathered money and bought their skipper a nice wristwatch. "He saved our rear end a lot of times," said Boats Eimermann, who presented the watch to Underwood along with a little speech. Now that he would be back in the Washington bureau, Captain Underwood told his men to write him if they ever needed something.

Reporting aboard as his replacement was a veteran skipper, Commander William Joseph Germershausen, Jr., USN, who had made three previous patrols in the war zone, two in command. Bill Germershausen had grown up in Baltimore and received his Bachelor of Science from the Baltimore Polytechnic Institute. He was enlisted for a year in the Naval Reserve before entering the U.S. Naval Academy in Annapolis on appointment, at large, on 19 June 1931. While there, he was a star boxer along with Slade Cutter, a classmate who would very ably command another proud Mare Island boat, *Seahorse*. He first met future Vice Admiral Charles Lockwood while in the Academy. "He was the head of the Seamanship Department when I was a midshipman," he recalled. "He was a commander at the time and he actually did the instruction. He had a prestigious job at the Academy, teaching midshipmen how to sail because it went right to the heart of a sailor's business."Once commissioned as an ensign on 6 June 1935, Germershausen had served two years as a junior engineering officer aboard the battleship *Nevada*. From June to December 1937, he went through submarine school at New London. He joined the submarine *Nautilus* in January 1938 and served as Torpedo Officer through January 1941. "It was the biggest boat we had," Germershausen recalled.[9]

He was serving on board *Nautilus* when she suffered a crankcase explosion at Pearl Harbor. A fellow officer, John Reeves Pierce—who was later lost as skipper of the old *Argonaut* when she was sunk by Japanese destroyers—was hospitalized and another sailor was killed. Following his time on *Nautilus*, Germershausen "went from the biggest to the smallest" submarine for duty.

Although "not really pleased" with his new assignment, Germershausen reported to the Navy Yard, Philadelphia, where the submarine *O-6* was in drydock, being demothballed and fitted out. "My mother and father drove up to Philadelphia from Baltimore with me," he said. "They saw this thing and they couldn't believe I was actually going to go to sea on it!"[10]

O-6 was so small that she had only two officers—her skipper, Arnold Henry "Ike" Holtz, and Bill Germershausen. "I was the Executive Officer, Chief Engineer, Navigator, and First Lieutenant. I had all the administrative paperwork. They don't cut down the paperwork with the size of the ship." *O-6* was used as a training boat on the East Coast for submarine school. After Holtz was transferred on, Germershausen served as the commanding officer of *O-6* from 27 May 1942 until December 1943.

"I had to do a lot of screaming and shouting to get off the boat to get out to the Pacific the next year," he recalled. In January 1944, while *Spadefish* was being launched, Germershausen finally received orders to the Submarine Force, Pacific Fleet for PCO School.

"I began to feel that the war was passing me by," he later wrote. "Classmates were returning from the Pacific and putting new fleet boats in commission. I requested destroyer duty, thinking it would be an easier route to combat. I was promptly ordered to Prospective Commanding Officers School at New London."[11]

For his PCO cruise, he was assigned to Commander John Paul "Beetle" Roach's *Haddock* (SS-231) for her ninth war patrol, which departed from Pearl Harbor in early March 1944. In May, Lieutenant Commander Germershausen assumed command of the submarine *Tambor* (SS-198). For *Tambor*'s eleventh war patrol, from 16 July to 1 September 1944, he received a Letter of Commendation, with Ribbon and Combat "V" from CincPac. In spite of cold weather and fog in the area, he pressed home three torpedo attacks, sinking the 2,324-ton freighter *Toei Maru* and damaging a second freighter.[12]

The second small freighter was not hit, and fortunately so. According to Germershausen, she was Russian, which could have touched off an international scandal. He later commented, "I knew she was Russian, but she didn't have proper markings. I thought it sank but I must have missed."[13]

Upon returning to Pearl Harbor, he found that "this Russian had reported and Moscow had protested to Washington." Met by Admiral Lockwood, Germershausen was instructed to go see Admiral Chester Nimitz, Commander in Chief, Pacific Fleet. "He wanted to know what happened." After explaining that he had not seen any marking on this "crummy looking old hulk," he related how he had fired and missed. Prepared for the worst, Germershausen was relieved to hear Nimitz, say, "Well, I'm glad to see you're back safely, son." Although excused from any repercussions from this incident, Bill Germershausen and Russian shipping had not seen the last of each other.[14]

He was awarded the Silver Star Medal for "conspicuous gallantry and intrepidity" for commanding *Tambor*'s twelfth war patrol, from 3

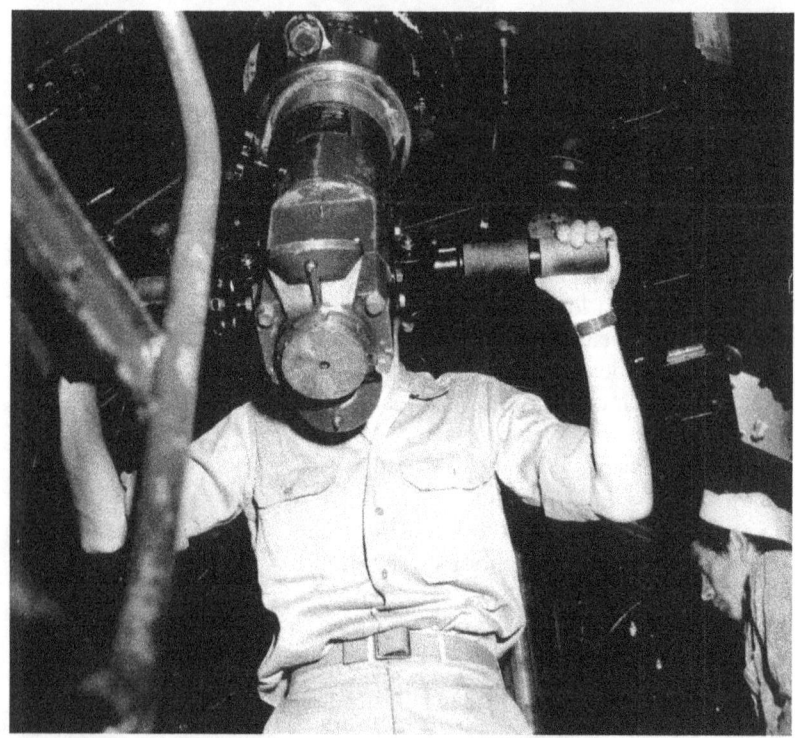

Captain Bill Germershausen, the new skipper of *Spadefish*, seen manning her periscope in the conning tower while on war patrol in 1945. Fire controlman Walter Charles is in the background. *U.S. Navy photo, National Archives.*

October to 30 November 1944. "Commander Germershausen expertly directed his ship in carrying out bold and aggressive attacks against the enemy to sink three Japanese vessels totaling over 5,000 tons and damaged an additional 200-ton craft." After firing torpedoes unsuccessfully at a Japanese patrol vessel, Germershausen battle-surfaced his *Tambor* and sank the craft, the 95-ton ex-picket boat *Taikai Maru*, and took two prisoners. Before sinking, the PC fired back and seriously wounded one of his sailors.[15]

Tambor was an old boat plagued with problems. "We had all four engines break down while I was making an approach on an enemy ship," he recalled. "I recommended that she be pulled out of service." *Tambor* went back to Mare Island to be a training boat, and Germershausen was relieved. He was then ordered out to Guam to Submarine Division 202 as a replacement skipper. When Commander Underwood received his orders to the Bureau of Ships, "I was ordered locally to command the *Spadefish* at Guam."[16]

Chief Paul Majoue, the unofficial photographer aboard *Spadefish*, found that Captain Germershausen's brother was a supply officer aboard one of the sub tenders at Guam. The new skipper's brother managed to supply Majoue with developer, a developing tray and several 25-foot strips of film for use on patrol. Shooting with a 3F model Leica camera that is still functional as of this writing, Majoue used the officer's mess as his developing room during patrol.

When he took command, Germershausen went over his new boat with Underwood. "He was a good skipper," Germershausen later reflected. During his familiarization tour with the outgoing skipper, one item of interest stood out to him. "I asked Gordon what that thing was up there on the bow. It was a big transducer."

Underwood nonchalantly explained, "That's called FM sonar. But don't worry about that. You'll never have to use it."

Germershausen had no idea at the moment just how quickly that statement would be proven wrong.

Soon after taking command of *Spadefish*, Commander Bill Germershausen paid his first visit to ComSubPac. Admiral Lockwood had moved his office from Pearl Harbor out into the Pacific to Guam in January 1945 to be closer to the action.

Advised by former skipper Gordon Underwood not to worry about the FM sonar gear installed aboard his boat, Germershausen suddenly learned that it was now a priority. "I was summoned before Admiral Lockwood and told I'm going to have to use that FM sonar and go map the minefields up in Tsushima Strait," he recalled. "So, I learned something about it real quick!"[17]

Spadefish's FM sonar gear had sat virtually dormant for many months. During this time, Admiral Lockwood had continued to install new FM sets in other subs, still seeking to achieve a safe means to penetrate Japan's Inland Sea once again. In December 1944, he was pleased that *Tinosa*, the second boat installed with FM gear, had successfully used her sonar to chart minefields around Okinawa prior to that island's invasion.[18]

Following his elation from *Tinosa*'s success, Lockwood was disappointed with the performance of two new FM sets aboard the submarines *Bowfin* and *Tunny*, which reached the Pacific in January 1945. Lockwood found that "circuits overheated; tubes gave inferior performances; and there were no electronic technicians on hand trained to handle this new, complicated, and temperamental gear."[19]

Summoning Dr. Harnwell back in California for help, Lockwood asked him to send his best FMS specialist for troubleshooting.

Professor Malcolm Henderson and two assistants reached Saipan during early March to assist. Prior to their arrival, Lockwood used the other most qualified FMS troubleshooter in the Pacific, *Spadefish*'s CRT Neal Pike.

Recently promoted to chief petty officer, Pike now had RT1c Joe Case and RT2c Bill Keeney, a new hand, aboard to stand the radar watches. Regardless, he was frequently answering the call of "Pike to the conning tower!" while on patrol. "Somebody would pick up something or something would go wrong and the captain would want me to look at it," he recalled. During battle stations, he would still man the sonar gear in the conning tower or the audible sound gear in the forward torpedo room. Now, ComSubPac himself was asking Chief Pike to troubleshoot the FM sonar on the new boats that were coming out to Guam and Saipan. "Admiral Lockwood knew that I had the first set and probably knew more about how to fix it that anyone else out there," said Pike. "I made two or three trips with him on his airplane. We would fly out to wherever the other boat was that was having trouble and we would fix it."

Pike recalled:

> Admiral Lockwood was becoming impatient to get U.S. submarines into the Sea of Japan and he took a personal, hands-on interest in making it happen. Therefore, as technicians on the other boats became stuck and could not fix their equipment, Admiral Lockwood would get in his plane, pick me up and take me to the other boat that was in trouble with its new sound gear. I was able to solve the problems as they came up and, fortunately, we got all the boats into operation and Admiral Lockwood was not embarrassed by not being able to solve a problem with the new equipment.[20]

On 2 March, Lockwood flew in his little Beachcraft from his office at Guam, where *Spadefish* was stationed, to Saipan. He routinely borrowed the Beachcraft from Vice Admiral Johnny Hoover, Commander Marianas. Commander George Pierce's new boat *Tunny* had just arrived and was tied alongside the sub tender *Fulton*. Professor Malcolm Henderson and his two California-based sonar experts also arrived, and *Tunny* was put to sea for tests during the next two days. After testing *Tunny*, Lockwood flew to Saipan with Professor Henderson to check out *Tinosa*, the next FM-equipped boat to arrive. *Tinosa*, of course, had received the second-ever FM set after *Spadefish*. Installed in September 1944, *Tinosa*'s set and all those installed after *Spadefish*, were keel-mounted to protect the units.[21]

Bill Germershausen found that ComSubPac was more than just a

Lt.(jg) Edward La Croix (right) receiving award from Captain Lewis Parks on 3 March 1945 in Apra Harbor, Guam. The division officer in center of photo beyond podium is Lt. Dick Fellows, who joined *Spadefish*'s wardroom three days later on 6 March from Parks' staff. *Courtesy of Submarine Force Museum, Groton, Connecticut.*

little involved in the FMS minefield penetration idea.

Admiral Lockwood was busy as a bird dog, going to sea daily with as many of the FMS boats as he could handle in turn, sizing up their men and equipment, and personally teaching the operators how to peak up their equipment and get the most out of their electronic detectors. I have never before or since seen a flag officer so well acquainted with the people and ships he commanded as was this great leader.[22]

Moored in a nest of submarines along the port side of *Proteus*, *Spadefish* had an awards ceremony on 3 March. The *Spadefish* crew returned aboard from rest camp at 1030. George Cook and Boats Eimermann mustered the crew on deck at 1100 and found no absentees. Captain Lewis S. Parks, Commander Submarine Squadron Twenty, had already come aboard at 0930 to inspect the refit being performed by Submarine Division 201. An awards ceremony commenced on deck at 1130, with Captain Parks presenting combat pins to officers and crew for *Spadefish*'s third patrol and higher medals to select officers and crew.

The week of 5-12 March was spent with intensive training to prepare *Spadefish* for her next patrol, involving a special assignment with her FM sonar. This training period was overseen by Captain Eugene Thomas Sands, Commander Submarine Division 201. *Spadefish* held torpedo practices on a multiple target group, while she was surfaced and while submerged, firing seven practice torpedoes. Chief Jake Lewis' gunners received a workout with battle surface rehearsals and firing on targets.

In addition to a new skipper, *Spadefish* received another new officer, Lieutenant Dick Fellows, who was assigned to engineering and electrical duties. Front row (l-r): MoMM1c John Taylor, CEM Emerson Ordway, EM1c Roy Moody and EM2c Billy Pigman. Rear row (l-r): unknown, CEM Carl Schmelzer, FC3c Walter Charles, CMoMM Charles Griffith, and Lt. Fellows. *Walter Charles collection, courtesy of Argyle Charles.*

Completing her training period on 12 March, *Spadefish* spent the next three days preparing for sea. Her wardroom had two new faces, including new skipper Bill Germershausen. Lieutenant Gus Laundy, a plankowner and the TDC operator, was transferred to ComSubPac's staff at Pearl. In return, *Spadefish* received another senior officer from SubDiv 202, Lieutenant Richard Decatur Fellows. Born in Spokane, Washington, Dick Fellows was an "old man" for the sub service at 29 years old. He had attended Beloit College in Wisconsin for two years before graduating from the industrial engineering program at the General Motors Institute in 1939. He was working as an engineer for General Motors at the time he joined the war effort in 1941.

Fellows was a diesel plant inspector before being assigned to *USS Griswold* (DE-7) for her fitting out and commissioning. He had reported to Submarine School in April 1944, but had since served in relief crews until being assigned to *Spadefish*. Fellows became *Spadefish*'s assistant engineering officer. To replace Laundy on the TDC, Lieutenant Dan Decker would serve as her torpedo and gunnery officer. Lt.(jg) Ed La Croix took over Decker's duties as first lieutenant. Ensign Bill Ware, the engineering and diving officer, would serve as Decker's assistant gunnery officer. Don Martin would serve as com-

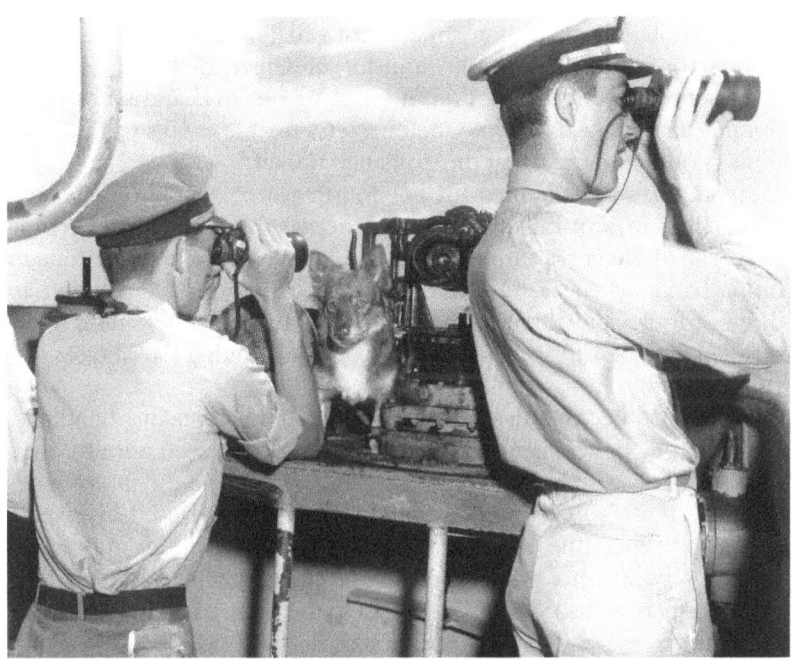

Lt. Dan Decker (left) and Lt.(jg) Ed La Croix in their dress caps on the bridge with one of the ship's mascots near the TBT as *Spadefish* enters port. Although grown, Seaweed is still a small dog. Loved by most aboard, Seaweed had more of a temper streak than his mother, Luau. *Courtesy of Thomas Miller.*

missary and assistant electrical officer, while Charles Johnson would be assistant communications officer to Perry Wood. In the commissary department, *Spadefish*'s StM1c Solomon was transferred. In his place, she received steward William Bynum, who had been aboard the old *R-14* and then had made patrols on *Burrfish* in 1944.

Fellows and Ware had another assistant engineering officer in Warrant Machinist Dutch Falconer, who had just joined the mustang club by being promoted on 14 March from chief motor machinist's mate. "Dutch was such a good person," recalled motormac John Brewer. "He just seemed so out of place, having to bunk with the officers now." On the positive side, Falconer's thorough knowledge and association with *Spadefish*'s black gang made him a perfect fit to assist Fellows, as Bill Ware took on more time with the assistant gunnery officer duties. With Dutch Falconer, the wardroom was now up to ten officers, plus two from previous patrols.

As was customary, the ship lost a number of key men to transfers, including chiefs "Silent Runnin' Carl" Biberdorf and senior torpedoman Harry George. Charlie Griffith, *Spadefish*'s original Fuel King, was promoted to chief motor machinist's mate, filling the void in the engine rooms created by the transfer of Chief Biberdorf. Griffith found out about his promotion upon going on R&R and had eagerly donned his new cap. "Stinky Schmelzer gave me a CPO pin to use until I could go buy one at the exchange myself."

Spadefish's complement for her fourth patrol was 86 officers and men, ship's mascot Luau, and her son Seaweed. "Weed" had become a favorite of the crew, although he was a little temperamental, prone to nip at hands when he was tired of being picked up. "He couldn't go three or four feet without someone picking him up and petting him," recalled Chief Griffith, "so Seaweed would get kinda nasty and snap at you sometimes."

At chow time, Seaweed was everyone's shipmate, taking handouts, the only time he was not picky with his friends. Seaweed went through the engine rooms "like a brown blur" to avoid one of the motormacs. This machinist's mate loathed the little dog that had used his engine room for relief one too many times. Occasionally, this motormac would "play possum" when Weed came sneaking through toward the after compartments. When the dog got to the point of no return, something usually came flying in his direction.[23]

The safety of the maneuvering room usually found a friendly hand ready to pat Seaweed. It is with little wonder, then that Seaweed made friends with the electricians there, particularly Chief "Stinky" Schmelzer and, later, Jim Cole. "Our chief electrician's mate had the personality of a drunken Tasmanian devil. That's probably why Seaweed liked him so much," recalled Pat Kelley. "He followed Schmelzer everywhere."

Spadefish got underway at 0600 on 15 March 1945 from alongside the tender *Proteus* at Guam in the Marianas Islands. She proceeded northeast in company with *Devilfish* and an escort to the nearby island of Saipan, where Admiral Lockwood was still at work testing the new FM sonar sets. *Spadefish* reached Saipan at 1745 and moored along the port side of the tender *Fulton* (AS-11), receiving fuel and minor voyage repairs in Tanapag Harbor.

After returning to Saipan from his test aboard *Tinosa*, Lockwood found "*Spadefish* was champing at the bit to get away on patrol." The admiral and Professor Henderson thus left *Tinosa* in port and returned to do some tests with *Spadefish*. "Vice Admiral Lockwood and Dr. Henderson came aboard," recorded JOOD Don Martin on 16 March. "0805, underway maneuvering, en route to operating area."[24]

With ComSubPac and his FMS specialist aboard, *Spadefish* passed through Tanapag Harbor's protective torpedo nets and headed out to test her sonar. "Uncle Charlie" found that Germershausen's first tests with his FM sonar had been "replete with disappointment, adjustments and cussing, but on the 16th, with a rough sea, when sonar conditions could be expected to be unfavorable, we got good ranges, actually, the best we had ever got." Lockwood gave full credit to the work of *Spadefish*'s talented operators. "This pioneer set, now improved by the latest alterations, performed beautifully. P. [H.] Majoue and Ch. Radio Tech. N. Pike, were especially adept and her set was in excellent adjustment."

Spadefish moored alongside *Fulton* at 1347. Lockwood and Henderson departed, satisfied with her FM set. They returned for further testing aboard Captain Dick Latham's *Tinosa*, which Lockwood planned to send out right behind *Spadefish* on patrol. Lockwood gave Captain Germershausen orders to sail the following Monday on a mission which included establishing the southern limits of the Tsushima Straits mine field. ComSubPac really needed to know where the mine field started in order to continue to plan out his penetration of the Sea of Japan.

"I also instructed Germershausen and Latham, as well as all skippers who followed them, to pick up—forcibly if necessary—prisoners from the Yellow Sea and near Tsushima Straits," wrote Lockwood.[25]

Admiral Lockwood knew that such prisoners rarely came aboard voluntarily. Swimming teams were formed on some boats to go drag them in. In *Spadefish*'s case, a boarding party was formed which would drag a prisoner back aboard if necessary.

Lieutenants George Cook and Dan Decker would head this team. They selected several other key crewmen to assist them with boarding duties: Chief Gunner's Mate Shakey Jake Lewis, gunner Bernie Massar and new Chief Torpedoman Red Wells. The boarding party found their new skipper was eager to carry out Admiral Lockwood's new orders to capture a prisoner.

While serving as a PCO on Captain Beetle Roach's *Haddock*, Bill Germershausen had come close to boarding an enemy vessel. During *Haddock*'s return from a patrol in the Okinawa area, she received an Ultra to intercept a small supply boat which was taking food and classified documents to Wake Island. Roach and Germershausen made plans to try and capture the small ship intact and sail it back to Pearl Harbor. "We thought we'd take the whole ship, depending on how heavily armed she was," said Germershausen.[26]

"I proposed to the captain that we try to take the ship intact and that I would take a prize crew and sail her into Midway," Bill Germershausen later wrote. "The chief engineer of *Haddock* was a gung-ho character and he wanted to take on the job. We were still arguing about this when we intercepted the ship."[27]

Admiral Lockwood, however, had also sent this Ultra to another submarine in their area, *Tuna*. Before *Haddock* could send a boarding party onto this vessel, *Tuna* came up and sank the ship, later identified as *Takima Maru*, with her deck gun. "She had it in flames on the surface by the time we came up on it," recalled Germershausen.[28]

Haddock put a rubber boat in the water with one of her officers and enlisted men to collect classified papers, books and other documents that were floating out from the sinking supply ship. "I was officer of the deck at the time," Germershausen remembered. "I asked the captain if I could join the fellas over the side and he said, 'yes.'"

With that, he stripped to his skivvies and dove overboard to begin collecting books and papers. "Meanwhile, people from the *Tuna* were doing the same thing. We were all in the water together, the Japanese, ourselves, the floating documents and the sinking ship." *Haddock* hauled two Japanese prisoners aboard, returning these and some sixty documents over to the intelligence center at Pearl Harbor upon her return. During the recovery efforts, *Tuna*'s chief of the boat, John Kirkman Huff, fell overboard and disappeared, possibly a victim of his own inability to swim.[29]

"When I climbed back aboard *Haddock*, the CO asked me who had the deck," wrote Germershausen. "I had assumed he had relieved me, so we had been operating without an OOD. I sheepishly said, 'Me.'"[30]

Now in command of *Spadefish*, Commander Germershausen would not be opposed to using his own boarding party to retrieve intelligence from enemy ships if such an opportunity presented itself.

After working with *Spadefish*, Lockwood returned to Guam that afternoon. He found to his surprise that Admiral Nimitz was at his headquarters to pay a visit. When Nimitz and Lockwood met on Guam on the following day, Sunday, 16 March, Lockwood informed his boss that he had just completed FMS training runs on *Spadefish*. "She sails tomorrow," he explained to his boss. "She's got an excellent set with fine technicians and one outstanding operator. We are sending her to locate the southern limits of that Tsushima mine field—and it is an important mission. I'd like permission to go with her."[31]

Nimitz told Lockwood that he knew "too damned much about our future plans" and that he could not go on patrol. He did agree to let Lockwood run sonar tests of different gear.

Despite ComSubPac's best efforts, he was again denied the chance of making a war patrol aboard *Spadefish*.

15

"Beyond Test Depth"

Fourth Patrol   *17 March–6 April, 1945*

Captain Bill Germershausen was on the bridge of his new command, calling out commands over the rumbling of *Spadefish*'s diesels. Having commanded two previous submarines, he had no difficulty pulling away from the tender nest in Saipan's Tanapag Harbor and getting his boat underway at 1336 on 17 March.

His boat was putting to sea under ComSubPac's Secret Operation Order Number 65-45. "The primary mission of my first patrol was to map mine fields," Germershausen recalled. "We were headed to Tsushima Strait." Admiral Lockwood was sending three boats out into Nishi Suido, the East China Sea and parts of the Yellow Sea, two of which were FMS-equipped. Command went to Commander Dick Latham, who had just returned from a successful mine field mapping patrol off Okinawa, for which Lockwood awarded him the Navy Cross for his FMS work.[1]

The third boat sent out from Saipan, separate from *Spadefish* and *Tinosa*, was Lieutenant Commander George Levick Street's *Tirante*, making her first war patrol. The three boats would operate as a wolf pack nicknamed "Latham's Locators," although more independently than previous wolf packs *Spadefish* had worked with. *Tinosa* and *Spadefish* proceeded out from Saipan under guard of escort *SC-775*, which departed their company at 2000.

After a month at Guam and Saipan on refit and then in training, the *Spadefish* crew was itching to get back into action. While on leave in February, two of the boat's plankowner chiefs extended their service agreement with the U.S. Navy. CBM Willard Eimermann and CCS Francis Scherman both signed on for another three year enlistment to continue fighting the war.

Scherman, boss of the galley aboard *Spadefish*, also served as the pointer for the 5-inch deck gun crew. His gun, of course, had seen no action during *Spadefish*'s first three runs, which was just fine with

Seaweed below *Spadefish*'s 5-inch/25 caliber deck gun. The two tubes above Seaweed's head are counter-recoil cylinders containing hydraulic damper pistons and six springs, used to recoil the main barrel (above these cylinders) back to its original position. The barrel and breech assembly could recoil up to 22 inches in distance when fired. *Courtesy of Paul Majoue.*

Scherman. "His contention was that sometime the sampans are used as decoys for submarines and are really outfitted with suitable weapons," wrote gunner's mate Bernie Massar. Scherman worried that men would be needlessly lost in a close gun duel or that the ship could be fatally holed. Regardless of his opinions, however, he stood ready to join the fight if the new skipper gave the nod.

Although the 5-inch gun had not been used against enemy targets, the small arms and 20mms aboard *Spadefish* had successfully destroyed many enemy mines. All weapons were kept on the ready, and fired in practice whenever practicable. "There were a few times we took our two shotguns to practice shooting while at sea," wrote Massar. "We did not have any clay pigeons or a thrower to fling any out. So, we used coffee cups thrown into the air. Once thrown, they were lost—hit or missed. Chief Scherman found out about this and the practice came to a halt to save his treasured coffee cups."

Massar and the chief gunner's mate, Shaky Jake Lewis, had every indication that Bill Germershausen was prepared to call for a battle stations surface on this run. "Captain Germershausen used to see me cleaning the guns all the time," recalled Massar. "he said, 'Gee, I'm sick and tired of watching you clean those guns all the time. We've gotta get you some business.'"

During the training period prior to patrol, the new skipper drilled his crew with the 5-incher. Midway through the firing exercise, the deck gun had a misfire. "In peace time, a misfire is treated as a hang fire and the shell is left in the gun for a period of time for safety's sake," related first loader Massar. The *Spadefish* gunners' mates knew during wartime to remove the bad shell before it could ruin their deck gun.[2]

Massar released the breech and Chief Lewis took the 5-inch shell out. "He turned it over to check the primer cap to see if it was struck," wrote Massar. Fellow shell loader Buck Miller noted Captain Germershausen on the cigarette deck shouting at Lewis to throw it overboard.

Lewis hurriedly heaved the shell toward the ocean, but not far enough. *Bong!* The sixty-five pound explosive caromed off the bulge of *Spadefish*'s hull and bounced into the ocean, fortunately without exploding.

Seemingly undisturbed and ready to continue the firing practice, Shaky Jake called, "Permission to commence firing, sir?"

"Give me a few minutes to get over this first!" Germershausen snapped.

The near tragedy avoided, deck gun firing practice resumed. Buck Miller could only think, "He should have let Harry Brenneis—very athletic—toss it."

With the promotion of Dutch Falconer to warrant officer and with Ensign Johnson now being qualified as a JOOD, Exec George Cook now had eight junior officers qualified to stand watch. For the fourth patrol, he opted to change the deck watch rotations from four-hour shifts to two-hours shifts to keep everyone fresh. Each officer team would stand deck watch for two hours, be off for six hours and then return for another two hour shift. Each team thus stood three watches in a 24-hour period.

Among the 84 officers and men aboard *Spadefish* for her fourth patrol was one man temporarily assigned for duty. Under orders from Commander Task Group 17.7, Photographer's Mate 1/c Robert Hamilton Rymer reported aboard for duty on the morning of departure. Although Chief Majoue had ably performed as the unofficial photographer during *Spadefish*'s first three runs and would continue to put his Leica to good use, Admiral Lockwood put photographer's mates aboard his FMS boats for their next runs. Rymer had already seen his

Reporting aboard *Spadefish* for temporary duty on her fourth patrol was photographer's mate Robert Hamilton Rymer (left). Having previously documented Army bombing missions and life aboard Navy carriers, some of Rymer's submarine photography (such as this submergence shot above) would be used postwar in the documentary film *Silent Service. Courtesy of Mrs. Ilona Rymer.*

share of action in the Pacific, having previously gone to sea on a carrier and making hops aboard B-29s for bombing missions.[3]

Shortly after *Spadefish*'s escort ship had departed, the radar screen lit up at 2047 with pips of eleven ships. Captain Germershausen stationed his tracking party to monitor what was obviously an Allied task force. *Spadefish* went to flank speed to avoid this unexpected group, as several destroyers came very close. Tracking was secured at 2150, well clear of the task force.

Once well clear of Saipan, Captain Germershausen read his secret patrol orders to the crew. In his journal for 17 March 1945, torpedoman Hugo Lundquist scrawled, "Capt. said we were to chart mine fields in Korean Strait between Kyushu and Korea—entrance to Sea of Japan."

The next two days were spent in training new crewmen en route to the patrol area. Newer unrated hands assisted with duties in the galley and in the endless washing of clothes in salt water. "They would wash our jeans and stretch them out over the engine covers to dry them out," related motormac John Brewer.

Spadefish submerged at 0903 on 18 March for trim and training, resurfacing at 0935. She ran the remainder of the day on the surface, save a practice plane dive at 1455. The tracking drills and practice dives continued throughout 19 March.

To break the monotony, some of the more seasoned crew members never missed a chance to have a good time by pulling pranks, even on the officers. On one particular occasion, Lieutenant Dan Decker and his cigar were the victims. A longtime cigar smoker, Decker would smoke one inch of his cigar whenever the smoking lamp was lit. "During submerged patrolling, all hands were allowed one cigarette every two hours," he recalled. When he would finish his one inch, he would place a chalk mark on his cigar and ration it for his next smoke break. He would simply leave the extinguished cigar in the nearest ash tray and proceed with his duties.

Shaky Jake Lewis, the leading gunner's mate, and his accomplices borrowed the abandoned cigar on this particular occasion and headed back to the auxiliary room. They bored out the cigar's center, refilled it with gunpowder that Lewis had removed from a 20mm shell, then packed in the shell's propellant. Stuffing some of the tobacco back in the tip, they returned the cigar to its ashtray and waited eagerly for the next smoking break.

"When I lit up again, I noticed a sputtering sound," remembered Lieutenant Decker. "I extended the cigar for an inspection, when it exploded all over the control room. I had a couple of blackened fingers, but was not burned." Those in the know about the control room —who had carefully backed as far away as possible—erupted into cheers. "Even the skipper thought this event was amusing."

At 1100 on 19 March, while holding tracking drills on *Tinosa* as her target, *Spadefish* sighted a periscope 800 yards abeam. Evasive maneuvers were made and a contact report was sent out to both *Tinosa* and ComSubPac. This submarine was likely still in the area the next day as *Spadefish* continued with training exercises. At 2128, radar contact was made at 30,000 yards. Captain Germershausen commenced tracking but soon lost his contact. He secured tracking at 2157, as contact could not be regained. This was believed to be due to a submarine that had dived and disappeared from radar.

At 0300 on 21 March, *Spadefish* passed *Bluefish* (SS-222), exchanging calls and recognition signals. Lookouts sighted an Army B-29 bomber at 1145. This was the fifth day out of Saipan, and *Spadefish* was steaming on the surface. At 1235, an aircraft was spotted at 8 miles, but it did not close the distance. Four minutes later, a Betty two-engine bomber was spotted. At first thought to be another friendly Army bomber, this pilot was now coming out of a cloud only 3 miles away, not appearing too friendly with his intentions!

Lt.(jg) Perry Wood was the OOD with Lt. Dick Fellows, making his first war patrol, as his JOOD. Wood immediately sounded the diving alarm and cleared the bridge. *Spadefish* made a crash dive, pulling a flare as she went down. As she reached 45 feet, a bomb exploded overhead. In two consecutive patrols, *Spadefish* had now been bombed by aircraft while en route to her station.

The explosion did not seem too terribly close, so Captain Germershausen kept her down until 1355, surfacing after the skies seemed clear of "friendly" aircraft. Upon surfacing, a bomb fragment was found on deck. "We found a piece of the bomb near our deck gun and realized it was closer than we thought," wrote gunner's mate Bernie Massar. "This fragment was recovered and we kept it on display in the crew's mess."

At 1638 on 21 March, Lt.(jg) La Croix took *Spadefish* down to 180 feet to conduct a test of her FM sonar set in preparation for her mission of mapping enemy mine fields. Chief Pike practiced with his equipment for about twenty minutes, but had no luck in picking up the triplane.

The following afternoon, 22 March, *Spadefish*'s crew again put the triplane and buoy over the side and commenced maneuvering for tests with her sonar equipment. Dan Decker took the boat down and made two runs on the triplane with Neal Pike on the FM set. In just under an hour, *Spadefish* was back on the surface at 1515, maneuvering to pick up the buoy and triplane. "En route [to] area, put triplane over the side several times and made trial runs on it," wrote Germershausen. "Definite contact on the triplane was never made."[4]

At 1710, Ed La Croix announced that his high periscope watch had sighted sister sub *Tinosa*. *Spadefish* and *Tinosa* remained on the surface, running at flank speed on all four main engines as they transited Colnett Strait from 2300 to 0300 on 23 March. Passing through Colnett Strait brought the two FM boats into the East China Sea. Bordered on the north by Kyushu, Japan, and the southern tip of Korea, the East China Sea's eastern boundary touched the Ryukyu Islands (Nansei-Shoto chain). The western boundary of the East China Sea, appropriately enough, was mainland China. Southeast of Shanghai and Kagoshima lay the 100-fathom curve, water considered safely deep enough for submarine operations. Depths north of this curve averaged only 60 fathoms.[5]

Having transited Colnett Strait and entered the East China Sea during the early morning hours of 23 March, *Spadefish* made contact with enemy shipping on her first day in this patrol area. Admiral Lockwood had sent out an Ultra to Bill Germershausen, directing him exactly where he would pick up this Japanese convoy. "We were headed up to Tsushima Strait when we got this Ultra," recalled the skipper. He found that ComSubPac's intelligence was perfect as to the enemy shipping's course and location. "It was right on the money. I just had to wait there."[6]

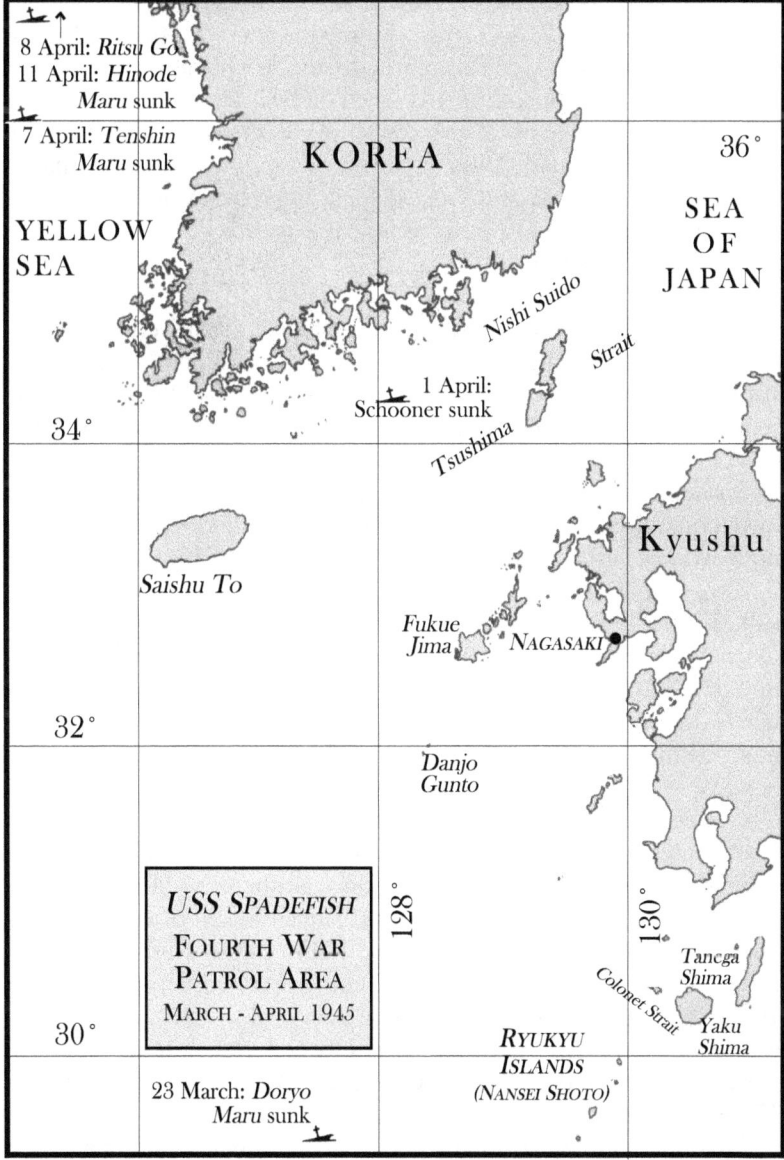

The high periscope watch spotted four large ships at 1530, distance 20,000 yards, and Lt. Decker called the skipper to the conning tower. This convoy was destined for Okinawa to reinforce the battle that was raging for control of this island group. *Spadefish* was leading wolf pack commander Dick Latham's *Tinosa* as she entered the East China Sea. "We were supposed to make coordinated attacks on this convoy, but we were far ahead of him and we had picked up the convoy at the point where it was supposed to be," Germershausen recalled.

Knowing that *Tinosa* was some distance behind, Captain Germershausen prepared for a torpedo attack. His desire for his first kill in command of *Spadefish* was egged on by his junior officers. "The 'Old Man,' at the age of 32 or so, was the conservative member of the group," he later related. "The junior officers on the boats were maybe 25." Now confronted with this golden opportunity on 23 March, Germershausen found his wardroom eager to attack.[7]

"Captain, let's shoot."

"Let's get her!"

With his officers ready and willing for the fight, Bill Germershausen did not hesitate to move. He found the Okinawa-bound convoy consisted of four troop transports and five escort vessels. During the initial setups on this convoy, lookouts spotted a floating mine at 1612 and OOD Ed La Croix maneuvered *Spadefish* to avoid it.

Spadefish submerged for an attack approach at 1616. Inside her busy conning tower, some of the roles had shifted. Germershausen now worked with Exec George Cook to orchestrate the attacks. Leading signalman Jim Schuett continued to serve as the periscope jockey, calling out bearings from the scope's dials upon request. Dan Decker had moved up to the TDC, with Perry Wood handling his former role as plotting officer. Chief Pike continued to handle radar needs during battle stations, torpedo. The JP and JK sound gear were manned during attack approaches by Chief Majoue and "Little Fox" Sergio.

Germershausen settled upon the leading ship in column, a large troop transport, as his target. From the information called out by the skipper, the approach party flipped through the ONI-208J book and settled upon *Koei Maru*, with an approximate weight of 6,700 tons.

Talker Vic Ives passed the word to TM1c Emery Kreher's forward room to open the outer tube doors. The prescribed depth setting was 10 feet, due to the deep draft of these heavy ships. Each forward tube was loaded with a Mark 18.1 wakeless torpedo. Despite facing rough seas, *Spadefish* was in firing position and commenced shooting at 1710, firing tubes 1, 2, 3 and 4, in order.

In the forward torpedo room, Kreher's men suddenly had their

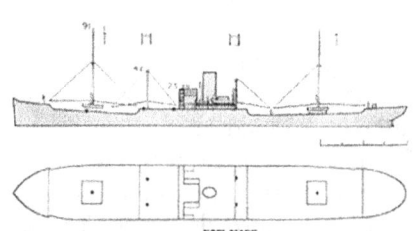

The target ship of *Spadefish* on 23 March 1945 was identified by her tracking party as *Koei Maru*, a 6,600-ton freighter shown here from the ONI-208-J recognition manual they used. *ONI 208-J (Revised).*

hands full with a problem. "We fired a torpedo and one of the poppet valves stuck," recalled motormac John Brewer. "The poppet valve was only supposed to stay open long enough to allow water to come in and fill the tube to compensate for the weight of the torpedo we had fired. But the water kept coming in."

Torpedoman 3/c Wallace McMahon stayed at his station, setting the torpedo gyros on all four fish, even as the water sprayed in. McMahon later related his experiences under water pressure.

> Between the six torpedo tubes was what we called the "Mickey Mouse." It was a little hand-operated device which directed or changed the angles of the torpedo while it was still in the tube. The actual angle the torpedo was going to be fired came down from the conning tower. This Mickey Mouse was not actually connected, so I had to sit in between the tubes and hand-set the wheels, one on each side, to match the angle shown on the needle from the conning tower.
>
> So, when the poppet valve went, I happened to be in this particular station. When the poppet went, it was like I dove into salt water. But I never left my station. I kept those damn needles matched while the ocean water was spraying in until we finished firing our torpedoes. Some time later, I happened to be passing by the wardroom and the captain said, "Nice work, McMahon." That was like the hand of God.

Making a submerged daylight attack, Captain Germershausen found that the alert Japanese escorts had spotted his periscope during the time he was firing his torpedoes. "The escort was too close to us and headed right for us," he said. "He must have been 1,000 yards away when I spotted him, so we had to go down."

"Take her to 400 feet," the skipper called. With plenty of deep water at this spot, he opted to try and take *Spadefish* below the depth that the onrushing destroyer would likely set her depth charges. At 1711 and fifteen seconds, the sound of *Spadefish*'s first torpedo exploding could be plainly heard. One second later, a second torpedo explosion announced to all that the attack had been a success. Paul Majoue had tracked the torpedoes to the target on his sound gear. He now announced that the target ship's screws had stopped. These explosions were followed "by several minutes of loud breaking-up noises, plainly audible through our hull," as recorded in the patrol report.

Lieutenant Dan Decker had dropped down to the control room to handle the duties of diving officer after the torpedo attack. Yeoman Kreinbring and Chief Lewis had already assumed their posts as battle stations planesmen. The ship was rigged for silent running, and Decker was initially ordered to take her down to 400 feet. The Japanese destroyer skipper this day was quite good, for the first round of depth charges were very close when they exploded at 1715. "The depth charge attacks were the most accurate and prolonged we experienced in our five patrols," wrote Decker.[8]

Standing duty in the maneuvering room, electrician Ken Sigworth felt that the first charges exploded alarmingly close. He heard the captain call out, "Take her to 450!"

Diving officer Decker had Lewis and Kreinbring ease the boat down to 450 feet, hoping to duck below the depth which the destroyer had set her first charges. The next string of explosions was still too close for comfort, so the diving officer eased her down another fifty feet to 500 feet. Other escorts converged upon the scene and apparently had an easy time picking up *Spadefish* on sonar this day. "One would listen on sonar while the other two made an X pattern above us to drop depth charges where the sound gear had picked us up," Sigworth explained.

The destroyers hung on to *Spadefish* doggedly and continued unloading depth charges each time they had a good fix on the submarine. The destroyer churned overhead and dropped another string of depth charges. Gunner's mate Bernie Massar, standing by as a relief behind Chief Lewis on the bow planes, recalled "getting a hell of a thrashing with many depth charges."[9]

Even as *Spadefish* dropped down from 450 to 500 feet, the enemy charges were exploding disturbingly close. "I was holding a depth of 500, I think the deepest we had ever been to evade a careful attack," said Decker. "The Japanese destroyer skipper was good." The next string of ashcans exploded directly overhead with enough force to slam the neutrally buoyant submarine straight down.

This blast "forced us down past 600 feet," recalled Massar. "I do not know of the actual depth before we stopped and gained control." Ken Sigworth remembered that before the descent could be checked, "we had gone 150 feet or better beyond test depth."

As *Spadefish* was blown down to the 600 foot depth, there were a few frantic seconds of trying to bring her back to the ordered depth. According to Sigworth, Captain Germershausen had called, "Stop her at 500 feet." When the concussion drove the ship down, he heard the skipper holler, "Goddamnit, stop her somewhere!"

Lieutenant Decker shouted back up that he had been at 500 feet, but that the high pressure force of the blasts had driven her deeper. "It took a bit of doing to work our way back to 500 feet," he recalled. With the hydraulic pump off for silent running, the planesmen labored heavily to rotate the control wheels by hand. The ship's unofficial history noted, "This was the deepest the boat would ever go."[10]

"Full rise on the bow planes," Decker ordered.

Shaky Jake Lewis twisted the wheel to have *Spadefish*'s bow assume a 15-degree up angle. Decker maintained standard speed with the planes pushing the boat upward to prevent even further submergence.

In the pump room, auxiliaryman Dick Gamby was worried as the ship's depth flew past 600 feet. "We ended up well past our test depth." Nervous eyes watched the valves and gauges for water leaks as the pressure squeezed the boat tightly. "I would put a wrench on the valves and just keep tightening them," said Gamby. "As the pressure built up on them, then I'd let them off."

While Decker and his planesmen struggled to bring the ship back up to 500 feet, a call from forward announced why *Spadefish* was more negatively buoyant than usual: "Flooding in the forward torpedo room!"

Irv Kreinbring, laboring with the stern planes, noted this extra challenge that posed itself during the depth charge attack.

> The one thing I remember most vividly about our fourth patrol was our first ship contact and torpedo firing, followed by the order to "take her down" to 450 feet. We stopped our descent at 612 feet only by holding a 10 degree up-angle on the boat and increasing the prop rpms. An error in the forward room flooded the bilges and we were nose-heavy.[11]

Kreher's torpedomen had managed to bang the poppet valve closed again after firing the torpedoes, but the extra seawater had flooded the forward bilges and made *Spadefish* nose-heavy. Under silent running, the electric pumps could not be used to pump out the excess water. As *Spadefish* descended to depths previously unexplored, the pressures on her hull were intense. "They put me down in the bilge room with a big monkey stetson wrench," said motormac John Brewer. He was ordered to relieve pressure on the induction valves, but found the sudden jarring blasts of depth charges quite uncomfortable. "Those depth charges would go off and it would pull the valve I was holding right out of my hand."

While at deep submergence during the depth charging, *Spadefish* also developed a leak in the circulating water suction to her No. 2 compressor, evidently caused by internal corrosion. After the boat's last refit, two nipples had been replaced on this line. The leak was found to be "under several layers of friction tape, heavily covered with green paint." Captain Germershausen noted in his report that "this is considered poor engineering practice to say the least."

Captain Germershausen's log notes that from 1715 to 1812, a total of 52 depth charges were dropped, "most of them close." Some were dropped with "shaking precision." Some crewmen tried to keep count of the depth charges as they went off. Ship's cook Ed Graf, stationed in the galley at the time, later wrote, "I had the exact count at one time. Then I sent my shorts to the laundry and lost the count." In his little journal, torpedoman Hugo Lundquist scribbled, "Cans dropped depth charges fast and close, about 50."[12]

In this case, the multitude of depth charge explosions caused severe turbulence and extensive gas bubbles. The searching destroyers likely found new echoes on their ranging gear. These disturbances, plus *Spadefish*'s extreme depth, allowed her to sneak away from her attackers.

In spite of frequent and close depth charge explosions, *Spadefish* received no serious damage from this attack. "The depth charge attack lasted for about one hour and we received a real good pasting with some block-busters," wrote Germershausen in his patrol report. "Again first team work. One ship was left with us as remainder could be heard in the vicinity of the sunken ship, probably picking up survivors."

It was not until 1900, almost two hours after firing on the transport convoy, that it was secure enough for the forward gang to reload their torpedo tubes. Although periscope observations had led the skipper to believe his victim was in excess of 6,000 tons, postwar credit by several sources all agreed that this ship was the 2,274-ton transport *Doryo Maru*. Japanese records show that *Doryu Maru* was hit in her No. 2 hold and sank in thirty seconds, taking down sixty crewmen and 262 Navy passengers with her.[13]

One destroyer remained above *Spadefish* long enough to keep her down and let the convoy escape from any further attacks. "Finally, it was dark, when we could come up and get everything squared away," recalled John Brewer. "I didn't think we were ever gonna get out of that one."

After the counterattack ceased, *Spadefish* surfaced at 2022. Captain Germershausen headed for the predicted midnight position of the convoy but was unable to reestablish contact during the night.

At 2100, *Spadefish* received orders from Commander Latham to form a scouting line with *Tinosa* to continue searching for the convoy. At 2110, *Spadefish* informed *Tinosa* that she had attacked and sunk one ship, and gave the last known position of convoy.

Recalling this Ultra-directed attack, Germershausen regretted that he had not waited on *Tinosa* to make a coordinated strike.

> Latham was senior. I should have waited for orders from him. I should have trailed and given him contact reports so that we could get on their quarters and make night attacks on it. I apologized all over the place about it. He didn't get a chance to make any attacks at all.
>
> When we surfaced to report to Latham, the convoy had disappeared and we were unable to regain contact on it. Had we held our fire and waited, we may have gotten two ships or more. As it was, we got only one.[14]

Dick Latham's *Tinosa* had endured her own tense moments on 23 March. While making a routine dive, her bow planes failed to rig out. He took her to 150 feet to assess the situation, but soon found a strong current taking the boat toward land. Just as the executive officer asked for periscope depth to take a navigational fix, *Tinosa* ran aground on a shoal just off the island of Amami-O-Shima. Latham was able to back his boat off the shoal, suffering little more than the loss of one forward torpedo tube due to a jammed outer door. One of *Tinosa*'s crewmen noted in his diary, "Submarine warfare—never a dull moment."[15]

Spadefish's Bendix log, an underwater device for measuring the submarine's own speed, was out of commission after the heavy depth charging. To get an accurate navigational fix, she ran in to pick up Yokoate Shima, then moved back to continue following the convoy track.

At 0543 on 24 March, *Spadefish* submerged 30 miles north of Iwo Shima, and ran north along the troop transport convoy's track, starting at its predicted noon position. No shipping contacts were made. The periscope watch sighted two enemy fighter planes at 0750. Ducking under, the watch heard two distant explosions at 0759.

After a fruitless day of submerged searching, *Spadefish* surfaced at 1520 and set course for her assigned area west of Kyushu. At 0028 on

Sunday, 25 March, the APR radar detector picked up enemy radar interference. This was followed by a pip at 8 miles on the SD radar. The combination of the radar bogey and the APR signal indicated a Japanese radar-equipped snooper, so OOD Ed La Croix ordered the ship submerged. *Spadefish* returned to the surface at 0110 and continued on her course for Kyushu.

Her consistently impressive radar made contact at 0350 on Uji Shima, at a distance of 59,000 yards (33.5 miles). Some of these extreme ranges on early radar were possible due to the "skip distance" of the radar waves over the ocean's surface. Running on the surface after sunrise, *Spadefish* had a very close call with another floating mine. At 0656, Bernie Massar, standing lookout atop the port side of the periscope shears, spotted the hellpot almost dead ahead, just slightly to port. "Mine ahead!" he shouted.

The officer of the deck, Dan Decker, maneuvered the ship to avoid the mine and only narrowly avoided colliding with it. Massar noted that the ultimate order for hard right rudder ended up putting "the mine on our port side and it came alongside of the boat as we went forward. The mine was a few feet off our port beam and bobbing along our side. I was looking down at the mine as we went forward and hoping for the best!"

Fortunately, Massar's alert watch standing had helped avoid this potential disaster. "It was left astern, but we sweated that one out—a near miss." In the patrol report, Captain Germershausen wrote that this mine was "cleared by five feet."

The remainder of this watch and the 8 to 12 went without incident. At 1215, an SD radar contact, followed quickly by a lookout's visual sighting, was made on an inbound aircraft at 150 feet. "Clear the bridge!" shouted Perry Wood as he pulled the diving alarm. *Spadefish* made a crash dive and elected to remain down in safer water for a while.

At 1510, Neal Pike turned on his FM sonar for its first test on plotting Japanese mines off Saishu To. At 1520, three mine contacts were made and plotted. The ranges at the time of detection were 300, 500 and 600 yards. At 1542, another mine contact was made at 225 yards. These four contacts were made at periscope depth, but the mines were not visible.

Spadefish surfaced at 1609 and moved toward one of the areas off Nishi Suido she had been ordered to test for enemy mines. At 1729, another plane contact was picked up on SJ at 8,950 yards, forcing her down before Captain Germershausen would have preferred. He took her to 150 feet and proceeded with his planned FMS testing.

Just over a half hour later, at 1804, the FM gear suddenly reported

48 mine contacts! The clear sound of hell's bell rang out from the conning tower speakers and Neal Pike's screen showed light discs at the appropriate shape and size. Germershausen had his helmsman carefully maneuver through the field of mines that showed on the PPI screen. In his report, he noted that the ship altered her depth between 80 and 175 feet. Ranges on the mines showed from 400 yards to 25 feet.

Germershausen later related this hairy episode to Admiral Lockwood, who wrote: "With mines before and behind, on bow and quarter, and with the bottom of the sea below, Germershausen decided that there was but one place for him to go in order to solve the deadly but fascinating mystery that confronted him."[16]

"Take her up," he called to the control room. "Fast! Blow bow buoyancy. Blow main ballasts."

The diving officer brought *Spadefish* straight up to the surface at 1834 with her diesels stopped until the mines could be spotted. OODs Ed La Croix and Don Martin, their lookouts and the captain raced up the ladder to the bridge and swept the seas on all sides of their submarine for the deadly hellpots. To their shock and great relief, they found that the FM sonar had played tricks on them.

"No mines in sight. Not a single one. Nothing," wrote Admiral Lockwood. "The mystery was never solved. Likeliest explanation: a school of fish."[17]

In his report to Lockwood covering 25 March, Captain Germershausen described this strange contact.

> Made contact with 48 apparent mines. All gave a good visual and tonal indication. Wind 2, sea 1. When surrounded by these contacts—many within a radius of 100 feet—secured the FM gear and surfaced. No physical contact was made. The water was very dirty and full of suspended matter. Evidently something was giving false contacts because search was made by periscope for the close ones.[18]

While those familiar with the equipment still held respect for its capabilities, not all of the *Spadefish* crew was feeling very confident about entering a mine-filled area with a finicky sonar set. "We got in the middle of a minefield, and the thing crapped out," recalled motormac Dick Gamby. "I don't know how we did it, but we surfaced and came out of that minefield without hitting anything. It was a miracle."

Torpedoman Don Anderson agreed. "I didn't think the gear was all that it was cracked up to be. On the fourth run, we were charting minefields going into the Sea of Japan. I'd rather do a lot of other things than that. We made it out of there all right, but I was nervous."

Spadefish set course for a night patrol in a convoy lane south of Tsushima Strait. Undeterred by the hair-raising mine episode, Captain Germershausen continued on with his orders to pinpoint mine fields in this area. He submerged his ship at 0554 on 26 March, approaching the suspected mine field at 90 feet. At 0650, Chief Pike switched on his FM sonar and *Spadefish* went to 180 feet to conduct her special mission.

The mine plotting was rudely interrupted by Japanese patrol boats which were sweeping the area of Tsushima Straits. The pinging of echo-ranging was picked up at 0750. Germershausen changed course to avoid these ships and continued on his special FMS mission. In his report, he concluded that the pinging was from an anti-submarine sweep, "common in this area."

In spite of the patrol boats, the skipper kept *Spadefish* on her mine searching mission. He was close to the suspected minefield area and still "intended to survey as much as possible, since weather and seas were ideal."[19]

At 0920, Pike's screen went blank as the FMS suddenly went out of commission. "At this time, four A/S vessels were pinging close," wrote Germershausen. Discontinuing his special mission, he now "reversed course and evaded." As he tried to move back out of the area, he "tried to evade pingers, who picked us up and went to short scale."

The OOD, Ed La Croix, logged, "Sound reports four sets of pinging and one set of screws, heavy and slow. Rigged ship for depth charge." Fortunately, the patrol craft did not attack and *Spadefish* crept away from them submerged. She returned to periscope depth at 1210. Pinging could still be heard from the anti-submarine sweep, but no ships were in sight. At 1240, one distant explosion was heard, followed by another at 1310. At 1452, a third distance explosion was head. *Spadefish* continued patrolling at periscope depth through the day while the technicians worked on the FMS gear.

At 1711, *Spadefish's* sonar operators could again hear the echo ranging. Intrigued, Germershausen headed down the true bearing of the pinging and one hour later he sighted three anti-submarine vessels, small trawler-types, searching. He prudently avoided these small death-traps and surfaced at 1923. *Spadefish* dived at 0529 on 27 March—4 miles southwest of the suspected minefield—manning her FM gear and heading into Nishi Suido for her third attempt to map out the enemy mine field. Germershausen took her down to 180 feet again as he approached the suspected area. At 0700, the FM sonar overheated and cut out once again.

Captain Germershausen was frustrated, and rightfully so. He hoped to map the minefields, get the hell out of there and get back to his primary goal of sinking ships. "There we were, blind," he later said. "We didn't know where the mines were and we had to come out and repair the gear."[20] Chief Pike, along with his radar technicians Joe Case and Bill Keeney, spent the remainder of the day affecting repairs and making adjustments to the sonar gear while Germershausen conducted a submerged patrol at periscope depth. Numerous explosions were heard throughout the day and during the night patrol.

By mid-day, the technicians had the finicky sonar repaired. Captain Germershausen took his boat back toward the mines again, writing later of his latest difficulty on 27 March.

> At 1500, FM gear was operating again. Ran it for one hour at 65 feet, went to 180 feet and operated gear for two hours. It appeared to be operating normally, except that there was a blank space on the screen from 020° to 050°. Cause of this is still undetermined.[21]

At 0255 on 28 March, *Spadefish* sighted a properly lighted hospital ship and avoided her. Neal Pike's team was satisfied that they had the FMS functioning properly again, so at 0545, *Spadefish* submerged to 180 feet while 11 miles south of the mine area. Pike again manned the FM sonar gear as his boat headed into Nishi Suido to look for mines. Germershausen found the sonar was again picking up false contacts. "350 to 400 contacts were made, similar to those made on the 25th, although the operators stated that they were exactly like contacts made during training."

Chief Pike and his team knew that these contacts could not be real mines, despite the clear sounds of hell's bells and their properly shaped image on the PPI screen. His technicians had found during the previous day's inspection while topside that the training shaft had been bent. This bent shaft—caused either by rough seas or the 23 March depth charge attack—was causing the training motor to overload. Due to this damage, coupled with the hundreds of false contacts, Germershausen "decided to make a report to ComSubPac and abandon the mission."[22]

At 0937, Germershausen secured the FM gear and resumed his normal patrol for the remainder of the daylight hours. Once again, numerous explosions were heard throughout the day. At 1047, Ens. Bill Ware reported that a periscope had been sighted and that screws were picked up by sound at 1,500 yards. This vessel was avoided. *Spadefish* surfaced at 1923 and cleared to the westward at full speed in order to make a radio transmission to ComSubPac, reporting on the failures so far to map any enemy mine fields. At 2305, Germershausen ordered flank speed and headed south to a new patrol station near Nagasaki. Three minutes later, a small ship was sighted at 8,000 yards. The tracking party was stationed and *Spadefish* began closing the distance. At 7,000 yards, however, the contact was identified as a small patrol craft and the decision was made to avoid her.

Spadefish ran at flank speed toward her new patrol station. She passed between Fukae Shima and Danjo Gunto. She dived at 0745 on 29 March at a point 25 miles west of Naga Shima. At 1917, she surfaced, clearing to the westward. At 2100, *Tinosa* made contact and she was given *Spadefish*'s position. At 2256, an SJ radar contact was made at 10 miles, closing to 7 miles in one minute. *Spadefish* dived at 2258 to avoid this contact. She returned to radar depth at 2340 and quickly made radar contact at 1,000 yards. Captain Germershausen elected to stay down. His JP sonar operator, Neal Pike, heard screw noises. Through the periscope, Germershausen could only see a white light from some sort of escort vessel, but no depth charges were dropped.

The skipper had decided to attack whatever this ship was that was displaying the white light. He ordered battle stations at 0000, Friday, 30 March. Although Captain Germershausen's patrol report makes no mention of the event, torpedoman Hugo Lundquist's journal for 30 March includes the following entry: "One torpedo came across our bow."

Chief Pike would never forget the event. "My battle station submerged was in the forward torpedo room, listening on the directional crystal head JP audio gear," he said. "We were at periscope depth, making an attack approach, when we were fired on by another submarine."

Captain Germershausen had already ordered Emery Kreher's men to open the forward torpedo tubes as the range on the target vessel narrowed. Moments later, Pike sent a chilling report to the conning tower. "I'm listening through my headphones, and suddenly I hear the distinctive big rush of compressed air of a torpedo being fired," he recalled. "I reported into my headset, 'Torpedo No. 1 running hot, straight and normal.'"

Germershausen, quite aware that no torpedo had been fired by his ship, instinctively shouted down to diving officer Dick Fellows, "Take her deep!" The second thing Neal heard the skipper say was, "I haven't fired yet."

Although in an approach position on a potential target, the skipper had blindly called for a dive based on Neal Pike's report. As *Spadefish* plunged downward, Pike continued to monitor the torpedo sounds on his JP hydrophone. "I tracked it coming in toward us," he said. "As it

Chief Radio Technician Neal Pike receiving the Bronze Star Medal on Majuro from Rear Admiral John Herbert "Babe" Brown for his service as radar operator during *Spadefish*'s first war patrol. During the fourth patrol, Pike alerted the skipper that another submarine had fired a torpedo at *Spadefish*, which she was able to dodge. *Courtesy of Neal Pike.*

came over our bow, I couldn't get any bearings for a moment, because it was right over us. As it passed on by, I continued to track and call the torpedo's bearings."²³

Many of *Spadefish*'s crew would remain blissfully unaware that their lives had very nearly been taken. Neal Pike would always be impressed by "the Captain's trust and trigger-like reactions without a two-minute drill asking questions. If the skipper would have stopped to ask me questions, we would all be dead."²⁴

The knowledge that *Tinosa* was very close in the same area may have given the skipper reason to think that he had been fired on by a "friendly." *Tinosa*, however, did not fire any torpedoes on her ninth war patrol. The torpedo had thus been fired by a Japanese submarine, likely alerted to the U.S. submarine's presence by the radar plane which had driven *Spadefish* down an hour prior. "That was probably the closest call we ever had," related Pike.

Bill Germershausen cautiously brought his boat back up moments later, but there was no sight nor sound of an enemy submarine. *Spadefish* surfaced at 0200 to clear the immediate area. No shipping contacts were made, but for the next hour the lookouts could see blinking lights on various bearings. The radar, however, had no pip. *Spadefish* attempted to close one light but nothing developed. At 0111, she exchanged radar recognition signals with *Tinosa*, who was also chasing potential contacts on the surface.

At 0122, an SJ contact was made on a ship at 10,000 yards. The tracking party investigated, and *Spadefish* closed the distance. This vessel was quickly identified as *Tinosa*. Germershausen sent Commander Latham all relevant information of his patrol to date. He then headed west of Danjo Gunto en route to Nishi Suido to try to complete his boat's special FMS mission, cruising on the surface at full speed.

Germershausen had advised ComSubPac of his difficulties with his FM gear in his first four attempts to plot minefields on this patrol. Orders had come back from Lockwood for him to make another attempt, and that he would this night. At 1055, *Spadefish* submerged for another test of her FM gear. "Put triplane over," wrote Germershausen. "Tested at periscope depth. Picked up at 150 yards. This was considered good, but could not pick it up at 180 foot depth."[25]

At 1220, she was back on the surface, heading for an area west of Tsushima. At 1439, she sighted two aircraft at close range and submerged. She returned to the surface at 1543 and headed for the area of her special mission at flank speed.

At 1700, *Spadefish* submerged 5 miles south of Nishi Suido and once again headed into an area where intelligence knew mine fields to exist. Chief Pike manned the FM gear as the ship went to 180 feet. This time her sonar worked as planned. *Spadefish* was able to locate and plot a mine field in Tsushima Straits. The boat covered 12 miles of this area during the next 4.5 hours as her FMS operators listened for hell's bells. "Very sticky business," noted the patrol report.

"We marked the latitude and longitude on a chart," recalled the skipper. "We had to approach it to the point where we were able to get a range on a couple of lines of mines. It was a hairy thing to do. Those mines were contact mines. You had to hit them" to detonate them.[26]

The special testing carried on through 2100, at which time Captain Germershausen reversed course to clear the area. The boat returned to the surface at 2355 and cleared the area to the southwest to charge batteries, intending to be in a position for a dawn dive in the same area.

At 0456 on 31 March, an SJ contact was made at 7,000 yards. This looked like a plane, so Lt.(jg) Wood dived the ship. She resurfaced at 0519 and went to flank speed. The radar planes were still in the area, however, for her SJ radar picked up another contact at 0525, distance 5,000 yards. Two minutes later, the SJ contact was at 2,500 yards. "Should have been able to see this in the dawn light, but could not," logged Germershausen. "At flank speed, it was closing."

Spadefish made a crash dive at 0529. She was within 12 miles of where she was next scheduled to map a minefield, so Germershausen went to 180 feet and turned on his FM gear. This time, it went out of commission before *Spadefish* could reach the mine area. "Headed south and conducted periscope patrol while effecting repairs," he wrote.

Neal Pike's gang discovered the sonar trouble during the day, but alerted the skipper that they were unable to fix it due to lack of spare parts. The high voltage transformer in the power unit was causing fuses to blow each time the power switch was thrown. The FM gear was thereby out of commission for the rest of the patrol. "We had made three attempts to get in there, but we kept having trouble with the gear," recalled Germershausen. "I reported the trouble I was having."[27]

At 1908, *Spadefish* surfaced to conduct a night patrol along the 34°N latitude. While surfaced, Captain Germershausen received orders from Admiral Lockwood which advised that *Seahorse* was to move into the area and take over the mine hunting from *Spadefish*.

At 2227, she submerged to effect repairs on her SJ radar and SD antenna hoist. She resurfaced at 0120 on April Fool's Day, with repairs complete on the radar. Radio reports this day would bring news of the U.S. landings taking place on Okinawa. At 0420, the SJ came back to life, picking up a contact at 10,200 yards. The tracking party was called to the conning tower and an approach was commenced on this target. From the size of the pip believed this to be a small patrol craft.

The potential was lost at 0433, when the SD picked up an aerial contact at 4 miles. *Spadefish* was forced to submerge southwest of Reisui Kaiwan, and she began conducting a submerged patrol between Kanjo Gan and Koku To. At 0914, she sighted a schooner. Three minutes later, another schooner was spotted through the periscope.

Various small sailing craft were sighted during day. By 1410, *Spadefish* had seventeen different sailing craft in sight. Two were within 2,000 to 3,000 yard range. Having seen very few shipping targets on this patrol thus far, Captain Germershausen finally decided to fire one torpedo at the nearest two-masted, 150-foot schooner. At 1550, he fired bow tube Number 6, from the point-blank range of 700 yards, with a 90° track. This Mark 18.2 torpedo, set for six feet, was seen to broach and miss ahead.

Spadefish turned and fired stern tube Number 7 at the same target at 1559, range 550 yards. Through the periscope, Germershausen could see his torpedo all the way as it broached the surface. "Watched the ripples all the way. Believe shallow water accounted for the broaching, as it looked like a porpoise all the way. The sea was flat calm." This second warfish slammed home in the middle of the little target and the Japanese schooner literally disintegrated in the resulting Torpex explosion. Shipping targets had truly become scarce for *Spadefish* to expend $40,000 worth of torpedoes against such a small vessel.

Captain Germershausen had decided to destroy another of the larger schooners. He immediately turned to port to fire at the second clos-

A two-masted, 150-foot Japanese schooner seen through the *Spadefish* periscope on 1 April 1945. Moments later, she was torpedoed and sunk. *Hugo Lundquist collection, courtesy of Jeane Lundquist.*

est vessel. *Spadefish* fired bow tube No. 4 at 1605, from a range of 650 yards. This torpedo did not run after leaving the tube but sank and exploded on the bottom. The skipper turned again, fired his stern tube No. 8 at 1610 at the same target, range 750 yards. The torpedo ran hot, but missed. By now, the Japanese crewmen were diving over the side of the schooner as they abandoned ship.

"Today's patrol station should have been productive of some worthwhile targets, as we were in coastal traffic lane off Korean east coast." Irritated at the poor performance his torpedoes were giving him this day, Germershausen decided not to waste any more fish. He secured his crew from battle stations at 1612 and cleared this area to the south.

"Like Pirates of Old"

Fourth Patrol   *7-21 April, 1945*

Spadefish surfaced and ran through the night. The second of April passed with no better luck on enemy shipping. The only sighting of interest was a floating mine spotted at 0617. By the time *Spadefish* came upon another drifting mine at 1515, Captain Germershausen decided to give his gunners a little practice, allowing Zombie Gallagher and Whitey Harbison to explode it with their 20-mm guns.

The SJ radar joined the FM gear in going out of commission at 2004, so *Spadefish* submerged to effect repairs. She resurfaced at 0105 on 3 April, with the SJ still out of commission. She sent a message on the wolf pack frequency, informing *Tinosa* and *Tirante* that her radar was out and giving her position.

Dick Latham's *Tinosa* had plotted its first minefield on 25 March in the Nansei Shoto chain south of Kyushu. Her FM gear remained in service and she had successfully plotted several other mined areas during the next few days. Latham was then ordered to report to Guam with his intelligence. After only twenty-seven days at sea with no sinkings, *Tinosa* arrived and Latham handed over charts with plotted mine positions in the Ryukyus. In spite of no sinkings, Admiral Lockwood rated *Tinosa*'s ninth patrol as successful. With *Spadefish*'s FMS out of commission, Lockwood then handed the mission of mine plotting over to two other FM boats, *Seahorse* and then *Crevalle*.[1]

After wrestling with repairs for six hours, Ens. Martin, Chief Pike and the *Spadefish* radar gang finally reported their SJ to be back in full service at 0334 on 3 April. At 0414, the refurbished SJ made a contact at 23,000 yards and *Spadefish* commenced tracking. At 0445, a plane was picked up on the SJ at 13,000 yards. "Believe this to be the target we were tracking," the skipper noted wryly in his patrol report. Perry Wood promptly submerged the boat to avoid this flying "contact."

Spadefish surfaced at 0519, assuming that the aircraft had moved on. Gunner's mate Bernie Massar and his buddy Irv Kreinbring were among the 0600 watch duty going on duty. Massar's keen vision may very well have saved *Spadefish* this particular morning, as he recalled.

> The dawn was just starting to break as we relieved the watch. My friend took the port side and I was on the starboard side of the periscope shears. I took one look around and it was clear. Then, I ran my glasses back to the bow section to make another sweep and I saw this plane coming in. It was a Japanese floatplane. It was low-winged, with floats. It was so close, I could see the guide wires on it. It was coming in under our radar, which hadn't even picked it up. I was the only one who had spotted him, so I hollered, "Plane coming in close, dead ahead!"[2]

Spadefish records show that an enemy aircraft was sighted at 0601 and a crash dive was made. Perry Wood and Dick Fellows were just turning the watch over to Dan Decker and Dutch Falconer when the enemy plane was sighted. "Perry Wood gave the command to clear the bridge and sounded the alarm," remembered Massar. "He was dancing up and down as the lookouts scrambled down the hatch. I never saw a plane this close."

Spadefish dropped toward deeper water. Fortunately, the first bomb did not drop for two minutes, indicating that the pilot may have circled around. At 0603, the bomb exploded "pretty close," by Captain Germershausen's estimation. Two minutes later, the pilot dropped his second bomb, which the skipper felt was "closer" than the first. There was no serious damage to *Spadefish* but it had "shook up a few people."

She returned to periscope depth at 0623 and continued her submerged patrol through the day. She surfaced at 1420 and headed north and east for a night patrol west of Koshiki Retto. She was heading east by 2100, intending to pass between Kusakaki Shima and Uji Gunto. The SJ picked up another aircraft at 18,000 yards at 2147. At 2148, the plane was determined to be coming in, so *Spadefish* dived and cleared the area to the westward.

"Decided to patrol tomorrow at 100 fathom curve north of Koshiki Retto," wrote Germershausen. At 0212 on 4 April, an SJ contact was made at 21,000 yards and tracking was commenced. This "target" was lost from radar three minutes later. "Probably another plane," the skipper noted.

At 0308, the SJ made contact on another plane at 13,000 yards and the OOD dived ship. *Spadefish* resurfaced within the hour and headed toward Kami Koshiki, diving at 0535 when 15 miles east. She surfaced that night 20 miles west of Oniki Saki, patrolling east and west, southeast of Fukae Shima.

At 0115 on 5 April, an SJ radar contact was made at 10,000 yards. *Spadefish* commenced tracking and soon had SJ radar interference. At 0125, she exchanged calls and information with Captain George Street's *Tirante*. Thus far, *Tirante*'s luck had been no better than *Spadefish*'s. She had similarly sunk two small vessels, both with torpedoes. Captain Germershausen received orders during the night from ComSubPac to shift to the Yellow Sea upon departure of boats now patrolling there. "This was a welcome order, since all our contacts in this area seem to be radar planes."

Spadefish also received a radio message from Commander Latham's *Tinosa*, which was en route to Guam with his minefield intelligence. In his journal for 5 April, torpedoman Hugo Lundquist wrote: "Prisoner picked up by *Tinosa* from troopship we sank [on 23 March, *Doryo Maru*] said there were 1,400 soldiers aboard."

The radar-equipped Japanese aircraft that had plagued *Spadefish* the past few days continued to dog her as she approached the Yellow Sea in the early hours of 5 April. At 0218, SJ made radar contact at 19,000 yards. A quick search with the SD aerial radar confirmed a contact at 9 miles. This plane was also coming in, so Bill Ware cleared the bridge. Due to the heavy load of plane contacts, Captain Germershausen's bridge crew was becoming quite adept at crash dives. "The boat at this point was making consistent 38-second dives."

Radar officer Don Martin had his operators direct their radar to seaward. The Japanese had many direction-finding (DF) radar stations ashore and could get a fix on enemy submarines by simple triangulation. The aircraft were then directed out to the submarine's location.

At 0300, *Spadefish* surfaced and began clearing the area to the westward, between Danjo Gunto and Fukae Shima. At 0544, SJ radar contact was made at 12,000 yards. This again checked with the SD air search radar. The aircraft moved in to 4 miles, before Perry Wood ordered yet another crash dive. The boat returned to the surface at 0631 and continued opening to westward but the yo-yo diving game did not end.

Another aircraft was sighted at 1250 and *Spadefish* submerged for an hour. At 1355, one minute after surfacing, another SD contact confirmed the decision to stay down a little longer. She resurfaced at 1409, and one minute later had another SD contact, this one at 29 miles out. Captain Germershausen elected to stay up this time. He had his radar operator continue keying the SD until the plane contact was lost at 31 miles out. "The SD radar was used only on surfacing and during low visibility to check APR signals for plane contacts," he recorded.

The skies were overcast in the Yellow Sea this day and the seas were running very rough. Photographer's Mate Robert Rymer, temporarily assigned to *Spadefish* to photograph her minefield plotting mission, had been scheduled as a regular lookout by Chief Eimermann. When one particularly large wave hit the bridge, he was caught off guard and very nearly washed overboard. Still clutching his 7x50 binoculars, Rymer fanned out his elbows like a butterfly and saved himself by snagging the conning tower railing.[3]

At 1525, *Spadefish*'s bow planes were accidentally rigged out in these heavy seas while the ship was going full ahead. The starboard rigging gear was instantly carried away, as its universal joint, located in the superstructure, broke from the sea's pressure. Officer of the deck Dan Decker immediately realized the seriousness of the situation, which would adversely affect *Spadefish*'s handling during dives.

In the control room below, gunner Bernie Massar and yeoman Irv Kreinbring were dressing in foul weather gear as they prepared to relieve the topside watch at 1530. As they dressed, they sat on the benches alongside the bow and stern planes, with their backs to the levers behind them.[4]

Word was suddenly received from the bridge that the bow planes had been rigged out and were damaged. Lieutenant Dick Fellows entered the control room and approached Kreinbring and Massar as they dressed. "He bellowed out that I had rigged out the planes and was responsible, pointing his finger at me," Massar recalled.

Kreinbring later wrote, "My thought is that the U-joint, that was found later to be broken, just let go and allowed the planes to drop and in so doing also caused the shaft to twist and bend. I'm sure that neither Bernie nor I rigged out the planes at the wrong time."

Both men protested to Lieutenant Fellows that they had not touched the lever for rigging out the planes. The lever in question was located between and behind the two men, and required a particular motion to activate it, beyond what just a simple bump could have done. "For many years, it bothered me and I wondered how this had happened," related Massar.

Twenty-three years later, he would find out that TM1c Emery Kreher in the forward torpedo room was the responsible person. At the time Massar and Kreinbring were dressing in the control room, Kreher had been demonstrating a procedure to rig out the bow planes from the torpedo room. In the process, he had accidentally rigged them out in the heavy seas.

Leaving Dutch Falconer to oversee the lookouts, Lt. Decker led a repair party out on deck at 1530 to inspect damage, in spite of the frequent plane contacts. One of the repairmen, Dick Gamby, noted, "The horizontal shaft that connects the bow planes with the machinery inside broke. The collar on the shaft sheared where it was held on by a grift pin. We had to take the shaft off."

At 1550, a scouting patrol plane was sighted 8 miles out and everyone scrambled below as *Spadefish* dived. She returned to the surface at 1735 and at 1755 sent the repair party back out on deck to rig in the planes with a jury rig. Seas were increasing and pounding the planes badly. To effect the necessary repairs, a party of officers and machinists went topside into the superstructure during the night.

"We all knew that the repairs involved the crew working in the forward superstructure without timely warning of another search or attack aircraft," recalled Decker. "The submarine might have to dive immediately, leaving the repair crew unable to reach an open hatch to the submarine."

The repair party worked out signals with the bridge crew, so that they could be alerted if anything was spotted. Barring a fast-approaching enemy plane, they felt that they should have sufficient time to clear the deck if something was spotted.

The repair gang took the broken shaft off and carried it down into the engine room. "We brazed it together again and put it back up," said Gamby. A key was constructed to repair the main shaft. The key consisted of two half-inch CRS bolts put through the coupling and shaft, and brazing (soldering with a metal having a high melting point) the ruptured section of the coupling. "The coupling, a bronze casting, was carefully examined and found to contain air bubbles," wrote Captain Germershausen. "This is believed to have been a contributing factor to the casualty."

The jury-rig was arranged, whereby the bow planes were secured in a rigged-in position, thus disabling them for the remaining dives.

While the repair work went on, *Spadefish* exchanged calls with *Sea Devil*, who was vacating the Yellow Sea area after sinking three marus on 2 April. *Spadefish* patrolled during the night southwest of Saishu To.

At 0621 on 6 April, an SJ contact was made at 12,000 yards, increasing out to 19,000 quickly. This was duly noted to be another of the pesky aircraft contacts. At 0906, the watch sighted a ship and commenced tracking. *Spadefish* tracked this vessel all morning with the high periscope. It proved to be a small patrol vessel headed for Kokusan. *Spadefish* remained to the westward of Kokusan and Daikokusan until 2000, in expectation that an enemy patrol was sweeping this area for an outgoing convoy.

At 2200, Germershausen sent his repair crew back out on deck to complete proper repairs to the bow plane shafting. *Spadefish* came to a halt, lying to, while the work continued on her bow planes. This job was particularly hard on the workers as it required standing in near freezing water. In spite of this, and the fact that it might be necessary to dive at any moment, there were more than enough volunteers to take care of the frequent reliefs.[5]

Lieutenant Decker was in charge of the repair party, which included CMoMMs Charles Griffith and Rebel Rewold—who had just received word of his promotion to chief on 2 April—and auxiliarymen Johnny Peel, Buck Miller and Dick Gamby. Three hours was spent drilling and installing dowels in the broken universal joint. Gamby recalled the efforts he and his fellow machinists made that night.

> It was at night and we were on the surface. You had to go up the ladder in the torpedo room and then you climbed down into the superstructure. It was right near the torpedo skid, where they skid the torpedoes into the torpedo room during reloads. We climbed through the superstructure to get hold of that shaft to take it out. It was a little cold! You're standing in hip-deep water to get that damn heavy shaft out of there. We brought her back to the engine room and did some more brazing on it.

The night's work was frustrating indeed when the sea carried away three hours worth of work. With nothing to show for the hard effort put into making the bow planes functional, Lieutenant Decker and his gang opted to just secure them for the time being. The crew removed a seven foot section of rigging shaft and took it below for additional repairs.

For the time being, the bow planes were cranked up out of the water. "We cabled them right to the ship, so we couldn't use them anymore," said Gamby. At the ends of the bow planes, the tag on the ends of them was cabled directly to *Spadefish*'s superstructure. The diving planes would no longer be able to be dropped down, but at least they would not stay permanently rigged out.

By 0400 on 7 April, Lieutenant Decker's repair party had completed the removal of the shaft and the cabling of the bow planes. For the repair crews, the work had been exhausting. The damaged parts were now below decks where the auxiliary gang could mend them.

For the bridge lookouts, their night had been difficult, knowing that every second counted should a plane or ship be spotted. The lives of their fellow men in the superstructure had depended upon their vigilance. *Spadefish* made a successful trim dive at 0452, resurfacing at 0512. For the weary repair gang, their work was far from over. The broken parts that had been removed needed repair. Once this was complete, there remained the task of crawling into the cold, wet superstructure yet again in enemy waters to attempt a permanent repair.

"Smoke on the horizon!"

The call from the high periscope watch at 1220 on 7 April was most welcomed. Since blasting the small schooner a week prior, *Spadefish* had endured nothing but rough seas, broken bow planes, drifting Japanese mines, and irritating enemy radar planes.

Duty messenger Buck Miller found his new skipper eager for more info upon being informed of a sighting. "Captain Germershausen pulled his pants on and headed for the conning tower, asking me questions about how far away and ship make-ups," recalled Miller. "All I could do was repeat my order, 'Smoke on the horizon. Captain to the bridge.'"

At 1250, *Spadefish* submerged and commenced an approach on this distant ship's smoke from ahead. This target proved to be a large 190-ton three-masted Chinese junk, a flat-bottomed ship with battened sails and a high poop deck aft. This junk had her foresail rigged but was smoking heavily from her stack, indicating that she must be burning soft coal. After a long approach and careful survey of the area, Captain Germershausen decided that this ship would offer his crew a good chance for action.

"Prepare for battle stations, surface."

As the orders went out over the 1MC at 1441, the gun crews raced to prepare for their first ever battle surface action where their powerful 5-inch deck gun might be used in anger. Actually, Bill Germershausen had ideas of gathering intelligence from this ship, just as he had done aboard *Haddock* on his PCO run the previous year. "Intended to board the junk without firing if possible," he logged.

At 1500, *Spadefish* battle surfaced for the first time at 2,000 yards from the ship. The surfacing was almost trouble. In the control room, new Warrant Officer Dutch Falconer was serving as the diving officer. Nearby, Tom Miller stood by torpedo and gunnery officer Dan Decker, as both members of the gun crew waited for *Spadefish* to pop to the surface. Miller suddenly noticed that "we were attempting to blow all ballast and surface with our vents open." Miller quietly whispered to the duty chief, Red Wells, "so as not to embarrass him and the diving officer, Warrant Officer Falconer, and Wells shut them

The *Spadefish* 5-inch deck gun crew stands by for action in hostile waters. *Courtesy of Thomas H. Miller.*

without orders, to Falconer's surprise." Miller noticed only a chuckle from Lieutenant Decker when he "observed what took place."[6]

Upon battle surfacing, the first of the gun crew swarmed out from the gun-access trunk. Gun captain Shaky Jake Lewis, pointer Francis Scherman on the left side of the gun, and trainer Rebel Rewold, seated on the gun's right side, took their positions. Ship's cook Ed Graf, the hot shellman, had his elbow-length asbestos gloves ready to handle the sizzling hot shells that would be fired as they popped out of the breech of the 5-incher. From the magazine to the gun, the four ammunition passers would move the 60-odd pound projectiles up to fire.

As *Spadefish* hit the surface, everyone poured out onto deck to unlimber the gun. At 1511, one of the battle lookouts suddenly reported a periscope sighting in the vicinity of the target ship. *Spadefish* opened out at flank speed to 5,000 yards while the gunners were sent scrambling below. Buck Miller, one of the shell handlers, had the responsibility to count heads as they cleared the deck through the gun access hatch. "As I closed the hatch, water was over the deck," he wrote. "Too close for my comfort!"[7]

At 1518, the gunners were ordered back out on deck. This time, the bow tubes were on the ready in case of another submarine report. At 1519, the 5-inch gun commenced firing.

Standing near the hatch, MoMM3c Harry Brenneis, making his first patrol aboard *Spadefish*, took the shells as they were passed up

Spadefish attacked a Chinese junk on 7 April 1945 in the Yellow Sea. After severely damaging the vessel with her deck guns, *Spadefish* put a five-man boarding party aboard her to collect intelligence and a prisoner. Many small Chinese and Japanese vessels were either involving in making supply runs or served as picket boats to radio warnings of approaching Allied fleet units. This Chinese junk was photographed by *Bullhead* (SS-332) in early 1945. *Official U.S. Navy photo, National Archives.*

through the ammunition hatchway from the ammo locker in the mess hall below. "I was in good shape then," he recalled. "It wasn't tough for me then, but I wouldn't want to do it now!"

Brenneis passed the shells to the next handler. En route to the gun, they were set to fire. Gunnery officer Dan Decker was in charge of the gun crew during surface actions. Wearing headphones, he stayed in communication with his spotter, Ens. Bill Ware, on the bridge. Decker repeated the director's signals to the pointer and trainer. They would yell, "Set!" before the pointer, Chief Scherman, fired the gun each time.

Graf, with his asbestos gloves, still preferred not to actually catch the shell casings if he could help it. On a previous firing exercise, he received a nasty burn on his arm in spite of the gloves. Buck Miller recalled: "As they hit the deck, I booted them over the side with the outside of my foot, utilizing my soccer ability. I was captain of my high school soccer team. It never made sense to Graf and I to try to catch them."

Gunner's mate Bernie Massar was the first loader for gun captain Jake Lewis. "I was to take over as gun captain if he became disabled. I carried a spare firing pin for this gun." Tom Riley, the feisty fighter turned baker, had bored with having no real battle station. Captain Germershausen had gladly taken his offer to serve on the battle surface team, and "Mother" Riley became the shell loader on Hugo Lundquist's .30-caliber machine gun.

At 5,000 yards range, the firing was very inaccurate, so the 5-incher was ordered to check fire at 1526. From the longer range, about 30 rounds of 5-inch had been fired with only one hit and several near misses. *Spadefish* began closing to 2,000 yards, the range she had first approached the junk before the periscope report had thrown her off.

As the range reached 2,500 yards, *Spadefish*'s deck gun resumed firing at 1530. They fired 27 more rounds of high capacity 5" shells with "8 or 10 good hits." Chief Lewis' crew kept up a rapid reload and firing pace. In his patrol report, Captain Germershausen noted that "only two duds were observed."

At the closer range, the bridge crews also fired considerable .50 caliber and 20mm shells. In comparison to the large 5-inch diameter shells, the 20-millimeters shells were about one inch in diameter and the .50-caliber shells were roughly one-half inch in diameter. "As she was disabled by our 5-inch gun, we drew closer and then opened up with the small arms," recalled gunner's mate Bernie Massar. "We raked them with the .50 caliber and 20mms."[8]

Whitey Harbison, Zombie Gallagher, Don Anderson and Billy Pigman manned the fore and aft bridge 20mms. Torpedoman Anderson served as loader for Gallagher's gun. "He was the gunner and I was supposed to be the loader, but sometimes he would let me shoot the darn thing and he'd load it. It was kinda fun," remembered Anderson. Gallagher, who had shot up his share of floating mines on previous patrols, finally had a chance to pump some lead into a ship. "This was the only time I ever got to man a gun against a real target ship. It was a junk, a wooden hull ship. They had hauled down their sail to be less conspicuous," Gallagher related. "After they had fired the 5-inch at it, then we started firing bursts of 20mm into it." One of the 20mms jammed after seven rounds, but was quickly cleared and resumed firing.

Within moments, the vessel was holed near the water line by ten more 5-inch shells and her decks were nearly awash. The deck crew

Chief Torpedoman Francis "Red" Wells, seen here with ship's mascots Luau and Seaweed, was among *Spadefish*'s five-man boarding party during the fourth patrol. *Courtesy of Jim Cole.*

had fired 57 total high-capacity rounds at the junk. At 1537, "Cease firing!" was ordered, and Germershausen "called away boarders." Postwar research would show that this junk was the 198-ton *Tenshin Maru No. 3.*[9]

Spadefish maneuvered to the bow of the junk. The crew of *Tenshin Maru* obligingly passed over a line to the *Spadefish* sailors, who secured their sub bow to bow with the junk. At 1638, the *Spadefish* boarding party went aboard the slowly sinking hulk while her decks were awash. It consisted of Lt. George Cook, Lt. Dan Decker, CGM Shaky Jake Lewis, CTM Red Wells, and GM3c Bernie Massar. The boarders were well armed. "We had submachine guns, rifles, pistols, and hand grenades," said Massar. "We wanted to make sure we got back aboard *Spadefish*." Assistant gunnery officer Bill Ware was out on deck with one of the .45-caliber Thompson sub machine guns, ready to come to the aid of the boarding party.

Most of *Tenshin*'s crew had survived the shelling and were now on their knees on deck, bowing and begging for mercy. George Cook headed aft with Dan Decker toward the conning area of the ship. Lewis, Wells and Massar rounded up the other Korean men on deck and checked to make sure that they were unarmed. Massar noted that some of the Koreans assumed that they were going to be brought aboard the submarine.

As lieutenants Cook and Decker approached open hatches or areas of suspicion, they fired a round or two into them to insure their own safety. Each officer was carrying a standard .45 caliber Navy issue pistol. Upon entering the conning structure, they found that the Japanese skipper had his living space nearby. Lieutenant Decker later recalled:

> A quick look inside showed that someone was hiding under some covers on the bunk. We both fired before the concealed person could shoot back. Carefully, we checked, but the skip-

Warrant officer Dutch Falconer (left) and Chief "Hocks" Majoue hold up a Japanese "meatball" flag captured on *Spadefish*'s fourth patrol. *Courtesy of Thomas Miller.*

per was not breathing. He was not armed, but how did we know? If the skipper had simply showed himself, hands up, he would have been okay."[10]

The *Spadefish* officers then searched through the navigating area of the ship and found some charts of mine fields. They, and the other members of the boarding party, removed several Japanese flags "and all the souvenirs that they could pocket."[11] The boarders retrieved various ship's papers, and about thirty charts of Japanese Empire waters. Some of these included mine field charts, "which turned out to be much like our own intelligence," recalled Decker. "Like pirates of old!"

Germershausen, in fact, would use the captured charts while his boat was in the Yellow Sea. The attacks on trawlers and other small craft by *Spadefish* and other submarines were done to help end the war. "They were carrying rice or other food stuffs from Korea to Japan, probably transshipped to the war zone for their troops," wrote Decker. "On their return to Korea, we can only guess that they carried manufactured goods in payment for the rice."[12]

The cargo of this junk was primarily grain to support the war effort. The boarding party seized the ship's mate, the only other Japanese man aboard, as a prisoner of war. Pat Kelley and other members from the *Spadefish* crew brought cans of fuel oil over to the boarding party to finish the destruction of *Tenshin Maru*. Concentrating on the after compartment and hold, the men doused the vessel in fuel oil as the dozen Korean sailors hastily abandoned ship in their rafts.

As the fuel was spread, Lt. Decker was atop the cabin of the sinking junk trying to cut loose a large raft for the Koreans. "He was working on kicking this life raft over while they were setting the junk on fire," recalled bridge gunner Jack Gallagher. "Captain Germershausen was yelling at him to get out of there and come back aboard."

The fuel oil was ignited at 1700 and the boarding party reboarded *Spadefish* with their Japanese prisoner. *Spadefish* then pulled clear at 1703 and watched her target vessel burn. The boat's main deck was awash and her topside was blazing. Captain Germershausen cleared the area to the southward at full speed, aware that all of the gunfire and the blazing, slowly sinking hulk would attract both PCs and aerial trouble.

"This was the first time *Spadefish*'s guns were fired in anger," noted Germershausen in his report. "The action and subsequent piracy were enjoyed by all hands."

Chief Wells had the prisoner taken below to Torpedoman 1/c Si Barnes' after torpedo room. The Japanese mate's limited English was enough for the submariners to find out some basic information. "The prisoner stated that the junk was en route [from] Dairen to the Empire [Kyushu], and that its tonnage was 190 and carrying rice," wrote Germershausen.[13]

Having endured one angry Japanese POW aboard ship in the past, the *Spadefish* crew treated their new "guest" with caution at first. "We didn't chain him, but we put him down in the bilges," stated John Schumer, a member of the after torpedo room. "We lifted up the grating and put him down there."

At first, Schumer and others used intimidation on their prisoner to make sure he did not try anything dangerous to himself, the ship, or any crewmen. "We had some fun with him. I'd take my .45 out and hold it on him. He would say, 'No! No!' But it was empty." Schumer and the after gang quickly realized that their young prisoner was very well-behaved and had no intent to rebel. The *Spadefish* crew soon began to take a liking to their new visitor. "I'd take him up and get him some ice cream," recalled Schumer. "He liked it pretty well."

The prisoner offered what intelligence he knew of, which mainly pertained to his own ship. "I don't think he really knew anything," said Schumer. "He was probably just a dumb seaman like I was!"

Si Barnes put the young Japanese sailor to work in his after torpedo room and nicknamed him "Joe." Motormac Pat Kelley remembered that Barnes "was one big walking sign. Barnes was the type of guy who would go ashore and get a tattoo, while everyone else would go ashore and get a drink."

Aboard ship, Gus Cuthbertson in the forward room and Barnes in the after room doubled as *Spadefish*'s barbers. Barnes found Joe to be a great helper in his barber shop. "Old Si Barnes was a jolly good fella," said Chief Charles Griffith. "He'd give Joe a foxtail and a dustpan and have him sweep up the hair after Barnes gave us haircuts."

Torpedoman Barnes enjoyed having a good time with his excitable prisoner, and he made the most of a little English/Japanese translation book he had acquired. Pat Kelley watched one of these events. "He would take the book out of his pocket, and say a word or two. Joe would just go into a fit, because Barnes had spoken Japanese to him."

Soon after *Spadefish* pulled away from the blazing *Tenshin Maru*, her lookouts sighted a ship on the horizon at 1740 and tracking was commenced. At 1830, two more ships were sighted, but all three were identified as small sampans. Leading signalman and assistant navigator Jim Schuett—on the bridge to take navigational readings with Exec George Cook—noticed an enemy plane and shouted, "Aircraft!"

"Clear the bridge!" shouted Bill Ware as he pulled the diving alarm.

Ware, JOOD Charles Johnson, Schuett, Cook, and the three lookouts all dropped through the conning tower hatch in an instant as *Spadefish* made a crash dive. Lookout Bernie Massar dropped down from the shears and ended up taking station at the trim manifold in the control room.

After a number of minutes passed quietly, the diving officer quipped, "It was probably just a sea gull!"[14]

About that same instant, at 1852, two distant explosions were heard as this aircraft dropped its bombs.

"It just took a shit!" Jim Schuett remarked to the diving officer.

Spadefish resurfaced at 1941, her blazing junk still in sight and afloat. She made a wide sweep around it to the south and west, working to the northward when clear. *Spadefish* cleared the area during the night, headed for old hunting grounds, the northeastern corner of the Yellow Sea. She patrolled on the surface during the forenoon hours of 8 April between Daisei Gunto and Tokuseki Gunto.

At 1345, the watch sighted a mast on the horizon and the tracking party was called to the conning tower. This ship was cautiously running between ports during the daylight, hugging the safety of the 10-fathom curve. *Spadefish* submerged at 1428 and commenced an approach. The target ship was identified as a small, engines aft freighter making about 5 knots on a steady course. *Spadefish* failed to get into attack position because of an error in estimates of angles and ranges and because this little ship managed to cut back inside the safety of the 10-fathom curve.

Captain Germershausen secured the crew from battle stations at 1621. He ordered his ship to the surface at 1757 and headed northwest toward Daisei Gunto to try to regain contact. At 1937, the SJ radar made contact at 27,470 yards and tracking was commenced. This tar-

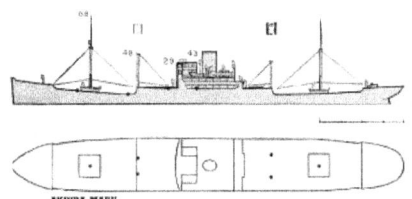

Spadefish expended ten torpedoes to mortally damage the freighter *Ritsu Go* on 8 April 1945. Her tracking party identified their target ship as *Akiura Maru*, shown here from the ONI-208J recognition book they used. *ONI 208-J (Revised)*.

get, however, was a single ship, passing southeast opposite the course of the early afternoon's contact.

Observing the masts and details of this maru, the bridge crew called out details to the tracking party in the conning tower. The night was bright enough that the ship was plainly visible. Using ONI-208-J, the identification party settled on the 6,800-ton *Akiura Maru*, with a central composite superstructure, to be the target ship. The depth of the water in this area of the Yellow Sea was 21 fathoms.

Captain Germershausen ordered Emery Kreher's gang to open the forward torpedo doors and set their Mark 18s at eight feet depth. Between 2047 and 2049, *Spadefish* fired four bow torpedoes, range 2,500 yards, with a 90° starboard track. Although the maru was on a steady course, making 9 knots and tracking perfectly, no hits were obtained.

Undeterred, Germershausen opened out and continued tracking her. At 2059, *Spadefish* came in for a second attack with her two remaining bow tubes. At 2120, both bow fish were fired at ranges of 1,600 and 1,300 yards, respectively, both set to hit, depth setting now 6 feet, track 110 starboard, 30° left gyro. Again, however, no hits were observed.

Kreher's forward torpedo crew moved swiftly to prepare the forward tubes again. Six misses did not please him in the least. "Kreher, our first class torpedoman, was from an old German family," recalled TM3c Wallace McMahon. "When he got real excited on a reload, he would drop right into German language on us!"

Germershausen, now completely frustrated, swung *Spadefish* to starboard to bring his stern tubes to bear and fired four stern torpedoes with 10-second intervals. Si Barnes' after crew methodically dispatched tubes 9, 10, 7 and then 8 at this nice freighter. Each torpedo was again set to run at six feet. The target freighter had slowed to 4 knots during this time. The range was 1,100 to 1,300 yards for each torpedo, with a 90° starboard track, gyro angles ranging between 0° to 4°. At the point of firing, the target's speed was judged to have been reduced to 3 knots now. To cover the full range of possibilities, Captain Germershausen had TDC operator Dan Decker use a full 200% spread with the torpedoes. Two of the four torpedoes should hit the target and one should miss her fore and another aft.

Finally, at 2124, one torpedo was seen from the bridge to hit aft. *Spadefish* opened out to westward and reloaded her after tubes. "Evidently our electric torpedoes [Mark 18-1s] are performing erratically and we suspect they are running slow. Injection is about 42° in this area."

TDC operator Decker agreed with his skipper on the poor torpedo performance. "We timed the hit accurately, and it had run at 20 knots, somewhat below its designated speed of 29 knots."[15]

At 2212, with the after tubes reloaded, *Spadefish* headed in for yet another attack. The target freighter now began steering wildly erratic courses toward the beach, and *Spadefish* could not get in for another attack due to the proximity of the shoals.

Ten torpedoes had been fired against this single contact to obtain one good hit. Germershausen secured his tracking party and began clearing the area. His target ship was getting very hard to track by radar at 14,000 yards range, and was apparently trying to beach herself.

Germershausen was completely discouraged in the Mark 18s, and he recommended that tests be run on them in cold water. "The injection averaged 38 to 42 degrees in the Yellow Sea. Though excuses do not sink ships, it is believed that Mark 18 torpedoes do run erratic in cold water," he wrote.

Perhaps the 8-foot settings on the original torpedo spread had been too deep for this ship, which proved to be smaller than what the bridge crew had believed her to be. Although this ship was running for the beach, postwar analysis showed that she did not make it. *Spadefish* claimed only damage to a 6,800-ton freighter, but JANAC would give her credit with sinking the 1,853-ton cargo ship *Lee Tung*. Researcher Roger Allan later found that the *Lee Tung* was the original Chinese name for this ship. Japanese sources revealed that this freighter was 1,834 tons and had been renamed *Ritsu Go* by April 1945. Ultra intelligence indicates that some of *Spadefish*'s dud torpedoes had actually opened seams on *Ritsu Go* and ultimately caused her to sink.[16]

At 2351, as *Spadefish* cleared the area of the shallow water, the watch began picking up lights of sampans and fishing vessels. Germershausen set course for a submerged day patrol off Chosan Kan. At 0445 on 9 April, an SJ contact was made on three ships and the tracking party was stationed again. The initial contact showed that all three ships were stopped, distance 32,000 yards. By 0531, it was getting light and *Spadefish* submerged 12 miles from Chosan Kan and closed to within 15,000 yards of these targets. At 0540, battle stations sounded.

At 0612, the targets were sighted by periscope. They were one three-masted schooner and two small fishing boats, all lying to. "The phenomenal range at which we contacted these small wooden-hulled vessels was hard to believe," wrote the skipper, "but we learned later to be surprised at nothing in this area in regard to radar performance."

At 0613, Germershausen secured his crew from battle stations. He commenced a submerged patrol 5 to 10 miles off Chosan Kan, watching for traffic in the strait between that point and Hakurei To. No contacts were made except for numerous small craft and sampans.

At 0732, a Jake twin-float reconnaissance seaplane was sighted. During the late morning and early afternoon, many explosions could be heard in the distance. This was later discovered to be the sound of escorts depth charging pack mate *Tirante* after she had robbed them of a 5,000-ton tanker. *Spadefish* surfaced at 1932. Four minutes later, her SJ had a contact at 52,000 yards, which was down to 35,000 yards by 2000. Two minutes later, another SJ contact was made at 16,850 yards. This second target was soon identified as a sampan, so tracking was commenced on the original, larger SJ target. Both *Spadefish* and *Tirante* continued to pursue radar contacts during the next few hours, but to no avail. *Tirante* contacted *Spadefish*, informing her that she had sunk a maru and an escort that morning, and had been the object of the depth charge attack heard earlier.

Another SJ contact was made at 0030 on 10 April, this one at 72,000 yards. It remained on the screen and a rough navigational plot showed this contact to be stopped. "Decided to investigate this one," wrote Captain Germershausen. *Spadefish* closed at standard speed in the direction opposite to her previous contact that evening.

At 0135, she started tracking, range 30,000 yards, with two targets now on radar. At 0205, the target started fading at 18,000 yards. At 0212, Germershausen sent his crew to battle stations and closed the latest target with tubes ready, "just in case this one is not a phantom." At 0213, *Spadefish* lost contact on one target at 13,000 yards but continued tracking the second one.

At 0230, the bridge finally sighted one target, a small sampan with her sail rigged. "Six sane and sober witnesses saw this at 2,000 yards," reported a disappointed skipper. "Secured from battle stations and headed for day submerged patrol position off Daisei Gunto."

Spadefish submerged at 0539 and patrolled 5 miles off the islands. Nothing of note was found during the day, other than a sampan sighted at 1705. After surfacing at 1942, Lieutenant Decker's repair crew was sent back into the superstructure at 2200 to commence installing the bow plane rigging shaft that had failed the week before.

The repair party worked until 0240 on 11 April, when repairs were completed and the bow planes were tested. The auxiliary gang and motormacs had done a first rate repair job on this equipment, as the planes could once again be rigged in normally for the balance of the ship's time on station.

Hoping to find an area with more enemy action, Germershausen set his course for the day to do a submerged patrol between Daisei Gunto and Tokuseki Gunto. At 0614, *Spadefish* sighted two planes "and they sighted us." She dove northwest of Kokureppi Retto and stayed down throughout the day. At 1947, minutes after surfacing for the night, an SJ contact was made on two ships at 66,000 yards. Between this time and 2025, the SJ picked up three contacts that looked like ships, at ranges from 25 to 35 miles. *Spadefish* headed for each one in turn only to lose contact upon closing.

At 2155, *Spadefish* exchanged calls with *Tirante*. At 2230, an SJ contact made on two ships at 10,000 yards. These two contacts plotted in as the two ships picked up at 1947. "We had been steering a course equal to the last bearing before contact had been lost," wrote Germershausen. "Navigational plot showed them to be on course 100°T, at a speed of 7 knots, when first picked up."

At 2281, he called George Cook, Perry Wood, and Dan Decker to the conning tower to track this latest contact. The target's course and speed as solved for by plot and TDC were 105°T, speed 6. The skipper made mention of this in his patrol report, "in view of the remarkable accuracy of the bearings and ranges at 66,000 yards on the original contact."

At 2302, *Spadefish* went to battle stations. Three forward tubes were made ready as the submarine closed her prey on a 90° starboard track. The radar pips were small, but the tracking party believed they might be small freighters. At 2310, the bridge lookouts sighted the targets and described them as small anti-submarine vessels, similar to PC boats. Captain Germershausen decided to fire his forward torpedoes with the targets overlapping at close range, depth setting zero, and all fired to hit (no spread).The first PC was at 1,500 yards and the second PC was overlapping at 2,900 yards at the time of firing.

At 2319, *Spadefish* fired three torpedoes, with gyro settings of 5° right. No hits were observed from the bridge. At 2325, however, one explosion resulted, followed by one more at 2326. Whether these flashes were torpedo explosions, gunfire, or depth charges could not be determined. Germershausen believed all three torpedoes had performed "erratic due to the cold water." *Spadefish* began to clear the area as one of the targets turned toward her but did not speed up. This target turned on a red light.

"Like Pirates of Old" 293

Spadefish fired three torpedoes at two Japanese patrol craft on the night of 11 April 1945. She was later credited with sinking *Hinode Maru No. 17*, a converted minelayer similar to this vessel.

At 2342, radar contact was lost at 12,000 yards. The ships at this time had come together to give a single pip. What had happened this night is unknown, but Japanese intelligence later showed that the 400-ton patrol craft *Hinode Maru No. 17* was lost in this area. This former merchant vessel had been converted to a minesweeper. Researcher John Alden found that three sources—two Japanese sources on warship losses and the independent research of Roger W. Allen in Tokyo—all agreed that the patrol craft *Hinode Maru* was lost the night of 11 April 1945 in the area that *Spadefish* occupied.[17]

Spadefish's patrol report claimed only a possible dud hit. Perhaps this hit was enough to cause damage to the patrol craft that resulted in her eventual explosion. Perhaps it was a low level explosion. Germershausen wrote: "A flash was seen on the bearing of the targets at the time of the first explosion, but it is not believed to have been a hit, since targets of this size should disintegrate when hit by a torpedo, and give unmistakable evidence."

At 2347, *Spadefish* heard a loud explosion, thought to be a depth charge, as she cleared the area of the PCs. Captain Germershausen sent a message to ComSubPac this night, "informing him that we were down to 3 torpedoes and having rotten luck and advising boats coming to Yellow Sea to carry steam torpedoes."

Germershausen would not know for years that his erratic torpedoes had actually sunk two more vessels than he had claimed.

During the early morning hours of 12 April, *Spadefish* headed southeast for a submerged patrol off Gaien Retto. During the early hours, half a dozen small pips, judged to be pesky sampans, were picked up on radar and avoided. She dived for the day before sunrise at a point 5 miles off Gaien Retto. Two distant explosions were heard at 0750, but the day's patrol was without contacts.

At 1903, *Spadefish* heard five loud explosions while still submerged. These blasts sounded close, but nothing was in sight. At 1932, the sonar watch could hear pinging from an enemy ship's echo-ranging gear, but still nothing was in sight. At 1935, another three loud explosions were heard, closer than the last ones. At 1936, Germershausen ordered his crew to battle stations. He needed to surface to charge his batteries and get some fresh air in the boat, and he was determined to fight it out with the phantom attacker. After nearly fifteen hours below, the air in the boat had gotten quite stale.

At 1942, *Spadefish* surfaced and cleared to the westward at flank speed to escape whatever was dropping the explosives. No radar contacts were made and whatever it was did not approach. The crew was secured from battle stations at 1948 and the ship continued to clear the area.

During the night, Chief Majoue's radio gang received orders from ComSubPac which ordered *Spadefish* to return to Guam for refit. This was a big disappointment to the crew, since it had been more than six months since they had seen Pearl Harbor. Before departing the area, Admiral Lockwood's staff ordered *Spadefish* to first search until dawn for a Japanese submarine reported to be in her area.

No enemy submarine contact was made. During her submerged exit from the area on 13 April, *Spadefish* heard fourteen distant explosions. She surfaced at 1527 and headed south to clear the area. At 0044 on 14 April, a green flare was sighted. At 0109, an SJ contact was made at 27,500 yards and she started tracking. Another SJ contact was made at 0117, distance 51,000 yards. At 0125, a third SJ contact was made at 55,000 yards. By 0230, *Spadefish* had a total of seven targets on radar, ranging from 11,000 to 50,000 yards, all widely spaced, all stopped. The closest target appeared to be a sampan. Germershausen decided all must be sampans or fishing boats, and secured his tracking party, clearing the area.

At 0310, the SJ had a new target dead ahead, range 69,000 yards. This pip was stronger than the previous signals, so *Spadefish* closed at full speed. When the range dropped to 20,000 yards, the tracking party was stationed at 0420. At a range of 16,000 yards, "this vessel put her stern to us and began making an end-around on us. We had been getting SJ interference from the bearing since first making contact, futilely challenging," wrote Captain Germershausen.

Finally, at 0521, *Spadefish* was challenged by this target. The radar gang exchanged calls with the submarine *Trutta*, which was informed by SJ keying that *Spadefish* was her target. Captain Germershausen later recalled "trying to exit the Yellow Sea and being tracked by the *Trutta*, who didn't acknowledge our recognition signals and was preparing to attack us. I sent him a radar signal, 'Lay off, you son of a bitch,' and he did."[18]

Torpedoman Wallace McMahon recalled, "We kept sending our call sign over the sound wave, 'We are your target! We are your target!' It didn't stop him." In his journal that night, another forward torpedo room crewman, Hugo Lundquist wrote, "Tracked all a.m. by *Trutta*. Persistent cuss."

Battle lookout Bernie Massar later recalled this uncomfortable exchange with *Trutta*.

> One of our own boats was giving chase. He was chasing and we were running. They wouldn't break off and did not identify us as friendly. I was on after lookout and Capt. Germershausen was pacing the after cigarette deck. He ordered the after tubes flooded and prepared to fire. Fortunately, the other sub finally realized we were friendly and broke off contact. They didn't know how lucky they were. It was close as to who would fire.[19]

Spadefish continued her run out of the Yellow Sea, sighting three different floating mines during the early morning. At 0922, a ship was sighted by high periscope dead ahead. It looked like a destroyer escort, so tracking was commenced. At 0931, SJ contact was made on two ships at 26,000 and 22,000 yards. At 0936, the APR picked up an enemy radar signal on 155mcs. This announcement was followed by an SD radar pip at 4 miles. *Spadefish* submerged and continued to move toward these targets. Sonar could hear pinging, but still nothing was in sight.

At 1040, six distant explosions were heard. At 1056, Germershausen resurfaced and continued closing his targets on their last true bearing, but to no avail. At 1216, *Spadefish* was forced to dive when a Betty bomber was sighted. She returned to the surface at 1410, only to be driven back under five minutes later by another aircraft. *Spadefish* continued submerged through the afternoon, resurfacing at 1745. The Japanese were obviously well equipped with radar in this area, for by 1822, another plane was spotted inbound. The OOD cleared the bridge and took her down to 150 feet, rigged for depth charge.

Three minutes after the plane had been spotted, a bomb exploded near *Spadefish* after she had reached 150 feet. The plane apparently stayed in the area, for a second explosion was logged at 1834. After one of the closer explosions, radioman Paul Majoue heard a distinct

Spadefish's prisoner of war on the fourth patrol was kept in the after torpedo room. The after room's sinking record of eleven kills was painted as little Japanese maru flags on the signal gun ejector piping (used to fire special cartridges that ran through the water) leading to one of the torpedo tubes. *Hugo Lundquist collection, courtesy of Jeanne Lundquist.*

scream come from the direction of Si Barnes' after torpedo room. Germershausen asked the talker to find out what was going on back there. "That was Joe," came back the reply. "He got a little excited, but we calmed him down." Barnes had picked up a crescent wrench and convinced his Japanese prisoner that the explosions of the depth charges were not really worth screaming about.

Spadefish returned to periscope depth at 1837, and secured from depth charge at 1844. At 1934, two fairly close explosions rocked the ship again. *Spadefish* went back to 100 feet and rigged for depth charge. Clearly, the enemy knew she was trying to leave the Yellow Sea and had plans to prevent her from doing so. At 1952, another bomb exploded close. The ship went down to 150 feet and yet another close bomb rocked her at 1956. At 2002, a third bomb went off, this the closest of the three. "These planes must have been equipped with something new," wrote Captain Germershausen. "Suspect magnetic detectors." Some of the bombs had fallen well after sunset on a dark night while the ship was below periscope depth.

Darkness had finally settled in on the surface, and the crew felt more at ease as the radar planes ceased their bombing for the night.

Spadefish was secured from depth charge at 2305, and she surfaced at 2311 after hours of bobbing up and down and being bombed. The SJ picked up interference at 2323, and at 2328, she exchanged calls with *Tirante*, and made contact with her.

Spadefish found that *Tirante* had been busy on 14 April. Directed by a ComSubPac Ultra to attack an important transport, Captain George Street found that she had holed up for the night in a small island's harbor about 100 miles south of the southwestern tip of Korea. Street boldly took *Tirante* into the harbor in 60 feet of water. With his Exec, Lt. Cdr. Edward "Ned" Beach, manning the TBT binoculars on the bridge, Street carried out the night attack from the conning tower. He fired three torpedoes at the anchored freighter and she blew up with a massive explosion. Instead of heading for deep water immediately, Street paused to fire more torpedoes at two frigate escorts. Both blew up and sank while *Tirante* raced at flank speed out of the shallow harbor.[20]

In addition to this brave harbor entry on his first patrol, George Street was credited with sinking eight Japanese ships with torpedoes—six of which survived postwar analysis. *Tirante* sank two more small vessels with her deck gun and brought in four prisoners of war. Street later received the Congressional Medal of Honor and his exec Ned Beach received a Navy Cross.

Spadefish and *Tirante* exchanged other calls during the night as they retired from their patrol area. *Spadefish* surfaced at 0235 on 15 April and went to flank speed, heading for the passage between Fukae Shima and Danjo Gunto. At 0303, an SJ radar contact was made on Saishu To, distance 51 miles. After clearing the area, she submerged for the day at 0522, about 40 miles west of the passage. Several distant explosions were heard during the late morning hours.

At 1325, a mine was sighted dead ahead and avoided. Mindful of the persistent bombings endured the previous afternoon by the radar planes, Captain Germershausen kept his boat down until 1944, when he surfaced 16 miles southwest of Fukae Shima and transited this passage. "Two weeks ago, we got away with going through here in daylight on the surface," he wrote, "but things seem to be getting tougher. Jap radar is in evidence in great profusion."

Spadefish continued south on 16 April in the East China Sea, passing Danjo Gunto. At 0122, she received SJ interference from another submarine, which was challenged and identified as *Bonefish*. At 0539, while leaving her patrol area, lookouts sighted an airplane. *Spadefish* submerged, headed for the passage between Akuseki Jima and Kodakara Shima.

During this time, the bitter battle for Okinawa was underway. The latest world news was typed up by Chief "Hocks" Majoue in his 16 April "Maru's Bull Sheet" newsletter, officially the "4th Patrol, 11th Issue." Among other news, the State Department in Washington announced that American submarines had sunk the *Awa Maru*, a vessel which was carrying supplies to American troops and Allied war prisoners. Tokyo Radio had made its first comments on the death of President Franklin D. Roosevelt and "hoped that his death would shake the security of the United Nations."

The job of continuing to plot minefields in Tsushima Straits had been passed to another four-boat wolf pack consisting of *Bowfin*, *Seahorse*, *Bonefish* and *Crevalle* after *Spadefish* and *Tinosa* had retired from that area. This wolf pack had success with its FM sonar and was able to make excellent reconnaissance of the mines of Tsushima, plotted for future penetration of this minefield. *Seahorse*, another Mare Island boat, successfully plotted several fields through 16 April before returning to her patrol.

She was spotted by two destroyer escorts on 18 April, and tried in vain to outrun them. As the escorts narrowed the distance and their gunfire drew alarmingly close, Captain Harry Greer took *Seahorse* down to evade the inevitable depth charging. She was just passing 150 feet, when eight very accurate ashcans literally blew the boat to the bottom, pushing her down into the muddy ocean bottom at 470 feet. The escorts remained in the area for eighteen hours, continuing to drop depth charges, some very close. *Seahorse* finally surfaced that night in a rain storm and limped away, badly battered, with a long list of damage and listing 15 degrees.[21]

Seahorse was so badly damaged that she would not be able to make the trip into the Sea of Japan, the special mission Admiral Lockwood had long been planning—and the purpose for her minefield probing. Upon reaching Guam, her undamaged FM sonar was removed and placed aboard another submarine, *Sea Dog*, who would take her place for the impending FMS mission.

Five miles past the center of the island passage, *Spadefish* surfaced again at 1941. She received orders from Admiral Lockwood to search for a downed aviator on her track, 340 miles distant. "Informed ComSubPac of our delay due to enemy planes," wrote Germershausen.

Further adding to his boat's delay, *Spadefish* was forced to dive again at 0047 on 17 April as a plane contact was picked up at 9 miles,

Firemen Tom Shaw and Cleveland Hord in a cribbage game during their off duty hours. *Hugo Lundquist collection, courtesy of Jeanne Lundquist.*

coming in. She returned to the surface at 0122 and proceeded on out from the East China Sea, sighting one floating mine during the morning. Shortly after lunch, the prospect of using the last torpedoes looked hopeful when the watch sighted what looked to be the mast of a ship, hull down on the horizon. The tracking party was stationed, but at 1259 the SJ picked up another plane contact at 9 miles. One minute later, the plane had closed to 6 miles, so *Spadefish* dived.

At 1336, she returned to the surface with the distant target now in sight. It looked like a sail this time. At 1350, Germershausen closed this target with his 20mm bridge guns manned. At 900 yards, the target was identified as a large Japanese type sea buoy. The skipper secured his gun crews and continued en route to Guam.

Spadefish was forced down again at 1602 by another closing plane contact. She eased back to periscope depth at 1636, but found the plane still out there at 6 miles. Germershausen elected to remain down until all was clear at 1728. Upon surfacing, the bow planes rigging gear failed again. Germershausen and his officers decided to keep the planes permanently rigged out and continue on toward Guam, where they could be properly repaired.

At 0040 on 18 April, an SJ contact was made at 8,000 yards. This was soon identified as another submarine, *Cero*. Another SJ contact was made at 17,000 yards and the tracking party was stationed. At

0436, a plane passed overhead with its running lights burning. *Spadefish* was now in the vicinity of the reported downed aviator. At 0437, a second plane came in at 4 miles, forcing *Spadefish* to submerge. Below, she continued to head toward the SJ contact. At 0454, her soundmen could hear pinging, and at 0500, a U.S. destroyer was sighted at 8,000 yards. She was challenged by sound, but no reply was received.

At 0520, *Spadefish* fired two recognition signals. No answer was received by sound, so she fired two more. At 0527, Germershausen finally elected to surface. As lookouts scrambled onto the bridge, the signalmen challenged the destroyer by searchlight and identified her as *USS Fanning*. Thankfully, mutual identification was made.

Fanning informed *Spadefish* that she was searching for the lost aviator. At 0752, a Navy PBM was sighted approaching in a hostile manner from 8 miles. The OOD pulled the bridge flare and submerged. *Spadefish* returned to the surface at 0812, with an all clear. Just to be certain, the SD radar was keyed, using IFF.

A pair of B-29s were sighted at 0950, but *Spadefish* did not see any sign of the downed aviator, leaving *Fanning* to continue the search. The next two days en route to Guam passed uneventfully.

At 0431 on 21 April, *Spadefish* joined up with her escort, *Osmus* (DE-701), a destroyer escort named for an aviator captured and killed at the Battle of Midway, Ensign Wesley Frank Osmus of Torpedo Squadron Six. *Spadefish* pulled into Apra Harbor, Guam, at 0830 and concluded her fourth war patrol.

She was again refitted by Submarine Division 21 and the sub tender *Proteus*. Upon mooring alongside the tender, a waiting detail of Marine guards came aboard to take "Joe," the polite Japanese prisoner of war *Spadefish*'s boarding party had taken from the sinking junk. "He was in no hurry to get off," recalled torpedoman John Schumer. "He had found a home, I tell you. Life for him was better aboard a submarine."

Spadefish was officially credited with two ships sunk for 4,127 tons, plus the three smaller vessels. As vessels under 500 tons were not counted as ships sunk, the tonnage was not officially credited to *Spadefish*. At the end of this patrol, however, she only claimed three ships sunk, including the junk, a schooner, and the 6,667-ton *Koei Maru* class freighter. Germershausen also claimed the 6,804-ton *Akuira Maru* class freighter as damaged.

Submarine Division Two Commander Eugene Thomas Sands, in his patrol endorsement, gave *Spadefish* credit for sinking three ships and damaging a fourth, for a collective 13,736 tons in enemy shipping destroyed or damaged. Germershausen was awarded the Bronze Star

Spadefish crew, including Luau and Seaweed, on her forward deck following their fourth war patrol. This photo was taken on 21 April 1945 alongside the tender *Proteus* in Guam's Apra Harbor. *Walter Charles collection, courtesy of Argyle Charles.*

Medal for *Spadefish*'s fourth war patrol. The citation said that he "launched four aggressive torpedo attacks and one gun attack which resulted in the sinking of a freighter, a cargo-carrying junk and a schooner, and the damaging of a freighter." In turn, Germershausen recommended Lieutenant Cook for the Navy's Letter of Commendation for his "excellent judgement and thorough knowledge of attack problems" as assistant approach officer.[22]

In reality, *Spadefish* had sunk a 2,274-ton transport ship, an 1,853-ton freighter, the 100-ton schooner, and the 180-ton junk, the latter two not officially tabulated by JANAC. Further, although Germershausen thought that she may have only been struck by a dud torpedo, the 400-ton patrol craft *Hinode Maru No. 17* was later credited to *Spadefish*. All told, the submarine had destroyed five enemy ships for 4,827 tons, evidence of how scarce Japanese shipping targets were becoming.

Because of the poor torpedo performance—which had caused the boat to use ten torpedoes on one ship alone—the run had lasted only 36 days, with 25 in the patrol area and fourteen days submerged. In his patrol report, Captain Germershausen listed all of the failures his FM sonar had encountered. Among them was the failure of the shaft which was supposed to rotate the sonar head, the same shaft that had been damaged in July off Hawaii and during August in the typhoon. Germershausen wanted the thing fixed properly before he went to sea again with it.

He recommended the fix to be installation of a stronger training motor. When not in use, the FM should be housed to protect the "strain from sea pressure and heavy surface seas." Germershausen felt that the "FM sonar gear in this vessel has a history of unsatisfactory operation during four war patrols."[23]

It would be more than a month before *Spadefish* went out on patrol again. Her original FM sonar set would indeed be fully repaired. In fact, its operation would be imperative for what Uncle Charlie Lockwood had planned for *Spadefish*'s next foray.

USS *Spadefish* Fourth Patrol Summary

Patrol Area:	Yellow Sea
Time Period:	15 March - 21 April 1945
Number of Men Aboard:	86 (76 enlisted and 10 officers)
Total Days on Patrol:	36
Days on Station:	25
Days Submerged:	14
Miles Steamed:	8,790.6
Fuel Used:	103,047 gallons
Number of Torpedoes Fired:	21
Ships Sunk, ComSubPac credit:	1 ship/7,000 tons
JANAC Postwar Credit:	2 ships/4,127 tons
Total sinkings, all size ships:	5 ships/4,827 tons
Limiting Factor of Patrol:	Torpedo performance

17

Operation Barney

Refit and Departure: Fifth Patrol   *21 April–27 May, 1945*

The refit period was longer than usual this time, but for good reason. *Spadefish* was being prepared for a patrol like no other.

"Training out of Guam in those days was quite an experience," wrote Captain Germershausen. "Japanese kamikazes were out in force around Okinawa and the Ryukyus. It seemed that at least one smashed destroyer limped into the port of Guam daily to be made seaworthy for the long trip back to Pearl Harbor or the West Coast for repairs." The most astounding to survive was the destroyer *Laffey*, which reached Guam under her own power on 22 April, the day after *Spadefish*'s arrival. *Laffey* had been attacked by twenty-two Japanese planes. She was hit by four bombs and six kamikazes which crashed into her and suffered damage from near-misses and strafing.[1]

Ashore at Guam, the reliable *Spadefish* softball team had occasion to clean up again. Chief Eimermann was taking a saltwater shower ashore when another CPO asked him, "What boat you on?"

"The *Spadefish*," Eimermann replied.

The other sailor said, "We've got $5,000 that says we'll beat your ass playing softball."

Knowing that he had a great team on his side, Eimermann told the petty officer from the other sub to wait while he rounded up some bets. Most of his crew was out of money by this point, but he did wager $200 of his own money, hoping to make up for some of his gambling losses on previous patrols. Pulling together his best players, Eimermann played the con as though they would try their best. In the end, the *Spadefish* team cleaned up and Boats made some easy money. "We beat 'em nine to nothing!"

Spadefish had a beer party on Tinian one day while on R&R. This was on a beach which had been Japanese-held only shortly before. The Marines had cleared the area, but there were still wires on the ground and people worried about someone stepping on a mine that might still

The winning *Spadefish* softball team during R&R at Guam. Front row (left to right): Lt.(jg) Perry Wood, Tony Dunleavy, Jim Fletcher, Joe Ring, pitcher Boats Eimermann and catcher Billy Pigman. Back row (l-r): Roy Moody, Harry Brenneis, Jim Cole, Ed Graf, Ken Sigworth and Buck Miller. *Hugo Lundquist collection, courtesy of Jeanne Lundquist.*

be buried in the sand. Several people took long canes and poked around the wires, making sure no lives mines were below the wires. Quartermaster Don Scholle noticed messcook William Bynum trying to dig things up out of the sand with one of the canes. "Why don't you go down the beach somewhere before you find a mine or something?" Scholle worriedly cautioned him.

Submarine Division 201's relief crew took over while the *Spadefish* crew enjoyed two weeks of R&R on Guam once again. The ship went into drydock to complete voyage repairs and to prepare for her next patrol. Now that entering enemy minefields had become part of her patrol routine, the mine-guard cables remained around her propellers and any topside protrusion. While in drydock, the boat's faulty bow planes were properly repaired as well.

In the customary process of transferring veteran personnel off for the benefit of other subs, Captain Germershausen found that he was officially overstaffed in the area of gunner's mates. Striker Maurice Noonan was promoted to GM3/c and Bernie Massar was advanced to GM2/c. "*Spadefish* was only supposed to have just so many rated men in their own rate aboard ship," recalled Massar. "Lewis had already made chief." Both Edgar Lewis and Massar were transferred to Submarine Division 201 during late April. "It was the only way I was able to get an upgrade to second class gunner's mate," wrote Massar, who was re-rated aboard the tender *Proteus*. "So, we had three rated gunner's mates now."

Shaky Jake Lewis and Massar were both received back aboard *Spadefish* on 6 May. This transfer "trick" was not uncommon among boats which wanted to keep key personnel aboard despite any regulation that might be encountered. Another crew's favorite, motormac Rebel Rewold, went through the same shuffle after the fourth patrol. Promoted to CMoMM on 2 April, Rewold was among those transferred to SubDiv 201 on 21 April in order to become advanced in rating. When the time came to draw replacements for the fifth patrol, Chief Rewold was received back aboard *Spadefish* on 6 May.

Another plankowner, electrician's mate Jack Gallagher, found that a change in duties cost him his position aboard *Spadefish*. "I was in the intercommunications gang under Chief Ordway. Dependahl wanted to get in the I.C. gang, and I wanted to go to the main power gang. We asked if we could change places, and they said, 'sure.'"

Len Dependahl remained with the I.C. gang, but Gallagher found that chief electrician Carl Schmelzer still remembered a little run-in the two had had a year prior.

> We were in Mare Island, loading the boat with spare parts. I was working with Emerson Ordway. He was down below in the maneuvering room. I was carrying this equipment down these ladders, working really hard. It was pretty hot down there and I was dripping sweat. Ordway says, "Why don't you go up on deck and take a smoke and cool off?"
>
> So, I went up on deck and I lit a cigarette. Next thing I knew, Schmelzer came aboard and said, "Get off your ass!" I was a young kid and I made a smart remark. I don't know what I said, but I didn't move. So, he went down below to find Ordway. A little later he came up and I was still sitting there. He glared at me and didn't say anything. He just walked off. So, I forgot about it. All that time—I guess it was a year later when I shifted gangs from Ordway to the main power gang under Schmelzer. That's when he put me off the boat.

The *Spadefish* wardroom had some new faces before time came to depart. The fun-loving Exec, George Cook, received new orders to a new boat, *Remora*, and was transferred on. Instead of advancing another officer from aboard, a new senior officer was pulled to replace Cook.

Reporting aboard was Lieutenant Richard Morgan Wright, an Academy man from the class of 1941. A California native, Wright had

Captain Bill Germershausen (left) with his new Exec, Lt. Richard Morgan "Dick" Wright. They are seen here after the fifth patrol with Paul Majoue's new battle flag. *Official U.S. Navy photo.*

been inspired to join the Navy since visiting the fleet at Long Beach with his father at age ten. Growing up around Los Angeles and Hollywood, Wright was also inspired by his older brother, who received an appointment to West Point. Dick Wright attended the Army West Point Preparatory School at San Francisco. "I figured that going there could best prepare me for competitive examinations for congressional appointments to the Naval Academy," he recalled.[2]

Wright received appointments to both West Point and the Naval Academy. "I chose the Naval Academy because that put me in line with my ambitions from childhood." After graduating from the Academy in February 1941, Ensign Dick Wright was assigned to the battleship *Tennessee*. He was aboard her in Pearl Harbor on 7 December, when the Japanese attacked America. He helped direct his ship's gunfire against enemy aircraft that morning.

> Actually, I was not an anti-aircraft battery officer. That guy was ashore and there was no other officer that was on deck. When I passed it on the way to my battle station, which was unimportant in the action, I just said to myself, "An officer is needed here and I guess I'm it." The exposed spot gave me a good observation point. I did see the *Arizona* blow up, and I did see the *Oklahoma*, which was forward of us, capsize, and I did see the *West Virginia* go down.[3]

Wright returned Stateside with *Tennessee* to repair her damage. Afterwards, the battleships conducted cruises between the States and Hawaii, but did not operate with the carrier fleet. "It looked like the war was going on and I wasn't going to be in it," thought Wright. "I applied for a transfer to submarines."

His request was eventually accepted and he went to Sub School in early 1943. He first served aboard *Pogy*, making five successful war patrols aboard her. *Pogy* destroyed eight enemy ships while Wright was aboard, including a destroyer that was torpedoed in a down-the-throat shot. He then transferred from *Pogy* to *Parche*, aboard which he made her fifth patrol in the Okinawa area. Upon return, he received new orders. "There was a submarine out in Guam getting ready for special patrol when their exec had to be relieved," recalled Wright, "so I was detached from the *Parche* and sent to the *Spadefish*."[4]

Wright would become known to the *Spadefish* crew as a strict officer, where Germershausen allowed Wright to keep a close hand on the crew's affairs. "The Exec's job is the administrator, disciplinarian, and he actually runs the affairs internally," explained Lieutenant Dan Decker. "It was normal Navy doctrine to keep the Skipper the good guy and to have the Exec carry out his wishes. After easy-going George Cook, I'm sure some of the crew viewed Wright as a change."[5]

Lt. Dan Decker would continue as the TDC operator with Ens. Bill Ware—both plankowners—as assistant torpedo and gunnery officer. Lt. Dick Fellows and Warrant Machinist Dutch Falconer, the latter another four-patrol *Spadefish* veteran, continued to handle the boat's engineering, diving and electrical officer duties. Lt.(jg) Ed La Croix stayed on as first lieutenant and Lt.(jg) Perry Wood, another plank owner, remained over the radio gang as communications officer.

Spadefish received two new junior officers, Ens. Raymond E. Dix and Harry Jacob Buncke, Jr., both making their first war patrol. Dix would replace Don Martin as radar officer, responsible for much of the ship's delicate electronics.

When Ensign Harry Buncke reported aboard from the *Proteus* relief crew, he already felt comfortable with his new ship. He had been over *Spadefish* while she was in the *Proteus* drydock, where he had helped check her hull inside and out during the refit. Aboard *Spadefish*, he became both the youngest and tallest officer. At age 22, Harry Buncke stood nearly six foot three inches. In Sub School at New London, he had trained on old O-boats, which he found to be difficult to maneuver through.

"My nickname was Big Stoop because I had to bend down all the time," he recalled. "I usually had scabs on my head from bumping into the overhead valves and all the machinery that hung down from the ceiling." Coming aboard with Lieutenant Wright, Buncke found the new Exec to be "a real tough nut. He had a brother who was in the Bataan Death March. Boy, he was really aggressive. He wanted to sink a lot of ships to avenge his brother's death."

Ensign Buncke, being the most junior aboard was now the wardroom "George," receiving the most junior duties. "My primary duty

The other two new *Spadefish* officers for her fifth patrol were Ensigns Raymond E. Dix (above left) and Harry Jacob Buncke, Jr. (right). *Hugo Lundquist collection, courtesy of Jeanne Lundquist.*

was commissary officer, but I was also assistant torpedo officer, assistant communications officer, and assistant everything."

Harry Buncke admittedly "knew nothing about food." Fortunately for him, *Spadefish*'s chief commissary steward, Francis Scherman, was an old pro. Scherman and Ensign Buncke made the rounds to the food warehouses, where Scherman hand selected what he felt were the best cuts of meat to bring aboard. "I can remember looking at the dates on these frozen beef and lamb," said Buncke. Some of the meat had been frozen for many years, which concerned him.

"Frozen meat, don't worry," advised Chief Scherman. "You take it and cut off an inch or so of freezer burn, and you've got good frozen meat on the inside."

Using some of the ship's petty cash, Buncke purchased sardines and other special treats for the wardroom that he intended to use to toast ship sinkings. "Having our fancy foods was a real celebration."

Aside from the wardroom additions, *Spadefish* had received her usual number of new hands during the required transfers. Among those coming aboard her was one familiar face, QM3c Don Scholle, who had commissioned *Spadefish* and made the first three runs. Caught in the required personnel transfer after the third patrol, he had remained at Guam aboard the tender *Proteus* in the relief crew.

"The second class quartermaster, Fugett, was first in the relief crew and he went aboard *Bonefish* when she came in," Scholle recalled.

"When *Spadefish* came in next, they asked for me and I went aboard *Spadefish* again." Scholle felt both guilty and relieved in being second in the pool, for neither quartermaster Mack A. Fugett nor *Bonefish* would return from their next war patrol.

Si Barnes, a plankowner who was in charge of the after torpedo room, was transferred. His replacement was TM1c Vernon Joseph Kite, a veteran of patrols aboard *Sunfish*, one of *Spadefish*'s former wolf pack mates. Kite had also been in charge of *Sunfish*'s after torpedo room and had been awarded the Silver Star for his assistance in sinking ships during his boat's successful ninth war patrol.

Torpedoman Wallace McMahon, now eighteen years old, had been the youngest sailor aboard *Spadefish*. When Seaman 1/c Charles Alfred Graff reported aboard, McMahon happily became "the second youngest sailor on the *Spadefish*. He was 17, younger than I was, and he earned the nickname 'Baby Graff.'"

Another new crewman coming aboard from *Proteus* was EM3c Albert George La Rocca. He had joined the Navy at age seventeen in 1943, but had been aboard *Proteus* as a relief crewmember for six months at Midway before she sailed for Guam. "Electronics was my hobby, so they had a hard time letting me go," he said. "Whenever they had a problem with something, I'd eat it up."

Al La Rocca at least knew one of his new crew members, a fellow electrician, EM3c Jim Casey. Like La Rocca, Casey had been aboard *Proteus* for more than six months. Having qualified for submarine duty aboard the old *S-43*, Casey had advanced to third class electrician aboard her. While in Pearl Harbor before patrol, however, Casey was badly burned by a battery short. *S-43* sailed without him while he recovered in sick bay. Joining the *Proteus* as a relief crewman, he soon found that Captain Pruitt "didn't have to advance you in pay grade, unless you made a war patrol." Eager for better pay, Casey felt that it was an eternity before he was finally transferred to *Spadefish*. "As the relief crew, you had to be the first ones in and the first ones out. With me, I was the last one in and the last one out!"

Both La Rocca and Casey would become valuable new additions to the electrical gang of chiefs Schmelzer and Ordway. Both also rotated into the lookout pool's watch section. "They raised my tail as far as they could get it, I guess," Casey felt from his vantage point atop the periscope shears.

The new hands got in plenty of practice. F1c James Douglas Cole, received from *Proteus,* was rotated in among the watch standers. When not on watch, he found himself assigned to many daily tasks, including the ship's laundry. "We had to watch water usage and conserve everything," remembered Cole, "so a couple of us were assigned to washing clothes part-time. We had a tub in the head and washed them by hand. To dry them, we spread them on the covers to the Fairbanks Morse diesel engines in the engine rooms."

On 7 May, PhoM1c Robert Rymer returned to CincPac's advanced headquarters, his temporary assignment aboard *Spadefish* for her fourth patrol completed. In his place, PhoM2c Edward Armstrong reported aboard on 13 May. Prior to the fifth patrol, *Spadefish* transferred sixteen men and received seventeen in return.

Spadefish to date had been more fortunate than most Pacific boats in retaining so many of her plank owners, with more than one-third of her men having made all patrols. Counting the upcoming fifth war patrol, the ship's twenty-two officers and chief petty officers could boast to have collectively completed 150 patrols.

Officers	No. Patrols
Cdr. W. J. Germershausen, Jr., USN	5
Lt. R. M. Wright, USN	7
Lt. D. D. Decker, Jr., USN	5
Lt. R. D. Fellows, USNR	2
Lt.(jg) E. J. La Croix, USNR	3
Lt.(jg) P. S. Wood, USNR	5
Ens. W. J. Ware, USN	11
Ens. R. E. Dix, USN	1
Ens. H. J. Buncke, Jr., USNR	1
Machinist L. D. Falconer, USN	8

Chief Petty Officers		No. Patrols
CBM	W. C. Eimermann, USN	13
CGM	E. L. Lewis, USN	10
CTM	F. A. Wells, USN	10
CRM	P. H. Majoue, Jr., USNR	5
CRT	N. Pike, USNR	5
CMoMM	C. C. Griffith, USN	12
CMoMM	R. C. Rewold, USN	10
CMoMM	J. R. Peel, USN	5
CEM	C. T. Schmelzer, USN	12
CEM	E. L. Ordway, USN	5
CPhM	V. L. Ives, USN	5
CCS	F. J. Scherman, USN	10

The level of experience aboard *Spadefish* was undoubtedly the strongest asset the ship would have as she prepared to depart on her most dangerous mission.

From first visiting the University of California Division of War Research team in April 1943, Charlie Lockwood has spent two years preparing for the ultimate submarine mission. He had approved the installation of the first FM sonar unit aboard *Spadefish*, and had been aboard her to see it in use. He approved the installation of more FMS units in more submarines and had been to sea on these boats to test the gear. During the previous month, he had used some of these FM boats—*Spadefish, Seahorse, Tinosa, Bowfin* and *Bonefish*—to map out Japanese minefields in the East China Sea and Tsushima Strait.

The intelligence gathered by their FMS operators was critical to the scheme that Vice Admiral Lockwood had been working on tirelessly since moving his advance base to Guam. He had appointed one of his staff, Commander William Bernard Sieglaff, to head up the task of planning a successful return mission into the Sea of Japan, an area that had not been exploited by U.S. submarines since the loss of Captain Mush Morton and his *Wahoo* in September 1943.

Barney Sieglaff, a veteran sub skipper, took over the training and planning for the new Sea of Japan mission, which became known as "Operation Barney" in his honor. *Wahoo* had been lost trying to exit the Sea of Japan through La Pérouse Strait, an area heavily patrolled by aircraft and surface vessels. Within Japan's Inland Sea, Sieglaff and Lockwood believed there to be a multitude of Japanese ships forced to retreat from U.S. submarines and carrier task forces.[6]

The Sea of Japan ran the length of the largest Japanese islands of Honshu and Hokkaido. Aside from the northern passage of La Perouse Strait, there was another passage between these two main islands known as Tsugaru Strait. This narrow central passage was mined and considered too dangerous to attempt. The widest passage into Emperor Hirohito's "private pond" was through one of the straits on either side of Tsushima Island at the southern end of the Japanese chain near the tip of Korea. Although also heavily mined, Tsushima Strait was judged by Barney Sieglaff and his boss to be the best entry point. There was also the advantage of the 3-knot Kuroshio Current which would help ease a submarine's entry through Tsushima, versus a boat struggling against such a current submerged during an exit through these straits.

Operation Barney was envisioned by Commander Sieglaff and Lockwood's Operation Officer Dick Voge to comprise three separate wolf packs of three submarines each. One pack of three boats could work off the coast of Korea, another pack along central Honshu, and the third could work north from Tsugaru Strait to La Perouse. The three groups of boats would enter the Sea of Japan through the minefields of Tsushima Strait using FM sonar on three successive nights.

Selecting the submarines to make this historic mission was simple. Only nine subs were currently available to Lockwood's staff at Guam which were FM equipped and trained: *Spadefish, Sea Dog, Crevalle, Tunny, Skate, Bonefish, Flying Fish, Bowfin,* and *Tinosa. Sea Dog* had only just received her FM sonar set from the badly damaged *Seahorse,* whose skipper had originally been designated by Barney Sieglaff to be the pack leader for Operation Barney. By war's end, only twenty-one U.S. submarines had the FMS installed, *Spadefish* being the first.

Collectively the nine FM-equipped boats were code-named "Hellcats," for their planned run through the hellpots of Tsushima. Each group of three boats was its own wolf pack, with a separate pack name, each headed by the senior skipper. As it turned out, Bill Germershausen knew each of the other eight skippers very well.

> We were all old friends. All had been contemporaries at Annapolis. All had served together in the peacetime squadrons of the Submarine Forces. [George] Pierce had a particular grudge against the Japanese. His older brother had been killed in action as Commanding Officer of the submarine *Argonaut* in the Solomon Islands area in 1942. Hydeman, upon whom fell the mantle of command as the senior officer, was well fitted to the task.[7]

Special training was part of *Spadefish's* extended rest period before the fifth patrol. With her refit completed on 5 May, post-repair trial runs and training were conducted from 10 to 14 May. Supervised by the Commander, Submarine Division 201, this training period consisted of day and night torpedo approaches on a multiple target group. *Spadefish* conducted both surface and submerged attack approaches, firing four exercise torpedoes during this training period. Captain Germershausen also ran his gunnery crew through battle surface drills, including firing his 5-inch deck gun.

Following the torpedo and gunnery drills, *Spadefish* and the other Hellcat submarines went through extensive FM sonar training and practice sessions through 24 May. Chief Pike rounded up spare FM sonar parts, sensing that all of the minefield mapping done in April had not been done without good reason.

On the evening of 23 May, a conference of all nine sub skippers was held aboard Admiral Lockwood's flagship *Holland.* For the early part of the meeting, the skippers were allowed to bring as many of their officers and FMS operators as the operations room on *Holland's* top deck could accommodate.[8]

From the San Diego laboratory, a training film had been prepared by Harnwell, Henderson and Dr. Kurie, the scientists familiar to the

Spadefish crew due to their development of the FM sonar. The film showed the training and operation of the FM gear, including the PPI screen's visual blobs which indicated mines and the tell-tale bell-like "hell's bells" tones.

After the film, Captain Germershausen was allowed to keep only new Exec Dick Wright and Communications Officer Perry Wood for the balance of the meeting. ComSubPac Operations Officer Dick

Vice Admiral Lockwood's Hellcats Wolf Packs Entering the Sea of Japan		
"Hydeman's Hepcats"		
Sea Dog	SS-401	Cdr. Earl Twining Hydeman
Crevalle	SS-291	Cdr. Everett Hartwell Steinmetz
Spadefish	SS-411	Cdr. William Joseph Germershausen
"Pierce's Polecats"		
Tunny	SS-282	Cdr. George Ellis Pierce
Skate	SS-305	Cdr. Richard Barr Lynch
Bonefish	SS-223	Cdr. Lawrence Lott Edge
"Risser's Bobcats"		
Flying Fish	SS-229	Cdr. Robert Dunlap Risser
Bowfin	SS-287	Cdr. Alexander Kelly Tyree
Tinosa	SS-283	Cdr. Richard Clark Latham

Voge then went through the plans for Operation Barney with twenty-seven officers from the nine Hellcat boats. Voge detailed how the wolf packs would enter the Sea of Japan through Tsushima Strait and then exit through La Perouse Strait.

The meeting lasted well into the night. Barney Sieglaff next went into specific details, passing out charts, intelligence reports and operation orders to Bill Germershausen and his fellow commanders. *Spadefish*, one of the three boats of Commander Earl Hydeman's "Hepcats," would be in the first wolf pack to enter the Sea of Japan, starting before daylight on 4 June.

A former submarine skipper who had never been able to fire on any enemy vessel in anger, Lockwood wished his skippers the best of luck in the Sea of Japan. "I would give a right hind leg to go with you," said Lockwood. "God bless you and good hunting."[9]

Spadefish was loaded with a combination of Mark 14-3As and the newer Mark 23 steam torpedoes. It is interesting to note that most of the Hellcat skippers had elected to load up with Mark 14s for the Sea of Japan patrol, even after the terrible failures experiences with the Mark 14s by such top boats as *Wahoo*. Admiral Lockwood's staff had finally resolved the faulty firing pin issue, and the Mark 14s had been restored to favor. They were generally preferred because they could run up to 50 mph, versus the slower 34-mph speed of the new electric

Mark 18s. The slower speed of the Mark 18s meant, generally speaking, that they were too slow to be shot at an angle where they would have to overtake an enemy ship making moderate speed which was steaming away from the submarine.

After disappointing luck with the Mark 18s on *Spadefish*'s fourth war patrol, Bill Germershausen wanted no part of such a finicky torpedo once his boat entered Japan's Inland Sea. As part of Hydeman's Hepcats, his boat would be the first to enter the Sea of Japan and also part of the first wolf pack to depart Guam.

The first section of Hydeman's Hellcats was ready when the departure hour arrived on 27 May 1945. The sun was hot and strong over Apra Harbor that morning as Vice Admiral Lockwood held a last-minute ceremony to see his first Hellcat skippers off. ComSubPac's staff held a buffet lunch for Hydeman and his fellow skippers aboard *Holland*. As a special surprise, Lockwood's staff had rounded up half a dozen girls—a Red Cross representative and five Navy nurses. "It was to celebrate the departure of the first echelon Hepcats to dare the hellpots of Tsushima," wrote Lockwood.[10]

The women knew nothing about the top-secret mission that the nine submarine crews were about to embark upon. They had just been asked to join the admiral in bidding a cheerful farewell to a group of men about to lead an important mission. The skippers enjoyed lunch with ComSubPac's staff and the ladies before taking a launch back to their boats. Lockwood watched from the *Holland*'s boat deck as mooring lines were taken in and crews mustered on deck for the departure.

Spadefish's diesels had already been idling for some time when Captain Germershausen came back aboard and prepared to depart at 1500. Ensign Harry Buncke recalled Admiral Lockwood—repeating his statement made to the nine Hellcat skippers the previous week—remarking to the crew as they were about to leave Guam, "I'd give my right arm to be going with you men."[11]

Somebody topside, in earshot of Buncke, mumbled in a stage whisper, "Right arms are pretty cheap these days."

Spadefish's rudder was put over and the engine went to back two-thirds, then ahead one-third as she twisted away from her spot near *Holland*. At 1517, the first three boats to head for the Sea of Japan were underway in Apra Harbor. Hydeman' Hepcats—*Sea Dog*, *Crevalle* and *Spadefish*—passed the old British battleship HMS *King George V* and they formed a single column as the threaded their way through the ships in the harbor. After all of the preparation, *Spadefish* was finally underway for what Bill Germershausen "knew would be a highly exciting cruise."[12]

After slipping through Apra Harbor's protective torpedo nets into the open sea, the Hepcats were met by the patrol boat *PC-549*. This vessel would lead them north along the coast of Guam to the submarine safety lane, code-named "Smokestack." *Spadefish* followed *Sea Dog* and *Crevalle*. Line abreast and five miles apart, the three subs pressed northwestward toward Japan, some 2,000 miles away, at a cruising speed of 13 knots.[13]

Before turning the subs loose, *PC-549* came alongside *Crevalle* and picked up a civilian technician who had remained aboard to continue working on the sub's finicky electronics gear.[14] The escort vessel was released at 2100 and *Spadefish*, *Sea Dog* and *Crevalle* proceeded independently, conducting training exercises and practice dives while en route on 27–29 May.

The other two three-boat packs, Pierce's Polecats and Risser's Bobcats, would leave port on 28 May and 29 May. This way each of the three boats would transit the strait on successive nights.

Aboard *Spadefish*, only Captain Germershausen, Dick Wright and Perry Wood had been in the secret ComSubPac briefing where Operation Barney had been detailed. The rest of the crew could only guess at the importance of this wolf pack's mission. All, however, could sense that something "big" was up with this patrol. The scuttlebutt had been rampant. Admiral Lockwood had been ever-present during the preparations stages, and another Navy photographer, Edward Armstrong, was temporarily assigned to the ship. The extensive FM training was also a sign that something big was up.

Each Hepcat skipper had his own way of informing his crew of their mission. *Spadefish* was not far out from Guam when their skipper let the cat out of the bag. Over the boat's 1MC speaker system, Germershausen changed up the usual delivery by letting his chief of the boat, Boats Eimermann, brief the crew on their destination.

Eimermann took the patrol orders and began to read through them over the 1MC as the captain stood beside him. Germershausen held down the microphone key as Boats began reading orders that were completely new to him. He immediately, however, began stumbling over some of the Japanese names. The chief of the boat found the experience embarrassing, as the captain had to chime in to help pronounce some of the foreign locations. "I had enough trouble with English words, much less Japanese places!" said Eimermann. Exasperated, Germershausen finally took over the 1MC duties and finished reading the orders.[15]

Commander TF 17's Operation Order No. 112-45 directed *Spadefish*'s wolf pack to steam toward the Sea of Japan at normal two engine speed. Cdr. Earl Hydeman decided not to have his Hepcats conduct the normal inter-ship training exercises en route to station. He did not want to slow their progress, as they were scheduled to be the first three boats to enter the Sea of Japan on 4 June, "Fox Day."[16]

Operation Barney's orders further detailed that each of the three sets of subs would be given a specific area to patrol inside the Sea of Japan. "Mike Day" was set as sunset on 9 June, the date when they could begin firing on targets. Since *Spadefish*'s pack would make the transit during the early hours of 4 June, they would have to remain undetected for the next five days before Mike Day commenced. All nine boats then had orders to exit the Sea of Japan through La Perouse Strait on 24 June ("Sonar Day") either surfaced or submerged, at Commander Hydeman's discretion. "The initials FMS were used to designate 'Fox Day,' 'Mike Day,' and 'Sonar Day,'" wrote Bill Germershausen. Respectively, these code name stood for the "day of penetration of the minefields, day of 'commence fire' and day of exit of La Perouse Strait. Fox Day was, of course, different for each sub group, but Mike and Sonar were identical for all."[17]

The crew was at least finally removed from the suspense which always tightly gripped the men while sailing under sealed orders. The trip to Tsushima Strait would take eight days, and all hands would have plenty of time to debate what exactly would happen in the Sea of Japan. The narrow channels leading into Japan's backyard were heavily mined. If American subs could bypass these fields, Admiral Lockwood speculated that they could sever the last remaining lifeline to the Japanese Empire.

Although the usual multi-boat training exercises had been eliminated en route to the Tsushima Strait, Captain Germershausen drilled his crew for other scenarios they might face on this patrol.

> We occupied ourselves with training exercises and gunnery drills supervised by Lt. Dan Decker, Torpedo and Gunnery Officer. [Commander] Hydeman had elected to conduct the exit through La Perouse Strait as a high speed dash on the surface. We did not know this in advance, but expected that would be his decision. Our intelligence indicated that the strait was seeded with moored anti-submarine mines watching at about 45 feet. A run on the surface meant we had to be prepared to shoot it out with the deck guns if we encountered opposition. Hence the emphasis on gunnery.[18]

En route to the Sea of Japan, Captain Germershausen ran on the surface as much as possible to keep time. The new Exec, Dick Wright, held field days every afternoon to keep the crew on their toes. "No matter what we were doing, at 1600, he'd go through the compartments and check," recalled Jim Cole. "Hell, we kept a clean boat." Gunner Bernie Massar also found the new Exec to be a real stickler for detail. "He was strictly military." Although his shirt may have been stenciled "R. M. Wright," he became known to some of the enlisted men as "I. M. Wright."

Dick Wright was equally demanding on his junior officers. He found communications officer Perry Wood to be too friendly with the enlisted men. "He was always balling me out," recalled Wood. "'You're too nice to the crew,' he would tell me. 'You have to make 'em hate you, so they will obey you in an emergency.'" Wood disagreed, feeling that the *Spadefish* crew was made up on intelligent young men who "understood the necessity of an order and did it."

To torpedoman Olaf Olson, the new XO was "a strict disciplinarian." When Lieutenant Wright held field day, Olaf's buddy Gus Cuthbertson would protest by making as much noise as he could. "When they would pull field day, we would start cleaning the torpedoes. When you used high pressure air in the torpedoes, they would squeal like a pig. Gus had a big bass voice. So, he would sit on the air flask with a bat and hammer and sing 'Yah-hah, yoke-noke!' and pound on that air flask with his hammer."

The new hands were checked out, most of whom were not yet fully qualified in submarines. As always, school of the boat was conducted throughout the patrol as time allowed for the new hands to become qualified to wear the coveted submariner's dolphin patch. In the maneuvering room, new electrician Al Rocca felt right at home. While surfaced, his crew would take hydrometer readings to check the voltage levels of the charging batteries. When the boat made a dive, the diesel engines were shut down and there was an air trip that had to be hit to shut off the oxygen to the diesels. "The electricians were always quick to make the trip," La Rocca recalled. "We'd try to hit the air trip before the enginemen could get it."

Chief Eimermann worked the new hands into lookout duty, sonar and radar watches. Fireman Jim Cole was assigned to Chief Griffith's forward engine room, where Sam Pierce served as the leading oiler. "You only needed an engineer and an oiler in each engine room, so with three watch sections you then had four extra people in each engine room," Cole explained. Extras like Cole rotated into the lookout watch sections. Cole also doubled as a member of the torpedo reload crew and watched over the trim manifold in the control room.

"We had three lookouts positions on the periscope shears, with one man standing by as relief," said Cole. "We split up the sky and sea search so that everything was covered. When you were relieved from one station, you would go to the next until you went down to the helm in the conning tower."

Spadefish's old hands knew all the tricks for passing time en route to station. Some of the more adventurous were quick to acquire the necessary ingredients to cook up a good batch of gilly juice for the

Spadefish's first watch section, fifth patrol. Front (left to right): EM3c Jim Casey, SC2c Ed Graf, SM1c Jim Schuett, S1c Olaf (Sandleben) Olson, QM2c Jim Fletcher, EM3c Dick Bassett (with Luau), TM3c Wallace McMahon, RM3c Tom O'Neil, and S1c Bill Terboss. Standing (left to right): FCS1c Andy Olah, TM2c John Nesnee, MoMM2c Buck Miller, GM2c Bernie Massar, TM1c Emery Kreher, CBM Willard Eimermann (holding Seaweed), unknown, S1c Roger Paulson, RT2c Bill Keeney, S1c Howard Melstrand, and MoMM2c Edwin Cunningham. *Hugo Lundquist collection, courtesy of Jeanne Lundquist.*

Spadefish's second watch section. Front (left to right): MoMM3c Melvin Mullen, EM2c Herman Cruze, unknown, RM3c Ken Powers, MoMM3c Harry Brenneis (with mustache), MoMM1c John Taylor, TM3c Thad Barton, F1c Cleveland Hord, CPhM Victor Ives, and EM3c Warren Asher. Standing (left to right): MoMM3c Tony Dunleavy, F1c Maurice Babb, MoMM1c Vic Holeman, unknown, CEM Carl Schmelzer, CMoMM John Peel, TM2c Gus Cuthbertson, and unknown.

Spadefish's third watch section, fifth patrol. Front (left to right): EM1c Roy Moody, MoMM2c John Brewer, EM2c Billy Pigman (with cigarette), (unknown in front), QM3c Don Scholle, Y1c Irv Kreinbring, MoMM2c Pat Kelley (in white T-shirt), FC3c Walter Charles, EM3c Al La Rocca (leaning forward in back), S1c Hugh Carney, MoMM2c Dick Gamby, F1c Jim Cole, and RM1c Mike Sergio.
Standing (left to right): RT1c Joe Case, SC1c Tom Riley, EM3c Tom Shaw, MoMM2c Nick Pelliciari, CTM Red Wells, MoMM2c Joe Ring, TM2c Hugo Lundquist, S2c Robert Mikesell, and CRM Paul Majoue.
Hugo Lundquist collection, courtesy of Jeanne Lundquist.

R&R period that would celebrate this historic patrol. New junior officer Harry Buncke found that his crew was crafty.

"One of my jobs aboard was to take care of the only official booze aboard. We had Absolut ethyl alcohol for cleaning and drying optics and connectors on the electronic equipment," Ensign Buncke said. "I had a five-gallon can of that, which was kept under my bunk under lock and key. As the assistant communications officer, it was my job to guard that. I don't know how they did it, but the crew got to it. That five gallons was gone in a couple of weeks!"

Hell's Bells

Fifth Patrol   *27 May–5 June 1945*

The trip to the Sea of Japan was broken up on 30 May when an American Ventura reconnaissance plane circled above *Spadefish*, requesting the sub to search for survivors of a downed U.S. aircraft. A Boeing B-29 Superfortress bomber from the Sixty-first Bomber Squadron, based on Guam, had gone down while returning from a incendiary raid against targets in Osaka, Japan's second largest city. The crew had been forced to bail out into the ocean near Sofu Gan, the 300-foot rock pinnacle which was a well-known mariner's landmark. One of the eleven-man crew had been lost during the bail out.[1]

Just hours after Lieutenant William Orr's B-29 crew had ditched, a Navy PBY had seen them in the ocean. The PBY could not land in the rough seas, but circled until a Boeing B-17 could drop the men a Higgins rescue boat, which had a hand-cranked "Gibson Girl" SOS radio transmitter aboard.

Spadefish increased speed to flank and headed for the reported position of the downed aviators. Captain Germershausen informed Earl Hydeman on *Sea Dog* that *Spadefish* was headed to search and she was joined by *Sea Dog* and *Crevalle*. The three boats reached the reported area at 0445 on 31 May and commenced scouring the seas. By 1100, there had been no sight of the aviators, so Hydeman abandoned the search and ordered his submarines to continue on.

Fortunately for Lieutenant Orr's crew, six more Hellcats were following behind Hydeman's Hepcats. Commander Risser's Bobcats next converged on the area and searched diligently on 2 June, assisted by aircraft. At length, Dick Latham's *Tinosa* sighted the Higgins boat at 1244 and brought aboard the ten surviving aviators.

Spadefish and her sister boats moved through the Nansei Shoto island group on 1 June, passing south of Akuseki Shima. *Spadefish* ran on the surface, sighting one floating mine at 0634 and a Betty bomber at 0910, distance 15.5 miles. She submerged at 1800, some 40 miles east of Yaku Shima for a quick test of her FM sonar. Between 1807 and 1824, three false target shells were fired to test the gear's tracking ability. The shells were fired out of the underwater signal tube from the after torpedo room and the resulting fizzy bubble mass was detected on the PPI screen and rang the hell's bells. Once resurfaced at 1956, she headed for Tokara Kaikyo at flank speed. The APR-1 reported sweeping radar signals from the Japanese ashore.

By 0100 on 2 June, *Spadefish* and her two packmates completed passage of Colnett Strait. They continued north in the East China Sea heading toward the Sea of Japan, with a planned rendezvous and final instructions on the approach to the straits. During the late morning, Captain Germershausen had Chief Pike test his sonar again, firing a false target shell for tracking. *Spadefish* surfaced again at 1136, and passed within sight of the island of Danjo Gunto. In the quartermaster's log SM2c Zelbert Gouker recorded at 1548, "Passed dead body in water. Looked like flyer." *Spadefish* passed between Danjo Gunto and Fukae Shima. At 2042, Perry Wood dived ship after an SJ radar contact was made on an aircraft at 8,000 yards.

Spadefish was back on the surface within two hours, approaching the island of Saishu To. The Japanese aircraft were still very active. At 0052, both SJ and SD radar showed a contact at 4 miles. Officer of the deck Dan Decker made a quick dive to 150 feet, ordered right full rudder, and rigged the ship for depth charge. Easing back to radar depth a half hour later, the ship made a quick sweep with both her SD and SJ, received an all-clear and then resurfaced at 0133. The radar planes seemed to be at work again this night, for at 0231, an SD contact was made on an aircraft at 5 miles. The ship dove again and remained down for more than a hour, hoping to give the pesky flyers time to move on. "The ease with which the aircraft found us was a result of direction-finding triangulation from ashore, followed by vector direction to the closest aircraft," explained Lieutenant Decker. *Spadefish* resurfaced at 0342, charging her batteries for another hour before she made her necessary submergence for the day at 0450.[2]

At 1253 on 3 June, two unidentified light bombers were sighted. Fast approaching the scheduled time to transit Tsushima Strait, Captain Germershausen had Neal Pike test his FM sonar for the third straight day. He took the boat down to 150 feet at 1324, and commenced an FMS drill. During the testing, *Spadefish* fired five false target shells on different bearings for her operators to track. The tests were deemed successful and the boat secured from FM drills at 1450. *Spadefish* surfaced and continued her run toward the scheduled rendezvous point for the next night's transit.

One floating mine was sighted and avoided. At 1545, Tsushima

Captain Bill Germershausen, standing at the base of the conning tower ladder, oversees EM3c Al La Rocca and S1c Hugh Carney on the diving planes in the control room as *Spadefish* passes 71 feet. *Courtesy of Al La Rocca.*

Island was sighted through the high periscope at 35 miles. The persistent enemy air patrols continued to threaten the secrecy of the Hepcats' approach. "Aircraft contact!" shouted the sailor on the SD radar watch at 1606. The bridge lookouts quickly had a visual on the Japanese aircraft, which they reported at 12 miles and closing.

"Clear the bridge!" shouted Decker, whose watch hours seemed to be most prone to include these radar-directed aircraft. He followed junior officer of the deck Dutch Falconer and their three lookouts down the ladder in an instant. *Spadefish* stayed down until well after dark. It was critical at this point that *Spadefish* not be detected as she neared her entry point to the Tsushima minefields.

She surfaced again at 2008 and headed for Hydeman's Hepcats' rendezvous position, south of Tsushima Strait. At 2223 on 3 June, an SJ contact was made, which was soon identified as Commander Hydeman's *Sea Dog*. *Spadefish* maneuvered to fall in 4 miles astern of *Sea Dog*. As the wolf pack was beginning to form up, sonar watch in the forward torpedo room could hear distant explosions somewhere in Tsushima Strait. In the quartermaster's notebook, Don Scholle logged at 2302: "Forward room reports hearing 4 explosions, believed to be depth charges."

Contact was also established with Commander Steinmetz's *Crevalle* shortly after *Sea Dog* had been identified. Before the early dawn, they were to run the passage. Each boat reached the area without any serious incident, although *Sea Dog*'s radar set was acting up.[3]

Shortly after midnight, as the early morning hours of 4 June 1945 ticked away, the three submarines comprising Hydeman's Hepcats were in close proximity on the surface at their rendezvous site south of Tsushima Strait for the run into the Sea of Japan. Commander Earl Hydeman called his *Sea Dog*, *Spadefish* and *Crevalle* together for a last-minute exchange of plans.

At 0025, *Spadefish* came to "all stop" as she nestled up close to her sister subs. From their bridges, Hydeman, Bill Germershausen, and Everett Steinmetz ran through the plan for transiting the minefields. The passage of Tsushima Strait was tricky enough in the daylight, without the additional mines to dodge. The area between the East China Sea and the Sea of Japan was called the Korea Strait, which divided the Korean mainland from Japan. In the center of this strait lay Tsushima Island, which runs north to south. To the left of Tsushima Island lay the deep but fairly narrow western channel known as Nishi Suido. To the right of Tsushima Island ran the fairly shallow eastern channel known as Tsushima Strait.

Tsushima Strait was cluttered with small islands and was a busy transit area for small shipping. The fact that more than a dozen lighthouses spotted the Tsushima area was evidence that these were tricky waters to negotiate. During wartime, the lighthouses were not blinking warning messages and the minefields within the strait forbid any shipping to pass which did not have proper mine charts.[4]

Both Tsushima Strait and Nishi Suido were mined, but Admiral Lockwood's planning staff had selected Tsushima as the safer of the two to transit. The 3-knot Kuroshio current, which flowed in the direction that the boats would be entering Tsushima Strait, was also a deciding factor for this entry choice. Of the nine boats selected to enter the Sea of Japan, *Spadefish*, *Crevalle* and *Sea Dog* would be the first to attempt.

Commander Hydeman briefed Steinmetz and Germershausen on his plans. Since his *Sea Dog*'s newer, keel-mounted FM gear had been acting up, he wanted *Crevalle* four miles on his port beam, in line abreast. *Spadefish*, the only boat with the original deck-mounted FM gear, would bring up the rear, four miles astern of *Sea Dog*.

The surface meeting took only five minutes, and was very much to the point. At 0034, nine minutes after "all stop" had been ordered, *Spadefish* was underway again. Hydeman's Hepcats moved northeast into the dark, starry night at 5 knots. He wanted his wolf pack to stay on the surface at 1/3 speed until the planned time of diving at 0300, or when *Crevalle* or *Sea Dog* detected a mine. Less than one hour into the Tsushima Strait transit, *Crevalle*'s radar picked up two Japanese picket boats at 0057. *Spadefish* picked up the two ships on radar, seen to be crossing Tsushima Strait from west to east at 15,000 yards. By 0117, the closest that signalman Zelbert Gouker had logged them to *Spadefish* was 12,000 yards. Fortunately, the picket boats moved away without further closing the distance.[5]

The trio of American subs put the patrol boats safely astern, continuing their 5-knot run as the moon rose at 0140. The plan for all three boats to dive at 0300 was fouled up when *Crevalle*'s radar picked up a Japanese aircraft at 9,000 yards, closing fast. Captain Steinmetz dove his *Crevalle* at 0210. Four miles astern, *Spadefish*'s SJ radar had the contact at 0212 at 8,000 yards and closing. Captain Germershausen ordered a crash dive to 150 feet and to rig the boat for depth charges, with all bulkhead doors securely dogged.

No explosions followed, but Germershausen and Steinmetz both opted to just stay down for the remainder of the Tsushima Strait passage, as the originally scheduled dive time was only 45 minutes and 4 miles away. *Spadefish* moved forward at 3 knots submerged, rigging in her starboard sound head at 0220. At 0222, Chief Neal Pike, the most experienced FM sonar operator aboard, took his position in the conning tower for what would turn out to be a very long shift. The QB sound head, rigged in, was manned for a listening watch as was the JP sonar in the conning tower.

Before diving, Germershausen had radioed *Sea Dog* to warn Commander Hydeman of the aircraft contact. Hydeman's boat did not pick up the contact on radar, nor did his lookouts see anything. He had shifted from long-range SJ search radar to his short range ST periscope radar. Not sensing an immediate threat, Hydeman kept *Sea Dog* on the surface, diving at 0300, just as planned.[6]

Moving through Tsushima Strait at 3 knots would give Chief Pike and his fellow FMS operators good listening conditions. At this rate, propeller noises would be low, while steering control was still effective. Finally, if a mine was spotted dead ahead, an emergency reverse would kill *Spadefish*'s headway almost immediately.

Captain Germershausen put TM3c Olaf Olson on the helm in the conning tower as *Spadefish* entered the straits of Tsushima. The helm duty would rotate during the long submerged passage to keep fresh hands on the wheel. GM3c Maurice Noonan, a plank owner and state trooper from New Jersey, was among the steady-handed helmsmen used during 4 June. Conning the ship through the minefields this day would require precise execution. "It scared the hell out of me, because you couldn't see anything," recalled Olson. "You're going dead slow speed and, of course, at that speed the boat didn't respond very fast. In your mind, you would picture yourself running into these damn mines all the time."

Another of the helmsman during the day was gunner Bernie Massar. He remembered that only a few men were selected to man the helm. "We were not to drift off course more than 1 to 2 degrees. This was pretty difficult when you travel at slow speed. When you did start to drift, you had to check it quickly. You also ran the risk of oversteering and swinging in the opposite direction."[7]

Aboard *Sea Dog*, the radar officer fired a false target shell through the underwater signal tube to test that his FM gear was truly working. The resulting fizzy bubbles from the test shell were picked up on the PPI screen and heard on the speakers, giving Hydeman assurance that his FM set was working properly.[8]

In *Spadefish*'s conning tower, Neal Pike watched the FM gear. The conning tower was cleared of non-essential men, leaving Pike, Captain Germershausen, Lt.(jg) Perry Wood on the plotting table, a sound man, the duty quartermaster, and the duty helmsman.

Because his FM head was mounted on the deck, Germershausen had been directed to go deeper than the other two subs with keel mounted FM sonar. *Spadefish* was ordered to make the minefield transit at 150 feet. Germershausen would stick to the agreed upon 3-knot speed, with course being 035° T, like the other boats. His course paralleled the prevailing northerly drift of the sea's current in this area. Although the Kuroshio current was as strong as 3 knots in places, Germershausen noted in his secret report that the drift this day was "a favorable current of one knot."

Bill Germershausen took liberty to revise his orders slightly, although he reported his depth at 150 feet in his secret report.

> Lockwood wanted us to stay close to the surface so we could pick up these mines. I didn't carry out my orders to the letter. He wanted us to take an angle of maybe 3 or 4 degrees, so if this sonar gear was tilted, it would have a better line on the mines we were watching on the surface. I didn't trust this gear because of the experience I'd had on the previous patrol. I went down to 180 feet and leveled off and went through at that depth.[9]

Chief Pike recalled his skipper ordering the 180 foot depth. "We were trying to go low enough that we were below the mines," he said. Pike's year of experience working with *Spadefish*'s often finicky frequency-modulated sonar would pay off now. Ensign Harry Buncke later recalled, "We were all very happy Pike was aboard because he was the one who really knew how to keep the equipment running properly."

After experiencing so much trouble with the FMS on *Spadefish*'s fourth run, Pike had scrounged many spare parts from the tender *Proteus* while in Guam. He had found that the power amplifier was apt to burn out at the worst possible moment. Pike had to keep the electronics stack in the forward torpedo room as cool as possible. The stack, containing five drawers of circuitry, consumed 1250 watts of power and generated lots of heat. The forward torpedo room was certainly not a cool place to keep such finicky gear, as temperatures submerged often exceeded 100 degrees. Carl Schmelzer and Emerson Ordway's electricians had mounted two small fans blowing on the set to keep the tubes from overheating during the transit. While Pike manned the FM console in the conning tower, RT1c Joe Case oversaw the rack and the sonar head in Emery Kreher's forward torpedo room.[10]

Spadefish had rigged in both sound heads and her Bendix log upon diving to avoid any other items protruding that could snag a mine cable. Chief Majoue would maintain listening watches throughout the long transit on both the QB hydrophonic sonar—even though its head was rigged into the ship—in the forward torpedo room and the JP sonar in the conning tower. Fortunately, Majoue had Little Fox Sergio, Bill Keeney, Tom O'Neil, Ken Powers, and other qualified radiomen strikers who could alternate the watches on both listening devices during the long submerged transit.

Silence was maintained throughout the boat. It was ordered but certainly not necessary. In Chief Johnny Peel's pump room, Dick Gamby and Whitey Harbison and the other members of the auxiliary gang watched their gauges and pumps, although most of the equipment was shut down. "We kept it very quiet going through that day," recalled Gamby.

The first half hour was quiet. The first FM sonar contact was logged at 0302, but this was not the first row of mines expected. Another hour passed before Pike's screen showed more contacts. Three contacts were logged between 0416 and 0419, although *Spadefish* had still not yet reached the space where rows of mines were known to be planted. The cause of these individual contacts could have been a random mine, a false return, or even a large fish. During this time, a Japanese

Ship's mascot Luau perched atop the deck-mounted FM sonar transducer, the electronics device which would enable *Spadefish* and eight other submarines enter the Sea of Japan in June 1945. This photo was taken in 1945 in Tiburon Bay upon *Spadefish*'s return to California. Left to right are Jim Cole, "Buck" Miller, Bernie Massar, and Ken Powers. *Courtesy of Bernie Massar.*

patrol boat could be heard above on the surface, pinging and moving around. It was not until 0455 that all pinging and screws were lost from sound. The submariners could only silently wonder if the Japanese knew that American submarines were slipping through their protected passages.

Chief Pike called out his fifth FM contact at 0508. Although the enemy surface craft had passed on by, sounds similar to depth charges were picked up a short time later. "Heard several fairly close explosions," logged quartermaster Jim Fletcher at 0535. "All clear on sound." The worst fear was that *Crevalle* or *Sea Dog* had found a mine. There would be no way to find out until surfacing hours later.

Another FMS contact was made at 0556. As *Spadefish* moved ever closer to the point in Tsushima Strait where the bulk of the mines were expected, her crew could hear a number of very distinct explosions. At 0618, Fletcher noted that "12 fairly close explosions" rocked the boat, although all was clear on sound. These blasts were even louder and closer than earlier ones.

Aboard *Crevalle*, Captain Steinmetz wrote, "Sounded like depth charges or bombs." Steinmetz thought that perhaps the explosions came from American B-29s dropping bombs on Pusan, Korea, to the west of Tsushima Strait. At 0626, three more explosions were heard through the subs. "We didn't know if one of the other two boats was getting depth charged or not," recalled Bernie Massar. At 0710, Fletcher logged three more explosions. Some of the submariners later thought that the explosions might have been from blasts at a rock quarry on Tsushima Island, just to the west. Despite the unnerving blasts, *Spadefish* and her sister subs pressed on. The patrol orders explicitly detailed that even a non-functioning FM sonar gear "will not be considered sufficient cause to delay the transit of any ship."[11]

Neal Pike called out three more FM contacts between 0714 and 0735. Throughout the boat, many men not on watch simply stayed in their bunks to keep the ship especially quiet. It was just after 0800 when *Spadefish* approached the first two distinct lines of mines, some five and a half hours after being forced to dive for the night.

"Hell's bells!" sang out Pike at 0808 as FM contact No. 10 of the day tolled in his ears. The distinct half moon shaped blob appeared perfectly on his PPI screen at the same moment. Captain Germershausen had him flip on the speakers in the conning tower.

The sound of hell's bells came more frequently now. The second mine was picked up five seconds after the previous one. Lieutenant Dan Decker recalled, "I could definitely hear the sonar echoes from the mines as we approached the first row. Then very shortly, I could hear the companion row." Intelligence had warned that the Japanese mines were in three rows. "It turned out that each row was double and a few miles between them," recalled Decker.

Chief Pike watched two more blobs appear on his PPI screen at 0829 and 0833. "I called out the ranges and bearings, such as '30 yards, 3 degrees to starboard. Twenty yards at 2 degrees to port," remembered Pike. "If my bearings had been off by 20 or 30 feet, we would have hit a mine."

Captain Germershausen began issuing orders to his helmsman to weave the boat. In the control room, Lieutenant Dick Fellows had to maintain a steady 180 feet. Despite whatever enormous pressures gripped him internally, Germershausen remained a rock during the passage. He later stated that although *Spadefish*'s FM gear worked beautifully this day, the range at which the mines were spotted offered little opportunity for maneuvering.

All was quiet for a short while. Another row of mines was encountered at 0914, and the hell's bells tolled seven times in seven minutes. Running at 180 feet, *Spadefish* stayed on a steady course for the first six mine contacts. The seventh consecutive contact and twentieth total FM contact for 4 June was logged at 0921. It was dead ahead.

"Left full rudder!" Germershausen ordered.

The helmsman dodged this contact and then settled back on course 035° T. Other than contacts directly in *Spadefish*'s path, the skipper believed that unnecessary steering around the mine contacts would potentially expose more of her hull to other mines. At 180 feet, Germershausen felt that he was below the depth of the Japanese mines. Rather than hitting a mine head-on, the greater risk at this depth was snagging a cable and pulling one down.

An hour passed before *Spadefish* found her next row of mines. Already eight hours into his shift, Chief Pike remained hunched over his PPI screen diligently. Nearby, Perry Wood sat at his plotting table, making careful note of the ship's progress, plotting all mine contacts that were called out. Lieutenant Dick Wright called up from the control room at one point, offering to spell Wood on the plot. "No, Perry's doing a good job," replied Captain Germershausen. "I don't want to change him."

Germershausen, as he later wrote, did let his XO take charge for half of the stressful transit hours. "I split the watch with the executive officer, Lt. Richard M. Wright—a fighting man of the highest order—and got some shut-eye."[12]

In the control room, well into the minefield transit, auxiliaryman Buck Miller also decided to get some sleep as his watch ended. "Well, my watch is over," he announced to Lt.(jg) Ed La Croix. "I guess I'll hit the sack."[13]

"Hit the sack?" asked La Croix. "How could you sleep while we're in the middle of a minefield?"

"What would be the difference whether I stay here and worry with you or in the sack?" replied Miller. "We're loaded with twenty-four torpedoes plus ammunition. If we hit a mine, I won't make any difference."

With that, Miller headed for his bunk and crawled in "for sure not to sleep but to pray."

Quartermaster Don Scholle logged FM contact No. 21 at 1025, followed by two more in the next half minute. *Spadefish* now entered a fairly heavily mined area of distinctive rows. Hell's bells rang out frequently, with eighteen more mines detected by 1101. In spite of the nervous tension that prevailed, the crew took the danger of passing through the Japanese minefields in stride. "At eighteen years of age, you didn't know any better," recalled electrician Al La Rocca. "You thought you were invincible."

Once clear of this large minefield, *Spadefish* continued steering on course 035° T, making 65 turns on her screws. The sound watch reported "fairly loud" screws from an enemy ship above at 1130, but these quickly faded on another course. The fourth distinct line of mines that had been foretold of by intelligence was picked up at 1248. Pike's screen showed four different mines during the next half hour. All was quiet for more than an hour before another contact was made. *Spadefish*'s fiftieth FM contact of the day came as the hell's bells rang at 1440 on 4 June.

During the midday and early afternoon hours, two more distant explosions were logged, possibly the sound of an escort dropping an occasional depth charge. Neal Pike remained at his FMS on the alert as *Spadefish* continued to clear the area of the last reported minefield. In the later afternoon, three more questionable FM contacts were made between 1826 and 1828. "We wondered how many more were out there," recalled Lieutenant Decker. "The few false echoes were enough to keep us alert." Jim Fletcher logged the last contact of the day as Number 55.

Two hours later, Captain Germershausen felt confident that his boat had safely cleared Tsushima Strait's minefields and prepared to surface. The transit was quite tense for the skipper, as he would later report to Admiral Lockwood.

> Regarding the mine fields—the most important part of the patrol, I am afraid, was hair-rising but uneventful.
>
> When our FMS picked up a mine—and we picked up a lot as we went along, with many long waits in between—there was no doubt about it.
>
> When you heard hell's bells ringing, it did not sound like a tri-plane practice target, a school of fish, or even like a dummy mine. You knew it was the real thing. And it gave you the creeps.
>
> The feeling those sounds gave us baffles description. But what can one say—except that it made the mouth dry and ran prickles up and down your spine as a piano player might run the scales.
>
> The passage itself was taken by all hands rather fatalistically. I don't think anyone was very trustful of the FM sonar gear, particularly since the mines we detected were picked up at such short ranges that we would not have been able to maneuver around them. We made the passage at 180 feet, at which depth we apparently under-ran the moored mines.[14]

The transit took nearly nineteen hours, and Chief Pike had remained glued to his little round green PPI screen throughout it. "I was on the FM for more than eighteen straight hours that time," he later said. "There was the mental strain, as well as the physical, of being up there the whole time."

The crew was exhausted from the mental strain, as well. The air in the boat had gotten stale as the carbon dioxide levels rose from the lack of fresh oxygen. The amount of carbon dioxide a man could safely breathe in varied on the person and the conditions. "We were down more than eighteen hours," said Jack Brewer, stationed in the forward engine room. "They had never kept us down that long." Radar-directed planes had kept *Spadefish* down some fifteen hours on her fourth patrol, but this was her longest submerged period in enemy territory.

Chief Pharmacist's Mate Ives passed through the boat sprinkling sulfite powder to absorb the CO_2 and purify the air. "Of course, the smoking lamp was out," said Brewer. "I didn't smoke, but after so long without good oxygen, you couldn't keep a cigarette lit anyway." A sailor striking a match would have the sulphur fizzle without actually flaming up. Vic Ives distributed the pungent-smelling carbon dioxide-eating chemical powder throughout the boat. "When they spread this powder around, it was supposed to absorb the CO_2, but all it did was make you sneeze and cough," said torpedoman Wallace McMahon.

In his secret journal in the forward room, torpedoman Hugo Lundquist wrote for 4 June, "Went thru Tsu-shima straits, submerged through mine field from 2 a.m. till 10 p.m. Heard lots of depth charges." The main patrol report of *Spadefish* gives little more detail of the passage, showing only this entry at 2054 on 4 June: "Completed passage of Tsushima Strait."

Sea Dog's FM set had been known to act up, and during her minefield transit, it only detected six mine contacts in seven hours. When a false target shell, however, was fired and tracked at 1600, it tracked fine out to 800 yards. *Crevalle* also made her 3-knot transit without serious incident.[15]

Diving officer Bill Ware brought the boat up to 65 feet at 2045 for the first periscope observations in many hours. With no enemy planes or ships in sight, *Spadefish* manned both her SD and SJ radar at 2052 and went all ahead full. Per Don Scholle's quartermaster log, the boat surfaced at 2053 and went all ahead on her engines while charging her badly depleted batteries. According to her crew, she was the first of the nine Hellcats to actually surface in the Sea of Japan.

Motormac Dick Gamby recalled proudly, "We were the first submarines to get into the Sea of Japan since the *Wahoo!*"

The only trouble that stuck in everyone's mind was that Mush Morton's famous *Wahoo* had not come home from her second trip into the Sea of Japan.

Upon surfacing past the Tsushima minefields on the night of 4 June, *Spadefish*'s operators keyed the SJ radar every two minutes. At 2058, they picked up an unidentified interference bearing 189° T. This first contact soon faded away and was believed to be a Japanese surface craft. The SD-4 air-search radar flooded out at 2100, leaving the ship blind to aerial contacts. Ensign Ray Dix and his radar gang went into action. The base plug was removed, the bottom of the SD mast was thoroughly cleaned, and the head was sealed with copaltite. The results proved satisfactory and the SD radar was repaired in two hours. During that time, *Spadefish* continued to run on the surface and monitored her SJ surface-search radar reports. Captain Germershausen stationed his tracking party at 2114. A second radar contact at 2123 was soon identified as Commander Hydeman's *Sea Dog*.

Since he had elected to stay on the surface until 0300, Hydeman had outdistanced *Crevalle* and *Spadefish*. During the transit, though, *Spadefish* had switched positions with Captain Steinmetz's *Crevalle*. *Spadefish* ended up being the second boat in line and she was now 3 miles off *Sea Dog*'s port beam. *Crevalle* was bringing up the rear, 8 miles behind, having been kept down until 2211 by pinging antisubmarine craft.[16]

Dix's radar gang announced that the SD radar was back into commission at 2304. Hydeman's Hepcats cleared the Tsushima Strait area on the surface into the early morning hours of 5 June. At 0137, *Spadefish* made SJ contact on land, Utsuryu To, at 75 miles. At 0204, the ship's amazing SJ picked up one of its longest range contacts, Oki Retto, at 130 miles. *Spadefish* submerged for the day at 0410, running at 2/3 speed all day until resurfacing at 2024.

Three more Hellcats passed through Tsushima Strait on each of the succeeding two nights. All made it through successfully, although not without a few gray hairs. On the night of 5 June, *Tunny*, *Skate* and *Bonefish* made the transit. *Tunny* logged 180 FM contacts, 82 of which were believed to be mines. Most of the mines *Spadefish* had encountered were at least 100 yards apart. *Skate* found herself in a field of mines less than 50 feet apart, barely offering enough room for a sub to squeeze through. *Skate* then ran against one of the mine cables, and it scraped the length of the submarine, fortunately not snagging.[17]

Spadefish and her fellow Hepcats made the transit on the night of 4 June without notice. One or more of the Polecats, however, was detected during the early hours of 5 June as they passed through Tsushima. Five sub chasers were sent out to investigate and one surfaced sub had been spotted at the southern end of Tsushima but no attacks were made.

The next group—*Flying Fish*, *Bowfin* and *Tinosa*—passed through Tsushima Strait during the early morning hours of 6 June without notice. The Bobcats chose to pass through farther to the west, within 12 miles of the Korean coast, before exiting the strait. Each of the three boats chose transit depths varying between 120 and 180 feet. *Flying Fish*'s FM gear had fits during the transit and went out of commission twice. Finally, in the latter stages of the transit, her FM crapped out completely. Captain Risser just stayed down and kept moving. Commander Tyree's *Bowfin* found one patch of mines only 45 feet apart, a tight squeeze for his 27-foot wide sub. Like *Skate* before her, *Tinosa* had a mine cable drag along her port side, scraping loudly for at least 60 seconds.[18]

Once inside the Sea of Japan, *Spadefish* and her sister subs had virgin hunting grounds. The water was deep, with some 900 miles between Tsushima Strait in the southwest to La Perouse Strait in the northeast. Between Japan's island of Honshu and Vladivostok in Siberia, the sea reached its widest measurement of about 250 miles. The principal mission of Admiral Lockwood's Hellcats was to disrupt Japanese supply lifelines and to sink as many Japanese ships as possible. Not only would a serious romp in Hirohito's backyard cripple the supply line for the Japanese people, but it would be a serious blow to public morale as well.[19]

Captain Germershausen and the other eight Hellcat skippers had been therefore ordered to torpedo anything and everything Japanese that came into their periscopes. Other small vessels, such as fishing sampans, sea trucks, trawlers, or other sailing vessels should be sunk with gun fire, if possible.

Things in the Sea of Japan were about to change. "The Japanese sailed across that as though it was their private lake, which indeed it was," recounted Exec Dick Wright.[20] "We were under orders not to fire anything until all nine had gotten inside the Sea of Japan and each one of the nine had time to reach a port of significance."

Per Admiral Lockwood's orders, absolutely no skipper could shoot at anything until the Bobcats and Polecats had reached their stations as well. "Mike Day" would be 9 June. If all boats held fire until that date, ComSubPac hoped that enemy shipping could be caught inside anchorages, with attacks starting in sync. The only exception to the rule was the chance to catch a major man-of-war before that date.[21]

This meant five days for *Spadefish*, *Crevalle* and *Sea Dog* to pass time undetected in the Sea of Japan, idly watching targets go by!

"It Was a Real Turkey Shoot"

Fifth Patrol *5-12 June 1945*

After passing his first 24 hours in the Sea of Japan with little to see, Bill Germershausen soon found bountiful targets. He found that Japanese marus became more and more plentiful the deeper that *Spadefish* penetrated into Emperor Hirohito's protected home waters.

It was hard to believe that there was a war on. The Japanese ships were blithely sailing back and forth without air or surface escorts. They steered straight courses and burned running lights—something I had not seen in three and a half years. "But," I said to myself, "we'll fix that!" And we sure did.[1]

Spadefish completed her overnight battery charge at 0400 on 6 June and made a quick dive at 0407. She remained submerged, moving ahead at two-thirds speed. At 0604, a small Japanese freighter was spotted crossing the Japan Sea 5,000 yards ahead, en route to the Korean coast. "Did not attempt to attack because of patrol orders," wrote Captain Germershausen.

When no further shipping came into sight, *Spadefish* surfaced at 1238. Her next contact was after dark, at 1830, when radar and sight contact was made on a contact at 15,000 yards. It turned out to be a medium freighter, unescorted, and on a steady course toward the Korean coast. "Did not attempt attack," he logged.

Germershausen submerged at 1831 to look over this target. The ship passed within 2,500 yards astern of *Spadefish*. Germershausen hoped to have his new photographer's mate Edward Armstrong take pictures of the ship "but there was not enough light."

Each of enemy ships was found to be unescorted, running a straight course, and burning running lights as well. They seemed to feel perfectly secure and were totally unaware that an enemy submarine was watching them. There were no anti-submarine patrols nor patrol

Captain Germershausen taking a smoke break on the bridge in the Sea of Japan during *Spadefish*'s fifth war parol. *Courtesy of Joe Marasco.*

planes to hamper activity. Sunset on 9 June was the magic hour and it could not come fast enough.

Spadefish surfaced again at 2048 on 6 June and made radar contact shortly before midnight on a ship at 16,900 yards. This vessel was also tracked until contact was lost. During the early morning hours of 7 June, another SJ radar contact was made at 0105 at 17,400, but contact was soon lost. *Spadefish* proceeded on the surface throughout the day toward her patrol station, the west coast of the Japanese island of Hokkaido.

Spadefish continued on the surface toward her patrol station on 8 June, sighting Shakotan Misaki, Hokkaido, at 0304, distance 23 miles. *Spadefish*'s area extended from Ahakotan Misaki off the port of Otaru, north along the coast of Hokkaido and Sakhalin to the Russian border. At 0312, Germershausen took her down for a day patrol on the approaches to the port of Otaru on Hokkaido. After sunrise, he spotted a small freighter at 18,000 yards at 0807. She stayed in sight for about fifteen minutes, again being allowed to pass on under the no-fire rules.

Another medium freighter was sighted at 1152, distance 18,000 yards. This was the sixth enemy shipping contact since entering the Sea of Japan. By 1240, the scope watch had smoke on the horizon and Germershausen exercised his crew at a mock battle stations on this ship, but again without making a real attack. The new exec, Lieutenant Dick Wright, was eager to make his first kill. His skipper, however, reminded Wright that orders were orders and wait they must.[2]

At 1317, the smoke from two freighters was spotted on the horizon. This time, PhoM2c Armstrong was able to take some periscope photos of the closest freighter, the only other option to making an attack. Germershausen secured the crew from battle stations at 1333.

At 1458, the periscope watch spotted a heavy bomber or transport flying toward the airfield at Sapporo. At 1555, smoke was sighted on the horizon. At 1615, smoke was again sighted on the horizon, this from another ship passing. At 1725, yet another freighter was sighted at 9,000 yards. Germershausen stationed his tracking party for practice and worked on tracking these ships.

Spadefish surfaced at 2015 to recharge her batteries and provide some fresh air in the boat after another long day submerged with no action. One minute later, the SJ made contact at 7,600 yards. *Spadefish* started tracking and soon spotted a medium freighter. Contact was lost at 2045 and the tracking party was again secured. Another SJ contact was made at 2322 on a ship at 21,700 yards. Once again, the tracking party worked on the courses and approach setup for a ship that could not be attacked for another 24 hours.

As midnight approached at 2322, Captain Germershausen took his boat in toward Hokkaido to look for shipping. Utilizing the theory that the best shipping would be hidden along the protection of coastal harbors, he opted to sneak *Spadefish* up close to the enemy's mainland for a reconnaissance.

Spadefish eased into Ishikari Wan, a bay on Hokkaido's western coast. Nestled deep within the Japanese bay was the shipping port of Otaru. The harbor was protected by a cape labeled on the charts as Takashima Misaki. Atop the bluff was a lighthouse with a bright search light. Thus, after arriving at his station, Germershausen used the early morning hours of 8-9 June to snoop around this bay and harbor for potential targets for the following night's "open season."

Germershausen took *Spadefish* in toward Otaru harbor for a trial run to see what resistance he might face the following night. He closed to within 15 miles from the harbor entrance and identified navigational lights. To his sheer delight, he found no patrol boats, no aircraft patrols and no radar interference. Tomorrow night should just be like shooting fish in a barrel.

Spadefish patrolled in Ishikari Wan on the surface, reconnoitering Otaru Harbor during the early morning hours. At 0013 on 9 June, a flashing light was seen, which was identified as the Takashima Misaki light, burning with normal characteristics.

The shipping contacts would be plentiful this day near Otaru. The first came at 0025, as a small patrol craft was picked up by SJ at 5,000 yards and avoided. *Spadefish* retired from Otaru harbor at 0036 at standard speed to ride out one more uneventful day, submerging before the sun could dance over the water. It was a long and again uneventful day as the crew counted the hours until hunting season opened that evening. The SJ picked up another ship at 0239 at 7,500 yards, which was also avoided. *Spadefish* dove 32 miles north of Maruyama Saki at 0251 on 9 June to begin her daylight patrol. A freighter was sighted by periscope at 0730 at 10,000 yards and avoided. Another small freighter was sighted at 0847 at 16,000 yards. Continuing to run submerged through this last day of peace in the Sea of Japan, *Spadefish* next sighted a fishing boat at 1325 at 6,000 yards.

The journal entry of torpedoman Hugo Lundquist is indicative of how all aboard felt at this point: "To date, we let 16 ships and 1 sampan go by since entering Sea of Japan. Orders not to fire until sunset of 9th."

Another fishing boat was sighted at 1530 at 4,000 yards. At 1640, the sixth cargo ship of the day passed within 10,000 yards of *Spadefish*. The crew went to battle stations again and commenced an approach.

The gonging of the klaxon sent men racing to their stations. For those new to submarine patrols, there was an extra thrill. Ensign Harry Buncke was still learning to deal with the klaxon. The tallest man aboard ship, his head had found the bunk above him on several occasions when the klaxon went off. "It took about four or five alarms like that before you get a conditioned reflex to know not to sit up," recalled Buncke. "You'd learn to *roll* out of your bunk and then get up."

Other than make another practice approach on this vessel, Bill Germershausen could do nothing. The log entry for 1705 indicates the frustration level aboard *Spadefish*: "In attack position, but we still have two hours before shooting time. Almost let go at this one, but thought better of it in the last minute." The crew was secured from battle stations at 1707.

Only after the sun finally slipped behind the horizon did *Spadefish* at long last rise from periscope depth and begin what her crew hoped would be a destructive romp through the bay of Ishikari Wan. When darkness settled in and *Spadefish* surfaced at 1955, she was about 15 miles from Otaru harbor. She headed shoreward on her Fairbanks Morse diesels at 15 knots at 2000, charging her batteries and planning to destroy any shipping anchored outside the breakwater of Tarukawa Basin. "From the volume of traffic seen in the vicinity the last few days, expected that there would be many ships at anchor both inside and outside the breakwater," Germershausen logged.

The stone wall breakwater protecting this little harbor would be far too dangerous to penetrate. There were no escorts evident here, but Germershausen knew that nearby Sapporo airport would be able to send military planes after him quickly, once discovered. Germershausen stepped up to his favorite platform, the fold-up platform on the starboard side of the bridge with his binoculars. From the conning tower, the night periscope and radar were used to look into Otaru harbor for potential victims.[3]

At 2100, the SJ radar picked up a contact at 6,200 yards.

"Station the tracking team," the skipper ordered.

A small vessel contact developed, but contact with her was lost at 7,300 yards at 2142. Three minutes later, the light at Takashima Misaki with its long and short flashes was sighted. By 2204, the light at Ishikari, which used short and long flashes, was also visible.

By 2215, *Spadefish* was only 10 miles from the harbor. Germershausen nodded to Dick Wright, "Sound battle stations."

The bells of St. Mary's bonged through *Spadefish* as she prepared to enter the Japanese harbor. The light rain that had commenced falling made the harbor lights barely distinguishable, "but otherwise everything was in our favor," the skipper logged. The rain cut down visibility of the harbor, but also served to help disguise *Spadefish* as she advanced toward the Japanese coast.

"There was a light rain, harbor lights were barely distinguishable and overall, things seemed in our favor," wrote CRT Pike. "We received a start when the eastern sky suddenly lit up. We were relieved when it was determined that the Sapporo airfield had turned its light on to let an aircraft land that was circling over the field."[4]

The Sapporo airfield first lit up at 2239 during *Spadefish*'s approach and a plane could be seen circling over the field. "Sighted running lights of aircraft," logged Don Scholle. At 2242, the bridge 20mms were manned as *Spadefish* moved in. Billy Pigman, Whitey Harbison and the other bridge gunners took their stations at the 20mm gun platforms, just in case. It was a very uneasy feeling for some of those topside to see the lights of Sapporo airfield on Hokkaido turned on as four-engined military planes appeared for landing. Landing lights would beam brightly into the rainy night sky only long enough for the planes to land before being extinguished again.

"You could smell the shore," recalled Bernie Massar, who was standing his normal battle station lookout spot with his buddy Irv Kreinbring. "You could see the lights from shore and planes would fly right over us with their landing lights on. If they would have caught us in there, we were dead to rights."

The fact that enemy aircraft were passing by overhead was actually comforting to Bill Germershausen in this instance. "Planes, presumably transports, could be seen landing and taking off. They caused us no concern. We were, in fact, reassured to see business being conducted in routine fashion."[5]

Spadefish's radar picked up three ship contacts at 2252, at 13,000 yards, dead ahead. Much to Germershausen's disgust, Perry Wood and Dan Decker soon announced their plot showed these targets to be within the section of Otaru harbor known as Tarukawa Basin. *Spadefish* stole closer. Multicolored town lights soon became visible and white harbor lights soon shone brightly from the drizzling rain.[6]

The SJ radar soon identified the breakwater at 2320 as *Spadefish* moved closer. Neal Pike:

> From my electronic vantage point on the SJ radar, it looked as though we were sitting alongside the dock in Otaru Harbor. On a six-inch diameter Plan Position Indicator radar screen, distances tended to get compressed and we seemed closer than we were. I had visions of harbor searchlights suddenly illuminating the harbor and artillery opening up on us, helpless alongside the dock.[7]

Various white harbor lights and town lights were visible but the port was fairly well dimmed out. At 2332, SJ radar picked up a ship contact at 9,100 yards, ahead. Five minutes later, Captain Germershausen sighted the entrance lights to the harbor's breakwater on either bow. At 2340, Pike's SJ radar made contact on another ship at 6,800 yards ahead.

"Make ready all tubes." Germershausen passed the word at 2344 and Chief Ives relayed the word to the forward and after torpedo rooms. Three minutes later, a third enemy ship was picked up by the SJ radar at 6,250 yards.

As the night passed into the early minutes of 10 June, a huge four-engined Japanese military plane suddenly made right for *Spadefish*. She was sweeping in low to land at Sapporo airfield, with lights glaring. The pilot was easing back on his throttle and lowering flaps to slow his landing speed, coming in at very low altitude over the harbor. It was a landing procedure the pilot had doubtlessly performed hundreds of times before as he made his approach to land on Hokkaido's mainland.

The only difference this night was that the Japanese aircraft was sweeping in directly over a United States submarine that was creeping up on an unsuspecting shipping port.

Germershausen, Wright, Dan Decker, Dutch Falconer, and the bridge lookouts were caught on the bridge as the glaring landing lights from the low flying plane suddenly illuminated them and their submarine. Everyone ducked and tried to cover their night vision as the lights finally passed them by as the large plane roared over their heads.[8]

After passing overhead, the Japanese plane swung into a wide circle to make an into-the-wind approach on the airfield.

"I wonder if those pilots saw us?" the skipper said aloud. "They had enough light on us to make movies!"

"Don't think so," said Wright. "They are still heading for the field."

Skipper Germershausen was unaware at the time that the entire ship's crew had heard the roar of the airplane and the ensuing conversations. The 1MC bridge microphone had been left on, so that all hands heard the drama that had unfolded. Bill Germershausen later related to Admiral Lockwood that his chief of the boat, Willard Eimermann, approached him the next day. Making his thirteenth patrol, Eimermann advised the skipper that leaving on the bridge mike when *Spadefish* was sticking her neck out too far "was pretty strong medicine for the new hands" aboard. The chief reckoned that the drama broadcast over the 1MC that night may have caused some extra "wet spots around the deck."[9]

Plane or no plane, Germershausen pushed forward along the edge of the harbor's mouth. As *Spadefish* approached the breakwater, he could see two thin white lights which marked the narrow gap. He wondered why one was not the standard green and the other red. Germershausen had given the two forward lookouts special instruction to keep their eyes on the station ship in the harbor. *Spadefish*'s low, dark hull or faint bow wake were certainly within spotting range of enemy lookouts now.

To the skipper's great disappointment, he did not find a harbor laden with fat merchantmen or prized vessels. At this point in the war, there were simply not that many left. What *Spadefish* found were disappointingly small cargo vessels. Even worse, one of these smaller vessels had just left its anchorage and was standing out to sea. Germershausen felt that: "The results of this long-planned operation began to fade into nothing at this point. All ship contacts in the harbor outside the breakwater were small."

Even still, he thought about it years later. "I have always regretted not having entered Otaru Harbor and firing all ten tubes at random and setting the whole damn town ablaze. Legalized arson."[10]

Germershausen decided to temporarily pass up the moving freighter and set his crosshairs on the harbor's station ship. She was lying about 1,500 yards off near the edge of a spread of fishing nets. Even though it was also a fairly small ship, he was willing to invest a couple of torpedoes. Orders were orders. He was to sink anything and everything he could on this patrol, regardless of size.

The station ship, apparently a small trawler, was showing running lights and lying to. Her hull was invisible behind a rain curtain at 0018 when *Spadefish* fired two forward torpedoes—each set at 6-foot depth, with a run of about 1,600 yards. She was now less than a mile from the harbor's breakwater.

Paul Majoue and Little Fox Sergio waited on the sonar, as the seconds were counted down on the torpedo runs. The bridge crew braced themselves for the explosions that would surely wake up the entire harbor. But they never came. The torpedoes apparently passed harmlessly under the little vessel's hull and never exploded.

Disgusted with the miss and his rotten luck in finding such poor targets after taking extreme risks, Captain Germershausen cleared Otaru harbor at flank speed. His ship hauled clear, still undetected along Hokkaido's coastline, but still bloodless. He would now make chase against the little freighter that had slipped away.

The little freighter was passing between Takashima Misaki and Shakotan Misaki, about 5 miles off the beach on a steady course. *Spadefish* spent the next hour chasing this freighter to gain position. Germershausen sent his crew to battle stations at 0130, once the range had come down to 8,000 yards, with the angle on her bow 60°.

Germershausen passed the visual data on the shipping targets to Ensign Harry Buncke, who had assumed recognition officer as one of his new duties. "The captain would describe a ship, the shape of the mast, the stern and so on and I'd flip through the recognition books we had," Buncke recalled. "If you had the height of the mast, then you could tell how far the ship was away by simple triangulation."

As the new assistant communications officer, Ensign Buncke held several assisting roles during attacks on the fifth patrol. He was Lt.(jg) Perry Wood's assistant plotting officer, assigned to work the Mark 8 angle solver. This piece of equipment had been replaced by the TDC, but was still used for the manual plotting, as the TDC had its limits. "My wristwatch today is more complicated than that great big machine was," said Buncke.

From the bridge on this night surface attack, the Japanese ship was clearly visible through the TBT binoculars. At 0152, *Spadefish* fired three bow tubes at a medium freighter, heavily loaded, range 1,350 yards, 80° starboard track. The Mark 23 steam torpedoes with their lethal Torpex explosive were set at 46 knots speed and 5 feet depth. One minute later the bridge crew heard and saw three hits. The target disintegrated and sank in less than one minute.

Quartermaster Gouker logged the hits at 0153.30, 0153.37 and 0153.44, one right after another. This first victim of the fifth patrol was the 1,999-ton cargo freighter *Daigen Maru No. 2*. The forward crew used the block and tackle to prepare three more warfish for tubes 1, 2 and 3. Each was decorated with little messages to Emperor Hirohito. F1c Jim Cole, a new member of the crew, was among those assigned to torpedo reload. "It was all basically hand work, outside of the block and tackle once we got them lined up," he explained.

While reloading the tubes and only ten minutes after their first kill of the patrol, a radar contact was made at a range of 18,000 yards. Captain Germershausen ordered his crew to commence tracking and *Spadefish* went to battle stations again at 0215.

At 0230, the target was sighted, another medium freighter, rounding Shakotan Misaki and heading for Otaru. At 0234, *Spadefish* fired three bow tubes at a range of 2,000 yards. Using a ten-second firing interval, Emery Kreher's gang fired first a Mark 23, then a Mark 14-3A from tube No. 2, and finally another Mark 23 torpedo. The range to target was 2,400 to 2,470 for the torpedo runs. One minute after *Spadefish* had fired her third fish, the bridge crew saw and heard two hits and saw the target blow up and sink. This second victim was later identified as the 1,293-ton *Unkai Maru No. 8*. Captain Germershausen headed away to clear the firing point and to reload his forward tubes. This second ship had been destroyed less than forty minutes after the first one.

The early morning of 10 June proved to be very busy indeed for *Spadefish* in the Sea of Japan. "Before we could secure from battle stations, we had another contact," wrote Bill Germershausen. Within ten minutes of sending her second victim of the night to Davy Jones' lock-

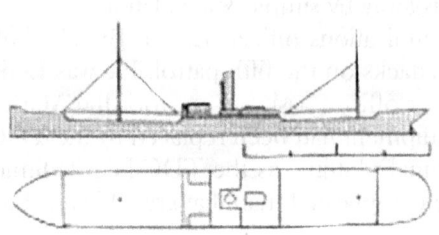

Unkai Maru, a 1,293-ton, 218-foot passenger/cargo ship built in 1924 in Japan, was one of three ships sunk by *Spadefish* torpedoes during the early morning hours of 10 June 1945. *ONI 208-J (Revised).*

er, radar had a pip at 0244, this time at a distance of 10,000 yards. The tracking party immediately commenced working out the numbers.[11]

It was going to be a long night!

"Got a quick set-up as the first streaks of dawn were just starting to show, and closed at flank speed," recorded the skipper. "Submerged at range of 6,900 yards and closed track at full speed."

"Clear the bridge! Take her down," Germershausen ordered at 0253.

The three lookouts quickly slid down from their perches on the shears and disappeared through the conning tower hatch. They were followed by the officers and finally Germershausen. As he slid down the ladder, the waiting quartermaster dogged the hatch. The battle stations tracking party was a well-oiled machine as they worked out their respective duties relative to sinking another ship. Dick Wright stood ready as the assistant approach officer, Perry Wood was at the plotting board, and Dan Decker was on the TDC. Elsewhere about the conning tower were Hocks Majoue and Little Fox Sergio on the sonar sets, leading signalman Jim Schuett assisting with the periscopes, Neal Pike standing by for radar checks, Vic Ives as battle talker on the headphones, Zelbert Gouker as the duty quartermaster and the helmsman. In the control room, diving officer Dick Fellows monitored the planesmen. Boats Eimermann had the Christmas tree, F1c Jim Cole stood watch over the trim manifold and Irv Kreinbring and Jake Lewis had the planesman duties.

The skipper moved to the periscope to begin observations as *Spadefish* closed the distance underwater. This target was identified as a medium freighter. At 0300, Germershausen ordered his ship up to 45 feet to check the periscope radar range against the old reliable ST surface radar. They checked.

The target was opening the distance, so Germershausen ordered three tubes readied forward. The torpedo track was 126° port, which placed *Spadefish* well abaft the target's port beam. Motioning to Jim

Spadefish's TDC operator, Lt. Dan Decker, receives his second Silver Star at Mare Island, California, in October 1945 for the fifth war patrol. His operation of the TDC during the Sea of Japan patrol resulted in six ships being sunk by torpedoes. Ribbons on his uniform denote Decker's previous awards for the Bronze Star, Silver Star and Presidential Unit Citation. *Courtesy of Dan Decker.*

Schuett to raise the scope, he rode it up for one last peek. The skipper checked bearing and then called out: "Fire one!"

The first fish left at 0310. Using ten second intervals, two more were dispatched, at a range to target of 1,990 yards. At 0311, the first torpedo hit. The ship settled about ten feet on an even keel. Ten seconds later, the No. 3 torpedo slammed into her. The target broke in two and sank immediately. Breaking up noises could be heard on the sound gear. This victim was later identified as the small 994-ton cargo ship *Jintsu Maru*. *Spadefish* reloaded again.

"Unless they heard the explosions, there is a strong possibility that we are as yet undetected by the citizens ashore, as all three ships sank so rapidly that there was no chance for spreading an alarm," wrote Germershausen.

Spadefish cleared the area submerged and commenced a daytime patrol 4 to 5 miles off Shakotan Misaki. The exhausted tracking party and all at battle stations could now finally settle down to a hearty breakfast and some rest. Germershausen decided that his best option was to hang around this target-laden area. Although the merchant ships here were disappointingly small, his targets had been steady during the night. There was no indication that the small ship he missed in Otaru harbor had sighted his torpedoes, so *Spadefish*'s presence in the area was still likely unknown.

"All ships sank so rapidly that the crews had no chance to signal an alarm," wrote Neal Pike. "I didn't know it then, but among those citizens were some that years later would become my friends and still are."[12]

Pike later lived in Japan for two years while working on the technical staff of the Computer Sciences Corporation. His company was contracted by the Air Force to implement a new telecommunications system interconnecting all U.S. bases in the Tokyo Area. During his time in Tokyo, Pike made a trip with his wife in September, 1967, to the island of Hokkaido to visit a family at Sapporo (the town that *Spadefish* had approached while submerged in 1945). He and his wife visited a family that lived in Otaru, whose house was on a hillside near the very harbor that *Spadefish* had attacked.

During our conversations, we were told that because of the danger of staying in Tokyo, the entire family had spent the war years in the Otaru home. Though it was not discussed then, it is now obvious the family had been at home in this house on the night of June 9, 1945, and I had been only a few miles away in Otaru Harbor on the *USS Spadefish*. To this day I often wonder, of all the remote harbors in the world that I might have visited by chance, why was it Otaru Harbor to which I returned?

"I was pooped," Captain Germershausen recalled of his boat's four straight torpedo attacks. "Since the area appeared so active, I elected to do business on the same corner that night, and ran a daytime submerged patrol clear of the bay to afford all hands a chance to rest up for the night's dirty work."[13]

At 0620, *Spadefish*'s periscope watch sighted a sea truck at 10,000 yards, headed for Kamui Misaki on Hokkaido. *Spadefish* commenced an approach but broke off at 0702 when Germershausen decided "this small vessel was not deemed worthy of attack. Heavy seas made prospect of hitting doubtful, and misses might cause routing of heavier traffic around this point."

Remaining submerged during the day on 10 June, a junk was sighted at 1308 at 6,000 yards and avoided. When *Spadefish* surfaced at 1957, she found a thick fog and haze, but no targets in sight. She set course for a night patrol between Kamui Misaki and Ofuyu Misaki. At 2217, SJ radar contact was made on a target at 12,000 yards. This appeared to be the same size as the targets sunk that morning. The Japanese ship suddenly reversed her course at 2235 and headed for Ofuyu Misaki, making radical maneuvers. Her range was about 8,000 yards.

Spadefish commenced an end around. Suddenly, at 2300, radar interference was noticed from this vessel. Visibility was only 1,000 yards, but radar said what vision could not: this was no freighter, but apparently an armed patrol boat.

Germershausen ordered full speed and pushed *Spadefish* in toward this target on the surface. Tubes were made ready at 2308, headed in on a 120° port track. Chief Wells and Emery Kreher's forward gang prepared tubes 4, 5 and 6, while Vernon Kite's after crew prepared tubes 8, 9 and 10. Intending to fire when within 2,000 yards, "unless he attacked us first," Germershausen felt that this ship "looked very suspicious." By 2311, *Spadefish* was in firing position.

Without warning, the target swung around and headed for *Spadefish*. The Japanese sailors definitely had her on their own radar.

At 2313, three bow tubes were aggressively fired down the throat at 1600 yards. As soon as the third torpedo swished out, Germershausen reversed course at full speed. The enemy escort was rushing full speed down upon *Spadefish*.

The torpedoes missed. One large explosion was noted at 2316 on the target's bearing, but was believed to be an end of run explosion. The range was closed to 1,300 yards, and the enemy ship straddled *Spadefish* with 40mm fire. Red slashes of gunfire ripped the night sky as the missiles whistled by overhead. The shots moved closer, until the enemy's gunners were straddling *Spadefish*. It might be tempting to send the 5-inch deck crew to fire back at this pursuer, but the risk was unacceptable in these conditions. With a sizable sea running, and the sub apt to take sharp evasive maneuvers while under fire herself, crewmen might be lost overboard before the 5-incher could even be cast loose.

"Clear the bridge!" Germershausen bellowed as more shells screamed by overhead.

Gunner's mate Bernie Massar was in the process of bringing up a replacement 20mm gun, in case a surface action was needed once the torpedoes found their target. Once the war fish missed and the call of "Dive! Dive!" rang out, Massar had to move quickly. "I had this damn 20mm in hand and I had a hell of a time getting it down the hatch in a hurry!"

The lookouts and officers didn't need to be told twice to get the hell below. *Spadefish* dove sharply as the enemy patrol boat raced in. Germershausen had hoped to evade on the surface, but he found that the "shots were too close."

QM3c Don Scholle dogged the hatch as Germershausen chased the last of the lookouts down the ladder into the conning tower. Expecting these depth charges to be close, the skipper ordered, "Go to 400 feet. All unnecessary personnel clear the conning tower." Not needing a second invitation, Scholle said, "I was the first one out!"

At 2317, Scholle logged in the quartermaster's notebook, "Going to 400. Rigged ship for silent running and depth charge." The first ashcan exploded at 2320 and fifty seconds. Five seconds passed. Click—*wham*! Fifteen more seconds passed. Click—*wham*! Five more seconds passed. Click–*wham*!

Harry Buncke, the recognition officer during the attack, now stood at the bottom of the ladder in the control room by the little desk. "There was a big desk where five or six people could stand around comfortably at elbow level, drink coffee, shoot the breeze and smoke cigarettes," he said. The first depth charges shook the boat mightily, causing some light bulbs to burst and showering cork insulation on people.

Spadefish worked to evade her attacker at deep submergence, running at 80 rpm. During the next three minutes, a total of eighteen depth charges exploded in her vicinity. For those like Buncke who were waiting out their first enemy attack, it seemed an eternity between explosions.

At the control room desk, Ensign Buncke muttered to Warrant Officer Dutch Falconer, "Jesus, you feel so defenseless. I wish there was something we could do."

Falconer, a veteran of countless depth charge attacks in his seven previous war patrols, turned to Buncke and said, "Well, Harry, why don't you start counting the depth charges?"

Spadefish remained at 400 feet, as her soundmen listened to the screws racing around on the surface above them. The pinging continued from the angry escorts, but *Spadefish* slowly increased her rpms and cleared the area.

The depth charging soon ended, but the escort continued to ping the area, hoping to home in on her quarry. No serious damage resulted from the depth charging other than a flooded head suffered by the XCLA sonar. Although the submarine's presence had been kept secret the previous night, the Japanese knew for certain of *Spadefish* being in their "pond" now.

The torpedo shooting had been easy during the first two days in the Sea of Japan. "We had a field day," recalled motormac John Brewer. "We stayed in there and just played havoc with them."

"Man, it was a real turkey shoot out there for a couple of days," agreed Harry Buncke.

Transbalt

Fifth Patrol   *11–14 June 1945*

About an hour after the new hands experienced their first depth charge attack, Captain Germershausen began easing *Spadefish* back to periscope depth at 0102 on 11 June. She reached 65 feet at 0111, and after a quick sweep showed the area to be clear, the skipper secured his crew from depth charge and silent running. *Spadefish* then eased up to 45 feet for the SD and SJ to make radar searches. Those not on watch took advantage of the quiet to return to their bunks. Echo ranging could still be heard astern from the anti-submarine vessel.

One minute after surfacing, radar watch at 0116 called out contacts at 3,400 yards and 6,000 yards. The aggressive anti-sub vessel was still astern and these new contacts were ahead. Germershausen commenced tracking these ships, both of which were on a southwesterly course, making about 6 knots. "Thought they might be friends of the boy who worked us over, so decided not to attack," he wrote. "Needed a battery charge, too, so opened out and headed for a daylight surface patrol, position 30 miles west of Kamui Misaki, letting Ishiwari Wan cool off."

The radar contacts had all faded by 0154 as *Spadefish* cleared the area and jammed juice in her depleted batteries. The next radar contact came at 0849, distance only 2,300 yards. There was such a thick fog, however, that visibility was only 1,000 yards, so Germershausen opted to avoid this unknown vessel. Another radar contact was made at 0953 at 4,100 yards and also avoided. The rest of the day passed without any visual sightings. A third small radar contact was picked up at 1957, distance 6,000 yards, and deemed unworthy of attack.

The Japanese were alerted as to the Americans' presence by 11 June. Radar-equipped patrol planes were put out to search for the subs, and a command was issued on 11 June restricting shipping to operate within a 50-mile radius of Nanao, Fushiki, Naoetsu, Niigata and Sakata during the daytime. If this directive were followed, the

Quartermaster Jim Fletcher stands near the deck guns holding the *Spadefish* battle flag. Fletcher was asked by Captain Germershausen to sew a Japanese flag, which was flown into battle on 12 June as *Spadefish* took on four small vessels with her guns. *Courtesy of Betty Fletcher.*

Japanese shipping would essentially hug the coastlines and force the U.S. subs to steal into shallower water to press home attacks.[1]

By 2023, *Spadefish* began closing the coast of Hokkaido. Several contacts on small craft were picked up by the SJ on the way in. The sea was calm but still foggy. An hour later, a new radar contact was made at 2130, distance 6,000 yards. This time, a side light was spotted. By this time, *Spadefish* was 7 to 8 miles from Iwanai and had picked up no larger ships inshore, so she commenced tracking this ship. *Spadefish* worked around astern and to seaward of this vessel but soon decided that he was too small for a torpedo attack. The contact was completely lost by 2227, at which time tracking was secured.

The power of the radar never ceased to amaze on *Spadefish*. Quartermaster Don Scholle logged at 2335: "Small radar contact, bearing 038° T, range 2,600 yards. Believed to be bird." The "contact" shifted bearing around, and finally disappeared from radar three minutes later.

During the early morning of 12 June, *Spadefish* headed north for her patrol area south of Rebun Shima and Rishiri Shima. The fog and haze persisted during the night. At 0256, SJ made a contact at 4,000 yards. Three minutes later, the bridge watch sighted the SJ contact, an unidentified small vessel, believed to be a fishing craft. Lieutenant Decker changed course to avoid it. The Japanese fishing craft and small vessels in this area were numerous.

At 0312, a motor sampan with sails rigged was sighted during morning twilight at around 5,000 yards distance. Captain Germershausen decided to give his gun crews some action. "Battle stations, surface," was ordered as *Spadefish* closed the distance. The ammunition lockers were opened and the men began passing the ordnance topside. The sampan was judged to be about 70 feet in length. At 0318, the two bridge 20mm guns were fully manned and ready, as well as one .30-caliber machine gun.

Germershausen called quartermaster Jim Fletcher to break out his recently-completed Japanese battle flag and rig it out on the *Spadefish* bridge as she went into action. "I was always impressed by sea stories I'd read of days of sail when men of war and privateers captured prizes and the whole crew shared the wealth," reflected Germershausen later. "I guess I still had the same romantic notions when I asked Jim Fletcher to fashion a Japanese man-o-war flag, which we flew in the Sea of Japan when approaching gun targets."[2]

"All ahead full," the skipper ordered at 0321. Bending on three engines, *Spadefish* narrowed the range quickly. At 0330, Whitey Harbison, Billy Pigman, Hugo Lundquist and the other bridge gunners opened up with their 20mms and .30-caliber machine gun fire. As the

During the first of four gun attacks on Japanese ships on 12 June 1945, *Spadefish* used only her bridge 20mms and machine guns. Torpedoman Hugo Lundquist is seen here manning one of *Spadefish*'s air-cooled .30-caliber machine guns. Assisting as loader for the .30-cal ammo belt this day is S1c Charles "Baby" Graff, a gunner's mate striker who is wearing ship's cook Ed Graf's jacket. *Courtesy of Thomas Miller.*

Ensign Bill Ware, assistant gunnery officer, on the bridge of *Spadefish* spotting for the gun crew as they attack a Japanese sea truck on 12 June 1945 in the Sea of Japan. The "gun" on her forward deck was found to be made of wood. *Courtesy of Joe Marasco.*

ship closed to 500 yards from the sampan, the gunners obtained about 50% hits while expending nine magazines of 20-mm and 580 rounds of .30 caliber. The firing was ceased at 0345, and the sampan was destroyed, left on fire and sinking. This target was listed as a 100-ton sampan in the patrol report.

At 0340, *Spadefish* rang up all stop, as men retrieved items from the water. Zelbert Gouker recorded in the log that the submarine moved about the area, stopping again at 0356. "I remember that Dick Wright, our executive officer, went overboard and swam out to retrieve a floating Japanese glass fishing ball," recalled quartermaster Don Scholle. After quickly backing to retrieve her swimmer, *Spadefish* briefly came to "all stop" and then "all ahead standard" at 0400.

The bridge gunners went below as *Spadefish* cleared the area, moving northward. At 0705, the SJ picked up Rebun Shima and Rishiri Shima at 50,000 yards. As the morning progressed, the visibility worsened and the SJ was manned continually as of 0715. At 0725, the topside lookouts picked up an enemy vessel. "Sighted fishing vessel, range 8,000 yards," logged Lt.(jg) Ed La Croix. "Commenced maneuvering to attack."

Spadefish 5-inch deck gun crew preparing for action against a Japanese sea truck on 12 June 1945 in the Sea of Japan. Lt. Dan Decker is just visible, center aft, wearing earphones. Left of Decker is CGM "Shaky Jake" Lewis, the gun captain. Right of Decker, wearing heavy gloves is SC2c Ed Graf, the hot shellman. Seated on the gun directly in front of Decker is the pointer, CCS Francis Scherman. Seated on the opposite side of the gun is the trainer, CMoMM "Rebel" Rewold. The other members of the *Spadefish* gun crew this day are (left to right): TM2c John Cuthbertson (looking out to sea); GM2c Bernie Massar; MoMM3c Harry Brenneis (smiling at camera); TM1c Emery Kreher; FCS1c Andy Olah (looking toward trainer Rewold) and MoMM2c Tom Miller. *Courtesy of Joe Marasco.*

Spadefish closed, but the vessel did not show up on radar. The lookouts soon identified their prey as a 135-foot steam trawler or "sea truck" of about 200 tons. The bridge gunners were ordered topside at 0728 to man the 20mms again. *Spadefish* closed for attack and ordered the 5-inch deck gun crew out for action at 0732. The men stood by for half an hour as *Spadefish* closed the distance. At 0749, she went all ahead flank to close the distance before opening up with the big after deck gun.

Chief Jake Lewis' deck gun crew would get quite a workout this day. Lewis served as gun captain, while Lieutenant Dan Decker wore headphones and served as the range setter, taking information from Bill Ware and the bridge spotters. On the gun, Chief Francis Scherman was the pointer, and Chief Rebel Rewold was the trainer. Standing by

Spadefish's gunners score a direct hit on this 100-foot lugger, her fourth gun victim of the day, shortly after 1230. *Courtesy of Joe Marasco.*

with heavy gloves was ship's cook Ed Graf as the hot shellman, ready to catch the ejected shells.

GM2c Bernie Massar was the first shell loader and alternate gun captain, standing by with a spare firing pin. Torpedoman Gus Cuthbertson served as the second shell loader. Motormac Buck Miller was the fuse setter at the end of the shell handling line. Motormac Harry Brenneis, fire controlman Andy Olah and torpedoman Emery Kreher were the other three main shell handlers topside.

Below decks, another line of sailors and the mess attendants passed the ammunition topside to the shell handlers. Thus, the firing of *Spadefish*'s main deck gun was no small undertaking, with eleven men out on deck, supported by many more below decks and on the bridge. "Our point of aim was what looked like a machine gun in the bow of the target," recalled gun director Dan Decker. "We later found the 'gun' to be a wooden mock-up."

At 0805.50, the 5-incher opened fire on the 200-ton trawler. The first hit missed its mark, as spotted by Bill Ware on the bridge. Ware estimated the splash at 100 yards short and called down to Decker, "Up 100." Decker took a quick look through the telescopic sight and put the cross hairs on the intended point of aim. Scherman and Rewold automatically followed the signals and when they matched the indicators, yelled, "Set!"

The third victim of *Spadefish* gunfire on 12 June 1945, this 170-foot steam trawler is left sinking in the Sea of Japan shortly after noon. *Courtesy of Joe Marasco.*

Gun captain Jake Lewis then called, "Fire!" The deck gun boomed, sending its second shell right as aimed. "The second shot hit close to the fake gun," Decker wrote. "Our point of aim was then shifted to the waterline amidships, which did the job." Don Scholle logged this second shell fired in the quartermaster's notebook as "first hit." Ten seconds later, the next 5-incher was logged as a hit. *Spadefish* circled around the target as Chief Lewis' gun team pumped shells into their target. By 0815, a cease fire was called, after lobbing 26 heavy shells at the hapless vessel.

As the range was closed to 200 yards, Whitey Harbison and Billy Pigman expended eleven magazines of 20-mm fire to finish the destruction of this target. This sampan was left on fire and sinking, with only a small part of her superstructure still above water.

Germershausen secured his crew from battle stations surface at 0836. The weather began clearing during the next two hours and Perry Wood's high periscope watch could identify two islands on the horizon at 0931. Smoke was twice spotted on the horizon during the later morning hours, but both contacts proved unworthy of attack. This area of the Sea of Japan was literally crawling with boats, as *Spadefish* neared Rishiri Island.

At 1057, the bridge lookouts sighted a ship on the horizon, which was identified as a small vessel. The decision was made to make an

Two additional views of the *Spadefish* 5-inch gun crew loading and firing at Japanese ships on 12 June. In top view, Chief Scherman is in the pointer's seat as Buck Miller prepares to load another shell. Gus Cuthbertson, with beard and cap, looks on. As Jake Lewis makes final inspection before firing, Miller covers ears and walks away, following gunner Bernie Massar. Standing by at left in bottom photo is Andy Olah and behind the gun mount to catch the casing is Ed Graf, in the hooded jacket.
Carl Schmelzer collection, courtesy of Don and Maury Martin.

attack approach submerged. "Clear the bridge!" The lookouts, Bill Ware and Perry Wood scurried below at 1103, as the ship made a quick, 39-second dive to 50 feet. Battle stations submerged was called and *Spadefish* moved ahead at two-thirds speed toward her target.

She moved ahead steadily, planing up to 55 feet for radar sweeps as she advanced. Two forward torpedo tubes were made ready at 1135. Ten minutes later, however, the primary target was close enough to identify as another trawler type vessel, appearing to be larger than the 200-tonner sunk earlier in the morning. Unworthy of a torpedo, she was at least on Bill Germershausen's plans for a surface attack.

Easing up to 45 feet, he had radar make a sweep for all clear. As *Spadefish* eased back down to periscope depth at 1155, he passed the word to prepare for a battle surface. At 1204, assistant diving officer Dutch Falconer brought her up quickly and Shaky Jake Lewis' gun crew streamed out on deck. Waiting for the boat to pop out of the water could be tense for the gunners. TM3c Wallace McMahon later reflected on the battle surface.

> I had the .50-caliber on the port side and Tony Noonan, one of the gunner's mates, was my loader. Four of us were

crammed into the forward room escape trunk with two .50 caliber machine guns and several cans of ammo for the battle surface. They would pass the words through the battle phones once *Spadefish* had hit the surface and somebody below us would tap a signal to us with a hammer that it was safe to open the hatch. I will admit I wondered when we opened the hatch —would there be air or water coming in?[3]

New hand Jim Cole was among those in the escape hatch with Noonan and McMahon, hauling up the starboard .50-caliber with his loader. "We brought those up from below and set them alongside the bridge when we battle surfaced," Cole explained. "The 20mms were permanently mounted on the bridge, but we had to bring the .50-calibers up and place them in fixed stanchions."

As *Spadefish* began closing the distance from 8,000 yards, the target was judged to be a 170-foot steam trawler of about 300 tons. Lewis' 5-inch crew opened fire at 1213. This time, five rounds of the 5"/25 ammunition at 500 yards range were sufficient to start this target sinking. Closing the range, *Spadefish* let her 20-mm and .50-caliber machine guns complete the destruction on this sampan. Firing was secured at 1217, only four minutes after opening up. *Spadefish* turned, raced back in and then gave the gunners another clear pass at her. All guns opened up at 1219, and by 1221, the target was engulfed in flames. Torpedoman Lundquist, manning one of the machine guns with ship's cook Tom Riley as his loader, wrote in his journal, "Got myself a Jap with .30 caliber." Three survivors were seen in the water, but another target was judged to need attention at the moment.

Quartermaster Gouker logged this target's sinking as 1223. *Spadefish* went all ahead flank to clear the area. Captain Germershausen was intent on training his guns on a second ship which had appeared. This one was a trawler type of fishing vessel, steam driven.

The distance was closed rapidly and Chief Lewis' deck gun crew opened fire on its fourth Japanese ship of the day at 1232. This vessel now appeared to be a little smaller than the others, and was judged to be a 100-foot wooden trawler or lugger of about 100 tons. Firing conservatively as the submarine was conned into the best positions, the 5-inch crew only fired five rounds, but they connected well. Closing in further, the 20mm and .50-caliber gunners opened up, as well. At 1239, the deck gun was secured as the lighter caliber bridge guns blazed away.

A three-minute cease fire was maintained as *Spadefish* maneuvered again for a good close position. The machine guns then opened up again and sprayed the hulk until she was left on fire and sinking. Germershausen ordered his crew secured from battle stations surface and cleared the area. These last two trawlers had absorbed ten rounds from the deck gun, plus eight magazines of 20-mm, 1,700 rounds of .50 caliber and 400 rounds of .30 caliber.

Spadefish's gunners saw more action this day than they had on any previous patrol. With four small vessels downed by gunfire, *Spadefish* could now claim to have already destroyed seven enemy vessels within the Sea of Japan after only three full days of being able to shoot at will.

The Japanese had not wounded any *Spadefish* sailors with return fire. The only injuries came to two of Chief Lewis' 5-inch crew. Chief Francis Scherman, seated on the left side of the gun as the pointer, had his right eardrum perforated from the blasts. Ship's cook Ed Graf, the hot shellman, suffered a perforated left eardrum. Chief Victor Ives, the ship's "doc," treated both men.[4]

"Several more small craft were sighted during the afternoon," wrote Germershausen, "all heading for the beach. Decided we had expended enough ammunition for today, so did not attack any of these." He would reserve his remaining sixty-four 5-inch shells for better targets another day.

At 1451, an SD contact at 7 miles caused *Spadefish* to dive quickly to 150 feet. Ensign Harry Buncke, learning the ropes of being qualified as JOOD, counted his lookouts as they scrambled below behind Captain Germershausen. "Then I jumped down the hatch, practically riding on the shoulders of the last man, while holding the wooden toggle on the cable that pulled down the hatch," he recalled. "I was about 188 pounds, solid muscle. As we all hit the deck in the conning tower, the cable snapped and the hatch popped up."

Fortunately, Ensign Buncke was able to jump up, grab the wheel, and pull down the conning tower hatch. "But I couldn't turn it since I was hanging in mid air! Fortunately, the Captain, who was standing by the scope, knew that even though we didn't have a green board, it was okay to continue the dive. Once we had a few tons of water on top of the hatch, it was an easy thing to spin it closed, and later repair the cable."[5]

Spadefish returned to 65 feet at 1525 and continued with a submerged afternoon patrol. At 1645, a seaplane was seen to be circling the area, apparently out to investigate the cause of all the morning's excitement. The scope watch had this snooper in sight for fifty minutes before it departed. *Spadefish* surfaced at 1957 and headed north for a patrol area off the west coast of Karafuto.

Radar contact was made just after midnight (0036) at a range of 22,000 yards 50 miles west of La Perouse Strait. The tracking party was stationed in the conning tower. A second SJ contact was made at 0042 on 13 June, range 19,730 yards. The first contact was stopped, apparently waiting for daylight before going through the mine-filled strait. The second radar pip was making 10.5 knots on a southwesterly course. "Pips look like large ships," the skipper noted in his patrol report.

Captain Germershausen elected to leave the sitting duck and go after the moving ship. He would come back after the other later. At 0101, he commenced an attack approach. The sea was calm, but the night was very dark. The weather was unsettled. Mists alternated with rain and fog, reducing visibility from 1,500 to 800 yards. A favorable firing position was soon obtained on this target ship, but the firing was withheld because of doubts as to this ship's nationality. This target was moving unescorted, without any lights.

"Information furnished this vessel concerning Soviet shipping routes shows westbound route from La Perouse Strait to Vladivostok to be due west to the Siberian coast," wrote Captain Germershausen. This ship "was headed southwest," which to *Spadefish*'s officers meant that she could be making for the Russian port of Vladivostok "but it could also have been Karafuto-Empire-Korean route."[6]

Germershausen found this ship to be rounding Regun Shima, not following a designated Soviet route. The waters in this area were used by Soviet shipping. The Russians were not at war with the Japanese so their ships were supposed to follow the rules used by hospital ships. Their merchant vessels were to follow designated routes and burn identification lights for their own safety.

Visual sighting of the vessel for recognition was impossible. Captain Germershausen and his lookouts were unable to make out any running lights. The skipper called Dick Wright to the bridge, and he agreed that no running lights could be seen. Recognition officer Harry Buncke did not have any silhouettes to look up in his ONI-208-J book this time. There simply was not the visibility. He recalled that Captain Germershausen determined that her actions indicated she was out of place. "He said, 'If it's not where it's supposed to be, it's an enemy target.'"

Germershausen himself later stated that he had at least some concerns over this ship's nationality. He was afraid that it could be Russian "because it was on a route that looked like it could have been going to Vladivostok." He found his junior officers eager to attack. "The boys were right behind me saying, 'I can't see any lights on that thing.' 'It can't be a Russian.' 'Captain, let's shoot!' So, I shot."[7]

Bill Germershausen elected to close in on her starboard beam and fire two bow torpedoes. "The torpedo supply was running low and so we reduced the number per salvo," related the skipper. The torpedoes were fired on a 125° starboard track, at 1,300 yards range, at 0133. In a confidential report to Admiral Lockwood submitted 1 July 1945, Germershausen reported:

> Commanding officer considered that identification lights, had they been carried, would have been easily seen at this range. Before torpedoes hit, range closed to 1,100 yards without either hull or lights being seen. The fact that the target was on a steady course and unescorted was not considered a factor since up to this time at least fifteen Japanese freighters had been seen, all on a steady course and unescorted.

The firing was been done on radar bearings, without any visual sighting. The explosion of the first torpedo was seen from *Spadefish*'s bridge. Both hits were heard and both were seen on radar. Quartermaster Gouker logged the first hit at 0134.32 and the second at 0134.41. "Target seen to be hit on S-J radar," he added. The target ship slowed to a stop and sank from radar in eighteen minutes.

Although there was some suspicion as to the nationality of this ship, *Spadefish* would claim to have sunk a 4,000 ton Japanese freighter. During the course of the next week, however, it would become evident that she had actually torpedoed a Russian freighter. According to a Tokyo radio broadcast on 17 June, the Russian ship *Transbalt* was sunk at a spot 30 miles south of the position at which *Spadefish* made her attack. According to this broadcast, the majority of *Transbalt*'s crew was rescued by a Japanese patrol boat. Subsequent information received from the U.S. naval attaché at Moscow would confirm that *Transbalt* had been sunk on 13 June. The specific hour of sinking and other key details were not given, only that Rebun Island bore 237° distant 15 miles from *Transbalt*'s last position.[8]

The Soviet ship *Transbalt* was an old vessel, originally launched on 10 May 1899 as the German passenger vessel *Belgravia* for the Hamburg America Line. She was originally a 10,155 gross ton ship, 501 feet in length and capable of accommodating 2,700 passengers. In 1900, she was rebuilt to 10,982 tons. *Belgravia* commenced her last passenger voyage between Hamburg and Baltimore on 9 February 1905. Sold to the Russian Navy, she was renamed *Riga*. The Navy sold *Riga* to the state shipping company, Sovtorgflot, in 1920 and she was renamed *Transbalt*, serving as a hospital ship from 1920-1923. *Transbalt* then served as a passenger/cargo ship and had made voyages to the United States during World War II.[9]

Lieutenant Dan Decker, the TDC officer in the conning tower this

The 10,982-ton Russian ship *Transbalt*, a former German passenger liner, seen in an American dock during World War II. Running through La Perouse Strait without running lights, she was attacked and sunk by *Spadefish* on 13 June 1945. *Courtesy of Al La Rocca.*

night, recalled:

> Years later, I found out why there had been no serious repercussions from the government of all three nations involved. We made our attack with repeated observations that the ship was not showing running lights. That was the information that we all had. Come to find out, the Japanese had forbidden the Russians from using La Perouse Strait from sunset to sunrise. The reports show that other Russian ships remained clear of penetration, but this skipper decided to chance it, dowsing his running lights and tried to continue to Vladivostok. The Russian was at fault and the Japanese probably told them, "We told you so."[10]

Captain Germershausen and his *Spadefish* crew would slowly learn of what ship they had sunk in the early morning of 13 June 1945. At that moment, however, they were more concerned with making their attack upon the next vessel. At 0135, two minutes after firing on *Transbalt*, *Spadefish* made an approach on the second ship, which was still stopped west of La Perouse Strait at a range of 17,000 yards. The tracking party continued to follow the first ship that had been attacked, which was shown on radar to gradually come to a stop. By 0152, the first target ship sank, at a range of 5,000 yards, as the break of dawn was approaching.

At 0209, while closing the second target, Germershausen spotted running lights on the second ship at 8,000 yards distance. By 0216, he had identified her as a large Russian freighter, showing proper identification lights, so he broke off the attack.

Two minutes later, radar contact was made on another ship at 16,000 yards. This vessel was making 7 knots on a southeasterly course, heading for La Perouse Strait. At 0232, *Spadefish* commenced closing this target at flank speed, trying to beat the dawn's early light. She submerged to 60 feet at 0242 and continued closing the track at 7 knots as twilight commenced. *Spadefish* made periscope observations every ten minutes as she approached. "Open outer doors forward," was ordered at 0254. By 0256, one white light could be seen on this vessel, range 3,000 yards. "Target identified as Jap," logged Zelbert Gouker in his quartermaster's notebook.

By 0300, Germershausen was ready to shoot on a 90° starboard track, range 1,500 yards. On his final look, however, he saw Russian identification lights on this merchantman and broke off the attack. "Target re-identified as Russian ship," logged Gouker. Captain Germershausen noted in a confidential report to Admiral Lockwood, "White lights were seen at 3,000 yards submerged and colored identification lights at 1,500 yards."

He secured the crew from battle stations and continued the submerged patrol. He kept the scope up long enough to shoot pictures of the Russian ship. He then heading north at two-thirds speed for the vicinity of Maoka, Karafuto.

After finding that these other ships were Russian, there was at least some mild thoughts as to what *Spadefish* had sunk earlier in the night. "There was some suspicion among us crew that she had been a Russian," recalled electrician Jim Casey. Bill Germershausen had actually fired upon a Russian ship previously while commanding *Tambor*, but had missed that one. He now belonged to an exclusive club with three other U.S. sub skippers who had sunk Soviet ships during World War II.

Spadefish spent 13 June submerged in the Sea of Japan, moving north into the Straits of Tartary closer to the port of Maoka, Karafuto, making occasional radar searches. She came up at 1957 and started a battery charge on the No. 1 and 2 main engines. At 2234, a white light was sighted that was identified as the Maoka Ko light. Cruising along near the coastline, other lights along the shore could be made out shortly. "Sighted what appeared to be a train," logged Don Scholle at

2314. Two minutes later, "sighted an airfield."

At 2352, *Spadefish* went to battle stations and started closing the harbor of Maoka Ko on range lights in the harbor. By 2355, there were still no contacts, but Captain Germershausen ordered the torpedo tubes readied, just in case.

At 0010 on 14 June, while approaching the harbor of Maoka submerged, contact was made on a small craft at 3,200 yards. Range to the beach was 3,000 yards. Many lights were visible, including railway, town and navigational lights, but no shipping at anchor or underway could be seen. *Spadefish* changed course to the westward and opened out at standard speed. The crew was secured from battle stations at 0016.

At 0200, the radio gang transmitted a message to group commander Earl Hydeman giving results and recommendations as required by her operational orders. At 0212, *Spadefish* reversed course and closed the coastline east of Karafuto for a daylight submerged patrol off Maoka harbor, diving at 0330 before the early dawn.

At 0545, a ship was sighted at 16,000 yards lying offshore near Maoka. *Spadefish* went to battle stations at 0549 and headed for the target freighter, which tracked as either lying to or at anchor. At 0659, Captain Germershausen took a good look at the target at 5,000 yards range. "She was a loaded freighter very similar to the ship on the left side of page 211, ONI 208-J (Revised)," he wrote. This target was later identified as the 2,018-ton Japanese freighter *Seizan Maru*.

"Open door, tube 8," talker Irv Kreinbring called to Vernon Kite's after torpedo room at 0710. The range was 2,000 yards as *Spadefish* swung right and brought her stern tubes to bear on a 90° starboard track. She had only four fish aft and two forward. At 0715, Germershausen ordered one torpedo fired from after tube No. 8 at a 5-foot depth setting, distance 1,800 yards.

At the order to fire, Ensign Harry Buncke reminded the skipper to film the attack. "The forward, number 1 periscope had a camera on it," said Buncke. "The captain would get so excited when we were sinking a ship, I'd have to pat him on the back and remind him to put up the forward scope. 'We've gotta take the moving pictures,' I reminded him."

As the torpedo bored in, *Spadefish* shot color kodachrome movies of the resulting explosion. One minute after firing, the Mark 14-3A torpedo hit *Seizan Maru* aft and exploded. The ship listed and settled slightly. The Japanese sailors tied down her whistle as an alert that she had been attacked. "The ship was only one mile from town and the weather was bright and sunny, so the citizens going to work must have had a grandstand seat for this one," logged the skipper.

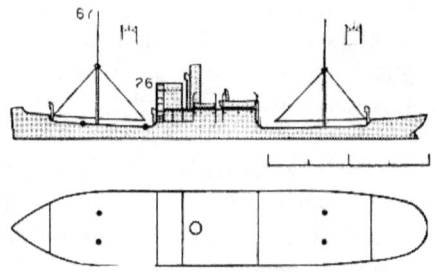

Seizan Maru, a 2,018-ton double-masted freighter, was sunk by *Spadefish* in the Sea of Japan on 14 June 1945. The date marked the one-year anniversary from *Spadefish*'s departure from California for the war zone. *ONI 208-J (Revised).*

"Stand by to fire another," called Germershausen as he noted that the maru was not going under.

Dan Decker announced that everything still checked on his TDC.

"Fire two!" called the skipper at 0719 as Dick Wright hit the firing key in the conning tower. In the after room, Vernon Kite manually fired tube No. 9. Set at the high-power speed of 46 knots, the second Mark 14 raced through the water at a 5 foot depth toward the damaged freighter. This one was aimed just forward of amidships, range 2,150 yards.

With the movie camera still rolling through the No. 1 periscope, this torpedo exploded at 0720 at a point one-third the length from *Seizan Maru*'s bow. The freighter was seen to begin releasing all of her life boats immediately and she began to capsize. The JK sonar operator, Mike Sergio, reported heavy breaking up noises. "I made a movie record of this with a periscope camera," recalled Germershausen, "but in the excitement of the attack it did not turn out to be a very professional picture."[11]

At 0722, *Seizan Maru* sank in 25 fathoms of water. She was the fourth Japanese torpedo victim and eighth Japanese shipping victim of *Spadefish* of the patrol. "Target submerged," logged Jim Fletcher.

In his journal, TM2c Lundquist noted, "Out of States 1 year." His ship's latest sinking was thus an appropriate celebration of the first anniversary of *Spadefish*'s 14 June departure from Mare Island for the war zone.

Mighty Mine Dodgers Return

Fifth Patrol   *14 June–4 July 1945*

Spadefish was the hottest Hellcat in the Sea of Japan thus far as she cleared the scene of her latest sinking at two-thirds speed on the morning of 14 June. At 0737, five or six small craft were spotted in the vicinity of *Seizan Maru*'s sinking, evidently picking up survivors. At 0743, *Spadefish* went to 150 feet to avoid the possibility of expected air searches, as there was a known airfield near the town of Maoka.

Spadefish conducted a submerged reconnaissance off the next seaport of Honto during the day, dodging two echo ranging PCs late in the late afternoon. She surfaced at 2015 and ran south along the coast past Honto, 6 miles offshore. No shipping was found outside this harbor, so she headed for a new station off Benkai Misaki, Hokkaido. "Intend to run surface patrol tomorrow if possible," Germershausen wrote.

Spadefish made 160 rpms (12 knots) as she headed for Hokkaido. New orders came in from Commander Hydeman during the night to instead shift to a new patrol plan. Germershausen was infuriated with the wolf pack commander's new orders, feeling that Hydeman was trying to take over *Spadefish*'s productive area. Radio silence was golden, so any words he had for Hydeman would have to wait until after the patrol. In the meantime, Germershausen would have to show up *Sea Dog*'s skipper by having his *Spadefish* snoop out worthwhile targets in Hydeman's former area.

Some aboard *Spadefish* did not look too favorably upon wolf pack leader Hydeman's orders to change patrol areas. *Sea Dog* had sunk two freighters on "Mike Day," but since had sunk only a 753-ton freighter on 11 June and an 887-ton maru on 12 June. After two more days without torpedo-worthy targets, Hydeman ordered *Spadefish* to trade patrol areas with *Sea Dog*.

"Headed south to trade areas with *Sea Dog*," wrote Hugo Lundquist. "They hadn't made out. New area off northern Honshu." *Spadefish* spent 15 June patrolling on the surface, zigzagging south in the Japan Sea, without contact. *Sea Dog* did sink a ship on 15 June, after making Germershausen trade areas, but it was another small ship of 884 tons. Occasional radar interference was picked up from islands *Spadefish* passed by. At 1645, the high periscope watch could see the peak of Hokkaido Island at a range of 35 miles. She moved at 10 knots through the night for her new patrol station.

Spadefish made a submerged passage off Okushiri Kaikyo while en route to her new station on 16 June. At 1115, the watch sighted smoke on the horizon and battle stations was ordered. Making a submerged approach, this ship could not be overtaken and contact did not develop. Unable to close his prey, the skipper secured the crew from battle stations at 1236.

Spadefish ran south along the coast 1,500 to 2,000 yards from the beach. At 1500, a sampan was sighted at 1,500 yards and avoided. Another sampan appeared only 1,000 yards away at 1547. Although tempting, Germershausen opted to let these little fish go in favor of larger game. He had already removed four of the small vessels with his deck gun. With four torpedoes remaining, he did not want to draw undue attention to his boat at this point.

Echo ranging was picked up at 2050, so the SD and SJ radars were manned. *Spadefish* surfaced at 2054 to investigate. Two minutes later, radar contact was made on a small vessel at 11,350 yards and the tracking party was called. By 2105, radar had made contact on four more vessels at ranges from 12,360 to 15,750 yards. Two of these vessels were identified as probable escorts. They were patrolling between the other ships and *Spadefish*, steering by constant helm.

Captain Germershausen headed north at full speed, planning to follow this Japanese convoy through Okushiri Kaikyo. Moments later, he decided to change his plans. He would take *Spadefish* to seaward of Okushiri Kaikyo and then attempt to regain contact with this shipping north of the pass. There was insufficient sea room in this strait and a bright moonlight was silhouetting *Spadefish*. Two escorts were also in the way of the original route. The convoy's speed was only 7 to 8 knots. Running at full speed, *Spadefish* would easily gain position ahead of the enemy ships before they reached the other side of the island. Germershausen predicted the time of contact north of the island to be 0100.

At 2225, radar contact was lost and tracking was secured. *Spadefish* continued north at full speed as the night passed into 17 June. "All four main engines on propulsion, making 260 turns [19.5 knots]. All ahead flank," logged Jim Fletcher. Germershausen went to flank speed in the late minutes of his run toward the point where he expected to reestablish radar contact with the ships. The lights of both Inabo Misaki and Motsuta Misaki lights were burning with normal characteristics as *Spadefish* raced past.

Five minutes earlier than had been expected, the SJ radar picked up a bogie again at 0055, range 15,850 yards, and tracking was resumed. The moon had now set and everything looked good for an attack. By 0102, a second ship contact was made at 10,380 yards. Five minutes later, a third ship was picked up at 13,340 yards. At 0108, *Spadefish* went to battle stations to track these ships. "The first contact was the largest ship, heading up the coast close inshore," wrote the skipper. "The second and third were possible escorts, patrolling on the port bow of the target. Commenced approach on the first target."

Spadefish closed on the port beam of the first ship, which was headed for Motsuta Misaki, about 3,000 yards from the shore. The bridge was manned with lookouts and Ensign Bill Ware on the TBT. Germershausen felt that his target was due to change course away from *Spadefish* after passing Motsuta Misaki light, so he opted to act quickly. Lieutenant Dick Wright remained in the conning tower to oversee the tracking party and take periscope observations.

The target freighter was visible from 4,000 yards as *Spadefish* narrowed the range. She was seen to be a medium sized, engines aft freighter. Germershausen called for the forward doors to be opened and the torpedoes to be set at 6 foot depths. Perry Wood's plot and Dan Decker's TDC solutions all checked perfectly, so at 0141, came the order, "Fire one!" Eight seconds later came, "Fire two!"

Spadefish shuddered as each 2,800-pound warfish departed and sped on its way toward the unsuspecting Japanese ship. They were fired on a 120° port track, with their gyro angle zero, and a range to target of 2,100 yards. Signalman Jim Schuett counted down the seconds of the torpedo run. One of the two torpedoes exploded at 0142, just over a minute after firing.

The ship, later identified as the 2,274-ton cargo ship *Eijo Maru*, lost all headway quickly. She was seen to circle and come to a stop as she began settling. *Spadefish* opened out to seaward as *Eijo* abandoned ship. By 0146, the freighter had disappeared from the radar screen and had been seen to sink by the bridge crew. Torpedoman Hugo Lundquist wrote in his journal for 17 June, "Picked off freighter which sank in 4 minutes. Big explosions on way out—evidently exploding boilers."

At 0153, *Spadefish* changed course to the northwest to intercept the remaining ships. At 0156, she picked up an escort on SJ radar which was headed for *Spadefish* at 14 knots. Captain Germershausen put him astern and abandoned his chase. The sky was getting light and it would not have been possible to get in firing position before they should reach Shakotan Misaki, then turn into Otaru Harbor.

By 0226, *Spadefish* had lost contact with the escort. She continued on a southerly course, heading down her assigned patrol lane.

Germershausen received orders from Group Commander Hydeman that afternoon to rendezvous the Hepcats at 2100, so he set course for that position.

At 1820, another submarine was sighted. *Spadefish* closed and identified her as *Crevalle*. The submarines exchanged greetings and information at 1900 via searchlights and SJ keying as they continued en route toward their rendezvous site. At 2024, SJ radar contact was made at 34,650 yards on another ship. Upon closing the contact, it was identified via blinker tube as *Sea Dog*. At 2153, *Spadefish* went alongside *Sea Dog*, ringing up all stop for a few minutes while supplementary patrol orders were received from wolf pack leader Earl Hydeman. At 2214, *Spadefish* had cleared *Sea Dog* and set course for the west coast of Honshu as ordered. By 2239, she had lost contact with both of her sister subs as they went their separate ways.

During the day on 17 June, Radio Vladivostok had transmitted a radio bulletin about the torpedoing of a Russian ship in the Sea of Japan. The 10,000-ton food-freighter *Transbalt* had been sunk in the Soya Straits between Hokkaido and Karafuto. The radio bulletin, relayed by the Domei News Agency in Japan, concluded that "it is beyond doubt that the submarine responsible was American."[1]

Unbeknownst to *Spadefish*, the *Transbalt* sinking made it to Admiral Lockwood via these Radio Tokyo intercepts. He fired off his own message, requesting exact information concerning the time and position of the sinking of *Transbalt*. A flurry of radio activity between the Pentagon and Pearl Harbor ensued with command trying to determine what had happened. The Japanese had managed to rescue 99 Soviet sailors from *Transbalt*.

"We got a message from Lockwood asking if anyone had fired at a ship in this particular area," recalled Bill Germershausen. Realizing the likely situation, the skipper radioed "guilty" back to his boss on Guam. *Spadefish*'s message, as relayed to Admiral Lockwood, stated: "*Spadefish* (SS411) reports—At 0130 13th June sank large ship, position of attack 45-44 N., 140-48 E. Closed to 1100 yards. Neither ship nor lights seen. 30 minutes later identified another vessel as Russian at 8,000 yards by recognition lights."[2]

When the Soviets later protested the sinking, Germershausen recalled that "they blamed it on a reactionary U.S. submarine skipper." At the time of firing, however, there had been no clear indication that this was not a Japanese ship. "That Russian was just a few hours from her destination—Vladivostok."[3]

Spadefish closed the west coast of Honshu during the morning of

18 June, heading for Henashi Saki at 15 knots. Henashi Saki was sighted at 20 miles distance at 0310. She submerged before daybreak at 0345 and continued closing Honshu's shoreline. The periscope watch sighted smoke on the horizon at 0630. The ship went to battle stations and commenced an approach, hoping to use the last two torpedoes aboard. By 0713, this ship had been identified as a small engines aft freighter. The target was tracking at 7 to 8 knots, going south between Henashi Saki and Sago Saki.

At 0750, Germershausen took an observation and found her to be at 3,000 yards, with a 120° starboard angle on the bow. "While debating whether situation could be improved," he wrote, "looked all around and sighted ship at 8,000 yards coming round Henashi Saki with zero angle on the bow. It looked like a destroyer at first glance. Reversed course and got off the track of new target and headed for deep water. Heard no pinging."

At 0805, Germershausen motioned Jim Schuett to raise the scope for another peek. He identified the target as a small freighter. The angle on the bow was estimated at 30° starboard, and she was at a range of 3,500 yards. With too great a distance, Germershausen swung *Spadefish* in and closed on the enemy maru. By 0820, distance to the freighter's track was 1,000 yards. *Spadefish* then swung around again to bring her stern tubes to bear on a 90° starboard track.

"Open outer doors," yeoman Kreinbring repeated over the headset to Vernon Kite's after torpedo gang. Perry Wood's plot was dead on and everything check with Dan Decker's TDC.

"Fire one." called Germershausen at 0824. Dick Wright smacked the electric plunger and Kite's crew fired manually, as well.

"Fire two." *Spadefish*'s second to last torpedo departed with a range of 1,450 yards to target and a 5-foot depth setting.

Bill Germershausen watched in disgust as he saw the smoke of one of his torpedoes pass under the stern of this target. He then could see the telltale torpedo wake on the far side of his target. He felt that this ship was light and it looked "as if the fish under-ran it." The target continued on at the same course and speed, apparently unaware that her life had just been spared.

Checking the setup again quickly, Germershausen ordered the last torpedo aboard his sub fired at this ship at 0826. The depth setting remained at 5 feet but the target's speed was reduced by one knot to counter a turn away. The range at firing was 1,800 yards. This lucky little maru had a good luck charm working in her favor, as she managed to turn away and avoid being hit.

Battle stations were secured at 0832 and *Spadefish* set course to open out for surfacing. She sighted sampan at 0923, and another at 1012. At 1217, the periscope watch sighted a plane at 8 miles. At 1312, a destroyer was sighted at 8,000 yards and his pinging could be heard on the sonar. At 1637, *Spadefish* surfaced 14 miles west of Henashi Saki and opened out at full speed. At 2100, Germershausen informed Commander Hydeman that he was out of torpedoes and requested permission to hunt gun targets in the vicinity of Musei Tai. He waited for a reply but did not get one this night. "Here we were, out of torpedoes and Sonar Day was six days hence," he later wrote. "We rested, cruised leisurely about, conducted daily trim dives, and played poker."[4]

At 2200, *Spadefish* converted her No. 3 and No. 4 fuel ballast tanks to main ballast tanks. John Brewer, Red Dunleavy, Buck Miller, and two other motormacs went into the superstructure to conduct the dangerous, wet job. Jim Schuett logged at 2209 that "five men on topside for conversion of #3 and #4 fuel ballast tanks." By 0245 on 19 June, the tank conversion was successfully completed and the fuel gang went back below decks with a new appreciation of life.

Spadefish and the other Hellcats all received a message from ComSubPac that evening, as Hugo Lundquist recorded in his journal: "Received congratulatory radio message from Admirals Nimitz and Lockwood to Japan Sea wolf pack. Also heard all 9 boats made Tsushima Strait O.K."

Spadefish cruised on the surface in her area during the morning hours of 19 June, awaiting permission from the group commander to shoot sampans. When no word came by early afternoon, Captain Germershausen impatiently sent another request to Hydeman, seeking permission to attack Japanese ships with his deck gun.

Spadefish continued patrolling on the surface into 20 June, awaiting orders. She had an enemy plane contact at 0528, distance 10 miles, which convinced Germershausen to dive for the day. He returned to the surface at 1710 and continued patrolling the western edge of his area, passing within high periscope view of Hokkaido Island. As the day of exiting the Sea of Japan neared, a test of the FM sonar gear showed that it had crapped out.

CRT Neal Pike and a repair party of several motor machinist mates was sent topside at 2200. The FM transducer was mounted on the port forward deck, rising about three feet high. "Our instructions were, if a plane came over, they were going to dive without us," recalled Pike. The unit's crystal head had flooded out following the 10 June depth charge attack. Chief Pike conferred with the skipper and they agreed that it should be brought below for repairs.

"We had wire ropes that hooked onto our belts so that they could pull us back aboard if we fell over," said Pike. Joe Case manned the radar to keep an expert eye out for enemy planes during this nervous operation. The team successfully removed the sonar head and took it below to the forward torpedo room. "It was flooded out, so I took it apart and dried it all out," Pike said. With the help of his repair gang, Pike worked through the night cleaning, drying and reassembling the finicky head. In its place, a blank flange was secured to the shaft topside until the head could be replaced.

During the early morning hours of 21 June, Commander Hydeman finally answered Germershausen's gun request with a negative. After two wasted days without permission, he was angry that his pack commander would not let his aggressive crew sink more small vessels. Germershausen set course for her pre-exit rendezvous. At 0335, her lookouts sighted a submarine. Despite repeated attempts, they were unable to identify her but believed her to be *Sea Dog*. The contact was thus avoided.

While running on the surface during the evening of 21 June, Neal Pike and his repair team replaced the FM sonar head at 2200 that they had removed the previous night. "We had gotten her back together and we spent that next night back up on the surface getting it put back on," recalled Pike. The set was found to work normally on a test using a false target shell. At 0258 on 22 June, Gouker logged, "FM back in commission." For repairing the tricky sonar head on the surface in the Sea of Japan and for guiding the ship through the minefields on 4 June, Pike was later awarded the Silver Star.

During 22 June, *Spadefish* patrolled on the surface at 10 knots, working generally northward toward her exit rendezvous. The watch sections kept a high alert with high periscope watches, but had no enemy shipping or plane encounters. *Spadefish* dove to 100 feet at 2001 to test the newly repaired FM gear, firing two false target shells.

Radar watch kept track of the passing islands as *Spadefish* narrowed the distance to her exit from the Sea of Japan the following day. She continued running on the surface at two-thirds speed. An enemy ship was sighted 16,000 yards away on the horizon at 1410. Captain Germershausen closed the contact and stationed his tracking party at 1416. He made a quick dive and pushed forward at two-thirds speed submerged, calling for battle stations at 1424. He closed the vessel until, at 1449, he could positively identify her as Russian. Battle plot was secured and Germershausen had moving pictures shot of the ship.

Hugo Lundquist logged for 23 June: "Battle stations. Turned out to be 8,000 ton Russian Freighter. Passed 200 yards to starboard."

Out of torpedoes, *Spadefish* proceeded toward her rendezvous point with her Hepcat packmates. This night was designated as the night they would depart the Sea of Japan. Their romp had been quite destructive. More than fifty Japanese vessels of all sizes had been destroyed or damaged by gunfire and torpedoes from the Hellcats. The smallest vessels had been sampans, schooners and sea trucks

Shipping Sunk in the Sea of Japan by Hellcats Wolf Pack: 9-20 June 1945

Date	Submarine	Ship Attacked	Tonnage	Type	Sunk by
6/9/45	Tinosa	Wakatama Maru	2,211	AK	Torpedo
	Sea Dog	Sagawa Maru	1,186	AK	Torpedo
	Sea Dog	Shoyo Maru	2,211	AO	Torpedo
	Crevalle	Hokuto Maru	2,215	AK	Torpedo
6/10/45	Spadefish	Daigen Maru # 2	1,999	AK	Torpedo
	Spadefish	Unkai Maru # 8	1,293	AK	Torpedo
	Spadefish	Jintsu Maru	985	AK	Torpedo
	Skate	I-122	1,142	SS	Torpedo
	Flying Fish	Taga Maru	2,220	AK	Torpedo
	Crevalle	Daiki Maru	2,217	AK	Torpedo
6/11/45	Flying Fish	Meisei Maru	1,893	AK	Torpedo
	Bowfin	Shinyo Maru # 3	1,898	AK	Torpedo
	Crevalle	Hakusan Maru	2,211	AK	Torpedo
	Sea Dog	Kofuku Maru	753	AK	Torpedo
6/12/45	Spadefish	unknown	100	sampan	Gun action
	Sea Dog	Shinsen Maru	887	AK	Torpedo
	Spadefish	unknown	200	trawler	Gun action
	Skate	Yozan Maru	1,227	AK	Torpedo
	Skate	Zuiko Maru	887	AK	Torpedo
	Skate	Kenjo Maru	3,142	AK	Torpedo
	Spadefish	Daido Maru	300	XPkt	Gun action
	Spadefish	unknown	100	trawler	Gun action
	Tinosa	Keito Maru	873	AK	Gun action
6/13/45	Bonefish	Oshikayama Maru	6,892	AK	Torpedo
	Crevalle	unknown	75	lugger	Gun action
	Crevalle	unknown	25	lugger	Gun action
	Bowfin	Akiura Maru	887	AK	Torpedo
	Skate	Hattenzan Maru	1,180 *	AK	Torpedo
6/14/45	Spadefish	Seizan Maru	2,018	AK	Torpedo
6/15/45	Flying Fish	unknown	30	schooner	Gun action
	Flying Fish	unknown	30	schooner	Gun action
	Flying Fish	unknown	30	schooner	Gun action
	Flying Fish	unknown	30	schooner	Gun action
	Flying Fish	unknown	30	schooner	Gun action
	Flying Fish	unknown	30	schooner	Gun action
	Flying Fish	unknown	30	schooner	Gun action
	Sea Dog	Koan Maru	661	AK	Torpedo
	Flying Fish	unknown	30	schooner	Gun action
	Flying Fish	unknown	30	schooner	Gun action
6/17/45	Spadefish	Eijo Maru	2,274	AK	Torpedo
6/18/45	Tinosa	Wakae Maru	2,000 **	AK	Torpedo
6/19/45	Sea Dog	Kokai Maru	1,272	AK	Torpedo

6/20/45	Sea Dog	Shinei Maru # 3	958 *	AK	Torpedo
	Bonefish	Konzan Maru	5,488	AK	Torpedo
	Tinosa	Kaisei Maru	880	AK	Torpedo
	Tinosa	Taito Maru	2,726	AK	Torpedo
	Tinosa	Sanjin Maru	2,500	AK	Torpedo

Unofficial total: 47 ships sunk for 62,156 tons

Russian Shipping Sunk by Hellcats: 9-20 June 1945

Date	Submarine	Ship Attacked	Tonnage	Type	Sunk by
6/13/45	Spadefish	Transbalt	11,439	AK	Torpedo

Ships Damaged by Hellcats Wolf Pack: 9-20 June 1945

Date	Submarine	Ship Attacked	Tonnage	Damaged by
6/10/45	Tinosa	Unknown AK	4,000	Dud torpedo hit
6/12/45	Sea Dog	Kaiwa Maru, AK	1,045 *	One torpedo hit
6/12/45	Skate	unknown AK	4,000	2 hits claimed
6/13/45	Bonefish	Takakurasan M., AK	1,885	claimed sunk
6/14/45	Bowfin	schooner	20	gun damaged
6/15/45	Flying Fish	harbor tug	50	gun damaged
	Flying Fish	harbor tug	50	Damaged with gun
6/22/45	Crevalle	Kasado, DD	870	One torpedo hit

Unofficial damage total: 8 additional ships, 11,920 tons estimated

Source: Alden, *U.S. Submarine Attacks During World War II*. All sinkings as credited by JANAC, except as noted. Also Alden, *United States and Allied Submarine Successes in the Pacific*, D349-56.

* Per research of Roger W. Allan and also *The Imperial Japanese Navy in World War II*, 1952 compilation (IJN).

** Credited by IJN source only.

destroyed by gunfire. *Bonefish* had sunk the largest ships, a 5,488-ton freighter and a 6,892 troop transport. *Skate* had managed to catch a Japanese submarine on the surface and sink it. *Tinosa* had been the first to sink a ship on "Mike Day," 9 June 1945. *Crevalle* had made the last successful attack in the Sea of Japan, torpedoing the Japanese destroyer *Kasado* on 22 June.

Exiting the Sea of Japan was just as potentially deadly as entering it had been for Admiral Lockwood's Hellcats.

La Perouse Strait had been selected by Admiral Lockwood's staff for the departure from the Sea of Japan. Russian ships used this strait to safely enter and exit the area. Commander Earl Hydeman had this as his first option, to either pass through submerged or to run out on the surface. Should he find enemy anti-submarine resistance too stiff, he could always head north through the shallow Strait of Tartary, or head south and pass back through the mine fields of Tsushima Strait.[5]

Lockwood himself was deeply worried over the submariners he had put into the Sea of Japan. His notes for 22 June 1945 included this: "We are all holding our breath till those boys come out—and I pray to God they will all come out. Years will be lifted from my shoulders."[6]

After filming the Russian freighter, *Spadefish* had remained submerged another hour. She hit the surface at 1556 on 23 June and went all ahead full on course 340° T. Visibility was poor after sunset, so the SJ radar was used continually. Hydeman's Hellcats were scheduled to rendezvous on the surface well west of Soya Strait this evening to discuss their exit from the Sea of Japan the following night.

Radar interference was picked up at 1944, and minutes later the lookouts spotted another submarine at 7,500 yards distance. Switching the conning tower sound gear onto the speakers, the watch soon identified her as *Crevalle* and communications were opened with her using SCR. At 2024, radar contact was made with *Sea Dog*.

Commander Hydeman then ordered Germershausen to link up with the southern group of subs, Bob Risser's Bobcats. *Spadefish* changed course and moved out as directed. Radar interference was picked up at 2146, which was quickly identified as *Bowfin* at 9,850 yards. At 2210, radar contact had also been made with *Flying Fish*. The third sub of this wolf pack, *Tinosa*, was identified by *Spadefish* at 2242. After making contact with all three, Germershausen changed course and moved back toward Hydeman's rendezvous spot at two-thirds speed during the closing minutes of 23 June.

While *Spadefish* was grouping the southern pack, *Sea Dog* and *Crevalle* had been joined at 2200 by *Tunny* and *Skate*, all that was remaining of the Polecats wolf pack. Their third sub, Commander Larry Edge's *Bonefish*, did not make the rendezvous. There was much concern about staying behind to keep trying to contact *Bonefish*, but Hydeman refused this.

The last time *Bonefish* had been seen was at 0600 on 18 June, when Pierce and Edge exchanged information with each other on the surface. Captain Edge asked pack commander Pierce for permission to take his *Bonefish* into Toyama Bay to check out targets. *Tunny's* skipper reminded Edge that this bay had been mined by B-29s and of the dangers of its shallow waters. The two subs then separated, the skippers bidding each other the customary "good luck and good hunting." *Bonefish* would never be heard from again.[7]

Bonefish made her final attack on a 5,488-ton freighter, sinking her but apparently becoming the victim of a Japanese ASW hunter-killer group. These destroyers depth charged a submerged target and reported debris and an oil slick. There is no conclusive evidence that these destroyers finished off *Bonefish*, however, as she became another of the fifty-two American submarines lost during World War II, many of which simply vanished with all hands. Bill Germershausen had lost a classmate and friend in *Bonefish*'s Commander Larry Edge.

The eight remaining Hellcats gathered on the surface together for their pre-exit conference with Commander Hydeman aboard *Sea Dog*. He spoke with each of the skippers via VHF radio. Hydeman believed that the newly laid mines in La Perouse Strait would have been placed deep to catch subs. After polling all seven other skippers, he found them in agreement. Making a surface run out was preferable to trusting the FM sonar units again for a submerged exit.[8]

Hydeman heard from his fellow skippers that Japanese anti-submarine forces had been weak in the Sea of Japan. He did not expect a fleet of destroyers. Having seen Russian ships transit La Perouse, and noting the area they used, he was willing to try a surface exit from the Sea of Japan. Further, his own FM sonar was out of commission, so would do him no good submerged in locating mines. Knowing that American subs were loose in the Sea of Japan, it was reasonable to expect that new mines would be laid in La Perouse Strait.

Around 0300 on 24 June, the eight subs submerged for the day and slowly made their way eastward on a 90° track. They would rendezvous again on the surface that night at 2000. The crew made plans for the exit during the day as *Spadefish* proceeded submerged at one-third speed. She was no longer with her Hepcats packmates, but had joined the southern group of *Flying Fish*, *Tinosa* and *Bowfin* for the exit, placing four subs in each departure group.

The day's transit was quiet, and *Spadefish* surfaced at 1955. The Hellcats rendezvoused again to prepare for the Sea of Japan exit. It would not be a quick one. From the center of La Perouse Strait—where depths up to 30 fathoms existed—to the safety of the 100-fathom curve to the east was about a 70 mile distance. At four engine speed, this would take four to five hours.

For the transit, Hydeman elected to form his ships in two columns of four each. The interval between columns was 2,000 yards and the distance between ships was 1,200 yards. In one column lined up were *Sea Dog*, followed by *Crevalle*, *Tunny* and *Skate*. The other column had *Flying Fish* in the lead, followed by *Tinosa*, *Bowfin* and *Spadefish*, each boat spread about 1,200 yards apart.[9]

At 2030, Hydeman led his group of subs eastward toward La Perouse Strait. The sea was calm and there was a full moon overhead, and for once the visibility was greater than they would have liked. *Spadefish* grouped up with the southern column of subs, but it took nearly another 90 minutes before they were properly formed up with *Sea Dog*'s column. *Sea Dog* led them on their way at 2126 on 24 June.

Some of the sub skippers elected to have their crews wear their Mae Wests for safety. Motormac Pat Kelley recalled, "We even wore life jackets in the engine rooms during the exit from the Sea of Japan." In his remote area of the ship, "I think we all imagined more than what really happened." Although the life jackets had been ordered to be worn, "it wasn't enforced," recalled Don Scholle.

The firepower of the Hellcats would be quite strong. They had eight 5-inch deck guns, plus another twenty or more 20mm and 40mm guns on their bridges. Against the smaller picket boats that had generally been encountered recently, they would be a formidable match. The deck gun crew stood ready below the gun-access trunk for the order to man the guns. At full speed, the crew would not go topside unless necessary. Any man who happened to fall overboard here would be left behind forever.

"Our gun crews, with ammo ready, gathered just below the hatch leading to the gun mount," recalled gunnery officer Dan Decker. If a mine was hit, men would not swim long in these waters. Death would come quickly in the near freezing water. Lookouts were tense. The mess attendants, Sie Brooks and William Bynum, kept hot coffee on constant supply to the bridge.

"Between eight submarines, we figured we could put up a good gun battle if we were challenged," recalled electrician Al La Rocca. In his journal, torpedoman Hugo Lundquist wrote that *Spadefish* was going "through pass at battle stations, standing by all guns."

The eight subs began their four-engine run through the strait after dark. Should an enemy ship appear, the subs would be forced to dive. Lockwood's intelligence had told the skippers that the mines were generally set a depth of about 45 feet to protect the Russian shipping which passed through. "We blew all of the ballast tanks as dry as possible," recalled Chief Charles Griffith, to keep *Spadefish* running as high on the surface as possible.

Any diving sub, however, was certain to connect with one of these. To avoid the risk, the Hellcats would not dive, no matter what happened. The little armada, bunched in tight, would simply have to shoot it out with whatever surface or air threat that greeted them.

Spadefish opened the transit at standard speed at 2139, increasing to full speed at 2147, making 18 knots. At 2230, she increased to flank speed on all four main engines. The eight subs had barely gotten underway when *Sea Dog*, leading the northern column, had her finicky radar go out of commission again. Hydeman quickly relayed the news to Commander Steinmetz and had his *Crevalle* pull into the lead. *Sea Dog* then fell in just astern of *Crevalle*.

Captain Germershausen had Chief "Stinky" Schmelzer open her up to maximum speed. Quartermaster Don Scholle recalled that Schmelzer "taped up some boards, wrapped them together and put them against the electrical panel to keep the breakers from kicking out." Schmelzer had opted to use a little ingenuity to achieve maximum speed this night, not wanting to use his feet as he and Roy Moody had done on the second patrol while escaping enemy destroyers.[10]

As the subs progressed, the visibility began to drop as fog began to set in. Half an hour into the run, *Crevalle*'s radar picked up an enemy ship at 17,000 yards. On the SJ, the ship showed up as a good-sized pip. It could be a destroyer or it could be a Russian ship in these waters. Germershausen ordered the tracking crew to stay on this ship. Below decks, Jake Lewis, Chief Scherman, Rebel Rewold and the 5-inch crew stood by the gun access trunk just in case the deck crew was ordered out on deck.

Tracking soon announced that the radar pip was on an opposite course to the U.S. subs and that she would pass to port. She had not made any indication of moving toward the eight oncoming submarines. "Turn three," Captain Steinmetz called over the radio to his column. This signal was for all boats to turn 30° to port in an effort to put a little more water between the American subs and the passing ship.[11]

Minutes later, the ship was in sight for those on *Spadefish*'s bridge. Quartermaster Don Scholle logged at 2354, "Sighted light from bridge. Identified as Russian ship." The lookouts clearly made her out to be a Russian ship with all of her running lights burning. Perhaps the loss of *Transbalt* the week before had convinced the Russians to warn their skippers about traveling without lights.

At least one reassuring thought went through some minds. Those who had feared running out on the surface could at least be reassured that Russian shipping was safely using the exact same lane. Still running at 18 knots, the U.S. subs began to pass by the Russian ship at a range of 6,000 yards. Just as she was nearly abeam, she suddenly opened up with a 24-inch searchlight which played up and down the columns of subs. The long, white finger of light turned on the southern column, sweeping back from *Flying Fish* to *Tinosa* to *Bowfin*. The spotlight finally came to rest on *Spadefish*. Germershausen and his bridge crew were suddenly on center stage, illuminated by the searchlight.

"We were the last boat in the column. We were going through at maximum speed," recalled Bill Germershausen. When the Russian spotlight lit up his *Spadefish*, he called for 20mm gunners Whitey Harbison and Billy Pigman to prepare to shoot out the light. "It was a big 24-inch, I guess, searchlight they turned on. They flashed it along the line of boats and it came to rest on the *Spadefish*. You should have heard my language!"

Although the spotlight only rested on his submarine for what Germershausen guessed was "about fifteen seconds," it seemed an eternity. With his 20mm gunners on the bridge, Captain Germershausen was just prepared to have them open fire when the light suddenly snapped off. The gunners went back below and the skipper was saved from having a chance to further damage international relations by firing on his second Russian ship of the patrol.[12]

Soon after midnight, the eight subs reached La Perouse Strait's charted entrance. Running on a southeasterly course, they would pass over as many as three lines of enemy mines. The fog had set in dense as the diesel subs maintained full speed and raced through the strait. The lookouts strained to see the other subs in a fog that dropped visibility to a few hundred feet.[13]

The wolf pack passed over the first minefield at 0035 on 25 June. Captain Germershausen ordered battle stations surfaced manned at that moment and increased speed to flank. At 0102, *Spadefish*'s SJ radar picked up a ship contact, range 9,350 yards ahead of *Spadefish*'s southern group. They were nearly halfway through La Perouse at this point, and this contact was believed to be a small radar-equipped patrol boat or a minelayer at work. The radar operators plotted her at zero speed, indicating that she was stopped, possibly using her sonar or maybe just anchored for the night. In any event, the sub skippers held their breaths and avoided the SJ contact as they plowed through the strait. *Spadefish* lost contact with her at 0134.[14]

The expected enemy attacks never happened. No ships. No planes. Not one shot was fired at the departing American submarines. No one could understand why it had been so easy, but it had been a tense transit nonetheless. At 0200, the SCR circuit lit up as the subs congratulated each other on having safely cleared the last known row of mines. It had taken the boats four hours to cruise from one side of La Perouse Strait to the other, but it had been safe.[15]

Captain Germershausen secured his tracking party at 0340. She was bringing up the rear. *Tinosa* was now in the lead, 6,550 yards ahead of *Spadefish*. *Flying Fish* was 3,990 yards ahead, followed by *Bowfin*, just ahead of *Spadefish* by 1,510 yards. The visibility through the entire passage was not much better than 600 yards. *Spadefish*'s radar operators kept watch on her sister subs as they continued on the surface at full speed through the early morning hours.

In his patrol report, Bill Germershausen gave no details whatsoever about the exit through La Perouse Strait. "The details of the exit were highly classified because Admiral Lockwood intended to continue the penetrations if the war lasted long enough," he later wrote.[16]

The crew felt an enormous sense of relief as battle stations were secured. Wolf pack commander Hydeman shortly thereafter released

Crewmembers aboard the U.S. submarines which penetrated the minefields of Tsushima Strait and invaded the Sea of Japan in late 1945 were awarded a "Mighty Mine Dodger" certificate by Vice Admiral Lockwood. *Courtesy of Albert G. La Rocca.*

the subs from their two groups and directed them to proceed homeward, some 3,800 miles to Pearl Harbor.

Bill Germershausen, much relieved to be out of the Sea of Japan and now en route toward home, ordered Chief Ives to break out the medicinal brandy for anyone who was interested. An appreciative torpedoman Hugo Lundquist wrote in his journal for 24 June, "Skipper thought a grog line was in order."

The Hellcats hauled clear of La Perouse Strait without event until about 1000 on 25 June, when a cable guard came loose aboard *Crevalle* and fouled her starboard screw. Earl Hydeman's *Sea Dog* fell behind to help *Crevalle*, who sent a diver overboard to try and clear the cable. *Crevalle* finally shook the cable by alternately backing down and going ahead until the cable came loose.[17]

Captain George Pierce of *Tunny* asked permission to remain behind near the exit to La Perouse to keep trying to contact *Bonefish*. Hydeman gave him two days, but then *Tunny* was to move on. As these three submarines dropped behind, *Spadefish* took the lead of the Hellcats and moved on out of the area of La Perouse Strait.

Captain Germershausen felt that his classmate Pierce made "a gallant try" to continued raising Larry Edge's *Bonefish* "while the rest of us balled the jack for Midway."[18]

At 1300 on 25 June, all ship's clocks were set ahead one hour as *Spadefish* passed into another time zone while clearing La Perouse. Admiral Lockwood listened intently for word on his Hellcats, but got no radio messages on 25 June. It was not until 26 June that *Sea Dog* opened up and sent the word of their glorious destruction in the Sea of Japan. Commander Hydeman also sent the bad news that *Bonefish* had failed to join up again. Lockwood sent back a congratulatory message to all of Hydeman's Hellcats. He concluded with, "Admiral Nimitz desires congratulate you on daring and aggressiveness to which ComSubPac and all submariners add three rousing cheers."[19]

Lockwood's messages also brought further news on the Russian ship *Transbalt* that had been sunk in the Sea of Japan. "Received word from ComSubPac that Russian freighter of 11,000 tons had been sunk in Sea of Japan at western end of La Perouse Strait," wrote torpedoman Lundquist in his journal. For many aboard *Spadefish*, there was at least some suspicion that their boat had brought about the end of this Soviet freighter.

Spadefish continued to run on all four main engines throughout the day. Seaman 1/c Norval Ingberg, striking for quartermaster, began his turn on the daily watch at maintaining the quartermaster's log. One of his entries for 27 June shows that two men were sent out on deck at 1911 "to cut mine cables from bow planes." The special mine-clearing precautions had served their purpose in preventing any mines from snagging on *Spadefish* during her 4 June entry through the minefields. Rough seas had caused both mine clearing cables to part, thus creating the need to cut them loose altogether.

Bill Germershausen later wrote of the return from the Sea of Japan.

> In *Spadefish*, we saw no reason to tarry. Our four main engines were kept on the line, and we didn't slow down a single knot until we reached Midway on June 29. This was one day ahead of the next boat in. We made only one contact before we picked up our escort at Midway. This was the U.S. submarine *Pogy*, Comdr. John Bowers commanding. *Pogy* was on her way to the Sea of Japan to start another cycle—independent patrols in the Emperor's lake.[20]

According to Ensign Harry Buncke, *Spadefish* was forced to crash dive during her run in toward Midway to avoid "an over-zealous Army Air pilot who dropped a bomb. We were all fortunate that he was a poor shot." *Spadefish* celebrated 29 June twice as she crossed the

Spadefish enters Midway upon return from Sea of Japan, flying her newest battle flag atop her periscope shears. FCS1c Andy Olah is standing in the shears. Along the edges of the conning tower (from left to right) are: Lt. Dick Wright, Captain Bill Germershausen, CPhM Vic Ives (wearing talker's headset), Ens. Bill Ware, Lt. Dick Fellows, and Ens. Harry Buncke (with binoculars around his neck). *Official U.S. Navy photo, courtesy of Bernie Massar.*

International Date Line, the 180th Meridian, at 0809 on the day that started as 30 June. The high periscope watch sighted Kure Island at 1302 on the second 29 June. Twenty minutes later, radar picked up her escort ship approaching. As *Spadefish* approached Midway, a motor launch came alongside at 1638 to transfer a pilot over to guide her in. *Spadefish* had continued to run on the surface en route to Midway and she arrived well ahead of any other Hellcats.[21]

News of the nine-submarine foray into the Sea of Japan was known to the command at Midway. To celebrate the occasion, Captain

Germershausen had his quartermasters deck out the topside with flags as *Spadefish* made her way through the passage in the reef and up the channel. Ashore, the usual throngs of gooneybirds, for which the atolls had been nicknamed, could be seen as the maneuvering watch prepared the lines topside.

The boat moored her port side to pier S-10 at 1750 on 29 June at Submarine Base, Midway. The maneuvering watch was secured at 1754 and John Brewer's fuel gang began overseeing the refueling process. Chief Scherman and Harry Buncke took care of ordering more provisions. Commander Johnny Waterman, first skipper of the successful sub *Barb*, met Captain Germershausen as *Spadefish* was docking at Gooneyville. In his deep Louisiana drawl, Waterman called out, "How come you got here so fast, Bill? You must really run scared, eh, boy?"[22]

At Guam, Admirals Lockwood and Nimitz drafted a message of congratulations to the Hellcat subs. They were thanked for sinking a large number of ships, for demonstrating faith in their new electronics equipment and in making "a shambles out of Hirohito's private ocean."[23]

The other Hellcats pulled into Midway behind *Spadefish*. *Tunny*, which had stayed behind at La Perouse trying to contact *Bonefish*, arrived a day later. *Spadefish* only remained at Midway overnight. Her diesels were rumbling in the morning as her crew itched to return to the Royal Hawaiian Hotel, which they had not seen in nine months. *Spadefish* got underway at 0916 on 30 June, cleared Midway's breakwaters by 0926 and headed for Hawaii.

The days between 30 June and 4 July were spent running toward Pearl Harbor. The yeomen, Irv Kreinbring and his assistant Roy Potting, worked on typing up the patrol report and on the paperwork for the men who had been newly qualified in submarines or advanced in rating. Since Spadefish had departed on her fifth patrol until the time she reached Hawaii, ten enlisted men had been promoted, including Potting.

Name:	New Rating:	Date Effective:
Barton, Thad R.	TM3c to TM2c	1 July 1945
Bynum, William T.	StM1c to St3c	1 July 1945
Carney, Hugh P.	S1c to TM3c	1 July 1945
Ingberg, Norval O.	S1c to QM3c	1 July 1945
LaFose, Murphy	F1c to F2c	1 June 1945
Mikesell, Robert E.	S2c to S1c	1 June 1945
Morrison, James W.	S1c to RM3c	1 July 1945
Paulson, Roger F.	S1c to F1c	15 June 1945

Motor machinist's mate Tom "Buck" Miller and gunner's mate Bernie Massar (right) display Chief Majoue's latest *Spadefish* battle flag en route home from their historic fifth war patrol into the Sea of Japan. *Courtesy of Thomas Miller.*

Potting, Roy C.   Y3c to Y2c   5 July 1945
Powers, Kenneth C.   RM3c to RM2c   1 July 1945

Heading in toward Pearl, Lieutenant Dick Wright made the announcements that only a certain number of men would be advanced in ratings. EM3c Jim Casey had qualified in *S-43* previously, but Wright made him requalify aboard *Spadefish* during her fifth patrol. "I stood lookout and did electric repairs for Bassett, EM3c, who was the auxiliary electrician," wrote Casey. "He would relieve me, I'd make the repairs, and then go back to being a lookout."[24]

Casey soon found that "at the end of the patrol, word was out that Bassett was to be rated as second class electrician." With the inevitable transfer of qualified men to other boats, Wright offered his men a chance to request transfers before he made his choices. "They wanted to know who wanted off the *Spadefish*, so I put my name in for a transfer," said Casey. Lieutenant Wright required that any sailor requesting a transfer must state a reason. Jim Casey felt that his reason was solid. "I stated that I had been a third class electrician longer than Bassett had been in the Navy!" Wright looked into Casey's record and promised he would rate him if he stayed aboard. "So both of us were rated," recalled Casey, both within two weeks of each other, Casey on 1 September 1945.

The fun-loving nature of the enlisted men returned as the ship drew closer to Pearl. Chief Griffith, a veteran of all *Spadefish* patrols, was on duty in the control room one day while Ensign Harry Buncke was on the bridge qualifying as an officer of the deck. Among the routines upon surfacing and taking the bridge was verifying that all systems checked out properly.

Before preparing for a dive, the OOD would call down to the control room and run through a sequence of checks, hoping to hear that the safety negative ballast tanks were properly filled, the air banks were serviced with air for proper buoyancy, and the proper equipment had been secured.

"Bridge, control," Buncke called down to the control room to verify all was normal.

In a fun mood, Chief Griffith called back, "Bridge, control. Air in the banks, water in the tanks. Everything tested, and nothing works."

Ensign Buncke called back, "Repeat?"

In a deadpan, Griffith calmly repeated his "disaster."

"Very well," came back the reply from Buncke, who had apparently picked up on the ruse from the amused faces looking toward him on the bridge.

At 0530 on 4 July, Independence Day, *Spadefish* made a rendezvous with *Flying Fish, Tinosa, Skate, Bowfin,* the destroyer *Pruitt* and *PC-782.* A full day ahead of Commander Hydeman and the other three Hellcat boats, they made the run in toward Pearl Harbor's channel on the surface with all flags proudly flying. From *Spadefish*'s shears, Captain Germershausen had Jim Fletcher rig up his Japanese rising sun flag in addition to the Stars and Stripes. From the top of her shears stretched to the aft railing of the cigarette deck fluttered three Japanese "rising sun" man-of-war flags and a string of meatball flags for each merchant ship sunk. In *Spadefish*'s case, she had so many flags for her sinkings there was an additional "short string of meatball flags that ran from the barrel of the 5/25 deck gun to the deck," recalled

Five Hellcats returning from the Sea of Japan. In foreground is *Flying Fish*, with *Spadefish* visible just behind her. Approaching Pearl Harbor on 4 July 1945, the other submarines in this photo are *Bowfin, Skate* and *Tinosa.*
Official U.S. Navy photo.

Bernie Massar. All of the officers and crew not required below decks went topside to enjoy the historic return.

Admiral Lockwood had organized a full-fledged reception for them. Bands, photographers and many well-wishers crowded the piers at the Sub Base at Pearl. Each sub steamed proudly up the channel with their battle flags and tally pennants fluttering. *Flying Fish* was first to tie up. Bags of mail, fresh fruit, and Admiral Lockwood himself came aboard to congratulate the first boat back from the Sea of Japan. "Admiral Lockwood had flown back from Guam and was on the pier wearing a grin that was a lot broader than La Perouse Strait," wrote Germershausen.[25]

As Lockwood was congratulating Captain Risser, *Spadefish* moored directly alongside *Flying Fish* and another brow was put across. Aboard came the mail bags, fresh fruit and Uncle Charlie. In short order, all five subs were moored alongside each other, with gangplanks from one deck to the next. Still cameras and movie cameras alike captured the grand entrance of the boats which had slipped through enemy minefields into Japan's own back yard.

"It was quite a good time," recalled auxiliaryman Dick Gamby. Fireman Jim Cole noted the women among the welcoming crowd on the docks. "That was the first time we had seen any women in I don't know how many months."

The following day, *Sea Dog* and the other boats made their way into Pearl, whereupon they were also greeted with a large reception.

Spadefish's fifth war patrol had lasted thirty-nine days, twenty days of which were at sea and eleven days submerged. She claimed 26,050 tons of shipping sunk, totalling ten ships. This included the gun targets: one motor sampan for 50 tons, a steam trawler of 200 tons, another steam trawler of 300 tons, and a wooden trawler of 100 tons. In the JANAC postwar assessment, *Spadefish* was credited with sinking five Japanese ships above 500 tons with torpedoes for a collective 8,578 tons. She had also destroyed four smaller vessels with her deck gun, plus one large Soviet ship.

Officially, JANAC would credit the Hellcats with twenty-eight ships sunk for 54,784 tons. Of course, this did not count the numerous vessels under 500 tons which had been sunk, including four by *Spadefish* with her deck gun. Every submarine of the wolf pack, with the exception of *Tunny*, had contributed to the total.[26]

Counting all of the smaller vessels, the wolf pack had sunk at least forty-seven Japanese ships for 63,959 tons, one Russian ship and had damaged or sunk nine other Japanese ships of varying tonnage. The majority of the shipping was merchant shipping, although one Japanese destroyer had been damaged and an I-class submarine had been sunk. In total, the Hellcats racked up more than 70,000 tons of enemy ship-

Spadefish returns to Pearl Harbor on 4 July 1945, flying Jim Fletcher's large Japanese rising sun flag and smaller pennants for each ship claimed sunk while on patrol. The men on the bridge are (left to right): SM1c Jim Schuett, Lt.(jg) Ed La Croix (behind Schuett), GM2c Bernie Massar and SM2c Zelbert Gouker (seated on rail). At lower left are EM3c Jim Casey and FC3c Walter Charles. *Courtesy of Joe Marasco.*

Tinosa viewed arriving at the sub base at Pearl Harbor on 4 July. She is viewed over the weathered deck of *Spadefish*, whose crew is gathered around her after 5-inch gun watching *Tinosa's* arrival. Note Luau on deck aft of the 5-inch gun. Emery Kreher is standing above Luau. Just forward of Kreher is John Taylor (with his head turned back). Continuing forward, Wallace McMahon and Dick Gamby (facing camera) converse with Whitey Harbison (seated on safety wire beside mess attendant Si Brooks). *Spadefish* is moored alongside *Flying Fish*. Courtesy of Joe Marasco.

Spadefish crew seen on deck in Pearl Harbor following their Sea of Japan patrol. The officers standing in second row are (left to right): Lt. Dan Decker, Lt. Dick Fellows, Lt.(jg) Bill Ware, Lt.(jg) Ed La Croix, Captain Bill Germershausen, Lt.(jg) Perry Wood, Warrant Machinist Dutch Falconer, Ens. Ray Dix and Ens. Harry Buncke. Chief Carl Schmelzer later recalled that his "Exec insisted all hands be in uniform" for this picture for the first time. *Hugo Lundquist collection, courtesy of Jeanne Lundquist.*

ping sunk or damaged in their unprecedented romp through the Sea of Japan.

Captain Bill Germershausen would be awarded the Navy Cross for the fifth patrol. The citation read in part that he had "directed his vessel deep into the shallow water of an enemy harbor to launch torpedo and gun attacks which resulted in the sinking of six hostile ships and four small craft for a total of 26,050 tons."

Due to his successful patrol, Germershausen was able to award commendations to other officers and enlisted men for their key roles in bringing the boat home once again from a highly successful patrol. Warrant Officer Dutch Falconer received a Bronze Star Medal for "showing skillful ability at his post of junior officer of the deck."

In his patrol report, he gave high marks to Dick Wright:

> Much of the credit for the success of this patrol is due to the devotion to duty and unquenchable fighting spirit of the executive officer, Lieutenant R. M. Wright, USN. Lieutenant Wright possesses to a high degree that quality which is necessary for

USS Spadefish Fifth Patrol Summary	
Patrol Area:	Sea of Japan
Time Period:	29 May - 4 July 1945
Number of Men Aboard:	87 (77 enlisted and 10 officers)
Total Days on Patrol:	39
Days on Station:	20
Days Submerged:	11
Miles Steamed:	9,949.8 miles
Fuel Used:	109,570 gallons
Number of Torpedoes Fired:	24
Ships Sunk, ComSubPac credit:	6 ships/26,100 tons
JANAC Postwar Credit:	5 ships/8,578 tons
Total sinkings, all size ships:	9 ships/11,321 tons (plus one 10,982-ton Russian freighter, *Transbalt*)

success in submarine warfare—an overwhelming desire to destroy Japs. He is recommended for early command of a fleet submarine.

Dick Wright, making only his first patrol aboard *Spadefish*, was proud of his ship's success in the Sea of Japan. "That was a big patrol of the war—the last big patrol—and I felt lucky to have been in on that."[27]

Admiral Lockwood's staff and members of the press gathered at the Pearl Harbor Sub Base to welcome back the "Hellcats" wolf pack on 4 July 1945. Lined up from left to right are *Flying Fish, Spadefish, Tinosa, Bowfin* and *Skate. U.S. Navy photo, courtesy of Thomas Miller.*

22

"Cease Offensive Operations"

Refit and Pre-Sixth Patrol   *4 July-2 September, 1945*

Returning to Pearl Harbor for R&R for the first time in nine months was cause enough to celebrate. The additional euphoria of being greeted by the press to celebrate an historic mission gave the *Spadefish* crew added energy to burn. Submarine Division 102 put a relief crew aboard while the officers and crew departed for Honolulu and the Royal Hawaiian Hotel. Instead of the customary two weeks of leave, Admiral Lockwood gave the Hellcat boats three weeks of R&R in Hawaii. "The Fourth of July celebration at the Royal Hawaiian Hotel that night was rather wet," recalled Captain Germershausen.[1]

Chief Boats Eimermann, who had "fifteen gallons of 180 proof in my room," soon became a popular person to visit. Among the eager visitors was one of the junior officers, whom the chiefs challenged to drink straight shots of the hard liquor. Before the night was out, Eimermann, along with Chief Paul Majoue, had to take this officer "each by an arm and drag him" back to his room to sleep it off. Thad Barton and Whitey Harbison, both sporting brand new cowboy boots, posed for pictures on the roof of the Royal Hawaiian with Dick Gamby and Harry Brenneis.

Gunner's mate Bernie Massar managed to buy four bottles of whiskey from a CPO who was hawking them for $20 a bottle. He sold three and kept one for himself. "Later, Red Dunleavy and I went looking for the chief to buy more. We couldn't find him, but ended up in the officers' section of the hotel. At one room, we were invited in by the officers from another boat and joined their party. They had the bathtub full of iced beer."

The parties were wild for those who indulged. Some non-drinkers, such as Chief Neal Pike, found other ways to pass their time on the island. Electrician Al La Rocca, another non-drinker, met up with his brother-in-law, who was stationed at Hawaii with the Army. "While the other guys were hitting the bars and getting arrested, I just toured the island," La Rocca said.

During the crew's R&R period, there was a big ship's party complete with hula dancers in a house with gardens on the other side of Oahu. "There was a 10 p.m. curfew," recalled Jim Cole. "We had buses to take us back to the Royal Hawaiian. We got wound up pretty good and a group of us missed the last bus." Realizing they had missed their last ride back to the Pink Palace, the *Spadefish* sailors set out on foot. Along the hike, one beer-toting crewman walked past a fire call box and pulled the alarm. "Fire trucks responded and, as they went by, he threw the bottle at a fire truck," recalled Bernie Massar. "Shore patrol wagons also answered and started to pick up crew members walking along the road."

"I suggested we jump over the wall to hide. Instead, the reaction was to go along with the Shore Patrol and get a free ride back to the hotel." The *Spadefish* sailors were packed into the overcrowded van. "I made a suggestion, at the next stop and pick-up, when the door opened, we should jump out and overturn the van and run. Evidently, the SP's heard me and when the door opened, they were standing with drawn .45s. So, we all went to the brig."

Torpedoman Wallace McMahon didn't make it past the shore patrol either. "Never try to hide in a sugar cane field," he said. "Every move you make, it makes an awful loud noise. We spent a few hours in the brig, but the Exec came and got us out."

Jim Cole and his buddy managed to avoid the SPs. "We were carrying half a case of beer from the party. We saw them getting picked up and we hid." Cole and his crewmate eventually hitched a ride into town aboard an Army truck, arriving just at curfew time. "So, now we're screwed—in downtown Honolulu with all this beer, it's almost ten o'clock and we've got no way to get to Waikiki Beach!" said Cole.

In desperation, they flagged down a cab. "When it pulls up, who's in the back but one of our electrician's mates, Roy Moody, with a Hawaiian girl!" They made it to the Royal Hawaiian's gates just as some SPs were pulling up. "We were the only two of our bunch that didn't make the brig that night," laughed Cole. "As soon as the SPs left, we went back outside and sat down on the curb with our beer."

"At the brig, the most unruly were put in a padded cell," said Massar. One man shouted, "You can't do that to my buddy!" He, too, was added to the special cell, until Dick Wright eventually arrived to straighten everything out. "We were eventually taken back to the hotel, minus some watches and money from our wallets, taken by the brig personnel."

Upon returning to the Royal Hawaiian, "most of us were upset, needless to say," recalled Massar. When he returned to the room he shared with Red Dunleavy, Buck Miller and Ken Sigworth—number 488—he busted many of the slots out of the door in frustration. When

Spadefish plankowners viewed on deck at Pearl Harbor, taken early August 1945 following fifth patrol.

Front row, left to right: Tom Miller, Bernie Massar, Hugo Lundquist (with Luau), Torr Riley, Tony Dunleavy, and Chief Charles Griffith.
2nd row: Chief Paul Majoue, Chief Emerson Ordway, Ken Sigworth, John Brewer, Melvin Mullen, Billy Pigman (white hat), Maurice Noonan (white hat), and Ken Powers (white hat).
3rd row: Chief Neal Pike, Joe Harbison (partially obscured), Len Dependahl, Vic Holeman, Dick Gamby, Joe Case (white hat), Warren Asher, Wallace McMahon, and Chief John Peel (partially obscured).
4th row, standing: Irv Kreinbring, John Nesnee, Lt. Dan Decker, Lt.(jg) Perry Wood, Warrant Officer Dutch Falconer, Andy Olah (white hat holding corner of flag), Thad Barton, Ed Graf and Roy Moody. *Top:* Jim Schuett seated and Emery Kreher holding battle flag, standing. *Courtesy of Bernie Massar.*

he checked out on 19 July, the hotel thanked him with a bill for the damage. Massar finally went to sleep. The next day, he and the gun crew were to report for a three-day instruction on 40mm guns at Barbers Point. The two new 40mms would replace *Spadefish*'s old 20mms. After the three days of training, Massar returned to his room to retrieve his ship's whites and found that his broken door had been repaired. Noting a guard standing by his floor, he asked what was up. "He told me that some gunner's mate was raising hell on the floor and that I should watch out for him," said Massar. "I explained that I was that gunner's mate!"

While the crew raised hell during the first few nights back, Admiral Lockwood and his submarine skippers held several meetings. Barney Sieglaff had secured the base theater for the event. Lockwood and his staff first debriefed the eight commanders on the Sea of Japan patrol, along with officers from Naval Intelligence. More subs were scheduled to go into the Sea of Japan, and everyone wanted all the details. Then, the admiral held a long press conference in the theater. Each submarine skipper was present to answer questions. The reporters were free to question Lockwood and all eight skippers, although their stories were delayed several weeks from being published for security reasons.[2]

Captain Germershausen related *Spadefish*'s adventures in stealing up on the Japanese harbor in search of shipping and in sinking three ships in her first night of attacks. He also related the trawlers and sampan his boat had destroyed with her deck gun. What he did not convey to the reporters was his own ire at Commander Hydeman for not allowing *Spadefish* to continue to attack targets with her deck gun during the last days in the Sea of Japan. Whereas Germershausen's noted "limiting factor" for not sinking more ships on the fourth patrol had been poor torpedo performance, his noted limiting factor on the fifth patrol was his "operation order."

Germershausen was sore at his wolf pack commander for trading patrol areas with his boat and for refusing to allow *Spadefish* to shoot up any more sampans after she had run out of torpedoes. So, after a few drinks one night at the Royal Hawaiian, he decided to enlist some volunteers to pay Captain Hydeman a visit. Joined by one of his tall, husky junior officers, Germershausen—as recalled by Wallace McMahon—"came up to our room one morning at the Royal and asked for volunteers to go down and visit Comdr. Hydeman." Bernie Massar also recalled his skipper's mission.

Spadefish undergoing refit in drydock. Courtesy of Bernie Massar.

Captain Germershausen visited the *Spadefish* crew's hotel rooms and requested us to follow him to the *Sea Dog*'s rooms. Tom Miller and I were chosen, along with the biggest crew members. The Captain said we were going to have "blows" with the crew. He had a bottle of booze with him. He knocked on one of the *Sea Dog*'s door. When it was opened up, he stated that the crew was not at fault with the exchanging of patrol areas. The officers were. The captain did offer a drink to the *Sea Dog* crew at our visit prior to moving on. He headed to the officers' quarters to even the score. This is when some of us decided we were not about to tangle with officers.[3]

Although the crewmen scattered, Germershausen and his junior officer soon found Earl Hydeman and one of his big officers in the hallway. Chief of the boat Eimermann later heard that Hydeman "had his big boy over there. He comes up to our guy and sticks one in his gut, and our boy says, 'That's it?'" According to Jim Cole, the *Spadefish* officer then "hit the other officer and drove him out of the elevator." In the ensuing brawl, Captain Germershausen broke the fifth metacarpal in his hand and would later have it set in a cast. To protect their skipper, the crew managed to keep the whole confrontation very hush-hush.[4]

The three weeks of R&R at Hawaii helped everyone unwind. Buck Miller was amazed to find that submarine sailors could be picked out just by their smell. "Bernie Massar, Ken Sigworth, Reds Dunleavy and I went to the Air Force Base in Honolulu in clean dungarees, freshly showered, and feeling as great as youth could ever feel," wrote Miller. Upon stopping at a soda stand, they were asked, "You're off submarines, right?"[5]

Miller was amazed, as none of his group had rates, markings or the telltale dolphins on their clothing. "We had no I.D. whatsoever showing, so we asked him, 'How do you know we're off subs?'"

"There's a certain smell about sub sailors," was the reply.

"We were crushed," recalled Miller. "That diesel oil must have been part of our skin."

ComSubPac's staff was busy during this time using the intelligence from the freshly returned Hellcat submarines to prepare the next round of submarines that would enter the Sea of Japan. The next seven boats Admiral Lockwood sent out in late July were *Stickleback, Pargo, Piper, Torsk, Sennet, Jallao* and *Pogy*. Each sub made an independent run through the minefields and operated in the Sea of Japan until V-J Day. Lieutenant Decker's younger brother, EM3c Richard W. Decker, was aboard the FM-equipped *Jallao* for this patrol. She managed to sink a 5,795-ton freighter on 11 August, two days after the second atomic bomb had been dropped.[6]

The *Spadefish* crew had no idea how close the end of the war was as they returned from their parties ashore. The ship still had thirty-eight men aboard who had made all five war patrols, a rarity in the submarine force with the required transfers. Beginning 26 July, a number of *Spadefish*'s plank owners were moved on to other assignments, including CBM Boats Eimermann, CGM Shaky Jake Lewis, CMoMM Rebel Rewold, CEM Carl Schmelzer, CPhM Victor Ives, EM2c Dick Bassett, TM1c Gus Cuthbertson, MoMM2c Nick Pelliciari, and RM1c Mike Sergio. In Eimermann's place, one of the new senior chief petty officers reporting aboard, CPhM Robert Gillespie, took his job as chief of the boat. The wardroom lost a plankowner, Lt.(jg) Bill Ware, as well as Lt. Dick Fellows. In their place, Lt.(jg) James D. Wall reported aboard.

Also departing was CCS Francis Scherman, who had been a key member of Shaky Jake's 5-inch gun crew. The new chief commissary steward coming aboard was Louis Strong, who had commissioned the new submarine *Torsk* and just made her first patrol. Chief Strong was one who never went through the regular sub school but had instead qualified aboard the *S-31*, operating out of New Caledonia. Strong had switched to submarines in 1943 after surviving the sinking of two different destroyers, *Benham* off Guadalcanal and *Gwin* off Kolombangara.

Fireman 1c Wayne Greening, a farm boy from Quanah, Texas, came aboard from the submarine tender *Sperry* to join *Spadefish*'s electrical gang. "They probably expected a great big Texan when I reported aboard, but I was just five foot seven," he said. "The ship had just come out of repairs and the crew had come back aboard from a luau at the Royal Hawaiian."

When he reported aboard to Lieutenant Commander Wright, the newly promoted Exec, Greening found that his boat was preparing to go through degaussing near Ford Island. "They literally ran a big cable around the boat to remove static electricity, so that we could penetrate minefields," he explained. One of Greening's buddies in the electrical gang was another new hand to *Spadefish*, EM3c Everett Shearer Jr., who had previously served aboard Dick O'Kane's *Tang* through her fourth patrol. "Everett got off her right before she was lost on her next patrol," recalled Greening. "His hair nearly turned white when he found out about her loss."

The transfer of the senior torpedoman in the after room, Vernon Kite, was filled by TM1c Willard Battenfield, who had made six war patrols aboard *Pogy*. "I was serving on the destroyer *Ralph Talbot* when the Japanese bombed Pearl Harbor on December 7, 1941. So, I was in Pearl Harbor when the war ended and when it had started."

With the transfer of Chief Lewis, *Spadefish* received GM1c Bill Noblit, who had made seven runs on the successful *Silversides*, as her leading gunner. While in drydock, the ship had been fitted with an additional 5-inch, 25 caliber deck gun, placed forward of the conning tower. She now sported one forward and one aft and would require two gun crews. "Torpedo targets were getting scarce for subs, so we they put more guns on us to prepare us to go after smaller targets that were not worth a torpedo," said gunner Bernie Massar. "We were to add 100 more rounds of 5-inch shells aboard, for a total of 200 rounds." *Spadefish*'s 20mm bridge guns were replaced with more powerful 40mm mounts. With the two deck guns, Massar was slated to move up to after 5-inch gun captain, while Noblit was to be gun captain of the new forward 5-inch gun.

During the refit period, Massar, GM3c Maurice Noonan and Lt.(jg) Perry Wood had gone through special training on the new guns and other ideas aimed at destroying smaller Japanese vessels. Among the special training they received was a flamethrower school put on by the Marines. "We were supposed to draw alongside and squirt the sampan with the flamethrower," recalled Massar. "Instead of the boarding party going aboard sampans and risking injury, we were to use the flamethrower to set it aflame. They mounted a new flamethrower aboard *Spadefish*." Lt.(jg) Wood and Massar also attended underwater damage control school. "I had always wanted to get into deep sea diving. We put on a diving helmet and we'd work underwater," said Massar.

Spadefish spent two weeks of training in preparation for her next war patrol. Several Marines came aboard for the trials to help the gunner's mates practice with their new flamethrower equipment. She was preparing to make another patrol into the Sea of Japan when news

Spadefish received an additional 5"/.25 deck gun and two 40mm Bofors in preparation for her sixth war patrol. Seated at the new 40mm on *Spadefish*'s cigarette deck are Ken Powers (left) and Jim Cole. Standing behind them are Buck Miller (left) and Bernie Massar. *Courtesy of Bernie Massar.*

came of the first atomic bomb being dropped on Hiroshima on 6 August 1945. "We were loaded and literally on our way out to patrol the next day when we got word of the atomic bomb," remembered Wayne Greening. "That held us up for two days while Naval Intelligence monitored events." On 9 August, Nagasaki was blasted with another A-bomb. The subs continued to operate, and *Spadefish* was prepared to go back into the Sea of Japan.

Rumors circulated about the war's end. The 11 August issue of the *Honolulu Star-Bulletin* boldly announced "SIRENS WILL SIGNAL V-J DAY." That night, a false alarm that war was officially over started the V-J Day festivities. Across the harbor, ships erupted into celebratory gunfire. Chief Neal Pike was ashore in the bleachers watching a ball game when the news made the rounds. "Every ship in the harbor started shooting," he recalled. Ships opened up with their heavy guns all over Pearl Harbor. "Shells were flying all over the place. I said, 'To hell with this!' I went down to the *Spadefish*, went aboard and got into my bunk. I had an inch of steel around me there. I figured I had lived through the war, and I wasn't about to get shot on armistice night."

Also in Pearl Harbor preparing for another patrol was Commander George Grider's successful boat *Flasher*. Even as every admiral in the harbor was flashing orders to the warships to stop their unauthorized pyrotechnics show, Grider and one of his crewmen joined the fun by firing flares from the signal gun on *Flasher*'s cigarette deck.[7]

By morning, however, it became clear that negotiations continued with Japan. *Spadefish* continued to prepare for her next war patrol. *Torsk* was the last U.S. submarine to sink Japanese ships in World

War II with torpedoes, as she destroyed two patrols boats in the Sea of Japan on 14 August. Five hours later, *Balao* became the last U.S. submarine of the war to sink a Japanese vessel with her guns. Two hours later, at 1700 on 14 August 1945, President Harry Truman announced the news of Japan's unconditional surrender. "Cease offensive operations against Japanese forces," was passed among the fleet by Admiral Nimitz. "They called us to quarters on deck and announced that the war was over," recalled Willard Battenfield.

Fireman Jim Cole had the below decks duty watch when the news spread about the war's end on the evening of 14 August. He went around waking everyone up to break the news to them, including the Exec, Dick Wright. "I don't know if he thought I was spoofing or what," recalled Cole. "I told him the war was over. The first thing he said was, 'It better be over, or it's over for you!'"

"Of course, all hell broke loose," recalled motormac Dick Gamby. "Everybody was happy."

Ensign Harry Buncke recalled that there were several false alarms before the official word came of the war's end. "There were three days of constant parties," he remembered. "You could walk out any place, on any street in Honolulu, and the front door was open. The parties were open. The war was over and everyone was just whooping it up."

Fifteen years later, Buncke visited the Royal Hawaiian Hotel with his wife and kids during Christmas time for a big submarine reunion party. He was amused when the German maitre d' recognized the wildhearted diesel boat sailors and remarked to him, "You guys really destroyed this place!"

Charles Griffith, Carl Schmelzer, Dutch Falconer and several others went into one bar. "We didn't know it, but they had free beer," recalled Griffith. His buddy Schmelzer "was tight with a buck." When the beers came, Schmelzer quickly excused himself with, "I've gotta go to the head, guys."

The second round came with the same story. After a couple more rounds, his buddies finally stopped him from heading for the bathroom. "Wait a minute, now, Schmelzer. It's your turn!"

With beer only ten cents apiece, he threw down a dollar and proclaimed, "I've really gotta got to the head this time."

When he returned, he demanded, "Where's my change?"

"Schmelzer, it's been free beer all day!" his buddies exploded.

"He went off like a rocket!" recalled Griffith.

On 25 August 1945, as the United States worked out the details of a formal surrender ceremony with Japan, *Spadefish* was recognized for her highly successful first two war patrols. Captain Germershausen had the entire ship's company form on deck for an awards ceremony, which this time included Admiral Lockwood presenting the boat with the Presidential Unit Citation—which was given by Secretary of the Navy James Forrestal for the President of the United States. *Spadefish* was awarded the coveted PUC "for extraordinary heroism in action during the first and second war patrols against enemy Japanese forces in the restricted waters of the Pacific."

Orders soon came for the large number of submarines idly sitting in Pearl Harbor to begin returning Stateside. Departing on 28 August was *Flasher*, followed by *Sea Owl*, *Flying Fish*, *Finback*, and *Bowfin* on 29 August. On 30 August, *Atule*, *Whale*, *Cero* and *Gunnel* departed the Hawaiian Islands for home.[8]

During the final days in port, several other *Spadefish* sailors received transfers. The new senior gunner's mate, Bill Noblit, was transferred to other duty, now that *Spadefish* would not be using her second 5-incher or flamethrowers against sampans. Bernie Massar now became the leading gunner's mate aboard. Lt.(jg) Perry Wood received transfer orders, but managed to work out a deal with Captain Germershausen to ride the boat home to his new duty as a passenger. Left behind at Pearl was Boats Eimermann, the chief of the boat during all five patrols. Transferred weeks earlier, he felt as if he was being left behind as his shipmates prepared to head home. Although he understood his need to move on to other duties, he felt "they could have at least taken me back to the States first!"

Spadefish backed away from the Pearl Harbor Submarine Base, steamed down the channel past Ford Island and headed out from Hawaii toward California. The date was 2 September 1945. Across the Pacific on this very day, Admiral Lockwood was standing aboard the battleship *Missouri* in Tokyo Bay for the surrender ceremony of Japan. Also anchored in Tokyo Bay was the submarine tender *Proteus*, moored to which were several Japanese submarines large enough to carry floatplanes. Two former *Spadefish* sailors, electrician Jack Gallagher and signalman Al Gibson, were both aboard *Proteus* and they proudly watched the hostilities against Japan come to a close officially.

As Oahu faded over the horizon, the *Spadefish* crew had thoughts of loved ones and liberty on their minds. She had remained at Pearl for almost two months since ending her successful fifth patrol. "We were anxious to get home," said Chief Griffith. "We had been in Hawaii so long guys started thinking we were going to become the pineapple Navy!"

Even more welcome than the sight of Hawaii fading away was the appearance of the Golden Gate Bridge days later. She was at long last

War is over for "Lu" and "Weed!" *Spadefish* mascots Seaweed and Luau and relaxing at the Royal Hawaiian Hotel in July 1945. *Courtesy of Joe Marasco.*

returning home, to the Mare Island Navy Yard. It was back to the yard that had built her and to the wives and families that had been left behind fifteen months previously.

Of the original crew who had placed *Spadefish* into commission, there remained only two officers—Dan Decker and passenger Perry Wood—and 26 enlisted men. During the return trip from Hawaii, Captain Germershausen had Decker and Lt.(jg) Jim Wall write up an unofficial "Ship's History," based on the patrol reports. Although completed on 1 October 1945, it would remain classified for some time. In this writeup, *Spadefish*'s return to California is triumphantly documented. "None were more proud when the boat sailed up Mare Island Strait—the war over, the record complete—than these men who had watched the ship from conception to near retirement."[9]

Returning to Mare Island, *Spadefish* was one of the top submarines to return that the shipyard had built. Arriving in port that day, there was none of the fanfare that had greeted them after the Sea of Japan patrol. "It was raining, and there were only a few line handlers on the dock," recalled Jim Cole. "It wasn't much of a greeting!"

The crew began taking well-earned thirty-day leaves upon return to Mare Island, and this more than made up for the lack of any large scale celebration. They were a veteran crew with a record that could be matched by few.

Spadefish had turned in two of the Top 10 war patrols in terms of enemy tonnage sunk. Once the Joint Army-Navy Assessment Committee (JANAC) reviewed sinking claims for all submarines, they would report that of the 258 American submarines participating in World War II, only five were successful enough to sink more than twenty enemy ships weighing more than 500 tons. *Spadefish* was offi-

Spadefish returns to Mare Island after the war. This view was taken on 20 December 1945, approaching the Mare Island causeway. *Courtesy of Joe Marasco.*

cially tied for fourth place in this category. In terms of tonnage of enemy ships sunk, she was sixth best of the war.

Counting all enemy ships destroyed, including those by gunfire, the efficiency of *Spadefish* was astounding. Every war patrol made had been successful. She had sunk twenty-nine total Japanese vessels during her 220 days actually spent on war patrol. This meant that *Spadefish* sunk an enemy ship, on average, for every 7.59 days on patrol. *Tang*, another hot Mare Island boat, slightly edged *Spadefish* by downing an enemy ship on an average of every 7.52 days.

Other U.S. submarines ranked among the top twenty in total sinkings had spent as many as 701 days on patrols to amass their records. *Spadefish* and *Tang* were the only two submarines to sink more than twenty enemy ships in less than 250 days on patrol. Among the elite top twenty group, there was only one boat commissioned as late as 1944 to still rank among the ultra efficient, *USS Spadefish* (SS-411).

Charged at commissioning to "Spade 'Em Under," she had done just that—in record time!

Epilogue

Upon arrival at Mare Island, Chief Paul Majoue was inspired to do something for his shipmates. He had designed the latest version of the *Spadefish* battle flag, and decided to try and make copies for his fellow crewmen. "I went over to the Sail Loft with my dirty-looking, beat-up battle flag with 29 merchant Japanese flags and three man-of-war Japanese flags on it."

Majoue found the woman in charge of Mare Island's sail loft and immediately began negotiating with her. Showing her his *Spadefish* flag, he explained that he wanted her to make replicas of the original.

"Just make each one about two feet long, and let the height fall where it may. Like the signal flags, I want it on wool bunting. Now, I want eight flags made that are double-sided. Then I want 82 that–"

"What?" the lady snapped.

"Wait, wait," Majoue calmed her. "Let me finish!"

In return for making ninety copies of his *Spadefish* flag, Majoue bartered with the woman in charge. He promised each of her three seamstresses fifty pounds of coffee and a fifteen-pound canned ham. "In those days, coffee was like gold!" he recalled. For the supervisor, he offered her two 15-pound hams and 100 pounds of coffee.

"When do you want 'em?" she countered.

"Cumshaw" was the Navy term for how chief petty officers dodged bureaucracy. "Cumshaw is how the Navy is run outside of the orders," said Harry Buncke. "The chief petty officers are the guys who really handle things." So, with a little sly bartering with Navy rations, Hocks Majoue had his *Spadefish* flag replicas produced within a few days by the Mare Island Sail Loft. Several officers and chiefs received the six double-sided versions, while the remaining crew received the single-sided flags.

Many *Spadefish* veterans still have their flags framed at home. At least a couple have been donated to the Submarine Museum at New

London. Majoue gave the original *Spadefish* flag to an ailing ex-shipmate, torpedoman Don Bird, who had not been aboard when the copies were made. His wife Connie made a large hook rug replica of the original, which still hangs on the Majoue home wall.

Captain Germershausen was relieved in December 1945 to take command of the submarine *Razorback*. Lieutenant Commander Dick Wright assumed command of *Spadefish*. "My captain got transferred. That left me as commanding officer, which delighted me," recalled Wright. "But it was short lived because we were putting the ship out of commission."[1]

A final ship's party for the *Spadefish* crew was held 14 January 1946 at Spengers Ferry Boat in Benicia, California. The U.S. Navy found that there was simply a surplus of fleet submarines soon after the close of hostilities in World War II. *Spadefish* and many other ships were ordered to go into the "mothball" fleet, whereby their fighting ability would be preserved until the vessels were called into action again. This process involved deactivating her engines and laying up beside a sub tender in Tiburon Bay for a complete overhaul. "Putting *Spadefish* into mothballs was a terribly difficult job," related Ensign Buncke. "Every piece of equipment had to be cleaned up, tuned up and greased up for storage in case the ship had to be put back into service at some point."

Electrician's mate Al La Rocca recalled spending much time filing down copper contacts in the battery compartments. At least California offered recreation during off time. "We could take a motor launch into San Francisco for five cents to Market Street," he said.

The two ship's dogs, Luau and Seaweed, were quality entertainment during the days at Tiburon Bay. "They used to run around the conning tower and sometimes they'd slide off and plop into the water," recalled leading gunner's mate Bernie Massar. "Dog overboard!" someone would call. Due to swift currents in Tiburon Bay, one of the crew would run to the fantail and hold another man to reach down for the flailing dog. "We'd have to grab the damn dogs as they swam alongside the sub and fling them up on deck," said Massar. "Then, they would shake themselves off and run around again. It didn't bother them a bit."

The crew ended up offering Luau to electrician Jim Casey because of how much she favored him. "I got her crated up, got her shots and sent her back to Alabama to my sister," he said. Luau lived out her final days on Casey's sister's place in Alabama.[2]

On 3 May 1946, Lieutenant Commander Wright read the decommissioning papers as *Spadefish* was placed in reserve, just twenty-six months after she had been commissioned. Fourteen crewmen were still aboard who had helped to commission her and had made all of her war patrols: Thad Barton, Len Dependahl, Dick Gamby, Charles Griffith, Whitey Harbison, Vic Holeman, Hugo Lundquist, Bernie Massar, Buck Miller, Roy Moody, Maurice Noonan, Johnny Peel, K. C. Powers, and Ken Sigworth.

Following the decommissioning, final chief of the boat Robert Gillespie acquired Seaweed since he had orders to remain stationed at the Mare Island Dispensary. "He turned out to be quite a car chaser," recalled Gillespie. Radioman Joe Marasco said, "Seaweed took on a vehicle and lost." Gillespie was riding in his model A Ford pickup at the time with Seaweed with the windows open. "He spotted a dog running loose," wrote Gillespie. "I stopped at a used car lot on Midway Drive. He jumped out on a chase for the dog across the street and was struck and killed." According to Marasco, Seaweed was buried "in a weighted tool box since he was a veteran of three patrols. It was the closest thing to a burial at sea for Seaweed."[3]

Like many other proud World War II boats, *Spadefish* would lay in mothballs for more than twenty years. Plans came for her to be transferred to the Turkish Navy, but this never materialized. Her name was stricken from the Navy list on 1 April 1967 and she was sold for scrap for $50,180 to Union Minerals & Alloys Corporation of New York on 17 October 1969.[4]

The Navy launched a second *Spadefish* in 1968 to carry on the original boat's proud name. More than thirty former SS-411 crewmen attended the 1969 commissioning of the nuclear-powered *Spadefish* (SSN-668). *Official U.S. Navy photo, courtesy of Carl Schmelzer collection.*

Veterans of the World War II diesel *Spadefish* gathered at the commissioning of the nuclear-powered *Spadefish*. Front: Don Bird (with paper in hand), Louis "Red" Chiavacci (in sunglasses), unknown, Frank Alvis, Nick Pelliciari (head turned), Tom "Buck" Miller, Ken Sigworth, Perry Wood (with bow tie), Harry Brenneis (with beard), Warren "Pappy" Asher (with glasses), Captain Bill Germershausen, Bernie Massar, Wayne Powell, Ken Powers, Don Scholle (kneeling), and Len Dependahl. Rear row: Olaf Olson, Emery Kreher, Jim Cole, Tony Dunleavy, Maurice Noonan, Hugo Lundquist and Dick Bassett. *Courtesy of Bernie Massar.*

Her name did not remain off the Navy list for long, however. The nuclear powered fast attack submarine *Spadefish* (SSN-668) was built by Newport News Shipbuilding and Drydock Company. Her keel was laid December 21, 1966, and she was launched May 15, 1968. The new *Spadefish* was commissioned 14 August 1969, and would serve for twenty-seven years. More than thirty original SS-411 *Spadefish* crewmen, including Captain Germershausen, were present for the commissioning of the nuclear *Spadefish*. Jim Cole actually went out on the new *Spadefish* for her sea trials and became the only man to serve aboard both *Spadefish* submarines. Bernie Massar and Emery Kreher was also present for the "nukie" *Spadefish*'s commissioning. It was there that Massar finally learned that Kreher had been responsible for rigging out the bow planes on the fourth patrol.

The new *Spadefish* was 292 feet long and displaced 4,600 tons submerged—twice that of the original *Spadefish*. Her primary wartime mission was to detect, track and destroy enemy submarines with her high-tech electronics and weapons systems. *Spadefish* veterans were guests aboard the nuclear *Spadefish* a number of times. Former officer

Jim Cole, seen aboard the nuclear-powered *Spadefish* in 1970, was the only crewman who had also served aboard the original diesel-powered World War II *Spadefish*. *Courtesy of Jim Cole.*

Dick Fellows attended a change of command ceremony for SSN-668 in April 1989 at the Norfolk Navy Yard. His former SS-411's top five finish in sinkings during the war meant something to the new *Spadefish* crew. "To substantiate this feeling of pride and inspiration by the 411, the 668 displays the 411 battle flag in the crew's mess," Fellows wrote after attending the ceremony.[5]

In 1996, *Spadefish* left Norfolk Naval Base on 24 May on her final deployment prior to inactivation and decommissioning. She made an around-the-world deployment that terminated in Puget Sound, Washington. During her career, the ship was deployed twenty times and twice supported national level joint military operations in Grenada in 1982 and Haiti in 1994.

The battle flag of the USS *Spadefish* (SS-411) was displayed aboard the "nukie" *Spadefish* since her commissioning. When *Spadefish* (SSN-668) was decommissioned, four SS-411 *Spadefish* veterans attended the decommissioning reception: Don Scholle, Olaf Olson, Dick Fellows and Jim Cole. Captain C. W. Puryear Jr. was the final commander of the nuclear *Spadefish* when she was decommissioned after 27 years of service. "The new crew, from the captain to the lowest rate, treated us with respect and awe over the accomplishments of the SS-411," recalled Jim Cole.[6] "The funny part of it is, we were in commission almost twenty-seven months before they put us in mothballs. They were in commission twenty-seven years, one year for every month we were in commission."

When the original *Spadefish* was preparing to go into mothballs in early 1946, many of her crewmen were given discharges. Bernie Massar did not yet have enough points to be discharged, so he stayed in the service long enough to help decommission the submarine *Aspro* after leaving *Spadefish*.

Some *Spadefish* veterans careered in the Navy after World War II. Jim Casey retired from the Navy as a chief electrician in 1961 after twenty years' service, mainly aboard submarines. Jim Cole also retired as a senior chief after twenty-five years between regular and reserve service. Don Bird also stayed in the Navy, serving on four other submarines after making *Spadefish*'s first two patrols. Fellow torpedoman Wallace McMahon ended up spending twelve years in submarines. Radford "Reb" Rewold put in twenty years in the Navy, serving through the Korean War. All of his service was aboard submarines. After his death, Rewold's ashes were scattered off the coast of San Diego by the nuclear powered submarine *Pogy* (SSN-637).

Pat Kelley put the new sub *Dogfish* in commission in 1946. Like Dutch Falconer aboard *Spadefish*, Kelley became a mustang, making warrant officer on *Dogfish*. He served in the Navy for thirty-two years, through a tour in Vietnam on river duty, and finally retired as a lieutenant commander. Charles Griffith also became a mustang and stayed in the Navy through 1960. Wallace McMahon stayed in the service but switched to the Air Force postwar, retiring in 1968.

Chief of the boat Willard "Boats" Eimermann stayed with the Navy until 1947, making eleven years in the service. He ran doughnut and bakery delivery routes for several years before getting on with American Motors, the company he eventually retired from in Milwaukee. Neal Pike had a long career in electronics and telecommunications, including research and development postwar in radar at MIT laboratories and work as a supervisory engineer for the Federal Communications Commission in Washington.

A large number of *Spadefish*'s crew members returned to their home towns after the war to pursue their individual careers. Motormac John Brewer returned to Brunswick, Georgia, where he made captain of the local National Guard and ran a Goodrich retail store for many years. Electrician Jack Gallagher worked for thirty-seven years as a telephone installer in Oakland, California. Torpedoman John Schumer

Veteran *Spadefish* torpedoman Bert Spiese meeting with author in October 2004 in Dallas, Texas.
Author's collection.

became a "pole climber," an electric lineman. Bert Spiese, another *Spadefish* torpedoman, worked almost forty years as a train conductor for a railroad company. Wayne Greening returned to farming in rural Quanah, Texas, and since has only "made one big move, about fifteen miles!"

Seaman Cameron Snider became a dentist and practiced in the Erie, Pennsylvania area for thirty-five years. Quartermaster Jim Fletcher went on to college after the war and became a lawyer in Kentucky. Electrician Billy Bob Pigman became a congressman in his home state of Oklahoma. Auxiliaryman Buck Miller dedicated a total of twenty-nine years of service to the Pennsylvania Building and Construction Trades Council and a total of forty-seven years to the Labor Movement, both locally and nationally.

Paul "Hocks" Majoue, *Spadefish*'s unofficial photographer, retired in his home state of Louisiana, where he continued shooting high school sports photos and other projects for many years. Radioman Tom O'Neil worked as a communications officer, coding and decoding messages at the United Nations and the Foreign Service Division. His international assignments included Beirut, Saigon, Paris and Helsinki, Finland.[7]

Electrician Al La Rocca retired from the Navy and returned to civilian life in New York. He has built a number of radio controlled model submarines, including a 1/48 scale model of his *Spadefish* which actually dives and surfaces, fires torpedoes and is equipped with sound effects. He and fellow submarine veteran Frank Chietro also spent two years constructing a 1/12 scale, 26 foot model fleet submarine model,

Dr. Harry Buncke, a former *Spadefish* officer, is now commonly known as the "father of microsurgery." The techniques he developed have enabled his doctors to transplant missing muscle tissue, bones, fingers, scalps, and even an eyelid that had been lost in a mauling. *Courtesy of Dr. Harry Buncke.*

appropriately named *Spadefish*, which they use for parades and other memorials.

Dan Decker was transferred from *Spadefish* at Mare Island to help commission the new boat *Sarda*. Upon returning to New London following *Sarda*'s shakedown cruise, Decker found his previous request for flight school had been approved. He was sent to Grand Prairie, Texas, for training and later served in a seaplane ASW squadron outfit in Bermuda. Decker retired from the Navy in 1964 as a commander. Bill Ware also retired from the Navy in 1957 as a commander. During one three-year duty as Personnel Officer at SubAd Mare Island, Ware's boss was none other than Captain Bill Germershausen.

Dick Fellows returned to work as an engineer with General Motors and later served with two other companies as a quality control engineer. Mustang Dutch Falconer remained in the Navy through 1955, serving as engineering officer aboard several ships and also recruiting in his home state of Iowa. Frank Alvis was employed by the Navy Department in the Pentagon, later retiring as a full commander.

Harry Buncke, the most junior officer on the fifth patrol, was married at Mare Island. "We both applied to medical school after we were married and put ourselves through on the GI bill," he said. His wife practiced dermatology, while Harry went into plastic surgery. He spent years of his life perfecting the technique of sewing blood vessels back together that were only one millimeter in size. His Buncke Clinic in San Francisco became the most experienced microsurgical transplantation and replantation center in the country, training doctors from around the world.

Dr. Buncke and his colleagues were the first surgeons to perform many microsurgical procedures, including the first great toe-to-thumb transplant in the U.S., the first successful scalp replant in the U.S., the first four-finger replant in the U.S., and the first successful tongue replant in the world. The recipient of many awards, Buncke is commonly called "the father of microsurgery." Most recently, he was awarded the Jacobson Innovation Award of the American College of Surgeons on June 11, 2004, for his innovations in the field of surgery.

Ted Ustick, the first *Spadefish* executive officer, commanded the submarine *Searaven* (SS-196) for five months during the war but *Searaven* was designated as a training boat at Pearl Harbor before Ustick could take her out on a war patrol. He then went on to command the submarine *Rock* until May 1946. "I was in command of the *Rock*, heading for the Sea of Japan, and was halfway past Wake Island when the first A-bomb was dropped," recalled Ustick. "I never got to fire a torpedo of my own before the war ended. I was always helping someone else firing torpedoes."[8] Ustick later commanded two more submarines, taught Marine Engineering at the Naval Academy for two years, commanded *USS Pictor* (AF-54) for one year, and worked for the Navy Department in Washington, D. C. before retiring as a captain in 1959.

George Cook, the second Exec, served as executive officer of *Remora* and *Tusk* (SS-426) before receiving command of his own sub, *Sea Owl* (SS-405) in April 1950. He retired as a captain after having held various staff positions and commanding submarine squadrons. In a strange twist of fate, Cook helped rescue *Spadefish*'s third Exec in a postwar accident.

Lieutenant Commander Cook was XO of the submarine *Tusk* on 25 August 1949 during a training exercise with sister submarine *Cochino* in the Barents Sea north of Norway and Siberia. The executive officer of *Cochino* was Lieutenant Commander Dick Wright, whose boat had been one of the first to receive a Guppy conversion, which allowed it to recharge its batteries without surfacing. "We were snorkeling, which means you have a very small part of the ship, about the size of a fire hydrant, above the surface of the water," Wright explained. The snorkel was submerged, causing the valve to snap shut and the diesel engines to begin pulling a suction on the air pressure within the boat. This was not too uncommon, except that a defective switch caused a hydrogen explosion.[9]

A deadly fire resulted in the forward battery compartment below the officers' quarters. *Cochino* came to the surface to fight the fire, but the forward battery continuing generating hydrogen to the after battery, making the fight almost impossible. Wright nearly lost his life trying to race in and shut off the fire's source.

> I did try to go into that compartment and open a battery disconnect switch, which would have terminated the generation of hydrogen. But just as I got inside of the compartment, there was

another explosion. It blew me out of the battery room and burned all or most of the clothes off of me.

Wright was horribly burned and *Cochino* had no morphine or sterile ointment aboard to treat him with. The torpedomen in the after room where he was carried used torpedo grease to cover his severe burns. "That's not known for being antiseptic, so in addition to the burns, they saw to it that I was thoroughly contaminated with torpedo grease," recalled Wright.

Tusk pulled alongside *Cochino* late in the day and the *Cochino* crew crossed over a plank to their sister sub shortly before their own boat sank from the explosions and fires that had ravaged her. Dick Wright spent fifteen months in hospitals for rehabilitation and skin grafts. For his bravery in trying to save *Cochino*, he was later awarded the Navy and Marine Corps Medal for Valor. Wright, *Spadefish*'s final skipper, eventually retired as a captain in 1969, after having commanded another submarine, two destroyers, a troop transport, and a submarine squadron in New London, among other assignments.

Spadefish's second skipper, Bill Germershausen, also retired with the rank of captain, on 1 July 1954. Following his brief postwar command of the submarine *Razorback*, he was detached in March 1946 for six months duty under postgraduate instruction in Naval Administration at Stanford University. Germershausen served as Captain of the Yard at the U.S. Naval Station, Pago Pago, Tutuila, from September 1946 until May 1948. He was also assistant governor of American Samoa during this time.[10]

Germershausen returned to the United States and served in Washington as Assistant Director, Island Governments until May 1950. He served as Operations Officer of Submarine Division Two aboard his flagship *Sarda* for one year and then served a year as Commander, Submarine Division 21. During the mid-1950s, he was a staff officer at Mare Island, an instructor at the Naval War College in Newport, Rhode Island, and commanded the *USS Castor* (AKS-1) for one year. On 23 August 1957, Germershausen was detached for duty in Korea as Chief of Staff and Aide to the Chief, U.S. Naval Advisory Group, Republic of Korea. After retiring from the Navy, Bill Germershausen spent his remaining years in San Jose, California. He had received both the Navy Cross and the Bronze Star Medal with Combat "V" for his two patrols commanding *Spadefish*.

Spadefish's first skipper, Gordon Underwood, had been assigned to the Bureau of Ships in March 1945, following his third command patrol. He was Force Engineer on ComSubPac's staff from March

USS Underwood (FFG-36), named for Captain Gordon W. Underwood, first skipper of *Spadefish*. *Official U.S. Navy photo, courtesy of USS Underwood.*

1947 to February 1950. He spent more than three years at the San Francisco Naval Ship Yard, first as Repair Superintendent and then as Captain. Underwood subsequently held commands in Guam, Charleston and Washington during the next decade. He retired from the Navy in July 1962 when he was diagnosed with colon cancer. After treatment, he worked in the defense industry until his retirement.

During World War II, Gordon Underwood was the third best U.S. submarine skipper in terms of enemy tonnage destroyed. He was awarded the Navy Cross for his first patrol in command of *Spadefish* and gold stars were added for each of his next two patrols as he earned additional Navy Crosses. Captain Underwood resided in San Jose, California, until his death in 1978. In his honor, the Navy commissioned the guided missile frigate *USS Underwood* (FFG-36) on 29 January 1983.

Perhaps the Navy will once again commission another *Spadefish* in honor of the proud original World War II warrior. Until then, her fighting spirit lives on in her remaining crewmen, who stay in contact with each other through reunions and their newsletters, dubbed the "Luau" in honor of the original ship's mascot. The first issues were edited by former *Spadefish* radioman K. C. Powers. After his death,

Although slightly creased, this copy of the *Spadefish* battle flag, belonging to Joe Marasco, is one of 90 copies made at Mare Island in 1945 under the direction of CRM Paul Majoue. The five stars above the fish represent the five successful World War II patrols of *Spadefish*. The Japanese "meatball" flags indicate the twenty-nine merchant ships that *Spadefish* claimed to have destroyed. The tri-colored pennant below represents the Presidential Unit Citation awarded for the ship's first two patrols. The three Japanese "rising sun" ensigns at the bottom of the flag indicates three warships sunk by *Spadefish*, including the aircraft carrier *Jinyo*. Photo by Michael Johnson.

former officer Dick Fellows was temporary editor until Buck Miller took charge of "Luau," which he and Peggy Ellis continue to write four times a year.

Spadefish earned four battle stars for her World War II service. For her first two patrols, she earned the Presidential Unit Citation. She was officially credited by JANAC with sinking twenty-one Japanese vessels for 88,091 tons. Paul Majoue's final battle flag shows thirty-two kills for *Spadefish*, twenty-nine merchant ships and three men of war.

In regards to this wartime claim, *Spadefish* certainly did damage or sink at least thirty-two ships. Using Commander John Alden's more modern research compilation in addition to the original JANAC cred-

Spadefish 1989 crew reunion in Reno. *Seated left to right:* Wallace McMahon, Tom O'Neil, Don Scholle, Don Bird and Jim Casey. *Middle row officers, left to right:* Dick Fellows, Bill Ware, Ted Ustick, Captain Bill Germershausen, Dan Decker, and Perry Wood. Standing, left to right: Paul Majoue, Ed Graf, Bernie Massar, Tony Dunleavy, Pat Kelley, Si Barnes, Roy Moody, Robert Jackson, Neal Pike, Buck Miller, and Jim Cole. *Courtesy of Thomas Miller.*

its, it appears that *Spadefish* sank a total of thirty ships during World War II, twenty-nine Japanese and one neutral Russian freighter. In addition, she damaged two other ships

In one of his earliest "Luau" newsletters, *Spadefish* veteran Ken Powers offered some interesting facts about his ship.

> None of the 155 men who sailed in *Spadefish* for one or more patrols was lost in action either on her or on any other ship.
>
> *USS Spadefish* (SS-411), tied for 4th in number sunk and 6th in tonnage sunk, was the only U.S. submarine with a hull number above 400 to be included in the Top 25 in ships sunk and tonnage category.
>
> *Spadefish* was the only submarine commissioned in 1944 to be in the Top 25 in terms of number of enemy ships sunk.
>
> All U.S. World War II submarines with hull numbers ending in eleven were Top 25'ers in terms of tonnage of enemy ships sunk: *Gudgeon* (SS-211), *Archerfish* (SS-311) and *Spadefish* (SS-411).

To these statistics can be added the tremendous efficiency rate of *Spadefish*. Among the top producers, *Barb*, *Tang* and *Spadefish* were the most effective U.S. submarines in operation during the war. Viewing sinking efficiency by number of total days out on war patrol, these three boats managed to sink, on average, an enemy ship for each week on patrol. *Spadefish*, by sinking thirty ships in 220 days on patrol, topped the efficiency list by destroying a ship every seven and one-third days.

Appendix A
Top U.S. Submarines of World War II by Tonnage Sunk (JANAC Credit)

Top Submarines By Tonnage of Ships Sunk
(According to JANAC figures.)

	Boat	Skippers	JANAC Tonnage
1.	Flasher	R. T. Whitaker, G. W. Grider	100,231
2.	Rasher	Hutchinson, Laughon, Munson	99,901
3.	Barb	Waterman, Fluckey	96,628
4.	Tang *	O'Kane	93,824
5.	Silversides	Burlingame, Coye, Nichols	90,080
6.	Spadefish	Underwood, Germershausen	88,091
7.	Trigger *	Benson, Dornin, Harlfinger, Connole	86,552
8.	Drum	Rice, McMahon, Williamson, Rindskopf	80,580
9.	Jack	Dykers, Krapf, Fuhrman	76,687
10.	Snook *	Triebel, Browne	75,473
11.	Tautog	Willingham, Sieglaff, Baskett	72,606
12.	Seahorse	Cutter, Wilkins	72,529
13.	Guardfish	Klakring, Ward	72,424
14.	Seawolf *	Warder, Gross	71,609
15.	Gudgeon *	Grenfell, Stovall, Post	71,047
16.	Sealion II	Reich, Putman	68,297
17.	Bowfin	Willingham, Griffith, Corbus, Tyree	67,882
18.	Thresher	Anderson, Millican, Hull, MacMillan, Middleton	66,172
19.	Tinosa	Daspit, Weiss, Latham	64,655
20.	Grayback *	Saunders, Stephan, Moore	63,835

* Boat lost in action during World War II.

Appendix B
Top U.S. Submarines of World War II by Ships Sunk (JANAC Credit)

Top Submarines By Number of Ships Sunk
(According to JANAC figures.)

	Boat	Ships Sunk	No. of Patrols	Total Days on Patrol	JANAC Efficiency (sinking per)
1.	Tautog	26	13	584	22.46 days
2.	Tang *	24	5	203	8.46 days
3.	Silversides	23	13	701	30.48 days
4.	Flasher	21 (tie)	6	330	15.71 days
5.	Spadefish	21 (tie)	5	220	10.48 days
6.	Seahorse	20	8	407	20.35 days
7.	Wahoo *	20	7	253	12.65 days
8.	Guardfish	19	12	662	34.84 days
9.	Rasher	18	8	390	21.67 days
10.	Seawolf *	18	15	522	29.00 days
11.	Trigger *	18	12	552	30.67 days
12.	Barb	17	12	545	32.06 days
13.	Snook *	17	9	415	24.41 days
14.	Thresher	17	15	596	35.06 days
15.	Bowfin	16	9	390	24.38 days
16.	Harder *	16	6	220	13.75 days
17.	Pogy	16	10	490	30.63 days
18.	Sunfish	16	11	540	33.75 days
19.	Tinosa	16	11	443	27.69 days
20.	Drum	15	13	646	43.07 days

* Boat lost in action during World War II.

Appendix C
Efficiency Rating of the Top U.S. Submarines of World War II
(JANAC's Top 20 Boats Re-ranked by Total Enemy Sinkings)

Most Efficient Submarines by Frequency of Enemy Vessels Destroyed
(Includes smaller ships destroyed by submarine's gunfire and other ships not counted post-war by JANAC analysis.)

	Boat	Total Ships Sunk [2]	No. of Patrols	Total Days on Patrol	Sinking Efficiency (sinking per)
1.	*Spadefish*	30	5	220	7.33 days
2.	*Barb*	73	12	545	7.43 days
3.	*Tang* [1]	27	5	203	7.52 days
4.	*Wahoo* [1]	26	7	253	9.73 days
5.	*Bowfin*	38	9	390	10.26 days
6.	*Flasher*	28	6	330	11.78 days
7.	*Harder* [1]	18	6	220	12.22 days
8.	*Seahorse*	24	8	407	16.95 days
9.	*Sunfish*	30	11	540	18.00 days
10.	*Tinosa*	23	11	443	19.26 days
11.	*Tautog*	30	13	584	19.46 days
12.	*Seawolf* [1]	25	15	522	20.88 days
13.	*Rasher*	18	8	390	21.66 days
14.	*Snook* [1]	19	9	415	21.84 days
15.	*Pogy*	20	10	490	24.50 days
16.	*Silversides*	25	13	701	28.04 days
17.	*Trigger* [1]	19	12	552	29.05 days
18.	*Guardfish*	22	12	662	30.09 days
19.	*Thresher*	17	15	596	35.05 days
20.	*Drum*	16	13	646	40.37 days

[1] Boat lost in action during World War II.
[2] Includes vessels under 500 tons, which were not counted by JANAC's scoring. Some U.S. submarines sunk numerous small vessels with their deck guns or with boarding parties. *Barb*'s total includes 54 small vessels sunk by rocket, gunfire or other means. Adjusted ship sinking totals from John D. Alden's *United States and Allied Submarine Successes in the Pacific and Far East During World War II. Second Edition*, October, 1999, pp. S1-S51.

Appendix D
Other *Spadefish* Top 10 Statistics

Top 10 U.S. Submarine Skippers of World War II in Enemy Tonnage Destroyed
(According to JANAC figures.)

	Skipper	Boat	JANAC Tonnage	Ships Sunk
1.	Fluckey, Eugene B.	*Barb*	95,360	16.33
2.	O'Kane, Richard H.	*Tang*	93,824	24
3.	Underwood, Gordon	*Spadefish*	75,386	14
4.	Cutter, Slade D.	*Seahorse*	72,000	19
5.	Munson, Henry G.	*S-38, Crevalle, Rasher*	67,630	2
6.	Gross, Royce L.	*Seawolf, Boarfish*	65,735	14
7.	Whitaker, Reuben T.	*S-44, Flasher*	60,846	14.5
8.	Reich, Eli T.	*Sealion II*	59,839	9
9.	Enright, Joseph F.	*Archerfish*	59,000	1
10.	Triebel, Charles O.	*S-15, Snook*	58,837	14

Best War Patrols by Tonnage of Ships Sunk
(According to JANAC figures.)

	Boat	Patrol No.	Skipper	Ships Sunk	Tonnage
1.	*Archerfish*	5	Joseph Enright	1	59,000
2.	*Rasher*	5	Henry Munson	5	52,600
3.	*Flasher*	5	George Grider	6	42,800
4.	*Tang*	3	Dick O'Kane	10	39,100
5.	*Barb*	9	Eugene Fluckey	3	36,800
6.	*Sealion II*	3	Eli Reich	2	32,900
7.	*Albacore*	9	James Blanchard	2	32,000
8.	*Spadefish*	1	Gordon Underwood	6	31,500
9.	*Spadefish*	2	Gordon Underwood	4	30,400
10.	*Cavalla*	1	Herman Kossler	1	30,000

Appendix E
Best War Patrols by Number of Enemy Ships Sunk

War Patrols with Five or More Ships Destroyed
(According to JANAC figures.)

	Boat	Patrol No.	Skipper	Ships Sunk	Tonnage
1.	Tang	3	Richard H. O'Kane	10	39,160
2.	Wahoo	4	Dudley W. Morton	9	19,530
3.	Tang	5	Richard W. O'Kane	7	21,772
4.	Flasher	5	George Grider	6	42,868
5.	Spadefish	1	Gordon Underwood	6	31,542
6.	Silversides	10	John S. Coye, Jr.	6	14,141
7.	Tirante	1	George L. Street III	6	12,621
8.	Sea Dog	4	Earl T. Hydeman	6	7,186
9.	Ray	6	William T. Kinsella	5.33	12,645
10.	Rasher	5	Henry G. Munson	5	52,667
11.	Seahorse	2	Slade D. Cutter	5	27,579
12.	Bowfin	2	Walter T. Griffith	5	26,458
13.	Ray	5	William T. Kinsella	5	25,988
14.	Hammerhead	2	John C. Martin	5	25,178
15.	Tang	1	Richard H. O'Kane	5	21,429
16.	Pogy	5	Ralph M. Metcalf	5	21,150
17.	Snook	5	Charles O. Triebel	5	21,046
18.	Seahorse	3	Slade D. Cutter	5	13,716
19.	Seahorse	4	Slade D. Cutter	5	19,375
20.	Sandlance	2	Malcolm Garrison	5	18,328
21.	Guardfish	1	Thomas Klakring	5	16,709
22.	Triton	3	Charles Kirkpatrick	5	15,843
23.	Barb	8	Eugene B. Fluckey	5	15,472
24.	Harder	2	Samuel D. Dealey	5	15,272
25.	Haddo	7	Chester Nimitz, Jr.	5	14,460
26.	Spadefish	5	W. Germershausen	5 *	8,578

* *Spadefish* sank four other Japanese ships that were each under 500 tons, too small to be counted by JANAC.

Appendix F
Sinking List of USS Spadefish

Ship Name	Type of Vessel	Date	Tonnage
Patrol 1A—Cdr. G.W.Underwood			
1. Tamatsu Maru	Transport/Ex-auxiliary	Aug. 19, 1944	9,589
2. Hakko Maru No. 2	Tanker	Aug. 22, 1944	10,023
Patrol 1B—Cdr. G.W.Underwood			
3. Nichiman Maru	Cargo	Sept. 8, 1944	1,922
4. Nichian Maru	Cargo	Sept. 8, 1944	6,197
5. Shinten Maru	Cargo	Sept. 8, 1944	1,245
6. Shokei Maru	Cargo/Ex-transport	Sept. 8, 1944	2,557
Patrol 2—Cdr. G. W. Underwood			
7. Gyokuyo Maru	Cargo	Nov. 14, 1944	[1] 5,396
8. Jinyo	Escort aircraft carrier	Nov. 17, 1944	[2] 21,000
9. Osakasan Maru	Tanker	Nov. 17, 1944	[3] 6,600
10. Sub Chaser 156	Patrol craft	Nov. 18, 1944	[4] 100
11. Daiboshi Maru No. 6	Cargo	Nov. 29, 1944	[5] 3,925
Patrol 3—Cdr. G. W. Underwood			
12. Sanuki Maru	Conv. seaplane tender	Jan. 28, 1945	7,158
13. Kume	Frigate	Jan. 28, 1945	[6] 940
14. Tairai Maru	Passenger/Cargo	Feb. 4, 1945	4,273
15. Shohei Maru	Passenger/Cargo	Feb. 6, 1945	1,092
Patrol 4—Cdr. W. J. Germershausen			
16. Doryo Maru	Cargo/Ex-transport	March 23, 1945	2,274
17. Unknown	Schooner	April 1, 1945	[7] 100
18. Tenshin Maru No. 3	Junk	April 7, 1945	[8] 198
19. Ritsu Go	Cargo	April 8, 1945	[9] 1,834
20. Hinode Maru No. 17	Ex-minelayer	April 11, 1945	[10] 235
Patrol 5—Cdr. W. J. Germershausen			
21. Daigen Maru No. 2	Passenger/Cargo	June 10, 1945	[11] 1,999
22. Unkai Maru No. 8	Passenger/Cargo	June 10, 1945	1,293
23. Jintsu Maru	Passenger/Cargo	June 10, 1945	985
24. Unknown	Motor sampan	June 12, 1945	50
25. Unknown	Trawler	June 12, 1945	200

26. *Daido Maru*	Trawler, ex-picket	June 12, 1945	69
27. Unknown	Trawler	June 12, 1945	100
28. *Transbalt*	Soviet freighter, ex-liner	June 13, 1945	[12] 11,439
29. *Seizan Maru*	Passenger/Cargo	June 14, 1945	2,018
30. *Eijo Maru*	Cargo/Ex-minelayer	June 17, 1945	[13] 2,274

Total of Above (less *Transbalt*): 95,646 tons
Official JANAC total: 88,091 tons

Other Ships Damaged or Not Officially Credited as Sunk by Spadefish

31. *Niyo Maru*	Tanker	Aug. 22, 1944	[14] 10,022
32. Unknown	Patrol Craft	January 31, 1945	[15] 1500

Notes:

[1] This ship was damaged by one torpedo which hit her engine room from *Barb* (SS-220) on 12 November. *Gyokuyo Maru* was under tow of escort vessel *CD 8* on 14 November when *Spadefish* sunk her.

[2] JANAC lists the carrier as *Jinyo* (the name used by her crew), 21,000 tons. Japanese sources called her *Shinyo*, and gave her tonnage at 17,500.

[3] Credited to *Peto* (SS-265) by JANAC, as *Spadefish* only claimed damage to a 10,500-ton tanker during this attack. New research by Cdr. John Alden shows that *Spadefish* should have received full or partial credit for sinking *Osakasan Maru*, also known as *Aisakasan Maru*. Japanese convoy history shows that *Osakasan Maru* was hit by a torpedo at 2340 on 17 November in her No. 2 hold. *Peto*'s attack was made after 0100 on 18 November. See John Alden, *United States and Allied Submarine Successes in the Pacific and Far East During World War II. Chronological Listing.* Pleasantville, NY: Self-published, second edition, October 1999. D-280-81. (Hereafter referred to as Alden, *Submarine Successes*.)

[4] *Spadefish* listed this victim as a 1,700-ton destroyer. JANAC credited her with the small sub chaser based on an Ultra report receipt.

[5] Japanese also recognized this ship's name as *Taisei Maru No. 6,* but *Daiboshi Maru* was her correct name. (Alden, *Submarine Successes,* D-287.)

[6] JANAC listed *Kume*'s tonnage at 900, but three Japanese sources list her tonnage as 940. (Alden, *Submarine Successes,* D-309.)

[7] No JANAC credit due to being a small size ship under 500 tons.

[8] Name given by Alden, *Submarine Successes,* D-332.

[9] JANAC credited 1,853-ton *Lee Tung* to *Spadefish*. Researcher Roger Allan found that *Lee Tung* was her original Chinese name. The Japanese listed her as the 1,834-ton *Ritsu Go*. (Alden, *Submarine Successes,* D-332.)

[10] *Spadefish* claimed a 400-ton patrol craft as sunk. One Japanese source lists that this former minesweeper was sunk by submarine torpedo. (Alden, *Submarine Successes*, D-334.)

[11] Also known as *Taigen Maru No. 2*.

[12] *Spadefish* fired on radar bearing. *Transbalt* was a Soviet freighter, the former German passenger liner *Belgravia* and former Russian Navy vessel *Riga*. Originally 10,155 gross ton ship, she was rebuilt to 10,982 tons in 1900. John Alden gives her final tonnage in 1945 as 11,439. (Alden, *Submarine Successes*, D-351.)

[13] Hansgeorg Jentschura's *Warships of the Imperial Japanese Navy, 1869-1945* says that this ship had a 5,200-ton normal displacement and a converted minelayer also known as just *Eijo*. (Alden, *Submarine Successes*, D-353.)

[14] *Niyo Maru* did not claim any damage, although *Spadefish* crew heard a timed hit on her.

[15] *Spadefish* fired at three freighters and four escorts with six torpedoes. Ultra intercepts show that *Nanshin Maru* reported seeing torpedo tracks. One of the escort vessel was tracked to have intercepted one of the torpedoes. *Spadefish* reported loud explosion and her sound men heard breaking up noises, but no escort was reported as lost by the Japanese on this date. (Alden, *Submarine Successes*, D-310.)

Appendix G
Awards Given to *Spadefish* and Crew

Presidential Unit Citation

The President of the United States takes pleasure in presenting the PRESIDENTIAL UNIT CITATION to the

UNITED STATES SHIP SPADEFISH

for service as set forth in the following

CITATION:

"For extraordinary heroism in action during the First and Second War Patrols against enemy Japanese forces in the restricted waters of the Pacific. In bold defiance of strong hostile air and surface opposition, the U.S.S. SPADEFISH effected wide coverage of her assigned sector and entered perilously shallow waters to seek out her targets. With her presence disclosed to the enemy by radar-equipped escorts, she daringly penetrated the powerful screen of a large Japanese convoy and headed in for a surface attack, striking fiercely against a fully laden large escort carrier to sink the target together with the embarked planes and personnel. Vigorously depth-charged following the action, she promptly turned to bring stern tubes to bear and launched a second attack to complete an illustrious record of combat achievement in vital Japanese ships sunk or damaged. A gallant and aggressive fighter, operating dangerously far from home base, the **SPADEFISH**, by her own efficient performance of duty, implemented the skill, the splendid seamanship and courage of her valiant officers and men in blocking shipping lanes vital to the enemy's sustained prosecution of the war."

For the President,
(signed) James Forrestal
Secretary of the Navy

Battle Stars

Spadefish sailors received four battle stars on their Asiatic-Pacific Service Medal for participating in the following operations:

Western Caroline Islands Operation, assaults on the Philippine Islands: one star for first war patrol period of September 9-24, 1944; one star for second war patrol period of October 23 - December 12, 1944; and a third star for the third war patrol period of January 6 - February 13, 1945.

Okinawa Gunto Operation, assault and occupation of Okinawa Gunto: one star for patrol period of March 23 - June 21, 1945.

Individual Commendations

The following awards were also received by officers and crewmen for service aboard *Spadefish* in World War II.

NAVY CROSS:
Germershausen, Cdr. William Joseph	(Fifth Patrol)
Underwood, Cdr. Gordon Waite	(First Patrol)

GOLD STAR (in lieu of additional Navy Cross):
Underwood, Cdr. Gordon Waite	(Second Patrol)
Underwood, Cdr. Gordon Waite	(Third Patrol)

SILVER STAR:
Alvis, Lt. Frank Ryals	(First Patrol)
Bassett, EM3c Richard Harold	(Second Patrol)
Cook, Lt. George Carlton	(Third Patrol)
Decker, Lt. Daniel Delos, Jr.	(Third Patrol)
Laundy, Lt. Henry Howard	(First Patrol)
Martin, Ens. Donald Ernest	(Second Patrol)
Pike, CRT Neal	(Fifth Patrol)
Ware, Ens. William James	(Third Patrol)
Wood, Lt.(jg) Perry Satterthwaite	(Second Patrol)
Wright, Lt. Richard Morgan	(Fifth Patrol)

GOLD STAR (in lieu of additional Silver Star):
Decker, Lt. Daniel Delos, Jr.	(Fifth Patrol)
Ustick, Lt. Cdr. Theodore Montanye	(First Patrol)

BRONZE STAR:
Decker, Lt. Daniel Delos, Jr.	(First Patrol)
Falconer, WM Leroy Douglas	(Fifth Patrol)
George, TM1c Harry	(First Patrol)

Germershausen, Cdr. William Joseph	(Fourth Patrol)
Ives, CPhM Victor Leon	(Second Patrol)
Kreher, TM1c Emery Andrew	(Second Patrol)
Kreinbring, Y1c Irwin Henry	(Third Patrol)
Laundy, Lt. Henry Howard	(Third Patrol)
Majoue, CRM Paul Henry, Jr.	(Third Patrol)
Pike, CRT Neal	(First Patrol)
Schmelzer, CEM Carl Thomas	(Fifth Patrol)
Schuett, SM1c James Shirley	(First Patrol)
Sergio, RM1c Michael	(Third Patrol)
Ware, Ens. William James	(Second Patrol)
Wells, CTM Francis Arthur	(Fifth Patrol)
White, Ens. Ray Curtis	(Second Patrol)
Wood, Lt.(jg) Perry Satterthwaite	(Fifth Patrol)

NAVY LETTER OF COMMENDATION RIBBON:

Brooks, StM1c Sie	(Third Patrol)
Charles, FC3c Walter Joseph Jr.	(Third Patrol)
Cook, Lt. George Carlton	(Fourth Patrol)
Dependahl, EM3c Leonard Edward	(First Patrol)
Fletcher, QM2c James Wallace	(Fifth Patrol)
Griffith, CMoMM Charles Clain	(Second Patrol)
Kelley, MoMM2c William Patrick	(Second Patrol)
La Croix, Lt.(jg) Edward J.	(Third Patrol)
Majoue, CRM Paul Henry, Jr.	(First Patrol)
Massar, GM2c Bernard Adam	(Fifth Patrol)
Ordway, CEM Emerson Locke	(Fifth Patrol)
Scherman, CCS Francis Julian	(First Patrol)
Schmelzer, CEM Carl Thomas	(Second Patrol)
Solomon, St3c Henry Lewis	(Third Patrol)

Special thanks to Patrick R. Osborn of the National Archives for his assistance in researching awards for *Spadefish* officers and enlisted men. My apologies for any crewman's award which may have been overlooked.

Glossary

Acey-deucy. Sailors' version of backgammon.
AK. Cargo vessel.
AM. Minesweeper.
Angle on the bow. The angle between the fore and aft axis of the target ship and line of sight of the submarine, measured from the target's bow to port or starboard.
Annunciator. An electro-mechanical signaling device for sending orders to the maneuvering room, where electrician's mates select power from the generators for propulsion or battery charging. The submarine's diesel engines generate power through their attached DC generators directly to the maneuvering room.
AO. Oil tanker.
AP. Troop transport ship.
APR-1. Non-directional radar detector.
AS. Submarine tender.
Ballast tanks. Tanks used to submerge and surface a submarine by filling them with water or blowing them dry.
Banjo. Hand-held Mark XVIII angle solver used prior to advent of TDC. Served later as backup plotting device to TDC.
Betty. IJN Mitsubishi Type 1 (G4M) twin-engine medium bomber.
Bow planes. Pair of horizontal rudders at the submarine's bow, rigged out on diving to help give the initial down angle. Bow planes used in coordination with stern planes to control depth.
BT. Bathythermograph device. Used to record sea temperature and submarine depth and to show gradients, or abrupt temperature changes.
Can. Electrical storage batteries.
Chief of the boat. Senior enlisted man aboard a submarine, responsible for the enlisted crew's overall operation and maintainence of the boat.
Christmas tree. Hull opening indicator panel in the control room. A green board signals the diving officer to proceed with his dive.

CinCPac. Commander in Chief, Pacific Fleet.
CO. Commanding officer.
ComSubPac. Commander Submarine Force, Pacific. This was Vice Admiral Charles Andrews Lockwood during *Spadefish*'s patrol periods.
Conning tower. Horizontal cylindrical compartment above the control room, used for navigating and directing attacks.
CV. Fleet aircraft carrier.
CVE. Escort carrier.
CVL. Light carrier.
Dave. IJN Nakajima E8N1 Navy Type 97 single engine reconnaissance seaplane.
DD. Destroyer.
DE. Escort destroyer, smaller in size than fleet destroyer.
D-F. Direction finding technique of Japanese shore radar installations to box in the location of the transmitting submarine.
ECM. Electric Coding Machine. Standard submarine coding-decoding device.
Emily. IJN Kawanishi H8K four-engine seaplane.
Fathom. Length of 6 feet, used as a unit of measure for the depth of water or the length of a rope, chain or cable.
Fire control. The mechanisms of directing torpedoes or gunfire.
FMS. Frequency-modulated sonar.
Fox Schedule. Submarine radio communications network.
Gyro angle. The angle set into each torpedo's gyro so that its steering mechanism will bring it to the proper course to hit the point of aim.
IFF. Identification, Friend or Foe, signal.
IJN. Imperial Japanese Navy.
Jake. IJN Aichi Navy Type 0 (E13A) twin float reconnaissance plane.
JANAC. Joint Army-Navy Assessment Commitee. Official military body charged after World War II with according credit to submarines for enemy sinkings.
Jima. Japanese word for harbor.
JK-QC. Dual-head, passive/active retractable supersonic submarine sound gear.
JOOD. Junior officer of the deck.
JP. Passive, single fixed-head sound gear installed in submarines beginning in mid-1944.
Kaibokan. Japanese coastal defense vessels.
Kaku. Japanese word for point.
Kate. IJN Nakajima B5N torpedo bomber.
Kuroshio. The Japanese current.

Mark 14. Two speed, steam-powered torpedoes. Capable of running at 46 knots with a 4,500-yard range in high power or at 31.5 knots with a 9,000-yard range in low power.

Mark 18. Newer model, electric, wakeless torpedo with a speed of 29 knots and a range of 4,000 yards.

Mark 23. A series of two-speed steam-powered torpedoes similiar to the Mark 14s.

Maru. Suffix to the names of most Japanese warship and in submarine language, any Japanese ship other than a warship.

Mavis. IJN Kawanishi H6K four-engine flying boat.

Misaki. Japanese word for point.

Mustang. Former enlisted man promoted into officer's rank.

Negative tank. Floodable tank used to impart negative buoyancy to make a submarine dive rapidly or to adjust buoyancy.

Nell. IJN Mitsubishi Type 96 G3M twin-engine medium bomber.

1MC. Shipboard announcing system.

ONI-208-J. Office of Naval Intelligence recognition manual for Japanese merchant ships.

OOD. Officer of the deck.

Outer doors (shutters). Streamlined movable covers over the torpedo tube muzzles.

PC. Smaller patrol craft, about half the length of a destroyer escort.

Poppet valve. Valve in the torpedo rooms used to vent residual torpedo firing impulse air back into the boat to reduce telltale air bubbles on the surface.

Port. Left side of a ship.

PPI. Position Plan Indicator. Radar scope display showing own ship and her position relative to other radar contacts.

QC. The echo-ranging portion of a sound head.

R&R. Rest and recreation period in between war patrols.

Relative bearing. Bearing in degrees measured clockwise from own ship's bow.

Rufe. IJN Nakajima A6M2-N single engine fighter seaplane.

Sally. IJN Mitsubishi Ki-21 twin-engine heavy bomber.

SC. Submarine chaser.

SCR. Single channel radio. VHF transceiver which uses a small AC power supply instead of a motor generator.

SD. Non-directional air search radar.

SJ. Surface-search radar which shows range and bearing of contact.

Sonar. Device used to detect underwater objects by means of sonic waves deflected back from the object. Can be used in active (sending and listening) or passive (listening) mode.

ST. Miniaturized radar unit installed in periscope head.

Starboard. Right side of a ship.

Stern planes. Pair of horizontal rudders at the submarine's stern, used to control the angle on the boat. In coordination with the bow planes, the stern planes maintain or change ship's depth.

Susie. Nickname for the SESE fathometer.

SS. Submarine.

TBT. Target bearing transmitter, one forward and one aft on the bridge to receive binoculars for transmission of bearings to the conning tower.

TDC. Torpedo data computer. Analog device used to keep the range to target ship current and displays the respective aspects of target and own ship. Its angle-solver section computes the proper gyro angle and continually sets the angle into all torpedoes readied for firing.

Tin Can. Nickname for a destroyer.

Topsy. Imperial Japanese Army Mitsubishi Type 100 Ki-57 twin-engine transport plane.

Torpedo gyro. The heart of the torpedo's steering mechanism.

True bearing (T). Angle between actual (not magnetic) north-south line and line of sight, measured clockwise from north.

UHF. Ultra high frequency. Radio frequencies from 300 MHz to 3,000 MHz.

Ultra. A classified priority message with information derived from a decoded Japanese transmission. An Ultra often gave the exact course, speed and location of an enemy convoy or warship.

VHF. Very high frequency. Radio frequencies from 30 MHz to 300 MHz.

Wan. Japanese word for island.

Watch schedule. Sailors generally stood four hours of duty period, followed by eight hours off duty. Standard navy watches are: first watch 2000-2400; midwatch 0000-0400; morning watch 0400-0800; forenoon watch 0800-1200; afternoon watch 1200-1600; first dogwatch 1600-1800; and second dogwatch 1800-2000.

XO. Executive Officer (Exec), or second in command of the submarine.

Chapter Notes

Prologue

1. *Spadefish* "Luau" newsletter, issues 20 (June 1992) and 21 (September 1992). Hereafter referred to as *Luau*.

Chapter 1
Mare Island and Luau

1. LaVO, Carl. *Back From the Deep. The Strange Story of the Sister Subs Squalus and Sculpin.* Annapolis: Naval Institute Press, 1994, 19, 32, 46-47.
2. Ted Ustick audiotape, February 19, 1993, courtesy of Cdr. Perry W. Ustick, USN (Ret.).
3. Blair, Clay, Jr. *Silent Victory. The U.S. Submarine War Against Japan.* Philadelphia: J. B. Lippincott Company, 1975. Two-volume reprint, I:397.
4. Tuohy, William. *The Bravest Man. The Story of Richard O'Kane & U.S. Submarines in the Pacific War.* Phoenix Mill: Sutton Publishing, 2001, 245.
5. "Ship's History," 2.
6. Ibid, 2.
7. Scanlon, Val, QMCM(SS), U.S. Navy (Retired). *USS Spadefish in World War II.* Bennington, Vermont: Merriam Press, 1999, 55.
8. Ted Ustick biographical sketch, written by Perry W. Ustick, Cdr. USN (Ret.).
9. Ustick audiotape, February 19, 1993.
10. Miller to Cary Cochran, July 14, 2000, in *Luau*, Issue 53: September 2000. Massar to Miller, *Luau*, Issue 44: June 1998.
11. Mendenhall, Rear Admiral Corwin, USN (Ret.). *Submarine Diary. The Silent Stalking of Japan.* Chapel Hill, North Carolina: Algonquin Books, 1991, 71.
12. Blair, *Silent Victory*, I: 495-99.
13. Don and Maury Martin to author, July 2004.
14. *United States Submarine Veterans of World War II. A History of the Veterans of the United States Naval Submarine Fleet.* Dallas: Taylor

Publishing Company, 1984-1990. Four volumes, Vol. I:354 and III: 232. Hereafter cited as *U.S. Submarine Veterans*.
15. Leroy Douglas Falconer Officer Biography Sheet.
16. *U.S. Submarine Veterans*, I: 369.
17. Sergio to Miller, November 6, 1989, in *Luau*, Issue 10: December 1989.
18. Bird to Miller, May 31, 1993, *Luau*, Issue 24: June 1993.
19. Lucille Carpenter Butchofsky to author, May 21, 2004.
20. *U.S. Submarine Veterans*, III: 272.
21. Massar to Miller, *Luau*, Issue 44: June 1998.
22. *Luau*, Issue 39, March 1997.
23. Ted Ustick audiotape, January 22, 1999. First war patrol report.
24. McMahon in *Luau*, Issue 16: June 1991.
25. Sergio to Thomas Miller, March 23, 1992, in *Luau*, June 1992.

CHAPTER 2
UNCLE CHARLIE'S SECRET WEAPON

1. Http://www.bergall.org/deckguns.html. Accessed 9/23/04.
2. O'Kane, Richard H., Rear Admiral, USN (Ret.). *Clear the Bridge! The War Patrols of the U.S.S. Tang*. Rand McNally & Company, 1977, 26.
3. Blair, *Silent Victory*, I: 45-47.
4. Lockwood, Charles A., Vice Admiral, USN, Ret., and Hans Christian Adamson, Colonel, USAF, Ret. *Hellcats of the Sea*. 1955. New York: Bantam Books, 1988. Reprint, 18-19. Smith, Steven Trent. *Wolf Pack. The American Submarine Strategy That Helped Defeat Japan*. Hoboken, New Jersey: John Wiley & Sons, Inc., 2003, 125-26.
5. Lockwood, *Hellcats*, 18.
6. Smith, *Wolf Pack*, 129-30.
7. Smith, *Wolf Pack*, 135-37.
8. Lockwood, *Hellcats*, 20.
9. Smith, *Wolf Pack*, 136.
10. See O'Kane, *Clear the Bridge*, 31.
11. Ted Ustick audiotape, November 3, 1994.
12. Lockwood, *Hellcats*, 23.
13. *U.S. Submarine Veterans*, Vol. IV:176.
14. Pike to Dan Curran, February 12, 1993, published in *Luau*; afterwards cited as Pike to Curran.
15. Smith, *Wolf Pack*, 4.
16. Ibid, 137.
17. Ibid, 137.
18. Robert W. Ives to author, January 15, 2005.
19. Massar to Thomas Miller, December 31, 1998, in *Luau*, Issue 47: March, 1999. Story also related by Massar to author during March 28, 2004 interview.
20. Lockwood, *Hellcats*, 23-24.
21. Smith, *Wolf Pack*, 137.
22. "Ship's History," 2.
23. Lockwood, *Hellcats*, 24-25.

24. Ibid, 25-26.
25. Smith, *Wolf Pack*, 137.
26. Ibid, 137-38.
27. Decker to author, March 10, 2004.
28. Lockwood, *Hellcats*, 28.
29. Ibid, 28-29.
30. Ibid, 29.
31. Ibid, 29-30.
32. Ibid, 30.
33. Ibid, 30-31.
34. Smith, *Wolf Pack*, 138.
35. Lockwood, *Hellcats*, 40.
36. Smith, *Wolf Pack*, 138.
37. Pike to Dan Curran, February 12, 1993.
38. Davenport, Rear Admiral Roy M., USN (Ret.). *Clean Sweep.* New York: Vantage Press, 1986, 139. *Luau,* Issue 69: September 2004 says that Butchofsky hit Frazier and broke his nose.
39. First war patrol report, 60.
40. "World War II Torpedoes." Cdr. Daniel D. Decker. *USS Coghlan* (DD-606) Newsletter. Issue 115: April 1997, Part II.
41. Blair, *Silent Victory,* I:436-43.
42. Ibid, I:481-82.
43. "Wahoo Final Battle Report." http://www.emackinnon.com/wahoo home-frame.html. Accessed September 30, 2004.

CHAPTER 3
TYPHOON

1. Sterling, Forest J. *Wake of the Wahoo.* Philadelphia: Chilton Company, 1960, 70.
2. Blair, *Silent Victory,* I:511-13.
3. Ibid, I:513-16.
4. Ibid, I:517, II: 569-72.
5. Ibid, II:655-57.
6. Ibid, II: 653-655; Smith, *Wolf Pack,* 201-13.
7. Smith, *Wolf Pack,* 179.
8. Sasgen Peter T. *Red Scorpion: The War Patrols of the USS Rasher.* Annapolis, Maryland: Naval Institute Press, 1995, 74.
9. Michno, Gregory F. *USS Pampanito. Killer-Angel.* Norman: University of Oklahoma Press, 2000, 144.
10. First Patrol Report, 57.
11. Ustick speech of November 3, 1994. Audiotape courtesy of Cdr. Perry W. Ustick, USN (Ret.).
12. Miller in *Luau,* Issue 8: June 1989.
13. Sergio to Miller, *Luau,* Issue 16: June 1991.
14. Scanlon, *USS Spadefish in World War II,* 6.
15. "Ship's History," 3.
16. Galatin, Admiral I. J., USN (Ret.) *Take Her Deep! A Submarine*

Against Japan in World War II. New York: Pocket Books, 1988, 68-69. Michno, *USS Pampanito*, 37.
17. Sasgen, *Red Scorpion*, 61.
18. Massar to author interview and Massar to Miller, *Luau*, Issue 44: June 1998.
19. Tuohy, *The Bravest Man*, 17-18.
20. Parkin, Robert Sinclair. *Blood on the Sea. American Destroyers Lost in World War II.* New York: Sarpedon, 1995, 263-84. Ewing, Steve. *American Cruisers of World War II.* Missoula, Montana: Pictorial Histories Publishing Company, 1984, 55.
21. "Ship's History," 3.
22. Blair, *Silent Victory*, 2:676.
23. Blair, *Silent Victory*, 2:676. Anthony P. Tully. "Convoy HI-71 and *USS Harder*'s Last Battles." Copyright 1998. See http://www.combinedfleet.com/atully05.htm.
24. Blair, *Silent Victory*, 2:677.
25. Tully, "Convoy HI-71."
26. Sasgen, *Red Scorpion*, 213.
27. Decker to author, May 7, 2004.
28. Russell, Dale. *Hell Above, Deep Water Below.* Tillamook, Oregon: Bayocean Enterprises, 1995, 142-43.
29. "Ship's History," 3.

Chapter 4
"First Blood for Spadefish"

1. Tully, "Convoy HI-71."
2. Blair, *Silent Victory*, II:677-78, 964.
3. "Ship's History," 3.
4. Alden, Cdr. John D., USN (Ret.) *United States and Allied Submarine Successes in the Pacific and Far East During World War II. Chronological Listing.* (Hereafter cited as Alden, *Submarine Successes*.) Pleasantville, NY: Self-published, second edition, October 1999, D-217; Convoy HI-71 research of Anthony Tully to author, June 15, 2004.
5. Tully, "Convoy HI-71."
6. Laundy to Miller, July 16, 1998, in *Luau*, Issue 45: September 1998.
7. Tully, "Convoy HI-71."
8. Alden, *Submarine Successes*, D-220; *Yunagi* Action Report, courtesy of Anthony P. Tully; Tully to author April 12, 2004. Hereafter cited as *Yunagi* Action Report.
9. *Yunagi* action report.
10. Ibid.
11. Massar to author, January 28, 2005.
12. Decker to author, June 10, 2004.
13. *Yunagi* action report.
14. Scanlon, *USS Spadefish in World War II*, 12; Neal Pike interview.
15. *Yunagi* action report.

Chapter 5
Cat and Mouse Games

1. *Yunagi* action report.
2. "IJN Yahagi." http://www.combinedfleet.com/yunagi_t.htm. Accessed October 10, 2004.
3. *Yunagi* action report.
4. Ibid.
5. Ibid.
6. Ibid.
7. "Ship's History," 3.
8. Blair, *Silent Victory*, II:664; Lockwood, *Hellcats*, 42.
9. Moore, Stephen L. *The Buzzard Brigade: Torpedo Squadron Ten at War*. Missoula, Montana: Pictorial Histories Publishing, 1996, 191-92, 225-26.
10. Ted Ustick April 1997 audiotape.

Chapter 6
A Double-Barreled Patrol

1. Blair, *Silent Victory*, 2:679-80.
2. Massar to author, January 28, 2005.
3. Miller in *Luau*, Issue 46: December 1998.
4. Alden, *Submarine Successes*, D-229.
5. Ibid.
6. Ibid, D229-30.
7. "Ship's History," 4.
8. Miller in *Luau*, Issue 8: June 1989.
9. Eimermann interview, April 20, 2004.
10. Smith, *Wolf Pack*, 231.
11. Blair, *Silent Victory*, 2:680.
12. Smith, *Wolf Pack*, 231.
13. Ibid, 231-32.
14. O'Kane, *Clear the Bridge*, 203.

Chapter 7
Underwood's Urchins

1. Michno, *USS Pampanito*, 105-106.
2. "Ship's History," 3.
3. Hinkle, David Randall (editor). *United States Submarines*. New York: Barnes and Noble Books, 2002, 296-98.
4. Bernie Massar in *Luau*, Issue 60: June 2002.
5. Blair, *Silent Victory*, 2: 668.
6. Ibid, 2:747.
7. Sergio to Miller, March 14, 1991, in *Luau*, Issue 16: June 1996.
8. Blair, *Silent Victory*, I:380-81.
9. Ibid, I:420.

Chapter 8
"Shaken Up"

1. Blair, *Silent Victory*, 2:747.
2. Ibid, 2:748.
3. Blair, *Silent Victory*, 1:66-235; Sasgen, *Red Scorpion*, 49-50.
4. Ustick audiotape, February 19, 1993.
5. Alden, *Submarine Successes*, D-274.
6. Fluckey, Admiral Eugene B. *Thunder Below! The USS Barb Revolutionizes Submarine Warfare in World War II.* Chicago: University of Illinois Press, 1992, 187-92.
7. Alden, *U.S. Submarine Attacks During World War II*, 154. See also Alden, *Submarine Successes*, D273-74.
8. Ware in *Luau,* Volume I: Issue 2, December 1987.
9. Alden, *Submarine Successes*, D-274.
10. Decker to author, March 10, 2004.
11. Blair, *Silent Victory*, 2:748.
12. Ibid, 2:748-49.
13. Decker to author, March 10, 2004.

Chapter 9
Jinyo's Last "Banzai!"

1. *Fighting Ships of the World. An Illustrated Encyclopedia of Modern Sea Power*, pp. 294-95. Courtesy of Bernie Massar.
2. Tony Tully to author, July 15, 2004. Hackett, Bob, Sander Kingsepp, Allan Alsleban and Peter Cundall. "IJN Seaplane Tender *Kiyokawa Maru*: Tabular Record of Movement." See http://www.combinedfleet.com/-Kiyokawa%20Maru_t.htm. Accessed January 29, 2005.
3. Blair, *Silent Victory*, 2:749.
4. Escort composition courtesy of Tony Tully to author, July 15, 2004.
5. "Ship's History," 5.
6. Tully to author, March 23, 2004.
7. Alden, *Submarine Successes*, D-280.
8. Ustick to Thomas Miller, April 7, 1993.
9. "Ship's History," 5.
10. Ted Ustick also stated, "That carrier was gone in about thirty minutes or so." April 1997 audiotape.
11. Okamura to Miller, June 9, 1994. By this time, the "Club Thinking of *Jinyo*" to remember her loss consisted of three survivors from the sinking, 11 former *Jinyo* officers, and 5 persons who had observed her sinking from escort vessels. One of these survivors was sub-lieutenant Konno, who was discharging his duties to a fire control party when *Jinyo* was torpedoed at midnight. Okamura to Decker, 1993.
12. Ustick to Thomas Miller, April 7, 1993.
13. Powers in *Luau,* Issue 5: September 1988.
14. "Ship's History," 6.
15. Don Scholle interview. Powers in *Luau,* Issue 5: September 1988.

16. Powers, *Luau,* Issue 5, September 1988.
17. Ustick to Thomas Miller, April 7, 1993. This narrative also combines Ustick's November 3, 1994 speech to "SIRS" group.
18. Powers, *Luau,* Issue 5, September 1988.
19. Ibid.
20. Tony Tully to author, March 23, 2004 and August 10, 2004.
21. Ted Ustick audiotape, November 3, 1994.
22. Ustick to Thomas Miller, April 7, 1993.
23. Alden, *U.S. Submarine Attacks During World War II,* 157.
24. "Ship's History," 6.
25. Ted Ustick April 1997 audiotape.
26. *Luau,* Issue 39, March 1997.
27. Tony Tully to author, March 23, 2004.
28. Blair, *Silent Victory,* 2:750.

CHAPTER 10
LUAU'S LITTER

1. Miller in *Luau,* Issue 45: September 1998; also Issue 71: March 2005.
2. Bill Ware in *Luau,* Issue 2: December 1987.
3. 40th Bomb Group Association *Memories,* Issue # 15, May 1987.
4. Alden, *U.S. Submarine Attacks During World War II,* 161.
5. "Ship's History," 6.
6. Ted Ustick January 22, 1999 audiotape, courtesy of Cdr. Perry W. Ustick, USN (Ret.).
7. Eimermann interview, April 20, 2004. See also Smith, *Wolf Pack,* 13.
8. Blair, *Silent Victory,* 2:561.

CHAPTER 11
FRIENDLY FIRE

1. Kreinbring to Miller, August 30, 1989, in *Luau,* Issue 9: September 1989.
2. Schratz, Captain Paul R. USN (Ret.) *Submarine Commander. A Story of World War II and Korea.* Lexington, Kentucky: The University Press of Kentucky, 1988, 138-39.
3. Sergio to Miller, February 9, 1993. Also Sergio to Miller in *Luau,* Issue 44, December 2000, and Sergio to Miller, November 6, 1989, in *Luau,* Issue 10: December 1989.
4. Schratz, *Submarine Commander,* 140.
5. Ibid, 141.
6. Massar to author, August 23, 2004.
7. Schratz, *Submarine Commander,* 142.
8. "Ship's History," 6.
9. Sergio to Miller, November 6, 1989, in *Luau,* Issue 10, December 1989.
10. George Carlton Cook officer biography sheet. See also Blair, *Silent Victory,* 1: 173.
11. Eimermann interview, April 20, 2004.
12. Blair, *Silent Victory,* 2: 816.

13. Schratz, *Submarine Commander*, 142. Blair, *Silent Victory*, 2:816. "Ship's History," 8.
14. "Ship's History," 8.

CHAPTER 12
"A GOOD WORKING OVER"

1. Schratz, *Submarine Commander*, 144.
2. Michno, *USS Pampanito*, 168-69.
3. Decker to author, March 23, 2004.
4. "Napan Relates Exciting Tales of Life Aboard U.S. Navy Submarine." *The Napa Register*, Monday, February 15, 1943.
5. "Ship's History," 8.
6. Decker to author, June 23, 2004.
7. Alden, *Submarine Attacks*, 174. See also Alden, *Submarine Successes*, D-309.
8. Ruhe, Capt. William J., USN (Ret.). *War in the Boats. My WWII Submarine Battles*. McLean, Virginia: Brassey's Inc., 1994, 211-214, 234.
9. "Ship's History," 8.

CHAPTER 13
ICY HUNTING IN THE YELLOW SEA

1. Schratz, *Submarine Commander*, 151.
2. Alden, *Submarine Successes*, D-310.
3. Blair, *Silent Victory*, 1: 252-54; 2: 793.
4. Decker to author, March 17, 2004.
5. "Ship's History," 9.
6. Miller to Decker, December 7, 1989. Also Miller narrative in *Luau*, Issue 47: March, 1999.
7. Blair, *Silent Victory*, 2:816.

CHAPTER 14
GUAM AND GERMERSHAUSEN

1. Morrison, Samuel Eliot. *History of United States Naval Operations in World War II.* Vol. VIII: *New Guinea and the Marianas. March 1944 - August 1944.* Boston: Little, Brown and Company, 1958. Reprint, 1988, 382-401.
2. Blair, *Silent Victory*, 2:809-10; Tuohy, *The Bravest Man*, 386. Cline, Rick. *Final Dive. The Gallant and Tragic Career of the WWII Submarine, USS Snook*. Placentia, CA: R.A. Cline Publishing, 2001, 187.
3. Http://www.homestead.com/seafoxss402/bios.html as accessed on July 20, 2004.
4. Massar to author, August 23, 2004.
5. Lockwood, *Hellcats*, 42.
6. "Current Orders, Naval Operating Base, Guam." Hugo Lundquist collection, courtesy of Jeanne Lundquist.

7. Such gilly cookers are well described in O'Kane, *Clear the Bridge*, 464, and Michno, *USS Pampanito*, 102-103.
8. Decker to author, September 26, 2004.
9. Scanlon, *USS Spadefish in World War II*, 56. W. J. Germershausen interview with Clay Blair Jr., circa 1970s. Clay Blair Papers, Acc. 8295, Box 97. American Heritage Center, University of Wyoming. Hereafter cited as Germershausen/Blair interview.
10. Germershausen/Blair interview.
11. Germershausen, Capt. William J., USN (Ret.). "O Boat Duty." *Shipmate*, November 1990.
12. Scanlon, *USS Spadefish in World War II*, 57.
13. Blair, *Silent Victory*, 2: 671.
14. Germershausen/Blair interview.
15. Scanlon, *USS Spadefish in World War II*, 56-57; Blair, *Silent Victory*, 2: 766; Alden, *U.S. Submarine Attacks During World War II*, 156.
16. Germershausen/Blair interview.
17. Ibid.
18. Lockwood, *Hellcats of the Sea*, 43-44; Blair, *Silent Victory*, II: 764-65.
19. Lockwood, *Hellcats*, 48-49.
20. Pike to Dan Curran, February 12, 1993.
21. Lockwood, *Hellcats*, 55-56.
22. Germershausen, Capt. W. J., U.S. Navy (Ret.). "Sea of Japan Was Climactic Battle." *San Jose Mercury-News*, Sunday, June 6, 1965.
23. Joe Marasco to author, June 9, 2004.
24. Lockwood, *Hellcats*, 56-57. See also Lockwood, Charles A., Vice Admiral, USN, Ret. *Sink 'Em All. Submarine Warfare in the Pacific*. New York: E. P. Dutton & Co., Inc., 1951, 294.
25. Lockwood, *Hellcats*, 57.
26. Germershausen/Blair interview; see also Blair, *Silent Victory*, II:576-78.
27. Germershausen to Miller, March 21, 1998, in *Luau*, Issue 44, June 1998.
28. Germershausen/Blair interview; see also Blair, *Silent Victory*, II:576-78.
29. Ibid.
30. Germershausen to Miller, March 21, 1998, in *Luau*, Issue 44, June 1998.
31. Lockwood, *Hellcats*, 58-59.

Chapter 15
"Beyond Test Depth"

1. Blair, *Silent Victory*, II:765.
2. Recollections of Massar and Miller in *Luau*, Issue 47: March 1999.
3. Ilona Rymer to author, July 10, 2004.
4. W. J. Germershausen Jr. "Special Mission, Report on." Previously classified document of 14 April 1945 written to ComSubPac. Hereafter referred to as Germershausen, "Special Mission."
5. Sasgen, *Red Scorpion*, 259.
6. Germershausen/Blair interview.

7. Ibid.
8. Decker to author, March 10, 2004.
9. Massar to author, June 14, 2004.
10. "Ship's History," 10.
11. Kreinbring letter of August 30, 1989, in *Luau*, Issue 9: September 1989.
12. Graf to Miller, March 12, 1991, in *Luau*, Issue 16: June 1991.
13. Alden, *U.S. Submarine Attacks During World War II*, 187. See also Alden, *Submarine Successes*, D-327.
14. Germershausen/Blair interview.
15. Smith, *Wolf Pack*, 238-39.
16. Lockwood, *Hellcats*, 101-102.
17. Ibid, 102.
18. Germershausen, "Special Mission Report," 1.
19. Ibid, 2.
20. Germershausen/Blair interview.
21. Germershausen, "Special Mission Report," 2.
22. Ibid, 2.
23. Pike to author, November 9, 2004.
24. Joan and Neal Pike to Miller, July 23, 1999, in *Luau*, Issue 49: September 1999. Also Pike to author, November 9, 2004.
25. Germershausen, "Special Mission Report," 3.
26. Germershausen/Blair interview.
27. Ibid.

Chapter 16
"Like Pirates of Old"

1. Smith, *Wolf Pack*, 239-41.
2. Massar to author and Massar to Miller in *Luau*, Issue 44, June 1998.
3. Ilona Rymer to author, July 10, 2004.
4. Massar to author, June 14, 2004.
5. "Ship's History," 10.
6. Miller to Decker, December 7, 1989.
7. Miller in *Luau*, Issue 44, June 1998.
8. Calvert, James F., Vice Admiral, USN (Ret.). *Silent Running. My Years on a World War II Attack Submarine*. New York: John Wiley & Sons, Inc., 1995, 159.
9. Alden, *Submarine Successes*, D-332.
10. Decker to author, April 5, 2004.
11. "Ship's History," 10.
12. Decker to author, September 26, 2004.
13. "Ship's History," 10-11.
14. Massar to Miller, in *Luau*, Issue 44, June 1998.
15. Decker, "World War II Torpedoes," April 1997. Note of edit made here: Decker wrote 11 knots, but patrol report shows 20 knots.
16. Alden, *U.S. Submarine Attacks During World War II*, 191. See also Alden, *Submarine Successes*, D-332.

17. Alden, *U.S. Submarine Attacks During World War II*, 192.
18. Germershausen to Buck Miller, 14 December 1995, *Luau*, Issue 35, March 1996.
19. Massar to Miller, *Luau*, Issue 44, June 1998.
20. Blair, *Silent Victory*, II:816-18. Roscoe, Theodore. *United States Submarine Operations in World War II*. Annapolis: Naval Institute Press, 1949, 463-64.
21. Bouslog, Dave. *Maru Killer. War Patrols of the USS Seahorse*. Placentia, CA: R.A. Cline Publishing, 1996. Second Printing, 2001, 285-94.
22. Scanlon, *USS Spadefish in World War II*, 57.
23. Germershausen, "Special Mission," 3.

Chapter 17
Operation Barney

1. Morrison, *History of the United States Naval Operations in World War II*, XIV: 233-37.
2. Wright, Capt. Richard M. USN(Ret). Oral History Interview # 202. East Carolina University, J. Y. Joyner Library, Manuscript Collection. Transcription, 1-2. Hereafter referred to as Wright Oral History.
3. Wright Oral History, 2-8.
4. Ibid, 12-16.
5. Decker to author, April 5, 2004.
6. Blair, *Silent Victory*, II: 832.
7. Germershausen, "Sea of Japan."
8. Lockwood, *Hellcats*, 92-94.
9. Ibid, 94.
10. Ibid, 97.
11. Buncke to Miller, April 8, 1993.
12. Germershausen, "Sea of Japan." See also Smith, *Wolf Pack*, 2.
13. Lockwood, *Hellcats*, 97.
14. Smith, *Wolf Pack*, 3.
15. Eimermann interview, April 20, 2004. See also Smith, *Wolf Pack*, 6.
16. Smith, *Wolf Pack*, 8.
17. Germershausen, "Sea of Japan."
18. Ibid.

Chapter 18
Hell's Bells

1. Smith, *Wolf Pack*, 9-10.
2. Decker to author, September 26, 2004.
3. Lockwood, *Hellcats*, 102-103.
4. Ibid, 109.
5. Smith, *Wolf Pack*, 246. For 4 June 1945, Don Scholle's original June 1945 quartermaster's notebook was heavily relied upon for accurate times. See also Captain Germershausen's secret report of 4 July 1945, "Special information concerning War Patrol No. Five in Japan Sea."

6. Smith, *Wolf Pack*, 246.
7. Massar to author, June 14, 2004.
8. Smith, *Wolf Pack*, 247.
9. Germershausen/Blair interview.
10. Smith, *Wolf Pack*, 250.
11. Ibid, 247-48, 303.
12. Germershausen, "Sea of Japan."
13. Miller in *Luau*, Issue 58: December 2001.
14. Lockwood, *Hellcats*, 111.
15. Smith, *Wolf Pack*, 251.
16. Ibid, 251-52.
17. Ibid, 252-54.
18. Ibid, 256-58, 263.
19. Lockwood, *Hellcats*, 124-25.
20. Wright Oral History, 16-17.
21. Smith, *Wolf Pack*, 259.

Chapter 19
"It Was a Real Turkey Shoot"

1. Lockwood, *Hellcats*, 111.
2. Ibid, 166.
3. Ibid, 167.
4. Pike, "Deja Vu." Printed in *Luau*, Issue 5: September 1988.
5. Germershausen, "Sea of Japan."
6. Lockwood, *Hellcats*, 168.
7. Pike, "Deja Vu."
8. Lockwood, *Hellcats*, 168-69.
9. Ibid, 169.
10. Germershausen to Miller, 14 December 1995, *Luau*, Issue 35, March 1996.
11. Germershausen, "Sea of Japan."
12. Pike, "Deja Vu."
13. Germershausen, "Sea of Japan."

Chapter 20
Transbalt

1. Smith, *Wolf Pack*, 264-65.
2. Germershausen to Miller, March 21, 1998, in *Luau*, Issue 44: June 1998.
3. McMahon to Thomas H. Miller, April 20, 2000, printed in *Luau*, Issue 53: September 2000. Also McMahon to author, November 6, 2004.
4. Quartermaster's Notebook, 12 June 1945.
5. Buncke to author; also Buncke to Thomas H. Miller, January 14, 1999.
6. 1 July 1945 Report on Sinking of Freighter, William J. Germershausen Jr.
7. Germershausen/Blair interview.
8. Lockwood, *Hellcats of the Sea*, 174.
9. *North Atlantic Seaway* by N. R. P. Bonsor, Vol. I: 406. *Merchant Fleets*,

by Duncan Haws, Vol. 4: Hamburg America Line. Information courtesy of Albert G. La Rocca.
10. Decker to author, March 14, 2004.
11. Germershausen, "Sea of Japan."

Chapter 21
Mighty Mine Dodgers Return

1. Smith, *Wolf Pack*, 272.
2. Germershausen/Blair interview and Smith, *Wolf Pack*, 272-73.
3. Germershausen/Blair interview and Germershausen to Buck Miller, 14 December 1995, *Luau*, Issue 35: March 1996.
4. Germershausen, "Sea of Japan."
5. Lockwood, *Hellcats*, 238.
6. Ibid, 239.
7. Smith, *Wolf Pack*, 280.
8. Ibid, 282-83.
9. Ibid, 285.
10. Don and Maury recollections; Don Scholle interview.
11. Smith, *Wolf Pack*, 285-86. Dan Decker to author clarified that this command was more properly "turn three" versus "three turn" as recorded by Smith.
12. Germershausen, "Sea of Japan." See also Lockwood, *Hellcats*, 247, and Smith, *Wolf Pack*, 286.
13. Smith, *Wolf Pack*, 286.
14. *Spadefish* Quartermaster's Notebook, June 1945. Smith, *Wolf Pack*, 286-87; Lockwood, *Hellcats*, 240.
15. Smith, *Wolf Pack*, 287.
16. Germershausen, "Sea of Japan."
17. Lockwood, *Hellcats*, 248.
18. Germershausen, "Sea of Japan."
19. Smith, *Wolf Pack*, 291.
20. Germershausen, "Sea of Japan."
21. Buncke to Miller, July 23, 2003, in *Luau*, Issue 69: September 2004.
22. Lockwood, *Hellcats*, 249.
23. Ibid, 251.
24. Casey to Miller, March 21, 1998, in *Luau*, Issue 44: June 1998.
25. Germershausen, "Sea of Japan."
26. Blair, *Silent Victory*: II:838.
27. Wright Oral History, 17.

Chapter 22
"Cease Offensive Operations"

1. Germershausen, "Sea of Japan."
2. Smith, *Wolf Pack*, 292.
3. McMahon to Miller, April 20, 2000, in *Luau*, Issue 53: September 2000. Massar to author.

4. Buncke to Miller, July 23, 2003, in *Luau*, Issue 69: September 2004.
5. Miller in *Luau*, Issue 8: June 1989.
6. Roscoe, *United States Submarine Operations in World War II*, 486.)
7. McCants, William R. *War Patrols of the USS Flasher*. Chapel Hill, North Carolina: Professional Press, 1994, 422-23.
8. Ibid, 425.
9. "Ship's History," 14.

Epilogue

1. Wright Oral History, 19.
2. According to Casey, Luau's final days did not end peacefully. After going into heat, she was tied up to keep her away from other dogs, but managed to hang herself on the rope while running after another dog.
3. Gillespie to Miller, March 31, 1989. Courtesy of Thomas H. Miller.
4. Scanlon, *USS Spadefish in World War II*, 38.
5. Fellows in *Luau*, Issue 8: June 1989.
6. Jim Cole to Buck Miller, September 25, 1996, published in the *Luau*, Issue 38, December 1996.
7. *Luau*, Issue 9: September 1989.
8. Ustick audiotape of January 22, 1999.
9. Wright Oral History, 21-24.
10. Scanlon, *USS Spadefish in World War II*, 56-58.

Bibliography

DOCUMENTS, MANUSCRIPTS AND COLLECTIONS

Germershausen, Capt. W. J. Interview with Clay Blair Jr. for the book *Silent Victory*, taped during the 1970s. Clay Blair Papers, Acc. 8295, Box 97. American Heritage Center, University of Wyoming.

Luau. Newsletter of the *USS Spadefish* (SS-411), published by Kenneth C. Powers, originally, and later by Thomas "Buck" Miller. Copies of all issues were generously provided by Peggy Ellis and Buck Miller. Other copies of past issues were loaned out by Dan Decker and others.

Lundquist, Hugo C. Private journal secretly kept in *Spadefish*'s forward torpedo room. Courtesy of Mrs. Jeanne Lundquist and her son, William A. Lundquist.

Pike, CRT Neal. "Deja Vu." Writeup published in *Spadefish Luau* newsletter, Issue 5, September 1988, concerning fifth patrol in Sea of Japan.

Quartermaster's Notebook. *USS Spadefish*, June 1945. Original 5"x8" book made available for review, courtesy of Donald Scholle.

"Ship's History. *U.S.S. Spadefish* (SS-411). 27 May 1943 to 9 September 1945." Unpublished. Compiled by Lieutenant Daniel D. Decker Jr. with assistance from Lt.(jg) James D. Wall. 1997 revised edition also provided by Daniel D. Decker, which includes photographs provided by William F. Graf.

USS Spadefish War Patrols. Censured copies of original reports provided by Daniel D. Decker Jr.

Ustick, Theodore. "The Lost Boat Ceremony." Transcript of Spring 1999 speech given at 60th anniversary of U.S. Naval Academy Class of 1939. Courtesy of Claire Ustick Bagley.

Ustick, Theodore M. Biographical sketch by Commander Perry W. Ustick, USN (Ret.). A retired World War II naval aviator and younger brother of *Spadefish* executive officer Ted Ustick, Perry generously provided his brother's biography, copies of photos and audiotapes on which his brother recalls his submarine days. Audiotapes (referenced in chapter notes) are from: November 3, 1994 "SIRS" presentation at Auburn Elks Lodge; October 1992 World War II experience audiotape; February 19, 1993; and USNA Alumni speech given on April 2, 1997.

Wright, Capt. Richard M. USN (Ret). Oral History Interview # 202. East Carolina University, J. Y. Joyner Library, Manuscript Collection.

Yunagi Action Report, courtesy of Anthony P. Tully.

CORRESPONDENCE, TELEPHONE INTERVIEWS

Anderson, Donald C. Telephone interview June 9, 2004.

Battenfield, Willard E. Telephone interview August 6, 2004.

Brenneis, Harry J. Telephone interviews April 20 and June 24, 2004.

Brewer, John B., Jr. Telephone interview July 26, 2004.

Buncke, Dr. Harry J. Jr. Telephone interview May 8, 2004. Dr. Buncke also passed along copies of letters, newspaper articles, photos and other *Spadefish* memorabilia.

Butchofsky, Lucille Carpenter. Wife of the late Richard D. Butchofsky. Telephone interview May 21, 2004.

Casey, James D. Telephone interview April 15, 2004.

Charles, Argyle. Wife of the late Walter J. Charles, she kindly provided photos and other memorabilia from her husband's personal collection.

Cole, James D. Telephone interviews March 27, 2004 and October 30, 2004. Jim Cole also provided photos and copies of relevant articles concerning *Spadefish* and her crew.

Decker, Daniel D. Jr., Cdr. (Ret.) Telephone interview March 2, 2004. Correspondence with author of numerous dates spanning March 7, 2004 - May 2005.

Eimermann, Willard C. Telephone interview April 20, 2004.

Fletcher, Betty. Wife of the late James W. Fletcher, she shared her husband's *Spadefish* photo collection for use in the book.

Gallagher, Jack A. Telephone interviews August 17, 2004 and January 30, 2005.

Gamby, Orville R. "Dick" Telephone interview April 24, 2004 and January 30, 2005.

Gibson, Alvin W. December 5, 2004 telephone interview.

Greening, Wayne A. Telephone interview August 22, 2004.

Griffith, Charles C. Telephone interviews April 6, 2004 and July 30, 2004.

Ives, Robert W. Son of the late Victor L. Ives, Sr. Telephone interview May 27, 2004.

Kelley, William P. "Pat" Lt. Cdr. (Ret.) Telephone interviews March 20, 2004 and November 15, 2004.

La Rocca, Albert G. Telephone interview April 4, 2004.

Laundy, Henry. H. "Gus" Telephone interviews May 1 and May 5, 2004.

Majoue, Paul H. Jr. Telephone interview March 10, 2004.

Marasco, Ralph J. "Joe." Telephone interview May 26, 2004 and correspondence, June 9, 2004. Joe provided photos and graciously loaned out his *Spadefish* battle (without provocation) to insure that I had a good picture of it!

Martin, Don and Maury Martin. Grandsons of Carl T. Schmelzer, they sent many important papers, photos and recollections from Schmelzer's submarine service days.

Massar, Bernard A. Telephone interview March 28, 2004. Correspondence with author spanning from April 2004 through April 2005.

McMahon, Wallace F. November 6, 2004 telephone interview.

Miller, Thomas H. Correspondence with author beginning March 18, 2004. Tom and his girlfriend Peggy Ellis graciously spent copies of every issue of "Luau," the *Spadefish* newsletter, as well as countless letters, articles and photographs.

Olson, Olaf B. (His legal name was Olaf Sandleben during time of service on *Spadefish*.) Telephone interview April 9, 2004.

Pike, Neal. Telephone interviews March 4, July 18 and November 9, 2004.

Rolf, Charles. Telephone interviews June 12, 2004 and January 30, 2005.

Rymer, Ilona. Wife of the late Robert Rymer. She shared some of her husband's experience aboard *Spadefish* and sent along several of his photographs.

Scholle, Donald J. Telephone interview May 19 and December 5, 2004.

Schumer, John M. Telephone interview June 9, 2004.

Sergio, Michael. Telephone intervew April 9, 2004.

Sigworth, Kenneth L. Telephone interviews July 12 and 17, 2004.

Spiese, Albert L. Telephone interview July 22, 2004. Also personal interview with Bert Spiese, his wife Jean, his brother-in-law and sister-in-law while traveling through Dallas on October 12, 2004.

Strong, Margaret. Wife of the late Louis Strong. Telephone interview August 6, 2004.

Tully, Anthony P. Correspondence with author March 23, 2004.

Wood, Perry S. Telephone interviews March 21 and August 4, 2004.

ARTICLES

Decker, Cdr. Daniel D. "World War II Torpedoes." *USS Coghlan*

(DD-606) Newsletter. Part I: February 1997. Part II: April 1997.
Germershausen, Capt. William J., USN (Ret.). "O Boat Duty." *Shipmate*, November 1990.

———. "Sea of Japan Was Climactic Battle." *San Jose Mercury-News*. Sunday, June 6, 1965.

Hackett, Bob, Sander Kingsepp, Allan Alsleban and Peter Cundall. "IJN Seaplane Tender *Kiyokawa Maru*: Tabular Record of Movement." See http://www.combinedfleet.com/Kiyokawa%20Maru_t.htm. Accessed January 29, 2005.

"Hampton Roads bids Farewell to Spadefish." *The Flagship*, Thursday, June 13, 1996.

Mastin, Frank, Jr. "Sailor's Ashes to be Scattered in Pacific." *Montgomery Advertiser*, Thursday, November 14, 1996.

"Napan Relates Exciting Tales of Life Aboard U.S. Navy Submarine." *The Napa Register*, Monday, February 15, 1943.

Tully, Anthony P. "Convoy HI-71 and *USS Harder's* Last Battles." Copyright 1998. See http://www.combinedfleet.com/atully05.htm.

BOOKS

Alden, Cdr. John D., USN (Ret.) *U.S. Submarine Attacks During World War II*. Annapolis: Naval Institute Press, 1989.

———. *United States and Allied Submarine Successes in the Pacific and Far East During World War II. Chronological Listing*. Pleasantville, NY: Self-published, second edition, October 1999.

Beach, Edward L., Cdr., USN. *Submarine!* New York: Henry Holt and Company, 1946.

Blair, Clay, Jr. *Silent Victory. The U.S. Submarine War Against Japan*. Philadelphia: J. B. Lippincott Company, 1975. Two-volume reprint.

Bouslog, Dave. *Maru Killer. War Patrols of the USS Seahorse*. Placentia, CA: R.A. Cline Publishing, 1996. Second Printing, 2001.

Calvert, James F., Vice Admiral, USN (Ret.). *Silent Running. My Years on a World War II Attack Submarine*. New York: John Wiley & Sons, Inc., 1995.

Cline, Rick. *Final Dive. The Gallant and Tragic Career of the WWII Submarine, USS Snook*. Placentia, CA: R.A. Cline Publishing, 2001.

———. *Submarine Grayback. The Life & Death of the WWII Sub, USS Grayback*. Placentia, CA: R.A. Cline Publishing, 1999.

Connor, Claude C. *Nothing Friendly in the Vicinity...My Patrols on the Submarine USS Guardfish During WWII*. Mason City, IA: Savas Publishing Company, 1999.

Davenport, Rear Admiral Roy M., USN (Ret.). *Clean Sweep*. New York: Vantage Press, 1986.

Bibliography

DeRose, James F. *Unrestricted Warfare. How a New Breed of Officers Led the Submarine Force to Victory in World War II*. New York: John Wiley & Sons, Inc., 2000.

Ewing, Steve. *American Cruisers of World War II*. Missoula, Montanta: Pictorial Histories Publishing Company, 1984.

Fluckey, Admiral Eugene B. *Thunder Below! The USS Barb Revolutionizes Submarine Warfare in World War II*. Chicago: University of Illinois Press, 1992.

Galatin, Admiral I. J., USN (Ret.). *Take Her Deep! A Submarine Against Japan in World War II*. New York: Pocket Books, 1988.

Grider, George (as told to Lydel Sims). *War Fish*. Boston: Little, Brown & Company, 1958.

Gugliotta, Bobette. *Pigboat 39. An American Sub Goes to War*. Lexington: The University of Kentucky Press, 1984.

Hinkle, David Randall (editor). *United States Submarines*. New York: Barnes and Noble Books, 2002.

Holmes, Harry. *The Last Patrol*. Shrewsbury, England: Airlife Publishing Ltd., 1994.

Kimmett, Larry and Margaret Regis. *U.S. Submarines in World War II. An Illustrated History*. Seattle: Navigator Publishing, 1996.

Knoblock, Glenn A. *Black Submariners in the United States Navy, 1940-1975*. McFarland & Company, 2005.

LaVO, Carl. *Back From the Deep. The Strange Story of the Sister Subs Squalus and Sculpin*. Annapolis: Naval Institute Press, 1994.

Lockwood, Charles A., Vice Admiral, USN, Ret., and Hans Christian Adamson, Colonel, USAF, Ret. *Hellcats of the Sea*. 1955. New York: Bantam Books, 1988. Reprint.

Lockwood, Charles A., Vice Admiral, USN, Ret. *Sink 'Em All. Submarine Warfare in the Pacific*. New York: E. P. Dutton & Co., Inc., 1951.

Maas, Peter. *The Terrible Hours. The Man Behind the Greatest Submarine Rescue in History*. New York: Harper Torch, 2000.

Mansfield, John G. Jr. *Cruisers for Breakfast. War Patrols of the U.S.S. Darter and U.S.S. Dace*. Tacoma, Washington: Media Center Publishing, 1997.

McCants, William R. *War Patrols of the USS Flasher*. Chapel Hill, North Carolina: Professional Press, 1994.

Mendenhall, Rear Admiral Corwin, USN (Ret.). *Submarine Diary. The Silent Stalking of Japan*. Chapel Hill, North Carolina: Algonquin Books, 1991.

Michno, Gregory F. *USS Pampanito. Killer-Angel*. Norman: University of Oklahoma Press, 2000.

Moore, Stephen L. *The Buzzard Brigade: Torpedo Squadron Ten at War*. Missoula, Montana: Pictorial Histories Publishing, 1996.

Morrison, Samuel Eliot. *History of United States Naval Operations in World War II.* Vol. VIII: *New Guinea and the Marianas. March 1944 - August 1944.* Vol. XII: *Leyte. June 1944 - January 1945.* Vol. XIV. *Victory in the Pacific 1945.* Boston: Little, Brown and Company, 1958. Reprint, 1988.

O'Kane, Richard H., Rear Admiral, USN (Ret.). *Clear the Bridge! The War Patrols of the U.S.S. Tang.* Rand McNally & Company, 1977.

——. *Wahoo. The Patrols of America's Most Famous World War II Submarine.* Novato, CA: Presidio Press, 1987.

Parkin, Robert Sinclair. *Blood on the Sea. American Destroyers Lost in World War II.* New York: Sarpedon, 1995.

Roscoe, Theodore. *United States Submarine Operations in World War II.* Annapolis: Naval Institute Press, 1949.

Ruhe, Capt. William J., USN (Ret.). *War in the Boats. My WWII Submarine Battles.* McLean, Virginia: Brassey's Inc., 1994.

Russell, Dale. *Hell Above, Deep Water Below.* Tillamook, Oregon: Bayocean Enterprises, 1995. A torpedoman's story of life aboard *Flying Fish.*

Sasgen Peter T. *Red Scorpion: The War Patrols of the USS Rasher.* Annapolis, Maryland: Naval Institute Press, 1995.

Scanlon, Val, QMCM(SS), U.S. Navy (Retired). *USS Spadefish in World War II.* Bennington, Vermont: Merriam Press, 1999.

Schratz, Captain Paul R. USN (Ret.) *Submarine Commander. A Story of World War II and Korea.* Lexington, Kentucky: The University Press of Kentucky, 1988.

Smith, Steven Trent. *Wolf Pack. The American Submarine Strategy That Helped Defeat Japan.* Hoboken, New Jersey: John Wiley & Sons, Inc., 2003.

Sterling, Forest J. *Wake of the Wahoo.* Philadelphia: Chilton Company, 1960.

Stern, Robert C. *U.S. Subs in Action.* Carrollton, Texas: Squadron/Signal Publications, Inc., 1983.

Trumbull, Robert. *Silversides.* Chicago: P. W. Knutson and Company, 1990. Reprint of 1945 original by Henry Holt and Company, Inc.

Tuohy, William. *The Bravest Man. The Story of Richard O'Kane & U.S. Submarines in the Pacific War.* Phoenix Mill: Sutton Publishing, 2001.

United States Submarine Veterans of World War II. A History of the Veterans of the United States Naval Submarine Fleet. Dallas: Taylor Publishing Company, 1984-1990. Four volumes.

Wheeler, Keith. *War Under the Pacific.* Alexandria, Virginia: Time-Life Books, 1980.

Index

Italics indicates inclusion in a photo caption.

Alden, Cdr. John D., 161, 169, 292, 414
Allan, Roger W., 150-1, 290, 292
Alvis, Lt. Frank Ryals, 1, 8, 18, 22, 24, 26, 33, *34*, 35-6, 41, 49, *57*, 63, 68, 69, 71-2, 77, 92, *95*, *111*, 115, 122-3, 130, 138, 143-4, 150, 153, 180, *186*, 191, *195*, *406*, 410, 426
Alvis, Libby, *34*
Anderson, Benjamin Herschel, 2,
Anderson, Donald Carl, 2, 134-5, 162, 207, *233*, 236, 267-8, 284
Anderson, Howard T., 177
Apra Harbor (Guam), 108, 238, 247, 300, 315
Armstrong, Edward Richard, 2, 310, 316, 335, 337
Asher, Warren Jay, 2, 134, *233*, *319*, *393*, *406*
Aslito (Isely) Field, 108

Babb, Maurice Lee, Jr., 2, *319*
Balao class submarines, 9, 14
Barger, Clarence Randolf, 2, 32, 33, *34*, 64
Barnes, Silas Marion ("Si"), 2, 33, 94, 135, 148, 160, 168, 209, 222, 228, *233*, 286-7, 289, 296, 309, *415*
Barrel Club (Vallejo), 28-9
Barton, Thad Ralph, 2, 25, 33, 94, 135, *192*, 202, *233*, 237, *319*, 382, 391, *393*, 405
Bassett, Richard Harold, 2, 33, 150, 159-60, 164-5, 187, *233*, *319*, 383, 396, *406*, 426
Battenfield, Willard Elvas, 5, 397, 399
Beach, Capt. Edward L. (Ned), 297
Bieberdorf, Carl Christopher ("Silent Running Carl"), 2, 33, 197, *233*, 249-50
Bird, Donald William, 2, 25, 33, 94, 135, 197, 404, *406*, 408, *415*
Blanchard, Cdr. James William, 420
Bowers, Capt. John, 380
Brenneis, Harry Jerome, 2, 134, 153, 225-6, *233*, 255, 282-3, *304*, *319*, *353*, 354, 391, *406*
Brewer, John Belton, Jr., 2, 115, 134-5, 147, 174, 189, *190*, *192*, 202, 213, 225, *233*, 238, 249, *256*, 261, 263-4, *320*, 332, 348, 370, 382, *393*, 408
Brey, John E., 236
Brinkman, Gerald Adelbert Jr., 5
Bronze Star, 129-30, 164, 187, 196, 231, 271, 300, 388, 412
Brown, Capt. John Herbert ("Babe"), 61, *195*, 238, *271*
Brooks, Sie (n), Jr., 2, 229, *230*, *233*, 376, *387*, 427
Buncke, Ens. Harry Jacob Jr., 2, 307, *308*, 310, 315, 320, 327, 338-9, 342-3, 348, 358-9, 363, 380, *381*, 382-4, *388*, 399, 403-4, *410*, 411
Burns, R. O., 39
Butchofsky, Lucille Carpenter, 25-26
Butchofsky, Richard David, 2, 25-26, 33, 54
Bynum, William Thomas, 2, 249, 304, 376, 382

Caldwell, Capt. Robert Hugh Jr., 137
Campbell, Capt. Gordon, 38
Camp Dealey, 235-41
Camp Myrna, 190
Carney, Hugh Patrick, 2, *233*, *320*, *323*, 382
Case, Joseph Bennion, 2, 48, 76, 98, *233*, 237, 246, 269, *320*, 327, 370, *393*
Casey, J. C., 6, 36
Casey, James David, 2, 309, *319*, 362, 383, *386*, 404, 408, *415*
Cavite (Philippines), 16, 93
Charles, Walter Joseph, Jr., 2, *244*, *248*, *320*, *386*, 427
Chiavacci, Louis Joseph, 2, 33, *406*
Chietro, Frank, 409
Clawson, Meredith Thomas, 5
Code, Thomas Joseph, 5
Cohen, Solomon (n), 2, 47
Cole, James Douglas, 2, 250, *304*, 309-10, 317-8, *320*, *328*, 343-4, 357, 385, 392, 395, *398*, 399, 401, *406*, *407*, 408, *415*
Congressional Medal of Honor, 18, 61, 297
Convoy College, 48-9, 61, 64, 69, 85

Convoy HI-71, 76-8, 85-8, 93-4, 102
Convoy HI-81, 152-4, 156, 158, 160, 163, 169, 173
Convoy MI-27, 156, 158, 161, 169, 173-4
Convoy TAMA-24A, 93, 104
Cook, Lt. George Carlton, 1, 195-6, 207, 216, 220, 224-5, 227, 231, *233*, 234, 247, 251, *255*, 260, 285-6, 288, 292, 301, 305, 307, 411, 426-7
Cooper, Samuel (n), 2, 33, 44, 80, 134-5, 237
Counsell, Edward J., 236
Coye, Cdr. John Starr Jr., 421
Crane, Jeannie, 24
Cromwell, Capt. John, 18
Cruze, Herman Franklin, Jr., 2, 17, 33, 71, 191, *233, 319*
Cunningham, Edwin William, 2, *319*
Cuthbertson, John Marshall ("Gus"), 2, 33, 81, 83, 117, 135, 148, *190, 192*, 207, *233*, 287, 318, *319, 353*, 354, *356*, 396
Cutter, Slade Deville, 242, 420-1

Davenport, Cdr. Roy Milton, 54
Dealey, Cdr. Samuel David, 24, 60, 93, 102, 235, 421
Decker, Lt. Daniel Delos Jr., 1, 8, 9, 18-19, 24, 33, *34*, 35, 49, 56, *57*, 63, 72, 73, 80-2, 84, 87, 91, 97, 107, *111*, 112, 117, 128, 130, 139, 147-8, 151-2, 154, 157, 159-61, 163, 183-4, *186*, 191, 196, 198, 201, 204-6, 216, 218, 222, 231, *233*, 236, 238, 240-1, 248, *249*, 251, 257-8, 260, 262-3, 265, 276, 278-83, 285-6, 289-92, 307, 310, 317, 322-3, 329, 331, 340-1, 344, *345*, 350, *353*, 354-5, 360-1, 364, 367, 369, 376, *388, 393*, 396, 401, 410, *415*, 426
Decker, Jean Duncan, 18, *34*
Decker, Richard W., 396
De Loney, Adam (n), 2
Dependahl, Leonard Edward, 2, 33, 114-5, 130, *233*, 305, *393*, 405, *406*, 427
Depth charges,
Dickerson, Harold W., 177
Dix, Ens. Raymond E., 2, 307, *308*, 310, 333, *388*
Donaho, Cdr. Glenn Robert ("Donc"), 59-61, 64, 99, 105-6, 113, 123, 127
"Donc's Devils" wolf pack, 61, 127
Drew, Wesley Arthur, 2, 21, 33, *233*
Dunleavy, Anthony Jr. ("Red"), 2, 134, 140, *233, 304, 319*, 370, 391-2, *393*, 395, *406, 415*
Dykers, Capt. Thomas Michael, 129

East China Sea, 60, 142, 253, 258, 260, 297, 299, 311, 322, 324,
Edge, Cdr. Lawrence Lott, 314, 374-5, 380
Eimermann, Willard Christ ("Boats"), 2, 26-27, 33, 53-4, 59, 66, 72, 106, 115, 126, 131, 134, 137, 159-61, 163, 164, 179, 185, 191, *192*, 193, 195, 196, 200, 205, 224-5, *233*, 238, *239*, 240, 242, 247, 253, 278, 303, *304*, 310, 316, 318, *319*, 341, 344, 391, *395*, 396, 400, 408
Ellis, Peggy, 414
English, RAdm Robert Henry, 38
Enright, Capt. Joseph Francis,
Erck, Capt. Charles Frederick, 129
Ericson, Robert Alfred, 5

Falconer, WM LeRoy Douglas (Dutch), 2, 22, 33, 134, 229, *233*, 249, *255*, 276, 278, 281-2, *286*, 307, 310, 323, 341, 348, 356, *388, 393*, 399, 408, 410, 426
Farragut, Cdr. David, 13
Fautley, James Walter, 2, 134
Fellows, Lt. Richard Decatur (Dick), 1, *247, 248*, 249, *257*, 270, 276, 278, 307, 310, 329, 344, *381, 388*, 396, 407, 410, 414, *415*
Flaig, F. F., 6, 36
Fletcher, James Wallace, 3, *233, 304, 319*, 328-9, 331, *350*, 351, 364, 366, 384, *386*, 409, 427
Fluckey, Capt. Eugene Bennett, 143, 150, 152, 420-1
FM Sonar, 38-44, 46-53, 61, 73, 127-8, 231, 245-7, 250-3, 255, 258, 266-9, 272-3, 275, 298, 301-2, 311-5, 322, 324-34, 370-1
Ford, Raphael V., 177
Formosa (Taiwan), 61, 74-7, 91, 114, 115-6
Forrestal, James, 400
"Fox Day," 316-7
Fox schedules, 61-2
Frazier, Dale Wayne, 3, 33, 54, 80, 135
Friedell, RAdm Wilhelm Lee, *45*
Fugett, Mack A., 309

Gable, Clark, 15
Gallagher, Jack Ambrose ("Zombie"), 3, 21, 33, 44, *55*, 65, 71, 90, 96-7, 165, 179, 191-2, 205, 225, *233*, 241, 275, 284, 286, 305, 400, 408
Gallaher, Cdr. Anton Renki, 231
Gamby, Orville Richard (Dick), 3, 20-21, 33, 68, 72, 106, 108, 131, 133, 147, 163,

Index

190, 194, 205, *233*, 241, 263, 267, 278-80, *320*, 327, 332, 385, *387*, 391, *393*, 399, 405
Garrison, Cdr. Malcolm, 421
Gato class submarines, 9
Geisler, Rolland W., 177
George, Harry, 3, 25, 33, 94, 118, 130, 134-5, 160, *233*, 249, 426
Germershausen, Cdr. William Joseph, 1, 242-3, *244*, 245-8, 251-61, 263-74, 275-7, 279-81, 284, 286-95, 297-303, *306*, 307, 310, 312, 314-5, 317, 321-2, *323*, 324-35, *336*, 337-46, 349, 351, 355-70, 374-5, 377-80, *381*, 382, 384, *388*, 391, 394-5, 400-1, 404, *406*, 410, 412, *415*, 417, 421-2, 426-7
Gibson, Alvin Wilson, 3, 198, 212, 218, 225, 235, 400
Gillespie, Robert Wayne, 5, 396, 405
Gilly juice, 239-40, 318, 320
Gimber, Capt. Stephen, 198, 231
Goodhue, Theodore L., 236
Goro, Lt. Cdr. Iwabuchi, 93, 95, 99, 102-5
Gouker, Zelbert, 3, 322, 325, 343-4, 352, 357, 360, 362, 371, *386*
Grable, Betty, 24
Graf, Edward Frank, 3, 33, 54-5, 154, *233*, 264, 282-4, *304*, *319*, 351, *353*, 354, *356*, 358, *393, 415*
Graff, Benjamin Pennybaker Jr., 3, 134
Graff, Charles Alfred (Baby Graff), 3, 309, *351*
Gray, Elmo, 177
Greening, Wayne Albert, 5, 396-8, 409
Greer, Capt. Harry, 298
Gregory, Earl Owen, 3, 7, 21, 26, 33, 35, 41, 53, 54
Grider, Capt. George William, 398, 421
Griffith, Charles Clain, 3, 22, 30, 33, 56, 70, 109, 115, 132, 135, 140, *142*, 147, 171, 185, *192*, 193, 197, 199, 202, *233*, 237-8, *239*, *248*, 249-50, 280, 287, 310, 318, 376, 383-4, *393*, 399-400, 405, 408, 427
Griffith, Cdr. Walter Thomas, 421
Gross, Capt. Royce Lawrence, 420
Guam, 108, 228, 230-1, 235-41, 244-7, 252-3, 275, 277, 294, 299-300, 303-4, 308, 311-6, 321, 327, 382

Halsey, Adm William Frederick, 72
Hamilton, Paul Jackson, 5
Harbison, Joseph Albert ("Whitey"), 3, 19-20, 33, 131, 165, 190, 205, *233*, 275, 284, 327, 340, 351, 355, 377, *387*, 391, *393*, 405

Harnwell, Dr. Gaylord Probasco, 39-40, 245, 312
Harvell, John C., 177
Hatch, Carlton, 3
Hayworth, Rita, 24
Hellcats wolfpack, 312-5, 332-4, 365, 370-8, 379-91, 396
Hell's bells, 39, 43, 49, 51, 269, 272, 313, 329-31
Henderson, Dr. Malcolm Colby, 39-40, 42, 246, 250, 312
Hirohito, Emperor, 207, 311, 334-5, 343, 382
Hobbs, Jessie Burl, 3
Hokkaido, Japan, 311, 336-41, 346, 350, 365-6, 368, 370
Holeman, Victor Rolla, 3, 33, 189, *233*, *319*, *393*, 405
Holtz, Arnold Henry (Ike), 243
Honshu (Japan), 68, 183, 311, 334, 365, 368
Hoover, VAdm John Howard, 246
Hord, Cleveland Maybee, 3, *299, 319*
Houser, Gordon Lee, 5
Huff, John Kirkman, 252
Hydeman, Capt. Earl Twining, 312, 314, 316, 317, 321, 323-6, 333, 365, 368-9, 371, 373-6, 378-9, 384, 394-5, 421
"Hydeman's Hepcats" (wolfpack), 314-6, 321, 323-5, 333, 368-71, 374, 377-9, 384

Icenhower, Capt. Joseph Bryan, 198
Ingberg, Norval Owen, 3, *233*, 380, 382
Inland Sea, Japan, 246, 314
Isley, Capt. Robert H., 108
Ives, Victor Leon, 3, 44-5, 81-2, 89, 106-7, 174, 187, 197, 202, 207, 221, *233*, *239*, 260, 310, *319*, 332, 344, 358, 379, *381*, 396, 427
Iwo Jima, 110

Jackson, Robert Franklin, 3, 33, 134, *415*
JANAC, 129, 211, 231, 233, 290, 385, 402, 414, 421-2
Japanese merchant vessels:
Aisakasan Maru (*Osakasan Maru*: AK), 161, 170, 187, 422-3
Akitsu Maru (XAPV), 152, 170
Akiura Maru (AK), *289*, 300, 372
Anzan Maru (AK),
Arita Maru (AO), 170
Awa Maru (AK), 78
Awagawa Maru (AO), 156-7, 170
Chinkai Maru (AK), 170
Chuyo (CVL), 18

Daiboshi Maru No. 6 (Taisei Maru No. 6, AK), 181, 422
Daido Maru (XPkt), 372, 423
Daigen Maru No. 2 (AK), 343, 372, 422
Daiki Maru (AK), 372
Doryu Maru (AP), 264, 277
Edogawa Maru (AP), 159, 170
Eijo Maru (AK), 367, 372, 423
Eiyo Maru (AO), 77-8
Enki Maru (AO), 170
Genzan Maru (AK), 227
Gyokuyo Maru (AK), 149-51, 422-3
Hakko Maru No. 2 (AK), 93-4, *95*, 98, 99-100, 102-4, 422
Hakusan Maru (AK), 372
Hashidate Maru (AO/AP), 170
Hattenzan Maru (AK), 372
Hayasui (AO), 76, 78, 85
Hokkai Maru (AK), 78
Hokuto Maru (AK), 372
Irako (AK), 76, 78
Jinstu Maru (AK), 345, 372, 422
Kaisei Maru (AK), 373
Kaiwa Maru (AK), 373
Keito Maru (AK), 372
Kenjo Maru (AK), 372
Kibitsu Maru (AP), 170
Kiyokawa Maru (XAV), 170
Koan Maru (AK), 372
Koei Maru (AK), 260-1, 300
Kofuku Maru (AK), 372
Kokai Maru (AK), 372
Konzan Maru (AK), 373
Koshu Maru, 170
Kurosio Maru, 93
Lee Tung (Ritsu Go), 290, 423
Mayasan Maru (AK), 78, 156-7, 170
Meisei Maru (AK), 372
Mirii Maru (XAO), 168, 170
Nanshin Maru (AK), 217, 424
Nichian Maru (AK), 118, 422
Nichiman Maru (AK), 118, 422
Niyo Maru, 93-5, 98, 102, 423-4
Noshiro Maru (AP), 78
Noto Maru (AK), 78
Osakasan Maru (see *Aisakasan Maru*)
Oshikayama Maru (AK), 372
Otowasan Maru (AO), 170
Ritsu Go (AK), *289*, 290, 422-3
Sagawa Maru (AK), 372
Sanjin Maru (AK), 373
Sanuki Maru (XAV), 207, *208*, 211, 214, 422
Seisho Maru (AP), 159, 170
Seizan Maru (AK), 363, *364*, 365, 372, 423

Shinei Maru No. 3 (AK), 373
Shinsen Maru (AK), 372
Shinshu Maru (LS), 160-1, 170
Shinten Maru (AK), 120-1, 422
Shinyo Maru No. 3 (AK), 372
Shoho Maru (XAP), 170
Shohei Maru (AK), 228, 422
Shokei Maru (AK), 120-1, 422
Shoyo Maru (AO), 372
Taga Maru (AK), 372
Taikai Maru (XPkt), 244
Tairai Maru (Taidai Maru, AK), *222-3*, 225-6, 230, 422
Taisei Maru No. 6 (AK), 181, 423
Taito Maru (AK), 373
Takakurasan Maru (AK), 373
Takima Maru, 252
Tamatsu Maru (AP), 78, 87-8, 106, 422
Teia Maru (AK), 78, 85
Teiyo Maru (AO), 78
Tenshin Maru No. 3 (junk), 285-8, 422
Toa Maru (AO), 170
Toei Maru (AK), 243
Unkai Maru No. 8 (AK), 343, *344*, 372, 422
Wakae Maru (AK), 372
Wakatama Maru (AK), 372
Yozan Maru (AK), 372
Zuiko Maru (AK), 372

Japanese Navy (IJN) warships:
Asakaze (DD), 76-8, 93, 98
CD-8, 149-51, 423
CD-11, 78
CD-25, 104
CD-32, 105
CD-61, 170, 173
CD-134, 170
Daito (PF), 156, 158, 170
Etorofu (CD/PF), 78, 158, 170
Fujinami (DD), 76, 78, 88
Harukaze (DD), 100
Hiburi (DD), 78, 93
Hinode Maru No. 17 (PC), 292, 301, 422
Hirato (CD), 78
I-122, 372
Jinyo (Shinyo), 152-4, 155-6, 158, 160-1, *162*, 163, 168-70, 173, 187, 211, 422-3
Kasado (DD), 373
Kashi (DD), 158, 168, 170
Kume (PF), 158, 170, 207, 211, 214, 422-3
Kurahashi (CD), 78
Matsuwa (CD/PF), 78, 93
Mikura (CD), 78
Sado (CD/PF), 78, 93
Shinan (PF), 156, 158, 170

Shonan (CD), 78
Shinyo (see *Jinyo*)
Sub Chaser *156*, 169-70, 422
Sub Chaser *157*, 170
Taiyo (*Otaka*; CVE), 76, 78, 85
Tsushima (PF), 158, 170
Unyo (CVE), 60
Yunagi (DD), 76-8, 93-8, 99-105

Jerolmon, Walter Edward, 3, 134, *192*, *233*
Joe (Japanese POW), 286-8, 296, 300
Johnson, Ens. Charles C., 2, 196, 230, *233*, 249, *255*, 288

Keeney, William Jackson, Jr., 3, *28*, 246, 269, *319*, 327
Kelley, William Patrick ("Pat"), 3, 22, 28-31, 33, *54*, *65*, 140, *233*, 242, 250, 286, 287-8, *320*, 376, 408, *415*, 427
King, Adm. Ernest Joseph, 136
King George V, 315
Kinsella, Cdr. William Thomas, 421
Kirkpatrick, Cdr. Charles Cochran, 421
Kite, Vernon Joseph, 3, *67*, 309, 347, 363-4, 369, 397
Klakring, Cdr. Thomas Burton, 421
Knox, Frank, 32
Korea, 137, 142-3, 181, 206, 256, 258, 286, 297, 311, 324, 328, 334-5,
Kossler, Cdr. Herman Joseph, 420
Kreher, Emery Andrew, 3, *25*, 33, 81, 83, 135, 187, 197, 207, 216, 225, 231, *233*, 260, 263, 270, 278, 289, *319*, 327, 343, 347, *353*, 354, *387*, *393*, *406*, 427
Kreinbring, Irwin Henry ("Irv"), 3, 33, 59, 95-6, 134, 150, 159, *189*, 190, *195*, 198, 210, 231, *233*, 262-3, 275-6, 278, *320*, 340, 344, 363, 369, 382, *393*, 427
Kure Island, 138, 381
Kurie, Dr. Franz N. D., 39-40, 43-4, 46-8, 52, 312
Kuroshio Current, 311, 324, 326
Kyushu, Japan, 152, 155, 177, 256, 265-6, 275, 287

La Croix, Alvin Maurice, 5
La Croix, Lt.(jg) Edward J., 1, 196, 204, 218, 227, *233*, *247*, 248, *249*, 258, 260, 266-8, 307, 310, 330, 352, *386*, 427
LaFose, Murphy, 3, 382
La Perouse Strait, 57, 311, 314, 317, 334, 358-9, 362, 373-6, 378-80, 382, 384
Larkie, Arthur Edward, 3, 33
Larkin, Alfred Lawrence Jr., 5
La Rocca, Albert George ("Al"), 3, 309, 318, *320*, *323*, 330, 376, *379*, 391, 404, 409
Larsen, Maj. Henry L., 235
Latham, Capt. Richard Clark (Dick), 251, 253, 260, 265, 271, *275*, 277, 314, 321
"Latham's Locators" wolf pack, 253
Laundy, Lt. Henry Howard Jr. (Gus), 1, 11, 24, 25, 33, 37, 48, 56, 57, 63, 69, 80, 82, 84, 85, 90, 100-1, 105, 109-10, *111*, 117, 130, 136, 138-40, 150, 158, 160, 168, 176, 179, 183, *186*, 196, 198, 202, 204-5, 207, 219, 227, 231, 248, 426-7
Laundy, James, 110-11
Lester, Clifford Robert, 3
Leyte, 107
Lewis, Edgar Lycurgous ("Shaky Jake"), 3, 28-30, 33, 37, *45*, *65*, 95-6, 126, 133, 150, *159*, 183, 191-2, 194, 197, 210, 224-5, *233*, *237*, *239*, 247, 251, 254-5, 257, 262-3, 282, 284-5, 304-5, 310, 344, *353*, *355*, *356*, 357-8, 377, 396-7
Lockwood, VAdm Charles Andrews ("Uncle Charlie"), 9, 13, 38, *39*, 40, 46, 49-52, 57-61, 108, 123, 127-8, 137, 152, 156, 188, 224, 243, 245-7, 250-3, *255*, 258-9, 267, 272-3, 275, 294, 298, 302, 311-7, 324, 326, 331, 334, 341, 360, 362, 368, 370, 373-4, 376, *379*, 380, 382, *385*, *390*, 391, 394, 396, 400
Loughlin, Capt. Elliott, 137, 143, 152, 154, 156, 187
"Loughlin's Loopers" (wolf pack), 153-4
Luau (ship's mascot), 28-30, 32, *45*, *55*, 68, *111*, *120*, 129, 132-3, 167, *184*, 185, *186*, 194, 213, 231, *233*, *237*, *239*, *249*, 250, *285*, *301*, *319*, *328*, *387*, *400*, 404
"Luau" newsletter, 163, 413-5
Lundquist, Hugo Carl, 3, 33, 64, *67*, 68, 71, 81, 83, 103, 106, 110, 123, *125*, *133*, 135, 138, 146, 154, 161-2, 176, 179, 181, 183-4, 207, 213, 215, 225, 228, *233*, *237*, 256, 264, 270, 277, 284, 295, *320*, 332, 338, *351*, 357, 364, 365, 367, 370, 376, 379-80, *393*, 405, *406*
Luzon (Philippines), 61, 72, 79, 90-1, 93-4, 98, 99, 113, 117, 235
Lynch, Capt. Richard Barr, 314

MacArthur, Gen. Douglas, 89, 174
Mainard, Bill Jack, 3, 197, *233*
Majoue, Connie, 404
Majoue, Paul Henry Jr. ("Hocks"), 3, 17, 23-24, 33, 62, 66, 67, 77-9, 81-2, 87-8, 94, 97, 103, 107, 109-10, 112, 117, 130, 132, 134, 148, 174, 191, 194, 196-7, 201,

212, 215, 217, 219, 229, *233*, *239*, 245, 251, 260, 262, *286*, 294-5, 298, 306, 310, *320*, 327, 342, 344, *383*, 391, *393*, 403-4, 409, *414*, *415*, 427
Majuro (Marshalls), 108, 182, 184-7, 189-96, 198, 200
Mako (Pescadores), 76
Manila (Philippines), 76, 90, 93, 98, 152, 156
Manson, Robert Thomas, 3
Marasco, Ralph Joseph Jr., 5, 405, *414*
Mare Island Naval Shipyard, 13-17, 19, 21-32, 34, 37, 40, 43-5, 68, 73, 128, 242, 244, 298, 305, 364, 401-4, 410, *414*
Martin, Ens. Donald Ernest, 2, 46, 57, 62, 63, 75, 80, 105, *111*, 116, 117, 157, 184, 185, 187, 196, 206, 216, 220, *233*, 248, 250, 267, 275, 277, 307, 426
Martin, Cdr. John Croysdale, 421
Massar, Bernard Adam ("Bernie"), 3, 10, 14-18, 29, 33, 34-36, 37, 44, 45, 66, *67*, 68, 71, 73, 96, 106, 114, 128, *133*, 150, 159-61, 164, 185, *192*, 193, 194, 200, 210, 212-3, *233*, 236, 251, 254-5, 258, 262, 265, 275-6, 278, 284-5, 288, 295, 304-5, 317, *319*, 326, *328*, 329, 340, 347, *353*, 354, *356*, *383*, 384-5, *386*, 391-2, *393*, 394-5, 397, *398*, 400, 404-5, *406*, 408, *415*, 427
Maurer, Capt. John Howard, 193, 198, 200, 231
Maxwell, Robert Elmer, 3, 33, 80, *133*, *192*, *233*, *237*
May, Andrew Jackson, 8-9
McGregor, Lt. Cdr. Louis Darby ("Sandy"), 60, 73, 76, 123, 127
McLaughlin, Paul Francis, 3, 33
McMahon, Wallace Francis, 3, 25, 30, 33, 55, 82, 110, 117, 135, 146-7, 171-2, 184, 194, 207, 213, 221, 226, *233*, 237, 261, 289, 295, 309, *319*, 332, 356-7, *387*, 392, *393*, 394, 408, *415*
Melstrand, Howard Walfred, 3, *319*
Metcalf, Cdr. Ralph Marion, 421
Midway ("Gooneyville"), 61, 62-4, 108, 137-8, 251, 309, 380-2
"Mighty Mine Dodgers," 379
"Mike Day," 317, 334, 365, 373
Mikesell, Robert Edward, 3, *320*, 382
Miles, Milton E., 215
Miller, Thomas Harry ("Buck"), 3, 16-17, 19-20, 33, 41, 67, 106, 114-6, 126, 128, *133*, *146*, 163, 173, 176, 177, 183, 194, 223-4, 230, 255, 280-4, *304*, *319*, *328*, 330, *353*, 354, *356*, 370, *383*, 392, *393*,

395-6, *398*, 405, *406*, 409, 414, *415*
Mines, 47-53, 144, 151-2, 178, 203-5, 265, 272, 275, 311, 322-33
Mitzel, Joseph Emanuel, 3, 19-20, 22, 33, 114-5, 134
Momsen, Capt. Charles B. ("Swede"), 8, 60
Momsen lung, 8, 17
Moody, Roy Hubert, 3, 28-29, 33, 110, 171, *192*, *233*, *248*, *304*, *320*, 377, 392, *393*, 405, *415*
Morrison, James Walter, 4, 382
Morton, Cdr. Dudley Walker ("Mush"), 56-7, 142, 311, 332, 421
Mueller, Jack L., 177
Mullen, Melvin "C" ("Moon") 4, 135, 189, *233*, *319*, *393*
Munson, Cdr. Henry Glass (Hank), 85, 90, 420-1
Myrna Island, 190

Nagasaki, Japan, 270
Navy Cross, 129-30, 187, 195, 196, 231, 253, 297, 388, 412, 413
Nesnee, John, 3, 33, 135, *233*, *319*, *393*
New London Submarine Base (CT), 11, 13, 14, 16, 17, 19, 22, 24, 27, 42, 65, 66, 79, 242-3, 307, 403-4
Newport News shipyard, 20
Newton, Gerald Arthur, 4, 22-24, 33, 62, 148, 196-7
Nimitz, Capt. Chester William Jr., 421
Nimitz, Adm. Chester William Sr., 40, 108, 129, 132, 188, 243, 252, 370, 380, 382, 399
Nishi Suido, 253, 324
Noblit, William James, 5, 397, 400
Noonan, Maurice Anthony, 4, 33, 96, 133, 159, 210, *233*, 237, 304, 325-6, 356-7, *393*, 397, 405, *406*
Nordstrom, Edwin George, 4, 33, 133
Nudd, Alton George, 4
Nygard, Everett J., 177

Okamura, Nobuyuki, 163
O'Kane, Cdr. Richard Hetherington ("Dick"), 60, 128, 397, 420-1
Okinawa, 203, 246, 251, 253, 260, 273, 303, 307
Olah, Andrew, 4, 33, 117, *192*, *233*, *319*, *353*, 354, *356*, *381*, *393*
Olsen, Norman Androus, 4, 33
Olson, Olaf Bernard (Sandleben), 4, *67*, 197, 199, 207, 212-3, 229-30, *233*, 318, *319*, 325-6, *406*, 407
O'Neil, Thomas Patrick, 4, 197, *233*, *319*,

327, 409, *415*
Operation Barney, 311-2, 314, 316
Ordway, Emerson Locke, 4, 21, 33, 197, *233*, *239*, *248*, 305, 309-10, 327, *393*, 427
Orr, William, 321
Osaka, Japan, 321
Osmus, Wesley Frank, 300
Otaru Harbor, 337-46, 367

Paine, Lt. Cdr. Roger Warde Jr., 40
Palau, 13
Panek, Edmund Edward, 4, 23, 33, 62, 133
Parker, Billy Rice, 4, 33, 44-5
Parks, Capt. Lewis Smith, *142*, *172*, 247
Parscale, James Stewart, 4, 64, 80, 135, 165-6, 171
Partin, Doyle Burline, 4, 33, 94, 135, *192*, *233*
Paulson, Roger Francis, 4, *319*, 382
Pearl Harbor, 28, 44, 45-56, 59, 61, 108, 123, 127-37, 147, 182, 184, 185, 229, 238, 241-2, 245, 251, 294, 303, 306, 368, 379, 384-92, 397-400
Peel, John Richard, 4, 20, 33, 131, 147, *233*, *239*, 241, 280, 310, *319*, 327, *393*, 405
Pelliciari, Nicholas John, 4, 33, 135, *233*, *320*, 396, *406*
Pierce, Capt. George Ellis, 242, 246, 312, 314, 374, 379-80
Pierce, Sam Henry, 4, 318
"Pierce's Polecats" (wolf pack), 314, 316, 333-4
Pigman, Billy Bob, 4, 137, *233*, *248*, 284, *304*, *320*, 340, 351, *355*, 377, *393*, 409
Pike, Neal, 4, 33, 42-3, 47-8, 50-3, 76, 80, 86-7, 98, 113, 117-8, 120, 128, 130, 159, 168-9, 180, 224, *233*, 235-6, *239*, 246, 251, *258*, 260, 266-70, *271*, 272, 275, 310, 312, 322, 325-31, 339-40, 344-6, 370-1, 391, *393*, 398, 408, *415*, 426-7
Pirrung, Edward Nicklous ("Buckwheat"), 4, 33, 55, 154
Pizzini, Fabian Frank, 4, 134
Portwood, William Marshall, 4, 56, 109
Potting, Roy Christian, 4, 382-3
Powell, Wayne Hobart, 4, 33, *233*, *406*
Powers, Kenneth Clyde, 4, 23, 33, *42*, 62, 134, 148, 164-8, *204*, *233*, *319*, 327, *328*, 383, *393*, *398*, 405, *406*, 414-5
Prast, James Leroy, 5
Presidential Unit Citation, 185, 187, 400, *414*, 425
Price, James Edward, 4, 33, 134
Puryear, Capt. C.W. Jr., 407

Ramage, Capt. Lawson Paterson ("Red"), 60-1
Randall, Augustus Lockhart, 4, 134
Reich, Cdr. Eli Thomas, 420
Rewold, Denise, 29
Rewold, Radford Crowell ("Rebel"), 4, 23, 28-30, 33, 38, 133, 137, 191, 194, 196, *233*, *237*, *239*, 280, 282, 305, 310, *353*, 354, 377, 396, 408
Riley, Thomas Gordon ("Mother"), 4, 33, 55-6, 112, 154, 179, 196, 213, 231, *233*, 240, 284, *320*, 357, *393*
Ring, Joseph John, 4, *304*, *320*
"Risser's Bobcats" (wolf pack), 314, 316, 321, 334, 374
Risser, Cdr. Robert Dunlap, 314, 321, 334, 374, 385
Roach, Lt. Cdr. John Paul (Beetle), 243, 251-2
Roberts, Maj. Donald W., 177-8
Roberts, William Arthur, 4
Rolf, Charles Frederick, 4, 134, 167, *233*
Roosevelt, Pres. Franklin D., 298
Royal Hawaiian Hotel (Pink Palace), 131-3, 136, 190, 228, 382, 391-2, 394-6, 399
Rymer, Robert Hamilton, 4, *255*, *256*, 278
Ryukyu Islands, 258, 275, 303

SACO (Sino-American Cooperation Organization), 215
Sadamichi, RAdm Kajioka, 76, 85, 88, 90, 93
Saipan, 107-13, 123, 125, 127, 201, 203, 246, 250-1, 253, 257
San Diego, CA, 36, 38, 40-1,
Sandleben, Olaf Bernard (see Olson)
Sands, Lt. Cdr. Eugene Thomas, 247, 300
San Francisco, CA, 8, 9, 13, 15, 18, 21-26, 32-35, 44-5, 404
Scanland, Capt. Francis W., 32
Scanland, Mrs. Francis W., 10
Schraft, William Ernest, 5
Schratz, Lt. Cdr. Paul Richard, 193, 200
Scheerer, Robert Allen, 4
Scherman, Francis Julian, 4, 33, 38, 55, 68, 130, 136, 154, 179, 184, 194, *233*, *239*, 253-4, 282-3, 308, 310, *353*, 354, *356*, 358, 377, 382, 396, 427
Schmelzer, Carl Thomas ("Stinky"), 4, 21, 33, 54, 103, 126, 165-6, 171, *172*, 210, *233*, 238, *239*, 240, *248*, 250, 305, 309-10, *319*, 327, 377, *388*, 396, 399, 427
Scholle, Donald Joseph, 4, 33, 106, 109,

115, 135-6, 162, 168, *192*, 211, 230, *233*, 236, 304, 308-9, *320*, 323, 330, 332, 340, 347, 350, 352, 355, 362-3, 376-7, *406*, 407, *415*
Schuett, James Shirley, 4, 33, 64, 80, 82, 87, 109, 119, 130, 136, 157, 180, 198, 207, 216, 220, 222, *233*, *237*, 260, 288, *319*, 344-5, 367, 369-70, *386*, *393*, 427
Schumer, John Martin, 4, 134-5, *192*, 210, 224, 239, 287, 300, 408-9
Scott, Cdr. John Addison, 13
Sea of Japan, 57, 246, 251, 256, 267, 298, 311, 314-7, 321, 324, 332, 334-70, 373, 375, 379-81, 384, 388-9, 394, 396-7, 401
Seaweed (mascot), 194, 213, 231, *233*, *237*, *249*, 250, *254*, *285*, *301*, *319*, *400*, 404-5
Sergio, Michael ("Little Foxhole"), 4, 23-24, 31, 33, 49, 62, 67-8, 73, 77-9, 81, 88, 97, 103, 117, 139-40, 158-9, 177, 191, 194-5, 197, 217, 219, 231, *233*, 236, 260, *320*, 327, 342, 344, 364, 396, 427
Shaw, Thomas Eugene, 4, *233*, *298*, *320*
Shearer, Everett Jr., 5, 397
Shelby, Cdr. Edward Ellis, 137, 156, 182
Shephard, Cdr. Evan Tyler, 156
Sherman, Vernon Fred, 5
Sieglaff, Cdr. William Bernard (Barney), 311-2, 314, 394
Sigworth, Kenneth Leroy, 5, 15, 33, 54, 72, 103, *133*, 146, 147-8, 149, 162, 165-6, 212, *233*, 235, 237, 262-3, *304*, 392, *393*, 395, 405, *406*
Silver Star, 129-30, 164-5, 187, 231, 243, 345, 371
Simms, William Wallace Jr., 5, 35, 56, 81, 82-3, 88-9, 94, 117-8, 134-5
Smith, Irving W., 177
Smith, Raymond Charles, 5
Snider, Cameron Frederick, 5, 134, 409
Snyder, Gilbert L., 236
Sofu Gan ("Lot's Wife"), 68, 139, 183, 321
Solomon, Henry Lewis, 5, 33, 43-4, 56, 109, *233*, 249, 427
"Sonar Day," 317, 369
Spiese, Albert Lewis ("Bert"), 5, 14, 33, 44, 46, 53, 63, 67, 69, 71, 81-3, *89*, 97, 106, 109-10, 123, 132, 134-5, *409*
Stanford, Jack, 5
Steinmetz, Cdr. Everett Hartwell, 314, 324-5, 328, 333, 376-7
Stephenson, Arnold John, 5
Street, Cdr. George Levick III, 253, 277, 297, 421
Strong, Louis Edward, 5, 396
Sugo (Japanese POW), 226, 231

Sullivan, Charles W., 177
Swinburne, Cdr. Edwin Robinson, 40

Takao, 93
Tanapag Harbor (Saipan), 107-10, 113, 250-1, 253
Taylor, John Wright, 5, *248*, *319*, *387*
Terboss, Wiliam Frederick, 5, *192*, 197, *233*, *319*
Tiburon Bay, 328, 404
Tinian, 108
Tokyo, Japan, 110, 198, 204, 298, 346, 400
Tokyo Rose, 10, 69, 176, 203-4
Torpedoes: Mark 14 (XIV) steam, 56-7, 88, 109, 118, 122, 136-7, 150, 181, 314, 343, 363-4; Mark 18.1 electric, 56-7, 101, 136-7, 219, 221-2, 226, 228, 260, 289-90, 315; Mark 18.2 electric, 273; Mark 23 steam, 56-7, 101, 219, 314, 343
Transbalt (Russian AK), 360, *361*, 368, 373, 377, 380, 389, 423-4
Triebel, Cdr. Charles Otto, 420-1
Truman, Pres. Harry S., 399
Trupis, Anthony, 236
Tsugaru Strait, 311
Tsushima Straits, 251, 253, 268, 272, 298, 311-2, 314, 317, 322-34, 370, 374
Tully, Anthony, 160, 168
Tyree, Cdr. Alexander Kelly, 314, 334

Ultra, 149, 152, 217, 251-2, 259, 265, 290, 297
Underwood, Cdr. Gordon Waite, 1, 8, 9, 10-12, *13*, 14-15, 24, 26, 30, *32*, 33, *34*, 35, 36, 41-2, 44, *45*, 46, 48-55, 57, 59-64, 70-1, 73, 75-91, 94-6, 99-105, 107, *111*, 113, 115-25, 127-30, 136-40, 143-54, 156-61, 163-9, 172-5, 178-9, 181-3, *186*, 187, 190, 193, 195, 197-8, 200-4, 206-32, *233*, 242, 412-3, 417, 420-2, 426
Underwood, Marion Outerson, 11, *34*
"Underwood's Urchins" (wolf pack), 137-42, 150, 152-4, 174, 198, 201-3
United States warships:
Albacore (SS-218), 420
Alwyn (DD-355), 15
Apollo (AS-25), 238
Archerfish (SS-311), 415, 420
Argonaut (SS-166), 19, 242, 312
Arizona (BB-39), 15, 46, 306
Aspro (SS-309), 88, 408
Atule (SS-403), 193, 195, 198, 200-3, 207, 217, 231, 400
Balao (SS-285), 399

Index

Bang (SS-385), 201-2, 213, 229, 231
Barb (SS-220), 137, 143, 149-53, 156, 382, 416-21, 423
Barracuda (SS-163), 27
Benham (DD-397), 396
Billfish (SS-286), 113
Bluefish (SS-232), 77, 78, 85-6, 89, 257
Boarfish (SS-327), 420
Bonefish (SS-223), 297-8, 308-9, 311-2, 314, 333, 373-5, 379-80, 382
Bowfin (SS-287), 78, 245, 298, 311-2, 314, 334, 373-5, 377-8, 384, *390*, 400, 417-9, 421
Bullhead (SS-332), 198, 283
Burrfish (SS-312), 249
Bushnell (AS-15), 185-6, 190, 194-5, 198
Castor (AKS-1), 412
Cero (SS-225), 60, 299, 400
Cochino (SS-345), 411-2
Coghlan (DD-606), 18-19
Colorado (BB -45), 11
Crevalle (SS-291), 212, 275, 298, 312, 314-6, 321, 324-5, 328, 332-4, 368, 372-7, 379, 420
Devilfish (SS-292), 201-2, 230, 250
Dogfish (SS-350), 408
Downes (DD-375), 107
Drum (SS-228), 25, 417-9
Ellet (DD-398), 113
Enterprise (CV-6), 108
Fanning (DD-385), 300
Finback (SS-230), 22, 25, 400
Flasher (SS-249), 170, 398, 400, 417-21
Flier (SS-250), 63
Flying Fish (SS-229), 312, 314, 334, 372-5, 377-8, 384, 385, *390*, 400
Fulton (AS-11), 201, 246, 250-1
Grayback (SS-208), 60, 417
Griswold (DE-7), 248
Guardfish (SS-217), 417-9, 421
Guavina (SS-362), 196
Gudgeon (SS-211), 415, 417
Gunnel (SS-253), 400
Gwin (DD-433), 396
Haddo (SS-255), 78, 93, 98, 421
Haddock (SS-231), 25, 26, 54, 243, 251-2, 281
Halibut (SS-232), 22
Hammerhead (SS-364), 60, 421
Harder (SS-257), 24, 60, 78, 93, 102, 235, 418-9, 421
Henley (DD-391), 26
Holland (AS-3), 108, 110, *111*, 113, 230, 239, 312, 315
Hornet (CV-8), 20

Hull (DD-345), 73
Jack (SS-259), 417
Jallao (SS-368), 195, 198, 201, 229, 396
Laffey (DD-459), 303
Lexington (CV-2), 26
Lexington (CV-16), 108
Macaw (ASR-11), 63
Mississippi (BB-23), 11
Missouri (BB-63), 400
Monaghan (DD-354), 73
Narwhal (SS-167), 55
Nautilus (SS-168), 21, 25, 242
Nevada (BB-36), 242
New York (BB-34), 22
O-4, 25
O-6, 242-3
Oklahoma (BB-37), 11, 46, 306
Osmus (DE-701), 300
Otus (ARG-20), 196
Parche (SS-384), 60-1, 307
Pargo (SS-264), 60, 396
Patterson (DD-392), 26
PC-549, 315-6
PC-1077, 61
PC-1126, 201
Peto (SS-265), 137-8, 141, 144, 150, 152, 156, 159, 170, 174, 176, 178, 180, 182
Pictor (AF-54), 411
Picuda (SS-382), 59-62, 64, 70, 73, 75-6, 78, 91, 99, 105-6, 108, 113, 124, 126, 137, 153, 156-8, 170
Pintado (SS-387), 78
Piper (SS-409), 396
Pittsburgh (CA-72), 73
Plunger (SS-179), 57
Pogy (SS-266), 198, 307, 380, 396-7, 418-9, 421
Pogy (SSN-637), 408
Pomfret (SS-391), 170
Pompano (SS-181), 28
Pompon (SS-267), 195, 198, 200-1, 203, 206-7, 213-5, 231
Proteus (AS-19), 230, 235, 250, 300, 305, 307-9, 327, 400
Pruitt (DM-22), 384
PS-483, 127
Queenfish (SS-393), 137, 143-4, 152, 153, 156, 170
R-14, 21, 249
R-20, 14-15, 19, 21
Ralph Talbot (DD-390), 397
Ramsey (DM-16), 198
Rasher (SS-269), 77, 78, 85-6, 89-90, 417-21
Raton (SS-270), 77

Razorback (SS-394), 404, 412
Ray (SS-271), 421
Redfish (SS-395), 59-62, 64, 70, 73, 75-8, 105-6, 108, 113, 124-5,
Remora (SS-487), 305, 411
Rock (SS-274), 195, 411
S-13, 26
S-14, 26
S-15, 420
S-17, 20, 26
S-20, 24
S-27, 11
S-31, 396
S-34, 40
S-38, 420
S-43, 309
S-44, 420
Sailfish (SS-192), 107
Sandlance (SS-381), 421
Sarda (SS-488), 410, 412
Sargo (SS-188), 196
Savannah (CL-42), 19
Sawfish (SS-276), 57
SC-775, 253
Scorpion (SS-278), 63
Sculpin (SS-191), 18
Sea Devil (SS-400), 279
Sea Dog (SS-401), 298, 312, 314-6, 321, 323-6, 328, 332-4, 365, 368, 371-6, 379-80, 385, 395, 421
Sea Fox (SS-402), 235-7
Seahorse (SS-304), 14, 242, 273, 275, 298, 311, 417-21
Sealion (SS-195),
Sealion II (SS-315), 60, 417, 420
Sea Owl (SS-405), 400, 411
Searaven (SS-196), 26, 195-6, 411
Seawolf (SS-197), 417-20
Seid (DE-256), 47
Sennet (SS-408), 396
Shad (SS-235), 60
Shark II (SS-314), 128
Silversides (SS-236), 13, 19, 22, 54, 135, 397, 417-9, 421
Skate (SS-305), 14, 109, 312, 314, 333, 372-5, 384, *390*
Snook (SS-279), 26, 60, 142, 417-21
Spadefish (SS-411): commissioning of, 10-12; armament of, 14, 37-8; first patrol, 58-130; second patrol of, 131-88; third patrol of, 198-234; fourth patrol of, 250-301; fifth patrol of, 315-89; battles typhoon, 71-3; torpedo attacks by, 80-4, 87-8, 94-6, 102, 117-20, 122, 150-1, 159-63, 169-70, 181, 207-9, 216-7, 219-20, 222, 227-8, 260-1, 273-4, 289-90, 292, 343-5, 347, 359-64, 367, 369; gun actions of, 281-5, 351-8, 359-60; POWs transported by, 105-8, 224-6, 231, 286-8, 300; battle flags of, 109, 111, 350, 380, 384, 403-4; motor scooter smuggled aboard, 131-2, 147, 190, 241; chains drug against hull, 211-2; maps minefields, 267-73; fired on by another submarine, 270-1; boarding party of, 285-8; transits minefields submerged, 322-32; sinks Russian ship, 359-62; decommissioned, 405; sinking records, 417-23
Spadefish (SSN-668), 405-6, 407-8
Spence (DD-512), 73
Sperry (AS-12), 135, 185, 238, 396
Spot (SS-413), 14
Springer (SS-414), 14
Squalus (SS-192), 7-8, 18, 60
Steelhead (SS-280), 60
Stewart (DD-224), 55
Stickleback (SS-415), 14, 396
Sunfish (SS-281), 14, 137-9, 141, 143-4, 152, 156, 158-9, 170, 173-4, 176, 178-80, 182, 185, 309, 418-9
Tambor (SS-198), 11, 22, 243-4, 362
Tang (SS-306), 8, 14, 25, 60, 128, 397, 402, 416-21
Tarpon (SS-175), 15-16, 45
Tautog (SS-199), 417-9
Tennessee (BB-44), 306
Texas (BB-35), 22
Thresher (SS-200), 417-9
Tilefish (SS-307), 14
Tinosa (SS-283), 14, 60, 128, 245-6, 250-1, 253, 257-8, 260, 265, 270-1, 275, 277, 298, 311-2, 314, 321, 334, 372-5, 377-8, 384, *387*, 390, 417-9
Tirante (SS-420), 253, 275, 277, 291-2, 297, 421
Torqua, 40, 43
Torsk (SS-423), 396, 399
Trepang (SS-412), 14, 54
Trigger (SS-237), 14, 417-9
Triton (SS-201), 421
Trutta (SS-421), 294-5
Tullibee (SS-284), 14
Tuna (SS-203), 13, 24, 25, 252
Tunny (SS-282), 14, 245-6, 312, 314, 333, 374-5, 379, 382
Tusk (SS-426), 411
Underwood (FFG-36), *413*
Vega (AK-17), 11
Wahoo (SS-238), 14, 40, 56-8, 60, 142, 311, 314, 332, 418-9, 421
West Virginia (BB-48), 306

Whale (SS-239), 14, 29, 400
Yukon (AF-9), 25

University of California Divison of War (UCDWR), 39-40, 46, 48, 52, 61, 128, 311
Ustick, Claire Marie Parsons, 16, *34*
Ustick, Cdr. Perry W., 15
Ustick, Lt. Cdr. Theodore Montanye (Ted), 1, 8, 14, 15, *16*, 17-18, 24, 27, 30, 32, 33, *34*, 35-36, 41, 45, 46, 53, 56, 57, 63-4, 74, 80, 82, 87, 93, 100-1, 108-9, *111*, 117, *120*, 121, 130, 134, 136, 138, 149, 150, 160-1, 164, 167-9, 171, 180-1, 184-5, *186*, 193, 195, 411, *415*, 426

Vallejo, CA, 13, 16, 28-31, 55
Vladivostok, 334, 359-61, 368
Voge, Capt. Richard George ("Dick"), 61, 311, 314

Wake Island, 64, 100, 251
Waleszonia, Alexander John Jr., 5, 17, 25, 26, 33, 35
Wall, Lt.(jg) James D., 5, 396, 401
Warder, Capt. Frederick Burdett, 60
Ware, Ens. William James, 2, 26, 33, 55, 57, 63, 85, 105, *111*, 117, 136, 150-1, 159-60, 176, *186*, 187, *190*, 196, 205, 206, 209, 224, 231, *233*, 234, 248-9, 269, 277, 283, 285, 288, 307, 310, 332, *352*, 353-4, 356, 367, *381*, *388*, 396, 410, *415*, 426-7
Waterman, Cdr. John, 382
Way, Angus Park, 5
Weidner, Delbert Clinton Jr., 5, 33, 134
Wells, Francis Arthur ("Red"), 5, *239*, 281, *285*, 287, 310, *320*, 347, 427
Whitaker, Reuben Thornton, 420
White, Ens. Ray Curtis, 2, 26, 33, *34*, 57, 63, *111*, 116, 121, 159-60, 164-5, *186*, 187, 195, 427
Wolf packs, 59-61, 137, 198, 201, 23, 311-5
Wood, Lt.(jg) Perry Satterthwaite, 1, 8, 9, 22-23, 24, 32-33, *34*, 35-36, 41, 47, 57, 61, 62, 63-4, 68, 71, 80, 88, 100, *111*, 117, 122, 134, 138, 147, 154, 157, 159, 162, 183, *186*, 187, 196, 205, 216, 218, 228, 230, *233*, 239-40, 249, 257-8, 260, 266, 272, 275-7, 292, *304*, 307, 310, 313, 316, 318, 322, 326, 330, 340, 343-4, 355-6, 367, 369, *388*, *393*, 397, 400-1, *406*, *415*, 426-7
Wright, Lt. Cdr. Richard Morgan (Dick), 1, 305, *306*, 307, 310, 313, 316, 317-8, 330, 334, 337, 339, 341, 344, 352, 359, 364, 367, 369, *381*, 383, 388-9, 392, 397, 399, 404, 411-2, 426

Yangtze River, 142, 149, 151
Yates, Palmus Lamar, 5, 33, 134
Yellow River, 142
Yellow Sea, 142-52, 177-8, 187, 206-9, 215-32, 251, 253, 277-9, 286-90, 292, 295-6, 302
Yocum, David Pier ("Pappy"), 5, 33, 192-3, *233*

www.ingramcontent.com/pod-product-compliance
Lightning Source LLC
Chambersburg PA
CBHW060447170426
43199CB00011B/1127